MW00637496

"If you're looking for the most thorough and thoughtful look at positive psychology from a Christian perspective, this is it. Dr. Hackney combines his impressive knowledge of research, an incisive Christian appraisal of human flourishing, and outstanding communication skills to provide this excellent textbook on one of the most promising movements in contemporary psychology."

Mark R. McMinn, author of *The Science of Virtue* and coauthor of *Embodying Integration*

"Charles Hackney offers a Christian view of second-wave positive psychology. For the reader who wants to put a Christian understanding of positive psychology in historical, theological, philosophical, and psychological perspective, this is the definitive book."

Everett L. Worthington Jr., author of *Coming to Peace with Psychology: What Christians Can Learn from Psychological Science*

"I found Charles Hackney's book to be a beautiful overview and critique of positive psychology—both the movement and its many topics—viewed through a Christian lens. I very much appreciated the thoughtful integration of a huge body of psychological literature within a faith-based context. The book provides a great deal of food for thought, all packaged within bite-sized, well-organized, highly readable chapters. I would highly recommend this book as a resource for scholars and clinicians, and I would see it as an excellent choice for a Christian-focused undergraduate or graduate course on positive psychology."

Julie J. Exline, professor in the Department of Psychological Sciences at Case Western Reserve University

"With good will and a sweet sense of humor, Charles Hackney demonstrates in these pages a deep appreciation of positive psychology as well as an impressive familiarity with its findings and sensibilities. Even better, he offers a constructive critique of some of its themes and makes some surprising contributions of his own (e.g., there are chapters on sports and martial arts). Best of all, he has given us a readable yet sophisticated Christian interpretation of its major contributions so far, while advocating for a Christian version of the project. With such a far-reaching synthesis, some minor disagreements are unavoidable, but the breadth and depth of what he has accomplished is so well done and so enjoyable."

Eric L. Johnson, professor of Christian psychology, Gideon Institute for Christian Psychology and Counseling, Houston Baptist University

"Not only does Charles Hackney helpfully locate the field of positive psychology historically and theoretically, he provides well-researched treatments of a variety of the field's most intriguing topics (e.g., hope, mindfulness, wisdom, self-control, flow). All of this is done from a thoughtful and balanced Christian point of view that is not forced or heavy handed. Hackney's book is a comprehensive, thoroughly researched, and clearly written introduction to positive psychology for Christian undergraduate and graduate students."

Steven L. Porter, professor of theology and philosophy, Rosemead School of Psychology, Biola University

POSITIVE PSYCHOLOGY IN CHRISTIAN PERSPECTIVE

Foundations, Concepts, and Applications

CHARLES HACKNEY

Academic

An imprint of InterVarsity Press
Downers Grove, Illinois

InterVarsity Press
P.O. Box 1400, Downers Grove, IL 60515-1426
ivpress.com
email@ivpress.com

©2021 by Charles H. Hackney

InterVarsity Press® is the book-publishing division of InterVarsity Christian Fellowship/USA®, a movement of students and faculty active on campus at hundreds of universities, colleges, and schools of nursing in the United States of America, and a member movement of the International Fellowship of Evangelical Students. For information about local and regional activities, visit intervarsity.org.

All Scripture quotations, unless otherwise indicated, are taken from The Holy Bible, New International Version®, NIV®. Copyright © 1973, 1978, 1984, 2011 by Biblica, Inc.™ Used by permission of Zondervan. All rights reserved worldwide. www.zondervan.com. The "NIV" and "New International Version" are trademarks registered in the United States Patent and Trademark Office by Biblica, Inc.™

The publisher cannot verify the accuracy or functionality of website URLs used in this book beyond the date of publication.

While any stories in this book are true, some names and identifying information may have been changed to protect the privacy of individuals.

Cover design and image composite: Autumn Short
Interior design: Daniel van Loon
Images: rough white surface photo © Pawel Czerwinski / Unsplash.com
    abstract vector plant © ANASTASIIA DMITRIEVA / iStock / Getty Images Plus

ISBN 978-0-8308-2870-8 (print)
ISBN 978-0-8308-2871-5 (digital)

Printed in the United States of America ∞

InterVarsity Press is committed to ecological stewardship and to the conservation of natural resources in all our operations. This book was printed using sustainably sourced paper.

Library of Congress Cataloging-in-Publication Data
A catalog record for this book is available from the Library of Congress.

P	25	24	23	22	21	20	19	18	17	16	15	14	13	12	11	10	9	8	7	6	5	4	3	2	1
Y	42	41	40	39	38	37	36	35	34	33	32	31	30	29	28	27	26	25	24	23	22	21

For listening to my manic ravings about

positive psychology during the writing process,

and for reminding me that the world exists

outside of the writing process,

this book is dedicated to my very patient wife.

CONTENTS

Part One

THE BIG PICTURE

Chapter One

WHAT IS POSITIVE PSYCHOLOGY?

Life achieves its summit when it does to the
uttermost that which it was equipped to do.

JACK LONDON, *WHITE FANG*

WELCOME TO POSITIVE PSYCHOLOGY

A little over two decades ago, the president of the American Psychological Association, Martin E. P. Seligman, announced the beginning of a new direction in psychological research and practice. He called this movement "positive psychology," the "study of the conditions and processes that contribute to the flourishing and optimal functioning of people, groups, and institutions" (Gable & Haidt, 2005, p. 203). Since then, positive psychology has exploded in popularity and influence, spawning graduate degrees, research centers, international conferences, and academic journals. Positive psychology has been embraced by researchers and practitioners in every subdiscipline of psychology. Teachers have begun employing positive psychology in the classroom (Gilman, Huebner, & Furlong, 2009). Employers and business consultants have been applying positive psychology in the workplace (Froman, 2010). The US Army built the Comprehensive Soldier Fitness Program on a foundation of positive psychology (Casey, 2011). Politicians have discussed using positive psychology to shape public policy (Cameron, 2010).

Positive psychology has also seen application in the church (McMinn, 2017). Theologians (e.g., Charry, 2010) and biblical scholars (e.g., Strawn, 2012) have brought Christian ideas about happiness and flourishing to center stage. Many Christian colleges and universities have added courses in positive psychology to their roster. Biola University's Center for Christian Thought dedicated its 2013–2014 research theme to "Psychology and Spiritual Formation" (Crisp, Porter, & Ten Elshof, 2019), including the question, "How does positive psychology contribute to a Christian understanding of human flourishing?" Flourishing, it seems, is a hot topic all over.

WHY IS THERE A POSITIVE PSYCHOLOGY?

When Seligman launched positive psychology in 1998, he argued that the movement was necessary because the field had become unbalanced. Originally, psychology had a threefold mission: "curing mental illness, making the lives of all people more productive and fulfilling, and identifying and nurturing high talent" (Seligman & Csikszentmihalyi, 2000, p. 6).

However, events in the twentieth century led to the first of those missions being prioritized over the second and third, to the point that nowadays many people think *psychologist* is just another way of saying "one who cures mental illness."

Let's look at how that happened.

POSITIVE PSYCHOLOGY BEFORE POSITIVE PSYCHOLOGY

The title of the first official positive psychology book is *Authentic Happiness: Using the New Positive Psychology to Realize Your Potential for Lasting Fulfillment* (Seligman, 2002). Note the use of the word *new* to describe positive psychology. Similarly, Seligman's 2011 book is titled *Flourish: A Visionary New Understanding of Happiness and Well-Being.* Much of the excitement about positive psychology is the sense that it is a *new* direction for psychology. However, positive psychologists are aware that this approach is "new" only in that it is a revitalization of ideas that have been around for as long as psychology itself. The first positive psychologist was in fact the first North American psychologist, William James (Taylor, 2001). James's *Principles of Psychology* (1890) is primarily concerned with topics such as perception, memory, and the nature of thought, but James also discussed "positive" phenomena such as sympathy and altruism, the constructive drive, play, and aesthetic enjoyment. James's most extensive treatment of happiness and flourishing can be found in his volume on the psychology of religion, *The Varieties of Religious Experience* (1902). Here, James describes the effect of religious devotion on people's lives. His primary conclusion is that religion provides a "new

zest which adds itself like a gift to life" and an "assurance of safety and a temper of peace, and, in relation to others, a preponderance of loving affections" (p. 401). We will discuss more recent work on the psychology of religion and flourishing in chapter twenty-one.

Gordon Allport is considered the "patron saint of personality," having done more than any other scholar to establish the study of normal personality as a mainstream topic for psychological consideration (Nicholson, 2003). Early in his career, Allport found himself in Vienna and, in a fit of fanboyish enthusiasm, arranged for a meeting with the man himself: Sigmund Freud. Allport did not have anything prepared to talk about with Freud, so he tried to make conversation, including relating to Freud a story about a dirt-phobic boy whom Allport had seen on a train. Freud listened (I always imagine him stroking his beard as he did so), then asked, "And was that little boy you?" (Evans, 1971, p. 4). Allport's impression of Freud was that the great psychiatrist tended to read far too much into things and interpreted far too many observations as indicators of unconscious pathology. As his career progressed and he became a leading figure in the study of personality, Allport (1937, 1955) continued to criticize psychoanalysis for overemphasizing illness and infantile neuroses. He sought to compensate for this tendency by developing the scientific study of the mature personality. His description of psychological maturity emphasized self-acceptance, connections to other people, dedication to higher ideals, zest, security, a well-developed philosophy of life, and an equally well-developed sense of humor (Allport, 1961).

The largest mainstream movement in psychology to take a positive approach to the human condition is humanistic psychology. Humanistic psychology arose in reaction to the negative views of human nature among the Freudians and the behaviorists (Maslow, 1962). On one side, Freudians saw humans as neurotic bundles of pathology driven by sex and violence. On the other side were the behaviorists, who in their more radical forms denied human choice, purpose, and dignity. Humanistic psychologists seek to establish a "third force" within mainstream psychology, emphasizing the goodness that can be found in human nature and the possibility for growth and flourishing (Goble, 1970). Abraham Maslow (1962) put it this way: "It is as if Freud supplied to us the sick half of psychology and we must now fill it out with the healthy half" (p. 5).

Positive psychologists owe a great deal to their humanistic colleagues. Humanistic psychologists redirected the spotlight back onto questions of fulfillment and above-average functioning with their inquiry into topics such as self-actualization (e.g., Rogers, 1961), peak experiences (e.g., Maslow, 1962), and self-determination (e.g., Deci & Ryan, 1985). Indeed, Maslow's "mission statement" quoted above could easily be seen as the mission statement of positive psychology.

How Psychology Became Negative

Despite the positive psychology being carried out by earlier psychologists, the field as a whole took on a decidedly negative tone after World War II (Seligman, 1999). Twentieth-century warfare was historically unprecedented in its infliction of mental trauma on combatants (Grossman, 1995), and the existing American mental health system was overwhelmed by the number of soldiers returning with such trauma (Pohls & Oak, 2007). To help fill this need, the Veterans Administration (VA) turned to a small group on the margins of psychology: clinical psychologists. Clinical psychology before World War II was primarily focused on psychological tests and measures, with some emphasis also on children experiencing school-related difficulties (McReynolds, 1987). After World War II, though, the VA began encouraging clinical psychologists to expand their consulting work to help treat traumatized veterans, and they dedicated funding for nearly two dozen doctoral programs in clinical psychology. The field of clinical psychology rapidly expanded in popularity, prestige, and power, to the point that by 1962, practicing psychologists outnumbered academic psychologists in the American Psychological Association. Clinical psychology is now the dominant force within psychology.

When this shift in the field is viewed in light of Seligman's (1999) complaint that psychology had become too negative, it might appear that positive psychologists see the rise of clinical psychology as a bad thing. By no means. Thanks to clinical psychology's powerful position, we have made tremendous strides in helping those who are experiencing mental health problems, and hopefully we can look forward to further substantial progress over the next half-century. Wanting to help those who are hurting is a good thing. For any students reading this who are considering a career as a clinical psychologist, you have the possibility to do great good pursuing a noble calling. Further, if you want your doctoral training to be specifically shaped by a Christian worldview, there are several Christian universities that offer doctorates in clinical psychology. So do not let me dissuade anyone who wants to work within the "illness" approach to psychology.

That being said, the primary message motivating the positive psychology movement has been that studying illness is not enough by itself. It should be balanced with an equally strong emphasis on studying wellness. To grossly oversimplify things, some positive psychologists (e.g., Gable & Haidt, 2005) use the image of a numerical scale to get this point across. Think of a scale ranging from negative ten to positive ten, with negative ten being the lowest possible depths of misery, the zero point being neutral (neither doing poorly nor doing well), and positive ten being the happiest life possible. Currently, psychology is good at helping people who are around negative six or negative seven to make it up to the neighborhood of zero (maybe positive one on a good day). By contrast, we know very little about how to help people get from the zero point to positive seven.

SELIGMAN'S CALL FOR A NEW MOVEMENT

In 1998, Martin Seligman became president of the American Psychological Association. In his presidential address, Seligman laid out his vision for his tenure, and a major part of that vision was "a new science of human strengths." He pointed to psychology's post–World War II status as a field primarily dedicated to repairing damage, and he argued that psychologists should

reshape the field in a way that addressed the needs of the twenty-first century: "We can articulate a vision of the good life that is empirically sound and, at the same time, understandable and attractive. We can show the world what actions lead to well-being, to positive individuals, to flourishing communities, and to a just society" (Seligman, 1999, p. 560).

In addition to the power of his position as APA president, Seligman had the financial resources to support his new movement. With backing from the Templeton Foundation, he announced the establishment of the Templeton Positive Psychology Prize. This prize, the largest ever offered by the APA ($100,000), was to go to a psychologist who was doing excellent work within positive psychology (the inaugural prize went to Barbara Fredrickson, whose work on positive emotion we will cover in chapter four). Funding from the Gallup Organization helped establish a series of International Positive Psychology Summits in Washington, DC, which gathered hundreds of scholars to present papers and discuss this emerging science of strengths. The Manuel D. and Rhoda Mayerson Foundation supported the creation of positive psychology's first major reference volume, *Character Strengths and Virtues* (Peterson & Seligman, 2004), which we will discuss in chapter ten.

Positive psychology has taken off since 1998, and it has shown itself to be one of psychology's great success stories. In January 2000, *American Psychologist* dedicated a special issue to this new movement, and an interdisciplinary team of researchers (including Ed Diener, whom we will meet in chapter four) launched the *Journal of Happiness Studies*. Two years later, *Authentic Happiness* (Seligman, 2002), the first book about positive psychology, was published. In 2005, the University of Pennsylvania introduced a master's degree in applied positive psychology. The following year, the first positive psychology textbook (Christopher Peterson's *Primer on Positive Psychology*) was published and the *Journal of Positive Psychology* was launched. In 2007, the International Positive Psychology Association was formed and the first PhD programs in positive psychology were offered at Claremont Graduate University. In 2008, the US Army began its work on the Comprehensive Soldier Fitness Program (our topic for chapter twenty), applying positive psychology to military personnel. Despite some early claims that all this happiness stuff was just a fad, positive psychology is not showing any signs of going away.

THIS IS NOT HAPPYOLOGY

As is the case with everything else in this field, positive psychology has attracted its share of critics. Some of the criticisms that have been leveled against the movement have some teeth, as we will see in chapter twenty-four, while others do not. One of the first misconceptions one encounters in connection with positive psychology is the accusation that positive psychologists are shallow Pollyannas. The media does not help to dispel this. News stories and op-ed pieces about positive psychology are often accompanied by pictures of big yellow smiley faces (if you want to take a study break at some point, do a Google image search for "positive psychology," and count

the smiley faces that result). In 2016, *Time* magazine published a special issue on positive psychology, which they titled "The Science of Happiness." The entire cover was nothing but smiling emojis. In addition, if a positive psychologist is the focus of a news story, that person is often tagged with a silly nickname (a 2000 article on Barbara Fredrickson in the *Albany Times Union* began by instructing the reader, "Call her Professor Happy"). Critics like Barbara Ehrenreich (2009) equate positive psychology with the "positive thinking" promoted by Norman Vincent Peale (1952) and accuse positive psychologists of telling everyone to put on a smile and think happy thoughts until their lives get better.

While some positive psychologists do focus on happiness as an emotion, that is only one component of the field, and nobody here really thinks that anyone's lives will get better if they just repeat, "I'm happy I'm happy I'm happy" until they believe it. Positive psychology is about what philosophers call "the good life." It's about flourishing, or living well, or, to put it another way, doing a good job of being human. Some of that will involve cheerful emotions, and some of it will not. For example, in chapter twelve we will discuss hardiness, which involves having the mental strength to get through stressful situations without developing anxiety problems. In chapter twenty-three we will even address the idea that death-related existential terror has a role to play in the good life.

We are also not helped by the way the phrase "the good life" is misused in popular media and advertising. As we will see in more detail in chapter two, when someone is living the good life, they are doing what humans are designed to do and doing it well. This is not, however, the vision of the good life that we are frequently sold in the media. Not surprisingly, given the deep influence of consumerism in our society, we are often told that the good life involves material prosperity and comfort. In 1999, Sears department stores excitedly launched a new corporate slogan designed to encourage customers to purchase their merchandise: "The Good Life at a Great Price. Guaranteed." *Road and Travel* magazine ran an article in 2006 titled "Charter Your Own Yacht for a Slice of the Good Life." The computer game *The Good Life* by Immersion FX Games allows players the simulated experience of life as a wealthy tycoon on a tropical island.

The good life is also sold to us in terms of fitness and beauty. In his book *Living the Good Life,* David Patchell-Evans (2004) defines the good life as being physically fit and feeling energized and confident (Patchell-Evans is the founder and CEO of GoodLife Fitness, Canada's largest chain of health clubs). In 2014, Columbia University professor and television personality Mehmet Oz launched his magazine *Dr. Oz: The Good Life*, featuring articles on topics ranging from new weight loss products to makeup tips to the many uses of kale. And if the good life is not enough for you, you can take it up to the next level with *Best Life,* a men's magazine published from 2004 to 2009 offering tips for boosting testosterone, maximizing investment returns, and putting together a killer outfit (remember, guys, as ZZ Top taught us, every girl's crazy about a sharp-dressed man).

But positive psychology is not about always feeling cheerful. Positive psychology is not about thinking happy thoughts in defiance of a clear-eyed view of reality. Positive psychology is not about shopping at Sears or renting a yacht or living on a tropical island (not that I have anything against Sears or yachts or islands). Positive psychology is about understanding human flourishing and helping people become better than they were.

WHAT ABOUT THE HUMANISTIC PSYCHOLOGISTS?

As we saw earlier in this chapter, the positive psychology movement is in many ways a continuation of the humanistic psychology movement. Like positive psychologists, humanistic psychologists want to focus on flourishing and help people do better than the "zero point," and humanistic psychology also arose as a reaction against the "illness" orientation of mainstream psychology. So why did Seligman not simply announce that he planned to support humanistic psychology so that it could be powerful enough to accomplish its mission of bringing balance to the field?

When Seligman and Csikszentmihalyi (2000) introduced positive psychology in their *American Psychologist* article, they offered three reasons. First, they claimed that humanistic psychology "did not attract much of a cumulative empirical base" (p. 7), while positive psychology was to be a fully scientific approach. Second, they claimed that humanistic theories encouraged self-centeredness, emphasizing the cultivation of the individual and ignoring collective well-being. Third, they held humanistic psychology responsible for the myriad of touchy-feely self-help books clogging the "Psychology" section of bookstores.

The humanistic psychologists were less than pleased with this set of accusations. Bohart and Greening (2001) expressed a wish that Seligman and Csikszentmihalyi "had done a more scholarly job of investigating humanistic psychology" (p. 81). Humanistic psychology, they argued, did in fact have a solid empirical base, especially when it came to therapeutic outcome research. A closer reading of the great humanistic psychologists would show that their notion of self-cultivation had concern for others (not self-centeredness) at its core. And as for the lame self-help books, those were the result of misunderstanding humanistic psychology, so one could not responsibly hold the humanists accountable for other people's errors. When Seligman and Csikszentmihalyi (2001) replied, they brushed off Bohart and Greening's concerns, reiterating their claim that positive psychology was distinct from humanistic psychology due to positive psychologists being, "unblushingly, scientists first" (p. 89).

The current state of relations between positive psychology and humanistic psychology is complicated. Christopher Peterson (2006), a leading figure in early positive psychology, has since distanced himself from Seligman's position, saying the dismissal of humanistic psychology "now seems glib and mistaken" (p. 9). And some humanistic psychologists, such as those associated with self-determination theory (DeRobertis & Bland, 2018), have found a place of prominence within positive psychology. Others (e.g., Waterman, 2013), on the other hand, argue that certain differences in underlying philosophy (such as the prominence of phenomenology and social constructionism in humanistic

thought) have created a rift between the two fields that is not going away anytime soon.

WHY A CHRISTIAN POSITIVE PSYCHOLOGY?

The issue of differing philosophies brings us to the purpose of this book. Since the advent of the positive psychology movement, several positive psychology textbooks have been published. So why write another one? And why a specifically "Christian perspective" on positive psychology?

As Gordon Allport put it, "All psychology rests on philosophical presuppositions of some sort" (Evans, 1971, p. 87). Philosophy has consequences. For psychologists, our philosophical anthropology (philosophy of human nature) shapes the assumptions built into our theories. Those assumptions work themselves out in the way in which we put psychology into practice. Applied psychology founded on bad philosophy will produce bad outcomes. For example, Harvard psychologist Steven Pinker (2002) is sharply critical of the philosophical notion that there is no innate human nature (often called the "blank slate" view of humanity), making human beings infinitely malleable. One consequence of this belief is that parents may be told by psychologists that they bear almost total responsibility for their children's personality, mental health, and even intelligence. As Pinker puts it, this theory "has distorted the choices faced by mothers as they try to balance their lives, and multiplied the anguish of parents whose children haven't turned out the way they hoped" (p. x). Philosophical presuppositions are not simply matters for ivory tower academic debates. Philosophical presuppositions have concrete effects on the lives of real people.

Christians may find that some of the presuppositions guiding the creation and implementation of psychological theories fit very well within a biblically informed view of the human condition, while others are more problematic. Mary Stewart Van Leeuwen (1979), for example, finds behavioral psychology to be entirely congruent with a Christian view of learning, but she finds the claims of the radical behaviorists (such as B. F. Skinner) to be contrary to a biblically informed view of humans. Angela Sabates (2012) takes on the entire field of social psychology, endeavoring to bring the disparate findings of social psychologists into a unified structure founded on the Christian themes of creation-fall-redemption. For those who want an even bigger big-picture view, I recommend *Psychology and Christianity: Five Views* (Johnson, 2010) for an introduction to the question of how psychology in general might be fruitfully engaged with by Christian thinkers.

Many Christians who work in the field of psychology have argued for the importance of developing a Christian approach to positive psychology (e.g., Hackney, 2007, 2010a; Kaczor, 2015; Nelson & Slife, 2017; Titus & Moncher, 2009). Positive psychologists have their own sets of philosophical presuppositions, most of them connected with Aristotle (Jørgensen & Nafstad, 2004). In addition to the fact that Christians have a long history of scholarly engagement with Aristotelian thinking, positive psychology deals with topics that are highly relevant for believers, such as virtue, spirituality, love, wisdom, and meaning. As Mark McMinn

(2017) observes, many of the leading researchers on gratitude, forgiveness, and humility are Christians. However, Christian students are typically taught positive psychology using material written by psychologists who assume that life is meaningless and that the purpose of spirituality and the virtues is personal enjoyment. A Christian positive psychology will be distinct from the positive psychology of our non-Christian colleagues due to our differing ideas about basic human nature (our philosophical anthropology), our differing ideas about what flourishing is, our differing ideas about how flourishing happens, and our differing ways of understanding those who do not flourish.

Compared with mainstream positive psychology, Christian positive psychology is a better fit with Aristotelian philosophy (Hackney, 2007), includes a broader and more coherent view of the virtues (Hackney, 2010a), and better fits the reality of human nature (Hackney, 2014). We will examine these topics in more detail in chapters two and three. In addition to producing better psychology, this project also has benefits for Christians. As we will see, many of the tools positive psychologists have developed are useful in assisting Christians in our spiritual growth, helping us cultivate a more Christlike character and lead better lives as followers of God (Kaczor, 2015; McMinn, 2017).

THE STRUCTURE OF THIS BOOK
The general approach I will take in guiding you through this introduction to positive psychology will be neo-Aristotelian (what makes it "neo" will be covered in chapter two), set within a Christian vision of the

good life. Flourishing will be described in terms of the cultivation of a Christlike character, making us better able to fulfill God's purpose for our species. This process requires that we cultivate that which is good in human nature and struggle to defeat that which is evil in human nature, and this will involve both the work of the Holy Spirit and responsible human participation.

After covering some big picture philosophical and theological matters in chapters two and three, we will get into specific topics within positive psychology. The chapters are organized around broad themes. They include discussion of how these topics fit within a Christian view of flourishing and sometimes include practical exercises that can help you apply positive psychology in your own life. In this way, it is my hope that this book may be of some use to you in your own efforts to live well as a disciple of Jesus.

The first of these sections focuses on positive subjective states and features some of the foundational theories of the positive psychology movement. Chapter four focuses specifically on happiness and subjective well-being. In chapter five, the emphasis is on humor. In chapter six, we review Mihaly Csikszentmihaly's research on "flow" states.

The topic of the next section is the role of cognitive processes in a life well lived. In chapter seven, we examine Martin Seligman's theory of learned optimism, which is one of the foundations of positive psychology. Mindfulness, our topic for chapter eight, involves bringing one's attention to bear on the present moment and has been associated with beneficial effects ranging from stress reduction to improved interpersonal functioning. In chapter nine, we focus on current psychological research on wisdom integrated with philosophical and theological scholarship on the topic, as well as practical methods for becoming wise.

The next section features the role of personality in flourishing, beginning in chapter ten with a focus on *Character Strengths and Virtues* (the *CSV*), the first major reference volume published by positive psychologists. In chapter eleven we examine self-control as a core human strength. In chapter twelve the focus is on characteristics we might call "mental toughness," emphasizing hardiness and grit.

Humans are an inherently social species, so no description of flourishing is adequate if it does not include positive relationships. Chapter thirteen is about love and marriage. In chapter fourteen we turn our attention to theories and research involving gratitude. Chapter fifteen is about research on forgiveness, research that eventually led Christian psychologist Everett Worthington Jr. to testify before the South African Truth and Reconciliation Committee.

In the next section we focus more closely on specific applications of positive psychology. In chapter sixteen the focus is on helping behavior and empathy, as well as Philip Zimbardo's Heroic Imagination Project. Chapter seventeen is about sport psychology, including Christian perspectives on sport and exercise, and the martial arts as a venue for character development. In chapter eighteen we will see positive psychology applied in education. In chapter nineteen we explore positive psychology in the workplace. In chapter twenty the US Army's Comprehensive Soldier Fitness Program is examined in detail. Chapter twenty-one is dedicated both to the role of religion in flourishing and to efforts to apply positive psychology in church settings.

Our final section is the most unique to this book. Being a highly functioning human does not always involve happy feelings, but most positive psychologists tend to overlook this in their enthusiasm for the upside of life. A Christian perspective on flourishing, though, goes beyond the individual sense of gratification that comes from playing to one's strengths and provides us with tools for successfully handling the darker sides of the human experience. In chapter twenty-two I provide an example of this by arguing for the goodness of guilt as both a psychological variable and a component of Christian maturity. Chapter twenty-three goes even darker, featuring existential approaches to human flourishing and a positive psychology of death.

Having considered the positive in the negative, we turn to the negative in the positive for our concluding chapter, twenty-four. While we will be dealing with criticisms of the positive psychology movement at several points throughout the book (and indeed have already mentioned a few of them), in this chapter the critics get center stage. We will cover some of the major assaults that have been made on the house that Seligman built, as well as some of the responses that have been put forward by positive psychology's defenders. Finally, we look to the future of positive psychology. This text concludes with a look at possibilities for the future of positive psychology, as well as possibilities for a more fully formed Christian positive psychology.

SUGGESTIONS FOR FURTHER READING

Gable, S. L., & Haidt, J. (2005). What (and why) is positive psychology? *Review of General Psychology, 9*(2), 103-10.

Hackney, C. H. (2007). Possibilities for a Christian positive psychology. *Journal of Psychology & Theology, 35*(3), 211-21.

Kaczor, C. (2015). *The gospel of happiness: Rediscover your faith through spiritual practice and positive psychology.* Image.

McMinn, M. R. (2017). *The science of virtue: Why positive psychology matters to the church.* Brazos.

Seligman, M. E. P. (2002). *Authentic happiness: Using the new positive psychology to realize your potential for lasting fulfillment.* Free Press.

Seligman, M. E. P., & Csikszentmihalyi, M. (2000). Positive psychology: An introduction. *American Psychologist, 55*(1), 5-14.

Chapter Two

THE PHILOSOPHY OF FLOURISHING

*All psychology rests on philosophical presuppositions of some sort,
and I think students should realize that and know enough about those
presuppositions so that if one approach proves less fruitful
than the student anticipated, he can turn to another.*

GORDON ALLPORT

PHILOSOPHY HAS CONSEQUENCES

In the previous chapter, I introduced the idea that psychological theories rest on philosophical presuppositions about (among other things) human nature. Here we will delve into that topic in greater depth and introduce the philosophies that have shaped the positive psychology movement. We will also examine some criticisms that have arisen from these philosophical positions.

THE FALL AND RISE OF VIRTUE ETHICS

Anytime someone begins to talk about an admirable trait (honesty, bravery, and so on) or holds up another person as a model of "good character," that person is employing the language of virtue. Ideas concerning what types of character traits make one a "good person" are as old as moral thought itself, appearing across cultures, in all major religions, in classic works of philosophy, and in everyday conversations.

Scholarly attention to the idea of virtue, however, experienced centuries of decline and neglect. The period of Western history known as the Enlightenment (roughly the seventeenth through nineteenth centuries) saw a rejection of this line of thought by many prominent thinkers. As will be described below, virtue is based on a vision of the ideal life, and this did not fit well with Enlightenment philosophy. Enlightenment thinkers wanted to rely entirely on objective rational analyses that flowed from self-evident first principles, and a vision of an ideal life is neither objective nor self-evident (MacIntyre, 1988).

The Enlightenment saw a shift of focus away from the question of how to be a good person and toward the method-ological question of how to make good choices. Should a medical experiment be performed if there is a risk to the partici-pants? Should the death penalty apply to convicted murderers who have a cognitive impairment? Should young teenage girls be required to inform their parents before having an abortion? It is assumed that the central function of ethical theory is to provide well-grounded ethical principles for resolving these quandaries. In a quandary-centered approach, ethics are not required until one comes to an instance in which rival options are presented. The individual shifts into an ethical mode of thought, decides which solution is the right solution, and then shifts out of ethical mode and back to business as usual. While the resolution of dilemmas is necessary, one downside to this approach is that ethics becomes irrelevant to everyday life unless a specific problem arises, thus eliminating large portions of ethical "real life" in favor of an emphasis on ethical "borderline cases" (Meilaender, 1984).

The two major theoretical camps in Enlightenment-influenced ethics are deontological and consequentialist. Deontological ethical thought centers around the idea that problems will be resolved through the systematic application of the correct *rules* and is primarily associated with the philosophy of Immanuel Kant. If the proper rules of behavior can be specified (for example, "Psychotherapists should never sleep with their clients"), then ethical dilemmas can be successfully resolved. Consequentialist ethics is typically represented by utilitarianism, an approach most often associated with such thinkers as Jeremy Bentham and John Stuart Mill. This approach focuses on the *outcome* of an ethically relevant situation and the idea that the right choice is the one that produces "the greatest good for the greatest number of people."

Numerous objections have been raised to these ethical approaches (such as the proliferation of exceptions to ethical rules or our inability to accurately know all possible outcomes of an event). At a fundamental level, many have objected to the rationalist emphasis in both deontological and consequentialist ethics (Murdoch, 1970), arguing that a life of moral excellence is not achieved through the elevation of dutiful legalism or the robotic calculation of pros and cons over such concepts as wisdom (Nussbaum, 2001) or having a kind heart (Stark, 2004). As dissatisfaction has grown with these two dominant ethical approaches, numerous scholars in the past several decades have increasingly given attention to a third possibility: bringing back virtue ethics.

THE CONTRIBUTION OF ALASDAIR MACINTYRE

Many scholars have made great contributions to the revival of virtue ethics, but the figure most often viewed as central to the movement is moral philosopher Alasdair MacIntyre. In his book *After Virtue* (2007), MacIntyre traces current problems in ethics and public moral debate to the failure of the Enlightenment project to rationally justify morality. All our disagreements, the Enlightenment philosopher would argue, would go away if we could establish a way to objectively justify a universally binding morality based exclusively on rational analysis.

MacIntyre argues that the failure of the Enlightenment project was inevitable. Ethical theories require commitments to certain foundational premises about human nature and the nature of moral authority. Once these premises are accepted, rational deliberation about the elaboration and application of these principles is straightforward. But how do we choose which set of premises to accept?

Questions such as whether to adopt one set of rational premises over another, or even why to act ethically at all, exist outside of any particular theory's domain, so any choice made between rival ethical claims collapses into a nonrational act of emotional preference empowered by the personal will (Murdoch, 1970). This is why public policy disagreements in our modern societies are in their current chaotic condition. Unable to agree on first principles, we have no common ground from which to work toward agreement on specific moral issues (abortion, euthanasia, marriage, and so on). "Rightness" on such issues in modern context therefore becomes a question of securing and maintaining power by persuading the majority of voters to agree with you, persuading people in positions of authority to agree with you, or acquiring enough wealth to unleash hordes of lawyers on whomever stands in your way.

Having traced the failure of the Enlightenment project, MacIntyre advocates a return to Aristotelian virtue ethics. By returning to a broadly Aristotelian approach (Hursthouse, 1999, refers to this approach as "neo-Aristotelian," as it holds to Aristotle's basic conceptual structure but rejects such specifics as Aristotle's treatment of slaves and women), we are able to recognize that, by its very nature, rational analysis must take place within a community and a tradition of thought that support a vision of the ideal. This argument is in strong accord with recent work indicating that any scientific research presupposes a socially guided set of ideas about what makes "good science" and a "good theory" (e.g., Kuhn, 1996), that

political ideologies are grounded in a culturally embedded vision of government and human nature (e.g., Koyzis, 2019), and, most relevant for our purposes, that psychological theories carry an inextricable concept of ideal or praiseworthy mental states (e.g., Tjeltveit, 2003; Van Belle, 1980).

NEO-ARISTOTELIAN THOUGHT

The Aristotelian (and neo-Aristotelian) approach is teleological in nature. The Greek word *telos* is typically translated as "end," "goal," or "purpose," and it refers to the built-in functioning of some object. A description of the telos is the answer to such questions as "what is this for?" or "what does this do?" The telos of a knife is to cut. The telos of an apple tree is to produce apples. The telos of a school is to educate. A description of the telos also provides a standard for describing something as good or bad. A good object fulfills its purpose well. A good knife cuts well. A good apple tree produces many healthy apples. A good school educates students effectively.

Is there a human telos? Good question. The telos of an organism is grounded in what that organism does. It is about fulfilling a natural function that is characteristic of that species (Foot, 2001; MacIntyre, 1999). While a telos is singular, it can be multidimensional, and classic Aristotelian approaches to a good human life emphasize a combination of rationality and sociality (Fowers, 2012b). Aristotle believed that, since it is our rational capacities that set humans apart from all other animals, the human telos is to be found in the exercise of reason, so a good human is one who functions as a highly competent practical reasoner (MacIntyre, 1999, 2016). It is also common among virtue ethicists (e.g., Devettere, 2002; Foot, 2001; Hursthouse, 1999) to focus on our status as exceptionally social animals. This makes a good human one who successfully navigates our hyper-social world (Fowers, 2015). In the next chapter we will return to the question of the human telos in light of biblically informed ideas about human nature.

The good life is one spent in progress toward the telos, and the ideal person is one who is progressing toward the telos. Within the Aristotelian approach, *eudaimonia* is the term employed for the "good life" (the life spent moving toward the telos), and *aretē* ("virtue") refers to the characteristics of the "good person" (the person who is living in the state of *eudaimonia*). *Eudaimonia* is often translated as "happiness" and refers to "a complete human life lived at its best" (MacIntyre, 2007, p. 149). As this definition of happiness centers around completeness and fulfillment, it is distinct from a hedonistic conception of happiness (the state of experiencing more pleasures than pains). Work involving a eudaimonic approach to happiness typically employs such terms as "flourishing" (Murphy, 2005a), "optimal functioning" (King, Eells, & Burton, 2004), "the actualization of human potentials" (Ryan & Deci, 2001), or "fulfillment in living" (Waterman, 1993) to describe this concept. "To flourish," says MacIntyre (2016), "is to function well" (p. 29). This distinction between eudaimonic and hedonic happiness should not be overstated, though, since functioning well often feels good. Living morally "is itself a response to the natural human longing for happiness and fulfillment" (Mattison, 2008, p. 26).

This puts virtue ethicists in stark contrast with those who might think morality is about forgoing happiness in order to obey an arbitrary set of rules.

The word *aretē* is typically translated as "virtue." MacIntyre (2007) defines the virtues as "those qualities the possession of which will enable an individual to achieve *eudaimonia* and the lack of which will frustrate his movement toward that *telos*" (p. 148). Virtues are character traits that enable one to be a highly functioning person. André Comte-Sponville (2001) puts it more strongly: As the virtues are qualities of excellence for humans, the more virtuous one becomes, the more human one becomes.

Overall, the neo-Aristotelian approach may be considered a description of the ideal human life and the ways and means of moving from our current state toward this ideal state by developing and exercising specifically human powers. This approach has found an appreciative audience in a wide range of academic and applied fields. For example, Higgins (2003) employs MacIntyre's system in developing a virtue-centered philosophy of teaching. Chen (2015) and Hicks and Stapleford (2016) employ "virtue epistemology" to describe the practice of science. And some scholars in military ethics (e.g., Toner, 2006; Oh, 2007) have applied the neo-Aristotelian perspective to military personnel.

NEO-ARISTOTELIANISM AND POSITIVE PSYCHOLOGY

There are also neo-Aristotelian ways of doing psychology. Blaine Fowers, for example, is a professor in the Department of Educational and Psychological Studies at the University of Miami, and he has worked extensively to bring an explicitly neo-Aristotelian perspective to bear on a variety of topics in psychology. In *Beyond the Myth of Marital Happiness* (Fowers, 2000), he asks, "What is the *telos* of marriage?" (we will discuss this further in chapter thirteen). In *Virtue and Psychology* (Fowers, 2005), he recasts professional ethics in psychology in terms of the necessary virtues of an excellent psychologist, with a particularly strong emphasis on the cultivation of practical wisdom. In *The Evolution of Ethics* (Fowers, 2015), he presents his general theory of psychological well-being, drawing from neo-Aristotelian virtue ethics and evolutionary psychology. In his most recent book, *Frailty, Suffering, and Vice*, Fowers (2017) presents (along with Frank Richardson and Brent Slife) a positive psychology grounded in the idea that virtues enable us to flourish, even though we are weak and limited creatures (more on this in some later chapters).

The positive psychology movement has been shaped by neo-Aristotelian thinking since its beginning (Kristjánsson, 2013). Seligman's *Authentic Happiness* (2002) is shot through with references to Aristotle, and he says his purpose is to "provide a fresh and scientifically grounded answer" to Aristotle's "great question": "What is the good life?" (p. 121). Peterson and Seligman (2004) describe the *CSV* as "the social science equivalent of virtue ethics" (p. 89), guided by "the Aristotelian notion of *eudaimonia*" (p. 18). Jørgensen and Nafstad (2004) say that "the Aristotelian tradition is a core root of positive psychology. . . . Positive psychology strongly associates itself with the Aristotelian model of human nature," and they describe the positive

psychology movement as a "revitalization of Aristotelian philosophy" (p. 16).

But How Aristotelian Are They Really?

Despite the prominence of neo-Aristotelian concepts and references to virtue ethics we find in the positive psychology movement, there are many who believe that the philosophical foundation is precisely where positive psychology is weak. A message has been emerging from multiple corners of psychology and philosophy suggesting that the prominent figures in the positive psychology movement have not done their philosophical homework.

MacIntyre (2007) claims that "any adequate teleological account must provide us with some clear and defensible account of the *telos*" (p. 163), and many philosophical critics of positive psychology have questioned what telos is provided in positive psychology's articulation of the good life. Louise Sundararajan (2005a, 2005b) aims her criticism at Seligman and Csikszentmihalyi's (2000) claim that the mission of positive psychology is to "articulate a vision of the good life that is empirically sound" (p. 5) and Seligman's (2002) claim that positive psychology is value-neutral in its approach to the good life. In a much-criticized passage, Seligman has said:

> Imagine a sadomasochist who comes to savor serial killing and derives great pleasure from it. Imagine a hit man who derives enormous gratification from stalking and slaying. Imagine a terrorist who, attached to al-Qaeda, flies a hijacked plane into the World Trade Center. Can these three people be said to have

achieved the pleasant life, the good life, and the meaningful life, respectively?

The answer is yes. I condemn their actions, of course, but on grounds independent of the theory in this book. The actions are morally despicable, but the theory is not a morality or a world-view; it is a description. I strongly believe that science is morally neutral (but ethically relevant). The theory put forward in this book describes what the pleasant life, the good life, and the meaningful life are. It describes how to get these lives and what the consequences of living them are. It does not *prescribe* these lives for you, nor does it, as a theory, value any one of these lives above the others. (Seligman, 2002, p. 303)

Sundararajan (2005b) argues for a position similar to MacIntyre's (2007), that any description of flourishing requires a telos or else it is meaningless. Sundararajan says Seligman's positive psychology is "a model of the good life devoid of a moral map" (2005b, p. 36), claiming to describe a journey of personal growth without any reference to the goal of the journey. How does the traveler know which direction to take? Sundararajan also employs a few choice food metaphors in her argument, describing Seligman's "morally neutral" positive psychology as a "happiness doughnut" with no core or similar to chemically mass-produced wine—it may technically be wine, but who would want to drink it? The regional particularities are what give wines their unique and inter-esting characteristics, and oenophiles (wine lovers) would not want to live in a world in which wines did not have such a wide variety of "personalities." Similarly, descrip-tions of human flourishing will show the

"regional particularities" of the worldviews in which they "grew." As we will see in more detail as we continue, psychological theories differ in their assumptions about basic human nature, about the telos of growth, and about the process by which we become more highly functioning humans. A better approach, Sundararajan (2005a) suggests, is to acknowledge the cultural specificity of our visions of the good life and explore the ways these visions create a variety of psychological theories.

MacIntyre (2016) also points out that "in most cultures, perhaps in all, it is taken for granted that human flourishing is what it is taken to be in that particular culture" (p. 28). While Sundararajan focuses her criticisms on Seligman's attempts to create a positive psychology without a telos, others claim that Seligman has in fact endorsed a telos without being aware of it. Seligman's telos can be seen in his description of the good life in *Authentic Happiness*: "a life wrapped up in successfully using your signature strengths to obtain abundant and authentic gratification" (Seligman, 2002, p. 249). This emphasis on one's own subjective gratifi-cation shows that Seligman's implicit telos is grounded in individualistic notions of the self (Woolfolk & Wasserman, 2005), notions that are firmly embedded in modern Western culture.

Philosopher Charles Taylor, in his book *A Secular Age* (2007), examines how our ideas about God, self, morality, and society have changed across five centuries of Western history. One theme Taylor emphasizes is that residents of the 1500s saw the world as "enchanted," that is, open to influence by spiritual forces of good and evil and having meaning that transcends the material composition of objects. Through a mean-dering historical course (which Taylor argues bears no resemblance to the sim-plistic "subtraction stories" told by the more naive varieties of atheist), humanity erected a conceptual wall between the natural and supernatural, disenchanting the world and stripping objects of deeper intrinsic meanings. In a disenchanted world, every-thing must be understood within the "immanent frame," an autonomous natural order that may or may not have any con-nection to the divine. God created water, for example, but we need not refer to God in order to understand that particular combi-nation of hydrogen and oxygen.

This shift to the immanent frame influ-enced our view of human flourishing. One step in the secularization process was the development of "providential deism," the view that God created the universe for our benefit, wound up the clockwork (so to speak), then stepped back and let the clockwork run on its own. The immanent frame is self-contained, and so our explana-tions of the universe are expected to be self-contained. Psychologists who are guided by this worldview see human behavior as entirely natural (i.e., lacking a supernatural dimension) and governed by predictable natural laws. If humans are to be described within the immanent frame, then the good life for humans can also only be described within the immanent frame, in terms of mutual material and emotional benefit. The idea that flourishing could be defined any other way becomes difficult to grasp in a secular age.

Taylor (2007) describes our current milieu as an "age of authenticity." The shift in perspective that led us to define human life and human flourishing in immanent terms has pushed further, opening up the possibility of defining human life in terms of "expressive individualism" (p. 299). In this view, truth and goodness come from within ourselves, and human flourishing means that "each of us has his/her own way of realizing our humanity, and that it is important to find and live out one's own, as against surrendering to conformity with a model imposed on us from outside, by society, or the previous generation, or religious or political authority" (p. 475). The idea that a good life is self-defined is everywhere in our culture, including in the preponderance of therapies that "promise to help you find yourself, realize yourself, release your true self, and so on" (p. 475). Social relations are seen as good if they are self-chosen and contribute to individual happiness. A career is worth pursuing if it feels fulfilling to the self. Churches must cater to the personal tastes and preferences of individual attendees or else those attendees will start shopping for a new church (McCracken, 2017). For those enmeshed in this worldview, the idea that they might have to change themselves to conform to religious teachings, rather than the other way round, just doesn't compute (we will discuss this further in chapter twenty-one).

This individualism also shapes positive psychologists' vision of the good life, with happiness defined in terms of personal achievement and positive emotion (Uchida, Unkit, & Kitayama, 2004). Fowers (2012a) describes this set of assumptions within psychology as "individualist instrumen-talism": "Individualism takes the individual to be the ultimate social reality and views the autonomous pursuit and satisfaction of individually defined ends as the ultimate goods in life. . . . Individuals pursue their chosen goods instrumentally, which means that they have subjectively predetermined ends, and they select the best strategies, techniques, and skills to attain those ends" (p. 2).

What about those who think the good life is not all about the individual self? One of the most important concepts to come out of crosscultural social psychology is the idea that Western individualism is not the only way to think about one's life. In cultures that are more "collectivistic," an interdependent self-concept is more prevalent than that of an independent self (Markus & Kitayama, 1991), such that the definition of *me* cannot be separated from the definition of *we*. With the boundary between the self and others blurred, the good life becomes "an inter-subjective state that is grounded in mutual sympathy, compassion, and support" (Uchida, Unkit, & Kitayama, 2004, p. 226) rather than achievement and enjoyment.

As a demonstration of the power of cultural assumptions to shape positive psychology, consider what positive psychology might look like if it were created in a more collectivistic culture. Paul Wong (2009) sketches what a Chinese positive psychology might look like, inspired by Confucian, Taoist, and Buddhist notions of flourishing. Such a positive psychology would be based on the assumptions that fatalism is the optimal mindset in an uncontrollable and unpredictable world, that the good life requires a balance between suffering and enjoyment instead of the elimination of suffering and maximization of enjoyment, and that group

harmony and hard work are moral goals in themselves. The development of non-Western approaches to positive psychology is a project that is still in its infancy (Delle Fave & Bassi, 2009; Joshanloo, 2014), but it is a project that is greatly needed as we try to respond to Sundararajan's (2005a) call for an acknowledgment that our approach to positive psychology is culturally specific rather than universal and as we try to describe the good life in ways that do not focus exclusively on subjective enjoyment.

As I have pointed out elsewhere (Hackney, 2014), one downside of placing the individual at the center of positive psychology is that our attempts to better the human condition can overlook social systems as both causes of problems and focuses for our interventions. As Becker and Marecek (2008) put it: "Positive psychologists conceive of flourishing as something determined by individual choice and attained by private, self-focused effort" (p. 1777), and we will see this individualism on display repeatedly in later chapters as we address various areas of application for positive psychology. When we examine the Comprehensive Soldier and Family Fitness Program (the application of positive psychology in the US Army), we will see that this program focuses entirely on empowering individual soldiers to thrive while paying no attention to the policies, organizational structure, procedures, or cultural norms of the US Army. Educational applications of positive psychology are similarly about teaching individual students how to cultivate a positive mindset rather than reforming the education system. When positive psychology is applied in the workplace, we do not see attempts to change corporate climate, company policies, workload levels, or any other "structural" factors. Instead, we see individual workers taught how to flourish "even in the midst of their heavy workloads and the tyranny of impossible expectations" (Achor, 2010, p. 22).

CHRISTIAN VIRTUE ETHICS

Relying on individual subjectivity for a definition of the good life is inadequate for those who believe that "there is a way that seems right to a man, but its end is the way to death" (Proverbs 14:12 ESV), and Christianity contains an extensive tradition of virtue ethics from which we can draw in our attempts to understand a life well lived (Kotva, 1996). In our next chapter, we will take a closer look at the Bible and theology on the topic of human nature and human flourishing. What follows here is just a very brief sampling of some Christian thought on virtue across the centuries.

Ancient and medieval Christian thinkers often used virtue language to describe a good life. Prudentius's fifth-century allegorical poem "Psychomachia" (meaning "soul battle") was tremendously influential in shaping the early medieval view of moral growth (O'Sullivan, 2004). In the poem we see virtues and vices locked in allegorical struggle, with plenty of allegorical blood and guts (for example, Faith crushes the skull of Idolatry and gouges out the monster's eyes for good measure). Like Prudentius, Augustine of Hippo argued that there is a powerful tendency toward evil in human nature and that living well involves winning our internal war so that we love that which should be loved in the way it deserves to be loved, empowered by virtues such as courage, wisdom, justice, and temperance and placing the knowledge of God at the center of our journey of personal development (Stalnaker, 2006).

Thomas Aquinas, the thirteenth-century philosopher and theologian, placed virtue and flourishing at the heart of his moral thought. In his *Summa Theologiae,* Aquinas identifies the human telos as union with God, with properly functioning reason directing us toward that goal. Virtues direct us toward true happiness (Herdt, 2015), which involves living toward our function as well as "the fullest possible development of our active powers" (Porter, 2016, p. 184). Because these powers are part of our created nature, Aquinas saw the possibility of an imperfect (merely human) form of happiness for those who do not know God. The cardinal virtues (wisdom, justice, courage, and temperance) that empower the proper functioning of these natural abilities can make one better but cannot make one perfect (MacIntyre, 1988). Perfect happiness will come only on the other side of death when we are at last in the presence of God (Charry, 2010), and "merely human" happiness on this side of the grave requires grace from God. Contrary to what we saw with Charles Taylor (2007) on flourishing within the immanent frame, virtue for a Christian has both natural and supernatural dimensions (Keenan, 2016; Titus & Moncher, 2009), so a Christian positive psychology will take into account the role of the Holy Spirit in the life of eudaimonic growth (Hackney, 2010).

In the twentieth century, MacIntyre's *After Virtue* sparked a boom of virtue thought among modern Christian scholars (Murphy, 1997). While earlier work on the virtues certainly existed (e.g., Henry, 1957; Pieper, 1965; Hauerwas, 1975), it is Mac- Intyre who has provided the concepts and vocabulary that is shaping much of current Christian thought on topics as diverse as missions (Wilson, 1997), education (Smith, 2009), and politics (Smith, 2002).

One Christian virtue ethicist who strongly influenced this text is Nancey Murphy, currently senior professor of Christian philosophy at Fuller Theological Seminary (see Murphy & Hackney, 2011, for my interview with her). Murphy (2005a) argues that psychology can never be value-free, as any descriptions of health, dysfunction, abnormality, and so on make sense only in the context of a particular set of assumptions about ultimate reality, human nature, and the highest good toward which humans can strive. Psycho- logical theories are embedded in ethical and theological visions of the human condition. "If it is the case," she claims, "that all psychological research programs are in fact 'theology laden,' then Christian psychologists are not only entitled but *obligated* to attempt to work out the consequences of their theologies for psychology" (p. 26).

Murphy (2005c) connects this inte- gration project to MacIntyre's teleological conceptual structure, "rewriting" psycho- logical theories by looking at how Chris- tians and non-Christians approach the following three questions:

1. What is the character of untutored and ungraced human nature?

2. What is the character of ideal human existence?

3. What are the means by which the transition can be made? (p. 56)

As we will see in our next chapter, Christian theologians have quite a lot to say about these three topics. And the answers provided will profoundly impact the con- struction of a Christian positive psychology.

SUGGESTIONS FOR FURTHER READING

Dueck, A., & Lee, C. (Eds.). (2005). *Why psychology needs theology: A radical-refor- mation perspective.* Eerdmans.

Fowers, B. J. (2005). *Virtue and psychology: Pursuing excellence in ordinary practices.* American Psychological Association.

Kotva, J. J., Jr. (1996). *The Christian case for virtue ethics.* Georgetown University Press.

Kristjánsson, K. (2013). *Virtue and vices in positive psychology: A philosophical critique.* Cambridge University Press.

MacIntyre, A. (2007). *After virtue* (3rd ed.). University of Notre Dame Press.

Chapter Three

THE THEOLOGY OF FLOURISHING

Happy are the people whose strength is in you;
Whose hearts are set on the pilgrim's way.

PSALM 84:5 (BAS)

GOD WANTS US TO BE HAPPY

No, I am not about to start pitching the prosperity gospel or any similar "health and wealth" nonsense. As we saw in the previous chapter, we are not defining the good life in terms of perpetual cheerfulness, and we are not defining it in terms of yachts, sunny beaches, affordable household appliances, or a well-tailored suit. "Happy" in this context is about flourishing. It is about living the good life by doing what humans were designed to do. Philosophers approach this topic from the perspective of virtue ethics, asking what kind of people we are supposed to be and what characteristics we must acquire in order to live as that kind of person.

Philosophers are not the only ones who ask these kinds of questions about how humans are to live well. Historically, most Christian thinkers have understood the moral life to be the pursuit of happiness (Mattison, 2008). In this chapter, we will consider some of the contributions made by biblical scholars and theologians to the question of human flourishing and begin to sketch out what a Christian positive psychology might look like when constructed on a foundation of biblically informed ideas about the human condition.

HAPPINESS IN THE BIBLE

Some people have the impression that the Bible teaches "pie in the sky" while ignoring the present life. "Fast on bread and water now, feast on steak and lobster in the life to come" (Kaczor, 2015, p. 21). The reality is, though, that the Good Book has quite a lot to say about the good life in the here and now (Strawn, 2012). In contrast with the Stoic doctrine that the only thing required for happiness is virtue, and also in contrast with the heretical Gnostic doctrine that the material world is entirely evil (making happiness a matter of escaping the material world), a biblical understanding of happiness is grounded in the goodness of creation and in the belief that humans are meant to participate in God's joy in creation (Fretheim, 2012). A well-lived life as described in the Bible includes family and friends (MacDonald, 2012), a peaceful and well-ordered community, a joyful and prosperous home life, and lots of good food and drink (Lapsley, 2012). Christians "don't have to differentiate between spiritual and sensual happiness. They belong together" (Moltmann, 2015, p. 8). We were created to live the shalom of flourishing and delight, and the fact that we do not all enjoy such a life is a consequence of the fall (Plantinga, 1995), not of any inherent evil in material existence.

In the Old Testament, much of what we find on living well involves the Hebrew word *asher*, which may be translated as "happy," "blessed," or "fortunate." None of these English words, however, precisely capture what is meant by *asher* (Brown, 2012). Rendering *asher* as "happy" puts us back into the problem we covered earlier: our tendency to equate the word *happy* with positive emotional gratification. "Blessed" reminds us that the good life is a gift from God, but it does not adequately capture the human effort that also goes into living well. "Fortunate" makes it sound too much like the good life is a matter of luck, which lines up with Aristotle but not with the Bible (MacDonald, 2012; Nussbaum, 2001). When the Psalms tell us that "blessed is [somebody]" (e.g., Psalm 1:1), we are being given guidance about what we can do to contribute to a life well lived. Ellen Charry (2010) refers to her theology of happiness as "asherist," arguing that most of God's commands for us "outline an obedient, rewarding, and wise life that can be lived now despite grief from sin and life's contingencies" (p. 173).

The Greek word *makarios* functions in the New Testament similarly to how *asher* does in the Old Testament. *Makarios* has also been translated as "blessed" or "happy," and the same English-language difficulties apply (Holladay, 2012). One key passage relevant to this project is the Sermon on the Mount, specifically the Beatitudes (Matthew 5:3-12). The Beatitudes is a list of eight "blessed are those who . . . " statements, and the word "blessed" here is a translation of *makarios* (for this reason, the statements are called "makarisms"). Those who cultivate the characteristics described in these makarisms are living the kind of life that points toward the kingdom of God, which will be rewarded when the kingdom arrives in its fullest. These characteristics also help us toward true happiness in the present life (Harrington & Keenan, 2005). "To put it more simply, Aristotle's 'secular' *eudaimonia* becomes Christianity's spiritual *makarios*" (Pennington & Hackney, 2016, p. 3). We may therefore, as we attempt to construct a Christian positive psychology, look to the Beatitudes as one source of our ideas about living well (Roberts, 2000).

THEOLOGY AND FLOURISHING

As we saw in the last chapter, Nancey Murphy (2005c) proposes that we construct our Christian positive psychology by adopting MacIntyre's teleological conceptual structure, building our understanding of flourishing by asking three questions: (1) What is the character of untutored and ungraced human nature? (2) What is the character of ideal human existence? (3) What are the means by which the transition can be made from (1) to (2)?

This process of transitioning from the "starting point" of basic human nature toward the teleological goal of living fully as humans are meant to live is described by theologians as "sanctification" (Kotva, 1996). Hoekema (1987) defines sanctification as "that gracious operation of the Holy Spirit, involving our responsible participation, by which He delivers us as justified sinners from the pollution of sin, renews our entire nature according to the image of God, and enables us to live lives that are pleasing to Him" (p. 61). The word *sanctified* means to be set apart to something, with the additional meaning of one's character fitting that status as set apart (Procksch & Kuhn, 1964). Christians are set apart to God, and that should be reflected in our lifestyle and character as it already is in our status (Bavinck, 1899/2008). Although the Christian is a new creation, sin continues to be an active factor, so sanctification also involves a reduction of the remaining evil, as well as an increase in the new nature as a controlling force in our thoughts, feelings, and behaviors (Hodge, 1872/2001).

A complete exploration of theological anthropology is beyond the scope of this text, but readers are encouraged to continue their engagement with this topic, starting with the "doctrine of humanity" section of a good systematic theology or two (examples abound) and expanding from there into the scholarly theological literature on human nature (even more examples abound). We will not concern ourselves at this point with anthropological issues such as dualism versus monism, human origins and interpretation of Genesis 1–2, or the question of free will (even though all of these are psychologically relevant topics and worthy of further investigation). Here we will focus on two concepts: our creation in the image of God and our status as fallen creatures.

"To be human means to be made in the image of God" (Sherlock, 1996, p. 95). If there is any theological concept that must serve as a ground for the development of a Christian psychology, it is this one. What exactly our status as image-bearers entails, however, is not made clear in Scripture, and Grenz (1994) describes this issue as "perhaps the single most debated topic of Christian anthropology" (p. 168). A number of human characteristics have been put forward as definitive of the *imago Dei*, ranging from our rational capacity to our free will to our upright physical posture (Grenz, 1994; Hughes, 1989; McDonald, 1981; Sherlock, 1996). Horton (2011), however, argues (as have many recent Christian scholars) that attempts to locate the *imago* somewhere within the individual self are a mistake. We are inherently relational beings, so who we are will be found *between* rather than *within*. This theological approach also corresponds with many developmental and social psychological findings regarding the social nature of the self (Balswick, King, & Reimer, 2016; Harter, 1999; Morf & Mischel, 2012).

Stanley Grenz (2001) connects this relational *imago* to trinitarian theology. Grenz points to the renewal over the past several decades of the "social trinity," a way of looking at the triune God as three persons who, while continuing to be three distinct persons, exist in loving relational unity (the term used to describe this intimate unity of mutual indwelling is *perichoresis*). If this is the nature of the triune God, and we are created in God's image, then the functioning of our human nature will involve our own limited form of *perichoresis* (Knabb, Welsh, & Alexander, 2012), characterized by living "in communion with God and others in mutually giving and receiving relationships" (Balswick, King, & Reimer, 2016, p. 37).

Grenz (2001) calls this the "ecclesial self." This view of human nature will inform our project of constructing a Christian positive psychology.

One consequence of our status as created in the image of God is that humans are afforded tremendous value and dignity (McDonald, 1981). As God's creation, we have origins that are unambiguously good (Wolters, 1985). Further, as image-bearers, we have a special place in creation (Grenz, 1994) and an exalted status above the other animal species (Hughes, 1989). That goodness, though corrupted by the fall, is not entirely eradicated by it (Sherlock, 1996). Christian positive psychologists may therefore find themselves resonating with the idea that humans are built with "inherent growth tendencies" (Ryan & Deci, 2000, p. 68) and that flourishing involves discovering ways to foster that growth by providing nutritive and supportive environments (Browning, 1987; Dueck, 1995).

Since the *imago Dei* is not entirely eradicated, we remain relational beings created for covenant, so mature functioning will be found in mutually reciprocating covenant relationships (Balswick, King, & Reimer, 2016). This approach fits well with Christopher Peterson's (2013) claim that positive psychology's message concerning the good life is that "other people matter" (p. 127), as well as research concerning the deep power of relationships (Baumeister & Leary, 1995). Sabates (2012) claims that a Christian approach to social psychology would be grounded in the belief that "humans, by virtue of having been created in God's image, have an intrinsic relational nature that includes a genuine capacity for other-centered care" (p. 68).

That's the good news. Now for the bad news: the fall. Although we were created to exist in loving community with God and others, and so to cultivate God's shalom of flourishing and delight, we broke covenant, broke shalom, and in so doing broke ourselves (Plantinga, 1995). This failure and fallenness create the intense duality of the human condition: we are "a mixture of good and evil, of godly beauty and diabolical hideousness, of unlimited potential and of tragic failure. In theological terms, we are God's good handiwork, but we have fallen into sin" (Grenz, 1994, p. 181). So if someone asks whether Christianity is optimistic or pessimistic about human goodness, the answer is "yes." Positive psychologist Ellen Berscheid (2003) sees a fundamental conflict between a view of humans as either "teeming with innate malignancies toward other humans" or a view of humans as "eager to love other humans and to be loved by them" (p. 44). A Christian would respond to Berscheid by saying that the reality is not "either-or"; it is "both-and." The optimist is correct; we are born with innate goodness and a disposition toward growth and thriving, and these can be thwarted by unhealthy environmental conditions (the corruption of our social systems, for example, is also a result of the fall). But the pessimist is also correct; we are (post-fall) born with innate badness and a disposition toward shalom-breaking and failure, even in the presence of nutritive environmental conditions (Hackney, 2014). This explains "why humans can conceive of aesthetic ideals but not create them, can long for a perfect world but not fashion one, can hope for genuine love but seldom express or experience it, can remember and anticipate Paradise yet sense it eluding us" (Ellens, 1989, p. 41).

This situation is inescapable. The doctrine of original sin is the claim that humans are, from birth, characterized by "attitudes, orientations, propensities and tendencies which are contrary to God's law, incompatible with his holiness, and found in all people, in all areas of their lives" (Blocher, 1997, p.18). We are predisposed both to fall short of the shalom that God established for the flourishing and wholeness of creation and to resist divine restoration of shalom (Plantinga, 1995), leaving us chronically misoriented in our motivations and prone to failure in our attempts to attain moral goals (Delkeskamp-Hayes, 2007). We are "estranged from God in all our powers, indisposed to do what is right in God's sight, and deeply inclined to do what is wrong" (Shuster, 2004, p. 160), and we are incapable of eliminating this tendency by our own power (Horton, 2011).

This position will put Christian positive psychologists at odds with many of our secular colleagues. As I argue elsewhere (Hackney, 2014), mainstream positive psychology is characterized by an unbalanced optimism when it comes to the basic goodness of human nature. While some positive psychologists hold to a balanced view of human goodness and badness (e.g., Peterson & Park, 2003; Brown & Holt, 2011), many create a false dichotomy by placing optimistic and pessimistic views in opposition to each other, rather than holding them as complementary, and denigrating pessimism as somehow unscientific. Martin Seligman (2002) caricatures anthropological pessimism in *Authentic Happiness*, calling it "the rotten-to-the-core dogma" (p. x), blames its existence on the unfortunate survival of the religious doctrine of original sin in the modern world, makes the bold claim that "there is not a shred of evidence that strength and virtue are derived from negative motivation" (p. xi), and declares that "if there is any doctrine this book seeks to overthrow, it is this one" (p. x). Berscheid (2003) says psychology's emphasis on the negative is the result of "popular assumptions" that human nature is innately bad, and she argues that positive psychology's ability to understand humans depends on a willingness to jettison pessimistic "assumptions" of human nature and embrace "the *fact* that, far from being born predisposed to be hostile toward other humans, it appears that we are innately inclined to form strong, enduring, and harmonious attachments with others of the species" (p. 45, emphasis mine). Similarly, Dacher Keltner's contribution to positive psychology's "declaration of independence" in the *Handbook of Positive Psychology* (Snyder & Lopez, 2005) includes a dismissal of pessimistic psychological theories as "assumptions about human nature" and a claim that "positive psychology offers an alternative, *scientific* approach to human nature" (Snyder et al., 2005, p. 763, emphasis mine). Note the consistent message here: these positive psychologists claim that pessimism is the result of unscientific assumptions and premodern dogmas, while optimism comes from embracing modern scientific facts.

These strongly optimistic psychologists are not naive. They do not wish to ignore the reality of dysfunction and evil. But then where does the "badness" of humanity come from? Linley and Joseph (2004) claim that all evil can be explained by "the absence of facilitative social-environmental conditions, rather than as an inherent aspect of human nature per se" (p. 718). This idea that an innately good humanity is forced into evil by bad circumstances can be traced at least as far back as Rousseau in 1762, and it continues to influence the field of psychology. Examples include Deci and Ryan's (2000a) claim that self-determination theory can fully account for the "darker sides of human behavior" in terms of the effects of "need thwarting contexts" (p. 319) and Philip Zimbardo's (2004) belief that evil comes from bad situations causing good people to do bad things.

What does this mean for positive psychologists? I argue (Hackney, 2014) that the unbalanced optimism in mainstream positive psychology carries dark consequences, which we will consider in more detail in chapter twenty-four. One thing I will point out here is that a Christian positive psychology will emphasize combating the self as vital to flourishing, while our secular colleagues focus more on the cultivation of that which is good in humans. As Stalnaker (2006) puts it, "For beings like us, the cultivation of virtue requires the restraint and redirection of certain impulses, as well as the cultivation of others" (p. 20). We will explore this further as we consider topics such as self-control (chapter eleven) and guilt (chapter twenty-two).

Now we consider the telos, the end or goal of the journey of sanctification. A happy life is a life that is oriented toward the telos and is making progress toward that telos. It is therefore of central importance to ask at what telos we are aiming. As we saw in the previous chapter, any psychological theory that describes flourishing, happiness, mental health, or maturity will be based on a particular vision of the good life, whether the theorist acknowledges it or not. Much of our current positive psychology implies a telos of human functioning grounded in individualism and subjective gratification.

This subjective individualistic telos does not fit well with a Christian view of the human condition. We believe that humans were created for a purpose and that this purpose is not to please ourselves. For example, the Westminster Catechism includes the teleological question, "What is the chief and highest end of man?" The accompanying answer given is, "Man's chief and highest end is to glorify God and fully to enjoy him forever." This idea that humanity's purpose is found not in ourselves but in God runs across multiple Christian traditions. Just to give a few more examples, in the Heidelberg Catechism we are told that God created humans "so that they might truly know God their creator, love him with all their heart, and live with God in eternal happiness, to praise and glorify him"; in the Catechism of the Catholic Church God is said to have created us that we may "share in his own blessed life"; in the London Baptist Confession Adam and Eve are described as having been created for a "life to God" and equipped with everything they needed for that purpose.

N. T. Wright's (2010) take on that "life to God" is that the telos of humanity is for us to serve as God's "royal priesthood" (1 Peter 2:9). We fulfill the royal function when we reflect God's wisdom and goodness in ruling creation, and we are fulfilling the priestly function when we reflect creation's praise back to God. One should note that this royal priesthood function is not about forcefully exerting domination over the present world but anticipating and pre-paring for our rule over the eschatological earth. This telos connects back to human-ity's original (pre-fall) role as caretakers of creation (Grenz, 1994; Horton, 2011) and as agents of shalom (Plantinga, 1995). When the Lord establishes his new heaven and new earth (Revelation 21:1), we will finally do what we were designed to do, and we will finally do it right. Grenz (2001) con-nects this eschatological perspective to his social trinitarian view of the *imago Dei*. We were created, he argues, to live in loving community with each other and with God, and this will find its fulfillment when we are perfected in the likeness of Christ: "The humankind created in the *imago Dei* is none other than the new humanity conformed to the *imago Christi*, and the telos toward which the Genesis creation narrative points is the eschatological community of glorified saints" (p. 18). When we finally do what we were designed to do, we will finally be the image of God we were intended to be.

One particular psychological implication of this eschatological perspective is Wright's (2010) take on "authenticity." The idea that we should be "true to ourselves" has a high degree of cachet in our current society (Taylor, 2007), influenced in part by the humanistic psychologists' emphasis on self-actualization (e.g., Rogers, 1961) and existential psychologists' calls for authen-ticity (e.g., Wood et al., 2008). In current positive psychology, Seligman's (2002)

belief that the good life is about subjective gratification could be seen as another example of this. But the self-concept is multifaceted, containing many kinds of self-knowledge, as well as multiple "selves" (Swann & Bosson, 2010). So to which "self" should we be true? Wright (2010) argues that we should be true to our eschatological selves, the royal-priestly selves we will one day be when the kingdom of God is fully actualized. This form of authenticity is more about living in the present in a way congruent with the character we are becoming instead of congruent with whatever characterizes the present self.

"The final goal of sanctification," says Hoekema (1987), "can be nothing other than the glory of God" (p. 88), and the more a person progresses in sanctification, the better that person will perform the will of God for the glory of God (Ames, 1629/1968). The way we fulfill that ultimate goal is by living a life of love involving "fellowship with God, with one another, and with all creation" (Grenz, 1994, p. 446). And the way we become fit members of that community is by cultivating a Christlike character. Sin involves a perversion and destruction of the image of God in hu-manity, and sanctification involves a reversal of that corruption. Thus Hoekema (1987) refers to sanctification as "our renewal in the image of God" (p. 66; see also Colossians 3:10), and William Ames claims that the end of sanctification is "the purity of God's image" in the person (Ames, 1629/1968, p. 169).

The image of God finds its full expression in Jesus (Colossians 1:15, 19; Hebrews 1:3), which means that sanctification, the renewal of humans in the image of God, will involve ever-greater conformity to Christ (Grenz, 1994; Guthrie, 1981; Hoekema, 1987; Murray, 1955). Among the other reasons for Jesus' life, teaching, death, and resurrection, one of his purposes on earth was to show us true humanity. In Jesus we see "the complete structure of what it is to be man, in his threefold relationship to God, the neighbor, and nature. Here is also the highest quality of what it is to be man, as love and freedom. Here human existence has reached its full maturity and therefore has fully become God's partner and instrument" (Berkhof, 1986, p. 303). Christ provides a prototype of human flourishing, a prototype that we should look to as we construct a Christian psychology of flourishing. We look to Jesus for our definition of human nature as it could be if it realized its telos, and sanctification can be seen as the closing of the gap between living the life we live now and living the life Jesus demonstrated (Boice, 1986).

According to Murphy (2005b), a description of the Christlike telos should feature the self-renouncing actions of Jesus. Murphy makes use of the term *kenōsis* ("self-emptying"; see Oepke, 1964) to describe this self-sacrificial principle. In Philippians 2:5-7, we are told to have the same mindset as Christ, "who, though he was in the form of God, did not count equality with God a thing to be grasped, but emptied himself, by taking the form of a servant, being born in the likeness of men" (ESV). Murphy (2005b) embraces kenotic renunciation of self as her formal description of the primary virtue of the ideal human. Research proposed by Murphy (2005c) toward developing a Christian psychology of flourishing would involve an

examination of kenotic versus nonkenotic ways of thinking, feeling, and behaving. Examples of such research topics include leadership styles, forgiveness, nonviolence, altruism, and the undermining of materialism. Clements and Mitchell's (2005) discussion of minimally coercive parenting is an example of what this approach might look like, as is Laporte's (1997) use of the word *kenōsis* to describe psychological maturity. Knabb, Welsh, and Alexander (2012) claim that kenotic self-giving is how we move from self-centered individualism to a healthy interrelatedness in which we find our true relational self by living in community with others. We become ourselves by dying to self.

In addition to having a different vision of basic human nature than our secular colleagues and a different vision of the telos of flourishing, a Christian positive psychology will also feature a unique perspective on how flourishing is accomplished. As Becker and Marecek (2008) note, "Positive psychologists conceive of flourishing as something determined by individual choice and attained by private, self-focused effort" (p. 1777). In contrast, the process by which sanctification progresses includes both responsible human activity and divine sovereignty, and scholars who address sanctification strive to find an approach that adequately addresses both aspects. Sanctification is a work of the Holy Spirit (Philippians 1:6; 1 Thessalonians 5:23; 2 Thessalonians 2:13), not human effort. At the same time, though, humans are called to a life of strenuous exertion as they battle against the evil that remains in them (Galatians 5:17; Colossians 3:5-10; Hebrews 12:1) and strive toward the development of a more Christlike lifestyle and character (Acts 24:16; Philippians 2:15; 2 Peter 1:3-8; 1 Timothy 4:15-16). We can see this dual nature of sanctification in Philippians 2:12-13, in which Paul encourages believers to "work out your salvation with fear and trembling, for it is God who works in you to will and to act in order to fulfill his good purpose." When Revelation 19 describes the church as the bride of Christ, the bride is "given" fine linen by God, but we are told that this linen represents "the righteous acts of the saints" (Revelation 19:8 ESV).

Outside of Scripture, this dual nature is also seen in Calvin's *Institutes*. In dealing with sanctification, Calvin (in book three) urges Christians to strive "with continuous effort" toward a life of increasing goodness, but at the same time he reminds us that "in no respect can works serve as the cause of our holiness" (Calvin, 1559/1960, p. 783). If we overemphasize the work of God in sanctification to the exclusion of human effort, that leads to the errors of passivity (the idea that God will give me a Christlike character while I sit on my rump and do nothing) and antinomianism (the idea that, since nothing I do will make me holy, I might as well live as sinfully as I wish). Overemphasizing human effort to the exclusion of the Holy Spirit leads to errors of legalism and self-righteous pride (Berkouwer, 1952). Berkhof (1986) claims that a proper definition of sanctification needs to include both the "activation" (sanctification requires our earnest effort) and "relaxation" (sanctification occurs as organic growth regardless of effort) models simultaneously, using one to correct the other. Hoekema (1987) also takes the perspective that we must understand

sanctification as an act of God in which we also are active: "God works in us the entire process of our sanctification—both the willing of it and the doing of it. The harder we work, the more sure we may be that God is working in us" (p. 71).

What is the role for psychology in the process of sanctification? The immediate danger in developing a "psychology of sanctification" is that considering the psychological cultivation of character strengths and virtues in this context could fulfill Berkhouwer's (1952) criticism of the tendency to degrade sanctification into nothing more than moralistic self-improvement, with the accompanying "insidious self-esteem" (p. 129) of the Pharisee. Charles Taylor (2007) describes the degradation of spiritual transformation to mere moralizing as another outcome of secularization and the barrier it erected between transcendence and the immanent frame.

On the other hand, it would also be wrong to entirely ignore a potentially valuable resource. William Ames (1629/1968) considered it "testing God" to desire something good, but at the same time, to "relinquish ordinary means appointed by God and to expect him to provide for them at their wish" (p. 275) or to refuse "the means necessary for it, as a person does in this world who desires health and continuance of life and yet rejects medicine or food" (p. 276). While I share the desire to avoid the error of reducing sanctification to human effort, we are provided with both divine and mundane resources for the living of our lives. In keeping with Ames's examples, we see that healing is described in the Bible as a gift of the Holy Spirit (1 Corinthians 12:7-11), and we are told to pray for healing in times of sickness (James 5:14). We are also told not to worry about food, because God knows our needs (Matthew 6:25-26). That being said, we still seek out medical doctors when sick and restaurants when hungry. This is not a rejection of God as long as we give thanks and glory to God for healing when we recover and for the food he provides.

The same principle can be applied to the humanities and social sciences. Preaching the gospel is fully dependent on the power and guidance of the Holy Spirit (Mohler, 1992), but expositors can draw unproblematically from scholarly work in communication, psychology, cultural studies, and philosophy in the construction of effective messages (Chapel, 1994). The Spirit of God is a spirit of reconciliation, and many Christians pursue the practice of peacemaking and conflict resolution as a way of living in step with that Spirit (Swartley, 2007), but those Christians see no hypocrisy in employing theoretical and methodological resources that arise from non-Christian scholarship on conflict resolution (Kale, 2003). The growth of Christlike character in the believer is, as we have seen, first and foremost the work of the Holy Spirit, but the possibility exists that research into virtuous development might be useful in providing practical guidance for the "human effort" side of this process (Worthington, Griffin, & Lavelock, 2019).

The word *sanctify* means to set something apart, and sanctification involves cultivating the kind of life that flows from that set-apart status. Bavinck (1899/2008) points out that early Christians endorsed and practiced specific virtues, "aware that by these virtues they were distinguishing themselves from the world and called themselves the people of God" (p. 237). If the cultivation and exercise of Christian virtues makes us distinct from the world, as well as making us better equipped to glorify God and live in community with him, then this would satisfy both definitions of sanctification. A Christian approach to positive psychology would also fulfill both definitions, as it would be an approach that is distinct from the rest of positive psychology and an approach that equips us to better fulfill our roles as psychologists: attempting to understand the human condition and improve human lives.

SUGGESTIONS FOR FURTHER READING

Balswick, J. O., King, P. E., & Reimer, K. S. (2016). *The reciprocating self: Human development in theological perspective* (2nd ed.). IVP Academic.

Charry, E. T. (2010). *God and the art of happiness*. Eerdmans.

Dieter, M. E., Hoekema, A. A., Horton, S. M., McQuilkin, J. R., & Walvoord, J. F. (1996). *Five views on sanctification*. Zondervan.

Grenz, S. J. (2001). *The social God and the relational self: A trinitarian theology of the imago Dei*. Westminster John Knox.

Mattison, W. C., III (2008). *Introducing moral theology: True happiness and the virtues*. Brazos.

Strawn, B. A. (Ed.). (2012). *The Bible and the pursuit of happiness*. Oxford University Press.

Part Two

POSITIVE
SUBJECTIVE
EXPERIENCES

Chapter Four

HAPPINESS

My whole house is great; I can do anything good.
I like my school, I like anything, I like my Dad, I like my cousins,
I like my aunts, I like my Allisons, I like my Mom, I like my sister,
I like my hair, I like my haircuts, I like my pajamas, I like my
stuff, I like my room, I like my whole house! My whole house
is great! I can do anything good! Yeah yeah yeah yeah!

Four-year-old YouTube celebrity "Jessica"

Hedonic Psychology

Despite the importance that people give to feeling happy, happiness is one of the least examined emotions (Averill & More, 2000). Back in chapter one, I put some effort into establishing that positive psychology is not "happyology" or the psychology of smiley faces. However, this does not mean that positive emotion is outside the domain of positive psychology. When Seligman and Csikszentmihalyi (2000) introduced positive psychology, one of the three core topics they put forward as focuses of the field was positive subjective experience, stating that "the hedonic quality[1] of current experience is the basic building block of a positive psychology" (p. 8).

To begin with, we need to consider the place positive emotion occupies in our conception of the good life. Operating from a eudaimonist perspective, hedonic pleasure cannot itself be the telos of authentic happiness, but it can be seen as a legitimate component of a life well lived. "Pleasure," says Martha Nussbaum (2015), "is not identical with happiness, but it usually (*not* always) accompanies the unimpeded performance of the activities that constitute happiness" (p. 227). Emotion researcher Caroll Izard (1977) describes joy as something that "just happens" (p. 231) while we pursue other goals. Existential psychologist Viktor Frankl (1984) argues that pleasure finds its proper place as a "side effect or by-product" (p. 125) of a good life, not as its goal. Frankl's claim is supported by researchers who have found that, while experiencing happiness is often associated with well-being, pursuing happiness itself as a goal is associated with experiencing less happiness (Mauss, Tamir, Anderson, & Savino, 2011)

---

[1]Hedonic: "relating to pleasure"

and more loneliness (Mauss, Savino, Anderson, Weisbuch, Tamir, & Laudenslager, 2011), as well as increased severity of mood disorders (Ford et al., 2014; Ford, Mauss, & Gruber, 2015). So we begin this examination of happiness guided by the principle that happiness is important but is not itself the good life.

When Martin Seligman launched the positive psychology movement with his presidential address (Seligman, 1999), he announced the formation of the Templeton Positive Psychology Prize (the largest monetary prize in the APA at the time), intended to honor excellent positive psychology research. The first recipient of the prize was Barbara Fredrickson for her work on positive emotion.

WHAT IS HAPPINESS GOOD FOR?

One of the central questions that animates Fredrickson's research concerns the function of positive emotion. At a certain level, the functions of negative emotions are easier to discern. Anger, for example, involves marshaling our motivational energy toward the elimination of threats and frustrations; disgust helps keep us free from contamination; fear is our danger sense (Izard, 1977). Anger pushes us to attack, disgust to expel, fear to flee, and so on. But happiness does not really solve a problem, and the behaviors that are motivated by positive emotions are not nearly specific enough to be described as one-to-one reaction tendencies (Fredrickson, 1998; Fredrickson & Levenson, 1998). Instead, positive emotions tend to signal that a goal has been reached or that progress is being made toward a goal (Scheier & Carver, 1988; Carver & Scheier, 1990).

Fredrickson (2000) argues that positive emotions have in common the fact that they "all share the ability to broaden people's momentary thought-action repertoires and build their enduring personal resources, ranging from physical and intellectual resources to social and psychological resources" (p. 219). She refers to this approach as the "broaden-and-build" theory of positive emotion. Rather than equipping us to deal with situation-specific crises, positive emotions are about adding new cognitive, behavioral, and social "tools" to our psychosocial toolboxes in the form of new ideas, new and deeper friendships, creativity, exploration, cooperation, and play. These tools become useful later, when we have need of them in the pursuit of goals and solving of problems (Cohn & Fredrickson, 2009).

This approach has found support in a number of studies. Derryberry and Tucker (1994) review research on mood and attention, concluding that negative mood narrows our attentional resources, while positive mood broadens them. Positive emotion is also associated with more cognitive flexibility (Isen & Daubman, 1984) and creativity (Isen, Daubman, & Nowicki, 1987). Researchers have also found positive emotion to enhance our social functioning (Fredrickson, 1998; Harker & Keltner, 2001). People are more willing to trust others (Dunn & Schweitzer, 2005) and demonstrate fewer prejudicial biases (Isen, Niedenthal, & Cantor, 1992; Dovidio, Gaertner, Isen, & Lowrance, 1995; Johnson & Fredrickson, 2005) when they feel happy. In addition, people are more likely to respond favorably to those who appear happy (Harker & Keltner, 2001).

A Joyful Heart Is Good Medicine

Generally speaking, positive emotion is good for us (Fredrickson & Joiner, 2002). Lyubomirsky, King, and Diener (2005) reviewed the research literature and concluded that experiencing more frequent positive affect predicted better outcomes across a number of domains, including career success, relationship satisfaction, medical health, social engagement, and coping ability. One of the classic studies in this area is the famous "Nun Study" (Danner, Snowdon, & Friesen, 2001). As part of an ongoing longitudinal study, 678 members of the School Sisters of Notre Dame have undergone annual physical and mental assessments, allowing researchers access to their records and agreeing to donate their brains for study after their deaths. Of those, around two hundred joined the order during a time in which sisters were being asked to write their autobiographies. Danner and colleagues coded these narratives, recording the amount of positive emotion expressed in each. When compared against outcomes six decades later, autobiographical happiness predicted a longer lifespan. The most cheerful nuns tended to live around a full decade longer than the least cheerful nuns. This finding is of great scientific interest, since members of a religious order tend to have so much in common (same gender and marital status, same occupation and income, similar diets, similar activities, similar access to medical care, and so on) that many possible explanations for the relationship between emotion and well-being are controlled for.

Lefcourt, Davidson-Katz, and Kueneman (1990) found the expression of positive emotion to be associated with improved immune system functioning. Laughing resulted in increased production of antibodies, with greater effects seen in those with better senses of humor (but see Martin, 2001, and our discussion in the next chapter for reasons to interpret these findings with caution). Fredrickson et al. (2000) argue that another possible pathway by which positive emotion improves physical health is by "undoing" the deleterious effects of negative emotions. It is well-known that long-term experience of negative emotions increases the risk of medical conditions, ranging from heart disease to the common cold to longer wound-healing time (Booth-Kewley & Friedman, 1987; Leventhal & Patrick-Miller, 2000). Fredrickson and colleagues (2000) first created anxiety in their participants by requiring them to prepare a speech in a very short time, then followed that by showing them one of several possible film clips designed to elicit specific emotions (contentment, amusement, sadness, and neutral emotion). Compared to the sadness group and the neutral control group, the heart rates of the participants in the two positive-emotion groups returned to baseline more quickly, supporting the authors' claim that positive emotions help to undo the physiological strain put on our systems by negative emotions.

Can There Be Too Much Happiness?

In the Elizabethan epic *The Faerie Queene*, heroic knights serve as personifications of virtues (one character represents faith, another represents justice, and so on). Book Two involves the virtue of temperance (moderation and self-control) embodied in the character of Guyon.

At one point Guyon attends a dinner hosted by three sisters. One sister, Perissa, represents excess, stuffing herself with meat and wine, laughing without control, and cheating on one lover with another. The other sister, Elissa, represents deficient happiness. She finds no joy in food or drink, refuses love, and faces the world with frowns and scowls. Between the two is Medina, striking the virtuous balance between the two extremes. We will return to the virtue of temperance in chapter eleven; for now, consider the message that too much laughter and merriment is just as bad as not enough laughter and merriment. Is that right? Is there an optimal level of positive emotion?

Fredrickson and Losada (2005) had their participants report on their experiences of positive and negative emotion over a twenty-eight-day period. They calculated the ratio of positive to negative emotions and compared that ratio against measures of psychological and social functioning. They found that optimal flourishing tended to occur around a ratio of 2.9 (almost three positive emotions for every negative emotion). Dropping below three positive emotions for every one negative emotion was associated with worse outcomes. Fredrickson and Losada also found an upper limit, though. Above 11.6, the relationship between positive emotion and flourishing breaks down. So experiencing more than eleven positive emotions for every negative emotion could also be a problem. Medina (the virtuous middle sister) may be on to something.

Or maybe not. Fredrickson's work has come under heavy attack. Brown, Sokal, and Friedman (2013) criticized Fredrickson and Losada (2005) on multiple levels, accusing them of using inappropriate equations and using them poorly. Fredrickson (2013) countered that, while there might be problems with the mathematics involved, the evidence for an optimal positivity ratio remains solid. A partial retraction was given (Fredrickson & Losada, 2013), in which the authors stated that perhaps the thresholds were not exactly 2.9 and 11.6, but the evidence still supported the central claim of an optimal range of positivity. More arguing ensued, which can be found in the September 2014 issue of *American Psychologist*. While the answer to "how much happiness is the right amount" might not range exactly from 2.9 to 11.6, there is evidence that flourishing is found in that median range between excess and deficiency (Grant & Schwartz, 2011).

SUBJECTIVE WELL-BEING

Happiness can be considered as a trait as well as a state (Diener, 1984). While Barbara Fredrickson has focused primarily on happiness as a temporary emotion, others have wanted to know about happiness as a stable characteristic that varies between individuals. Who are the happy people? Why are some people happier than others? Is there anything we can do to make people happier? Psychologists who concentrate on these kinds of questions often define happiness in terms of subjective well-being (SWB), which Diener (2000) defines as "people's cognitive and affective evaluations of their lives" (p. 34). SWB, which is measured by a variety of instruments, consists of three components: "experiencing high levels of pleasant emotions and moods, low levels of negative emotions and moods, and high life satisfaction" (Diener, Oishi, & Lucas, 2009, p. 187). Within this approach to happiness, the focus is on "the satisfaction of a single general desire: the desire for our life overall to go as we want. To be happy is therefore to be satisfied with our life as a whole" (Mulnix & Mulnix, 2015, p. 5).

Like Martin Seligman (see chapter seven) and Philip Zimbardo (see chapter sixteen), Ed Diener "was a card-carrying member of the Dark Side before he helped define the field of positive psychology" (Larsen & Eid, 2008, p. 2), having spent a substantial part of the 1970s studying aggression and deindividuation (the psychology of dangerous mobs). In 1980, however, Diener surprised his colleagues and students at the University of Illinois by swerving his career into the understudied topic of happiness. Diener describes the eighties as a time when happiness was "a backwater research area" (Jarden, 2012, p. 88) that, to draw from the well of Rodney Dangerfield, didn't get no respect, no respect at all. Early in his career, Diener was talked out of working on happiness on the grounds that it was not worthy of scholarly attention (Biswas-Diener, 2009), and later several of his colleagues even tried to block Diener's promotion to full professor because they saw the topic as "flaky" (Diener, 2008).

Once the positive psychology movement got underway, though, Diener and his colleagues in happiness research found themselves increasingly the recipients of interest and attention. Today, Ed Diener is one of the leading figures in positive psychology and one of the most influential psychologists altogether, having been cited by others over 30,000 times (Jarden, 2012).

Ed's son, Robert Biswas-Diener, has gone on to become a prominent positive psychologist in his own right, contributing to our understanding of the role that culture plays in happiness (e.g., Biswas-Diener, Vittersø, & Diener, 2005) and publishing positive psychology books for professionals and the general public (e.g., Biswas-Diener, 2012). Happiness research is now "arguably the hottest topic of contemporary social science" (De Vos, 2012, p. 182).

SHINY HAPPY PEOPLE

A number of theories have been put forward to explain why some people are happier than others (Diener, Oishi, & Lucas, 2009). One question that might be asked is, are some people naturally happier than others? Subjective well-being scores are not strongly influenced by age, sex, or race (Myers & Diener, 1995). Certain personalities seem to bring with them a proclivity to higher or lower subjective well-being scores. Reviewing the research literature on the topic, Diener, Oishi, and Lucas (2003) argue that the primary traits linking personality to SWB are extraversion (correlated with positive affect) and neuroticism (correlated with negative affect).

Researchers have carried out a number of studies that provide us with evidence of a genetically influenced "set point" for our happiness level (warning—incoming dad joke: I am biologically inclined to low levels of happiness. My blood type is B-negative). Tellegen and colleagues (1988) carried out a twin study in which they found that 40% of the variability in positive emotionality and 55% of the variability in negative emotionality are due to genetic influences. In other studies, researchers' estimates of the genetic influence on subjective well-being and its components have been as low as 25% (Bergeman et al., 1991) and as high as 80% (Lykken & Tellegen, 1996). Lykken and Tellegen's findings led them to the rather strong claim that one's long-term happiness is firmly established by one's DNA, which means that "trying to be happier is as futile as trying to be taller" (p. 189). Other researchers, though, allow for a substantially larger influence of environmental factors and behavioral habits on long-term happiness (Lyubomirsky, Sheldon, & Schkade, 2005).

One possible environmental aspect that could influence happiness is the surrounding culture (Diener & Suh, 2000). Average subjective well-being scores do vary considerably from one country to another (Myers & Diener, 1995), and many researchers have attempted to figure out what variables are influential in making one culture "happier" than another. Examining cultures in terms of their relative individualism versus collectivism is a perennial favorite among crosscultural psychologists (Markus & Kitayama, 1991; Triandis, 2001). The relationship between individualism or collectivism and SWB is complex. The basis for evaluating one's life as a good one (the cognitive component of SWB) can vary from one culture to another. Those in more individualistic cultures are more likely to display a positive correlation between self-esteem and SWB, while those in more collectivistic cultures are more likely to derive their happiness from interpersonal relationships (Triandis, 2000). Suh and colleagues (1998) found that those in individualistic cultures were more likely to derive their satisfaction with life from their emotions, while those in more collectivistic cultures were more likely to balance emotion and group norms. The connection with culture becomes even more complex when we compare subjective well-being scores against more "objective" outcomes, with individualistic cultures scoring high on SWB but also displaying higher rates of suicide and divorce (Diener, 1996), as well as depression and bipolar disorder (Weissman et al., 1996).

MONEY AND HAPPINESS

We've all been told that money can't buy happiness. Is that true? Well, it's complicated. In 1974, economist Richard Easterlin claimed that while average income was rising, average well-being was not. This has become known as the "Easterlin paradox," and many economists and psychologists have attempted to confirm, rebut, or modify Easterlin's proposition. Brickman, Coates, & Janoff-Bulman (1978) compared the impact of both extremely positive gains (winning a lottery) and extremely negative tragedies (paralyzation after an accident) against an equivalent control group. While one might predict that winning a large amount of money would create substantial long-term gains in happiness, the lottery winners' happiness was indistinguishable from the control group's less than a year after winning. The money created intense short-term happiness but not enduring changes in SWB. Similarly, the accident victims' levels of happiness had also returned to average within a year of their accident, a pattern that positive psychologists call the "hedonic treadmill." As an example of this treadmill in action, Easterlin (1995) reported that, although income in Japan increased fivefold between 1958 and 1987, average happiness scores showed no increase during that same period. Crosscultural research has also shown that economically advantaged countries are not necessarily happier than more impoverished countries. As Diener (1984) puts it, "Japan is not much happier than India, and Latin American countries are in some respects happier than European countries" (p. 553). Diener, Horwitz, and Emmons (1985) sent questionnaires to one hundred of the 1983 *Forbes* magazine top four hundred wealthiest Americans (forty-nine agreed to participate). Average happiness scores for the very wealthy were only slightly higher than those of the general population. "People who go to work in their overalls and on the bus are just as happy, on the average, as those in suits who drive to work in their own Mercedes" (Lykken, 1999, p. 17).

Others have put forward a modified version of the Easterlin paradox, in which they do predict a positive relationship between income and happiness but only at the lower end of the economic spectrum (Myers, 2000). When basic safety and survival needs are not being met, an increase in income represents a step out of poverty and a reduction in the misery associated with poverty. For example, there is a positive relationship between income and happiness in India (Argyle, 1999) but little to no relationship in Canada (Inglehart, 1990). Once basic needs have been met (Frey & Stutzer, 2002, claim that the threshold is around $10,000, while Layard, 2005, believes it to be closer to $20,000), the slope of the relationship between income and happiness levels off, with subsequent

increases in income producing little to no additional increases in happiness.

Is there an actual "zero point" in this pattern of diminishing returns? Stevenson and Wolfers (2013) searched for evidence of a "satiation" point (a point at which increasing income produces no additional happiness at all) by calculating multiple comparisons between income and happiness across different data sets. In all cases, a linear logarithmic relationship was found between income and happiness, not a curved relationship, as the modified Easterlin paradox would suggest. Stevenson and Wolfers conclude that the existing evidence does not support the modified Easterlin paradox. If the paradox had been valid, they argue, the relationship between income and happiness should have been stronger at the lowest levels of income, weaker toward the higher levels, and eventually nonexistent. But instead the linear relationship held steady across all income levels. But wait. Stevenson and Wolfers (2013) found the relationship between income and happiness to be a linear *logarithmic* relationship. A logarithmic scale is one in which the value of a variable is shown in increasing orders of magnitude rather than simple addition. In Stevenson and Wolfers's case, they displayed income (both personal income and national gross domestic product) on a scale that doubled between every point (1, 2, 4, 8, 16, 32 . . .) but happiness on a simple one-to-ten scale. This means that every one-point increase in happiness is associated with an increase in income, but the amount of increase in income gets increasingly large for every additional corresponding one-point increase in happiness.

To illustrate what this means, let's say that doubling personal income results in a one-point increase in long-term SWB (this is for illustrative purposes only; Stevenson and Wolfers's regression analysis is more complex). If you make $20,000 per year, that means you need an extra $20,000 per year for that one point of happiness. But if you were making $200,000 per year, you would need an extra $200,000 increase for the same happiness boost. And if you made $20 million per year, the same amount of happiness would "cost" $20 million in additional annual income. So when the relationship between income and happiness is expressed in standard linear terms instead of logarithmic linear terms, we see that increasing one's income does in fact become less "cost-effective" at procuring happiness the wealthier one becomes.

Jebb and colleagues (2018), in their study of income and happiness across multiple countries, did find a satiation point, so the possibility exists that Stevenson and Wolfers (2013) are incorrect. But even if there is no satiation point, the only real challenge that Stevenson and Wolfers (2013) present to the modified Easterlin paradox is that their data support the idea that the relationship levels off without ever truly reaching "zero." More money may have the potential to make you happier, but the more you accumulate money, the amount of happiness money can buy becomes smaller and smaller until it becomes microscopic, eventually no longer worth the effort (Boyce, Daly, Hounkpatin, & Wood, 2017). Further, making the accumulation of wealth one's goal in life carries toxic side effects. Researchers (e.g., Kasser & Ryan, 1993; Kasser & Ahuvia,

2002; Ryan et al., 1999; Vansteenkiste et al., 2006) have found that those for whom money-related goals are central tend to have worse social functioning and worse mental health, and Kasser et al. (2014) performed a set of longitudinal and experimental studies in which they found that well-being improves the less materialistic one becomes.

Income may be considered a contributor to happiness but not the most important contributor (Biswas-Diener, 2008). This ambiguity in the research literature matches the ambiguity we see in Scripture regarding material wealth. As we saw in chapter three, the Bible's portrait of a happy life is a life lived in the material world of creation with material comforts and prosperity (Fretheim, 2012; MacDonald, 2012). The happy have full barns and abundant livestock (Psalm 144:13) and eat the fruit of their labor (Psalm 128:2). The "wife of noble character" described in Proverbs 31 is active in investment and trade. In the new creation, we are shown houses and vineyards (Isaiah 65:21-22), along with the wealth and splendor of the nations brought to the New Jerusalem (Isaiah 60:5; Revelation 21:24). However, the pursuit of wealth must not be an end in itself or it becomes the "love of money" that we are warned against in 1 Timothy 6:10, and money becomes a rival master, usurping the place of God in our lives (Matthew 6:24). When money is seen as a tool to be used for helping others (Dunn, Aknin, & Norton, 2008) or pursuing enriching experiences (Van Boven & Gilovich, 2003), then it finds its proper place in the pursuit of the good life.

NATIONAL WELL-BEING

It is common to claim that "one purpose of social institutions is to increase the happiness of the people" (Mulnix & Mulnix, 2015, p. 8). Despite the limited contribution wealth makes to a life well lived, quite a lot of our public policy has as its goal the promotion of economic prosperity at both the individual (e.g., personal income) and national (e.g., gross domestic product) levels. Diener and Seligman (2004) argue that we in the Western democracies have reached a point at which increases in our economic prosperity will contribute little to our well-being. Connecting back to the previous section, the majority of us are living beyond the "satiation point" identified by Frey & Stutzer (2002). If that is the case, then the time may have come to shift our public policy priorities toward other goals. This is not to say that economic indicators or economic policies should be disregarded, but rather that the set of indicators we use to guide policy should be expanded to include more of those things money cannot buy.

Reviewing the research literature on subjective well-being, Diener and Seligman (2004) point to studies on divorce rates, religiosity, social trust, economic indicators, democratic governance, membership in voluntary organizations, and other correlates. They conclude that "nations high in average well-being can be characterized as democracies with effective and stable governments, as well as societies that are high in social capital, are religious, and have strong economies with low rates of unemployment and inflation" (p. 7), along with promotion of physical and mental health and support for strong marriages and stable families. Public policies that support such things might be a good idea (Diener & Diener, 2011; Deiner et al., 2009; Layard, 2005).

Diener and colleagues (2009) even believe that subjective well-being indicators can themselves provide insight into the nature of the good society. This brings us to an aspect of flourishing we have not yet touched on. As humans are inherently social beings (created for community, as Stanley Grenz put it), we can flourish only as social beings (Balswick, King, & Reimer, 2016; Fowers, 2015; Sabates, 2012). Discussions of the good life for humans must therefore include the question of the social conditions that foster or impede flourishing (more on this in our chapters on positive environments). The good life requires the good society. Unfortunately, the question of the good society is just as contentious and complicated as the question of the good life for an individual human, especially since we are now introducing politics into the mix. Is the good society one that maximizes individual freedom, as in classical liberal or libertarian thought? Is it the stable tradition of the conservatives? Is it the future egalitarian utopia of the progressives? What about socialism? Nationalism? Some kind of hybrid, like the European "Christian Democracy" parties? Who should a Christian positive psychologist vote for?

Already we have seen that constructing a Christian positive psychology requires that we engage in interdisciplinary study involving philosophy, theology, and biblical studies. If the good life requires a good society (Stoner & James, 2015), then it seems that we must also add social sciences such as political theory, sociology, and economics to our reading list. Readers beware: embarking on the study of human flourishing may set one off on a course of ever-expanding lifelong learning (not that this is such a bad problem to have).

Not surprisingly, given the political implications of this line of thought, Diener's proposal to use subjective well-being scores to guide public policy has caused a bit of a stir. In 2010, UK Prime Minister David Cameron gave a speech in which he announced that the Office of National Statistics (ONS) was going to begin tracking British well-being, with an eye to implementing policies that would improve it (Cameron, 2010). Since then, the ONS has been posting publications on its website (www.ons.gov.uk/peoplepopula tionandcommunity/wellbeing) tracking trends in UK happiness. Pushback in the media was immediate, with some criticizing the idea for being nice but irrelevant, others claiming that Cameron would just use the project to support a partisan agenda, others claiming that the project was a waste of money, and so on. A number of scholarly critiques of Cameron's plan involve the question of whether the government has the ability to increase happiness through public spending (Bjørnskov, 2012) or whether the people's happiness is the government's job at all

(Schwartz, 2012). Mulnix and Mulnix (2015) worry about the potential threats to liberty and self-determination that come with governments claiming to know what makes people happy. Robert Nozick (2015) and Martha Nussbaum (2015) each criticize the philosophical incoherence of the definition of happiness behind SWB research, urging caution lest we blunder ahead doing more harm than good by shaping policy around ideas about happiness that do not make sense.

SUGGESTIONS FOR FURTHER READING

Diener, E. (1984). Subjective well-being. *Psychological Bulletin, 95*(2), 542-75.

Diener, E., & Seligman, M. E. P. (2004). Beyond money: Toward an economy of well-being. *Psychological Science in the Public Interest, 5*(1), 1-31.

Fredrickson, B. L. (1998). What good are positive emotions? *Review of General Psychology, 2*(3), 300-19.

Lyubomirsky, S., King, L., & Diener, E. (2005). The benefits of frequent positive affect: Does happiness lead to success? *Psychological Bulletin, 131*(6), 803-55.

Mulnix, J. W., & Mulnix, M. J. (Eds.). (2015). *Theories of happiness: An anthology.* Broadview Press.

Volf, M., & Crisp, J. E. (Eds.). (2015). *Joy and human flourishing: Essays on theology, culture, and the good life.* Fortress.

Chapter Five

A SENSE OF HUMOR

*A priest, a rabbi, and a horse all walk into a bar. The
bartender says, "What is this, some kind of joke?"*

The word *humor* has changed considerably
over the centuries. Originally, the word
referred to one of four bodily fluids in
Hippocratic medicine (yellow bile, black
bile, phlegm, and blood), with imbalances
in these fluids producing physical ailments.
The humors were also thought to influence
moods and cause psychological disorders
(melancholy, which we now call depression,
was blamed on an excess of black bile). The
second-century Roman physician Galen
famously gave us a personality theory based
on the humors, in which one's temperament
was determined by whichever humor was
predominant in one's physiological makeup.

Starting around the sixteenth century,
we began to use the term *humor* to refer to
the mood states themselves (Ruch, 1998). If
someone were grumpy, that person might
be described as being in a dark humor, and
humoring someone meant going along with
that person's mood. The idea of humoring
someone's passing fancy led to the seventeenth-century use of the word *humorist*
to describe someone who was odd or
eccentric in an amusing way. That in turn
produced the nineteenth-century usage
where *humorist* referred to someone who
intentionally produced funny things to

amuse others (e.g., Mark Twain) and
humor to refer to the funny thing that
amused (Martin, 2010). Remnants of these
varied uses continue. The anatomy of the
eye includes the "aqueous humor" and
"vitreous humor," which are fluids. We still
talk about "humoring someone" when we
let them have their way, and the Good
Humor ice cream company was formed
in the 1920s, its name grounded in the
unarguable logic that ice cream puts
people in a happy mood.

The point of this chapter, though, is to
focus specifically on laughter and mirth.
I will also use it as an excuse to break out a
few of my favorite bad jokes, so humor me:
René Descartes walks into a bar. The bartender asks him if he wants a beer. Descartes
says "I think not" . . . and disappears.

WHAT IS FUNNY?

One of the earliest attempts to understand
humor from a psychological perspective
came to us from Sigmund Freud and his
1905 book *Jokes and Their Relation to the
Unconscious*. Freud thought laughter was
an outlet for psychological energy. When
joking, we are able to release some of our
socially unapproved impulses in a way that

is deemed socially acceptable. I might not be allowed to knock someone to the ground, but I can enjoy watching that person slip on a banana peel. This approach is an example of the "tension relief" theories of humor, in which the pleasure of jokes is said to come from the alleviation of psychological strain (Keith-Spiegel, 1972).

In the 1970s, cognitive researchers such as Paul McGhee (1971) and Jerry Suls (1972) gave us information processing–based accounts of humor grounded in the creative resolution of incongruity. While this approach to humor may be based on cognitive psychology, it has philosophical roots reaching as far back as Aristotle, who claimed that the core of humor involved "a mixture of surprise and deception" (Forabosco, 2008, p. 46). According to Suls (1972), joke processing involves two stages: First, we are presented with something that surprises us and violates our expectations, and second, we reinterpret the situation in a way that reaffirms our expectations. Our pleasure in jokes is derived from success at resolving these incongruities.

Forabosco (2008) connects this process to cognitive dissonance theory but with a difference: while cognitive dissonance requires that discordant elements be integrated so as to avoid the unpleasantness of dissonance, humor maintains a playful balance and a light touch, allowing the punchline to simultaneously fit and not fit. McGhee (1979) similarly points to the importance of a "playful" state of mind in understanding and appreciating jokes, and Martin's (2010) general description is that "humor is best viewed as a form of play that comprises cognitive (nonserious incongruity), emotional (mirth), and expressive (laughter) components" (p. 114).

Uekermann, Daum, and Channon's (2007) review of neuroscientific research on jokes and incongruity includes the possibility that the two stages are handled by different hemispheres of the brain, with the left hemisphere detecting the incongruity and the right hemisphere creatively resolving it. Consider the following joke: A skeleton walks into a bar and orders a beer and a mop. When we are told that a skeleton orders a beer and a mop, the left hemisphere of our brain reacts with confusion. (Why would anyone order a mop from a bartender? That doesn't make sense.) But with further processing, our right hemisphere makes sense of the statement. (If a skeleton tried to drink beer, it would fall through its bones onto the floor. The mop is for the puddle. *Now* I get it.) Some of those who focus on the relief of tension in humor (e.g., Shurcliff, 1968) argue that the pleasure derived from jokes results from one part of the brain starting to feel anxious (so to speak) about the punchline not making sense and another part of the brain reassuring (neurologically) the first part that everything is actually all right. Of course, neurocognitive processes are actually far more complicated than anything we can capture in such a simple description; see Bartolo et al. (2006) for an fMRI study in which multiple neural structures were shown to be involved in the processing of humor.

Another major approach to the psychology of humor involves a variety of "superiority" theories (Martin, 2010). This approach also has a long philosophical lineage, one that includes Aristotle and Thomas Hobbes. Those who hold to this approach believe the pleasure in humor comes from perceiving another person as inferior in some way to oneself, in line with Aristotle's claim in the *Poetics* that comedy comes from the enjoyment of a character's ugliness or defect (Keith-Spiegel, 1972). For example, anti-Nazi jokes were common during World War II, providing a way to portray Nazis as inferior to those whom they were attacking and oppressing (Obrdlik, 1942; Stokker, 1991). In the Academy Award–winning 1943 Disney short *Der Fuehrer's Face*, Donald Duck has a nightmare about living in a Nazi-controlled dystopia, subject to a variety of negative consequences of Nazi domination (bad food, no coffee, poor housing, overwork, abuse, and so on). Much of the humor in the cartoon comes from portraying the Nazis as ugly and idiotic, and the song featured in the cartoon encourages the audience to fart in Hitler's stupid face. (When I show students this cartoon, I point out the number of times a swastika is incorporated into a patch on the seat of a fat man's pants. It is difficult to have any respect for Nazis as "worthy opponents" while associating their symbol with a blubbery bottom. Talk about being the "butt" of a joke.) The psychological effect of such humor is that it bolsters the self-esteem of those who enjoy the joke by denigrating outgroups (Middleton, 1959; Priest, 1966; Wolff, Smith, & Murray, 1934) and those seen as immoral (Gutman & Priest, 1969; Hackney, 2011). Sexist jokes and ethnic jokes also serve as examples of the superiority approach, as does most political humor. Peterson and Seligman (2004) remind us that an appreciation of the positive effects of humor must be balanced with an awareness of humor's antisocial "dark side."

So, according to superiority theorists, my enjoyment of watching someone slip on a banana peel does not come from pent-up aggressive impulses; it comes from the fact that it is someone other than myself who is slipping on the banana peel. This interpretation is supported by McCauley and colleagues' (1983) findings that more aggressive cartoons tend to be rated as funnier. Even self-deprecating humor can be seen in this light. If I tell a funny story about the time I stuck my finger in a broken light switch (resulting in a painful electric shock), the audience laughs because they feel superior to me, and I laugh because I learned something important that day (don't stick your finger in a broken light switch), which makes my present self superior to my past self. And if I make fun of my current foibles, I am still asserting a form of superiority because I am displaying a level of self-awareness that enables me to criticize a part of myself.

BENEFITS OF HUMOR

While much philosophical and psychological ink has been spilled over the years on the idea that humor comes from such dark places as aggression and a sense of superiority, there does exist a parallel scholarship emphasizing humor as positive (Lefcourt, 2004). Jeffrey Goldstein (1982) claims that the division was originally between philosophers and physicians. While devotees of Aristotle focused on laughter's power to denigrate others, devotees of Hippocrates were more likely to claim that a hearty laugh was good medicine for both body and soul. Richard Mulcaster wrote in the sixteenth century about the power of laughter to overcome melancholy and chills. In the nineteenth century, Professor Gottlieb Hufeland called laughter "one of the most important helps to digestion with which we are acquainted" and recommended that meals be taken in the presence of joyful companions, as "the nourishment received amid mirth and jollity is productive of light and healthy blood." James Walsh, an early-twentieth-century American physician, wrote about laughter as an antidote to tension, giving us this summary statement: "The best formula for the health of the individual is contained in the mathematical expression: health varies as the amount of laughter" (Goldstein, 1982, p. 22).

In regard to physical health, we need to remember to steer clear of exaggerated claims found in certain self-help books and stick to proper research. Martin (2008) reviews the medical research on the health benefits of laughter and points out that many supposed physiological effects of laughter have not been empirically tested (muscular relaxation, for example) or have produced null results when tested (such as the release of endorphins). There is some evidence (e.g., Berk et al., 1989; Lambert & Lambert, 1995; McClelland & Cheriff, 1997) that exposure to comedy increases production of various physiological substances that are involved in immune system functioning. Nevo, Keinan, and Teshimovsky-Arditi (1993) exposed participants to humorous videos, finding a positive correlation between how funny the participants found the videos and how well they could tolerate pain. Relationships between laughter and pain tolerance were also found by Cogan et al. (1987) and Weisenberg, Raz, and Hener (1998). However, Martin (2001)

cautions us that these studies generally show small effect sizes and are beset by methodological weaknesses and the existence of alternate interpretations (such as the effect being due to increased neurological arousal or general positive affect rather than laughter specifically).

Connections between humor and physical health may be tenuous, but connections between humor and positive mental health are a bit more solid (Lefcourt, 2004; Peterson & Seligman, 2004). Generally speaking, it is good for us to have a sense of humor and to frequently experience mirth. Higher humor scores (as measured using the Values in Action Inventory of Strengths that we discuss in chapter ten) are associated with higher levels of life satisfaction (Peterson, Ruch, Beermann, Park, & Seligman, 2007), and Kuiper and Martin (1998) have found sense of humor to be associated with greater personal growth and self-esteem, along with lower levels of anxiety and depression. The effects of humor on well-being are moderated by several possible factors rather than being direct causes, and Martin (2010) places the positive psychological effects of humor into three categories: "(1) the ability to regulate negative emotions and enjoy positive emotions; (2) the ability to cope with stress and adapt to change; and (3) the ability to establish close, meaningful, and enduring relationships with others" (p. 270).

The connection between humor and positive emotion brings us back to the discussion in chapter four of Fredrickson's (2000) "broaden-and-build" theory of positive emotion, as well as the research on correlations between positive emotion and desirable outcomes (e.g., Lyubomirsky

King, & Diener, 2005). Exposure to humorous material has been shown to produce positive mood states (Ruch, 1997; Szabo, 2003) and reduce negative moods (Moran, 1996). Vilaythong, Arnau, Rosen, and Mascaro (2003) exposed participants to humorous material and found that it produced increases in hopefulness. In a solid validation of Mary Poppins, Dienstbier (1995) found that participants who watched a comedy video and then engaged in a boring task found the boring task more interesting and enjoyable.

There is an extensive literature on the use of humor as a way of coping with stressful circumstances, going all the way back to the earliest work on the topic in the field of psychology. Freud (1905/1960) claimed that humor was "the highest of [the] defensive processes" (p. 233). In a later paper, Freud (1928) discussed the role of humor in comforting the ego in times of suffering, maintaining that humor is rebellious and liberating. By treating the troubling situation as something light enough to jest about, humor represents "the ego's victorious assertion of its own invulnerability. It refuses to be hurt by the arrows of reality or to be compelled to suffer" (p. 2). This idea was taken up by George Vaillant (1977; 1992) in his project of recasting defense mechanisms as cognitive coping mechanisms (Vaillant, 2000). Defense mechanisms can be relatively more or less mature, with their level of maturity depending on how closely one stays in contact with reality and how often one engages in self-deception. Vaillant (1977) found that the most emotionally mature and highly functioning adults tend to employ the most mature of the defense mechanisms when coping with

life's difficulties. Humor, "one of the truly elegant defenses in the human repertoire" (p. 116), does not deny that the stressful event is occurring or lie to the self about the fact that it is stressful. Many of Vaillant's healthiest participants in his longitudinal studies were described as having excellent senses of humor. Researchers have repeatedly found the use of humor to be a powerful and effective tool for coping with hard circumstances (Lefcourt et al., 1995). The employment of humor is well-established as a coping mechanism among those who work in difficult jobs, such as prison clinicians (Maier, Bernstein, & Musholt, 1989), staff in maximum-security psychiatric units (Kuhlman, 1988), firefighters (Sliter, Kale, & Yuan, 2014), and law enforcement personnel (Burns et al., 2008).

Elgee (2003) claims that the need to deal with our mortality is the motivational "first cause" of all humor. Humor allows us to reclaim a sense of control in the face of the inevitability of death by choosing how we will react to it, "going on the offensive against the very concept of death" (Thorson, 1985, p. 206) and robbing death of some of its power over us (Stevenson, 1993). Perhaps the truest representative of this is the form of joking known as "gallows humor," defined by Maxwell (2003) as "humor which makes light of life-and-death, terrifying situations, or very serious matters" (p. 93) and given a much more picturesque description by Thorson (1985) as "death personified with pie in its face" (p. 206). Viktor Frankl (1984) describes the "grim sense of humor" that characterized his experiences as a prisoner in a Nazi concentration camp, connecting it to the exercise of "the last of the human freedoms—to choose one's attitude in any given set of circumstances" (p. 75). Henman (2001) relates a similar use of humor among American prisoners of war in Vietnam, using jokes and mockery to build camaraderie, gain a sense of control, and "strike back" against their captors. Martin (2010) connects the psychological "distance" that humor provides between the joker and the situation to the superiority theories of humor that we covered earlier: "Thus, as a means of asserting one's superiority through playful aggression, humor is a way of refusing to be overcome by the people and situations that threaten one's well-being" (p. 283).

In 2008 I attended an academic conference in Toronto hosted by the existentially oriented International Network on Personal Meaning. The theme of the conference that year was death, and one of the keynote speakers was Irwin Barker, a Canadian comedian with terminal cancer. For his keynote address, Barker got up on stage and performed a comedy set about his cancer. While this was a bit awkward for the audience (exactly how loudly is one expected to laugh and clap for a funny joke about a tumor?), developing and performing this routine was Barker's way of coping with his situation, and he turned it into a nationwide tour that was the subject of a CTV documentary titled *That's My Time*. Barker passed away in 2010.

The third function of humor that Martin (2010) points to as valuable in promoting positive mental health is its social function. As we will see in chapter thirteen, close relationships are a vital component of a life well lived, and humor can act as a social "lubricant" (Martineau, 1972) "intended to initiate social interaction and to keep the machinery of interaction operating freely and smoothly" (p. 103), though it has the potential to act as an "abrasive" when it does not go well. The shared experience of positive emotion establishes and solidifies social relationships (Shiota et al., 2004), and "in-jokes" are a part of almost every culture (Fine & De Soucey, 2005; Martineau, 1972). Consider this one: Captain Jack Harkness and Clara Oswin Oswald both walk into a bar and die. Jack walks out of the bar, and Clara walks into a different bar.

If you don't get the joke above, I know that you are not a *Doctor Who* fan (and I won't bother explaining the joke to you). Of course, if you are a serious *Doctor Who* fan, you are probably wondering why I didn't work Rory Williams into the joke somehow. Joking assumes that group members have a shared set of references (what Becker and Geer, 1960, call "latent culture") that influences their identities and views of the world, and whether or not someone gets a joke can be a signal indicating whether that person really belongs to the group (Fine & De Soucey, 2005). Everyone from Saskatchewan has heard the one about Saskatchewan being so flat that you can spend three days watching your dog run away from home. If any of you reading this are students, then try these out on your psychology professor to show that you are one of us:

- Why did Solomon Asch become a social psychologist?
  All of his friends were doing it.

- Why did John Bargh become a social psychologist?
  He liked it immediately.

- Why did David Buss become a social psychologist?
  Chicks dig social psychologists.

Humor can also help make groups more cohesive, with shared mirth creating a rapport between group members (Holdaway, 1988; Vinton, 1989). When done well (see Alberts, 1992, for a look at how complex a process this is), this cohesion-facilitation effect extends even to more aggressive forms of humor, such as teasing and insults (e.g., Terrion & Ashforth, 2002). In the case of humorous insults, the behavior of the joker provides cues that the putdowns are all in good fun, and the target responds by providing cues that he or she is a good-natured person and the putdowns are being received as nonserious.

Humor can also facilitate social interactions by smoothing over conflict, treating disagreements as less serious and therefore resolvable. "Jokes both direct attention away from potential discord and make the case that, because we can laugh together, there is no *essential* discord present" (Fine & De Soucey, 2002, p. 9). A well-timed joke can de-escalate tension, signaling that a potentially conflict-creating behavior was not "really" serious, allowing all involved to save face (Long & Grasser, 1988; Palmer, 1993). Humor can serve as a form of social control as well, keeping group members in line with moral expectations by delivering criticism in a form that reduces the likelihood of rancor (Martin, 2010). Dews, Kaplan, and Winner (1995) conducted a series of experiments in which they found that criticism presented with an ironic delivery was perceived by participants as more amusing and less insulting. Haas (1972) observed the use of teasing and putdowns among high-steel ironworkers to test the competence and trustworthiness of new coworkers and to facilitate apprentices' on-the-job training. The "play" element of the teasing allowed criticism and correction to take place while limiting the likelihood of conflict.

WHERE'S YOUR SENSE OF HUMOR?

Of course, any discussion of the functions and benefits of humor is complicated by the fact that some people have a better sense of humor than others. In the *CSV,* humor is treated as a character strength, defined as "(a) the playful recognition, enjoyment, and/or creation of incongruity; (b) a composed and cheerful view on adversity that allows one to see its light side and thereby sustain a good mood; and (c) the ability to make others smile or laugh" (Peterson & Seligman, 2004, p. 584). Being seen as having a "good" sense of humor is a social asset, helping to instill a positive reaction from others (Martin, 2010). Derks and colleagues (Derks & Berkowitz, 1989; Derks, Kalland, & Etgen, 1995) found that participants formed more positive impressions of someone who made others laugh, and experimental inducements of humorous interactions have been shown to increase attraction between strangers (Cann, Calhoun, & Banks, 1997; Fraley & Aron, 2004; Grammer, 1990). Cann and Calhoun (2001) found that participants tended to assume that someone with a good sense of humor was also intelligent, imaginative, pleasant, friendly, and considerate, and Sprecher and Regan (2002) found that participants consistently rated sense of humor as one of the most important qualities to look for in a friend, dating partner, or potential spouse. Masten (1986) assessed children's sense of humor and found higher humor scores to be associated with better intellectual ability, motivation, and peer relationships.

Most of the research on sense of humor has involved humor and stress in an attempt to examine the possibility that a sense of humor may serve as a buffer against the negative psychological effects of difficult situations (Martin, 1996). Martin and Lefcourt (1983) found that those who had higher scores on sense of humor scales showed less of a relationship between negative events and mood disturbance, supporting the idea that sense of humor may moderate the effects of stressful situations on a person's life. Nezu, Nezu, and Blissett (1988) found similar results, with sense of humor scores moderating the relationship between stressful events and depression. Kuiper, Martin, and Dance (1992) even found that participants with high scores had a mild positive relationship between stressful events and positive emotional outcomes, which they interpreted as indicating that people with a strong sense of humor might find some stressful events "invigorating."

Researchers have also inquired into the relationship between sense of humor and the ability to effectively cope with difficult circumstances. Kuiper, Martin, and Olinger (1993) assessed students using the Coping Humor Scale and then asked them about an upcoming exam in their Introductory Psychology class. Those with higher CHS scores were more likely to see the exam as a challenge instead of a threat and also got better grades on the exam. Kuiper, Mc-Kenzie, and Belanger (1995) also found that

CHS scores predicted the likelihood of perceiving a stressful situation as a challenge instead of a threat, and they found that those with a more pronounced sense of humor were better at looking at stressful situations from a different perspective. Drawing from research such as this, Kuiper (2012) argues that humor may be seen as a vital component of psychological resilience.

So, if having a strong sense of humor has such potential to improve psychological functioning, the next question many psychologists ask is whether it is possible to influence someone to have a better sense of humor. Cherkas and colleagues (2000) found that genetics contribute very little to one's sense of humor. Most of the variation in humor scores appears to be the result of environmental influences, especially from the individual's family (Fisher & Fisher, 1981; McGhee, Bell, & Duffey, 1986). There have been some attempts to develop training programs to improve one's sense of humor, but the empirical research literature on these programs is limited and not promising at this time (Lefcourt, 2004; Martin, 2010). A humor training program remains a possibility for some very funny psychologist in the future.

HUMOR AND PSYCHOTHERAPY

In our coverage of the superiority approach to humor, we briefly touched on self-deprecatory humor as a form of superiority over self. Martin (2010) connects this to the use of humor in the therapeutic process; the ability to laugh at one's faults can help the process of learning to overcome them and provide a freedom from the burden of perfectionistic expectations. Many prominent therapists have employed humor as a component of their work with clients. Viktor Frankl (1967a) employed a method he called "paradoxical intention" in his practice of logotherapy. If a client was struggling with an anxiety-producing problem, Frankl would teach that client to establish a humorous detachment by planning to deliberately enact the problem twice as often as before. For example, Frankl once worked with a man who stuttered severely and found that the only time he did not stutter was when he was actively trying to stutter. So the solution was to adopt this attitude: "Next time, I am going to stutter. I will stutter so hard that the walls shake with my stuttering! It will be stuttering of such epic proportions that the very stars will shout from the heavens, 'Knock it off with the stuttering already!'" By exaggerating the problem to the point of being funny, Frankl found that his client gained sufficient distance and control that he was able to eliminate the problem. Albert Ellis, creator of rational emotive behavior therapy (which we will discuss further in chapter seven) frequently incorporated humor into therapy, often in the form of silly songs and jokes (Ellis, 1977, 1987), as a form of combating the extreme and rigid thinking that rational emotive behavior therapy (REBT) practitioners believe to be at the core of their clients' problems. Gordon Allport (1950) said that "humor may throw an otherwise intolerable situation into a new and manageable perspective. The neurotic who learns to laugh at himself may be on the way to self-management, perhaps to cure" (p. 104).

While the empirical research on humor as a therapeutic tool is scarce, some researchers have demonstrated that the skillful use of humor may have positive therapeutic effects. Cai and colleagues (2014) found humor-based interventions to be effective when treating clients with schizophrenia. In a series of studies, Australian psychologists tested the effectiveness of a program they called SMILE (Sydney Multisite Intervention of Laughter-Bosses and ElderClowns) among residents of elder-care facilities (Brodaty et al., 2014; Chenoweth et al., 2013; Goodenough et al., 2012; Low et al., 2013; Low et al., 2014) and found the program to be helpful in decreasing some negative psychological variables while increasing happiness.

Holy Jokes

Christian perspectives on humor have varied over the centuries, and the differences in attitudes have usually flowed from preferences for some version of tension relief theory or superiority theory. Those who historically saw superiority as the basis of laughter thought it was immoral to elevate the self and to denigrate others by mocking them. Early church fathers such as John Chrysostom and Basil the Great condemned laughter. Basil famously pointed out that nowhere in the Bible do we see Jesus laughing, and he argued that there is never a proper time for laughter; a cheerful smile is enough for a true follower of God (Silvas, 2005). Chrysostom did not even permit the smile (Marciniak, 2014). The Puritans were famously down on laughter, and the seventeenth-century Quaker Robert Barclay wrote:

> It is not lawful to use games, sports, plays, nor among other things comedies among Christians, under the notion of recreations, which do not agree with Christian

silence, gravity and sobriety; for laughing, sporting, gaming, mocking, jesting, vain talking, etc., is not Christian liberty nor harmless mirth. (Layman, 1982, p. 5)

On the other hand, humor had a powerful defender in the middle ages, as Thomas Aquinas considered amusement to be a valuable rest for the soul (Joeckel, 2014). Medieval Easter celebrations included the *risus paschalis* (Easter laugh), in which it was considered inappropriate *not* to fill the church with joyful mirth in celebration of Jesus' victorious resurrection (Wilkens, 2019).

Believers can find biblical support for either approach. The author of Ecclesiastes calls laughter "folly" (but to be fair, he says that about everything under the sun) and tells us that sorrow is better than laughter (Ecclesiastes 7:3). Morreall (2008) points out that the most common mention of laughter in Scripture involves mockery. In 1 Kings 18, Elijah mocks the priests of Baal; in Psalm 37, God laughs at the wicked; and in Isaiah 14, God invites Israel to taunt the beaten king of Babylon. The superiority-based view of laughter, though, is balanced by certain passages in which laughter is the sign of a happy heart. The people laugh for joy in Psalm 126 when God restores the fortunes of Zion, and although he has called it folly, the author of Ecclesiastes nevertheless does say there is a time to laugh (Ecclesiastes 3:4). Wilkens (2019) sees humorous themes running through much of Scripture, including political satire in Esther and bathroom humor in Judges.

For the most part, Christian thinkers in the early modern era were more likely to follow the "superiority" perspective. It was not until the eighteenth century that theories of humor emphasizing incongruity

and tension relief rose to great prominence (Morreall, 2008). With this conceptual shift in our ideas about the root of humor came a shift in the overall tone of Christian attitudes toward humor. Søren Kierkegaard (1941a/1846) was a fan of the incongruity approach and considered humor to be the second-highest level of existential awareness (just below the religious sphere). In fact, Kierkegaard considered Christianity to be "the most humorous world view in history" (Morreall, 2008, p. 228), with its adherents willing to live in the dynamic tensions of the immense incongruities of the human condition.

In the twentieth century, Reinhold Niebuhr (1946), also an incongruity fan, pointed to the use of irony in many of Jesus' teachings and said that "laughter is the beginning of prayer" (p. 111). Karl Barth (1961) saw self-deprecatory laughter as the only natural result of a proper under-standing of the extreme oddness that God would bestow honor on humans, an ap-proach that also parallels incongruity theory. "Is not the contrast between man himself and the honour done him by God really too great for man to take himself ceremoniously, and not to laugh at himself, in his quality as its bearer and possessor? . . . Humour is the opposite of all self-admiration and self-praise" (p. 665). Wilkens (2019) similarly points out that, as humor is based on ironies, juxtapositions, and unexpected punchlines, a God who turns Saul the persecutor into Paul the apostle, who features a pregnant virgin in his plan for cosmic salvation, who uses a vine-munching worm to make a divinely commissioned prophet look like a whiny teenager, and who creates such a mass of contradictions and oddities as the human race has a good sense of humor indeed. Fred Layman (1982) points to several ways in which humor fits well within a Christian view of life, pointing to such things as the playfulness of God, the instances of joyful laughter in the Bible, and the idea that the ability to laugh at ourselves "saves us from pretentiousness and pomposity" (p. 14), making it a healthy reminder of our creaturely finitude. Samuel Joeckell (2014) argues that salvation, with Jesus freeing us from our burden of sin, produces the laughter of joy. Once we adopt the perspective that humor can be virtuous when done right, as well as vicious when done wrong, laughter can be seen as the overflowing of a heart full of joy, a grateful response to the Lord's gifts, and a path toward humility and wisdom.

Now then: A monk, a clone, and a Ferengi decide to go bowling together . . .

SUGGESTIONS FOR FURTHER READING

Layman, F. D. (1982) Theology and humor. *The Asbury Seminarian, 38*, 3-25.

Lefcourt, H. M. (2004). Humor. In C. R. Snyder and S. J. Lopez (Eds.), *Handbook of positive psychology* (pp. 619-31). Oxford University Press.

Martin, R. A. (2010). *The psychology of humor: An integrative approach*. Elsevier.

Thorson, J. A. (1985). A funny thing happened on the way to the morgue: Some thoughts on humor and death, and a taxonomy of the humor associated with death. *Death Studies, 9*(3-4), 201-16.

Wilkens, S. (2019). *What's so funny about God? A theological look at humor*. IVP Academic.

Chapter Six

FLOW

A good martial artist does not become tense, but ready.
Not thinking, yet not dreaming . . . and when there is
an opportunity, I do not hit. It hits all by itself.

BRUCE LEE

You are in an ecstatic state to such a point that you feel as though
you almost don't exist. . . . My hand seems devoid of myself, and I have
nothing to do with what is happening. I just sit there watching it in a state
of awe and wonderment. And [the music] just flows out of itself.

COMPOSER INTERVIEWED BY MIHALY CSIKSZENTMIHALYI

Many of us have had the experience of becoming so absorbed in an activity that we lose track of time, of extraneous stimuli, even of self. I sometimes had that experience while writing this book. In the 1960s, Hungarian psychologist Mihaly Csikszentmihalyi became interested in stories of artists who became so single-mindedly engaged in painting that they forgot to eat, forgot to sleep, and forgot to pay attention to things like pain and discomfort (Nakamura & Csikszentmihalyi, 2005). Csikszentmihalyi called this state of mind "flow," and his work in this area is one of the foundation stones of the positive psychology movement (Rich, 2013).[1]

THE CONCEPT OF FLOW

Csikszentmihalyi (2009) defines flow as "a subjective state people report when they are completely involved in something to the point of forgetting time, fatigue, and everything else but the activity itself. . . . The defining feature of flow is the intense experiential involvement in moment-to-moment activity, which can be either physical or mental. Attention is fully invested in the task at hand, and the person functions at his or her fullest capacity" (p. 394). Athletes call this being in "the zone." Writers experience the words flowing through them onto the page. Musicians lose themselves in a performance. Those who

---

[1] The pronunciation of *Csikszentmihalyi* often causes confusion among students of positive psychology. I ask forgiveness from those who may object to a drug reference in a Christian text, but the mnemonic that I find helpful is to imagine a young woman offering me a marijuana joint. Csikszentmihalyi is pronounced "chick sent me high." I sometimes joke with my students that the ability to both pronounce Csikszentmihalyi and spell it without looking it up automatically qualifies one for a master's degree in positive psychology.

have such experiences often report them as being intense and wonderful, the sort of thing that Abraham Maslow (1962) might call a "peak experience" (see Privette, 1983, for a proper comparison of peak experiences and the flow state). Flow experiences are so enjoyable that people will throw themselves into activities that are dangerous, time-consuming, and difficult and that show no promise of concrete reward in order to achieve them (Csikszentmihalyi, 2009).

The flow experience has the following characteristics: (1) "intense and focused concentration on what one is doing in the present moment," (2) "merging of action and awareness," (3) "loss of reflective self-consciousness," (4) "a sense that one can control one's actions," (5) "distortion of temporal experience," and (6) "experience of the activity as intrinsically rewarding" (Nakamura & Csikszentmihalyi, 2005, p. 90). Let's look at each of these characteristics more closely.

(1) Intense and focused concentration on what one is doing in the present moment. Activities that are likely to promote flow tend to be challenging, and successful performance requires that practitioners not let their minds wander. Jackson and Csikszentmihalyi (1999) recount the experience of a long-distance cyclist: "I rode for four hours one day in the rain and sleet, and I don't think I remember anything other than the white line on the road, going underneath for four hours. And the guy's wheel in front of me. For four hours, that's all I remember" (p. 25). Non-physical activities can also produce this level of exclusive concentration. A chess expert who is easily beating a novice

opponent can afford to let his or her mind wander, but facing a tough challenger is a different situation. One chess player said the following: "When the game is exciting, I don't seem to hear nothing—the world seems to be cut off from me and all there is to think about is my game" (Csikszentmihalyi, 1975, p. 40).

(2) Merging of action and awareness. This type of concentration is often so absolute that the practitioner can lose track of the self. In the same way the chess master has no spare cognitive resources left to attend to the world, people who are experiencing flow might have no spare cognitive resources for thinking about themselves, and that includes awareness of the self making a decision to act. Questions like "What am I doing here?" and "Am I doing it right?" fade from awareness (Csikszentmihalyi, 1975), and there is the sense that the action almost springs into being from nowhere. A composer describes it in this way: "My hand seems devoid of myself, and I have nothing to do with what is happening. I just sit there watching it in a state of awe and wonderment. And it just flows out by itself" (Csikszentmihalyi, 2014a, p. 142). Athletes in the "the zone" talk about amazing performances happening "automatically" (Jackson & Csikszentmihalyi, 1999). As I was preparing the first draft of this chapter, UFC fighter Lyota Machida faced off against Vitor Belfort in UFC 224. Machida finished the fight with a front kick knockout, and for those of us who enjoy combat sports, it was a thing of beauty. Belfort dropped his lead hand ever so slightly, and Machida's foot was in motion at almost the same moment, sliding into the hole in Belfort's defense and tagging him on the jaw. In a postfight interview (Simon, 2018), Machida said the kick was unplanned. It earned Machida a $50,000 "Performance of the Night" bonus, and Vitor Belfort announced his retirement from the UFC.

(3) Loss of reflective self-consciousness. The loss of self-focus that characterizes flow can be so complete that practitioners lose track of their own self-concept. A rock climber whom Csikszentmihalyi interviewed said that "one tends to get immersed in what is going on around him, in the rock, in the moves that are involved . . . search for handholds . . . proper position of body—so involved he might lose the consciousness of his own identity and melt into the rock" (Csikszentmihalyi, 1975, p. 43). This loss of self-awareness may be part of the reason for the enjoyable nature of the flow state. Focusing completely on accomplishing a goal allows one to exclude any stressful or upsetting thoughts (Csikszentmihalyi, 2009), which can be a relief. Csikszentmihalyi (1975) interviewed a dancer who described it as "a feeling that I don't get anywhere else. . . . I have more confidence in myself than at any other time. Maybe an effort to forget my problems. Dance is like therapy. If I am troubled about something, I leave it out of the door as I go in [the dance studio]" (p. 41).

(4) A sense that one can control one's actions. Despite the sense that one is being "carried along" by the flow experience or that the moves are spontaneously generating, there is no sense that the individual is out of control (Csikszentmihalyi, 1990). In fact, people who have reflected on what it feels like to be in flow report a sense of power and mastery (Csikszentmihalyi,

2009). Athletes report feeling "unbeatable," as if "nothing can go wrong" (Jackson & Csikszentmihalyi, 1999, p. 26), and a chess player described the experience as "a tyrannical sense of power. I feel immensely strong, as though I have the fate of another human in my grasp" (Csikszentmihalyi, 1975, p. 44).

(5) Distortion of temporal experience. One of the most common things reported about flow is that one loses track of time. Csikszentmihalyi (1990) describes the case of a young lawyer who finds flow in legal research: "She spends hours in the library, chasing down references and outlining possible courses of action for the senior partners of the firm to follow. Often her concentration is so intense that she forgets to have lunch, and by the time she realizes that she is hungry it is dark outside" (p. 40). Others report an alteration in their perception of the speed of events, with time seemingly speeding up and slowing down at once. A cyclist said, "It felt like you'd slowed everything down and made sure everything was right, everything was fluent. . . . It felt really quick, but everything felt slow at the same time" (Jackson & Csikszentmihalyi, 1999, p. 29).

(6) Experience of the activity as intrinsically rewarding. Csikszentmihalyi (1975) uses the term *autotelic* to describe this. We have seen the word *telos* many times by this point, meaning end, goal, or purpose. An activity is "autotelic" if the goal of the activity is the activity itself. There does not need to be a reward beyond the activity. A poet and rock climber whom Csikszentmihalyi interviewed put it this way: "The mystique of rock climbing is climbing; you get to the top of a rock glad it's over but

really wish it would go forever. The justification of climbing is climbing, like the justification of poetry is writing; you don't conquer anything except things in yourself. . . . The act of writing justifies poetry" (p. 47).

These experiences can be had in almost any domain of activity (Csikszentmihalyi, 2014b) as long as three conditions are met. The first condition is a clear set of goals for the activity. This shifts one's attention away from the self and lends focus. The second condition is a perception that the challenges inherent in the activity and one's level of ability are evenly matched. Flow states are not likely to be achieved if the activity is either impossible and frustrating (which creates anxiety instead of flow) or mind-numbingly easy (which creates boredom) but instead can be found in the "sweet spot" boundary between the two (Csikszentmihalyi, 1990). The third condition for the flow experience is clear and immediate feedback between the person and the environment (Csikszentmihalyi, 2014b), such that the person knows what to do in any given moment and knows how well he or she is doing at the activity. At the place where challenge and ability meet, "the individual operates at full capacity" (Nakamura & Csikszentmihalyi, 2005, p. 90), and Csikszentmihalyi considers this state of optimal absorption in one's activities to be a core feature of the good life. More on that toward the end of this chapter.

Flow has been measured using interviews (e.g., Csikszentmihalyi, 1975), questionnaires (e.g., Csikszentmihalyi & Csikszentmihalyi, 1988), and a real-time assessment approach called the experience sampling method (Larson & Csikszentmihalyi, 1983) in which participants are given pagers and instructed to go about their everyday activities but to stop and answer a brief set of questions whenever the pager goes off.

WHO FLOWS?

While the flow state is available to anyone, some people are more likely to experience flow than others. Csikszentmihalyi (2009) refers to such people as having an "autotelic personality." Such people possess "a general curiosity and interest in life, persistence, and low self-centeredness, which result in the ability to be motivated by intrinsic rewards" (p. 93); they are thus more likely to enter into flow states, stay in these states longer, and find them more rewarding. Some researchers have attempted to describe the autotelic personality in terms of the five-factor model of personality. Ullén et al. (2012) found flow-proneness to be associated with lower neuroticism scores and higher conscientiousness scores, as did Johnson and colleagues (2014). The negative correlation with neuroticism is not surprising, as the flow state can be short-circuited by worry and negative emotion. Highly conscientious people may be more likely to experience flow states due to their willingness to put in the necessary practice at challenging activities, and they are also more likely to experience positive emotion and intrinsic motivation (Ullén et al., 2012). Ross and Keiser (2014) found the same pattern involving neuroticism and conscientiousness but also found flow-proneness to be associated with lower agreeableness scores. This finding may seem odd, but the authors interpret it as evidence that people who are more likely to go their own way rather than conform to the crowd are more likely to engage in autotelic activities. Mosing and colleagues (2012) found dispositional flow-proneness to be moderately heritable, and the genetic connection may involve structure and functioning of the dopaminergic neurons in the dorsal striatum (de Manzano et al., 2013).

WHAT FLOW DOES FOR YOU

In addition to flow being an intrinsically enjoyable experience, Csikszentmihalyi (1990) argues that seeking out more flow experiences will improve one's quality of life. To begin with, finding flow in one's daily activities tends to make those activities more enjoyable, which means that those who flow at work are more likely to enjoy their work, and students who flow at school are more likely to find school enjoyable. Csikszentmihalyi and LeFevre (1989) used the experience sampling method to measure the relative challenge-ability balance people experienced while at work and while engaged in nonwork activities such as reading, playing games or sports, socializing, shopping, and doing chores. They found that people were three times more likely to be in flowlike situations (an optimal balance between high-level challenge and ability) at work than during leisure activities, and that challenge-ability balance contributed the most to participants' of positive affect, sense of strength and creativity, concentration, and satisfaction. It did not matter whether they were at work or at play; what mattered was whether they experienced flow. Moneta and Csikszentmihalyi (1996) found something similar among high school students: challenge-ability balance enhanced the positive enjoyment of activities both inside

and outside school. Keller and Bless (2008) found that participants who played the video game Tetris at a level that matched their ability enjoyed the game more and were more involved in the game.

The enjoyability and intrinsic motivation of flow states increase motivation to continue with an activity (Keller et al., 2011), which facilitates commitment and the growth of skill in the activity (Nakamura & Csikszentmihalyi, 2005). Heine (1996) found that students who experienced flow during the first part of a math course performed better in the second half. Csikszentmihalyi et al. (1993) conducted a five-year longitudinal study of high school students and found that those who experienced more flow in an activity were more likely to stick with it for the long term. Jackson and Csikszentmihalyi (1999) report that athletes who experience flow are motivated to continue with the sport, and flow has been found to be associated with superior athletic performance (e.g., Jackson et al., 2001; Stavrou et al., 2007).

Csikszentmihalyi (1990) argues that personal growth is the key to flourishing and that finding flow is the key to personal growth. By embracing challenges and finding joy in the moment through pursuit of goals, individuals develop into "autotelic selves" (more on that term later) and live happy and meaningful lives. As Moneta (2004a) describes it, flow has both direct and indirect effects on happiness. Flow "has a direct impact on subjective well-being by fostering the experience of happiness in the here and now" and "has an equally important indirect effect on subjective well-being by fostering the motivation to face and master increasingly difficult tasks, thus promoting lifelong organismic growth" (p. 116). Csikszentmihalyi and Hunter (2003) found flow to be a powerful predictor of happiness, and Csikszentmihalyi and Wong (2014) found participants' happiness scores to be the highest when they were in a flow state.

These benefits are more likely to accrue for those who already possess certain pro-flow personality characteristics. Those who score high in internal locus of control (the tendency to believe that the outcomes in one's life are the result of one's own actions rather than fate or powerful others) are more likely to find the balance of challenge and ability intrinsically enjoyable (Keller & Blomann, 2008), as are those who are more dispositionally oriented toward intrinsic motivation in general (Abuhamdeh & Csikszentmihalyi, 2009). Demerouti (2006) found that certain job-related characteristics predicted more flow at work but that flow translated into improved workplace performance only for participants who had high levels of conscientiousness.

Crosscultural differences can also play a role (Moneta, 2004a). Csikszentmihalyi (1990) claims the flow experience to be a human universal, "reported in essentially the same words by old women from Korea, by adults in Thailand and India, by teenagers in Tokyo, by Navajo shepherds, by farmers in the Italian Alps, and by workers on the assembly line in Chicago" (p. 4), and there are studies in which we see support for this claim. Similarities in the flow experience have been reported in Japanese (Asakawa, 2004), Dutch (Bakker et al., 2011), and Taiwanese (Wu & Liang, 2011) samples. But there may also be differences in the way people from different cultures find flow (Csikszentmihalyi & Asakawa, 2016). Moneta (2004b) found that Chinese participants were more likely to experience intrinsic motivation in low challenge–high skill conditions rather than the high challenge–high skill conditions predicted by the standard flow model. He interpreted this as an indicator that Chinese culture fosters a preference for expanding one's capacities in a more incremental manner, within domains in which one already has a degree of mastery, rather than the riskier high challenge–high skill balance preferred by others. Landhäußer and Keller (2012) caution us that most research on the effects of flow suffers from conceptual and measurement problems, so these findings should be held lightly, and more research is clearly called for, whether we are talking about the benefits of flow or individual and cultural differences.

INCREASING FLOW

For those who wish to increase the amount of flow in their lives, there are number of possibilities, most of which focus either on flow-conducive circumstances or cultivating the personal characteristics that make flow more likely. Rich (2013) suggests that parents and teachers should be on the lookout for activities that young people find autotelic and that societies increase their offerings of affordable possibilities for meaningful engagement (e.g., volunteer groups). In addition to seeking out pro-flow activities, it is possible for us to redesign environments and activities to make them more pro-flow, ensuring clear goals, timely feedback, and an optimal challenge-skill balance. Rathunde (1996) examined the family lives of talented high school students using the experience sampling method. Students who experienced more flow and intrinsic motivation in their school activities tended to come from families that provided both high levels of challenge (children were expected to take on more responsibilities and develop their capacities) and high levels of support (parents created an environment that was stable and consistent). Not only does such a family environment promote the development of high levels of ability, but it also tends to repeatedly expose children to high challenge–high skill activities. A school in Indianapolis (sadly shut down in 2016) tested the effects of structuring the classroom around flow principles (Whalen & Csikszentmihalyi, 1991). The school included a "flow activities room" that contained a variety of books, puzzles, and board games, and students spent forty minutes in the room three or four times a week. The activities were challenging and required concentration, but intrinsic motivation was fostered by allowing students as much free choice in the activities as possible. Whalen and Csikszentmihalyi (1991) conducted a preliminary study of the school and concluded that students were consistently experiencing flow, as well as growing in intrinsic motivation and the ability to focus.

Flow research has also found application in the workplace (Bakker, 2008). Demerouti (2006) found that job characteristics such as autonomy, feedback, and task variety increased workers' experience of flow on the job, and Bakker (2005, 2008) found autonomy, feedback, and support to be predictive of flow. Increasing flow at work can carry positive benefits for the worker

(Bakker, 2008) and can also improve the workplace experience of colleagues and the overall well-being of the organization (Bakker, 2005; Salanova, Bakker, & Llorens, 2006). Several organizations have begun to implement flow-related ideas, including a Swedish police force and a Volvo plant (Csikszentmihalyi, 2009).

Jackson and Csikszentmihalyi (1999) offer many suggestions for athletes who wish to increase their experience of flow in sports. They argue that sports are well-suited to flow because of the many challenges with which athletes are presented and that opportunities abound to find the optimal challenge-skill balance for the individual athlete. What is necessary for the athlete who wants more flow is to find that proper balance, avoiding the boring and easy as well as the impossible. In my own limited experience doing judo competitions, I once had the misfortune (due to the small number of competitors at this tiny regional tournament) of being placed in a bracket with three other judoka who were bigger than me, half my age, and double my belt rank. There was no flow there; I just got trounced. So athletes who are not experiencing flow in their sport might want to reexamine the level of challenge, and coaches are encouraged to pay attention to the challenge-skill match that they present to their players. Athletes can also be coached to be less self-focused as they perform, directing their attention to the actions of the sport in the present moment instead of internal doubts and external distractions. Establishing clear goals and timely feedback is also important.

Finally, there have also been applications of flow in psychotherapy. Nakamura and

Csikszentmihalyi (2005) say that "a given individual can find flow in almost any activity . . . working a cash register, ironing clothes, driving a car" (p. 91), and therapeutic applications of flow tend to involve looking for ways to assist clients in finding or creating more flow-conducive conditions in their everyday lives. Massimini, Csikszentmihalyi, and Carli (1987) used the experience sampling method as a real-time indicator of moment-by-moment well-being, monitoring the daily experiences of forty-seven students in Milan. The times when participants experienced a high challenge–high skill balance were the times when they felt happy, active, open, intrinsically motivated, free, and excited. The authors recommend that therapists "stimulate psychiatric patients to perform activities that are challenging, while also requiring relatively high skills" (p. 549) in order to promote mental health and continuing personal development.

CAUTIONS AND CONCERNS

Flow theory and research has been the subject of criticism. As mentioned above, Landhäußer and Keller (2012) point to methodological limitations in the research. Reiss (2000) criticizes Csikszentmihalyi for overemphasizing the centrality of flow to human flourishing, pointing to numerous other intrinsic motives that are not connected to flow, and Smith (2000) criticizes Csikszentmihalyi's approach as overly individualistic, saying Csikszentmihalyi focuses far too much on the subjective experiences of individuals instead of communal and relational functioning.

Although in one brief article Csikszentmihalyi (2000) states, "I do not claim that flow is the only means of reaching happiness" (p. 1163), that statement is in response to criticism of an earlier article (Csikszentmihalyi, 1999), in which he claims fairly explicitly that "happiness depends on whether a person is able to derive flow from whatever he or she does" (p. 824) and that if people "can experience flow working on the assembly line, chances are they will be happy, whereas if they don't have flow while lounging at a luxury resort, they are not going to be happy" (p. 826). In a later publication, Csikszentmihalyi (2014c) makes the bold claim that the quality of one's experiences "determines whether and to what extent life was worth living. Optimal experience [by which he means flow] is the 'bottom line' of existence. It is the subjective reality that justifies the actions and events of any life history. Without it there would be little purpose in living, and the whole elaborate structure of personality and culture would reveal itself as nothing but an empty shell" (p. 209). Add that to Nakamura and Csikszentmihalyi's (2005) claim that "a good life is one that is characterized by complete absorption in what one does" (p. 89), and we have a strong set of claims here, with Csikszentmihalyi drawing connections between flow and the telos of human functioning.

The first problem with this is that "flow is essentially an amoral psychological state" (Rich, 2013, p. 48). It is entirely possible to experience flow while engaged in activities that violate moral standards and are destructive to self and society. Harari (2008) discusses flow in combat, including the possibility of soldiers experiencing flow states while committing war crimes or fighting to support a brutal totalitarian regime. Flow has also been reported by speeding motorcyclists (Chen & Chen, 2011), strippers (Barton & Hardesty, 2010), and marijuana users (Hathaway & Sharpley, 2010). Csikszentmihalyi (1990) describes flow as an energy that can be used for beneficial or destructive ends, and he cautions readers that we should seek to "enjoy everyday life without diminishing other people's chances to enjoy theirs" (p. 70). Beyond that guidance, though, Csikszentmihalyi is unwilling to weigh in on what goals are truly worthy of pursuit, leading Harari (2008) to accuse flow theorists of ignoring the well-established tendency of humans toward self-deception and ignorance regarding the true nature of happiness.

If flow can be used for evil, then flow cannot be the supreme human good. In many ways, this parallels our discussion in chapters two and three about Martin Seligman and the telos of flourishing. As we saw, Seligman (2002) wants to describe the good life but is unwilling to "impose" a moral vision on others, leading him to a place where he cannot say that murderers or terrorists are not living good and meaningful lives. Similarly, Csikszentmihalyi (1990) claims that all values are relative and that life is inherently meaningless but that value and meaning happen when we do that which we think is meaningful: "From the point of view of an individual, it does not matter what the ultimate goal is—provided it is compelling enough to order a lifetime's worth of psychic energy" (p. 215). Csikszentmihalyi considers discovering a cure for cancer to be equally meaningful (to an oncologist) as

having the best collection of beer bottles (to a bottle enthusiast), and he refuses to pass judgment on whether Napoleon or Mother Teresa led better lives.

The goal of flourishing, Csikszentmihalyi claims, is to develop into an "autotelic self." Earlier in this chapter, we saw the term "autotelic" used to describe specific activities. When one is experiencing flow, activities are autotelic in that they are engaged in for their own sake. For one who flows while playing chess, the point of chess is playing chess; for one who flows while rock climbing; the point of rock climbing is rock climbing. There is no goal (telos) beyond the thing itself. Csikszentmihalyi's vision of flourishing is that we become people who have "relatively few goals that do not originate from within the self" (p. 209), lining up perfectly with Charles Taylor's (2007) description of our current historical era's elevation of the authentic self.

As Christians, we would decline to endorse this vision of flourishing. If we reject the individualistic telos and hold to the belief that the telos of human existence is to serve as God's royal priesthood (Wright, 2010) as a people perfected in the likeness of Christ, then our choices of goals can be objectively right or wrong. And if God does in fact exist, then values are not relative and life does have an objective meaning (more on that in chapter twenty-three). So we can celebrate Mihaly Csikszentmihalyi's contribution to our understanding of the flow state and seek to increase our own experiences of flow as a way of enjoying life and developing our capacities. These goals fit perfectly well within a Christian vision of flourishing. But we must part ways with our colleague when he goes beyond the data and begins to speak about values and meaning, and remain committed to our understanding of the good life for humans.

SUGGESTIONS FOR FURTHER READING

The June 2004 issue of the *Journal of Happiness Studies* is dedicated to crosscultural issues in the experience of flow.

Csikszentmihalyi, M. (1990). *Flow: The psychology of optimal experience*. Harper & Row.

Engeser, S. (Ed.). (2012). *Advances in flow research*. Springer.

Nakamura, J., & Csikszentmihalyi, M. (2005). The concept of flow. In C. Snyder & S. Lopez (Eds.), *Handbook of positive psychology* (pp. 89-105). Oxford University Press.

Rich, G. J. (2013). Finding flow: The history and future of a positive psychology concept. In J. D. Sinnott (Ed.), *Positive psychology: Advances in understanding adult motivation* (pp. 43-60). Springer.

Part Three

POSITIVE
COGNITIONS

Chapter Seven

OPTIMISM AND HOPE

Always look on the bright side of life.
MONTY PYTHON

HOW MARTIN SELIGMAN DISCOVERED OPTIMISM

Martin Seligman, you will remember, is the ringleader of this "positive psychology" circus of ours, introducing the movement in 1998. One of the key turning points in his career that led him toward positive psychology was his work in optimism. What led him to optimism was his study of depression—and some very unhappy dogs.

The year was 1964. As he describes it in *Learned Optimism* (1990), Seligman had just embarked on his graduate studies at the University of Pennsylvania, doing research under the direction of Richard Solomon. The researchers found that when laboratory dogs were given the chance to escape painful electric shocks, they just whimpered and waited for it to be over. Why didn't they try to escape? What if, Seligman thought, the problem was that the dogs had learned that there was no escape from shocks? Solomon was skeptical. Remember that this was the mid-1960s and behaviorism was still the king of scientific psychology, so the notion that a dog could learn an abstract concept like helplessness was more than a little heretical. But Seligman and a colleague (fellow

graduate student Steven Maier) were given the green light to attempt to run a study exploring this possibility.

Seligman and Maier (with reluctance, having some moral unease over inflicting pain on innocent animals even in the name of science) set up a design in which dogs were exposed to shocks. One group of dogs could turn the shock off by pressing a panel with their noses, while another group had no such option. Later, they were all given the chance to escape the shocks by hopping over a short wall. The "escapable shock" dogs learned to jump fairly quickly. The "inescapable shock" dogs lay down and whimpered and did not try to escape.

They had done it. Seligman and Maier had shown that dogs can learn helplessness. They published their findings (Seligman & Maier, 1967) and in so doing made a lot of behaviorists angry. According to Seligman (1990), the great B. F. Skinner himself sent a note saying their article made him "physically sick," and Seligman was cornered in a men's room at a conference by an irate Skinnerian who took him to task for publishing nonsense about dogs learning concepts.

This experimental shot across the bow of behaviorism became known as "learned helplessness" theory, and the theory played a substantial role in the cognitive revolution (Peterson, Maier, & Seligman, 1993). In a number of studies (see Maier & Seligman, 1976, for an early review), it was shown that when organisms (including humans) are in circumstances in which their actions have no connection to outcomes, they learn that nothing they do matters. Helplessness leads to decreases in motivation, cognitive problems, and emotional disturbance. In humans, this can manifest as depression (Seligman, 1975). If life continues to kick us in the head (workplace problems, cash flow problems, relationship problems, health problems, and so on) no matter what we do, with no way to escape or make it better, we learn that nothing we do matters.

Learned helplessness theory was later revised to include the concept of attribution in the mix (Abramson, Seligman, & Teasdale, 1978). Attribution is the process by which humans explain the cause of an event. In regard to the learned helplessness theory of depression, Abramson and colleagues posit that when bad things happen, we generate three-dimensional attributions. The three dimensions are internal/external, global/specific, and stable/unstable. An attribution is internal if the cause of the event comes from inside the person (e.g., I slipped and fell because I am clumsy) and external if the cause of the event comes from outside the person (I slipped and fell because the road is icy). An attribution is global if the cause holds true in general (my attempt to ask someone out on a date failed because I am ugly) and specific if the cause holds true only for something particular (my attempt to ask

someone out on a date failed because there was a giant booger hanging from my nose). An attribution is stable if the cause is likely to persist over time (I got a bad grade on the psychology exam because I stink at psychology) and unstable if the cause is more short-lived (I got a bad grade on the psychology exam because I was exhausted that day).

Our attributions will be combinations of all three dimensions. For example, "My attempt to ask someone out on a date failed because there was a giant booger hanging from my nose" is internal (the problem is with me, not the woman I was asking out), specific (the problem is just with that one booger, not my entire appearance), and unstable (somebody get me a tissue, then the problem is solved). By contrast, a different attribution for the same event, such as "My attempt to ask someone out on a date failed because she is biased against Alaskan men," is external (the problem is with her, not me), global (her bias is general in nature), and stable (she will probably still find Alaskan men unattractive in the future).

We focus here on attributions for unhappy events because those tend to be stronger predictors of psychological outcomes than attributions for successes (Peterson, 1991). People who are in the habit of making internal, global, and stable attributions in response to failures or disappointments are more prone to depression (Peterson & Seligman, 1984; Seligman et al., 1979; Sweeney, Anderson, & Bailey, 1986). Seligman (1990) claims that "a pessimistic explanatory style is at the core of depressed thinking" (p. 58), and this approach to depression has resulted in therapeutic techniques intended to retrain people with depressive attributional styles toward something less pessimistic. Now, what does any of this have to do with positive psychology? Seligman also claims that people's lives can be improved by training them in the opposite of learned helplessness: learned optimism.

If failures and disappointments are consistently interpreted as being the result of internal, global, stable causes, then this establishes a generalized expectation that future events will also be the result of factors before which we are helpless (Seligman, 1990). That is pessimism. Optimism is the opposite. Peterson and Seligman (2004) define optimism as "thinking about the future, expecting that desired events and outcomes will occur, acting in ways believed to make them more likely, and feeling confident that these will ensue given appropriate efforts to sustain good cheer in the here and now and galvanize goal-directed actions" (p. 570). Optimists have a generalized expectation that future events will be the result of factors that are within their control.

OPTIMISM RESEARCH

Generally speaking (see below for exceptions to the "generally"), optimism is associated with good outcomes. Optimists tend to experience less distress in difficult circumstances ranging from entering college to dealing with AIDS (see Carver, Schier, Miller, & Fulford, 2009, for a review). Optimists tend to have more satisfying relationships (Fincham, 2000). Optimistic mothers-to-be are less likely to develop postpartum depression (Carver & Gaines, 1987). Optimists are better at sticking to diet and exercise plans

(Shepperd, Maroto, & Pbert, 1996). Optimistic politicians are more likely to get elected (Zullow & Seligman, 1990). Optimists tend to cope with crises in ways that are more problem-focused and engage in less denial and avoidance (Scheier, Carver, & Bridges, 2001). Optimists tend to be more successful in school (Peterson & Barrett, 1987), in sports (Seligman et al., 1990), and at work (Seligman & Schulman, 1986). So the message so far appears to be that optimism is good; therefore, be optimistic. Malouff and Schutte (2017) performed a meta-analysis on a variety of interventions and found them to be effective at increasing optimism. So what are some ways in which optimism can be cultivated?

One possible source of a person's attributional style is their upbringing. Some researchers (e.g., Seligman et al., 1984) have found that children's optimism tends to parallel the optimism of their mothers, and Franz et al. (1994) found that children who are raised in happy and supportive homes are more likely to be optimistic. This line of research fits well with the work done by attachment theorists (as we will see in more detail in chapter thirteen) showing that caregivers who are warm and responsive to their children teach them a basically optimistic stance toward the world (e.g., Bartholomew & Horowitz, 1991).

Seligman (1990) recommends that parents encourage an optimistic explanatory style in their children from an early age. This can be done by modeling optimism (for example, how the parents talk about their own failures and disappointments) and by phrasing criticism in an optimistic way (for example, "You got in trouble because you didn't listen when I told you not to do that" is both unstable and specific, while "You got in trouble because you're a rotten little monster" is global and stable). Muller and Dweck (1998) found that when teachers praised children based on internal, global, stable characteristics (e.g., "You're so smart"), it carried the potential to teach children that both success and failure are a matter of stable traits rather than effort.

Our efforts to increase optimism may be somewhat constrained by genetic factors. Schulman, Keith, and Seligman (1993) conducted a twin study to see if there is any heritability to optimistic explanatory styles. More than 140 twin pairs completed a measure of attributional style, and researchers found that the correlation in optimism scores for the monozygotic (identical) twins (r = 0.48) was substantially greater than the correlation for the dizygotic (fraternal) twins (r = 0.00). Peterson and Steen (2005) are quick to point out that this does not mean there is an "optimism gene" (we've had quite enough nonsense from the media about there being a "[fill-in-the-blank] gene," thank you very much). As we saw in chapter four, we come with a genetically influenced happiness "set point," so it might be the case that we are born with a certain proclivity toward optimism or pessimism. That genetically influenced starting point, however, is only a starting point. Experience (including training) can still create significant change in our cognitive styles.

How to Be More Optimistic

Seligman (1990) grounds his method for cultivating optimism in the techniques of

Albert Ellis. Ellis (1962) is the creator of REBT, which he developed after reading the ancient Stoic philosophers and being impressed by what he read. As I very briefly mentioned in chapter three, the Stoic view of the good life is that happiness is entirely disconnected from our earthly condition (wealth, social status, and so on) and what matters is virtue. In Ellis's version of this approach, what matters is rationality. Our sorrows in life, Ellis argues, are not due to the things that happen to us; they are due to the way we think about those events. This is called the ABCs:

A: Adversity. (This is sometimes called the "activating event," which helpfully also starts with *A*.) This is the thing that happens. For example, let's say I have a disagreement with my father about my decision to become a psychologist (he wanted me to be an engineer).

B: Belief. Our beliefs about ourselves and the world shape our reactions. Keeping the example going, I hold the belief that I absolutely must have my father's approval, and that I just can't live without his approval.

C: Consequence. Because I see not having my father's approval as beyond my ability to handle, the disagreement causes me to suffer an emotional breakdown. It is important to see here that *A* does not cause *C*. *B* causes *C*.

In REBT, we are told to look for the beliefs that shape the consequences. Rational beliefs will lead to healthy outcomes, while irrational beliefs will lead to unhealthy outcomes. Irrational beliefs are typically rigid and extreme, and they involve absolute demands and catastrophic consequences ("I *must* have my father's

approval, or else I just *couldn't live with it.*").
The next steps in REBT are the DEFs:

D: Debate. Irrational beliefs are to be
challenged. What reasons do we have to
hold them? What evidence is there to back
them up? Is it really the case that I *must*
have my father's approval? Why so absolute? Aren't there people all over the
world whose parents disapprove of their
career choices? They seem to be surviving.

E: Effective beliefs. Irrational beliefs are
replaced with more rational versions that
are less rigid and involve less catastrophizing. Perhaps it would be better to think,
"I would like to have my father's approval,
but I will get along okay if I do not have it."

F: Functional emotions. With the
irrational beliefs disputed and replaced
with rational beliefs, our emotional distress
greatly lessens. An argument with my
father is no longer a life-or-death melo-
drama; now it is merely irritating.

The methods of learned optimism follow
these same principles, with an emphasis on
attribution. An optimistic attributional
style can be cultivated if we identify and
debate pessimistic attributions, replacing
them with healthier alternate interpretations. An important thing to bear in mind
here is that learned optimism is not "positive thinking" in defiance of the facts;
rather it is a careful and reasoned consideration of the facts. Seligman (1990) does not
advise readers to apply optimism in all
circumstances. There can be times when
optimism is not called for. Instead, he
advocates for what he calls a "flexible"
optimism in which we adapt our explanatory style based on the specific needs of the
moment. Crafting a political speech is an
excellent time for optimistic explanations

(as we saw, more optimistic politicians
tend to get elected), but counseling people
who are suffering is the wrong time for
optimistic explanations. There should also
be a cost-benefit analysis when choosing
to employ optimism. Better to be pessimistic about one's ability to successfully
drive home drunk given the potential
outcomes.

REBT has had an interesting relationship
with religion, and Christians who are
interested in positive psychology may find
that this complicates our relationship with
learned optimism. However, this need not
be the case. REBT is based on the idea that
our emotional troubles are the result of
irrational beliefs, and in his early publications (e.g., Ellis, 1960), Albert Ellis claimed
that all religion belonged in the category of
"irrational beliefs" that lead to psychological
disturbance. This could lead Christian
psychologists to avoid REBT and, possibly
by extension, learned optimism. However,
a look at Ellis's writings on religion shows
us that his views became more nuanced
and tolerant over time (Hackney, 2010d).
By the time we get to the year 2000 (seven
years before his death), Ellis had accepted
that even devout and absolutist believers
could be highly functioning people. Many
religiously active psychologists have
embraced REBT, considering Ellis's personal antireligious attitudes to be a separate
issue from the quality of his theory and
method (e.g., Robb, 1988; Nielsen, 1994).
Nielsen (1994) claims that REBT is actually
quite good for religiously active therapists
and clients, since both religion and REBT
focus on the power of belief and the
importance of challenging wrong beliefs,
and Robb (1988) considers many aspects of
REBT to be congruent with scriptural

teachings regarding how to live well. Ellis's own issues aside, Christian psychologists have little to worry about when it comes to REBT or learned optimism.

THE PESSIMISTS STRIKE BACK

Seligman's (1990) approach to depression involves the central claim that pessimism is the road to depression while optimism is the road to health. The situation turns out to be more complicated than that. One of the recurring messages in this text is that positive psychology is not "happyology" but is about high levels of functioning. This includes the healthy employment of "negative" thoughts, feelings, and behaviors when appropriate (Kashdan & Biswas-Diener, 2014; Parrott, 2014a). Guilt can be good when we do it right (see chapter twenty-two). So can anger (Hess, 2014). Researchers have followed up on Seligman's original work on optimism and pessimism, showing that pessimism can also be good when we do it right (Norem & Chang, 2002). So if you find yourself to be one of the "Eeyores" of the world, forever seeing the possibility of failure and disappointment, you are not doomed to psychological dysfunction. In this section, we will talk about healthy pessimism.

The connection between optimism, pessimism, and health is not straightforward. Pessimists do tend to experience more emotional distress than optimists (Carver, Scheier, Miller, & Fulford, 2009), and Rasmussen and colleagues (2009) found optimism to predict better physical health. However, Watson and Pennebaker (1989) argue that there might be a methodological reason for findings such as these. People high in "negative affect" tend to complain and worry more, but they show

no objectively worse physical health outcomes than their more positive peers. So some of the findings that connect pessimism to poor health might be the result of using self-report measures of medical complaints. Shepperd, Maroto, and Pbert (1996) found that optimists were better at sticking to diet and exercise plans, arguing that optimists put forth more effort due to their belief that goals are attainable. However, Fontaine and Cheskin (1999) found that it was pessimists who were more likely to stick with a weight loss program. Their explanation for this was that pessimists are less likely to think they can lose weight through their own effort, so they are more likely to rely on the external supports offered by a formal weight loss program.

If researchers sometimes find pessimism to be associated with worse outcomes and sometimes find it to be associated with better outcomes, perhaps this is evidence that there is a right way to be pessimistic and a wrong way to be pessimistic. Julie Norem (2001, 2002, 2014) argues that, although optimism feels good, we should avoid the temptation to assume that something is good because it feels good. Optimists tend to be more cheerful people than pessimists, but when we look at objective outcomes, a pattern emerges showing that optimism and pessimism function as different tools for different jobs. There are some situations in which optimists do better than pessimists and some situations in which pessimists outperform optimists. Norem (2002) employs the term "defensive pessimism" to describe pessimism as a healthy cognitive strategy.

To begin with, we need to distinguish between defensive pessimism and depressive pessimism as examined by Seligman (1990) in connection with his learned helplessness theory. As we saw above, depressive pessimism is characterized by internal, global, and stable attributions in the face of failure or disappointment. Defensive pessimists do not show this pattern of depressive attributions (Norem, 2001). Defensive pessimists also show healthier patterns of coping than depressive individuals do (Showers & Ruben, 1990), and they do not engage in unhealthy strategies such as self-handicapping (Norem, 2001), which depressive individuals do tend to employ (Strube, 1986; Weary & Williams, 1990).

Norem (2001) defines defensive pessimism as "a cognitive strategy in which individuals set low expectations for an upcoming performance, despite having done well in similar situations in the past" (p. 77). This strategy helps the pessimist deal with anxiety since anticipated disappointments are less stressful than actual disappointments, and being emotionally prepared for disappointments makes them easier to handle. Defensive pessimists worry about the many ways a plan can go wrong, so they take steps to avoid those circumstances and prepare backup plans in case something unforeseen happens. With possible errors and accidents anticipated and prepared for, task performance is improved. The use of defensive pessimism is associated with superior athletic performance (Wilson, Raglin, & Pritchard, 2002) and superior academic performance (Eronen, Nurmi, & Salmela-Aro, 1998). Chang and Sivam (2004) found that

defensive pessimists in Singapore engaged in more preventive-health-related behaviors during a SARS outbreak, and Brower and Ketterhagen (2004) found that African American students at predominantly white universities who employed defensive pessimism (maintaining lower GPA expectations while working to surpass those expectations) were less likely to drop out.

The downside of defensive pessimism is that it is not as much fun (Norem, 2014). However, if you are a defensive pessimist, your best strategy appears to be to make use of the tool that works. Trying to make defensive pessimists into optimists does not seem to do any good. Norem and Cantor (1986) found that encouraging defensive pessimists to be more confident resulted in worse performance. Del Valle and Mateos (2008) obtained similar results using a mood induction: defensive pessimists' performance was made worse by putting them in a good mood. Louis Armstrong used to sing about people who were prone to the blues, telling them, "Just direct your feet on the sunny side of the street." It turns out Armstrong was a much better musician than psychologist. For the Eeyores, cheering up is not the path to success.

This contrast between optimism and pessimism reflects an ongoing issue that we have already seen and will persist throughout this text. Flourishing is less about everyone being cheerful and more about living well. Also, there is more than one way to flourish. Norem (2001) connects healthy optimism and healthy pessimism to enduring dispositions toward positive and negative affect. For those who find themselves more on the optimistic side of the scale, my practical advice would be to notice the difference between healthy optimism (which facilitates positive functioning) and unrealistic optimism (which undermines positive functioning) and work toward greater use of healthy optimism. For the pessimists, my practical advice would be to notice the difference between healthy pessimism (which facilitates positive functioning) and depressive pessimism (which undermines positive functioning) and work toward greater use of healthy pessimism. Just direct your feet on the highly functioning side of the street.

HOPE THEORY

A term that is often seen in the optimism literature is *hope*. While some positive psychologists (e.g., Seligman, 1990; Peterson & Seligman, 2004) treat optimism and hope interchangeably, others (e.g., Snyder, Rand, & Sigmon, 2005) see hope as a distinct entity in positive psychology. C. R. Snyder (2000a), the creator of "hope theory," argues that Seligman's take on optimism is focused on the past, especially on people being formed by their reactions to past failures and wanting to avoid those failures. Hope theory, on the other hand, focuses on how people think about the future. Hope is defined here as "the belief that one can find pathways to desired goals and become motivated to use those pathways" (Snyder, Rand, & Sigmon, 2005, p. 257).

Hope theory has several connections to other theories we have encountered so far (and some we will encounter later). Snyder (2000a) describes the "pathways thinking" of hope as envisioning a desired goal and producing a route from one's current point to that desired endpoint. In short, hope theory is teleological in structure. This puts it squarely within our neo-Aristotelian approach, as teleology is also about moving from one's current state toward a desirable end state. As we will see in chapter nine, envisioning a goal and producing a pathway to that goal are central to the virtue of practical wisdom. In order for hope to occur, goals must carry some uncertainty (Snyder, 2000a); nobody is hopeful about an outcome that is one hundred percent certain. Self-determination theorists (as we will see in detail in chapter eighteen) have also found that internalized motivation is improved when goals are challenging but not impossible (Deci & Ryan, 1985). People who are hopeful "prefer *stretch goals* that are slightly more difficult than previously attained goals" (Lopez et al., 2004, p. 389). In fact, if goals are too easy, people who are characterized by high levels of hope may deliberately make the task harder by imposing restrictions on themselves, such as a shorter time frame than is technically required (Snyder, 2002).

In addition to hope being characterized by "pathways thinking" and generating possible means to attain goals, it is also characterized by "agency thinking," the belief that one has the ability to move along these pathways toward goals (Snyder, 2000a), similar to Bandura's (1997) notion of self-efficacy. Agency thinking is especially important when one encounters obstacles, as it provides the motivational force to overcome or circumvent blockages in one's pathways (Snyder, 2002).

Similar to what optimism researchers have found, it is generally the case that being hopeful is associated with a number of good outcomes. People who score high on hope measures tend to do well in school (e.g., Snyder et al., 1991; Snyder, et al. 1997) and in sports (Curry & Snyder, 2000; Curry et al., 1997). Hopeful people tend to cope better with physical ailments (e.g., Barnum et al., 1998) and are less likely to engage in risky behaviors that may endanger their health to begin with (e.g., Floyd & McDermott, 1998). Higher hope scores are also associated with improved psychological adjustment and reduced risk of depression (e.g., Snyder et al., 1991; Snyder et al., 1997). Hopeful people tend to have more supportive relationships (Crothers & Shaw, 1999) and gain greater enjoyment from being with people (Snyder et al., 1997).

Can hope, like optimism, be learned? Lopez et al. (2004) describe ways in which psychotherapists can bring hope into the therapeutic process, enhancing agentic and pathway thinking. One strategy, "hope finding," involves assessing clients' current levels of hope through means both formal (e.g., administering a hope measure) and informal (e.g., asking clients to talk about their pursuit of goals). This can help clients come to understand hope as a potential resource for change. Much like the name implies, hope enhancing involves increasing individuals' levels of hope using methods such as formal teaching about hope, working on goal setting and pathway identification, and reminders of previous successful goal attainments.

Snyder (2000b) discusses ways in which children learn pathways and agentic thinking. He points out that young children who are going through the "me do it" phase (loudly insisting that they and they alone should do things like dress themselves or stick the straw into the juice box) should be encouraged, as they are learning early lessons in agency. Parents should not be too quick to do things for their children, as this trial-and-error learning allows them to establish pathways (this action leads to that outcome). Similarly, when children encounter obstacles, this is also a time to gain in hopefulness, as struggling to overcome obstacles is a lesson in agency, so parents should not be too quick to swoop in and help. Let kids be frustrated; this is how they develop frustration tolerance. Maintaining a warm and responsive relationship with the child is also a way to develop hope, as secure attachments help children to see that people do listen and respond when they communicate (Snyder et al., 1997).

Teachers can help young people learn hope as well. In addition to the tips for parents given above, there are some specific strategies that have been shown to work in the classroom (Lopez et al., 2009). Setting goals that are specific rather than vague, helping to formulate multiple strategies and deal with obstacles, and breaking goals down into intermediate steps all serve to help students think in terms of pathways. Agency can be enhanced by helping students choose goals that are personally meaningful rather than chosen for them by others, "stretching" goals based on past performance to make them challenging, and helping students see the power of hopeful versus hopeless self-talk ("I'll keep at it" instead of "I can't deal with this").

HOPE AS A CHRISTIAN VIRTUE

Hope is also found, in Christian scholarly circles, among the "theological virtues," that is, virtues that directly concern God (Mattison, 2008). Despite being a theological virtue, hope is grounded in naturally occurring goal-directed orientation. In the *Summa Theologica*, Thomas Aquinas claims that even a dog has hope when it chases a rabbit. In that chase, "the dog's attention becomes fixed on a good that is not yet his, but might be—it is possible that he might catch the hare. Yet not without his effort, his pursuit" (Pinches, 2014, p. 350). As "natural hope" is common even across species, it is not surprising that we might see strong continuity between the theology of hope and the psychology of optimism and hope theory. Natural hope is future-oriented, focused on a goal that is challenging but attainable. "If the hare were lame and slow, we would not say the dog hopes to catch it" (p. 351). Similarly, Snyder's hope theory requires that there be some challenge (such as an obstacle or time limit) in our pursuit of goals (Snyder, 2000a). In both accounts of hope (the psychological and the theological), there is a rational assessment of one's ability to attain the goal (Pinches, 2014). Hope may also involve an assessment of someone else's ability. If I tell my children that we will have pizza for supper, they may hope for pizza based on their knowledge of my ability to successfully put frozen pizzas in the oven. If I tell my children that I will make the sky rain down pizzas, they will not hope for pizza because they know I lack that ability. (They will instead assume I am joking. Silly Daddy.)

While the theological virtue of hope has its roots in natural hope (for which reason a Christian positive psychologist can enthusiastically endorse both learned optimism and hope theory), it goes far beyond the mere expectation that good things will happen (Carver, Scheier, Miller, & Fulford, 2009) or

an optimistic attributional style (Seligman, 1990). Natural hope directs us toward challenging earthly goals and motivates us to attain them; theological hope directs us toward the highest of all goals—God. This brings us back to our earlier material (chapter three) on the telos of a human life. Christians describe true happiness in terms of living in a loving and blessed relationship with God, finally fulfilling our created role as a royal priesthood in a perfected eschatological state.

The eschatological nature of this telos puts humanity in a bind and shows us how far beyond mere optimism Christian hope is. Optimism and natural hope involve the realistic belief that one has the ability to attain goals, but Christianity holds out a goal that is unattainable by human effort (no salvation by works for us), and it stands in contradiction to a "realistic" assessment of the present situation (Moltmann, 1967). Because I cannot restrain myself from going off on a rant about this: In 1998, DreamWorks released an animated re-telling of the Exodus story (*Prince of Egypt*) that met with generally positive responses from Christians. While there was quite a lot about the movie that I liked, I was deeply irritated by the song "When You Believe," sung as the Hebrews are departing Egypt. The song (which won the 1999 Academy Award for Best Original Song) is filled with words about hope, but Stephen Schwartz (the writer and composer) completely missed the point, giving all agency for the release from slavery to the Hebrews, not to God. It includes lines such as "We were moving mountains long before we knew we could" and "Who knows what miracles you can achieve when you believe." In a story about the power of God to rescue his people, Schwartz gave us a song about the people's ability to rescue themselves by their own power. Argh.

Christian hope is not the same as a naive belief in "progress," the idea that the world is perfectible and can be made into a paradise if we just throw enough hard work at it (Wright, 2008). The only hope for the world (and for ourselves) is in the return and reign of Christ (Grenz, 1994). Christians see that the present world was made for fulfillment in God but is broken and corrupt. Despite what we see in the present, though, we believe God's promises about the future and trust that he will carry them out. Our hope is therefore grounded in God's ability, not in our own ability. Hope "trusts in the Divine assistance in moving forward toward what we know by faith is the rightful object of our existence, namely true and eternal happiness" (Pinches, 2014, p. 360).

This hope carries concrete psychological consequences. Hope "does not calm the unquiet heart, but is itself this unquiet heart in man. Those who hope in Christ can no longer put up with reality as it is, but begin to suffer under it, to contradict it" (Moltmann, 1967, p. 21). We long for the happiness that is to come but understand and can accept that we are not yet at our final destination (in chapter eight we will take a closer look at acceptance in positive psychology). Thus it does not

surprise us that our current happiness is always incomplete and that our hearts remain restless (Mattison, 2008). Suffering is something to be expected in a fallen world, but it is not the last word. Our journey toward complete happiness in Christ "is an exodus *through* the cross to a glory that is yet dimly perceived" (Horton, 2011, p. 708), and our hope that we will one day be brought to the end of that journey empowers us to face death without fear (Tomer, 2012) and "makes us ready to bear the 'cross of the present'" (Moltmann, 1967, p. 31).

SUGGESTIONS FOR FURTHER READING

Carver, C. S., Scheier, M. F., Miller, C. J., & Fulford, D. (2009). Optimism. In S. J. Lopez & C. R. Snyder (Eds.), *The Oxford handbook of positive psychology* (pp. 303-11). Oxford University Press.

Chang, E. C. (Ed). (2001). *Optimism & pessimism: Implications for theory, research, and practice.* American Psychological Association.

Norem, J. K. (2002). *The positive power of negative thinking: Using defensive pessimism to harness anxiety and perform at your peak.* Basic Books.

Seligman, M. E. P. (1990). *Learned optimism.* Knopf.

Snyder, C. R. (Ed.). (2000). *Handbook of hope: Theory, measures, and applications.* Academic Press.

Chapter Eight

MINDFULNESS

This one a long time have I watched. All his life has he looked
away . . . to the future, to the horizon. Never his mind on where
he was. Hmph! What he was doing. Hmph! Adventure. Heh!
Excitement. Heh! A Jedi craves not these things.

Yoda

Mindful Versus Mindless

In chapter six we discussed the concept of "flow," the experience of being so completely absorbed in an activity that one loses track of time. In this chapter we begin with a different form of losing oneself, one that has little to do with flow and is much less desirable. Have you ever had the experience of "zoning out" while carrying out an activity? Some drivers, for example, occasionally report the sudden realization that they have driven a substantial distance and have no recollection of having done so. Others have reported eating a meal and looking down at the plate to realize most of it is gone and they have no idea what it tasted like. Jon Kabat-Zinn (1990) describes this as our awareness of the present moment being carried away by our own thoughts. This kind of "mindless" loss of awareness could in fact be considered the opposite of flow. In the flow state, individuals lose track of time and experience diminished self-awareness because they are completely absorbed in the activity. Mindlessness, on

the other hand, involves a loss of awareness because individuals are disengaged from the activity, going through it on "autopilot" (Langer, 2009). When we go through life mindlessly, not paying attention to what we are doing, we deal with situations by unthinkingly applying rigid routines, robotic rules, and repetitive repetition. We evaluate events as being good or bad without considering context or nuance.

The opposite of being mindless is being mindful. Marlatt and Kristeller (1999) define mindfulness as "bringing one's complete attention to the present experience on a moment-by-moment basis" (p. 68), and Harris (2006) defines it as "consciously bringing awareness to your here-and-now experience with openness, interest and receptiveness" (p. 2). Mindfulness is characterized by openness to novelty, sensitivity to context, and engagement with the present moment (Langer, 2009). When one is mindful of the present, one is sensitive to the situation instead of being trapped in rigid routine and guided by the rules rather than robotically controlled by them. Shapiro, Schwartz, and Santerre (2005) provide the following list of qualities associated with a mindful state: nonjudging, nonstriving (lack of focus on achievement), acceptance, patience, trust, openness, letting go of one's thoughts and feelings, gentleness, generosity, empathy, gratitude, and lovingkindness. A large number of positive psychologists have endorsed training in mindfulness as an important tool in fostering well-being (Baer & Lykens, 2011; Ivtzan & Lomas, 2016). In this chapter we will look at the origins and theoretical foundations of mindfulness training, the benefits of mindfulness, and controversies that have surrounded this practice.

ACTing Up

Mindfulness training is often seen in the context of "third wave" therapies, such as acceptance and commitment therapy (ACT), and there are strong connections between ACT and positive psychology (Ciarrochi, Kashdan, & Harris, 2013). Those who employ this approach prefer that it be pronounced as the word *act* instead of A-C-T, because the emphasis is on "taking effective action guided by our deepest values and in which we are fully present and engaged" (Harris, 2006, p. 2).[1] While many people approach life with the assumption (often unspoken) that humans' natural state is to be happy and pain-free, ACT begins with the assumption that suffering is normal (Hayes, 2005). Unpleasant things happen in the real world, and it is healthier for us to embrace this reality rather than

escape or deny it (Fruzzetti & Erikson, 2010). Howell and Passmore (2019) found that training people in ACT principles was associated with improved well-being, and they promote ACT as a positive psychological intervention.

Here is an example. A few years ago, I was driving my car along the Trans-Canada Highway, heading toward Regina, Saskatchewan, where I was going to be teaching a class that evening. Somewhere between Regina and the middle of nowhere my car began to have engine troubles. My first inclination was toward denial ("No, no, no, not now, not here, no, no, no, no!") and conversations with the Lord not found in a typical prayer book ("Come *on*, God! Seriously? Here? In the middle of nowhere?"). I was able to pull over to the side of the highway before the vehicle completely died (and I mean *died*—the car was declared to be beyond repair when I finally got it hauled to a garage). Did I mention that this was in the middle of a blizzard? So there I was, stuck on the side of the highway at night somewhere outside of Regina, with snow piling up around my car and eighteen-wheelers driving by perilously close to me. This was not a good day. Now, as much as I felt like raging against the heavens and venting my spleen by pounding the steering wheel, what exactly would that have solved? Fighting the situation would accomplish nothing. The car was dead, and yelling would not make it undead. Loudly declaring that day to be the Worst Day Ever would not make it undead. Sitting on the side of the highway dwelling

---

[1]Hayes et al. (2012) also point to the side benefit that, since pretty much every other therapy uses acronyms (CBT, REBT, etc.), those who don't actually know anything about ACT are likely to call it A-C-T and thus betray their lack of knowledge.

on the good old days when my car worked would not make it undead. Daydreaming about how much farther along the highway I'd be if I had a car that worked would not make it undead. A better approach would be to accept that this was a thing that happened (and not an unexpected thing—the car was over twenty years old and had been on its last legs for a while at that point) and deal with it.

That's life. Cars break down. That's what they do (was I really expecting an immortal car?). The same thing happens in all sorts of areas of life. People get sick. Economies go up and they go down. Friends move away. The same can be applied to our emotional lives. Sadness happens. Anger happens. Stressful circumstances happen. Those who hold to acceptance-based approaches believe that trying to fight our emotional pain only makes it worse and traps us in it like mental quicksand (Hayes, 2005). What's more, researchers have found that trying to actively suppress unwanted thoughts and feelings actually increases their frequency (e.g., Clark, Ball, & Pape, 1991; Wegner, Schneider, Carter, & White, 1987). A more effective approach is to live with our pain and learn from it (Kabat-Zinn, 1990). We do this by realizing that we are not our thoughts and feelings (Harris, 2006). Instead, thoughts and feelings come and go, and we can develop the psychological flexibility to mentally "step back" (ACT practitioners refer to this as "defusion") and observe those thoughts and feelings as they come and go (Kabat-Zinn, 1994; Zettle, 2007). One core method employed by ACT practitioners for developing this flexibility is the practice of mindfulness (Ciarrochi, Kashdan, & Harris, 2013).

BECOMING MORE MINDFUL

The most common form of mindfulness training involves meditation. This version of meditation switches the practitioner's mindset from "doing" (preoccupied with activities and schedules and emails and thinking about activities and schedules and emails) to "being." In this mindset, practitioners are "simply allowing themselves to be in the moment with things exactly as they are, without trying to change anything" (Kabat-Zinn, 1990, p. 20), which, to an outside observer, looks a lot like just sitting quietly. This quiet sitting is psychological training, cultivating the ability to pay attention to what's going on without getting dragged away by the wandering mind. One way to do this is to focus on one's breathing. Zettle (2007) provides an example of a mindful breathing exercise:

1. Find a comfortable chair in which you can sit while practicing this exercise, preferably in a location that is relatively quiet and where you will not be disturbed.

2. Position your back straight and slightly away from the back of the chair. Rest your feet flat on the floor with your legs uncrossed. Rest your arms and hands in your lap or on the armrests of the chair.

3. Close your eyes and take up to thirty seconds to notice the parts of your body that make contact with the chair. See if you notice where you feel your legs and buttocks press against the chair, where your feet contact the floor, and the places on your arms and legs that touch either your lap or the armrests of the chair.

4. When you are ready to do so, shift the focus of your attention to your breathing.

5. See if you can notice the exact moment when the air begins to enter your nostrils.

6. Follow the breath as it enters your nostrils and travels down through your body and into your lungs.

7. Notice how your chest and abdomen gently rise upward and slightly inward with each breath that is inhaled.

8. Notice the point where the breath has reached its end and the process of exhaling begins.

9. Follow the breath as it comes from your lungs and leaves your nostrils.

10. See if you can focus your attention on the very spot and moment where the air leaves your nostrils. Notice that the air that leaves your nostrils is just a bit warmer than the air that enters.

11. Notice the sensations in your chest and abdomen as they move slightly downward and outward as the breath leaves your nostrils.

12. Continue to follow each breath as it enters and exists your nostrils.

13. If you become distracted at any point during the exercise, see if you can first notice what distracted you. Then gently bring your attention back to your breathing. There is no way to fail this exercise no matter how many times you might become distracted. Each time you become distracted is an opportunity to practice gently redirecting your attention back to your breathing.

14. Please spend at least five minutes on the exercise each time you practice it the first day. You may want to use a timer to signal the end of the practice time.

Increase the length of the practice time by two or three minutes each day so that you are practicing the exercise at least fifteen minutes twice daily. (pp. 274-75)

After writing that previous section, I gave it a try. I was grateful for point thirteen, because I became distracted quite a lot. What distracted me the most often was, as expected, my wandering mind. Instead of spending the entire five minutes focusing on my breathing, I experienced thoughts about what else I was going to write in the chapter, what was for supper tonight, an old episode of *Babylon Five* that I had recently watched, how much longer I had until the timer went off, how I was pretty bad at this, and so on. Symington and Symington (2012) developed what they call the "two-screen method" to help people deal with intrusive thoughts. Imagine that there are two TV screens inside your head, one in front and one off to the side. On the front screen is what is happening right now, while the side screen contains the fears, temptations, and threatening ideas that intrude on our thoughts. Neither screen turns off. Focusing on the side screen to try to fight intrusive thoughts only means giving those thoughts more control and distracts from the front screen. Accept that the side screen exists and allow the contents of that screen to play without watching them. Symington and Symington find that teaching this image to clients helps them to maintain an awareness that they are not their thoughts and frees them to choose to respond to life based on their values instead of anxieties and automatic reactions. To use a nontelevision metaphor that is beloved by mindfulness practitioners, if we think of our thoughts and feelings as the disturbances of the ocean's waters, "you can't stop the waves, but you can learn to surf."

While this form of "sitting meditation" is the one most commonly encountered, there are hundreds of other techniques that can be employed to cultivate mindfulness (Ciarrochi, Kashdna, & Harris, 2013). "Knowing what you are doing while you are doing it is the essence of mindfulness practice" (Kabat-Zinn, 1990, p. 27), and there are many things that we could be doing. The goal is to attend nonjudgmentally ("'The situation is what it is' rather than 'The situation is awful'"; Fruzzetti & Erikson, 2010, p. 349) to all stimuli in the internal and external environment while letting thoughts, feelings, and bodily sensations "come and go in the mind" (Segal, Williams, & Teasdale, 2002, p. 48). "Mindful yoga" involves being aware of one's breathing, emotions, and body movements while performing a set of stretches (Stahl & Goldstein, 2010). Shapiro and Mariels (2013) present a classroom-based exercise in mindful public speaking (and also mindfully listening to those who are speaking).

Kabat-Zinn (1990) also teaches a mindful eating exercise. In this exercise, participants are given three raisins to eat as slowly and attentively as possible. Even those who do not like raisins report this to be a very positive experience. Earlier in the chapter I gave an example of mindless eating. Many of us eat without taking the time to really taste what we eat, reaching for the next bite before we have even finished chewing the current bite. Take a moment to consider how different our diets would be (and likely how much less we would overeat) if we slowed down and paid attention to every bite. Framson et al. (2009) found that those who were more mindful about their eating tended to have lower BMI scores, and Dalen et al. (2010) found that obese participants who were trained in mindful eating lost weight and became better able to control their eating behavior. Mindful eating may also be helpful in the treatment of various eating disorders (Wanden-Berghe, Sans-Valero, & Wanden-Berghe, 2010).

One form of mindfulness that is reminiscent of Kabat-Zinn's mindful eating is savoring (Bryant & Verhoff, 2007). The term *savoring* refers to "processes through which people actively derive pleasure and fulfillment in relation to positive experience" (p. xii) and involves mindful attention to the experience, "being complexly aware of the experience of pleasure, delight, joy, contentment, awe, pride, or other positive feelings" (p. 13) in the savored moment. All kinds of experiences can be savored, including food, music, a warm bath, visual art, nature, watching one's children play in the yard on a beautiful afternoon, or the silence of the house when one's children are playing somewhere far away. Savoring shares many features with mindfulness, especially the process of attending to the present moment. By focusing on the experience, one treats internal states (sensations, thoughts, feelings) as if they were external to oneself, similar to the way in which connoisseurs of fine wine, beer, or food are able to consider their subjective experiences of the object as if from a distance (Bryant & Verhoff, 2007). In this way, what appears to be self-centered (the appreciation of an experience) can actually have an anti-ego component. This is reminiscent of the arguments that are put forward for the importance of beauty in human flourishing (Scruton, 2011). When we contemplate beauty, we become absorbed into the aesthetic experience, interested in the beautiful thing for what it is instead of what it can do for us. Beauty "makes a claim on us: it is a call to renounce our narcissism and look with reverence on the world" (p. 145).

If you wish to try this practice, Harrison, Smith, and Bryant (2013) recommend a "savoring expedition." Plan out an activity you wish to savor (a meal, a visit to a museum, a mountainside hike) and prepare for it ahead of time. Once you get to the activity, try to set aside whatever else may be on your mind and be fully in the moment. You may wish to write down the important features of the experience to be reflected on later. O'Brien and Smith (2019) had participants enjoy common activities in unusual ways (e.g., eating popcorn with chopsticks instead of fingers, drinking water with a spoon), and they found the experience more "immersive" and enjoyable because the unusual methods made it seem like new. Give it a try, and be creative.

EFFECTS OF MINDFULNESS TRAINING

Most studies on mindfulness have found it to be associated with better psychological functioning (Keng, Smoski, & Robins, 2011). Brown and Ryan (2003) developed a measure of how often individuals experience mindful states and found that greater mindfulness was associated with greater mental flexibility, engagement, self-esteem, optimism, life satisfaction, vitality, self-actualization, and medical health; it was associated with less self-consciousness, anxiety, depression, and hostility. Frewen et al. (2008) found that mindful people were less prone to negative automatic thoughts and were better at banishing those thoughts. Shapiro, Schwartz, and Santerre (2005) reviewed the research literature and concluded that the benefits of this practice encompass improved medical health, stress reactions, mood, cognitive ability, interpersonal functioning, creativity, self-esteem, empathy, self-actualization, and spirituality.

In experimental studies, researchers examined the effects of mindfulness training in a way that is more direct and powerful than correlational research. In an early study, Teasdale et al. (2000) found mindfulness-based therapy to reduce the likelihood of relapse among people with depression, a claim that was substantiated by meta-analyses conducted by Piet and Hougaard (2011) as well as Hoffman, Sawyer, Witt, and Oh (2010). Mindfulness training also appears to bolster positive outcomes. Anderson et al. (2007) found the training to produce improved emotional well-being, Oman et al. (2008) found it to increase forgiveness, and Grossman et al. (2010) found it to improve quality-of-life scores. Encouraged by findings such as these, many positive psychologists have embraced mindfulness training, with applications proposed for teaching mindfulness in schools (e.g., Miller, Nickerson, & Jimerson, 2009), at work (e.g., Lomas et al., 2019), in couples counseling (e.g., Carson, Carson, Gil, & Baucom, 2006), in sport psychology (e.g., Birrer, Röthlin, & Morgan, 2012), and in the military (e.g., Johnson et al., 2014).

CRITICISMS OF MINDFULNESS

Mindfulness is not without its critics, though. Some psychologists (e.g., Farias & Wikholm, 2015) argue that the recent push for mindfulness training is based on poor-quality research and an excess of media hype. But what about those experimental studies that we just looked at? We've been told that randomized experimental design is the "gold standard" for psychological research. Not so fast, say critics. For any readers who may happen to be my students, this is why I am continually yammering about the necessity of being familiar with research methods. Scientific studies stand or fall based on the rigor of their methodology. One central methodological criticism of the experimental mindfulness research is the problem of control groups. The goal of a properly designed experiment is for both groups (the control group and the experimental group) to be as close to identical as possible, with the exception of the variable that is being manipulated. In this case, we want the control group to be as similar as possible to the group that receives mindfulness training. Any systematic differences that exist between groups other than the manipulated variable make it difficult to know if the effect we see is due to the variable or to other differences.

How do mindfulness experiments stack up to this standard? Typically not very well. Astin's (1997) experimental group went through mindfulness training, while the control group did nothing. Anderson et al. (2007), Chambers et al. (2008), and Oman et al. (2008) put their control participants on a waitlist, where they did nothing. Farias and Wikholm (2015) examined 163

studies of the effects of mindfulness meditation and found that fewer than ten of those studies included an "active" control group in which participants did anything other than wait around.

This raises the possibility that the success seen in mindfulness training may be due to the mere fact that the participants are "doing something." Oman et al. (2008) found no difference between mindfulness and an alternative form of focused meditation. Miller, Kristeller, Headings, and Nagaraja (2014) compared participants who completed a mindful eating program against participants who completed a "Smart Choices" program of instruction that provided information about nutrition and goal setting. No significant difference was found between the two groups in terms of weight loss or blood glucose levels, and the Smart Choices group became significantly more likely to eat greater amounts of fruit and vegetables. When Farias and Wikhoklm (2015) examined the research on mindfulness training, they found that when active control groups were used (for example, people doing muscle relaxation rather than meditation), the mindfulness groups did not score any differently than the control groups. Mindfulness itself might not confer any advantages that could not be obtained through other activities.

Another major source of criticism has been the connections between mindfulness training and Buddhism. Mindfulness is based on methods of meditation found in Theravada Buddhism (Farias & Wikholm, 2015), and leading mindfulness psychologist Jon Kabat-Zinn (2003) describes mindfulness as the "heart" of Buddhist meditation residing at the "core of the teachings of the Buddha" (p. 145). Indeed, cultivating "right mindfulness" (*sammā sati*) is one part of Buddhism's noble eightfold path (Bodhi, 2011). However, what is taught in standard mindfulness training programs (and therapeutic approaches such as mindfulness-based stress reduction and mindfulness-based cognitive therapy) is a "secularized" mindfulness, presented without reference to its Buddhist roots (Kabat-Zinn, 1990; Siegel, Germer, & Olendzki, 2009).

But can a technique be uprooted from the conceptual framework that provides it with its inspiration, justification, coherence, and goal simply by not talking about the framework when it is employed? Does a technique from existential psychotherapy stop being existential if the therapist never mentions the word *existentialism*? People within the mindfulness community are divided over the question of whether "secular" mindfulness is truly secular, and they are also divided over whether that is a good thing (Farias & Wikholm, 2015).

Some see mindfulness as inherently Buddhist, no matter the manner in which it is taught. Many of the people in this camp are themselves Buddhists and celebrate the spread of Buddhist ways of reducing suffering, regardless of the title applied to it (Kabat-Zinn, 2011). Others are less sanguine about the secularization of Buddhist meditation and question whether mindfulness is authentically Buddhist (Bodhi, 2011). Wakoh Hickey (2010), a religious studies professor and ordained Zen priest, begins her critique of the mindfulness industry by criticizing Jon Kabat-Zinn's decision to present a Buddhism-free mindfulness as a possibly dishonest attempt to circumvent insurance policies (which may cover cognitive therapy but likely will not cover Buddhist studies) and avoid the possible association of mindfulness with New Age charlatans who peddle "alternative medicine" cures within the larger medical community. She goes on to argue that mindfulness for its own sake has never been a core Buddhist teaching, as Buddhism gives primacy to moral living and the pursuit of enlightenment.

Mindfulness training is also focused on the individual, while Buddhism upholds community. One implication of individualism that we have already discussed is that systemic sources of suffering are deemphasized in favor of individual meditation as the cure for what ails us. Hickey compares secular mindfulness training to the prosperity gospel: "If you are suffering, it is your individual psychological problem" (p. 175). Farias and Wikholm (2015) describe an encounter with a mindfulness teacher who rejects the psychologized forms of mindfulness, primarily because meditation for the purpose of enhancing personal happiness or empowerment is self-centered, while the purpose of Buddhist spirituality is the elimination of the illusion of self. Gebauer and colleagues (2018) conducted a study which seems to provide support for this criticism. In their study, Westerners who engaged in yoga or mindfulness meditation did display increases in well-being, but they also displayed increases in self-centeredness. Stripped of Buddhist teachings about overcoming the self, mindfulness practitioners might not find these meditative techniques useful in overcoming selfishness.

CHRISTIANS AND MINDFULNESS

The question of whether or not mindfulness training is separable from Buddhism can also present an area of difficulty for Christian positive psychologists. If it is accurate to say that "mindfulness is nothing but an introduction to Buddhism" (Farias & Wikholm, 2015, p. 224), then a Christian might decide to have nothing to do with mindfulness. If, on the other hand, mindfulness is really nothing but a particular way of learning to pay attention, then how could a Christian object to that, even if Buddhists invented it? Different possibilities exist for the Christian who wishes to deal seriously with this issue.

Some claim that it is possible for Christians to employ techniques from mindfulness, slightly modifying them so they are more reflective of a Christian worldview. Highland (2005) and Vandenberghe and Costa Prado (2009) argue for parallels between mindfulness and concepts found in the works of Augustine, possibly easing this translational process. Hathaway and Tan (2009) report a case study in which a Christian client was taught mindfulness, emphasizing God's unconditional love as a form of acceptance and meditation on God's presence during breathing exercises. They report that this approach to therapy resulted in improved emotional and relational functioning for the client. According to Tan (2011), a mindful Christian is one who learns to surrender his or her thoughts to God and cultivate an awareness of the "sacredness of the present moment" (p. 246). Garzon and Ford (2016) also adapt mindfulness methods by altering awareness of breath to include "resting in God's caring presence"

(p. 264) and adjusting lovingkindness meditation into a prayer of compassion. Hoover (2018) connects the "acceptance" part of mindfulness to the Christian notion of contentment in all circumstances.

Symington and Symington (2012) argue that "the underlying principles of mindfulness are not only compatible with Christianity but can also enhance the Christian spiritual journey and increase value-based behavior" (p. 71). Their version of Christian mindfulness involves mental states such as awareness of breath (recall the breathing exercise earlier in this chapter) as a gift from God, as well as awareness of God's presence. They put forward a three-pillar Christian model of mindfulness: (1) presence of mind, in which practitioners learn to experience the here-and-now moment; (2) acceptance, in which practitioners learn nonresistance toward unwanted thoughts and feelings; and (3) internal observation, in which practitioners learn to distance themselves from thoughts and feelings (for example, "I am having the experience of anxiety" as opposed to "I am anxious"). They claim that this practice will help Christians cultivate a greater appreciation for the miraculousness of ordinary life and free us to live according to biblical values rather than our fears and inner adversities. As an example of this freedom in action, Tan and Yarhouse (2010) found mindfulness to be useful when working with clients who were struggling with conflict between their Christianity and their sexual identity. Mindful Christians can learn that there is a difference between "I am having the experience of this attraction" and "I am defined by this attraction."

Many Christians find this approach appealing, as well as congruent with biblical teaching to be alert and sober-minded as we strive against evil (1 Peter 5:8). But for those Christians who remain uncertain about mindfulness, the alertness component is not the issue. What may trouble such believers is the nonjudgmental acceptance of one's thoughts and feelings. When practicing mindfulness, "The aim is not to change your thoughts, but your global beliefs about thoughts—essentially, you're expected to stop believing that your thoughts are true or important. This is where the Buddhist philosophy really kicks in: your thoughts are mere 'mental events'" (Farias & Wikholm, 2015, p. 88). That may be the sticking point. As Christians, we are explicitly told to believe that our thoughts and feelings are important. The Lord is pleased when the meditations of our hearts are characterized by righteousness (Psalm 19:14), and we are warned against evil thoughts (Matthew 15:19) and told to take every thought captive (2 Corinthians 10:5). In fact, psychological states such as wrath and lust are given moral weight equal to murder and adultery (Matthew 5:21-28). How can this be compatible with nonjudgmental acceptance? Shouldn't the Christian life be more like something out of Prudentius (last seen in chapter two), in which we constantly judge and grapple with (and beat the stuffing out of) our inner evil?

I emailed Scott Symington (half of "Symington and Symington") and asked him these questions. His response was that internal struggle operates according to different principles than external struggle (personal communication, February 12, 2013). Beating the stuffing out of physical threats in the external world might work just fine. Internal threats, however, become stronger as we give them more attention (recall Clark, Ball, & Pape, 1991, and Wegner, Schneider, Carter, & White, 1987), so combating evil thoughts requires a different set of tactics. Symington argues that focusing attention on unwanted thoughts is like giving them some of our mental energy, when what we should be doing is weakening them by denying them that energy. In the example of lust being equivalent to adultery (Matthew 5:28), there is a difference between a passing lustful thought and willful lusting. Passing thoughts happen, and accepting that they happen does not mean we endorse them. Passing thoughts become sin when we indulge those thoughts, imbuing them with our mental energy and letting them become part of us (Symington & Symington, 2012, describe this as a form of "fusing" with the thoughts). Symington also points out that "taking thoughts captive" does not imply the eradication of the thoughts. Captives, after all, are still alive; they have merely been disarmed and chained up.

Symington's distinction between passing sinful thoughts and willful mental sin fits with the arguments of a number of biblical scholars on passages such as those referenced above. When Jesus equates lust with adultery, he is not referring to fleeting attraction or noticing someone's beauty but to ruminating on the target with an eye toward possessing that person (Keener, 1999). The use of the present tense in the Greek indicates that we are talking here about a "studied looking with sexual intent" (Osborne, 2010, p. 196) rather than a passing thought. Similarly, when we see the inner process of temptation leading to sin in James 1:14-15, temptation itself is not sin (Moo, 2000) but merely desire (Davids, 1982). Jesus, as we know, was tempted but remained without sin (Hebrews 4:15). Desire leads to sin only "when the individual allows his or her mind to dwell on the temptation to the extent of *contemplating* sin" (Baker, 2004, p. 21). So maybe Symington and Symington (2012) are onto something here. Perhaps the best way to combat our inner evil and take thoughts captive is to refuse to dwell on those thoughts, allowing their force to pass by and leave us unscathed in a kind of psychospiritual aikido deflection.

Some forms of mindfulness training are more secularized than others, so another possible option for Christians might be to seek out certain streams of thought within the mindfulness literature while avoiding others. Some authors (e.g., Langer, 2009) take mindful nonjudgmentalism to extremes, saying that "what is considered evil, beautiful, good, folly, and wickedness are products of our mind" (p. 279) and nothing more. Others (e.g., Fruzetti & Erikson, 2010) take a more moderate position that some things (but not all) are to be accepted, and some problems (but not all) are due to evaluation. Further, when mindfulness is employed within ACT, practitioners are explicitly encouraged to use these methods to live life according to their deepest values (Wilson & Murrell, 2004), which for us would be Christ-centered values (Trammel, 2015). Brown and Ryan (2003) take no position at all on the issue, focusing only on mindfulness as a way of enhancing mental self-control. So perhaps this is less a

matter of accepting or rejecting mindfulness in its entirety, or even of adjusting mindfulness techniques to suit our preferences, and more a matter of exercising discernment concerning which version of mindfulness training to employ.

For those who remain unconvinced that the practice of mindfulness can be separated from its Buddhist roots, another option for Christians might be to seek the benefits of mindfulness training within Christian contemplative practices. As we saw earlier, one limitation of mindfulness research is that the benefits of mindfulness might also be acquired by doing other things, such as cognitive training, muscle relaxation, or nonmindfulness forms of meditation. Those who are interested in Christian spiritual practices as an alternative to mindfulness can draw from a considerable array of resources. Christianity has several well-established spiritual disciplines that involve quiet, sustained attention (Allen, 1997), including spiritual reading (e.g., Peterson, 2006) and many forms of prayer (Boa, 2001; Peterson, 2005). Cynthia Bourgeault's (2004) description of "centering prayer" as a contemplative method has many similarities to mindfulness meditation, including sitting silently and "letting go" of intrusive thoughts, and Knabb (2012) suggests centering prayer as a Christian alternative to mindfulness training. There is a small but growing body of research literature on the psychology of prayer (Spilka & Ladd, 2013), and Johnson et al. (2009) found some evidence that centering prayer might provide some emotional benefits to practitioners. Trammel (2015) combines approaches by incorporating prayer into her mindfulness breathing exercises and sees "mindful tea drinking" (a variant on the mindful eating described earlier in this chapter) as symbolic of receiving God's grace.

As is the case with many of the topics that we are exploring in these chapters, complexity abounds. There is no single Christian approach to mindfulness that can be called "the Christian approach." At the time of this writing, I admit that my own mind is not made up about which of the options I prefer. What is needed here is wisdom to sort through the difficult issues found within the range of possibilities that exist for the development of a Christian approach to positive psychology.

Suggestions for Further Reading

Farias, M., & Wikholm, C. (2015). *The Buddha pill: Can meditation change you?* Watkins.

Hayes, S. C, Follette, V. M., & Linehan, M. M. (Eds.). (2004). *Mindfulness and acceptance: Expanding the cognitive-behavioral tradition.* Guilford Press.

Kabat-Zinn, J. (1990). *Full catastrophe living: Using the wisdom of your body and mind to face stress, pain, and illness.* Delta Trade Paperbacks.

Kashdan, T. B., & Ciarrochi, J. (Eds.). (2013). *Mindfulness, acceptance, and positive psychology.* Context Press.

Spilka, B., & Ladd, K. L. (2013). *The psychology of prayer: A scientific approach.* Guilford Press.

Symington, S. H., & Symington, M. F. (2012). A Christian model of mindfulness: Using mindfulness principles to support psychological well-being, value-based behavior, and the Christian spiritual journey. *Journal of Psychology and Christianity, 31*(1), 71-77.

Chapter Nine

WISDOM

Wisdom is always an overmatch for strength.

PHAEDRUS, *FABLES*

Oh, a wise guy, eh? Nyuck nyuck!

CURLY HOWARD

"Wisdom is supreme; therefore get wisdom" (Proverbs 4:7 NIV 1984). In the biblical wisdom literature, we are urged to seek out and cultivate wisdom that we might see reality as it truly is, rightly give glory to God, and deal well with the challenges and quandaries of everyday life (Murphy, 2002). Eugene Rice (1958) calls wisdom "an ideal of twenty-two centuries" (p. 2), and Birren and Fisher (1990) report that the oldest known wisdom literature dates to a period in Egyptian history soon after 3000 BC. As the sages of the ages have considered this topic, wisdom has been given a wide range of definitions (Swartwood & Tiberius, 2019). When nineteen of the top twentieth-century scholars in the field got together to discuss the nature of wisdom (Sternberg, 1990), the result included more than a dozen definitions of wisdom, some of them quite divergent from each other. The general theme that emerged, though, was that wisdom is some form of knowledge. But what form?

As the positive psychology movement is guided by a vision of human flourishing that is shaped by classical Greek thought, we can begin there. Ancient Greek philosophers distinguished between three major forms of wisdom: *sophia* (transcendent philosophical wisdom), *phronēsis* (practical wisdom), and *epistēmē* (scientific knowledge; Robinson, 1990). Most scholars exclude scientific knowledge from their approaches to wisdom, considering it a separate area (e.g., Maxwell, 1984). Socrates believed that wisdom was obtained through moral development rather than acquiring naturalistic knowledge (Swartwood & Tiberius, 2019), and Plato believed that a person did not even necessarily need to be literate to be wise (Robinson, 1990). Leaving *episteme* aside as a possible foundation for a theory of wisdom, then, we turn to *sophia* and *phronēsis*.

When I discuss this topic with my students, I show them Raphael's *School of Athens*, a sixteenth-century fresco that can be found on one of the walls of the Apostolic Palace in the Vatican. The fresco is a portrayal of classic philosophy, featuring characters who represent great thinkers of that age, each doing something that symbolizes their own approach to philosophy. In the center are Plato and Aristotle. As Plato and Aristotle debate, Plato points upward, representing his view that wisdom can be found by focusing one's attention on transcendent eternal principles. Aristotle points outward, representing his view that wisdom comes from observing the world.

Plato's vertical finger may serve as our symbol of transcendent wisdom (*sophia*). Psychologists Paul Wink and Ravenna Helson (1997) conducted a study in which they examined people who were described as either transcendently or practically wise. In that study, they found that transcendently wise people were characterized by inner self-awareness, the ability to reconcile seemingly opposed intellectual concepts, and the search for answers to the meaning of life. These people demonstrated greater cognitive openness, intuition, and creativity.

Aristotle's horizontal hand symbolizes practical wisdom (*phronēsis*), which is obtained by observing the world. Alasdair MacIntyre (2007) defines *phronēsis* as the ability to exercise good judgment in particular cases. Wink and Helson (1997) describe the characteristics of the practically wise person in terms of good interpersonal skills, superior decision-making ability, and expertise in giving useful advice. People who possess *phronēsis* have demonstrated greater leadership ability, empathy, and concern for making the world a better place.

These two contrasting approaches to wisdom have wrestled their way through history. Some thinkers have tried to find a way to harmoniously blend the two, while others have maintained that they stand in irreconcilable conflict. Those who exclusively focus on transcendent wisdom and do not balance it with an emphasis on practicality often see material existence as a hindrance to be shunned or overcome in the pursuit of eternal truths. An example of this within the Christian tradition is Simeon Stylites, who spent thirty-six years living at the top of a pillar near Antioch (Latourette, 2000), while a Buddhist example might be the nine years that Bodhidharma is said to have spent staring at a wall in a cave in Henan Province (Maliszewski, 1996).

Moving from one extreme to the other, Eugene Rice (1958) considers Pierre Charron to be the ultimate example of the Renaissance humanists' "secularization" of wisdom. Charron's late-sixteenth-century treatment of wisdom divorces the temporal from the transcendent entirely, considering transcendent wisdom useless while enshrining *phronēsis* in an illustration as a triumphant goddess. Charron's pictorial presentation of *phronēsis* is a wholly humanistic one. She stands victoriously on a pillar, arms crossed as if embracing herself and looking into a mirror, for she needs no source of wisdom beyond herself.

It is my position that both of these are flawed and unbalanced approaches to wisdom. Wisdom must have both a transcendent and a temporal component, and devaluation of either component cuts us off from our ability to function as humans. Transcendent wisdom without practical wisdom produces the Platonized ascetic: Cut off from humanity and lost in contemplation, the person becomes isolated through retreat. Practical wisdom without transcendent wisdom produces Charron's self-absorbed humanist: Socially embedded but lost in her own reflection, the person becomes isolated through narcissistic self-encapsulation. As we have seen at the beginning of this text, we are operating within a vision of human flourishing that is grounded in our inherently social nature (e.g., Grenz, 2001; Horton, 2011; Hursthouse, 1999; MacIntyre, 1999), and both of these unbalanced forms of wisdom undermine relationships and communal functioning.

An approach to wisdom that avoids both of these would be one in which practical decision-making is grounded in transcendent ideas that provide necessary foundational concepts about human nature and social functioning. Renaissance thinker Justus Lipsius combined both aspects in his claim that "the wise man should have some ground in an elaborated philosophical system. He must be able to justify his convictions by means of an ethics which itself springs from a philosophical view of knowledge and nature" (Collins, 1962, p. 17). Renowned wisdom researcher Robert Sternberg (2019) describes a wise person as someone who is able to apply practical problem-solving skills in such a way that positive values are employed to balance the demands of multiple interests toward achieving the common good. But what values should be brought into play? And what exactly is the common good? Sternberg (1998b) has no answer, suggesting that we turn to moral philosophy and religion for these concepts, but he insists that without these value concepts, wisdom is not wisdom. Tyrants and dictators, Sternberg (2019) argues, may employ practical problem-solving skills to balance environmental variables and multiple interests, but if the agenda is evil, then the person is not wise. Pieper (1965) claims that "realization of the good presupposes knowledge of reality" (p. 10) and that practical wisdom consists of understanding the means toward the true ends of life. A "best" solution is one in which true ends are pursued in accordance with the principles of the real world. Transcendent wisdom allows us to intelligently consider what the nature of the real world is and what the true ends of life are.

THE PROCESS OF WISDOM

Of these two forms of wisdom, *phronēsis* has been the focus of the great majority of the work done by positive psychologists in this area. Psychologists associated with the Berlin Wisdom Project (e.g., Baltes, Glück, & Kunzmann, 2005) approach wisdom as "expertise in the fundamental pragmatics of life" and the wise person as someone who possesses "knowledge about the essence of the human condition and the ways and means of planning, managing, and understanding a good life" (p. 331). This approach is similar to the kinds of problem-solving research that students of psychology often encounter, but while that research may involve transporting hobbits in an orc-intensive environment or realizing new uses for common household objects, practical wisdom research involves problems such as how to advise a teenage girl who wants to marry her boyfriend right away or the decision of whether or not to accept a particular job offer. These kinds of problems are less well-defined and the procedures for generating the solutions more uncertain. Because of the ambiguity in circumstances (Schwartz & Sharpe,

2019), the role of moral emotions in decision-making (Tangney, Stuewig, & Mashek, 2007a), and the need to balance seemingly opposing truths when resolving thorny life problems (Staudinger & Glück, 2011), wisdom cannot be a mere exercise in technical decision-making.

Blaine Fowers (2005) describes wise decision-making as a three-step process. The first step is moral perception, the "capacity to discern the features of a situation that are the most important" (p. 118). Recall from chapter two that our approach here is teleological in nature, concerned with the telos (end, goal, purpose) of a thing, as well as movement in the direction of greater fulfillment of that telos. The telos of a knife is to cut, the telos of a human is to glorify God and enjoy him forever, and so on. We can also apply teleological thinking to understand social relationships and institutions such as marriage (see chapter thirteen) and education (see chapter eighteen). A situation can also have a telos, and our actions in these situations can be evaluated in terms of our progress (or lack of progress) in bringing about that telos.

It is now time to tell the story of the stupidest fight I ever got into with one of my brothers. Discerning the telos of a situation is not always easy. In the case of family conflict, sometimes the right goal to pursue involves staying true to one's convictions even if there is regrettable fallout in the form of strained relationships. In other cases, the goal should be family harmony, and in those situations, being right is less important than getting along. Far back in the mists of time, when my brothers and I still lived with our parents,

one of my brothers had a movie collection (VHS tapes, so you know this was a while ago). The problem was that he alphabetized his collection incorrectly. All right-thinking people understand that, when one is alphabetizing a movie collection, words like *the* and *a* at the beginning of titles are ignored (so *The Babadook* should go under B, not T, and *A View to a Kill* should go under V). But that is not what he did. He put movies with *the* in the titles with the Ts, and *a* in the titles with the As. I explained to him the depth of his error. Nevertheless, he persisted. At this point, a wise person would have accurately perceived that this was a situation in which family harmony was a more vital telos than being true to one's convictions and allowed him to organize his movies in whatever way he wanted. But that is not what I did. One day, when he was out of the house, I went into his room and "fixed" his movie collection for him. That was not a wise decision, and the result was a ridiculous and unnecessary quarrel. Mea culpa.

The need to discern the specific telos in specific circumstances is one reason that wisdom will not involve the mechanical application of one-size-fits-all rules. It is also possible to pursue more than one telos at once, making the decision even more complicated. Other central features of a situation include the characteristics of the people with whom one is dealing, as well as one's capacities and resources, time frame, past experience, and so on. Wise decision-making requires a certain degree of emotional maturity (Haidt, 2006; Schwartz & Sharpe, 2010; Schwarz, 2002) and understanding of the relevant values (Sternberg & Glück, 2019). It is also necessary to judge which features of the situation are important and which are not (one important feature of the situation with my brother was that the movies were his property, not mine. Not relevant was the fact that about half of them were Godzilla movies).

The second step in Fowers's (2005) description of practical wisdom is deliberation. Once one has perceived the essential features of the situation, one must consider how best to pursue one's goal. If we continue our consideration of family conflict as a source of examples, we see there are multiple options for resolving a dispute with a family member. Sternberg (1998a) categorizes options in terms of adapting oneself to the environment, shaping the environment to fit oneself, and selecting a new environment. The first option, resolving a family conflict by adapting oneself to fit the environment, is what I should have done with my brother's movie collection: kept my mouth shut, minded my own business, and let him have his way. Instead, I attempted to shape the environment to fit myself by rearranging his movies. That was unwise of me, but there are wise examples of resolving conflict by shaping the environment. One could shape the other person's behavior through reasoned discussion, for instance. Sometimes the best way to handle a family conflict is to remove oneself from the situation, selecting a new environment (I have noticed that my brothers and I argue far less frequently since I moved to Canada). And within those three general options, there are multiple specific plans that can be generated. This process of generating multiple ideas is known as "divergent thinking" by problem-solving

researchers. Divergent thinking plays an important role in creative problem-solving (Guilford, 1950; Runco & Acar, 2012), and successful problem-solvers are flexible in their deliberations regarding multiple possible solutions (Pretz, Naples, & Sternberg, 2003).

Deliberation leads to reasoned choice, the third step in the process (Fowers, 2005). In this step, the best option is selected from among the contenders. In his "balance theory of wisdom," Sternberg (1998a) describes the process of making wise choices as the pursuit of a three-part win-win-win solution involving intrapersonal, interpersonal, and extrapersonal interests. To illustrate this process, let's say I have been offered a new job at a faraway university, and I need to make a wise choice about whether to accept the position. Intrapersonal interests are the "what's in it for me" factor. A wise choice will never be a self-centered choice, but self-interest will play some role in the decision. What do I want out of this job? What is the salary? Does this job represent a step up in prestige? Who will my colleagues be? Do I want to live in this new location? Interpersonal interests involve what is good for those around me. Does my wife want to live in this new location? Are there opportunities for her at the new place? What educational opportunities exist for our children there? What quality of neighborhood would we be raising them in? Extrapersonal interests are bigger-picture goods and values involving community, country, and God. Do I feel a calling to this new position? Would my work involve something that benefits humanity?

Have You Tried . . . Not Being Stupid?

When it comes to navigating the ambiguous and complicated problems of life, IQ does not guarantee success (Richardson & Norgate, 2015; Sternberg, 2019; Wenke & Frensch, 2003), and earning the right to put the letters *PhD* after one's name does not make a person immune to displays of astoundingly bad judgment. A glance at the news will provide numerous examples of people one would assume to be intelligent making very bad decisions, both in their professional and private lives. Heuer (1999) focuses on failures among intelligence agencies in relation to international conflicts such as the Cuban Missile Crisis and the first Gulf War. As the term implies, one would expect professional intelligence analysts to be intelligent, but despite their cognitive abilities and academic training, sometimes these experts make terrible judgments, and geopolitical analysts' ability to predict outcomes are often no more accurate than random guessing (Tetlock, 2005). Moorhead, Ference, and Neck (1991) examined why NASA managers (also a high-IQ bunch) ignored the engineers who recommended that the space shuttle Challenger not go up on January 28, 1986. Halpern (2002) and Sternberg (2004) point out that President Clinton's intellectual background as a Yale graduate and a Rhodes scholar did not buffer him against poor judgment when it came to his interactions with young women.

Ray Hyman (2002) defines stupidity as "a failure of the actor to optimally use her abilities or cognitive capacity" (p. 2), making "stupid" a characteristic of an action, not a general trait of a person.

Stupidity occurs when there is a discrepancy between the decisions a person is capable of and the decisions that person ultimately makes. There are many things that explain why a smart person can do something stupid (and I recommend that you avoid these things). Stanovich and West (2008) demonstrated that intelligence has no connection to one's vulnerability to irrational biases such as framing and myside bias. Highly intelligent people may behave stupidly because they are just as likely as the rest of us to make irrational decisions (Aczel, 2019).

Dweck (2002) points to the difference between people who believe that intelligence is a trait one either possesses or does not possess (called "fixed" beliefs) and people who believe that intelligence can be developed over time ("incremental" beliefs). Those who hold to incremental beliefs about intelligence think that even geniuses need to work hard and have a lot to learn (Dweck & Leggett, 1988), while those who hold to fixed beliefs can make themselves behave stupidly by letting ego get in the way of learning (Kamins & Dweck, 2000) and may engage in defensive self-handicapping (Dweck, 2002). They might pass up opportunities to learn out of a desire to avoid embarrassment, put in less effort toward goals, refuse to put in the necessary practice, or engage in acts of self-sabotage ("I would have studied for the exam, but there was a *Deep Space Nine* marathon on TV and I just love that show").

Moldoveanu and Langer (2002) make a connection between stupidity and mindlessness. As we just saw in chapter eight, mindlessness is the opposite of mindfulness. When we are not mindful of the present, we go through life on "autopilot" (Langer, 2009), not paying close enough attention to what we are doing. Making wise decisions requires a proper perception and evaluation of the situation (Fowers, 2005), and that is impaired when we deal with situations unthinkingly and without considering context or nuance.

According to Ayduk and Mischel (2002), another factor that can produce stupid decisions is a failure of willpower (see chapter eleven). Schmeichel, Vohs, and Baumeister (2003) found that depleting participants' self-control capacity resulted in a range of intellectual impairments, including memory, reasoning, reading comprehension, and cognitive extrapolation, and Baumeister and Exline (1999) connect self-regulatory failure to a large number of moral failings. Superior self-control, on the other hand, predicts intellectual performance more strongly than IQ or academic qualifications do (Wolfe & Johnson, 1995; Duckworth & Seligman, 2005), and it is associated with better outcomes in domains that require wisdom, such as career decisions, interpersonal relationships, and health choices (Tangney, Baumeister, & Boone, 2004).

Sternberg (2004) prefers to avoid the term *stupid* in his examination of smart people's failures to be wise, opting instead for the more traditional (and more correct) term *foolish*. Sternberg explains foolish behavior by inverting his balance theory of wisdom into an imbalance theory of foolishness. If a wise decision is one in which the person balances intrapersonal, interpersonal, and extrapersonal interests in the pursuit of the common good, a foolish decision is one that veers away from

this proper balance. Smart people are especially vulnerable to this kind of foolishness, because they are prone to certain errors in thinking that involve their own ability, and these errors in thinking are magnified when the individual in question is in a position of power (see Claxton, Owen, & Sadler-Smith, 2015). Sternberg (2005) calls them the five fallacies of foolishness, characterizing them as a way of being locked into an adolescent mindset when making decisions. The five fallacies of foolishness are as follows: (1) unrealistic optimism, in which smart fools believe that all their plans will come out right in the end, so they need not worry about consequences; (2) egocentrism, in which smart fools think that their intrapersonal interests are more important than interpersonal and extrapersonal interests (with their own intelligence and powerful status being possible sources of their sense of importance); (3) a sense of omniscience, in which smart fools believe that they already know all they need to know and do not need to listen to advice; (4) a sense of omnipotence, in which smart fools believe that their power and brilliance are so great that they cannot fail; and (5) a sense of invulnerability, in which smart fools believe themselves to be shielded from the consequences of any mistakes. To put it another way: pride kills wisdom (Hackney, 2009a).

HOW TO WISE UP

Beginning with the earliest known wisdom literature, those who want to increase in wisdom have been advised to learn from those who have gone before (Wegner, 1999). One of the most direct ways of doing this is to read classic literature (McKee, 1990;

Sternberg, 2001; Bruya & Ardelt, 2018). For those who may be hesitant to venture into ancient texts, C. S. Lewis (2002) has these words of encouragement:

> There is a strange idea abroad that in every subject the ancient books should be read only by the professionals, and that the amateur should content himself with the modern books. Thus I have found as a tutor in English Literature that if the average student wants to find out something about Platonism, the very last thing he thinks of doing is to take a translation of Plato off the library shelf and read the *Symposium*. He would rather read some dreary modern books ten times as long, all about 'isms' and influences and only once in twelve pages telling him what Plato actually said. The error is rather an amiable one, for it springs from humility. The student is half afraid to meet one of the great philosophers face to face. He feels himself inadequate and thinks he will not understand him. But if he only knew, the great man, just because of his greatness, is much more intelligible than his modern commentator. The simplest student will be able to understand, if not all, yet a very great deal of what Plato said; but hardly anyone can understand some modern books on Platonism. It has always therefore been one of my main endeavors as a teacher to persuade the young that first-hand knowledge is not only more worth acquiring than second-hand knowledge, but is usually much easier and more delightful to acquire. (p. 200)

So if you have been operating under the assumption that only philosophers should read philosophy, take a lesson from Lewis. Whether your interest is Plato, Cicero, Augustine, or Aquinas, don't be afraid to go to the source. Read slowly and thoughtfully. If that means it takes you half a year to read a particular volume, that's just fine. It will be worth the extra time and effort. Connect the ideas with prior knowledge and experience. Do you agree with what is being said? Why or why not? Can you remember times in your own life when you have seen these ideas at work? How might you have made a different decision in a past situation if you were operating in line with the ideas being presented? Go beyond "reading through" a text and "think through" that text. The more you establish the habit of reading, the better you will be able to connect the thoughts of history's great minds to your life, and the closer you come to making their wisdom your own.

Given that human nature is inherently social, that human flourishing is inherently social, and that wise decision-making involves balancing one's interests with others', we would expect that the process of becoming a wiser person would also be social. Staudinger and Baltes (1996) tested this by assigning participants to different groups. One group was given a dilemma to ponder and asked to think it through alone. Another group was given the same dilemma and asked to work through it in discussion with a partner. As evaluated by a group of expert raters, the second group produced wiser responses than the first. Another group, though, was instructed to think through the dilemma alone but to imagine a dialogue with a wise person and consider what that person would say. This third group also produced wiser responses. Cultivating wisdom may be assisted by selecting a paragon of wisdom and asking yourself what that person would say when confronted with life's difficulties.

Seeking out an actual wise person for actual wise counsel might be an even better approach. Baltes and colleagues (1995) asked participants to provide wise advice in a set of difficult life circumstances (e.g., facing a decision that seemed to pit devotion to family against career advancement), and their responses were rated along five dimensions (such as richness of knowledge displayed and uncertainty management). Older participants from the community (average age sixty-four) who had been nominated by others as being wise performed just as well as experienced clinical psychologists at providing sage advice for handling tough dilemmas. Older participants who were not nominated as wise did not do as well, so gray hair by itself does not guarantee wisdom.

In Psalm 119:99-100, the psalmist says,

> I have more insight than all my teachers,
>   for I meditate on your statutes.
> I have more understanding than the elders,
>   for I obey your precepts.

Although personal wisdom comes from experience (Staudinger & Glück, 2011), researchers have found that there is no actual correlation between age and wisdom (Staudinger, Smith, & Baltes, 1992; Staudinger et al., 1998). In fact, Pasupathi, Staudinger, and Baltes (2001) found that the most crucial time in the development of wisdom is late adolescence and early adulthood (about age fifteen to twenty-five). Along those lines, most of the work on the deliberate cultivation of wisdom has focused on young people.

Practically without exception, scholars who have examined virtues have stressed the notion that the virtues tend to "intertwine with and reinforce each other" (Hursthouse, 1999, p. 232). We have already seen that growth in wisdom requires the virtue of humility. Park and Peterson (2008) describe the cultivation of wisdom as requiring the "development of a cascade of psychosocial virtues" (p. 60), and Huynh and colleagues (2017) found that participants who more stridently pursued the virtues endorsed wiser reasoning strategies when dealing with personal conflicts (both their own and others'). One way to foster wisdom is to become a more morally excellent person. Just as sin darkens our thinking (Moroney, 2000), preventing us from growing in wisdom, progress in combating sin should produce a "noetic sanctification" (p. 104), freeing our minds from that which twists them away from seeing ourselves and others as we truly are.

Pamela Bright (2008) points out that the Christian approach to cultivating wisdom is far more complex and nuanced than "the abstract formulation of patterns of instruction" (p. 168) given the fact that, for Christians, wisdom is a person: Jesus. As we see, for example, in 1 Corinthians 1:24, Christ is far more than someone who has the wisdom of God; he *is himself* the wisdom of God (Dunn, 1999; McCall, Waters, & White, 2015). *Logos,* the wisdom through which all things were created, became flesh (Guthrie, 1981). For Christians, growth in wisdom is inextricably connected to growth in Christlikeness, following the concrete example of Jesus' life, and Bright (2008) claims that Christians already have an extensive pedagogy to draw from for the teaching of wisdom in the form of spiritual disciplines and practices.

She provides examples ranging from Augustine's seven steps of wisdom to the Rule of Benedict of Nursia to Richard Foster's (1998) six traditions of spiritual formation. Further, growth in wisdom is paradoxically something that we are encouraged to strive toward and something that is entirely a gift from God (Bright, 2008), paralleling our earlier discussion of flourishing as sanctification: entirely a work of the Spirit but involving our responsible participation (see Hackney, 2010).

"Wisdom is supreme; therefore get wisdom" (Proverbs 4:7 NIV 1984). We do this by drawing nearer to the one who himself is wisdom. As we employ the theories and findings of positive psychologists toward the cultivation of wisdom, let us not lose sight of this truth.

Suggestions for Further Reading

Fowers, B. J. (2005). *Virtue and psychology: Pursuing excellence in ordinary practices.* American Psychological Association.

Schwartz, B., & Sharpe, K. (2010). *Practical wisdom: The right way to do the right thing.* Riverhead Books.

Staudinger, U. M., & Glück, J. (2011). Psychological wisdom research: Commonalities and differences in a growing field. *Annual Review of Psychology, 62,* 215-41.

Sternberg, R. J. (1998). A balance theory of wisdom. *Review of General Psychology, 2*(4), 347-65.

Sternberg, R. J. (Ed.). (2002). *Why smart people can be so stupid.* Yale University Press.

Sternberg, R. J., & Jordan, J. (Eds.). (2005). *A handbook of wisdom: Psychological perspectives.* Cambridge University Press.

Part Four

POSITIVE
PERSONALITY

Chapter Ten

CHARACTER STRENGTHS AND VIRTUES

Character is destiny.

Heraclitus

VIRTUE ETHICS AGAIN

You will recall from chapter two that the philosophical tradition that heavily informs the positive psychology movement is virtue ethics. At this point we will circle back around for a brief recap of our basic concepts. Like the positive psychology that came later, virtue ethics is concerned with human flourishing. Virtue ethicists ask questions about what kind of person we should be, what the ideal form of a human life looks like, and how we can move in the direction of becoming that ideal kind of person. With Alasdair MacIntyre (2007) as a primary inspiration, we define flourishing (*eudaimonia*) as growth from a starting point ("human nature as it happens to be") toward a teleological end point ("human nature as it could be if it realized its telos").

"To flourish is to function well" (MacIntyre, 2016, p. 29). Recalling the knife example I gave in chapter two (the telos of a knife is to cut), we have a way of describing good knives and bad knives in light of a knife's function. Good knives cut well; bad knives cut poorly. If we want to get more specific than that, we can talk about the characteristics of highly functioning knives. A good knife is sharp. A good knife is sturdy. A good knife has a well-built handle. Specific knives can then be evaluated in terms of the degree to which they possess these characteristics that empower proper functioning. If the specific knife I have in my hand is a bad knife, it is because that knife does not cut well. One explanation for why it does not cut well might be that it is not sharp. It lacks that characteristic of highly functioning knives. The solution, of course, is to increase the degree to which it has the desired characteristic (sharpen it). The characteristics that empower proper functioning are virtues (*aretē* in Greek), so "sharp" and "sturdy" would be two of the virtues of a highly functioning knife.

If the telos of a knife is to cut, what is the telos of a human? What is our function? What do we do that makes us "us"? Philosophical approaches to this question often involve some combination of humanity's social and rational nature (e.g., Foot, 2001; Fowers, 2015; Hursthouse, 1999; MacIntyre, 1999). Christian thought on human nature and flourishing includes social and rational functions (e.g., Kotva, 1996; Sabates, 2012; Vanhoozer, 2010), but those functions are directed toward a superordinate God-focused telos that could be described in terms of serving as a royal priesthood (Wright, 2010), loving God (Charry, 2010), and bringing glory to God (Hackney, 2007). This means that an anthropocentric telos focusing only on intellect or social functioning represents a diminished vision of human flourishing. Charles Mathewes (2015) argues that "we were never designed simply for human sociability, and attempts to reduce us to that mutilate our natural being" (p. 65). Given the roles rationality and sociability play in both approaches, we should not be surprised to see a certain amount of agreement between Christians and our secular colleagues on the good life. Given the differences between a vision of a good human life as excellent social-rational functioning and a vision of a good human life as glorifying God, we should not be surprised to see certain disagreements as well.

The function-centered teleological approach provides us with a way of describing good human lives and bad human lives. If a badly functioning knife lacks the characteristics that make a knife function well, a badly functioning human lacks the characteristics that make a human function well. If improving a knife involves increasing the degree to which it possesses the virtues of a good knife, improving a human will involve increasing the degree to which that person possesses the virtues of a good human. Virtues are character traits that enable one to be a highly functioning person. André Comte-Sponville (2001) puts it more strongly: As the virtues are human

qualities of excellence, the more virtuous one becomes, the more human one becomes.

MacIntyre (2007) defines the virtues as "those qualities the possession of which will enable an individual to achieve *eudaimonia* and the lack of which will frustrate his movement toward that *telos*" (p. 148). "The best definition of virtues is that they are character strengths that make it possible to flourish" (Fowers, 2017, p. 55). If the virtues of a highly functioning knife include such qualities as sharpness and sturdiness, what are the virtues of a highly functioning human? Plato is credited with presenting one of the classic lists of the virtues. In *The Republic*, he presents what are known as the four cardinal virtues—wisdom, justice, courage, and temperance—which he considers to be the psychological equivalents of the components of a properly ordered society. This approach has had a tremendous impact on moral philosophy through the centuries, including Christian thought on the virtues (Pieper, 1965). Other virtue theorists avoid the development of a definitive catalog of the virtues. MacIntyre (2007) avoids this, as did Aristotle.

The virtues that will be included or not included on one's list of necessary characteristics will vary depending on one's ideas about flourishing and the human telos (Hackney, 2010). For example, in the pagan worldview in which we encounter Aristotle, pride is not seen as a sin but a virtue (Casey, 1990). When Aristotle talked about the virtues, he described *megalopsychia*, which we typically translate as "greatness of soul" or "magnanimity" (Curzer, 1990), as one of the virtues. The *megalopsychos* ("great-souled man") is concerned with his own glory and desires the praise of others, and this motivates him to do great things that genuinely merit praise (the lesson here being that the best way to get glory is to do something glorious). Such a man will offer help to others because this demonstrates his strength and greatness, but he would be ashamed to receive help from others because this demonstrates inferiority (MacIntyre, 1999).

Aristotle's vision of the good life is that of the wealthy intellectual male aristocrat. A Christian's vision of the good life is that of the suffering servant, with Jesus showing us the human telos (Kotva, 1996; MacIntyre, 1988; Murphy, 2005b). This means that what we consider the necessary characteristics of a highly functioning human will differ from Aristotle's list. Humility, for example, is a Christian virtue but an Aristotelian vice. Aristotle used the term *micropsychia* ("smallness of soul") to describe the vice that marks those who do not think themselves worthy of glory (Osborne, 1979).

The greatest of all attempts to bring together Christian and Aristotelian thought on the virtues was undertaken by Thomas Aquinas (Foot, 1978). The good life that Aristotle calls *eudaimonia* Aquinas calls by the name *beatitudo* (MacIntyre, 2016), or "blessedness." The truly happy existence is one in which we come to fully know God, and the virtues are those characteristics that are necessary to move toward that blessed state (Charry, 2010). Aquinas gives us a list of seven virtues divided into the "cardinal" virtues and the "theological" virtues. The cardinal virtues are wisdom, justice, courage, and temperance (Plato's list), and they are built into human nature. But these "natural" virtues cannot make

one perfect (MacIntyre, 1988). Perfect development (and thus perfect happiness) requires the theological virtues: faith, hope, and love (see 1 Corinthians 13:13), which are given by the Holy Spirit.

VIRTUE AND PERSONALITY PSYCHOLOGY

Psychology has a long history of describing personality in terms of moral characteristics. Up until the late nineteenth century, one of the most common ways to describe someone's individual personality was in terms of "character" (Collini, 1985), emphasizing such things as "duty" and "integrity." In the early twentieth century, though, the growing desire for scientific objectivity in our understanding of humanity led to a shift away from talking about "character" to talking about "personality" (Susman, 2012). One key figure in this shift within scientific psychology was Gordon Allport (Nicholson, 1998). Allport (1921) argued that "character" and "personality" are distinct categories, with "character" referring to society's evaluations of one's moral qualities and "personality" referring to objective individual differences such as intelligence and temperament. As psychology is a science, moral terms should be excluded (Allport & Vernon, 1930), so in the name of value neutrality, there shall be no more talk about character in personality psychology (Nicholson, 1998).

This plan never worked. Despite his attempts to maintain morality and personality as separate categories, Allport was never able to create a value-neutral description of personality. His own description of the mature personality (Allport, 1937) included such concepts as devotion to higher ideals and concern for the social good, and his general approach was grounded in humanistic values (McAdams, 1997). The rest of personality psychology also never achieved real value neutrality. Erikson's (1963) theory of personality development includes "ego values" (p. 269) such as trust and a growing sense of justice. Even the rigorous data-driven five-factor model of personality (McCrae & Costa, 2003) includes agreeableness, which includes facets such as altruism and modesty, and conscientiousness, which includes dutifulness and self-discipline, as personality traits. Despite the best efforts of Allport and others, personality psychology remains value-laden (Tjeltveit, 2003). The importance of virtue seems inescapable.

THE CSV: A MANUAL OF THE SANITIES

With the positive psychology movement, personality psychologists admitted defeat (I'm actually the only one who puts it in those words) and began to "reclaim the study of character and virtue as legitimate topics of psychological inquiry and informed societal discourse" (Peterson & Seligman, 2004, p. 3). When Seligman and Csikszentmihalyi (2000) introduced positive psychology, they presented "positive individual traits" (p. 5) as one of the three major focuses of the movement. That same year, the Manuel D. and Rhoda Mayerson Foundation provided funding for the development of positive psychology's first major reference volume. Christopher Peterson headed up the project, collaborating with Martin Seligman and fifty-three other researchers (Niemiec, 2013), hoping to provide a first shot at a relatively comprehensive classification of the elements of good character. The result was *Character Strengths and Virtues: A Handbook and Classification* (Peterson & Seligman, 2004), and no positive psychologist's shelf should be without it. *Character Strengths and Virtues* was modeled after another of psychology's central reference volumes, the *Diagnostic and Statistical Manual of Mental Disorders* (American Psychiatric Association, 2013), commonly referred to by students and professionals as "the *DSM*." Manuals such as the *DSM* are valuable for psychologists because they provide a consensual classification that gives us "a common vocabulary for basic researchers and clinicians, allowing communication across professional groups as well as with the general public" (Dahlsgaard, Peterson, & Seligman, 2005, p. 203). Because *Character Strengths and Virtues* was intended to be an "anti-*DSM*," positive psychologists refer to it as "the *CSV*."

Peterson and Seligman (2004) describe the process by which they developed this volume. The working group started by brainstorming lists of psychological strengths, then a massive crosscultural interdisciplinary literature review was undertaken. Descriptions of virtues and strengths were assembled from a variety of sources, some of them deeply respectable (e.g., Confucius, Plato), and some of them . . . well, I suspect that some virtue lists were brought into the discussion because the researchers were having a bit too much fun (Hogwarts's four houses, the Klingon code of honor). Bringing Klingons into it earns them extra cool points from me at least. If a specific moral code was not technically a list of virtues, they eyeballed it to see if anything in there looked sufficiently closely virtue-adjacent. For example, when examining the Ten Commandments, the group decided that the prohibitions against murder, theft, and lying constituted an endorsement of the virtue of justice; adultery and covetousness were rooted in temperance; and the fact that these rules come from God involved transcendence (Dahlsgaard, Peterson, & Seligman, 2005). As they examined these religious and philosophical texts, they were looking for virtues that "recurred with a sort of pleasant tenacity" (p. 210), being endorsed across cultures and throughout history. They found six: courage, justice, temperance, wisdom, transcendence, and humanity. These will be described below.

What is unique to the *CSV* is that Peterson and Seligman (2004) do not focus on the virtues themselves. The members of the working group decided that virtues such as wisdom and courage were "too abstract and general" (p. 31) to be scientifically measured. Instead, virtues are treated in the *CSV* as broad categories that contain specific character strengths. Twenty-four specific strengths are identified and described, and these strengths are sorted into their respective virtuous categories. For example, the virtue "wisdom," which involves "the acquisition and use of knowledge" (p. 29), contains the character strengths of creativity, curiosity, open-mindedness, love of learning, and perspective. The primary measurement tool based on the *CSV* (also described below) therefore provides twenty-four scores rather than six. Peterson and Seligman's perspective is that all six of the virtues "must be present at above-threshold values for an individual to be deemed of good character,"

but also that "someone is of good character if he or she displays but 1 or 2 strengths within a virtue group" (p. 13). This is one of their ways of addressing the fact that there is a variety of ways one can be a good person. Everyone, for example, should be wise. But not everyone will be wise in the same way. Character strengths may therefore be thought of as "distinguishable routes to displaying one or another of the virtues" (Peterson & Park, 2004, p. 435).

Courage. One of the fundamental truths of the virtues is that they are corrective in nature, "each one standing at a point at which there is some temptation to be resisted or deficiency of maturation to be made good. . . . It is only because fear and the desire for pleasure often operate as temptations that courage and temperance exist as virtues at all" (Foot, 1987, pp. 8-9). Courage is grounded in our awareness of our vulnerability to injury and death (Pieper, 1965), counteracting the fear that springs from this awareness (Fowers, Richardson, & Slife, 2017). Peterson and Seligman (2004) define courage as "the exercise of will to accomplish goals in the face of opposition, either external or internal" (p. 199). The centrality of fear and vulnerability to the nature of courage forms the basis of the often-heard statement that courage is never to be understood as the absence of fear but as "doing the right thing in the face of fear" (Goud, 2005, p. 111).

Character strengths within the virtue category of courage are

- Bravery: Not shrinking from threat, challenge, difficulty, or pain

- Persistence: Finishing what one starts

- Integrity: Speaking the truth

- Vitality: Approaching life with excitement and energy.

Justice. Plato's masterwork *The Republic*, written in the fourth century BC, centers on the question, "What is justice?" Platonic thought on justice was grounded in the belief that "the universe is the manifestation of a single pervading law, and that human life is good so far as it obeys that law" (Nettleship, 1961, p. 10). Justice is therefore defined as a life lived in harmony with the moral structure of the universe. To be a just person within this definition is to be someone whose life "fits" in the order of the universe; when interacting with others, a just person treats those others in a manner that fits their place in the universe. This introduces the concept of desert into matters of justice, a perspective that continues to inform current thought on the matter. Cupit (1996) defines an unjust act as "an unfitting act; it is an act which fails to accord with the status of the person treated" (p. 2). If a person deserves a reward, justice is ensuring that the person gets that reward; if a person deserves punishment, justice is ensuring that the person is punished. Sterba (1988) claims that all major approaches to the concept of justice within the scholarly literature agree that justice consists of giving people what they deserve. The disagreements center around exactly what people deserve and how to give it to them. In the *CSV*, Peterson and Seligman (2004) define the virtue of justice in reference to "that which makes life fair" (p. 36).

Character strengths within the virtue category of justice are

- Citizenship: Working well as a member of a group

- Fairness: Treating all people the same
- Leadership: Encouraging a group of which one is a member.

Temperance. The temple of Apollo at Delphi reportedly had two phrases carved into its walls: "Know thyself," and "Nothing in excess." These maxims are connected in the Greek virtue *sōphrosunē* (North, 1979), which is commonly translated into English as "moderation" or "temperance." Peterson and Seligman (2004) classify temperance as the category of "positive traits that protect us from excess" (p. 431). The philosophical literature on temperance, however, provides a broader definition. Pieper's (1965) treatment of temperance as a virtue centers around the ordering of a person's self in accordance with the principles of reason. In this approach, the person does not merely engage in self-restraint, a definition of temperance that conjures up images of a tight-lipped abstemious killjoy, but understands the correct balance of laughter and sadness, work and play, firmness and gentleness that characterizes the ideal person. One who is intemperate engages in a "perversion of the true through excess or underdevelopment" (Jordan, 1989, p. 50). In chapter four, we briefly looked at a literary example of this principle in Edmund Spenser's sixteenth-century epic poem *The Faerie Queene*, which includes the characters Perissa (excess), Elissa (deficiency), and Medina (balance). One core character strength that falls within the virtue of temperance is self-control, and we will delve deeply into the scholarly literature surrounding this strength in chapter eleven.

Character strengths within the virtue category of temperance are

- Forgiveness/mercy: Forgiving those who have done wrong

- Humility/modesty: Letting one's accomplishments speak for themselves

- Prudence: Being careful about one's choices

- Self-regulation: Monitoring and controlling what one feels and does.

Wisdom. Wisdom stands alongside justice as a concept that has been hotly debated for millennia. In chapter nine we took a brief look at the many complexities involved in arriving at a proper definition for this virtue. Peterson and Seligman (2004) hold that wisdom encompasses character strengths "entailing the acquisition and use of knowledge into human affairs" (p. 40). Due to the amount of time we spent in chapter nine on wisdom, I will leave this section short and redirect readers back there for more information.

Character strengths within the virtue category of wisdom are

- Creativity: Thinking of novel and productive ways to conceptualize and do things

- Curiosity: Taking an interest in ongoing experience for its own sake

- Open-mindedness: Thinking things through and examining them from all sides

- Love of learning: Mastering new skills, topic, and bodies of knowledge

- Perspective: Being able to provide wise counsel to others.

Transcendence. Peterson and Seligman (2004) define transcendence "in the broad sense as the connection to something higher—the belief that there is meaning or purpose larger than ourselves" (p. 38). This can include religiousness and spirituality (see chapter twenty-one; see also Hill et al., 2000, for the complicated relationship between those two terms), but the approach to this virtue in the *CSV* is so loose that it includes optimism, an appreciation of beauty, and having a sense of humor (see Hackney, 2010d, for the difficulties in defining these kinds of terms in such a broad way). When this approach finds its application in the Comprehensive Soldier Fitness Program (chapter twenty), Pargament and Sweeney (2011) define "spiritual fitness" in terms of the capacity to "(a) identify one's core self and what provides life a sense of purpose and direction; (b) access resources that facilitate the realization of the core self and strivings, especially in times of struggle; and (c) experience a sense of connectedness with diverse people and the world" (p. 59).

In his book *Man's Search for Meaning*, Viktor Frankl (1984) claims that "the true meaning of life is to be discovered in the world rather than within man or his own psyche, as though it were a closed system. . . . Being human always points, and is directed, to something, or someone, other than oneself—be it a meaning to fulfill or another human being to encounter. The more one forgets himself—by giving himself to a cause to serve or another person to love—the more human he is and the more he actualizes himself" (p. 115). As we saw in chapter three, the vision of the good life around which we are centering this text sees the telos of humanity in glorifying God and in loving God and each other. Transcendence is therefore crucial to our understanding of flourishing.

Character strengths within the virtue category of transcendence are:

- Appreciation of beauty and excellence: Noticing and appreciating that which is admirable and aesthetically pleasing

- Gratitude: Being aware of and thankful for good things that happen

- Hope: Expecting the best in the future and working to achieve it

- Humor: Liking to laugh and tease

- Spirituality: Having coherent beliefs about the higher purpose and meaning of the universe.

HUMANITY

Peterson and Seligman (2004) define "strengths of humanity" as "interpersonal strengths that involve tending and be-friending others" (p. 29) and that tend to "manifest in caring relationships" (p. 293). This virtue category is most closely tied to Peterson's (2013) often-quoted claim that one of the core lessons of positive psy-chology is that "other people matter" (p. 127), and we will see more on this topic in chapter thirteen. Related concepts within psychology and philosophy include al-truism, compassion, love, care, and benevo-lence. C. Daniel Batson (1991) defines altruism as "a motivational state with the ultimate goal of increasing another's welfare" (p. 6). Virginia Held (2006), a central figure in care-based ethical theory, claims that "the central focus of the ethics of care is on the compelling moral salience of attending to and meeting the needs of the particular others for whom we take responsibility" (p. 10). If there is a need, the benevolent person seeks to see that the need is met. If there is an opportunity to make someone's

life better, the benevolent person takes that opportunity. If there is suffering, the benevolent person strives to alleviate it.

Within the Christian tradition, work on this virtue has typically involved the term *agape* and the paean to this virtue found in 1 Corinthians 13. The word *agape* was coined by the authors of the New Tes-tament to refer to a very specific form of love. It was translated into Latin as *caritas* and into English as "charity," though "charity" has acquired a connotation in the English-speaking world as synonymous with the activities of organizations such as the Red Cross or the United Way. *Agape* is a self-sacrificial form of love that equalizes all humanity as members of God's creation, equal recipients of God's love (Post, 2002). As God is the source of all value and all humans are beloved by God, then all humans are ascribed the tremendous value that this love carries with it. As God loves us, so we are to love each other.

Character strengths within the virtue category of humanity are

- Love: Valuing close relations with others

- Kindness: Doing favors and good deeds for others

- Social intelligence: Being aware of the motives and feelings of other people and oneself.

There is a third level to this classification. Just as there can be multiple ways of displaying and cultivating a virtue, there can be multiple ways of displaying and manifesting character strengths. "Situ-ational themes" are "the specific habits that lead people to manifest given character strengths in given situations" (Peterson & Seligman, 2004, p. 14). So if wisdom is a virtue category and love of learning is a character strength within that virtue category, a situational theme within love of learning might be an action such as joining a book club or listening to history podcasts. While the authors of the *CSV* believe that virtues are too broad to be scientifically examined, situational themes are simply too numerous and individual to be scientifically studied. Most of the work in positive psychology that is guided by the *CSV* happens at the level of character strengths.

Measuring Character Strengths

A number of measures have been developed based on the *CSV*'s classification of character strengths, but the most widely used is the Values in Action Inventory of Strengths (VIA-IS; see Ruch et al., 2010). At the time of this writing, the VIA-IS is available to take (free) at viacharacter.org, and I highly encourage all readers to take a few minutes and complete it. The output of the VIA-IS is a ranking of one's twenty-four character strengths from highest (most predominant, based on points scored) to lowest. One's "top five" on the VIA-IS are referred to by positive psychologists as one's "signature strengths" (Peterson & Seligman, 2004). Signature strengths "are strengths of character that a person owns, celebrates, and frequently exercises" (p. 18). Use of these strengths feels energizing, and one feels intrinsically motivated when engaged in activities employing these strengths. One tends to easily learn activities that involve this strength, and using these strengths makes one feel like "this is the real me." In case anyone is interested, my signature strengths are "love of learning," "spirituality," "judgment," "curiosity," and "perseverance."

Seligman (2000) considers the use of one's signature strengths to be a core component of the good life.

Practice Practice Practice

In chapter seventeen we will deal in more detail with MacIntyre's (2007) notion of a "practice." Put briefly, practices are activities through which we display and cultivate the virtues. This connects to the *CSV* at its third level of classification, situational themes. Those who wish to develop a character strength are encouraged to find habitual activities that allow them opportunities to exercise their virtue muscles.

Strengths-based interventions typically involve helping clients become aware of their strengths and explore ways to apply these strengths (Niemiec, 2013). Peterson (2006) recommends that readers use the VIA-IS to identify their signature strengths, pick one to focus on, and spend a week finding new ways to use it. Haidt (2002) provides a helpful list of suggestions (aimed at students) that can get you going. For example, if one of your signature strengths is "social intelligence," one suggested activity could be to "meet one new person each day by approaching them." Another possibility is to "go into a social situation in which you would normally feel uncomfortable and try to fit in." Martin Bolt (2004) also provides a number of suggested activities, and Rashid and Anjum (2005) list 340 suggestions, including movies that are well-suited to specific strengths. Seligman, Steen, Park, & Peterson (2005) had participants identify their top VIA strengths and spend a week trying novel ways to use them. At a six-month follow-up, participants who found new ways to use their strengths had higher happiness scores and lower levels of depression. Schutte and Malouff (2019) conducted a meta-analysis of signature strength interventions and found them to have a substantial positive impact on well-being.

What about those strengths that are down at the bottom of one's list? (My lowest three are "leadership," "appreciation of beauty," and "social intelligence.") Niemiec (2017) objects to calling them "weaknesses" on the grounds that the VIA-IS does not measure weakness, only strength, making the lowest-scoring traits one's "lower strengths" (p. 282), and he warns that thinking of them as weaknesses might result in a vicious cycle in which someone decides he or she lacks those strengths and simply gives up. Park and Peterson (2006) also point out that *weaknesses* are not the best description, as the VIA-IS ranks only the order of the strengths, with no indicator of the magnitude to which someone possesses those lower strengths. Just because a strength is at the bottom of your list, that does not mean you have low levels of it, only that the scores for the other strengths were higher.

Haidt (2002), on the other hand, has no problem using the term *weaknesses*. While Niemiec (2017) says it is better to focus on one's signature strengths than try to beef up one's areas of weakness, Haidt (2002) found that participants who tried to cultivate and display both strengths and weaknesses received just as much benefit as those who focused only on signature strengths, though focusing on signature strengths was a more enjoyable exercise. Rust, Diessner, and Reade (2009) similarly found that building up one's areas of weakness produced just as much improvement in happiness scores as

focusing only on strengths. As one of my weaknesses (or lower strengths) is "appreciation of beauty," I have been trying to better understand and appreciate art, architecture, and music (most poetry continues to baffle me). At this point I still remain a bit of an aesthetic blockhead, but there has been some progress, and I consider it well worth the effort.

In several different chapters throughout this book, we will look at ways to cultivate character strengths and virtues in such areas of life as school, the military, relationships, the workplace, and sports. Something that might get overlooked in all of this is the possibility that psychology itself can be seen as a venue for virtuous growth. The study of psychology as an academic field and an area of scientific research requires certain intellectual virtues that are grounded in "a deep and abiding love of truth, a desire to know and understand things as they really are" (Dow, 2013, p. 12) and the humility to realize that one still has a lot to learn (Krumrei-Mancuso et al., 2020). A flourishing researcher, as well as a student of psychology, needs the courage to reconsider previously held ideas in light of new evidence and new arguments, the carefulness and self-control to avoid sloppy errors in data analysis, the integrity to avoid plagiarism, and the humility to see truth as more important than one's ego. Chen (2015) talks about courage and honesty, as well as patience, but primarily focuses on the role of practical wisdom (*phronēsis* in Greek) in scientific research. The telos of scientific research is "producing scientific work that yields reliable, reproducible, and accurate knowledge that explains or describes natural phenomena"

(p. 79), and doing science well involves aiming at that goal. *Phronēsis* is the form of wisdom that involves making sound judgments in the face of practical and moral choices (see chapter nine), and doing good science involves making a multitude of sound judgments regarding issues that include "deciding upon a research question, planning and implementing experiments, interpreting and presenting data, examining others' work, and so on" (p. 86).

Blaine Fowers (2005) considers *phronēsis* to be "the heart of professional ethics" (p. 177) for applied psychology (i.e., the psychological undertakings of clinicians and counselors). A practically wise therapist will be able to choose and act well in relation to clients, pursuing the goals of reducing their suffering and facilitating their flourishing, a process that will also require the exercise of strengths such as warmth, fairness, honesty, and courage. In this way, pursuing excellence as a psychologist becomes a way to foster growth and flourishing for the psychologist as well as the client.

In chapter three we discussed connections between virtue ethics and Christian notions of flourishing (e.g., Kotva, 1996). While a Christian view of the human condition can enhance and focus our understanding and practice of positive psychology, Christians can also employ positive psychologists' theoretical and empirical work on the virtues with the goal of cultivating a Christlike character and empowering our spiritual formation (Kaczor, 2015). Mark McMinn (2017) argues that the findings of positive psychologists can help the church develop practical methods for fostering the virtues and figuring out exactly how the virtues function. We know that gratitude is the proper response to God (e.g., Psalm 107; 1 Thessalonians 5:18), but we can find help in knowing how to distinguish gratitude from other responses and how to become a more grateful person by reading the work of Michael McCullough and Robert Emmons (e.g., Emmons & McCullough, 2003, 2004). Those who are struggling with temptation can find helpful assistance in Baumeister and Tierney's (2011) book about cultivating self-control. If humans flourish to the degree that they are like Christ (Murphy, 2005b), and positive psychology can help us move toward that goal, then believers should embrace and employ the things that positive psychologists are learning about character strengths and virtues.

Suggestions for Further Reading

Comte-Sponville, A. (2001). *A small treatise on the great virtues* (C. Temerson, Trans.). Henry Holt.

Dahlsgaard, K., Peterson, C., & Seligman, M. E. P. (2005). Shared virtue: The convergence of valued human strengths across culture and history. *Review of General Psychology, 9*(3), 203-13.

Fowers, B. J. (2005). *Virtue and psychology: Pursuing excellence in ordinary practices.* American Psychological Association.

Fowers, B. J., Richardson, F. C., & Slife, B. D. (2017). *Frailty, suffering, and vice: Flourishing in the face of human limitations.* American Psychological Association.

Peterson, C., & Seligman, M. E. P. (2004). *Character strengths and virtues: A handbook and classification.* American Psychological Association.

Pieper, J. (1965). *The four cardinal virtues.* Harcourt, Brace & World.

Tjeltveit, A. C. (2003). Implicit virtues, divergent goods, multiple communities: Explicitly addressing virtues in the behavioral sciences. *American Behavioral Scientist, 47*(4), 395-414.

Chapter Eleven

CONTROL YOURSELF

He who conquers others is strong.
He who conquers himself is mighty.

Lau Tzu

Our Christian approach to positive psychology is one in which our vision of human flourishing is deeply connected to the theology of sanctification (Hackney, 2010b). Sanctification involves developing a Christlike character (Murphy, 2005b) and is a work of the Holy Spirit involving responsible human participation (Hoekema, 1987). Self-control is an example of this dual nature of sanctification. Self-control is a gift given to us by the Spirit (Galatians 5:23; 2 Timothy 1:7), and we are also called to actively cultivate self-control (Titus 2:1-6; 2 Peter 1:5-8). In this chapter, we will examine the overlapping concepts of willpower, self-regulation, self-control, and delay of gratification, with an eye toward employing the work of positive psychologists to facilitate our responsible participation in the process of sanctification.

As we saw in chapter ten, virtue ethicists treat self-control as a component of temperance. Pieper (1965) describes temperate people as those who order themselves in accordance with the principles of reason. This involves finding the moderate balance between "too little" and "too much" and being strong enough to keep the self in that healthy middle zone between excess and deficiency (Jordan, 1989). This principle of moderation applies to many areas of life. Too little food and we starve; too much and we become obese. Too little exercise and we remain weak; too much and we end up injuring ourselves. Comte-Sponville (2001) describes temperance as "that moderation which allows us to be masters of our pleasure instead of becoming its slaves. . . . The intemperate person is like a slave, all the more subjected in that his master—the monkey on his back—is with him wherever he goes. He is the prisoner of his body, of his desires or habits, of their strengths or weakness" (p. 39).

When psychologists approach the topic of self-control, they often use the term interchangeably with the term *self-regulation* (Baumeister & Exline, 1999). "Self-regulation refers to how a person exerts control over his or her own responses so as to pursue goals and live up to standards" (Peterson & Seligman, 2004, p. 500), and this capacity represents one of humanity's greatest strengths (Baumeister & Tierney, 2011), placing it firmly within our bailiwick as positive psychologists.

High levels of self-regulatory capacity predict a wide range of positive outcomes, including lower divorce rate, better childhood adjustment, better grades, better stress management, more popularity, more career success, better health, better relationships, better people skills, better money-management habits, fewer teen pregnancies, less criminality, and even healthier teeth (Moffitt et al., 2011; Tangney, Baumeister, & Boone, 2004). Duckworth and Seligman (2005) found self-control to be a more powerful predictor of academic performance than IQ. Strong self-control predicts so many desirable social outcomes that Baumeister and Exline (1999) consider self-control to be the supreme "moral muscle."

Aside from the fact that self-regulation is effortful and tasks our mental resources (Baumeister & Alquist, 2009), there seems to be no "downside" to high self-control. Zabelina, Robinson, and Anicha (2007) found that people with high levels of self-control are sometimes perceived by others as less spontaneous and extraverted. That's pretty much it for a disadvantage: Cultivate the virtue of temperance, and some people might think you're a bit "buttoned up" for their taste.

In the early twentieth century, though, very little work was being done by psychologists on the benefits of strong self-control. The decline of virtue ethics (which we covered in chapter two) and the desire of early personality psychologists to avoid talking about good moral character (which we covered in chapter ten) contributed to this "strengths-based" approach being seen as illegitimate. Another factor plays a role in the history of this concept, and that is the idea of the will as a "faculty."

FIRING AT WILL

Traditionally, self-regulatory capacity has been connected to the concept of willpower. For centuries, it was common to refer to the mind as having "faculties" (powers), with the will being one of those faculties. "Faculty psychology" became a prominent movement in the late eighteenth century and was applied in schools in a pedagogical approach known as "formal discipline" (Coover, 1916; Watson, 1961). The faculties were thought of as being like mental muscles; the more you used them, the stronger they became. A school was to be like an athletic center, providing students' brain-muscles with a good hard workout. And once those brains had developed a sufficiently Captain-America-like musculature, graduates could take that big brain into whatever career they chose, confident they had what it takes to succeed.

Support for the idea that the will is a vital faculty can be found among some of the key figures in late nineteenth-century psychology. Although he criticized faculty psychology as a theory, William James (1890) continued to use some of the faculty psychologists' key concepts, such as the education of the will. He even gave practical advice that paralleled the faculty psychologists', encouraging people to "be systematically ascetic or heroic in little unnecessary points, do every day or two something for no other reason than that you would rather not do it" (p. 82).

Faculty psychologist E. Boyd Barrett (1916) applied this idea specifically to improving one's will, both through deliberately constructed practice sessions and in everyday activities. Drawing directly from James's suggestion about small acts of systematic heroism, Barrett claims that willpower may be cultivated in everyday life, through such habits as keeping things tidy, exercising, getting up early in the morning, occasionally going without food, performing unpleasant or tiresome chores, and striving for excellence in one's area of specialization. Barrett also recommends that his readers perform daily five- to ten-minute exercises, such as keeping one's eyes fixed on a small object, submerging one's hand in cold water, drawing parallel lines, and (my personal favorite) writing out the sentence "I will train my will" fifty times.

The notion of training the will had started to become unpopular, though, in the early twentieth century. A series of empirical and theoretical criticisms (Kosits, 2004), not to mention the connections between faculty psychology and phrenology (the pseudoscience of "reading" someone's character by measuring that person's skull), dragged faculty psychology into the dreaded category of "discredited theory." It became unfashionable to talk about willpower. One thing I find fascinating about the history of psychology, though, is that certain ideas about human functioning tend to keep popping up long after they have been declared "discredited." We proclaim the debate to be over, the science settled, and the theory dead. Dirt is shoveled on the corpse of the theory and a headstone placed above it bearing the words "Nobody Thinks This Anymore." But on a dark and stormy night, under a gibbous moon, the dead theory starts to twitch. It pushes its way out of the grave to sink its teeth into the brains of a new generation of scientists, who find themselves thinking, "Well, maybe there was

something right about that theory after all. I should look into this." Between the work of those cognitive neuroscientists (e.g., Fodor, 1983) who gave us the concept of "modularity" and self-regulation researchers like the ones we are about to meet, a mutated form of faculty psychology is back. And so is willpower.

GIMME DAT MARSHMALLOW

One of the key figures in the resurrection of willpower research is Walter Mischel. Early in his career, Mischel had an opportunity to participate in some anthropological research in Trinidad, but he found himself sidetracked into studying children's ability to delay gratification (Lehrer, 2009). Delay of gratification is defined as "voluntary postponement of immediate gratification for the sake of more distant long-term gains" (Mischel & Ebbesen, 1970, p. 329). The ability to delay gratification is vital to success in many domains in life. Losing weight by sticking to a diet involves saying no to the short-term reward of ice cream in order to say yes to the long-term reward of fitting into smaller pants. Working a job involves delay of gratification, saying no to whatever you would rather be doing than working in order to get the desired paycheck. Education also is an exercise in delay of gratification, saying no to a multitude of short-term pleasures in the name of completing a degree and the long-term rewards for which the degree provides opportunities. Mischel's research has been about figuring out strategies that can help people exert self-control when facing a powerful stimulus. "Absent the availability and accessibility of such strategies, efforts to sustain delay of gratification and self-control are likely to be

short-lived and the power of the immediate situation is likely to prevail and elicit
the prepotent response—eat the cake,
smoke the cigarette, grab the money,
succumb to the temptation" (Mischel &
Ayduk, 2011, p. 83).

What are these strategies, and can they be
learned early in life? Mischel chose to study
this form of self-control in children using a
procedure that has come to be known as
"the marshmallow test." In earlier versions of
this test (e.g., Mischel, Ebbesen, & Zeiss,
1972), children were asked to choose
between a marshmallow and a pretzel. The
researcher then told the child that he or she
could have the nonpreferred snack now or
the preferred snack later (a fifteen- or
twenty-minute delay, depending on the
study). In the later, more well-known
versions of the test (e.g., Mischel & Baker,
1975), the children were offered a choice
between one marshmallow now and two
marshmallows later. The children were four
years old. Children below that age were too
young to really understand how the deal
worked, and the test did not reveal meaningful differences in older children (Mischel,
1996). The child's ability to delay gratification was measured by timing how long
he or she could wait for the larger reward. If
the child could not wait, there was a bell that
could be rung to summon the researcher
(and the child got only the smaller reward).

One of the things that makes this
research so interesting is the fact that
Mischel was able to do a longitudinal
follow-up with many of the children who
had participated in his early work.
Mischel's daughters went to the same
school as some of his participants, and he
would occasionally hear about how they

were doing (Baumeister & Tierney, 2011).
This inspired Mischel to track down as
many of his original participants as he
could. He compared their current status
with their performance on the marshmallow test and found that the ability to
delay gratification at age four predicted a
large number of desirable outcomes
(Mischel, Shoda, & Rodriguez, 1989).
Mischel, Shoda, and Peake (1988) sent
questionnaires to parents ten years after the
original studies and found that longer delay
times at age four predicted greater academic and social competence, frustration
tolerance, verbal fluency, rationality,
attentiveness, planfulness, and ability to
cope with stress. Shoda, Mischel, and Peake
(1990) followed that up with a more
detailed questionnaire packet for the
parents of these adolescents and found
delay time to be associated with higher SAT
scores, greater self-control in frustrating
situations, reduced likelihood of yielding to
temptations, less distractibility, and greater
intelligence. Impressively, Casey and
colleagues (2011) found that delay of
gratification times predicted neurocognitive outcomes in a laboratory study with
a forty-year delay. Those who had displayed
worse self-control back when they were
four years old produced more errors in a
perceptual task that required suppressing
their emotional reactions (basically, reacting to face images without letting the
emotions on the faces get in the way).
Functional neuroimaging also showed that
those who had displayed worse childhood
self-control showed reduced activity in the
inferior frontal gyrus (a brain region
associated with impulse restraint) an
increased activity in the ventral striatum

(part of the brain's reward system) during the perceptual task.

For those who want to cultivate self-control in children or enhance their own ability to stand up under temptation, we can take some practical techniques from this line of research. One technique for resisting temptation involves the power of distraction. Mischel and Ebbeson (1970) found that children were better able to wait when the rewards (cookies and pretzels in this case, rather than marshmallows) were removed from their sight (staring at a cookie makes it harder to resist the cookie). So get that tempting thing out of the room (or get yourself out of the room). Mischel, Ebbesen, and Seiss (1972) provided the children with distractions. They found that children were better able to wait for the larger reward if they were given a toy to play with (it was a Slinky, in case you were curious) or if they were instructed to think about some fun activity while they waited. The effect of distracting thoughts, though, was specific to fun activities; thinking about something sad resulted in significantly shorter wait times, as did thinking about the marshmallow. So, for those of you who are looking for temptation-resistance techniques, it's a good idea to find something to think about or do that distracts from the temptation (especially if it involves a Slinky).

A second technique for enhancing delay of gratification involves a distinction between what Metcalfe and Mischel (1999) call the "hot" versus "cool" cognitive systems. The hot cognitive system is emotional and impulsive, and it tends to get in the way of self-control. The cool system is emotionally neutral, contemplative,

analytical, and strategic, and it enhances self-control. The marshmallow test involves setting one system up against the other; the hot system wants the delicious marshmallow right now while the cool system strategically considers two marshmallows better than one marshmallow. Mischel and Baker (1975) put children into one of two experimental conditions intended to activate either the hot or cool systems. Children in the cool condition were told to think about the objects' stimuli features (marshmallows are white and fluffy, like little clouds), while children in the hot condition were told to think about how yummy and chewy marshmallows are. Children in the cool condition were much better at resisting the treats. So another practical tip we can adapt from this line of research is that, when faced with temptation, we can try to switch our thinking into a cool analytic mode of thought. Fujita and colleagues (2006) conducted a series of experiments in which they found that participants who had been instructed to think about abstract and higher-level cognitions, as opposed to more concrete and immediate cognitions, demonstrated greater self-control. Higher-level cognitions included big-picture thinking such as Why am I doing this? (versus How do I do this?) and the concept of cleanliness (versus "moving a broom around the floor"), so one specific form of cool cognition we might try is to think about the situation in terms of abstract principles rather than gut feelings.

BEEFING UP THE MORAL MUSCLE

The year was 1984, and an early career social psychologist named Roy Baumeister had no interest at all in the topic of will-power (Baumeister & Tierney, 2010; Storr, 2014). But that would soon change. One of Baumeister's primary areas of interest at the time was self-esteem, and like many people in the 1980s, he held to the notion that making people feel better about themselves would bring about positive outcomes in all areas of life. He soon found, though, that self-esteem is overrated (Baumeister, 1998). Aside from making people feel happy about themselves, raising people's self-esteem generally does not lead to better func-tioning and in fact can have negative side effects (Baumeister et al., 1996, 2003).

Self-control, on the other hand, showed itself to be more beneficial than self-esteem. Baumeister and his colleagues began to discover that the faculty psychologists (remember them?) may have been on to something all along. Willpower appears to be a real thing, and it appears to operate much like a muscle. The first thing they saw was that, like a muscle, the will is tempo-rarily weakened following exertion. Bau-meister and colleagues (1998) tested people's willpower by seeing how long they would persist at solving unsolvable puzzles. Before they did that, though, they were presented with a platter of chocolates, a platter of warm freshly baked cookies, and a platter of radishes. One group of partici-pants was told they could eat the chocolate or cookies, and the other group was told to eat radishes but not the chocolate or cookies. (For an extra dose of delightful evil, the cookies had been baked in that room, so the air was full of the scent of freshly baked cookies—that they were not allowed to eat. *Mwa-ha-ha-ha.*) The

researchers then left the room and watched through a one-way mirror. Everyone in the radish group successfully resisted the temptation and ate only radishes (though the researchers could see they were clearly struggling), but afterward the radish-eaters showed less persistence at the puzzles. This weakening of willpower was referred to as "ego depletion."

In another study, Muraven, Tice, and Baumeister (1998) induced ego depletion by assigning a number of tasks that required self-control (maintaining a straight face while watching an upsetting movie, trying *not* to think about a white bear,[1] doing math problems, and so on) and found that exerting self-control in one domain resulted in impaired performance in self-control in other domains (squeezing a hand grip, working on puzzles, keeping a straight face while watching a funny comedy routine). In subsequent studies, researchers found that ego depletion resulted in impaired intellectual perfor-mance (Schmeichel, Vohs, & Baumeister, 2003), increased alcohol consumption (Muraven, Collins, & Nienhaus, 2002), inappropriate sexual behavior (Gailliot & Baumeister, 2007a), reduced ability to restrain aggression (DeWall et al., 2007), increased impulse buying (Vohs & Faber, 2007), failure to stick to a diet (Vohs & Heatherton, 2000), and increased academic cheating (Mead et al., 2009). Hagger and colleagues (2010) conducted a meta-analysis of eighty-three ego depletion studies and found the effect to be robust and substantial regardless of the domain in which self-control was exerted.

---

[1] You're thinking about a white bear right now, aren't you? Stop it.

The fact that the effect crossed domains was mindblowing, as it did not fit most standard theories of self-regulation (there should have been no way that resisting cookie temptations would have an impact on puzzle solving). But it did fit the notion that self-control is a resource that operates like a muscle. And it gets better, because also like a muscle, self-regulatory strength grows when repeatedly exerted over an extended period of time. Muraven, Baumeister, and Tice (1999) did a repeated-measures experiment in which they assessed the weakening of self-control caused by an ego depletion task (a hand-gripping task, followed by efforts to not think of a white bear, followed by another grip test). They then assigned participants two weeks of self-control homework (trying to maintain good posture, trying to stay in a good mood, and maintaining a diary of all food intake). After two weeks of self-control exercise, participants came back and repeated the hand-grip and thought-suppression procedures. Compared to a no-homework control group, those who diligently practiced their self-control homework showed a reduced vulnerability to ego depletion. Gailliot, Plant, Butz, and Baumeister (2007) looked at self-control and reliance on stereotypes. They began by establishing that suppressing stereotypes (for example, by writing an essay about a day in the life of an obese or homosexual person without using any existing stereotypes of obese or homosexual people) produced ego depletion as measured using word puzzles. They then assigned two weeks of self-control homework (such as performing daily tasks using one's nondominant hand and not

starting any sentences with "I"). Similar to Muraven, Baumeister, and Tice (1999), they found that those who did their homework were less vulnerable to ego depletion in a follow-up session.

Other researchers have also found ways in which practicing self-control results in longitudinal gains in self-control strength. Lakes and Hoyt (2004) found that a three-month taekwondo course produced increases in self-control, and Oaten and Cheng (2006) found the same effect for a two-month program of regular physical exercise. Intellectual exercise also works, as Oaten and Cheng (2006, 2007) found a regular schedule of study to improve self-control.

PUTTING THE MUSCLE TO WORK

There are number of practical applications we can take from Baumeister's line of research (see Baumeister & Tierney, 2011). One lesson we can apply from the ego depletion research is that our capacity to self-regulate is finite, so it's a good idea to avoid overloading the system. Hofmann, Vohs, and Baumeister (2012) found that exerting willpower to resist everyday temptations reduced participants' ability to resist temptations experienced later that day; the greater the frequency, the worse the later performance. This is one reason so many people's New Year's resolutions fail. They fail because they are lists. Someone might start the year off with grand ambitions to "turn their life around," producing an impressive list of proposed self-improvements ("This year I resolve to stop smoking, stick to a healthy diet, get to the gym five days a week, read great literature, learn karate, teach myself French, cut my beer intake in half, and stop getting into pointless political arguments with pinheads on the internet"). Personally, I give that list four days, maybe five, before it is in tatters. Faced with multiple desires, our hypothetical person might successfully resist the lure of doughnuts, eat a healthy lunch, and get to the gym on day one. But what happens afterward when this person really really really wants a cigarette? With depleted resources to resist the desire, it is more likely that he will fail. And then he sees a comment by some pinhead on the internet. . . .

Studies of dieters (e.g., Herman & Mack, 1975; Polivy, 1976) have revealed that once a dieter has indulged and exceeded the day's calorie limit, there is a tendency to abandon restraint (Baumeister and Tierney [2011] call this the "what-the-hell effect"). Norcross and Vangarelli (1988) report that only 19% of those who make New Year's resolutions are successful in the long term. Our hypothetical person, after a couple of failures, is likely to see the list as "broken" and give up the plan entirely. So start by aiming low. Instead of making a massive list, pick one thing to work on at a time. Since most of Norcross and Vangarelli's participants were able to keep their resolutions for the first week, perhaps pick a short-term goal that can be met in a week (Jordan Peterson would probably suggest that you start by cleaning your room). In fact, starting with your room might help with subsequent resolutions, as Vohs et al. (2013) found that participants who were put in an orderly environment tended to make healthier and more prosocial decisions (the flipside was that people in a messy environment made more creative decisions). As Baumeister and Tierney (2011) put it, "Order seems to be contagious" (p. 252).

Nutrition may also play a role in self-regulation. The brain uses glucose to fuel its operations, and processes in the brain that are conscious and effortful, such as self-control, require extra glucose (Gailliot & Baumeister, 2007b). Fairclough and Houston (2004) found that exerting mental effort resulted in lowered glucose levels. Giving participants a glucose drink improves performance on attention tasks (Benton et al., 1987; Benton, 1990), while inducing low glucose levels impairs performance on such tasks (Smid et al., 1997). Gailliot and colleagues (2007) carried out a series of nine studies in which they found that exerting self-control reduced glucose levels and that increasing glucose levels (by giving participants a sugary drink, compared with a control group that got a sweet-tasting sugar-free drink) undid the effects of ego depletion. Masicampo and Baumeister (2008) found that glucose increased participants' rule-based reasoning, and DeWall and colleagues (2008) found it to improve prosocial behavior. Some researchers have challenged these findings (e.g., Beedie & Lane, 2012; Molden et al., 2012), leading Baumeister, Tice, and Vohs (2018) to admit that the situation might be more complicated than originally thought. However, the general relationship between glucose levels and self-control was upheld in Hagger and colleagues' (2010) meta-analysis.

So if you want strong self-control, eat something. Of course, this can be a problem for those who are trying to apply their self-regulatory powers to dieting. Baumeister and Tierney (2011) call this the "nutritional catch-22" (p. 226): You need willpower to not eat, and you need to eat to have willpower. One suggestion Baumeister and Tierney offer is to put less effort toward eating less food and more toward eating healthy food. Yaryura-Tobias and Neziroglu (1975) found that changing participants' diet to lower carbs and higher fat reduced aggressiveness, and Gesch et al. (2002) conducted a prison study in which they found that improving convicts' nutrition resulted in fewer disruptions. Studies like these provide evidence that improving one's diet may boost self-control strength.

Getting a good night's sleep is also important. Barber et al. (2010) argue that sleep helps restore self-regulatory resources, and Krizan and Hirshler (2016) provide a review of studies, showing that sleep deprivation and disruption are crippling to one's executive functions, impairing self-control and success in a wide range of domains. Emotional control, behavioral restraint, effortful mental focus, social interaction, and goal pursuit are all impacted. Hagger (2010) sees the deleterious effects of sleep deprivation on self-control to be one explanation for the link between sleep and physical health outcomes.

In this final practical tip, we come full circle, back to willpower as a faculty. It does not take a tremendous leap to see connections between the self-regulation homework of Baumeister and colleagues (1999; Gailliot et al., 2007) and the recommendations of William James and the faculty psychologists. Self-regulation homework such as maintaining good posture bears a striking resemblance to Barrett's (1916) recommendation of such tasks as keeping one's eyes focused on a specific object. We all know that a single pushup will not immediately transform one's musculature, but establishing a habit of thousands of pushups over time will enhance upper body strength. In the same way, one small act of self-control will not immediately produce an ironclad will, but establishing a habit of multiple small acts of will over an extended period of time has been shown to enhance self-regulatory capacities. I will repeat William James's (1890) advice: "Be systematically ascetic or heroic in little unnecessary points, do every day or two something for no other reason than that you would rather not do it" (p. 82). When we connect the work of self-regulation researchers to the importance of self-combat in sanctification (Stalnaker, 2006), it becomes clear how vital it is that we cultivate our ability to say "no" to ourselves.

SUGGESTIONS FOR FURTHER READING

Baumeister, R. F., Tice, D. M., & Vohs, K. D. (2018). The strength model of self-regulation: Conclusions from the second decade of willpower research. *Perspectives on Psychological Science, 13*(2), 141-45.

Baumeister, R. F., & Tierney, J. (2011). *Willpower: Rediscovering the greatest human strength.* Penguin.

Mischel, W., Shoda, Y., & Rodriguez, M. L. (1989). Delay of gratification in children. *Science, 244*(4907), 933-38.

Tangney, J. P., Baumeister, R. F., & Boone, A. L. (2004). High self-control predicts good adjustment, less pathology, better grades, and interpersonal success. *Journal of Personality, 72*(2), 271-324.

Vohs, K. D., & Baumeister, R. F. (Eds.). (2016). *Handbook of self-regulation: Research, theory, and applications* (3rd ed.). Guilford Press.

Chapter Twelve

TOO TOUGH TO QUIT

You oughtta thank me, before I die,
For the gravel in your guts and the spit in your eye.
JOHNNY CASH, "A BOY NAMED SUE"

HARDINESS

Once upon a time, a giant stretched its mighty arms across the American landscape, and that giant's name was AT&T. The giant was born when the Bell Telephone Company was launched by Alexander Graham Bell (among others) in 1877, which was followed in 1885 by the establishment of the Bell subsidiary American Telephone and Telegraph Company. AT&T merged with Bell in 1899 (with AT&T as the head of the conglomerate). Like the Borg in *Star Trek*, AT&T began to assimilate competitors, and by the 1920s, the Bell System operated as a virtual monopoly (by the 1970s, 95% of long-distance calls in the US were overseen by Ma Bell). But this monopolistic dominance did not last. Ma Bell had withstood a 1949 antitrust suit, but in 1974 the Justice Department took another swing at the giant and this time landed a knockout blow. The biggest corporation in American history was broken up into several smaller companies.

One of the "Baby Bells" carved out of the monopoly was Illinois Bell Telephone (IBT). The corporate reorganization was a time of chaos and confusion, and IBT looked for guidance to a University of Chicago research team led by Salvatore Maddi. Maddi (2002) describes the chaos thusly: "In barely a year, IBT decreased its workforce by almost half. One manager told me that he had had 10 different supervisors in one year, and that neither they nor he knew what they were supposed to do" (p. 174). As one might imagine, this was a time of terrible stress for employees. In 1975, Maddi and colleagues began a longitudinal study that lasted twelve years, investigating workplace stress in IBT. They wanted to know what the effects of the stress were, what contributed to stress, and what buffered against it. They found that those who could bear up under the strain and flourish in the face of chaos were characterized by a set of attitudes the research team called "hardiness" (Kobasa, 1979).

EXISTENTIALISM AND THE HUMAN DILEMMA

On more than one occasion in this book, we have dealt with the notion that psychological ideas cannot be separated from the philosophical (and theological) ideas that provide them with a foundation and superstructure. In order to understand what hardiness is, Maddi (2002) turned to existential psychology and what existentialists have to say about what it means to be human.

Although there is considerable variety among existential thinkers, there are certain common themes that connect them. One such theme is an emphasis on the experience of what it is like to be a human (Pervin, 1960). Ernest Becker (1973) said all humans have to deal with the paradox that we possess a mind that can contemplate the atom and the infinite, but we are also animals that will one day die (see chapter twenty-three for a fuller discussion of this topic). The author of Ecclesiastes calls it a "burden God has laid on the human race" (Ecclesiastes 3:10) that we have eternity set in our hearts but are finite in our ability to understand and just as mortal as any animal. Søren Kierkegaard (1844/1944) said we are trapped between imminence (the world, in which we are animals subject to death and the laws of nature) and transcendence (the spirit, in which we are free beings), living as a "synthesis of the infinite and the finite, of the temporal and the eternal, of freedom and necessity" (1849/1941, p. 146). Freedom of the will is also taken by existentialists to be one of the givens of the human condition (Yalom, 1980). We may be subject to the contingencies of material existence, but we at least retain the freedom to choose how we respond to them.

The human paradox produces anxiety, and this anxiety is the normal human state. "Who wants to face up fully to the creatures we are, clawing and gasping for breath in a universe beyond our ken?" (Becker, 1973,

p. 27). We are finite beings thrown into a world we did not create and do not understand, but as free beings we are responsible for the choices we make (Sartre, 1956). Our lives are the products of our choices, and this carries the dreadful realization that we, not anyone else, are the ones to blame for how our lives have turned out (Yalom, 1980). Facing this existential reality requires courage (Ostenfeld, 1972/1978; Pieper, 1965), and existential courage is Maddi's (2004) definition of hardiness.

BACK TO BELL

When Maddi and colleagues carried out their study of workplace stress at IBT, they found that the upheaval had substantially impacted employees' well-being. As IBT employees attempted to survive the fallout of the corporate breakup, two-thirds of Maddi's participants displayed evidence of severe stress. "There were suicides, violence in the workplace, divorces, depressive and anxiety disorders, heart attacks, strokes, and cancers." The other third, however, "not only survived, they actually thrived, feeling enlivened, deepening their relationships, and rising up in their company" (Maddi, 2004, p. 286). What was going on with this other third? What made them different from the others? Attempting to answer this question was the program of research that led Maddi and colleagues to develop their ideas about hardiness (Maddi, 1999; Maddi et al., 2002; Maddi et al., 2006; Maddi et al., 2009a; Maddi et al., 2011).

Hardiness is a mindset consisting of three connected attitudes that all (conveniently for us) start with a C: commitment, control, and challenge. Commitment "is expressed as a tendency to involve oneself in (rather than experience alienation from) whatever one is doing or encounters" (Kobasa, Maddi, & Khan, 1982, p. 169). Someone with a high degree of commitment embraces the existential reality that we are free beings whose choices shape our lives. Taking responsibility and living in that reality produces a sense of ownership of one's choices and activities, resulting in a feeling of engagement. These individuals are likely to live by the wisdom of Yoda ("Try not. Do, or do not. There is no try"); once they decide to do something, they do it wholeheartedly. When things get tough, they stay involved instead of detaching and feeling alienated from what they are doing (Maddi, 2013). They don't give up under pressure. Adopting this attitude requires courage. If there is "a time to search and a time to give up, a time to keep and a time to throw away" (Ecclesiastes 3:6), every bump in the road as we work toward our goals raises the question of whether now is the time to give up and whether we would be foolish to keep going. A hardy person will live with this uncertainty and keep pushing toward his or her chosen goals long after a less-courageous person has given up.

Control reflects an acceptance that our lives are shaped by our choices. This attitude is "a tendency to feel and act as if one is influential (rather than helpless) in the face of the varied contingencies of life" (Kobasa, Maddi, & Khan, 1982, p. 169). This is related to the idea of "locus of control" (Rotter, 1990); in fact, Kobasa (1979) used a locus of control measure in some early hardiness research. Julian Rotter (1966) introduced the idea of locus of control, which refers to a person's belief about the

cause of outcomes in life. Those who believe that events occur due to factors outside of themselves (luck, fate, powerful people, the alignment of the planets) are said to have an external locus of control, while an internal locus of control involves believing that events occur due to one's own behavior or characteristics. This is similar to the ideas that we encountered in chapter seven involving optimistic attributions (Seligman, 1990) and agency thinking (Snyder, 2000a). Like those similar constructs, internal locus of control has been shown to predict successful outcomes in a wide range of domains of life (e.g., Findley & Cooper, 1983; Strudler Wallston & Wallston, 1978). Maintaining an attitude of control over one's life "enhances stress resistance perceptually by increasing the likelihood that events will be experienced as a natural outgrowth of one's actions and, therefore, not as foreign, unexpected, and overwhelming experiences" (Kobasa, Maddi, & Khan, 1982, p. 169); this leads to actions aimed at transforming events into something consistent with one's life plan.

Instead of a focus on our status as free beings, challenge involves "the belief that change rather than stability is normal in life and that the anticipation of changes are interesting incentives to growth rather than threats to security" (Kobasa, Maddi, & Khan, 1982, p. 170). While some existential psychologists (e.g., Fromm, 1941; Yalom, 1980) connect this concept to the belief that life is meaningless, this philosophical move is not necessary (May, 1967). For our purposes it is enough to say that change happens and change can be scary. Humans have a deep need to seek meaning (see our discussion in chapter twenty-three), but if life is fluid, what does that do to life's meaning? Twenty years before writing this book, I was a single young man who had not yet been to graduate school and was living in the United States. As I type this, twenty years later, I am a married man, a father of three, a psychology professor, and living in Canada. So who am I? What is my life? Given how fast they are growing and changing, who are my children? The idea that my oldest daughter will be a teenager in a few short years is terrifying, but what's the alternative? Do I really want her to stay ten forever? Those with a low-challenge attitude are terribly uneasy with the idea that children grow up, people change jobs, the economy goes up and down, the political landscape lurches about, people die, people are born, people get married, technology marches on, and the BBC keeps changing the actor who plays the Doctor on *Doctor Who*. Those who have a high-challenge attitude accept that this is normal reality, see that change brings opportunities as well as risks, and choose to "learn continually from [their] experience, whether positive or negative, rather than playing it safe by avoiding uncertainties and potential threats" (Maddi, 2002, p. 174).

These three attitudes mutually reinforce each other (Maddi, 2004), and together they provide the courage to apprehend one's finiteness (Yalom, 1980), live with the accompanying anxiety, and take responsibility for one's responses (May, 1967). "To tolerate and resolve stressful circumstances, one must see them as (a) natural developmental pressures rather than catastrophic setbacks (challenge helps here), (b) resolvable rather than unmanageable (control helps here), and (c) worth investing in

rather than to be avoided (commitment helps here)" (Maddi, 2004, p. 288). Instead of seeing stressors as catastrophic, hardy people look for ways that stressors might be turned into advantages (Maddi, 2008).

HARDINESS RESEARCH

Suzanne Kobasa (1979) published the first hardiness study (her dissertation, in fact). In it, she compared IBT managers (all of whom were under considerable stress connected with the Bell breakup) who were suffering medical ailments against similarly stressed-out managers who were not showing the same negative outcomes. She found that those who showed higher levels of commitment, control, and challenge in their attitudes were less likely to see their stressful circumstances transformed into physical ailments. If they were hardy people, managers whose lives had been thrown into chaos maintained a clear sense of their abilities, values, and goals; threw themselves into the new situation rather than "passively acquiesce" to it; and continued to find meaning in their work. A hardy person "is not just a victim of a threatening change but an active determinant of the consequences it brings about" (p. 9). A series of studies followed in which Kobasa and colleagues continued to collect and analyze data from IBT employees. They found that hardiness buffered against the effects of stress, reducing the likelihood of stress-related health problems (Kobasa, Maddi, & Courington, 1981; Kobasa, Maddi, & Kahn, 1982; Kobasa, Maddi, & Puccetti, 1982) and increasing the likelihood of healthy coping (Maddi, 1999). In fact, Kobasa and colleagues (1986) found hardiness to be twice as effective as social support and physical exercise at buffering against the negative effects of stress.

Beyond IBT, researchers have found hardiness to predict better stress response and health outcomes in a variety of different contexts. Paul Bartone (1989) found hardiness to buffer against stress-related illness among bus drivers. He later published a series of studies in which hardiness was shown to provide buffering effects among military personnel (Bartone, 1998, 1999; Sandvik et al., 2013), reducing the likelihood of substance abuse (Bartone et al., 2015) and posttraumatic stress disorder (Escolas et al., 2013) resulting from combat stress (see our discussion in chapter twenty on military resilience). Kobasa (1982) found hardiness to predict healthier stress response among lawyers, and Keane et al. (1985) found a buffering effect of hardiness among nurses. In a meta-analysis, Alarcon, Eschleman, and Bowling (2009) found an inverse relationship between hardiness and workplace burnout.

Besides predicting better stress response, hardiness scores predict higher performance levels, especially in challenging situations. In addition to his work on stress response in the military, Bartone found hardiness to predict military leaders' adaptiveness (Bartone et al., 2013) and effectiveness (Bartone et al., 2009), as well as soldiers' likelihood of being accepted into an officer training program (Hystad et al., 2011) and completing special forces training (Bartone et al., 2008). Westman (1990) and Florian et al. (1995) found similar results in their studies involving the Israeli military. Lancer (2000) studied competitive swimmers and found hardiness

to be connected to the likelihood of being selected for the US Olympic team and better performance at the Olympics. Maddi and Hess (1992) found hardiness to predict superior performance among high school basketball athletes (with the exception of free throws, which Maddi [2013] interprets as evidence that hardiness has its strongest effects in stressful circumstances, since free throws take place during the few relatively calm moments of the game). Maddi and colleagues (2007) found hardiness to predict performance among firefighter trainees, and hardiness has been found to predict academic performance in a number of studies (e.g., Lifton et al., 2000; Maddi et al., 2009b).

Hardiness is also a predictor of a number of dimensions of healthy psychological and social functioning. Hardy people are less likely to abuse alcohol (Maddi, Wadhwa, & Heier, 1996) and tend to have lower depression scores (Funk & Houston, 1987). Maddi and Khoshaba (1994) found hardiness scores to be associated with a wide range of mental health variables, including negative correlations with anxiety, hysteria, dependency, and paranoia. Maddi et al. (2009a) found that hardy college students had more positive opinions of their lives, their schools, and the people around them, and Maddi et al. (2010) found hardy college students to have better coping processes and social interaction, as well as a greater sense of meaning in their lives. Given the research in which we see hardiness contributing to human flourishing, Maddi (2006) argues that hardiness research deserves a place within the positive psychology movement.

CULTIVATING HARDINESS

When hardiness researchers ask the question "Where does hardiness come from?" they tend to focus either on developmental factors or on deliberate training. Khoshaba and Maddi (1999) asked IBT managers about their early childhood memories to see if there were any hints there about developmental influences on hardiness. They found that hardy participants were more likely to report a childhood in which they faced significant stressors but were encouraged by family members to compensate and rise above the circumstances. Children grow to be hardy when they become convinced they have the ability to overcome the difficulties life throws at them.

Maddi (2013) points to a number of possible strategies parents can employ to foster hardiness in their children, organized around the three Cs. Commitment is encouraged "if the youngster's parents are generally loving and supportive, approving their child's interactions with them and others with encouragement and acceptance" (p. 26). As we will see in the next chapter, establishing a secure attachment style is an important foundation for children's ability to relate to others. By being there for the child in times of difficulty and by being a general source of everyday encouragement, parents help their children develop a generally optimistic view of themselves and a willingness to enter into relationships with others and stick with them when relationships hit their inevitable rough patches (Bartholomew & Horowitz, 1991). We will see that when children are ignored or treated as unimportant by their parents, they are more likely to turn into the kind of

adults who respond to difficulties by looking for escape.

Parents encourage control by putting children into situations that lead to a sense of mastery over their environment. Recall that in chapter seven we saw that viewing positive outcomes as within one's capacity to achieve is part of learning to be optimistic (Seligman, 1990). Self-determination theorists (e.g., Deci & Ryan, 1985) argue that one of humanity's fundamental needs is a sense of competence, the belief that one has the ability to effectively interact with the environment and attain goals. Whatever term one employs, one of the keys to fostering this attitude in children is to present them with tasks that are difficult enough to require effort but not so difficult as to be impossible (Maddi, 2013). We will discuss this in chapter eighteen when we talk about self-determination theory in educational settings.

Parents can help their children develop an attitude of challenge "by turning them on to the richness, rather than threats, of experiential changes" (p. 46). Children can be encouraged to think about the possibilities for new learning, growth, and experiences that come from changing circumstances and to look for alternate meanings of events beyond what the child might immediately assume. Children can see moving to a new location, for example, as a time of chaos and upheaval, leaving behind old friends and familiar streets. While this may be true, moving can also be a time to make new friends, experience what life in a new location has to offer, and enjoy the newness of the new house. It might be scary, but it is also exciting and fun.

Hardiness training is one of the major areas of emphasis for psychologists who specialize in this topic. Hardiness is an attitude, and attitudes can be taught. Maddi (1987) developed an in-house training program for IBT organized into twelve once-per-week small group sessions involving exercises intended to foster hardy responses to stressful situations. One such exercise is called "situational reconstruction" (Maddi, 2013). Trainees are told to imagine a stressful situation in their lives, then to think about how it might have been worse and how it might have been better. They are then asked to think about what they could do to reduce the likelihood of it getting worse and increase the likelihood of it getting better. This helps get the trainee thinking in terms of free choice having an impact on the way life turns out. Another exercise involves recognizing that perhaps this specific situation is beyond one's current ability to resolve. If this is the case, the trainee chooses a related situation that can be resolved and works on that (for example, a student might find that a stressful situation involving extracurricular activities is currently beyond his or her ability to control and choose to focus on academic improvement instead). Eventually, trainees develop a specific goal and a plan to attain that goal (Maddi, 1987). The results of carrying out the plan provide feedback, and learning from this feedback should increase the attitudes of control, commitment, and challenge.

Maddi (1987) found that those who went through the training program reported less anxiety and depression and also had lower blood pressure. Maddi, Khan, and Maddi (1998) tested the effectiveness of hardiness training with a controlled experiment. Participants (IBT managers) were assigned to either a hardiness training group, a relaxation and meditation group, or a placebo control group. Compared to the other two conditions, the participants in the hardiness training group reported fewer symptoms of strain and illness and higher levels of job satisfaction and social support from those around them. Hardiness training has also been shown to increase GPA among students (Maddi, Khoshaba, Jensen, et al., 2002; Maddi et al., 2009b).

Don't Just Be Hardy, Be Gritty

Hardiness shows a certain resemblance to a related line of research: grit. Research involving the personality construct of "grit" began with Angela Duckworth's studies of military cadets at West Point (Duckworth, 2016). The US Military Academy is highly selective, taking only students at the top end of the academic and physical distributions, but even then one out of five of these super-students drops out before completing his or her time at West Point. Military psychologists have expended quite a lot of effort to determine the reasons for this. Duckworth was a graduate student at the University of Pennsylvania, and in the course of her research (which formed the basis for her dissertation), she interviewed cadets about their attitudes toward themselves and toward the activities in which they were engaged. From those interviews came the idea of "grit" as the key psychological feature that separated the dropouts from the achievers.

Grit is the combination of passion and perseverance (Duckworth et al., 2007). People with a high degree of grit will work "strenuously toward challenges, maintaining effort and interest over years despite failure, adversity, and plateaus in progress. The gritty individual approaches achievement as a marathon; his or her advantage is stamina. Whereas disappointment or boredom signals to others that it is time to change trajectory and cut losses, the gritty individual stays the course" (p. 1087). Gritty people tend to develop a long-term passion for projects and goals, while the less gritty drift from one "interest" to another, letting new projects distract them from what they are currently working on (Duckworth & Quinn, 2009). Once gritty people have devoted themselves to a goal, they heed the words of Tim Allen's character in *Galaxy Quest* and "never give up, never surrender." They tend to prioritize the pursuit of meaning and engagement in absorbing activities over the hedonic pursuit of pleasure (Von Culin, Tsukayama, & Duckworth, 2014) and are diligent "hard workers" who are not discouraged by setbacks (Duckworth & Quinn, 2009). The "never-say-die" attitude of gritty people predicted West Point cadets' likelihood of sticking it out through "Beast Barracks," the intentionally harsh intensive summer program that marks the cadet's entry into the academy (Duckworth et al., 2007), as well as their likelihood of completing the entire four-year West Point program (Kelly, Matthews, & Bartone, 2014). The same predictive power was found among soldiers trying to complete an Army Special Forces selection program (Eskreis-Winkler et al., 2014). Grit predicts success at spelling bees (Duckworth et al., 2007, 2011), as well as long-term career retention and achievement (Duckworth, Quinn, & Seligman, 2009;

Eskreis-Winkler et al., 2014; Robertson-Kraft & Duckworth, 2014). Gritty adults show greater educational attainment (Duckworth et al., 2007), gritty high school students are less likely to drop out, and gritty husbands are less likely to abandon their wives (Eskreis-Winkler et al., 2014).

Achievement requires perseverance. Duckworth (2016) sees her research as a campaign against the idea that the primary thing necessary to do well in life is IQ or talent. Talent and raw smarts are great to have, but without the grit to stick to long-term projects, the gifted individual's potential will not be realized (Mozart may have been a genius, but he also spent his childhood in intense musical training, and Leonardo da Vinci spent many years toiling away as an apprentice). Eskreis-Winkler and colleagues (2014) found that it was grit added to intelligence and physical fitness that enabled Special Forces trainees to complete the course. Duckworth et al. (2007) found grit to consistently predict success above and beyond intelligence in different domains, leading to their conclusion that "grit may in fact matter more than IQ to eventual success in life" (p. 1099).

Training programs intended to foster grit are still in their infancy, largely relying on others' work in areas that are adjacent to and overlap with grit. Duckworth (2016) provides a number of suggestions in her book, including advice to explore one's interests to develop passion for a long-term project. O'Keefe and Dweck (2018) compared people who held the attitude that one's passion is something fixed (you either have it or you don't) against those who held that passions grow and develop over time. Those who held to the fixed belief were less likely to try new things and more likely to give up when they experienced obstacles. And passion grows as one goes deeper into an activity. A lesson to take from this is that you should not think that your passion in life is something you need to go find, expecting a fully formed blast of interest and competence once that special something is stumbled upon. Don't discover your passion; build it.

Duckworth (2016) also draws on research involving the practice habits of elite performers (e.g., Ericsson, Krampe, & Tesch-Römer, 1993). What some of us might mistake for genius is more likely the result of many hours of deliberate, goal-focused practice. So remember what I said about Mozart and put in the hard work of developing your skill. Duckworth (2016) also talks about the importance of seeking flow, pursuing meaning, and serving others in the development of passion. To develop persistence, Duckworth advises that readers look to theories such as Seligman's learned optimism, cognitive behavioral therapy, and developmental theories of healthy parenting.

While passion is certainly desirable, Credé, Tynan, and Harms (2017) claim based on their meta-analysis of the grit research literature that perseverance is what really drives the beneficial effects of being gritty. The perseverance in grit aligns well with the concept of persistence, defined in the *CSV* as a form of courage involving "voluntary continuation of a goal-directed action in spite of obstacles, difficulties, or discouragement" (Peterson & Seligman, 2004, p. 229). In the *CSV*, Peterson and Seligman review research on the effectiveness of persistence training programs,

as well as social variables (e.g., family environment) that lead to greater persistence. The common factor in these training programs and persistence-supportive social contexts is practice and reward. When people engage in tasks that require persistence and then receive positive reinforcements for their efforts, they become more likely to stick with tasks in the future (e.g., Eisenberger, 1992).

Grit and hardiness overlap in that both involve the courage necessary to deal with the struggles that characterize life in the real world (Maddi et al., 2013). In the *CSV*, courage is defined as "the exercise of will to accomplish goals in the face of opposition, either external or internal" (Peterson & Seligman, 2004, p. 199). The specific form of courage involved in hardiness, though, is not quite the same as that involved in grit, because the types of oppositions differ, as do the ways of exercising the will. Hardiness is a more reactive form of courage, in which the individual responds to stressful life circumstances by understanding that suffering and change are normal aspects of the human condition and taking responsibility for his or her choices in dealing with the situation. Grit is more proactive, in which the individual has "a dominant superordinate goal . . . tenaciously working toward it in the face of obstacles and setbacks, often for years or decades" (Duckworth & Gross, 2014, p. 322). A glance upward at our coverage of hardiness in this chapter will also show that Maddi's ideas about commitment as a facet of hardiness strongly parallel Duckworth's ideas about perseverance as a facet of grit.

Eugene Peterson (2000) reminds us that, in a society obsessed with instant gratification and passing fads, we have to remember that our lives as Christians are the "long obedience" of patient discipleship. And if any readers came to this text hoping to find a set of quick and easy tricks ("life hacks," to use a currently popular term) that would provide a shortcut to success and flourishing, you will not find any in this chapter. Living well is a marathon, and there really is no substitute for working hard and being tough.

SUGGESTIONS FOR FURTHER READING

Duckworth, A. (2016). *Grit: The power of passion and perseverance*. Scribner.

Duckworth, A. L., Peterson, C., Matthews, M. D., & Kelly, D. R. (2007). Grit: Perseverance and passion for long-term goals. *Journal of Personality and Social Psychology, 92*(6), 1087-1101.

Maddi, S. R. (2002). The story of hardiness: Twenty years of theorizing, research, and practice. *Consulting Psychology Journal: Practice and Research, 54*(3), 175-85.

Maddi, S. R. (2004). Hardiness: An operationalization of existential courage. *Journal of Humanistic Psychology, 44*(3), 279-98.

Maddi, S. R. (2013). *Hardiness: Turning stressful circumstances into resilient growth*. Springer.

Part Five

POSITIVE
RELATIONSHIPS

Chapter Thirteen

LOVE AND MARRIAGE

*Sonny, true love is the greatest thing in the world—except for
a nice MLT—mutton, lettuce, and tomato sandwich, where the mutton
is nice and lean and the tomatoes are ripe; they're so perky. I love that.*

MIRACLE MAX, *THE PRINCESS BRIDE*

Love and relationships are central to any consideration of human flourishing. In *City of God*, Augustine considered the core of moral growth to consist of increasing in one's love of that which is good and decreasing in one's love of that which is evil (less selfishness, more love of God and neighbor). In *On the Morals of the Catholic Church*, he defined all of the virtues in terms of how they function in relation to love. Freud said the only things one needs in order to live well is "to love and to work" (Erikson, 1963, p. 265). Baumeister and Leary (1995) argued that humans have a fundamental need to establish close relationships, and Christopher Peterson (2013) said the core message of positive psychology is that "other people matter" (p. 127). Balswick, King, and Reimer (2016) describe mature functioning in terms of our ability to engage in mutually reciprocating relationships. In a very real sense, love could be said to be the theme running through most (if not all) of this book. In chapter three, we looked at love as an essential feature of the *imago Dei*. In chapter ten, we looked at love

as a virtue. In chapters fourteen and fifteen, we will see love in action in the forms of gratitude and forgiveness. In chapter sixteen, we will see love in the form of altruism. And in chapter twenty-two, we will look at guilt, which often involves sorrow over the damage done to a relationship and the harm done to a loved one. So our task here is to narrow our focus down to a specific way of looking at love.

In this chapter, we will focus on marriage. As I said, love is a topic that encompasses many different kinds of relationships, but much of that is touched on in other chapters, and marriage is an especially good fit for our teleological approach. We will ask what makes such relationships flourish and thrive after we look at the role such relationships play in the good life. Naturally, this will take us into areas such as marriage and family therapy and couples counseling, and we can fill libraries with the books that have been written on how to make these relationships work. So this chapter will involve a brief survey of a few of the major theories and lines of research that tie most directly into our approach to positive psychology.

LOVE AND FLOURISHING

"A mountain of data reveal that most people are happier when attached than when unattached" (Myers, 2000, p. 62). There is a general consensus among researchers that close relationships such as marriage contribute to psychological well-being (Feeney & Collins, 2015a; Myers & Diener, 1995; Tao, 2019; Tomlinson & Aron, 2013). Those who are in relationships are better able to handle stressors (Cohen & Wills, 1985) and are more likely to be rated as "very happy" (Diener & Seligman, 2002). Couples provide each other with social support, both in times of crisis and in the pursuit of personal growth (Feeney & Collins, 2015b). Looking specifically at marriage, Gove, Hughes, and Style (1983) found that "the married are by far in the best mental health" (p. 125) compared to the never-married, widowed, or divorced, with marital status shown to be the most powerful predictor of participants' happiness, life satisfaction, and (lower) symptoms of psychiatric distress. Mastekaasa (1994) conducted an international study with more than 25,000 participants and found that marriage is associated with greater happiness around the world.

The benefits of love and committed relationships extend to physical health as well (Paxson & Shapiro, 2013). Negative reactions to threat and pain can be reduced by the mere act of holding a spouse's hand (Coan, Schaefer, & Davidson, 2006) or looking at the beloved's picture (Younger et al., 2010). Williams et al. (1992) found singles who were diagnosed with heart disease to have a lower survival rate than those who were married. In general, married people tend to live longer (Ben-Shlomo et al., 1993; Gower, 1973).

Before we start proclaiming marriage to be a universally beneficial experience, another factor we must take into account is the quality of the marriage. As Myers (1992) points out, research on the connections between marital status and well-being should lead us to conclude that "a bad marriage is worse than no marriage at all" (p. 158). When we differentiate between those whose marriages are going well and those whose marriages are going poorly, those in poorly functioning marriages report even less happiness than divorced participants (Myers, 2000), as well as equally bad levels of physical health and mortality (Lawrence et al., 2019). Marital troubles are also associated with a wide range of negative psychological outcomes (Kiecolt-Glaser & Newton, 2001).

This brings us to the question of what constitutes a good, highly functioning marriage versus a troubled or dysfunctional one. Many theories have been put forward by those who want to describe marriages and adult romantic relationships, helping people to avoid the less healthy versions and seek out better relationships (Hojjat & Cramer, 2013). In this section, we will focus on two of these theories: attachment theory and Sternberg's triangular theory of love.

ATTACHMENT THEORY

Attachment theory was developed by John Bowlby (1969) as an alternative to behaviorism and object relations theory in the study of relationships. The theory was originally created to explain the relationship between a child and the child's primary caregiver, but the principles of attachment theory have proved to be useful in understanding a number of human relationships, including those among workplace colleagues (e.g., Harms, 2011), in leadership (e.g., Davidovitz et al., 2007), and in politics (e.g., Weise et al., 2008), as well as the relationship between the believer and God (e.g., Kirkpatrick & Shaver, 1990).

Hazan and Shaver (1987) looked at adult romantic relationships as attachment bonds. The bond between an individual and an attachment figure typically features four patterns of behavior: (1) the individual is motivated to be in proximity to the attachment figure, (2) the individual tends to experience distress when separated from the attachment figure, (3) the individual looks at the attachment figure as a "haven of safety" to which he or she can turn when crises occur, and (4) the individual looks at the attachment figure as a "secure base" who provides everyday security and encouragement. Adult romantic relationships clearly show us all four of these patterns (Finley, 2016). People in love tend to spend a lot of time together and dislike separation. If the relationship is going well, they rely on each other when life goes horribly wrong (Collins & Feeney, 2000), and they are supportive of each other's endeavors, offering praise and words of encouragement (Feeney, 2004). Providing others with a haven of safety and a secure base facilitates their thriving (Feeney & Collins, 2015b), which is why marriage therapists who employ attachment theory seek to improve the degree to which family members fulfill the haven of safety and secure base functions

for each other (Byng-Hall, 1999; Brassard & Johnson, 2016).

Individual differences in attachment style affect relationships (Hazan & Shaver, 1987). Those who have a secure attachment style tend to be easier to get along with and more willing to rely on their loved ones in times of trouble, while those with insecure styles veer toward being either too clingy or too distant. Relationships with people who have secure attachment styles are more likely to be characterized by shared activities, a healthy balance of closeness and distance, open communication, and a style of interaction that is flexible and adaptive (Byng-Hall, 1999). Fortunately, while attachment style is a fairly stable individual difference variable, being in a long-term relationship with someone who has a secure attachment style (and is therefore more likely to provide the other person with a haven of safety and secure base) may help the partner's attachment style shift in a more secure direction (Feeney, 1999).

THE TRIANGULAR THEORY OF LOVE

Robert Sternberg (1986) claims that love has three components. The first component is intimacy, which involves "feelings of closeness, connectedness, and bondedness" (p. 119). In relationships characterized by a high degree of intimacy, the people involved are likely to experience warm feelings, sharing, emotional support, and a desire to promote the partner's welfare. The second component, passion, refers to "the drives that lead to romance, physical attraction, and sexual consummation" (p. 119) in a relationship. And the third component is commitment, which is "the decision that one loves someone else, and in the long term, the commitment to maintain that love" (p. 119).

These components vary in their importance depending on the type of relationship (for example, whether a relationship is meant to be long-term or short-term will influence the importance of commitment), and it is possible to describe a variety of relationships in terms of the degree to which they are characterized by these three components. A "liking" relationship will have a high degree of intimacy but low levels of the other two components. This is the kind of relationship one has with casual friends. Sternberg (1986) calls a passion-only relationship "infatuated love." Imagine a summer fling in which two lovebirds fall head over heels for each other and there is quite a lot of kissing, but they have nothing in common, so after a few intense weeks it's over and they go their separate ways (and John Travolta and Olivia Newton-John sing us a round of "Summer Nights"). If our lovebirds were to top off the summer with an impulsive marriage only to discover afterward that they didn't really like each other outside the bedroom and the bedroom passion then faded away, Sternberg would call that "empty love," characterized by commitment and nothing else. While the passion remained, though, this hypothetical pair would demonstrate both passion and commitment, the combination of which Sternberg calls "fatuous love." "Romantic love" occurs when there is a combination of intimacy and passion, with those involved having both a physical and emotional bond, though the lack of commitment prevents it from being something deeper. When the relationship partners are best friends (intimacy) with a

lifelong bond (commitment) but without passion, that is what Sternberg calls "companionate love." Best of all, though, is "consummate love," which is characterized by high levels of all three components.

Sternberg (1997) developed a scale to assess relationships in terms of his triangular theory. Intimacy was measured by the degree to which participants agreed with statements such as "I feel emotionally close to [person's name]," passion by statements such as "I find myself thinking about [person's name] frequently during the day," and commitment by statements such as "I view my relationship with [person's name] as permanent" (p. 318). Using an earlier version of this measure, Acker and Davis (1992) found that (as expected) those who were in "serious" relationships displayed higher commitment scores. Commitment was the strongest predictor of relationship satisfaction. In long-term relationships, women (but not men) tended to demonstrate a decline in passion scores, but intimacy scores tended to be higher for both genders. Grover and Helliwell (2019) found that the effect of marriage on well-being was about twice as large among those who described their spouses as their best friend. Whitley (1993) found that higher scores on all three components predicted relationship "survival."

A NEO-ARISTOTELIAN APPROACH TO THE GOOD MARRIAGE

In this book we have come back again and again to the question of the telos of human life. As we saw in chapter two, flourishing can be understood using MacIntyre's (2007) three-part teleological conceptual structure: (a) human nature as it currently is,

(b) human nature as it could be if it realized its telos, and (c) how to get from (a) to (b). Any proper account of human flourishing will involve all three components, and if a positive psychologist does not specify what ideas about human nature are upholding that psychologist's theory, that only means the psychologist is leaving those ideas unstated (but still present and influential). Also in chapter two, we saw that Martin Seligman (2002) endorsed a teleological view of flourishing influenced by modern Western individualism in which the telos is subjective gratification (Woolfolk & Wasserman, 2005); the good life is whatever the individual takes it to be, and discussions of flourishing involve selecting the optimal strategy for attaining that goal (Fowers, 2012a). Drawing from Christian theology and biblical studies, I presented an alternate view in chapter three, in which the telos of human functioning is found in God rather than self.

Blaine Fowers (2000) asks the teleological question about marriage. What is the telos of marriage? What is the purpose or function of this relationship? Answering this question is far more than a matter of academic debate, disconnected from "real life," since the telos of something not only describes its purpose but also provides a standard for evaluating it as good or bad. In previous chapters I have used the example of a knife. The telos of a knife is to cut; therefore a good knife cuts well and a bad knife cuts poorly, and the way to fix a bad knife is to increase its ability to cut well (by sharpening it, repairing a broken handle, and so on). If a person were to come to me and complain that he had a bad knife because he tried to pound a nail into a

board with it and it didn't work, my response would be to question his teleological beliefs about the knife. A knife cannot be a bad knife because it fails to pound nails, because the telos of a knife is not to pound nails. What we need here is a hammer. Similarly, I cannot complain about having a bad hammer if I try to cut a slice of bread with it and it doesn't work.

So what happens if someone complains about having a bad marriage? Fowers is a marriage therapist, and people generally do not go to marriage therapists because their marriages are doing well. They go to marriage therapists because their marriages are not working as they should. Saying that a marriage is not working as it should implies that we know how a marriage should work. Even the word *dysfunctional*, so often used to describe relationships when they go wrong, requires us to know the function. The teleological question is unavoidable.

Fowers (1998) argues that in the modern era, we have split apart the categories of "objective" and "subjective" and placed morality in the realm of the subjective and science in the realm of the objective. A result of this split is a vision of human life in which the world consists of "neutral matter to be shaped according to the individual's purposes" (p. 518). We have lost the ability to understand human flourishing as anything beyond personal fulfillment and relationships as anything beyond arrangements of mutual benefit, whether those arrangements are grounded in social contract or divine providence (Taylor, 2007). Marriage then comes to be seen as a way to pursue individual purposes, making subjective gratification the telos that defines a good marriage. "Within this dominant view of marriage, autonomous individuals choose to remain married largely on the basis of whether the relationship continues to provide the intimacy and mutual nurturance that will foster personal fulfillment and self-development" (Fowers, 1998, p. 518). Fowers (2000) calls this the "myth" of marital happiness: "the belief that the spouses' emotional fulfillment is the primary purpose of marriage" (p. 77), and he found that this myth lies behind many of the complaints put forward by those who seek out marriage counseling. The relationship is seen as dysfunctional because one or both spouses are "not happy" or "not satisfied" with the relationship, and if individual gratification is not forthcoming, divorce is seen as an acceptable "solution." Fowers claims that "most divorces are more a result of disappointment than of abuse, addiction, or infidelity" (p. 12). Because this is the dominant view of marriage in our culture today, most marriage therapists themselves endorse this myth and shape their methods around the goal of restoring or increasing the subjective emotional satisfaction experienced by spouses.

Consistent with the objective-subjective split, successful therapy is seen as centering around the application of "value-neutral," scientifically supported techniques for the achievement of the spouses' desires, with communication skills training the most common technique employed (Fowers, 2001). The science that supports these techniques is itself a reflection of this popular myth about the good marriage, with "satisfaction" considered the variable that defines a good marriage in most

studies and measures of satisfaction employed to quantify marital success (Fowers, 2000).

But what if the point of a successful marriage is not to "feel good" in the relationship but to "be good" in the relationship? Fowers (2000) develops his approach by making use of Aristotle's thoughts on friendship. Although there can be considerable overlap in these categories, Aristotle distinguishes between friendships that are based on mutual advantage (e.g., business partnerships), friendships that are based on mutual pleasure (e.g., those who share a hobby), and friendships that are based on virtue. This third kind of friendship (which Fowers calls "character friendships") involves two people functioning as partners who work toward important shared goals, who recognize that the other person possesses character strengths that are vital to realizing these goals, and who value the friend for his or her own sake. The two operate "side by side, absorbed in some common interest," to employ C. S. Lewis's (1960, p. 91) description of true friendship. Put in terms of our general neo-Aristotelian teleology, my friend and I can better actualize the good life by working together and employing each other's virtues, with enjoyment as a happy byproduct (Anderson & Fowers, 2020).

Fowers (2000) argues that a good marriage should be seen in these terms. Along with the passionate aspect (as seen in Sternberg's triangular theory of love), in a good marriage spouses are partners in the pursuit of shared valuable goals and the construction of the good life (Fowers & Owenz, 2010). As we saw in earlier chapters, a eudaimonic perspective does not devalue positive emotions but places them as byproducts of a life lived well. Similarly, a eudaimonic perspective on marriage will not cause us to advocate for marital misery but will cause us to see emotional gratification as an enjoyable and valuable side effect of the combined pursuit of a shared vision of the good life. Fowers and colleagues (2016) created the Relationship Flourishing Scale to assess the degree to which married couples are engaged in this kind of partnership, and RFS scores demonstrated substantial correlations with a wide range of measures of relationship quality and stability.

The pursuit of a shared vision of the good life requires the cultivation and exercise of virtues. Fowers (2000) discusses the roles that virtues such as loyalty, generosity, self-restraint, and justice play in the construction of a good marriage. As we saw in chapter ten, the cultivation of these virtues also ties into the development of the person as a highly functioning human, making a good marriage a "virtuous cycle." A good marriage helps develop the virtues, and developing the virtues helps make the marriage good.

Christians are likely to find much here with which we can agree. Like Fowers, Christians often criticize the artificial objective-subjective split (Evdokimov, 1985), as well as the idea that the purpose of marriage is emotional gratification (Lee & George, 2014). For Christians, marriages are "not about one's own desires and fulfillment, but are outwardly directed things, aimed toward the other person, toward growth, maturity, and deepened spirituality, for the benefit of the Church, and for the sake of children" (Jeal, 2010, p. xvii), and this fits

well into Fowers's approach. Fowers (2000), in fact, lists several of the same purposes as Jeal when he talks about possible goals for couples in marriage.

However, we are also likely to find some points of divergence. For one thing, Fowers (2000) does not take us too far beyond the error committed by Seligman that we saw in chapter two. Seligman (2002) is unwilling to specify a telos for human flourishing, resulting in a teleology that points toward subjective individual preference. In a later book (Seligman, 2011), he tries to get past this by claiming that a life can be objectively meaningful but ends up grounding the "objective" meaning in our collective subjective assessment (going from a life being meaningful because *I* say it is to a life being meaningful because *we* say it is). Fowers (2000) attempts to get past the objective-subjective split, encouraging couples to dedicate their marriages "to projects that take us beyond our narrow personal interests" and thus provide our lives with "richness, meaning, and dignity that go far beyond what is possible in the pursuit of individual happiness" (p. 218). That is certainly better than simple individualism, but it is still a shift from a subjective "because *I* say it is" to a mutually subjective "because *we* say it is," with the *we* being the married couple rather than the larger society. In chapter twenty-three we will have more to say about the pursuit of that which is objectively meaningful, but we have already seen in chapter three that a Christian positive psychology will be guided by an objective telos for human functioning.

A Christian view of marriage will fit within that vision. There is a tradition of

Christian thought on "character friendship" as described by Aristotle and Fowers. The twelfth-century monk Aelred of Rievaulx (1167/1977) made a distinction between friendships that is strikingly similar to Aristotle's, listing carnal friendships (grounded in pleasure), worldly friendships (grounded in hope of gain), and "spiritual friendships" that involve growth in the virtues and "a mutual conformity in matters human and divine united with benevolence and charity" (p. 61). Wesley Hill (2015) has recently taken up Aelred's project, promoting spiritual friendship in a society that has lost contact with the tradition.

Aelred of Rivaulx connects spiritual friendship to marriage, but in a Christian approach to marriage, marriage is both more specific and far larger than Aristotelian friendship (Thorne, 2010). Friendship-love can be a part of many relationships, including marriage (Lewis, 1960), but in marriage the couple becomes one flesh, a bodily union that is not found in friendship relationships (Lee & George, 2014). Girgis, Anderson, and George (2012) distinguish between the "conjugal" view of marriage, in which marriage is a physical, emotional, and spiritual bond between husband and wife that points toward family and lifelong fidelity, and the more recent "revisionist" view of marriage as an intense long-term emotional bond that points toward personal fulfillment. While much of the theorizing about marriage and flourishing within mainstream positive psychology will align with the second definition of marriage, a Christian positive psychology of marriage will align with the first, giving greater depth and significance to the institution of marriage. Grenz (1990) describes four major purposes of marriage that can be found in Christian scholarship on the subject: marriage as the proper venue for sexual expression, marriage as directed toward procreation, marriage as companionship, and marriage as a spiritual metaphor. While these purposes are all connected, Grenz places greatest emphasis on the fourth purpose, describing the marriage bond as "a picture of the divine will to community" (p. 56). Fourth-century church father John Chrysostom called marriage an "icon of the church," a corporeal revealing of divine truth. Ephraim Radner (2010) sees marriage as a mystery, parallel to the mystery of the incarnation of Christ. In one mystery, that which is different (the divine and the human) comes together, resulting in new life (the church). In the other, that which is different (male and female) comes together, resulting in new life (children). Even if the couple, for one reason or another, cannot or do not have children, the relationship remains oriented toward procreation in its basic nature (Girgis, Anderson, & George, 2012; Lee & George, 2014). Husband and wife becoming one flesh is an embodied image of the Trinity (Evdokimov, 1985), and marriage is an embodied image of the relationship between God and Israel in the Old Testament and Christ and the church in the New Testament (Grenz, 1990).

The strongest theological link between Fowers and Christian positive psychologists is found among those (e.g., Burke, 2015) who argue that the telos of marriage includes "the sanctification of the spouses themselves through their faithful grace-sustained love for one another" (p. 49). In order to be a good husband to my wife, I rely on the guiding and strengthening power of the Holy Spirit, and I must exercise the virtues, including wisdom, justice, and temperance. I also need courage to commit to a lifetime with this woman in the face of an unknowable future (see our earlier material on commitment and hardiness). Above all, I need Jesus' kenotic love to place her good above my own. So Christian positive psychologists can fruitfully employ Fowers's (2000) work on marriage as a kind of friendship, as that friendship does have a valuable place in marriage (Lee & George, 2014), while being aware that Fowers's treatment of marriage will be, in our eyes, theologically incomplete.

SUGGESTIONS FOR FURTHER READING

Cassidy, J., & Shaver, P. R. (Eds.). (2018). *Handbook of attachment: Theory, research, and clinical applications* (3rd ed.). Guilford Press.

Fowers, B. J. (1998). Psychology and the good marriage: Social theory as practice. *American Behavioral Scientist, 41*(4), 516-41.

Fowers, B. J. (2000). *Beyond the myth of marital happiness*. Jossey-Bass.

Hojjat, M., & Cramer, D. (Eds.). (2013). *Positive psychology of love*. Oxford University Press.

Jones, B. F. (2015). *Faithful: A theology of sex*. Zondervan.

Sternberg, R. J., & Weis, K. (Eds.). (2006). *The new psychology of love*. Yale University Press.

Chapter Fourteen

AN ATTITUDE OF GRATITUDE

Almighty God, Father of all mercies, we thine unworthy servants
do give thee most humble and hearty thanks for all thy goodness and
loving-kindness to us, and to all men. We bless thee for our creation,
preservation, and all the blessings of this life; but above all, for thine
inestimable love in the redemption of the world by our Lord Jesus
Christ; for the means of grace, and for the hope of glory.

BOOK OF COMMON PRAYER (1662)

The test of all happiness is gratitude.

G. K. CHESTERTON

CHRISTIANS ARE A BUNCH OF INGRATES

Receiving and responding to a gift is far more than mumbling polite words as one takes what is given (Visser, 2008). A gift creates a link between giver and receiver, carrying with it a weight of history and deep social meanings, as well as an obligation to respond. In the ancient world, gifts formed a circle from benefactor to beneficiary and back, a circle that must not be broken (Leithart, 2014). I give a gift to my friend, who reciprocates with his own gift, motivating me to continue the pattern with another gift, and so on, to our mutual benefit. A war chief honors the feats of those who fight under his banner with praise and a juicy portion of the plunder, and the warriors honor the war chief with loyalty and service. Worshipers offer the gods sacrifices that please them (in the *Epic of Gilgamesh*, the gods are shown to enjoy the smell of the burnt offerings), and the gods bestow favors on the worshipers. Parents give their children the gift of life, and children respond with reverence and obedience. The Roman system of patronage was based entirely on gifts and gratitude; wealthy patrons provided clients with favors, money, legal counsel, advantageous positions for clients' sons, advantageous marriages for clients' daughters, and so on. The clients would campaign for their patrons if they ran for office (and definitely vote for them), accompany them if they went to war, ransom them if they were captured in battle, praise them in public, and so on (Visser, 2008).

One theme that runs through most of these examples is that the benefactor is of a higher status than the beneficiary (gods and humans, parents and children, patrons and clients, etc.), and the grateful response is also asymmetrical (the lovely smell of a sacrificed sheep is not quite equal to the power and glory involved in a divine blessing). Aristotle took these status considerations very seriously in his vision of human flourishing. As we saw in chapter ten, Aristotle's ideal human was the *megalopsychos* ("great-souled man"), a wealthy male intellectual who is very concerned with his own greatness. The *megalopsychos* is a happy giver, because lavish gifts are demonstrations of his greatness, and he can show even more greatness by not being too concerned about whether or not the recipient gratefully responds with an equivalent gift. But the great-souled man hates being on the receiving end of generosity, because the one who bestows a gift is superior to the one who receives it (Leithart, 2014). If he must receive a gift, he will "close the circle" as quickly as possible, repaying the benefactor and clearing the metaphorical books, then moving on and trying not to think about the shame of having been lowered in status. If we view gratitude as repaying gift for gift, the *megalopsychos* is perhaps the most grateful person alive, but if we view gratitude as an emotional response that involves appreciating the giver, the *megalopsychos* seems more like the least grateful person alive.

Countering the classical "circular" view of gratitude is a "linear" view inherited from the Judeo-Christian tradition (Leithart, 2014), in which gifts do not require counter-gifts. God provides generously but tells us straight out that he gets no benefit from burnt offerings (Psalm 50:8-13;

Isaiah 1:11), breaking the circle of human-divine gift and gratitude. The ultimate example of this linearity, of course, is the gift of Christ, given out of pure love with no strings attached (Barclay, 2015). Instead of using gifts to carefully cultivate a network of advantageous clients, the wealthy are to give freely to those in need without consideration for their own gain or status (Leviticus 25:35-37; Deuteronomy 15:7-8), breaking the circle of human-human gift and gratitude. If there is any "circularity" to biblical teachings on generosity, it is that God promises to repay those who are generous either in this life or afterward (Psalm 41:1-3; Proverbs 19:17; Matthew 10:42). If a believer wants to "pay God back" for his provision, a righteous heart and righteous behavior will suffice (Hosea 6:6; 1 Samuel 15:22; Proverbs 21:3), and Christians handle "debts of gratitude" between each other not by paying each other off but by "acknowledging it, by feeling and expressing gratitude" (Roberts, 2007, p. 143). In this way, "linear" gratitude still establishes relational bonds between giver and receiver, but without demanding that we "close the circle" by satisfying the quid pro quo or being locked into considerations of status (Barclay, 2015).

This caused early Christians no end of bad publicity among their Roman neighbors (Leithart, 2014), who saw them as deeply ungrateful. Christians were not ashamed to depend on each other and were not (in their Roman colleagues' eyes) very good at playing the patronage game, often spending more time thanking God for a benefit than the human who handed it over. Even "worse," they had the nerve to live and work in cities that were overseen and protected by the Roman gods but were not grateful enough to offer even the smallest sacrifices at the altars to those gods.

Quite a lot of the ancient "circular" view of gratitude persists, even among believers. Barclay (2015) points to the medieval practice of nobles making grand donations to the church, expecting the Lord to reciprocate with blessings in this world or the next. Visser (2008) warns readers that accepting gifts can carry an obligation, giving the example of a wealthy man who bestows gifts "freely" on a young woman but pressures her to provide sexual favors "in return." (She even quotes from the musical *Guys and Dolls*, which earns her extra cool points in my book. "Take back your mink. Take back your pearls.") Generously tipping a waiter (a tip is often referred to as a "gratuity") is a way of displaying one's greatness while responding to satisfactory service. Despite the egalitarian ideals of our culture, patronage is firmly entrenched in modern politics:

> Everyone knows that gratitude is the lifeblood of politics. Senator negotiates with senator by calling in or imposing debts of gratitude: I will support your Medicare proposal if you lend aid to my tax plan. Congressman scratches the back of congressman so that he will later get a scratch himself. Legislators deliver truckloads of pork to constituents, who repay them with votes. (Leithart, 2014, p. 140)

Through the Christian influence (by way of Adam Smith), much of the "linear" view is mixed in, although as we have seen the "circular" view dies hard. Among psychologists, gratitude is considered to primarily be an emotional reaction, whether or not it results in tangible action to repay the giver

(Harpham, 2004; McCullough et al., 2001), showing the influence of the "linear" view in the psychology of gratitude.

DEFINING GRATITUDE

Psychologists approach gratitude as a moral emotion, one of those feelings "that are linked to the interests or welfare either of society as a whole or at least of persons other than the judge or agent" (Haidt, 2003, p. 853), and as connected to thoughts and behaviors that are morally praiseworthy or blameworthy (more about moral emotions in chapter twenty-two). McCullough and colleagues (2001) describe gratitude as "both a response to moral behavior and a motivator of moral behavior. People ('beneficiaries') respond with gratitude when other people ('benefactors') behave in a way that promotes the beneficiaries' well-being" (p. 250). They focus on the social function of gratitude to explain what this emotion does. Society holds together when we take care of each other and trust each other. Gratitude helps this happen by functioning as a moral "barometer," shaping our responses to other people's actions; as a moral motive, since grateful people are more likely to behave prosocially toward others; and as a moral reinforcer, since displays of gratefulness make the benefactors feel good, which encourages future prosocial behavior. Gratitude provides emotional support to the reciprocity norm, the principle that benefit should be requited with an equivalent benefit (Gouldner, 1960). As we have seen, though, gratitude goes well beyond mere reciprocity, binding people together in relationships with each other (Algoe, Haidt, & Gable, 2008).

Gratitude is thus connected deeply to the basics of human nature. Recall (from chapter three) that humans, created in the image of God, are inherently relational (Grenz, 2001). We are defined in terms of our connections to others, and the human telos involves living "in communion with God and others in mutually giving and receiving relationships" (Balswick, King, & Reimer, 2016, p. 37). Although this view of human functioning flies in the face of the Western (and especially American) individualistic assumption that happiness comes from autonomy and independence (Fowers, Richardson, & Slife, 2017), God created us to be dependent on each other (Roberts, 2007). We are born into a period of extended dependence in childhood, spend our adulthood in societies in which we rely on each other to survive and function (especially during times of injury and illness, which happens often to vulnerable creatures like us), and typically finish off in an old age that involves dependence on the younger generation and surrounding community. Alasdair MacIntyre (1999) refers to humans as "dependent rational animals," pointing out that even those qualities that empower "independent rational agency need for their adequate exercise to be accompanied by what I shall call the virtues of acknowledged dependence" (p. 8). "We flourish as human beings when we are excellent social animals," and that will involve the ability to be dependent well (Fowers, Richardson, & Slife, 2017, p. 85).

MacIntyre (1999) argues that Aristotle's *megalopsychos* fails (as many wealthy and powerful people do) to realize that he is not actually self-sufficient, and it is that perceptual deficiency that makes him so ungrateful and self-absorbed. Gratitude connects us to the reality of human existence and sustains the relationships within which human flourishing happens. Roberts (2007) extends this to our relationship with God. Human unwillingness to accept the reality that we depend on God's provision and God's forgiveness (which Roberts points out can be experienced by some as humiliating, just as the *megalopsychos* finds it shameful to depend on other humans) makes us prideful and foolish, unable to see reality as it is. The correct response to God is one of thankfulness.

GRATITUDE RESEARCH

Gratitude can be studied as a situation-specific emotion or as a character trait. Fredrickson (2004) takes the first approach, placing gratitude within her "broaden-and-build" theory of positive emotion (see chapter four). Feeling grateful broadens our perceptual horizons as we consider the many ways to reciprocate the benefit we have received, and feeling grateful builds our psychological and social resources as it strengthens relationships. Feelings of gratitude involve an increase in empathy, as grateful people recognize that the benefactor went to some effort to provide the benefit (Lazarus & Lazarus, 1994). Fredrickson (2004) points to a number of ways grateful emotions can enhance well-being and subjective enjoyment but notes that few empirical studies have been performed on gratitude as an emotion. In one such study, Stone and Watkins (2001) placed participants in control and experimental groups, manipulating some into feeling grateful. Grateful participants demonstrated increases in positive affect, showing that Fredrickson (2004) may be correct in that gratitude might contribute to the enjoyment of positive subjective experiences.

More common than research on gratitude as an emotion is research on gratitude as a trait. Gratitude is listed as a character strength in the *CSV* (Peterson & Seligman, 2004), and those with a high degree of this strength are described as having "a sense of thankfulness and joy in response to receiving a gift" (p. 554) that endures across time and circumstance. McCullough, Emmons, and Tsang (2002) describe the trait of gratitude as "a generalized tendency to recognize and respond with grateful emotion to the roles of other people's benevolence" (p. 112) that is made up of four components. First is gratitude intensity, with highly grateful people likely to feel gratitude more strongly than others when they perceive themselves to be the recipients of a benefit. Second is gratitude frequency, with highly grateful people experiencing gratitude a greater number of times per day. Third is gratitude span, with highly grateful people feeling grateful for a wider range of blessings (family, job, health, and so on). Fourth is gratitude density, with highly grateful people noticing a greater number of people who were involved in the provision of a given benefit. McCullough and colleagues measure this trait with a six-item gratitude questionnaire (the unimaginatively named GQ-6), which they found to be a valid and reliable assessment tool.

McCullough et al. (2002) looked at the personality correlates of gratitude using the five-factor model. Highly grateful people tend to have higher agreeableness, extraversion, and openness scores and lower levels of neuroticism. In general, women tend to be a bit more grateful than men (Kashdan, Mishra, Breen, & Froh, 2009). Grateful people are more likely to live in smaller towns (Park & Peterson, 2010) and tend to be more religious (McCullough et al., 2002; Watkins et al., 2003) and more politically conservative (Hanek, Olson, & McAdams, 2011).

The general theme that emerges from the research on gratitude is that gratitude is good for you (Watkins, 2014). Watkins describes gratitude as an amplifier, enhancing the goodness in people's lives by increasing their ability to perceive and appreciate it. Highly grateful people are more likely to recognize the value of a benefit when they receive it (Wood et al., 2008) and have a greater appreciation for beauty (Diessner et al., 2008). McCullough and colleagues (2002) found GQ-6 scores to be associated with a number of positive psychological variables, including more life satisfaction, more vitality, more hope, less anxiety and depression, more religiosity and spirituality, more empathy, less materialism, and less envy. Park, Peterson, and Seligman (2004) found gratitude to be "consistently and robustly" associated with greater life satisfaction, as did Wood, Joseph, and Maltby (2008). Watkins and colleagues (2003) found gratitude scores to be strongly associated with happiness, life satisfaction, and positive affectivity, as well as negatively associated with depression, hostility, and narcissism. Witvliet, Ludwig, and Laan (2019) found gratitude to be associated with greater happiness and hope.

Gratitude has also been shown to enhance moral functioning (Wood, Joseph,

& Linley, 2007). As we saw earlier, Mc-Cullough and colleagues (2001) classify gratitude as a moral emotion, claiming that gratitude serves three functions in sustaining healthy relationships and communities. The first function was that of moral "barometer" or "benefit detector" (McCullough, Kimeldorf, & Cohen, 2008). Gratitude enhances people's moral perceptual abilities, making highly grateful people more likely to notice when someone has benefited them (Watkins, 2014), which increases the possibility for emotional connections between people.

The second moral function identified by McCullough and colleagues (2001) is that of gratitude as a moral motive. People should be more motivated to behave prosocially (or at least restrain destructive impulses) when they feel grateful toward a benefactor. McCullough et al. (2002) found that dispositionally grateful people scored higher on empathy and were more likely to be described by peers as someone who is helpful and unselfish. Tsang and Martin (2019) found that inducing gratitude in experiments resulted in more prosocial behavior, and Giacomo Bono and colleagues (2019) found in a longitudinal study that young people who became more grateful over time also became more empathetic and engaged in more prosocial behavior. Researchers have also found that grateful participants responded to benefits from others with more helpfulness (Bartlett & DeSteno, 2006) and more generosity (Tsang, 2006).

The third moral function is gratitude as a moral reinforcer (McCullough et al., 2001). Because people are likely to repeat behaviors that result in expressions of

approval or affection from others (Skinner, 1953), "expressing gratitude to someone for his or her prosocial actions produces greater effort on the part of the benefactor to behave morally in the future" (McCullough et al., 2001, p. 253). In numerous studies (e.g., Clark, 1975; Moss & Page, 1972), researchers have found that simply thanking benefactors results in the benefactors being more willing to do more for others. Rind and Bordia (1995) found that, if restaurant servers wrote "thank you" on the bill, it resulted in larger tips from customers. In a dramatic example of the power of thanks, McGovern, Ditzian, and Taylor (1975) strapped participants in pairs (one male and one female) to electric shock generators and gave them control over which one would receive the painful zaps. The female "participant" (actually a confederate) would then ask the male participant if he would take the shock for her. The participants were split into two groups. In one group, the participant was thanked if he took the shock; in the other group, he was not thanked. Those who were thanked for the self-sacrificial act were more likely to volunteer to keep taking the shocks, while those who were not thanked became less likely to help.

Gratitude improves our ability to establish and maintain relationships, which connects it to the vision of flourishing that informs this book: Highly functioning people exist in mutually reciprocating covenant relationships (Balswick, King, & Reimer, 2016; Grenz, 1994; Sabates, 2012) and imitate Christ's love for others (Murphy, 2005b). People like grateful people (Watkins, 2014) and want to be in relationships with them.

Anderson (1968) gave college students 555 personality trait words and asked them to rate the "likableness" of someone with that trait. "Ungrateful" was way down the list at number 495, surrounded by such disliked traits as "cowardly" and "prejudiced," while "grateful" and "appreciative" were closer to the top, sharing space with "brilliant," "helpful," and "forgiving" (the top-rated traits were "sincere" and "honest," while the bottom two were "phony" and "liar"). Ungrateful behavior produces negative impressions on others (Suls, Witenberg, & Gutkin, 1981), while expressions of gratitude make the formation and positive functioning of a relationship more likely (Algoe, Haidt, & Gable, 2008). Algoe (2012) calls this the "find, remind, and bind" theory of gratitude (one has to appreciate a theory that rhymes), in that gratitude facilitates the establishment of relationships ("find"), orients attention toward existing relationships ("remind"), and joins the benefactor and beneficiary closer together ("bind").

In a number of studies, researchers have found evidence supporting the theory that gratitude promotes the establishment and maintenance of healthy relationships. Algoe, Gable, and Maisel (2010) had participants in romantic relationships complete a brief daily questionnaire for two weeks, with questions involving behavior (for example, whether or not the other person did something thoughtful for you today) and experiences of grateful emotions. Gratitude from everyday acts of thoughtfulness predicted increases in relationship closeness and satisfaction. Gordon, Arnette, and Smith (2011) also used a daily diary method and also found

gratitude to be associated with greater satisfaction among married couples. Gordon et al. (2012) found that romantic partners who felt gratitude toward the other person were more responsive to their partners' needs and were more committed to maintaining the relationship over the long term. So if you are in a relationship, take a moment today to notice some benefit that you have received recently from that person, and express your gratitude.

COUNT YOUR BLESSINGS, NAME THEM ONE BY ONE

Speaking of expressing gratitude, a number of interventions have been developed to help people cultivate gratitude. Like other virtues, gratefulness increases through practice, so these interventions involve becoming more grateful by expressing gratitude (Baumsteiger et al., 2019). Emmons and McCullough (2003) carried out a series of gratitude studies in which participants (university students) were randomly assigned to one of three conditions. One group was instructed to spend ten weeks writing a weekly gratitude journal, describing at least five things for which they were grateful that week (examples of things participants listed included parents, God, and music). The second group was instructed to keep a weekly journal in which they described hassles that bothered them (examples listed included bad grades, stupid drivers, and financial troubles). The third group (a control group) was instructed to simply write about things that happened (examples listed included attending a festival, taking a trip, and talking to someone). At the end of the ten weeks, the participants who kept a gratitude journal felt more gratitude, had a more positive view of their lives, were more optimistic about how the upcoming week was going to go, were more likely to help others, reported fewer physical ailments, experienced more positive affect, and got more exercise than participants in both the hassle group and control group. This effect has been replicated by Sheldon and Lyubomirsky (2006) and Froh, Sefick, and Emmons (2008), so if you are looking for a positive psychology intervention that is easy to do and has been shown to have a direct impact on well-being, keeping a gratitude journal could be a helpful practice for you to begin. Seligman, Steen, Park, and Peterson (2005) created a variant of the gratitude journal that they called "three good things." This version involves writing down every evening three benefits you received that day, along with an explanation of what caused this good event. They found that performing the "three good things" exercise resulted in increases in happiness scores that were sustained over a six-month follow-up period.

Seligman and colleagues (2005) also developed a more powerful and specific version of this exercise, the "gratitude visit," in which you select someone who has had a powerful positive impact in your life, write a letter in which you express your gratefulness (be specific), and then go visit the person and hand-deliver the letter. This activity produced a massive surge in happiness scores and a corresponding drop in depression scores. Seligman (2002) ran this as a "gratitude night" in which students invited people to come to a special dinner in which the invited guests were thanked using the "gratitude visit" format. To say

that the evening was emotionally powerful would be a tremendous understatement. There were tears. Several students said it was one of the best nights of their lives.

While the gratitude visit focuses on specific benefits received from specific benefactors, gratitude can be generalized to include an awareness of and appreciation for that which is positive in life (Peterson & Seligman, 2004; Wood, Froh, & Geraghty, 2010). Life itself is a gift from God. Frias and colleagues (2011) wanted to see if reflecting on one's mortality could be a method for cultivating gratitude, testing Steindl-Rast's (1984) claim that "only a heart familiar with death will appreciate the gift of life with so deep a feeling of joy" (p. 18). They separated participants into three groups. A control group was instructed to imagine a typical day, one experimental group was given the mortality salience manipulation from terror management research (see chapter twenty-three for more on terror management theory) in which they were told to think about their eventual death, and a second experimental group was instructed to imagine and reflect on a hypothetical scenario in which they died. Compared to the control group, the gratitude scores of those both in the mortality salience group and in the death reflection group increased.

There are also some inhibitory factors that make gratitude less likely, all of which involve a focus on self. Seligman (2002) says that seeing oneself as a victim and dwelling on hurts of the past undermine one's ability to appreciate the good things in life. Envy and resentment have a similar effect (Etchegoyen & Nemas, 2003). Narcissism (Watkins et al., 2003) and a sense of entitlement (McWilliams & Lependorf, 1990) also undermine gratitude, either because benefits are seen as simply one's due or because (like Aristotle's *megalopsychos*) one resents the implication of inferiority that accompanies the receiving of a benefit from another. Selfishness and gratitude exist in opposition to each other. The more one cultivates gratitude, focusing on the goodness of life and the good actions of other people, the more that combats self-centeredness. The more one focuses on the self, the greater the degree to which one loses the capacity to perceive and appreciate goodness outside the self.

Brother David Steindl-Rast (2004) considers gratefulness, which he calls "a celebration of undeserved kindness" (p. 284), to be the heart of prayer, and Schnitker and Richardson (2019) found gratitude exercises to be even more effective when they were structured as prayers. We are grateful when we react with wonderment to undeserved blessings, experiencing the simple joy of a child who just saw a rainbow (Steindl-Rast, 1984). When we are mindful of how all of life is gratuitous, an undeserved kindness bestowed by God, Steindl-Rast says we go through life fully alive to the gift of existence, responding with thankfulness to the divine giver who created it all. Our prayers of thanksgiving are the utterances of a grateful heart.

SUGGESTIONS FOR FURTHER READING

Algoe, S. B. (2012). Find, remind, and bind: The functions of gratitude in everyday relationships. *Social and Personality Psychology Compass*, 6(6), 455-69.

Emmons, R. A. (2013). *Gratitude works! A 21-day program for creating emotional prosperity.* Jossey-Bass.

Emmons, R. A., & McCullough, M. E. (Eds.). (2004). *The psychology of gratitude.* Oxford University Press.

McCullough, M. E., Kilpatrick, S. D., Emmons, R. A., & Larson, D. B. (2001). Is gratitude a moral affect? *Psychological Bulletin*, 127(2), 249-66.

Steindl-Rast, D. (1984). *Gratefulness, the heart of prayer.* Paulist Press.

Watkins, P. C. (2014). *Gratitude and the good life: Toward a psychology of appreciation.* Springer.

Chapter Fifteen

TO ERR IS HUMAN, TO FORGIVE DIVINE

One pardons in the degree that one loves.

LA ROCHEFOUCAULD, *MAXIMES*

In the movie *Forrest Gump*, the eponymous Gump spends his life wandering rather aimlessly from one situation to another, somehow finding himself at the center of several major events in mid-twentieth-century American history and eventually ending up as a wealthy shrimp magnate. In his autobiographical chapter in the book *Integrating Faith and Psychology: Twelve Psychologists Tell Their Stories*, Everett Worthington Jr. (2010) strikes me as the Forrest Gump of positive psychology. He did not plan to be a leading figure in forgiveness research and practice, it just kind of . . . happened. He originally trained as a nuclear engineer and joined the US Navy but then entered into graduate studies for psychology (he does not say why). He began his career doing research on self-control and pain but switched to marriage and family (he does not say why). While praying, he felt God leading him to assemble research articles on parental involvement in adolescent abortion decisions. He didn't want to but said "OK" and put together the stack, "and just like that" (he

said in a Forrest Gump voice) he was asked to testify before the Virginia legislature on parental involvement in adolescent abortion decisions. And then to present at a conference in Washington DC on the topic. And then to write articles and chapters on the topic. He hadn't planned on doing forgiveness research, but some of his graduate students wanted to and they dragged him along, "and just like that"[1] he was coauthoring a book on forgiveness. And then speaking before the Truth and Reconciliation Commission in South Africa. And then serving as executive director of the Campaign for Forgiveness Research (Worthington, 2019). Dr. Worthington chalks all this up to God working in surprising ways, and he encourages us to be willing to follow where the Lord leads, even if it bears no resemblance to our original plans.

DEFINING AND MEASURING FORGIVENESS

Worthington and Sandage (2016) describe forgiveness as a two-step process in which

---

[1] I emailed Dr. Worthington just to make sure he did not interpret these Gump jokes as mockery. No point in starting trouble when in fact I have the highest respect for the man and his work. He was cool with it.

one chooses to view the perpetrator as a person of value, forswears vengeance (decisional forgiveness), and replaces negative emotions toward the perpetrator with positive emotions (emotional forgiveness). As we embark on this tour of the forgiveness literature, we will see that there is more than one way to define forgiveness, but psychologists tend to agree on what forgiveness is *not*. Forgiveness "does not imply forgetting, condoning, or excusing offenses" (Exline, Worthington, Hill, & McCullough, 2003, p. 339). So we do not pretend that the offense never happened or try to explain it away. Instead, the offended party recognizes that the injury was a genuine injury and that it was unjust but "chooses to abandon his or her right to resentment and retaliation, and instead offers mercy to the offender" (Enright & Coyle, 1998, p. 140).

Some people are more forgiving than others. Robert Roberts (1995) describes this "forgivingness" trait as a virtue that involves "the disposition to abort one's anger . . . at persons one takes to have wronged one culpably" (p. 290) and replacing the perception of the perpetrator as evil or alien with more benevolent perceptions. Forgivingness is listed in the *CSV* as a character strength, defined as "readiness or proneness to forgive" (Peterson & Seligman, 2004, p. 446). People with a high degree of this strength "get over" their hurt feelings quickly and easily and are unlikely to hold a grudge or seek revenge.

While Worthington (2006) focuses on forgiveness as an attitudinal change within the victim, McCollough, Pargament, and Thoresen (2000) argue that forgiveness is both intrapersonal and interpersonal and the interpersonal aspect cannot be eliminated from consideration. As forgiveness involves one's attitude toward another person in response to an injury inflicted by that person, forgiveness is inescapably social. Baumeister, Exline, and Sommer (1998) point to the power of forgiveness to keep relationships and communities functioning. Since nobody is perfect, transgressions and injuries are inevitable as we interact with each other. Without forgiveness our supply of friends would rapidly dwindle, so forgiveness serves a positive social function. Social roles are also involved; forgiveness involves giving up the role of "victim," with its position of moral superiority and claims to the benefits of recompense, in exchange for the restoration of relational roles to their earlier state. This "social" approach to forgiveness, though, is less common than the "internal" approach, and most research and practice is guided by the idea that forgiveness is a process of inner attitudinal change.

FORGIVENESS RESEARCH

McCullough and colleagues (2009) claim that we can understand the variables that make forgiveness more or less likely in terms of the effects of these variables on three conditions: careworthiness, expected value, and safety. Careworthiness is the degree to which we consider the perpetrator to be a legitimate object of moral concern (i.e., someone about whom we should care). Expected value refers to our anticipated future interactions with the perpetrator and whether or not we think those interactions will be positive. Safety involves the perceived likelihood that the perpetrator will harm us again in the future.

Research on empathy and forgiveness shows the careworthiness condition in operation (see chapter sixteen for more on empathy and altruism). Batson and Ahmad (2001), using a prisoner's dilemma game, found that inducing empathy (making participants feel what the other person was feeling) reduced the likelihood that the participants would retaliate when betrayed. Fincham, Paleari, and Regalia (2002) found that empathy predicted husbands' willingness to forgive their wives' transgressions. McCullough, Worthington, and Rachal (1997) and Baskin and Enright (2004) found that forgiveness-promoting interventions worked when they increased empathy toward the perpetrator. Worthington (1998) includes humility with empathy as a vital component of the forgiveness process. Both empathy (by identifying with the feelings of the perpetrator) and humility (by seeing oneself as similarly in need of forgiveness) increase our perceptions of the perpetrator as someone who is inside of our circle of moral relevance.

While empathy and humility foster forgiveness, narcissism undermines it (Eaton, Struthers, & Santelli, 2006). Among those who research narcissism and forgiveness, personality psychologist Robert Emmons (2000) says that "the narcissistic personality is the antithesis of the forgiving personality" (p. 164). Rather than identifying with others, people with a high degree of narcissism elevate the self above others. This results in a sense of entitlement that impedes forgiveness by creating an exaggerated concern with the loss of status that comes with an injury and an exaggerated concern for restoring that lost status (Exline et al., 2004). Narcissists are more likely to see themselves as victims (McCullough et al., 2003), feel more anger over their injury, ruminate over it more, and feel less empathy toward perpetrators (Fatfouta et al., 2015), and they are more likely to seek revenge (Brown, 2004).

Forgiveness is more likely when we expect that we will have to continue to interact with the perpetrator. McCullough and colleagues (2009) argue that this is why we are more likely to forgive people with whom we are already in a relationship and are more likely to forgive relationship partners when we are strongly committed to the relationship. Researchers have found that relationship commitment increases the likelihood of forgiveness (Finkel et al., 2002), that we are more likely to forgive friends than strangers (Phillips & Brown, 2002), and that we are more likely to forgive coworkers we like than coworkers we find unlikeable (Bradfield & Aquino, 1999).

Our impressions of safety are also influenced by expressions of repentance and remorse (McCullough et al., 2009). Darby and Schlenker (1982) conducted one of the first experimental studies of forgiveness, examining how children aged six to twelve reacted to transgressions by manipulating specific aspects of a reported event (a child bumped into another child who was carrying a stack of dishes). Four kinds of apology were presented. The first group was told a story in which the perpetrator did not apologize, the second group's story involved a perfunctory apology ("Excuse me"), the third group's story involved an apology with remorse ("Excuse me; I feel badly about this"), and the fourth group's story involved an apology with remorse and an offer of help. The "better" the apology, the more forgiving the participants became. When a perpetrator confesses and shows remorse, that serves as a signal that this person is less likely to harm us in the future (Gold & Weiner, 2000), which increases the likelihood that we will forgive this person (Eaton & Struthers, 2006). Struthers and colleagues (2008), though, found that apologies only increased forgiveness when the transgression was unintentional. Saying "sorry" after deliberately hurting someone actually made it less likely that the victim would forgive the perpetrator. The researchers interpreted this as the victim perceiving the perpetrator's apology as dishonest; a liar is more, not less, likely to harm us in the future.

However, there are other theoretical options available besides this three-condition approach from McCullough et al. (2009). Several researchers have employed the five-factor model of personality, in which personality is described in terms of the individual's relative degrees of extraversion, neuroticism, conscientiousness, agreeableness, and openness (McCrae & Costa, 2003), in their attempts to understand the antecedents of forgiveness. Mullet, Neto, and Riviére (2005) reviewed the research literature on personality and forgiveness and found that researchers have tended to find relationships between four of the five factors and various aspects of forgiveness. Mullet and colleagues split forgiveness into three factors: resentment, vengefulness, and forgiveness. Agreeableness and neuroticism are the traits most consistently found to show correlations with all three forgiveness factors, with agreeableness predicting less resentfulness

and vengefulness and more forgiveness. Neuroticism consistently predicts more resentfulness and vengefulness and less forgiveness. McCullough and colleagues (2009) interpret this in terms of their three-condition approach, with agreeableness increasing our empathy toward transgressors (thus increasing their careworthiness in our eyes) and neuroticism producing greater emotional pain when harmed (thus making perpetrators seem less safe and giving our anticipated future interactions more of a negative valence). The other two sets of correlations, though, are more difficult to interpret in light of the three-condition approach. In some of the studies reviewed by Mullet and colleagues (2005), researchers found a direct relationship between extraversion and vengefulness, which Worthington (2006) interprets in terms of extraverts' need for excitement (revenge is exciting). Other researchers (e.g., Berry et al., 2001; Brown, 2003), though, found substantial positive correlations between extraversion and forgiveness but offer no theoretical explanations for these correlations. Conscientiousness showed no relationships with resentfulness or forgiveness, but several researchers did find positive correlations between conscientiousness and vengefulness (Mullet et al., 2005). Worthington (2006) explains that this relationship reflects highly conscientious people's concern for justice and duty. Highly conscientious people might pursue vengeful outcomes out of a sense of "law and order" rather than emotional reactivity.

Given the great importance ascribed to forgiveness in many religious traditions, it is not surprising that researchers have found strong connections between forgiveness and faith (McCullough, Bono, & Root, 2005). McCullough and colleagues present survey data showing that over 80% of US adults report that their religious beliefs "often," "almost always," or "always" help them to forgive and to feel forgiven by God. Self-reports of religiousness and of forgivingness as a general value and practice consistently show substantial positive correlations (e.g., Gorsuch & Hao, 1993; Mullet et al., 2003; Rokeach, 1973). Correlations between religiousness and people's reactions to specific transgressions, however, are generally weak (McCullough & Worthington, 1999), though that may be due to factors within the studies themselves, including psychometric issues and the complexity of religiousness as a variable (Tsang et al., 2005).

THE EFFECTS OF FORGIVENESS

Having engaged in a very brief survey of a few of the "input" variables that make forgiveness more or less likely, we now turn to some "output variables." What are the outcomes of forgiving? Forgivingness as a character strength is consistently associated with greater well-being (McCullough et al., 2009; Peterson & Seligman, 2004). Berry and colleagues (2001) found forgivingness to be associated with less anger and hostility, and Berry and Worthington (2001) found it to be associated with less relationship anxiety. Many researchers (e.g., Gismero-Gonzalez et al., 2020; Maltby, Day, & Barber, 2005; Toussaint & Friedman, 2009) have found the act of forgiveness to be associated with greater happiness and well-being. Forgiveness is associated with improved physical health as well; Witvliet

and colleagues (2001) found that thoughts about forgiveness resulted in lower stress and improved cardiovascular functioning, and Krause and Ingersol-Dayton (2001) present qualitative evidence that forgiving people enjoy improved health.

Worthington and Scherer (2004) explain the links between forgiveness and well-being by describing forgiveness as an emotion-focused coping strategy. Recall that Worthington (2006) approaches forgiveness as a process by which negative attitudes about the perpetrator are replaced by positive attitudes. The negative emotions involved in being unforgiving create stress, and the act of forgiving reduces that stress (Worthington & Scherer, 2004). This has led a number of psychologists (e.g., Bono & McCullough, 2006) to propose that forgiveness be brought into the process of psychotherapy.

As forgiveness is inherently social (Baumeister et al., 1998; McCullough et al., 2000), it is not surprising that forgiveness brings about positive relational outcomes. Forgiving a relationship partner results in greater commitment (Tsang, McCullough, & Fincham, 2006), and being forgiven also produces greater commitment (Wieselquist, 2009). Baumeister and colleagues (1998) point out that transgressions are inevitable as we interact with each other, and a lack of forgiveness locks us into a spiral of vengeance following vengeance. The process of forgiveness "may intercept a downward spiral started by the transgression, replacing it with a cycle of positive intent and action" (Exline & Baumeister, 2000, p. 136). Rusbult and colleagues (2005) review the empirical literature on forgiveness, showing that forgiveness is a vital component to the process of repairing a damaged relationship. Forgiving a perpetrator restores the lost pro-relationship motivation, promoting cooperation, willingness to sacrifice, relational adjustment, and happiness. Fenell (1993) conducted a survey of couples who had been married for more than twenty years, asking them what the keys to their marital longevity were. "Willingness to forgive and be forgiven" was in their top ten most important characteristics.

I should point out that the relationships between variables found by researchers in this area are neither simple nor straight-forward. The process of forgiveness is influenced by additional variables, in-cluding the nature of the offense, the nature of the relationship between perpe-trator and victim, the repentant (or unre-pentant) behavior of the perpetrator, and variables within the victim that increase or decrease the likelihood of forgiveness (many of which we covered above). Victims are more likely to respond with deep emotional pain when a transgression occurs in the context of a close committed relationship (Finkel et al., 2002) but are also more likely to forgive in those con-texts (Hannon, 2001). Forgiveness is more likely when the perpetrator communicates a sincere responsibility for the offense, offers a sincere apology, and makes a sincere attempt at atoning for the trans-gression (Rusbult et al., 2005). Exline and Baumeister (2000) point out a number of internal barriers to offering forgiveness, including fear that the transgression might be repeated, fear of appearing weak, and fear of losing the benefits that come with victim status. Forgiveness is also a process that takes time, so the temporal "distance" between the transgression and the present moment is a factor (McCullough, Fincham, & Tsang, 2003)

FORGIVENESS INTERVENTIONS

Methods for encouraging and guiding forgiveness have been incorporated into community-based interventions (Griffin et al., 2019) and into therapies for individuals (Malcolm, Warwar, & Greenberg, 2005) and couples (Gordon, Baucom, & Snyder, 2005) when clients are experiencing emotional and relational difficulties involving a past transgression. Enright and Coyle (1998) describe a therapeutic ap-proach that consists of twenty units grouped into four phases. The first phase of the process involves uncovering and understanding the nature and extent of the injury inflicted on the victim. The second phase is where forgiveness is introduced and discussed as a response to the trans-gression. In the third phase, the cognitive and emotional work takes place, in which one reconsiders one's thoughts about the perpetrator, enhances empathy, and alters one's emotions toward the perpetrator. In the final phase, the victim reflects on and deepens his or her understanding of the significance of the decision to forgive the perpetrator. This method has shown promising results in clinical (e.g., Hebl & Enright, 1993) and psychoeducational (e.g., Al-Mabuk, Enright, & Cardis, 1995) set-tings. Baskin and Enright (2004) conducted a meta-analysis of forgiveness-based interventions in counseling settings and found that their method not only en-couraged forgiveness toward the perpe-trators who victimized their clients but also produced improvements in mental health.

Worthington's (2001) REACH model gives us a five-step process for therapeutic forgiveness: Recall the hurt, Empathize with the other person, offer forgiveness as an Altruistic gift, Commit to the forgiveness (no taking it back), and Hold on to the forgiveness (through methods such as writing reminder notes to oneself about having forgiven the perpetrator). Wade, Worthington, and Myer (2005) carried out a review and meta-analysis of the empirical research literature on forgiveness interventions (including REACH), finding substantial effect sizes, which provides evidence of these methods' effectiveness.

But Is It Forgiveness?

As we saw at the beginning of this chapter, Worthington is himself a Christian. He sees his work on forgiveness as directly connected to Jesus' command that we forgive each other (Matthew 18:21-35). Although we are told to forgive, the Bible does not provide us with a step-by-step guide for the exact process of forgiving. This is where positive psychologists can be of assistance, carrying out research on the process of forgiveness and developing practical guides to help us forgive (Worthington, Sharp, Lerner, & Sharp, 2006).

While this argument fits well with my general approach to the relationship between Christian theology and positive psychology (e.g., Hackney, 2010), theology is also supposed to provide us with guidance in understanding the phenomena under consideration if we are to do positive psychology in a way that does justice to both psychology and Christianity. Despite Watts's (2004) claim that theological and psychological studies on forgiveness are

examples of examining complementary aspects of the same phenomena, many of us see substantive divergences between Enright's and Worthington's "therapeutic" takes on forgiveness and a vision of forgiveness that is grounded in Scripture and Christian theology.

One important difference is the telos (goal) of forgiveness. Why should we forgive? What is the purpose of forgiving? In a Christian view, we forgive because God is forgiving (Jones & Musekura, 2010). The Holy Spirit works to restore sinful humanity to communion with God and with each other. As creatures made in the image of God, this is our goal as well. For Christians, the telos of forgiveness is reconciliation. Although we must not collapse those two concepts entirely into each other (Bash, 2007; Coutts, 2016), forgiveness is "a means of seeking reconciliation in the midst of particular sins" (Jones, 1995, p. 5) and so should not be entirely divorced from the concept of reconciliation. But that is exactly what psychologists tend to do on the topic of forgiveness. Frise and McMinn (2010) conducted a survey of psychologists and theologians on the topic of forgiveness. They found that while theologians were more likely to describe forgiveness as a part of the reconciliation process, psychologists were more likely to see forgiveness and reconciliation as separate concepts. Worthington (2003) says forgiveness may motivate the victim to seek contact with the perpetrator for the purposes of reconciliation but that this step is entirely optional, and Worthington and Sandage (2016) say the idea that reconciliation is necessary is a "misconception" about forgiveness.

Forgiveness as described by psychologists is directed toward a telos of individual freedom and maximized health (Coutts, 2016). Pargament and Rye (1998) describe forgiveness as "a powerful method of coping for those interested in finding peace in their lives" (p. 70). Enright and Coyle (1998) say the purpose of forgiveness research and practice is the alleviation of misery. Worthington (2003) relates his struggles over forgiving his mother's murderer, admitting that in the end he forgave because he wanted to be free of his anger. While he encourages his Christian readers to forgive out of a desire to imitate God's character and cautions them against forgiving for selfish emotional reasons, he justifies this advice by appealing to the greater emotional benefits and personal growth potential that come from other-oriented forgiveness. Lamb (2002) and Jones and Musekura (2010) criticize forgiveness theorists and practitioners for "cheapening" forgiveness into therapeutic self-help. Despite any claims they might make along the way that forgiveness is an altruistic "gift" freely given to the perpetrator, the free gift is justified on the grounds of the benefit to the forgiver. If forgiveness is a gift, it is a gift the recipient does not necessarily receive. Theologian Anthony Bash (2007) points out that therapeutic methods of forgiveness do not involve any actual interaction with the perpetrator: "Victims are dealing with mental representations of wrongdoers, not real people" (p. 41).

Is forgiveness that does not aim at reconciliation actually forgiveness? One scenario in which this might be an issue involves a perpetrator who is unavailable or deceased. If, for example, one of my parents was abusive during my childhood but that parent is now dead, can I forgive that parent? Worthington (2003) would respond with a clear "yes," as he sees forgiveness as an inner alteration in one's disposition toward the perpetrator. So from his perspective, if I was angry and resentful over the abuse I suffered and through the therapeutic process let go of that anger, coming to see my absent parent in a more benevolent light, then of course I have forgiven that parent (Worthington applies this logic to his own situation, as they never discovered who it was that murdered his mother). If we are guided by Miroslav Volf (1996), though, and see forgiveness as "the boundary between exclusion and embrace" (p. 125), where we open our arms to the enemy and invite him into communion, can that invitation be delivered to an absent enemy? L. Gregory Jones (1995) considers it possible to engage in a modified form of forgiveness that is anticipatory rather than present. But even then, that forgiveness is grounded in a "hope for the possibility of reconciliation in the Kingdom" (p. 232) rather than a "mere discharge of a victim's angry resentment" (Volf, 1996, p. 122).

Another problem comes up in the case of an unrepentant perpetrator. What if the perpetrator is alive and could reconcile if he or she wanted to but has no interest in doing so? Worthington (2003) would apply the same logic as before; since forgiveness is an internal cognitive and emotional change disconnected from reconciliation, of course one can unilaterally forgive the perpetrator, even if they never speak to each other again in their lifetimes and even if one has no intention of tracking down the perpetrator to offer reconciliation. If we hold the telos of forgiveness to be reconciliation, though, that becomes a problem. Without repentance and at least the hope of reconciliation, there can be no true forgiveness. Donald Gowan (2010), in his examination of forgiveness in the Bible, says, "Because forgiveness in Scripture is never said to be meaningful without reconciliation, then it might be offered before the offender repents—as God in fact does—but it will not happen, it will not be real unless the offender finds it possible to accept it" (p. 209). Gowan argues that psychologists are studying "the forgiving spirit" but not "the completion of an act of forgiveness" (p. 210).

What does this mean for people who are suffering as a result of a victimization and are trying to be free from the anger and resentfulness associated with their past? Are we telling them that, because an inner emotional transformation is not "real forgiveness," they are simply out of luck and must go on suffering? Of course not. The Bible and Christian scholarship have alternative language to describe the situation of an unrepentant perpetrator. In Matthew 18, Jesus says that if you are sinned against by a fellow believer and the perpetrator is not interested in repentance even when the matter is brought before the church, then you are to "treat them as you would a pagan or tax collector" (Matthew 18:17). Jones (1995) argues that our approach to forgiveness must be guided by God's way of forgiving. God offers forgiveness to everyone, but many refuse that gift. Those people are therefore not forgiven and they remain enemies of God. Similarly, we are to hold out the possibility

of forgiveness to those who have harmed us, but not everyone who has harmed us will be interested in repenting and reconciling. Those people are therefore not forgiven and they remain our enemies. That sounds harsh until you remember what we are supposed to do with enemies: "Love your enemies and pray for those who persecute you" (Matthew 5:44). There can still be an inner transformation of our cognitive and emotional disposition toward an unrepentant perpetrator. Loving our enemies means abandoning vengeance, praying for them, wishing them well, and remaining open to the possibility (however slight) that they may one day repent. But that is not the same thing as a completed act of forgiveness (Jones, 1995).

We are also not leaving suffering people without therapeutic options in the case of an absent or unrepentant perpetrator. Most psychotherapies involve an inner cognitive-emotional transformation that produces a reduction in misery and opens the door for happiness and flourishing. In the case of my hypothetical abusive parent, a Gestalt therapist might assist me in dealing with the "unfinished business" of my past abuse and help me find closure. A rational emotive behavior therapist might help me change my beliefs about my abusive parent. An ACT practitioner might help me to accept that the abuse is a thing that happened, freeing me from the trap of ongoing anger and resentment. And so on. Criticizing forgiveness as a therapeutic technique does not mean withdrawing hope from clients.

Considering the difference between forgiveness as an emotional change that aims at inner peace and forgiveness as a "moral response to wrongdoing" (Bash, 2007, p. 3) that aims at reconciliation between people estranged by sin brings us to two additional areas of difficulty in forgiveness research and practice. Both of these areas are topics that students of forgiveness and positive psychology will encounter, and both present problems for our Christian perspective on forgiveness.

The first of these is the topic of self-forgiveness (Woodyatt, Worthington, Wenzell, & Griffin, 2017). Enright and colleagues (1996) define self-forgiveness as "willingness to abandon self-resentment in the face of one's own acknowledged objective wrong, while fostering compassion, generosity, and love toward oneself" (p. 115). Therapists may encounter clients who experience unhealthy forms of guilt (see chapter twenty-two for a discussion of healthy guilt) and are unable to stop obsessing over past misdeeds, sometimes resulting in self-punishing behaviors and severe emotional distress. One therapeutic goal with such clients might be to help them cultivate a less self-condemning attitude and forgive themselves for their wrongdoing (Worthington, 2013).

If forgiveness is an inner emotional change, then self-forgiveness makes perfect sense, and researchers have found self-forgiveness to be associated with greater well-being, especially for believers (e.g., Fincham & May, 2019; Fincham, May, & Carlos Chavez, 2020). But if we define forgiveness as a part of reconciliation, then the idea of self-forgiveness presents us with some basic conceptual problems, aside from the obvious hesitation that Christians (Twenge, 2006) might feel when reading Enright's call to greater self-love.

Worthington (2006) points out that "when people try to forgive themselves, they play two roles at the same time. They are simultaneously the wrongdoer and the forgiver" (p. 188), and he says this can make self-forgiveness difficult. Bash (2007) goes further, highlighting the logical difficulty in a perpetrator offering himself a gift that is rightfully the victim's to give. Self-forgiveness also seems inconsistent with Volf's (1996) description of forgiveness as the embrace of an offender by a victim that is motivated by the victim's self-giving love and done in imitation of Christ's forgiveness of those who crucified him, especially in light of Murphy's (2005b) employment of *kenōsis* (self-emptying) as the core characteristic of Jesus' love. Kenotic self-love appears to be a contradiction in terms, and self-forgiveness is found nowhere in Scripture (Gowan, 2010). Tangney, Boone, and Dearing (2005) summarize the empirical research on self-forgiveness, finding that people who are prone to forgive themselves "appear to be rather self centered, insensitive, narcissistic individuals, who come up short in the moral emotional domain, showing lower levels of shame, guilt, and empathic responsiveness" (p. 151). They worry that self-forgiveness may be far too self-focused to be helpful as a therapeutic goal. As with situations involving unrepentant perpetrators, there are a number of effective therapeutic approaches that might help a client who is struggling with unhealthy forms of guilt. So, again, we are not leaving suffering people without options in resolving their emotional difficulties.

This divergence between the two approaches to forgiveness reaches a crescendo when we begin to talk about the possibility of forgiving God himself. Julie Exline and colleagues have been engaged in research on the experience of anger against God (e.g., Exline et al., 2011; Grubbs, Exline, & Campbell, 2013). It is common to feel angry at God during unhappy circumstances, but some people struggle with prolonged unresolved anger toward God (Exline & Rose, 2005). Forgiveness pioneer Lewis Smedes (1984) suggests that people find peace by "forgiving [God] for the wrongs we suffer" (p. 83), and Exline, Yali, and Lobel (1999) conducted a study in which they found that forgiving God for one's suffering produced reductions in depression and anxiety.

As before, if we define forgiveness solely in terms on an inner change in our thoughts and feelings, then forgiving God makes sense. Anger at God is a normal phenomenon. Even in the Bible we have examples of people yelling at the Lord in their pain. In the Psalms, we see the psalmist accusing God of forgetfulness (Psalm 13:1; 42:9) and passive acquiescence to suffering (Psalm 35:17), and Job utters complaints of epic proportions against God during his time of misery. This anger, though, does not result in a rejection of God, and the biblical complainers resolve their anger against the Lord. The complaints against God in the Psalms are followed by words of trust and praise, and Job's complaints are mixed with affirmations of God's righteousness and praiseworthiness. It is also worth noting that God is not angry with Job; after reminding Job that his puny human brain is inadequate to the task of comprehending the divine plan, the Lord's anger is directed toward Job's

three friends for their false counsel. So we have biblical precedent for the idea that it is an acceptable part of the coping process to yell at God and then to get over that anger in a process of inner attitudinal change.

But is that forgiveness? Here we see very strongly the difference between forgiveness defined as an internal process through which people "give up their angry feelings and/or desires for retribution in the wake of a damaging act" (Exline et al., 1999, p. 366) and forgiveness defined as an interpersonal process in which "to forgive is a moral response to a morally wrong act" (Bash, 2007, p. 46). If forgiveness is a response to a morally wrong act, then forgiving God becomes an impossibility, as God commits no morally wrong acts. "Hence, though it might be psychologically comforting to 'forgive God' . . . that is a theological and ethical mistake" (Jones, 1995, p. 231). Due to these conceptual difficulties, Exline has backed away from the term *forgiving God* in her later work (Exline & Martin, 2005), preferring instead to approach the issue in terms of "resolving anger toward God" (p. 74). Christian counselors should assist their believing clients in working their way out of longstanding or irrational resentments toward God. Just don't call it forgiveness.

We are inherently social beings, created for community (Grenz, 2001). As such, forgiveness serves a vital function, restoring damaged relationships and breaking the cycle of vengeance (Baumeister et al., 1998). Further, we are beings created in the image of God, and we find our identities in the story of Jesus Christ (Volf, 1996). Jesus, with his self-emptying death and resurrection, makes forgiveness and reconciliation possible between humanity and God, so forgiveness is central to our life and identity as Christians, and our understanding of interpersonal forgiveness must be primarily set in the context of divine forgiveness (Coutts, 2016). Learning to live as forgiven and forgiving people is "an embodied way of life in an ever-deepening friendship with the Triune God and with others" (Jones, 1995, p. xii), requiring the exercise of practical wisdom (Roberts, 1995) and the work of the Holy Spirit. While Worthington describes forgiveness as a gift a victim gives to a perpetrator, Jones and Musekura (2010) point out that forgiveness properly understood is a gift given to us by the Lord. Forgiving is a practice, one in which we participate in Jesus' ministry of reconciliation by imitating his embrace of the enemy and the reciprocal self-giving of the triune God (Volf, 1996).

SUGGESTIONS FOR FURTHER READING

Bash, A. (2007). *Forgiveness and Christian ethics*. Cambridge University Press.

Enright, R. D., & North, J. (Eds.). (1998). *Exploring forgiveness.* University of Wisconsin Press.

Jones, L. G. (1995). *Embodying forgiveness: A theological analysis.* Eerdmans.

Jones, L. G., & Musekura, C. (2010). *Forgiving as we've been forgiven: Community practices for making peace.* InterVarsity Press.

McCullough, M. E., Pargament, K. L., & Thoresen, C. E. (Eds.). (2000). *Forgiveness: Theory, research, and practice.* Guilford Press.

Volf, M. (1996). *Exclusion and embrace.* Abingdon Press.

Worthington, E. L., Jr. (Ed.). (2005). *Handbook of forgiveness.* Routledge.

Worthington, E. L., Jr. (2006). *Forgiveness and reconciliation: Theory and application.* Routledge.

Part Six

APPLIED
POSITIVE
PSYCHOLOGY

Chapter Sixteen

HEROISM AND ALTRUISM

Everyone's a hero in their own way;
You and you, and mostly me, and you!

CAPTAIN HAMMER,
DOCTOR HORRIBLE'S SING-ALONG BLOG

On February 3, 1943, a US Army transport ship was torpedoed by a German U-boat. The *Dorchester* sank within twenty minutes. The *Dorchester* held a crew of over 900, but only 230 of those survived. Four chaplains were aboard the ship at the time: a Methodist minister (George L. Fox), a Reformed minister (Clark Poling), a Roman Catholic priest (John Washington), and a Jewish rabbi (Alexander Goode). As the ship sank, the four chaplains could be seen tending other people's wounds, calming the frightened, preaching courage, and praying for the dead and with the dying. One crewmember claimed that it was only due to the encouragement of these chaplains that he was able to survive in the icy waters and deadly debris. As the boat went down and people were moved topside, the chaplains took charge of lifejacket distribution. When the lifejackets were all gone, the chaplains removed their own jackets and gave them away to others without hesitation. As the ship sank beneath the waves, the four chaplains could be seen praying with their arms linked.

All four chaplains received posthumous honors, and on February 3, 1951, President Truman dedicated the Four Chaplains Memorial Chapel in Valley Forge (the chapel is now located at the Philadelphia Naval Shipyard). In his dedication speech, Truman said, "This interfaith shrine . . . will stand through long generations to teach Americans that as men can die heroically as brothers, so should they live together in mutual faith and goodwill." The full stories of the chaplains can be found at fourchaplains.org, the website of the Four Chaplains Memorial Foundation. In this chapter we will look at actions taken for the benefit of another by exploring the research literature on altruism. We will also take a close look at a specific project connected to altruism, Philip Zimbardo's Heroic Imagination Project, and what we can learn about resisting the forces that push us to stand aside when it is time to help others.

ALTRUISM

C. Daniel Batson (1991) defines altruism as "a motivational state with the ultimate goal of increasing another's welfare" (p. 6).

Batson's research has centered around the empathy-altruism hypothesis, which is the proposition that connecting with others' feelings results in an increased motivation to help (e.g., Batson & Shaw, 1991; Coke, Batson, & McDavis, 1978). Carse (2005) defines empathy as "the ability and disposition to imagine (as best we can) how others feel, what they fear or hope for, and how they understand themselves and their circumstances" (p. 170), and empathic feelings are typically treated as synonymous with compassion (e.g., Batson et al., 1995; Carse, 2005; Shapiro & Rucker, 2004). Empathy researchers have found that imagining oneself in another person's place results in a reduced desire to harm others (Miller & Eisenberg, 1988), more prosocial and moral behavior in general (Batson et al., 2005; Eisenberg & Miller, 1987), and more helping behavior specifically (Coke, Batson, & McDavis, 1978).

At a philosophical level, altruism is associated with the "ethic of care." Barbara Held (2006) lists five distinguishing features of the ethic of care: (1) it emphasizes that humans are dependent on each other and that a theory of ethics must not pretend that we make moral decisions autonomously, (2) emotions are considered an asset rather than a hindrance, (3) other scholars' emphases on increasing abstractness in moral reasoning are rejected, (4) public behavior and private behavior are not segregated from each other, and (5) humans' inherently social nature is made an integral part of the theory of care. We can see a good deal of resonance between Held's ethic of care and certain central aspects of the vision of human life that animates this text. We are created as

finite, so dependence is not something to flee or feel shame about (recall Aristotle's *megalopsychos* from previous chapters and how much a Christian understanding of the human condition clashes with this character's desire for self-sufficiency). Our approach to the *imago Dei* emphasizes the relational "between" of our inherently social nature. And although we see love as an act of self-emptying rather than warm fuzzy feelings, we are also not the detached intellects portrayed in Enlightenment ethical theories. God is compassionate (Psalm 86:15), and we are to emulate that.

ARE HUMANS REALLY ALTRUISTIC?

In chapter three we spent some time on the topic of basic human goodness. The question, recall, is whether or not human nature is inherently good (loving, rational, and cooperative) or inherently evil (selfish, foolish, and hostile). Applied to the topic of altruism, those who hold to a negative view of human nature will claim that what appears to be other-centered altruistic behavior is in fact egoistic, motivated by gene-preserving evolutionary forces or self-centered social-cognitive processes (Cialdini et al., 1997; Hamilton, 1964; Trivers, 1971). Even actions that appear to be entirely self-sacrificial can be interpreted in egoistic terms. For those of us who believe in an afterlife in which God repays us a hundredfold for our sacrifices (Matthew 19:28-29), even the loss of our lives (Matthew 16:24-25), martyrs come out ahead in that calculation. Even without heavenly rewards factored into the equation, it is possible to come up with egoistic interpretations for altruism.

Batson and colleagues have spent many years putting forward the alternate view that humans have the capacity for genuine selfless altruism (Batson, 1991). This can be seen as an argument for inherent goodness in human nature, with humans portrayed as "fundamentally social and moral" (Jørgensen & Nafstad, 2004) rather than purely self-interested. There is considerable evidence that empathy-fueled, other-oriented altruism does in fact exist (Batson, Ahmad, & Lishner, 2009; Batson & Shaw, 1991; Eisenberg & Miller, 1987), but the debate continues.

Sabates (2012) claims that, given a Christian view of humans as created good (which would incline us toward the empathy-altruism hypothesis) but fallen and corrupt (which would incline us toward the psychological egoism hypothesis), we should not be surprised to see self-oriented and other-oriented motivations coexisting in the same creature. To make this more complicated, not all self-oriented motivations are evil. As we saw in chapter three, our created nature is neither a disconnected nonrelational self nor an obliterated self without particularity and value but is a reciprocal self-in-relation (Balswick, King, & Riemer, 2016). Jesus, whose self-emptying *kenōsis* shapes our understanding of human flourishing, displayed a strong-willed independence (Kimball, 2005). Further, God does not hesitate to appeal to self-interest in the Bible, urging us to avoid punishment and seek blessing (Isaiah 1:18-20) without condemning the desire to seek blessing as inherently evil or immature. Also, many of the Bible's teachings can be seen in terms of the pursuit of happiness for the self as well as for others (Charry,

2010; Strawn, 2012). Batson and Shaw (1991) point out that the debate is not about all human motivation as purely selfish or purely selfless. Both altruistic and egoistic motivations can exist in connection to the same action, as behavior is typically motivated by a plurality of goals. The error here is to assume that any evidence for any egoism somehow proves that all altruism is a mere façade masking ultimate selfishness.

ALTRUISM RESEARCH

The ethic of care involves accepting personal responsibility for the safety and well-being of others. Batson (1991) refers to this consideration of others as morally relevant as the "scope" of empathy. But which others belong within the scope? Jesus answers that question in Luke 10. An expert in the Torah is quizzing Jesus about inheriting eternal life, and Jesus points him right back to the law, reminding him that love of God and love of neighbor are supreme. This expert then asks about the boundary between neighbor (someone within my circle of moral relevance) and not-neighbor (someone whom I have no duty to love), and Jesus tells him a parable about a Samaritan (a hated outsider) who treats a wounded Jew as a neighbor.

During the Holocaust, an estimated 50,000 to 500,000 Gentiles risked their own lives in defense of those who were not of their family, their religion, their ethnicity, or, in most cases, even their prior acquaintance (Fagin-Jones & Midlarsky, 2007). Monroe (1996) examined the motivations of those who risked their lives and those of their families to save persecuted Jews, as did Fagin-Jones and Midlarsky (2007). Both sets of motivational patterns found by these researchers fit well within an ethic of care and our examination of the literature on altruism. Fagin-Jones and Midlarsky compared the personalities of the rescuers to those of equivalent nonrescuers (those people, labeled as "bystanders" by the authors, who inhabited areas occupied by Nazi forces during the same time period but did not engage in any rescue activities) and similarly compared the situational aspects of these people's lives (marital status, geographic location and living arrangements, personal experience of persecution, and so on). Above all other variables, the feature that most strongly distinguished rescuers from bystanders was "their ability to subscribe to the personal norm that requires people to help others who are dependent on them without the expectation of gain, because it is the right thing to do" (Fagin-Jones & Midlarsky, 2007, p. 144), their ability to feel compassion for those who are suffering, and their willingness to take risks in expressing that compassion. Monroe's interviews with Holocaust rescuers indicate that the common thread for those who took altruistic action in defense of those whom the Nazis hunted was a sense of compassion derived from the perception of a shared humanity between Gentile and Jew. "Altruists," Monroe (1996) writes, "share a view of the world in which all people are one" (p. 198).

When experimentally studying altruism, researchers typically put participants in an empathic frame of mind by instructing them to imagine how the other person feels. Batson, Klein, Highberger, and Shaw (1995) performed a study in which they manipulated participants into feeling compassion,

resulting in a tendency to allocate resources in a way that favored those who were suffering. There also exists a body of literature in which altruism is approached as an individual difference variable, with some people being dispositionally more altruistic than others. Rushton and colleagues (1981) developed a twenty-item self-report altruism scale in which participants rate how often they tend to engage in altruistic behaviors (such as giving money to charity, holding a door open for a stranger, or helping push a stranger's car out of the snow). Participants who got higher scores on this measure were more empathetic, engaged in more prosocial behavior, and were more likely to have filled out an organ donor card.

Altruism is also a facet of the trait of agreeableness within the five-factor model of personality. Highly agreeable people are considerate and motivated to help others (McCrae & Costa, 2003), and the widely-used NEO PI-3 five-factor measure includes an altruism subscale (McCrae, Costa, & Martin, 2005; De Fruyt et al., 2009). There are strong connections between agreeableness and prosocial behavior (Graziano & Eisenberg, 1997), including volunteerism (Elshaug & Metzer, 2001; Carlo et al., 2005) and cooperation (Hilbig et al., 2013). Children who score highly on this trait are more likely to defend victims when confronted with bullying (Tani et al., 2003), and police recruits with high scores are more devoted (operationalized as low absenteeism rates) to their training (Detrick, Chibnall, & Luebbert, 2004).

In the *CSV*, altruism as an individual difference variable is covered under "kindness" as a character strength (Peterson

& Seligman, 2004). Strengths can be cultivated, and the induction of empathy is often used as a training tool in cultivating altruism. Barak (1990) created a "game" intended to increase empathy in counselors-in-training. Barak's empathy game involves evaluating statements written by hypothetical counseling clients. In the statements, the hypothetical clients describe various life situations (estranged daughter, extramarital affair, feelings of worthlessness, and so on). The trainees are given these statements and asked to imagine the thoughts, desires, emotions, and so on behind them. Barak focuses on four questions participants are to ask about the hypothetical statements: (1) What is the person saying about themself? (2) What emotions are being conveyed in the statement? (3) What do they think is the cause of their problem? (4) What do they think is the solution? The goal is that, in pondering these questions, counseling trainees will become more likely to feel increased empathy toward future clients.

Johanna Shapiro (Shapiro, Morrison, & Boker, 2004; Shapiro & Rucker, 2004) trains medical students at the University of California Irvine. Emphasizing the importance of empathy in physicians, she also focuses on the role stories play in its cultivation. Using an elective course on literature and medicine, Shapiro and her colleagues (Shapiro, Morrison, & Boker, 2004) engaged a group of medical students in reading and discussion groups involving short stories, poetry, and skits. These bits of literature all touched on topics that were related to medicine (pain, sexuality, lifestyle adjustments, examinations, and so on) and were intended to enhance empathy and com-passion in the reader. Reading and discussing these stories resulted in measurable increases in the students' ability to empathize. Movies can serve a similar function (Shapiro & Rucker, 2004). Although film typically presents us with a sanitized and simplified vision of reality, we may nevertheless carry away some of the sympathy and compassion inspired by the characters.

ZIMBARDO TURNS FROM THE DARK SIDE

Students of psychology will know the name of Philip Zimbardo, he of the infamous Stanford Prison Simulation (Haney, Banks, & Zimbardo, 1973; Zimbardo, 2007). Zimbardo has spent much of his career studying the many ways humans engage in evil acts. He did some of the early work in "mob psychology," looking at how deindividuation influences people to do cruel things when part of a crowd that they would never do alone (Zimbardo, 1969). He studied police brutality in Brazil (Huggins, Haritos-Fatouros, & Zimbardo, 2002) and cultists in San Francisco (Zimbardo & Hartley, 1985). Zimbardo's interest in prisons led him to consider psychological factors among murderers (Lee, Zimbardo, & Bertholf, 1977), executioners (Osofsky, Bandura, & Zimbardo, 2005), and those involved with the abuse scandal at Abu Ghraib (Zimbardo, 2007). He is known for his situationist approach to the psychology of evil (Zimbardo, 2004), in which he argues that the most powerful forces that move us to commit immoral acts are not within us but in the environment.

The idea that humans are morally weak and easily pushed around by external variables does have a certain resonance with a Christian understanding of the human condition (there is a reason the Bible calls us "sheep"), and we are given biblical admonitions to avoid social circumstances in which we would be pressured to do wrong (see Psalm 1:1-2; Proverbs 22:24-25; 1 Corinthians 15:33). So, although we also hold tight to the idea that sin is caused by our sinful inner disposition (Plantinga, 1995; Shuster, 2004), we simultaneously hold to the truth that "our sinfulness is also derived in part socially: We teach each other to sin" (Grenz, 1994, p. 205). Once again, Christians look at an "either-or" question and answer with a "both-and." Zimbardo's situationism is a useful way of looking at one side of the causes of evil. It is also a valuable lesson in humility, reminding us that the vast majority of people who engage in evil acts are thoroughly normal, just like you and me. The psychology of evil is not the study of Them (those monsters over there who ruin everything); it is the study of Us.

Later in his career, Zimbardo became interested in those cases in which individuals resisted the push of the environment and acted morally in defiance of social pressure. In his analysis of the Abu Ghraib scandal (Zimbardo, 2007), he describes the many environmental factors that contributed to the abuse (stress from constant mortar shelling, sleep deprivation, lack of training and supervision, pressure from superiors to break the prisoners, and so on), but he also wanted to know about the Army reservist who blew the whistle on the scandal despite the tremendous social pressures arrayed against him. "When the majority of ordinary people can be

overcome by [environmental forces]," Zimbardo (2004) writes, "the minority who resist should be considered *heroic*" (p. 47). Consistent with his situationist approach, Zimbardo places primary emphasis on the environmental factors that increase the likelihood that we will do evil. "We are not slaves to the power of situational forces. But we must learn methods of resisting and opposing them" (Zimbardo, 2007, p. 446).

HOW TO BE A HERO

As a part of this newfound interest in heroes, Zimbardo launched the Heroic Imagination Project (heroicimagination.org), where Zimbardo and his colleagues offer resources for those interested in the topic as well as training programs for the cultivation of heroism in the population. The first thing we need to do, say Franco and Zimbardo (2006), is get rid of the idea that heroes are a special elite. Throughout history and into the present, we have been presented stories of heroes who possess a unique attribute that is the key to their heroism. Theseus was half god. King Arthur was the chosen one of prophesy. Edmund Spenser's Redcrosse Knight was raised by the Fair Folk. Tarzan was raised by gorillas. Superman is a powerful alien. Batman spent a decade in training before donning his cape and cowl. Captain America was injected with the super-soldier serum.

While these are great stories, the downside is that they leave most of us out of the heroism game. I might do judo twice a week, but that doesn't make me Batman. Heroism is for the extraordinary people, right? Wrong. That kind of thinking is an excuse that allows us to assume that someone else will respond in emergency situations. If (as we see in the psychology of evil) the villains of the world are almost all ordinary people who, like you and me, have a potential for evil acts given the right circumstances, then the heroes of the world are almost all ordinary people who, like you and me, have the potential for good acts given the right circumstances. Heroism is for anyone. Corrie ten Boom, for example, was a middle-aged watchmaker. Without the aid of superpowered armor or ninja training, she bravely helped several hundred Jews escape from Nazi-occupied Holland and lived through incarceration in the Ravensbrück concentration camp (ten Boom, 1971).

Franco, Blau, and Zimbardo (2011) consider courage to be central to heroism, defining a heroic act as a social activity in service to others in need, engaged in voluntarily, with recognition of possible risks and costs, without external gain anticipated at the time of the act, and in which the actor is willing to accept anticipated sacrifice. Franco, Efthimiou, and Zimbardo (2016) connect heroism to eudaimonic well-being, as acting heroically requires *phronēsis* (practical wisdom) and an orientation toward the good. The likelihood that we will engage in heroic acts is empowered by the "heroic imagination," which Franco and colleagues (2011) call "a mind-set, a collection of attitudes about helping others in need, beginning with caring for others in compassionate ways, but also moving toward a willingness to sacrifice or take risks on behalf of others or in defense of a moral cause" (p. 111).

This heroic imagination can be cultivated in a number of ways, many of which are derived from social psychological research on the factors that pressure us to go along with evil. One method for resisting those factors involves simply knowing that social forces pressure us. Reactance researchers (e.g., Brehm & Brehm, 1981) have found that, if we perceive that someone is infringing on our freedom by trying to force us to engage in behavior X, we become more likely to react against that by choosing behavior Y. So being aware that we are pushed toward evil by the forces of conformity can trigger reactance, a refusal to go along with evil out of stubborn independence.

Speaking of conformity, many of us are complicit in evil not because we are the architects of devious schemes, but because we go along with crowd (like I said: sheep). In a classic study, Solomon Asch (1956) demonstrated that people will give blatantly wrong answers to a simple perceptual task if surrounded by other people (confederates of Asch's) who are all giving the wrong answer. However, if only one person goes against the crowd, participant conformity drops by 75% (Asch, 1955). Sometimes simply speaking out robs situations of their power. Recall the story of the emperor's new clothes.

We can also be pressured toward evil by authority figures, as Stanley Milgram (1963) showed in his infamous study. The majority of participants (again, perfectly normal people) were willing to shock someone into unconsciousness (maybe death) simply because an authority figure told them to (and an even larger majority, just over 90%, were willing to pass along an order for someone else to do the shocking). Zimbardo (2007) counsels us to be mindful of the difference between a just authority figure and an unjust authority figure. Obeying authority is not bad in and of itself, but we need to remember that we are responsible for our own actions. We see this same distinction in the Bible, with believers being instructed to submit to the governing authorities (Romans 13:1) but also willing to declare that, if there is a conflict between human authorities and the Lord, we must obey God even if it means defying the rulers (Acts 5:29). In a pattern reminiscent of Asch's (1955) findings, when Milgram (1965) included a single confederate who disobeyed the order to shock, participant obedience dropped dramatically. A single voice can be enough. And have I mentioned the emperor's new clothes?

Another force that pushes us away from heroic action is the bystander effect (Darley & Latané, 1968). Our willingness to help in an emergency is reduced by the number of people around us at the time (Latané and Nida, 1981; Fischer et al., 2011) due to the diffusion of responsibility. Put simply (and don't hold me to these exact numbers), if I am alone and witness an emergency, I feel something like 100% of the responsibility to do something about it. If one person is with me, I feel 50% responsible. If I am in a crowd of fifty, I feel only 2% responsible. What this translates to is fifty people standing around watching an emergency, all fifty thinking that someone should do something and wondering why nobody is doing anything. Zimbardo (2007) urges readers to adopt a mindset of personal responsibility to combat this. Fortunately, learning about the bystander effect has been shown to be effective in reducing the bystander effect (Beaman, Barnes, Klentz, & McQuirk, 1978), and a number of

training programs have been developed (such as anti-bullying programs; see Polanin, Espelage, & Pigott, 2012) that are specifically designed to increase bystander intervention. Connecting back to our altruism discussion, Bereczkei, Birkas, and Kerekes (2010) found that participants who scored higher on a "social cooperation" scale (a measure of traits such as empathy and compassion) were less vulnerable to the bystander effect.

Something specific we can do to increase our likelihood of helping is to learn useful skills. Cramer and colleagues (1988) found that registered nurses were immune to the bystander effect in a situation that involved a workman falling off a ladder. Huston and colleagues (1981) examined instances of real-world helping in emergencies and found that people were more likely to help if they had (among other factors) some sort of medical or law-enforcement training and were physically stronger. So if you do not know first aid, take a class. Hit the gym and lift some weights. Levine and Wilson (2016) review research that shows the powerful impact of social identity on willingness to help in emergencies. I make an argument in my book about positive psychology and martial arts (Hackney, 2010c) that those of us who enjoy studying new and interesting ways to beat people up should adopt the role of "protector" as a component of our self-concepts. Learning martial arts means not only that a person becomes someone with whom one does not mess; taking the ethic of care seriously means this person also takes on "personal responsibility for the safety of others" (p. 166).

Since Zimbardo's work, interest in heroism has grown. In 2015, Australian researcher Olivia Efthimiou launched *Heroism Science*, a new academic journal dedicated to the interdisciplinary study of heroism, with Scott Allison serving as editor-in-chief (Allison, 2016). The *Handbook of Heroism and Heroic Leadership* was published shortly thereafter (Allison, Goethals, & Kramer, 2017), and research articles on heroism have been appearing in some of psychology's top-tier journals (e.g., Kinsella, Ritchie, & Igou, 2015). The field is still small, with far more remaining for us to learn than we have so far discovered. But hopefully this growing interest means we will develop new and more effective ways to encourage prosocial behavior.

Now go out there and help somebody.

Suggestions for Further Reading

Allison, S. T., Goethals, G. R., & Kramer, R. M. (Eds.). (2017). *Handbook of heroism and heroic leadership.* Routledge.

Batson, C. D. (1991). *The altruism question: Toward a social-psychological answer.* Lawrence Erlbaum Associates.

Batson, C. D., & Shaw, L. L. (1991). Evidence for altruism: Toward a pluralism of prosocial motives. *Psychological Inquiry, 2*(2), 107-22.

Franco, Z. E., Allison, S. T., Kinsella, E. L., Kohen, A., Langdon, M., & Zimbardo, P. G. (2018). Heroism research: A review of theories, methods, challenges, and trends. *Journal of Humanistic Psychology, 58*(4), 382-96.

Chapter Seventeen

POSITIVE SPORT PSYCHOLOGY

Mens sana in corpore sano.
"A healthy mind in a healthy body."
Juvenal

SPORTS IN CHRISTIAN PERSPECTIVE

Sports and religion have always been deeply interconnected (Harvey, 2014), and Christians have struggled to find the proper approach to that relationship since the days of the early church (Higgs, 1995; Wittmer, 2008), with certain troublesome issues coming back again and again. Early Christians had to work out their relationship with Roman sports, with the ritual displays of pagan worship and brutal treatment of the athletes' bodies that were entrenched in those spectacles. In the year 314, the Council of Arles proclaimed excommunication for gladiators and charioteers, and Emperor Constantine banned gladiatorial fights in AD 325. Sports remained inextinguishably popular, though, throughout the Roman Empire's existence. Emperor Theodoris (fifth century) dealt with it by "Christianizing" the chariot races to the point that different racing teams were affiliated with different positions on doctrinal issues (Harvey, 2014).

In the medieval age, the church was an enthusiastic supporter of races and ball games (Ellis, 2019); it was tournaments that were the object of ecclesiastical consternation (Keen, 1984). Thirteenth-century bishop Jacques de Vitry accused tournaments of encouraging all seven of the deadly sins, and a series of popes issued condemnations against the tournaments. None of this clerical disapproval had much effect, however, and those who appreciated the tournaments saw them as "a step on the scale of chivalrous perfection" (p. 100), tests of character in which desirable qualities of mind and body could be cultivated and rewarded (Farrell, 2010).

During the Reformation, Martin Luther and Ulrich Zwingli considered physical education (including combat sports, such as wrestling and swordsmanship) to be essential components of developing good Christian character (Anglo, 2000). Puritan attitudes toward sports were complex and ambivalent (Baker, 2007; Ellis, 2019). In general, Puritans saw recreation and exercise as useful and healthy, part of a well-ordered and God-centered life (Harvey, 2014). But they did not approve if those sports took place on Sundays, were surrounded by a culture of gambling and vice, or were deemed to be too violent and bloody (Daniels, 2008; Hoffman, 2010).

Though boxing fell within the "too-violent" category, other combative sports, such as shooting, swordplay, and wrestling, were enthusiastically encouraged by North American Puritans, as they developed skills that were useful in times of conflict with surrounding Native populations (Baker, 2007). Puritans also did not like tennis, but that was because it was associated with aristocrats and Catholics (Daniels, 2008).

The "muscular Christianity" movement of the nineteenth and twentieth centuries forms the backdrop to much of our current deliberation on the relationship between Christianity and sports (Ladd & Mathisen, 1999; Mangan & Hickey, 2008; Mathisen, 2008). The nineteenth century saw a booming enthusiasm for the importance of health, and many Christians preached the importance of the body as the temple of the Holy Spirit, the importance of physical strength to carry out the work of the gospel, and the importance of sports as a potential venue for evangelism (Hoffman, 2010; Watson, Wier, & Friend, 2005). One dominant theme of this movement was the message that sports build character, promote good health, and foster patriotism (Mathisen, 2008). This message was opposed by Christians who saw the sporting organizations and events of the day as infested with organized crime, gambling, cheating, academic scandals, profanity, violence, drunkenness, consumerism, and egocentrism (Hoffman, 2010; Ladd & Mathisen, 1999). Despite these misgivings, today the partnership between Christianity and sports is stronger than

ever (Meyer, 2019). Robert Ellis (2019) sees sport as a type of play, part of God's good creation, and a means by which we can reach beyond ourselves.

In this chapter, we will examine sports from the perspectives of virtue ethics and positive psychology and attempt to gain some clarity on this complicated issue. I am an avid martial arts enthusiast and author of several scholarly works on the philosophy and psychology of the martial arts, so my go-to examples for this chapter will involve combat sports such as judo. Readers who are less enthusiastic about combat sports will just have to bear with me and mentally insert their own sporting examples.

A Philosophical Perspective on Sports and Flourishing

As I have mentioned (quite often by this point), my attempt at a Christian approach to positive psychology is heavily influenced by Alasdair MacIntyre's take on virtue ethics. Fortunately for us, MacIntyre has already exerted a strong influence on many scholars who are concerned with the moral status of sport[1] (Hardman & Jones, 2011; McNamee, Jones, & Duda, 2003). Those who work in this area employ MacIntyre's concept of a "practice" (sometimes referred to by scholars as a "moral practice," "social practice," or "eudaimonic practice") to describe the role that sports play in people's lives.

In *After Virtue*, MacIntyre (2007) argues that virtues always exist in a specific community context. A description of the telos for individuals, as well as for humanity in general, is developed through

---

[1]You will find "sport" and "sports" used mostly interchangeably in the scholarly literature, though British publications are more likely to contain references to "sport" as a general category of activity, while North Americans are more likely to call it "sports."

community members' interactions, and the actions by which virtues are cultivated are socially grounded. It is in discussing this socially grounded action that MacIntyre develops the idea of a "practice." MacIntyre provides this somewhat cumbersome definition of a practice: "any coherent and complex form of socially established cooperative human activity through which goods internal to that form of activity are realized in the course of trying to achieve those standards of excellence which are appropriate to, and partially definitive of, that form of activity, with the result that human powers to achieve excellence, and human conceptions of the ends and good involved, are systematically extended" (p. 187). This definition is commonly employed by scholars (e.g., Hackney, 2009; Hardman, Jones, & Jones, 2010; Kirk & Kinchin, 2003) who argue that athletic activities can serve as venues for the cultivation of the good life. Using one of my favorite sports (judo), let us examine this definition one piece at a time.

A practice is complex and social in nature. When someone enters into a practice, that person enters into relationships with other members of that practice. In doing so, the newcomer submits to the members' standards regarding the nature of the practice, the goal (telos) of the practice, and the standards of value that define excellence in the practice. Those who participate in sports enter into exactly such communities of practice (Kirk & Kinchin, 2003). A novice judoka is mentored by the coach and learns through interactions with fellow club members. Through such interactions, the student learns the skills, terminology, goals, and values of judo (Hackney, 2009).

MacIntyre (2007) also defines practices in terms of the "goods" toward which they aim, and he differentiates between the "internal" and "external" goods of a practice. External goods are those goods which one can obtain through engagement in a practice but which can also be achieved elsewhere, and these goods tend to be easily comprehensible to those who are not practitioners. Internal goods are more difficult for outsiders to understand and are specific to the practice. In combat sports such as judo, external goods, which may be acquired through other means, include an increased ability to defend oneself, physical fitness, the feeling of "living history" that comes from participation in a martial art with a rich tradition, and enjoyable competition. Judo may also be said to possess internal goods, which may not even be communicable to those outside of the practice. For example, the competitive camaraderie enjoyed by judoka who smile and shake hands after having just finished inflicting painful throws, chokes, and jointlocks on each other can be incomprehensible to those who prefer to experience such competition across a chess board. Hardman, Jones, and Jones (2010) describe these internal goods as "the precious gems of sport participation. They are what make sports unique and special" (p. 347). Achieving these goods is a core component of the telos of the practice. The telos of a judo match is an excellent judo match, in which the internal goods of judo are achieved.

Achieving these goods requires a certain kind of play and a certain kind of player. Sports have desirable character traits that must be developed for one to become an excellent practitioner and achieve the goods internal to the sport (Kirk & Kinchin, 2003). Jigoro Kano, founder of judo, specifically had character development in mind when he introduced it (Kano, 1986). He emphasized the development of mental as well as physical "efficiency" (thinking strategically in terms of maximum effect from minimum effort), and he argued that sparring (*randori*) cultivated quick thinking, decisiveness, self-control, sound judgement, and courage, "becoming neither cocky with victory nor broken with defeat" (p. 25). These qualities are characteristics of an excellent judoka. (For a negative example, I am reminded of the fighter Ronda Rousey, who shifted her career from judo to mixed martial arts [MMA], and who was quite cocky when she won and broken after losing her 2015 bout with Holly Holm. She has been the target of severe criticism for her arrogance and self-absorption.) For example, an indecisive judo player will hesitate to act when openings are perceived and so will frequently lose. Without self-control, anger can lead to stupid mistakes and more losses. To use Ronda Rousey as a negative example again, Rousey won the bronze medal in judo at the 2008 Olympics but was heartbroken that she did not win gold and so quit the sport. She was unable to come back from her 2015 MMA loss, and at the time of this writing has apparently given up MMA as well and gone into acting and professional wrestling. Who knows what heights someone with her athletic gifts may have reached in judo, or in MMA, had she been more true to Kano's principles?

The pursuit of excellence within a practice flows into individual flourishing and the good life for humans in general. It is through activity as a member of various practices that one develops the virtues that constitute one's character and empower human flourishing. I have argued (Hackney, 2009, 2010c, 2013) that if we define martial arts such as judo as eudaimonic practices, then we see that the kinds of virtues that enable a person to be an excellent judoka (courage, self-control, humility, and so on) are the same virtues that facilitate individual development into a more mature human being. In order to act boldly in the face of opposition, an excellent judoka must develop and display courage. In order to become more skillful, continuous practice is required, necessitating self-control. Humility enables a practitioner to submit to the coach's instruction and to serve as a good training partner to the other students. This maturity facilitates functioning in the broader context of society. A courageous, self-controlled, and humble person is better able to be a good citizen, a good neighbor, and a good friend. Kano (1986) used this logic in justifying his promotion of judo as a part of physical education: "The powers of attention and observation, of reasoning and judgment are naturally heightened [by participating in judo], and these are all useful attributes in daily life as well as in the dojo" (p. 23).

What makes an activity a eudaimonic practice rather than only a fun way to fill one's time is the fact that cultivating the qualities of excellence within the practice is connected to becoming a more highly functioning human being. So, do sports in fact cultivate those qualities of excellence? It is to this question that we now turn.

SPORTS AND PSYCHOLOGICAL WELL-BEING

The emotional benefits of an active and healthy lifestyle are indisputable (Mutrie & Faulkner, 2004). Thayer, Newman, and McClain (1994) compared ten behavioral methods of mood regulation, concluding that exercise was the most effective at changing a bad mood into a good mood. Berger and Motl (2000) reviewed twenty-five years of research and found exercise to be associated with both short-term and long-term improvements in mood. Activities they examined include aerobic dance, jogging, weight training, rock climbing, and cycling. Rejeski and colleagues (2001) found increased physical activity to be associated with increased subjective well-being, as did Stathi, Fox, and McKenna (2002) and Ginis et al. (2010). Exercise has been shown to reduce stress and anxiety (Long & Van Stavel, 1995; Petruzzello et al., 1991) and improve sleep (Kubitz et al., 1996). Physical activity has also been associated with reduced depression (Craft & Landers, 1998). Lawlor and Hopker (2001) performed a meta-analysis of studies involving exercise and depression and found regular exercise to be equal in effectiveness to cognitive therapy at reducing depressive symptoms, while Blumenthal and colleagues (1999) found exercise to be as effective as anti-depressant medication.

Physical activity clearly carries a feel-good effect (Biddle & Mutri, 2008), but it does matter that you do it right. Berger and Motl (2000), for example, found exercise to confer no benefits, and sometimes to make things worse, when the environment in which the exercise takes place is unpleasant,

when too much emphasis is placed on winning, or when the exercise is excessively intense. Self-determination theory researchers (e.g., Gagne, 2003; Kipp & Weiss, 2013; Stenling, Lindwall, & Hassmén, 2015) have found athletic participation to be associated with improved well-being when coaches and teammates create a healthy team environment in which psychological needs (competence, autonomy, and relatedness) are met, but the thwarting of those needs leads to worse outcomes, including increased athlete burnout (Quested & Duda, 2011; Adie, Duda, & Ntoumanis, 2012). Szabo (2000) reviewed the research on psychological correlates of physical activity and found that exercise can result in psychological hardship when novices (especially novices with high levels of pre-existing anxiety) are pushed too hard or when exercise is motivated by concern with an undesirable physical appearance. When carried out in a sensible and healthy manner, however, physical activities convey a wide range of emotional benefits.

What explains the emotional benefits of physical activity? As we saw in chapter four, one component of subjective well-being is the experience of frequent positive emotions, and many researchers have focused their work on the mood-enhancing effects of exercise (Biddle, 2000). The popular "endorphin hypothesis" (Hoffman, 1997) is the notion that exercise improves mood because the strain on muscles triggers a release of the body's pain-control chemicals (endogenous opioids). This is the explanation often given for the "runner's high" and the feeling of invincibility that can follow an especially good session of weight-lifting. There is some evidence supporting the endorphin hypothesis (e.g., Boecker et al., 2008), but methodological difficulties and inconsistent findings render it an uncertain explanation for the hedonic benefits of exercise (Dishman & O'Connor, 2009; Boecker & Dishman, 2013). Additional hypotheses include exercise boosting mood by way of its influence on monoamines (dopamine, noradrenaline, and serotonin; see Chaouloff, 1989, and Meeusen & De Meirleir, 1995) and the possibility that exercise produces mental and physical benefits by heating up the body, an idea that is referred to as the thermogenic hypothesis (Koltyn, 1997). Taking a more long-term approach, Dienstbier and Zillig (2005) argue that our nervous systems respond to repeated challenging activities (including regular exercise) with physiological changes that better equip them to handle challenging activities. These changes (such as increased serotonin production and faster recovery to baseline rates of nervous system arousal following a stressor) result in reduced anxiety, increased feelings of energy, improved stress tolerance, improved capacity to learn, and enhanced emotional stability.

Other explanations are more mental and less physiological. Hefferon and Mutrie (2012) review ways in which sports and exercise can serve as venues for positive psychological functioning, including opportunities to experience flow, cultivate resilience, engage in positive relationships, and improve one's self-concept. Feltz, Short, and Sullivan (2008) point to self-efficacy (the belief that one has the ability to effectively achieve goals; see Bandura, 1997) as a major contributor to high performance in sports, and performing well in sports can

lead to a general sense of confidence that one has the ability to achieve goals in life (Leith, Kerr, & Faulkner, 2011). Bahrke and Morgan (1978) argue that exercise helps relieve anxiety by providing a distraction from one's day. While individual effects will vary, Mutrie and Faulkner (2004) recommend around thirty minutes of at least moderate physical activity every day in order to receive the emotional benefits of exercise.

SPORTS BUILDING CHARACTER

What about the moral benefits of exercise? In this chapter, we are treating sports as practices (McNamee, 2008) as defined by Alasdair MacIntyre (2007). Becoming a high-level practitioner requires that we cultivate "important qualities of mind, body and character necessary both for excellent performance and for informed and accurate judgment about excellence in performance" (MacIntyre, 1988, p. 30). MacIntyre notes the role, for example, that justice plays in engagement in a practice, and this example applies to our approach to sports. Judging performance in a practice as excellent requires that the performance be evaluated and acclaimed according to the principles of merit, with the practitioner receiving exactly the level of accolade deserved. Self-control also plays a role in the practice, as a competitor must exert self-restraint to play within the rules and perform according to the applicable standards of excellence. Lawrence (2010) claims that fencing well requires courage. One must risk a hit to score a hit. So, at a conceptual level, it makes sense that pursuing excellence in sports should result in the cultivation of those moral qualities (like justice, self-control, and courage) that empower not only excellence in the sport but excellence as a moral agent and highly functioning human.

Is this borne out by the empirical literature? Not always. Beller and Stoll (1995) studied the moral reasoning of high school students and found athletes to function at a lower moral level (in terms of impartiality, reflectiveness, and consistency of moral thinking) than non-athletes. As is the case with the emotional benefits of sports and exercise, the moral benefits of sports largely depend on *how* one engages in the practice. What matters is that you do it right more than whether it is done at all. Quite a lot of work on this topic involves the role of coaches. From a behaviorist and social-learning viewpoint, moral improvement is a matter of reinforcing correct behavior and punishing incorrect behavior (Skinner, 1953), as well as modeling moral behavior for learners to observe (Bandura, 1973). Wandzilak, Carroll, and Ansorge (1988) found that "sportsmanlike" behavior increased among junior high school basketball players when such behaviors were rewarded and unsportsmanlike conduct punished by the coaches. Coaches who themselves display disrespect or rule-breaking are more likely to produce players who engage in the same (Treasure, 2002). Bolter and Weiss (2013) found coaches' modeling of sportsmanlike behavior to be predictive of players engaging in more prosocial behavior toward teammates and less antisocial behavior toward opponents. Players' moral behavior is also influenced by observation of physical education teachers (Gibbons & Ebbeck, 1997) and the moral or immoral

actions of professional athletes (Mugno & Feltz, 1985).

Coaches can create a "moral atmosphere" for their team that either fosters or inhibits virtuous growth (McNamee, Jones, & Duda, 2003; Stephens & Bredemeier, 1996). Stevens and Kavanaugh (1997) found that the best predictor of antisocial behavior among hockey players was their perception that aggression and cheating were normal for their team, and Stephens (2000) found the same patterns among soccer players. Several researchers (Guivernau & Duda, 2002; Shields, LaVoi, Bredemeier, & Power, 2007) have found that coaches, teammates, and spectators all contribute to the likelihood of immoral behavior by athletes, showing how moral atmosphere is constructed from multiple sources.

Self-determination theorists (e.g., Hagger & Chatzisarantis, 2007) argue that motivation in an activity depends on how well the environment satisfies the three basic psychological needs of competence, autonomy, and relatedness. When those needs are met, motivation to engage in the activity tends to shift away from extrinsic motivation (motivation based on the external rewards and punishments attached to a behavior) toward intrinsic motivation (motivation based on enjoyment of the activity itself). Satisfying those needs and facilitating intrinsic motivation is associated with greater enjoyment, well-being, and flourishing in a wide range of domains of life (Ryan & Deci, 2000), including sport and exercise (Ryan & Deci, 2007). One way coaches and physical education teachers can create a healthy sporting environment is through autonomy-supportive approaches (such as allowing athletes to make choices, rewarding initiative, and explaining the "why" behind rules) rather than controlling approaches (such as "shut up and do it" or "because I said so; that's why") (Bartholomew et al., 2009, 2011), as well as by interacting with players in a warm rather than harsh or disconnected manner (Van den Berghe et al., 2014). Need-supportive coaching has been shown to be associated with more moral behavior, more sportsmanship, less "moral disengagement" (justifying immoral actions through such mechanisms as euphemistic labeling, rationalization, and blaming others), and fewer antisocial attitudes (Ntoumanis & Standage, 2009; Hodge & Lonsdale, 2011).

The undermining of psychological needs is also associated with athletes pursuing extrinsic goals such as fame, pride, and winning at all costs (Hodge & Lonsdale, 2011). Recall that earlier in this chapter we looked at MacIntyre's (2007) distinction between the "internal" and "external" goods of a practice. Kirk and Kinchin (2003) argue that rewards such as the fortune and glory that come with success in the realm of professional sports constitute the external goods of sports, and it is the prioritization of these external goods over the internal goods that cause athletes to engage in immoral and unhealthy behaviors such as drug use, cheating, and overtraining to the point of injury. A review of the research on the effects of moral atmosphere on athlete behavior supports this MacIntyrean perspective.

MARTIAL ARTS AS A PATHWAY TO FLOURISHING

I have been a student of the martial arts since 1995, with a background that includes hapkido, Bujinkan Budo Taijutsu, Brazilian jujitsu, traditional jujitsu, European medieval martial arts, bartitsu, and judo. Way back when I was an undergraduate student, the first psychology study I ever designed and ran involved personality and martial arts. I have had martial arts on the brain for a while now.

I argued earlier in this chapter that judo fits very well within MacIntyre's (2007) definition of a eudaimonic practice, but the same can be said for the other martial arts, including those arts that are more traditional and less competitive in nature (Hackney, 2009, 2013). In this section, I return to this topic that I am passionate about and argue that training in the martial arts is associated with an increase in positive psychological variables and a decrease in negative psychological variables. A MacIntyrean perspective on the martial arts (Hackney, 2010c) allows us to see the training as a venue for character development and flourishing.

Zivin and colleagues (2001) found that youth who participated in a kenpo program demonstrated improvement across twelve different variables, including happiness, attentive ability, and schoolwork performance. Kurian and colleagues (1994) examined taekwondo practitioners' personalities, concluding that "belt rank is associated with a pattern of enthusiastic optimism and self-reliance" (p. 905). Martial arts training has also been associated with increases in positive self-image (Finkenberg, 1990; Richman & Rehberg, 1986) and self-control (Focht, Bouchard, & Murphey, 2000).

Martial arts training has also been found to be associated with the reduction of negative characteristics, including aggressiveness (Harwood, Lavidor, & Rassovsky, 2017), and anxiety-related characteristics (Kurian, Caterino, & Kulhavy, 1993; Layton, 1990; Ozer & Bandura, 1990), such as neuroticism (Layton, 1988), as well as feelings of vulnerability (Madden, 1990, 1995), nightmares (Slater & Hunt, 1997), and symptoms of PTSD (David, Simpson, & Cotton, 2006). Because of these psychosocial benefits, some have advocated for the martial arts as an adjunct to traditional psychotherapy (e.g., Gleser et al., 1992; Weiser, Kutz, Kutz, & Weiser, 1995) and as a way of encouraging the reform of delinquent youth (e.g., Trulson, 1989; Twemlow & Sacco, 1998; Zivin et al., 2001).

MARTIAL VIRTUES

Like any other practice, pursuing excellence in the martial arts requires characteristics that are deemed to be desirable by martial artists. In my book (Hackney, 2010c), I engage in a crosscultural review of a variety of literatures on "warrior virtues" to see what qualities of excellence keep recurring across the centuries and around the world, covering sources as far-ranging as Plato's *Republic*, the chivalric literature, Bushido, the *hwarang* tradition in Korea, and the work of fifteenth-century swordmaster Fiore dei Liberi. Combining these and many other sources, I found that five virtues consistently emerge across history and across cultures as necessary characteristics of an excellent warrior: courage, justice, temperance, wisdom, and benevolence (see chapter ten for a detailed discussion of the definitions of these virtues). These five virtues not only facilitate victory in self-defensive encounters but are also characteristic of highly functioning people. Liberi, for example, considers "audacity" (a form of courage involving the ability to act swiftly and decisively in the face of fear) to be the crowning virtue of his art, enabling the fighter to take immediate advantage of openings in opponents' defenses. Audacity can also empower everyday acts of courage, such as standing up for one's beliefs in the face of peer opposition or taking altruistic action when situations call for it (Hackney, 2006). Here are some ways in which martial training can facilitate growth in these virtues:

Courage is the virtue most easily associated with the martial arts. Peterson and Seligman (2004) define courage as "the exercise of will to accomplish goals in the face of opposition, either external or internal" (p. 199). The most obvious example of opposition in the martial arts is one's opponent. Training in the martial arts also involves risk, and courage empowers swift action in the face of fear (Hackney, 2006), as well as the ability to continue in spite of pain and fear. For a personal example, there is a particular throw in judo (*seoi nage*) that consistently scares me—at one point in the throw, the person being thrown is upside down and airborne. Continuing to show up and let people throw me can be seen as a small exercise in courage.

Justice can be cultivated in the martial arts through concepts such as honor (Westhusing, 2003) and obligation. A highly functioning martial artist will treat others with the honor they are due and take seriously the obligations that come with the various roles found in the dojo. For example, in some Japanese arts, the term *uke* is used to describe the one who plays the role of attacker when practicing a technique, while *tori* is used to describe the one who responds with the technique being practiced. Both have to perform their roles in order for the training to go well (Hatsumi & Cole, 2001; Ledyard, 2002).

As we saw in chapter ten, temperance includes character strengths such as self-control and humility. The martial arts provide ample opportunities for the cultivation of both humility and self-regulatory strength. Training in the martial arts involves frequent failures and frustrations, exposure to others who are more highly skilled than oneself, and the necessity of obeying one's instructor. Lakes and Hoyt (2004) examined the possibility of martial arts training enhancing self-regulation. This study was done using traditional experimental methods and involved a school-based taekwondo program. Half of the two hundred participants were assigned to a four-month program of Moogong Ryu taekwondo training, while the other half engaged in standard physical education classes. Compared to the control group, the students in the taekwondo group demonstrated improvements in their cognitive, emotional, and behavioral self-control.

As we saw in chapter nine, it is common in wisdom research to distinguish between transcendent and practical wisdom (Robinson, 1990). Both can be found in the martial arts. One example of cultivating transcendent wisdom can be found in the traditional martial arts that maintain a strong connection to Buddhist thought and practice, including kendo (Kiyota, 2002) and kyudo (Hoff, 2002). The seventeenth-century English swordmaster George Silver provides an example of practical wisdom in the martial arts. Silver's approach to training emphasizes cultivating the ability to quickly and accurately perceive situations (including the opponent's distance and position) and make use of that information in response to attacks. Silver's description of a fighter's judgments lines up well with Fowers's (2005) description of practical wisdom.

Benevolence as a warrior virtue may strike some as odd, but it fits well with Virginia Held's description of care-based ethics: "The central focus of the ethics of care is on the compelling moral salience of attending to and meeting the needs of the particular others for whom we take responsibility" (Held, 2006, p. 10). In this case, one who studies the martial arts is adopting the responsibility to protect others, meeting their needs for safety (Hackney, 2010c). Benevolence toward opponents is also found within the martial arts themselves. One example of this is the teaching that violent force is only to be used as a last resort, which finds practical application in karate with the requirement that the opponent be the first one to attack. "It isn't accidental," says Shotokan karate master Teruyuki Okazaki, "that, while training, the first move we make from shizen tai (ready/natural position) is a block, and that each kata begins with a blocking technique" (Okazaki, 2006, p. 45).

Suggestions for Future Research

It seems to me that a strong argument can be made for martial arts as a venue for virtuous development. But, unfortunately, examples abound of martial artists who have spent years engaged in the practice but display low moral character. In the 2008 Olympics, Cuban taekwondo competitor Angel Matos argued with a referee and then kicked that referee in the head (earning a lifetime ban from all World Taekwondo Federation events). In the tenth season of *The Ultimate Fighter*, MMA competitor and coach Quinton "Rampage" Jackson threw a temper tantrum when one of his fighters lost a match, demolishing a gym door while emitting a stream of profanities. In 2014, a California karate instructor was arrested in connection with more than 500 counts of child molestation. As we saw with other research on participation in sports, engaging in a practice does not guarantee moral development. Coach behavior and the moral climate of the team influence the likelihood that the person who participates in the practice will cultivate the virtues associated with excellence in the practice. I referred to the possibility that martial arts teachers moderate the effect of training on flourishing as the "Kreese-Miyagi effect" (Hackney, 2013), after the characters in the 1984 *Karate Kid* movie. While there is some research in which we see a connection between martial arts training and personal growth, to my knowledge no study has included a measure of the coach's character or training style.

Another area of research that remains relatively unexplored is the possibility that different styles of martial arts might have different influences. Martial arts vary widely in the relative emphases given to defensive and offensive tactics, striking and grappling, the use of weapons, the importance of politeness, and the importance of winning competitions. One major division

between styles is that of "traditional" martial arts versus "combat sports." Traditional martial arts (such as aikido) feature the practicing of techniques without active resistance, the memorization of forms (kata), little or no sparring, and a focus on techniques that are intended to be applicable in "real-world" self-defense situations rather than competitions. Combat sports (such as kickboxing) emphasize competitive sparring within a set of rules, training with opponents who actively resist, and employing either no forms or very few. Some arts combine elements of both. Judo, for example, has roots in traditional jujitsu and formal kata but is also an Olympic sport. Traditional and competitive versions of karate and taekwondo exist. MMA is primarily sporting in emphasis but is not entirely divorced from the traditional martial arts (MMA fighter Lyoto Machida has a background in Shotokan karate, and Anderson Silva and Anthony Pettis got their starts in taekwondo).

It is reasonable to predict that the ratio of traditional to sporting elements found in a martial art might have some relationship with the psychological effects of training. One of the very few studies that have included this angle was conducted by Trulson (1989), who found that taekwondo students whose training emphasized traditional aspects demonstrated reduced aggressiveness, while those whose training emphasized the combative and competitive aspects demonstrated increased aggressiveness. Harwood and colleagues (2017), on the other hand, found that martial art type had no bearing on the relationship between training and aggressiveness. Researchers who want to investigate the possibility of martial arts as a pathway for personal growth should be sensitive to the differences among martial arts and aware that the results of a study examining one martial art might not generalize to others.

◆ ◆ ◆

In one form or another, sports have presented problems for Christians since the days of the early church due to their vulnerability to idolatry, immorality, and degradation of the human body (Higgs, 1995; Hoffman, 2010; Koch, 2012), but arguments that these problems render sports irredeemably toxic for Christians (e.g., Higgs, 1995) have been countered by arguments that sports can be a venue for bringing glory to God, advancing the gospel message, and building Christlike character (Ladd & Mathisen, 1999; Lixey, 2012; Weir, 2008). In one form or another, these same arguments continue today, with some (e.g., Higgs, 1995) claiming that we have turned sports into a deeply anti-Christian phenomenon that amounts to a quasi-religion that worships victory, profit, and self-aggrandizement and fosters a range of vices. Shirl Hoffman's (2010) description of the corrupting elements of sports sounds quite familiar after our brief historical flyover: "Variously described by those inside it as narcissistic, materialistic, self-interested, violent, sensational, coarse, racist, sexist, brazen, raunchy, hedonistic, body-destroying, and militaristic, the culture of sports is light years removed from what Christians for centuries have idealized as the embodiment of the gospel message" (p. 11). Hoffman, however, is not dismissive of sports in their entirety. He believes that sport provides great potential for personal and spiritual growth, provided we can learn to avoid the aforementioned corrupting elements and think carefully about how to be genuinely "Christian" in our approach. What little research has been done on the role of the Christian faith in sport psychology has shown us that navigating this complexity is not an easy task (Egli & Hoven, 2019). Bringing together theological, philosophical, and psychological work on the role that sports (including the martial arts) can play in the good life can help provide some guidance for this process.

SUGGESTIONS FOR FURTHER READING

Hackney, C. H. (2010). *Martial virtues.* Charles E. Tuttle Publications.

Hagger, M. S., & Chatzisarantis, N. L. D. (Eds.). (2007). *Intrinsic motivation and self-determination in exercise and sport.* Human Kinetics.

Hardman, A. R., Jones, C., & Jones, R. (2010). Sports coaching, virtue ethics and emulation. *Physical Education and Sport Pedagogy, 15*(4), 345-59.

Hoffman, S. J. (2010). *Good game: Christianity and the culture of sports.* Baylor University Press.

Hoven, M., Parker, A., & Watson, N. J. (Eds.). (2019). *Sport and Christianity: Practices for the twenty-first century.* Bloomsbury Publishing.

Mutrie, N., & Faulkner, G. (2004). Physical activity: Positive psychology in motion. In P. A. Linley & S. Joseph (Eds.), *Positive psychology in practice* (pp. 146-164). John Wiley & Sons.

Rice, S. M., Purcell, R., De Silva, S., Mawren, D., McGorry, P. D., & Parker, A. G. (2016). The mental health of elite athletes: A narrative systematic review. *Sports Medicine, 46*(9), 1333-53.

Chapter Eighteen

FLOURISHING STUDENTS

*The purpose of education is to allow each individual to
come into full possession of his or her personal power.*

JOHN DEWEY

In 2011, the University of Nevada Las Vegas decided to eliminate the entire philosophy department. The president of the university explained that this decision was due to budget cuts, and he framed the decision in terms of the university's mission, which was "to build a globally competitive and highly educated workforce that can attract new industries and build a more diversified economy" (*Las Vegas Sun*, 2011, March 8). Philosophy was not seen as an important part of that goal, as very few people get rich by doing philosophy. Fortunately (for those of us who value philosophy), the peasants revolted, and UNLV faced vociferous public objections. Philosophy was taken off the chopping block.

One of the central organizing principles of this book is neo-Aristotelian teleology (see chapter two). Something is described as good or bad by referring to the telos of that thing. We applied this line of thinking to human flourishing by asking what the human telos is, and our answers come from Christian theological sources involving human nature and sanctification. In chapter thirteen, part of our foray into the psychology of love was the question of the

telos of marriage. In chapter seventeen, we looked at sports from a teleological perspective, including the telos of a judo match. In this chapter, we will turn our eyes toward education.

What is the telos of education? Recall that someone may hold to an implicit telos and that we can discern that telos if we look at the goal this person is trying to achieve and the standards employed to evaluate the goodness or badness of the thing under discussion. Looking at the story of UNLV and the imperiled philosophy department, we can see that the telos guiding their decision to cut the philosophy department was economic in nature. Their purpose of education was apparently to shape students into economic agents, producers, and consumers who would take their places as the next generation of participants in the marketplace.

This is a very common telos, and you are likely to see it all over the place now that you have been made aware of it. In 2009, President Obama gave a speech in which he praised certain countries in Asia, the leaders of which were reducing their support for the humanities in high school in favor of greater emphasis on preparing students for jobs in technology-oriented fields. He said, "They are spending less time teaching things that don't matter, and more time teaching things that do" (Nussbaum, 2010, p. 138). Such a statement shows the economic telos living loudly in Obama's mind. In 2018, President Trump proposed that the US Department of Education be merged with the Department of Labor, creating a "Department of Education and the Workforce." See if this sounds familiar: The move was justified by the White House (in a proposal posted online at whitehouse .gov) using the claim that the Department of Education and Department of Labor "share a common goal of preparing Americans for success in a globally competitive world through family sustaining careers." There's that economic telos again.

The president of the Association of American Colleges and Universities criticized Trump's proposal as "an attempt to reduce higher education to work-force development at the expense of a liberal arts education" (Kreighbaum, 2018). The liberal arts tradition is the other most commonly encountered camp in these debates. Instead of an economic telos, we see a political telos for education (Kimball, 1986). The Romans used *liberalis* to mean "of or relating to free men" (p. 13), and a liberal arts education became connected with the goal of shaping students into the kinds of people who would function well as free citizens (Nussbaum, 2010). As someone who appreciates the political telos at the heart of the liberal arts curriculum, I see the basic mistake of the University of Nevada Las Vegas (and Presidents Obama and Trump) in the assumption that the

worth of an academic program rests on its economic results. It may be true that nobody gets rich doing philosophy, but that is not the point.

A Christian vision of education will similarly be teleological but grounded in the overarching telos of "transformation into Christ's likeness" (Zimmermann, 2017, p. 2). In the same way that we talked about sports as practices that shape athletes into certain kinds of people, schools are communities of practice (Smith & Smith, 2011) in which students are shaped into certain kinds of people. Rather than shaping students into economic agents or democratic citizens (although those goals may be realized as beneficial side effects), a central goal for Christian educators is to facilitate the transmission of the faith to the next generation in a manner that demonstrates both intellectual and spiritual integrity (Houston & Hindmarsh, 2013). This will involve the combined employment of faith practices (e.g., corporate worship) and academic practices (e.g., close reading of texts), such that "faith practice orients academic practice" and "academic practice enriches faith practice" (MacInnis-Hackney, 2017, p. 109), and the virtues associated with each are cultivated. The recent surge in enthusiasm among Christians for classical education (Bauer & Wise, 2016; Reynolds, 2009) is an example of this.

Positive psychologists have also weighed in on the formative power of schools.

> With all the pressures on educators to foster academic achievement, it is too often forgotten that schools are more than learning factories—they are *contexts for child and adolescent development.* Children learn more than "reading,

'riting and 'rithmetic" in schools; they also learn about authority, industry, social relationships, and how they are perceived and valued by others outside the home. Schools shape the *development of the whole child,* affecting intellectual outcomes as well as motivation, self-concept, and the vitality and integrity of self-development. (Ryan & Deci, 2017, p. 353)

Researchers have looked both at how schools can serve as venues for positive development and at how the findings of positive psychologists might be employed to improve students' performance and adjustment (Gilman et al., 2009; Wade et al., 2015). Many of the topics within positive psychology that we have already covered in this book are represented here, with educational applications flowing from researchers' more general theoretical and empirical work. For example, based on what we have seen regarding the value of positive subjective states, many teachers have begun encouraging happiness and flow (Baylus, 2004). Conoley and Conoley (2009) suggest that educators increase flow among students by assigning work that is optimally challenging, meaningful, and intrinsically motivating. We will begin our coverage of positive education by looking at a specific positive psychological theory that has been applied at multiple levels of education and then cover some programs that are grounded in theories we have seen earlier in this text.

SELF-DETERMINATION THEORY

Self-determination theory (SDT) "is an empirically based, organismic theory of human behavior and personality development" that "is centrally concerned with

the social conditions that facilitate or hinder human flourishing" (Ryan & Deci, 2017, p. 3). Although SDT predates the advent of the positive psychology movement with its emphasis on well-being, personal growth, and improved performance, SDT has found a natural home among positive psychologists (Ryan & Deci, 2000; Sheldon & Ryan, 2011). SDT is an "organismic" theory, meaning that it begins with the assumption that humans actively engage with their environments, integrating their experiences into a coherent and growing self (Deci & Ryan, 1985). This connects SDT to humanistic psychology (see chapter one), with the belief that human nature is inherently good and growth-oriented.

If humans are naturally inclined toward growth and flourishing, why are so many of us not flourishing? Self-determination theorists place the responsibility for both positive and negative outcomes on the environment. We might employ a botanical metaphor to understand this. I have a garden at my home, and as all gardeners know, we do not have the ability to *make* our plants grow. If I were to go to my garden, grab a tomato plant, and start yanking on it, that would not make the plant grow any larger (in fact, it is more likely that I would destroy it). What I can do is provide my plants with a nutritive environment, with sufficient sunlight, water, and fertilizer. Growth is built into the plants' DNA, so growth will happen on its own if the environment is right. Similarly, I cannot make my children grow taller by grabbing their ears and pulling upward. If I provide a sufficiently healthy environment for my children, they will grow as a part of the natural maturational process (and go through shoes like crazy). According to self-determination theorists, this same principle that applies to the physical growth of plants and children applies to the development and flourishing of a human personality. Personal growth and well-being happen through an innate process of self-actualization as long as the social environment satisfies their basic psychological needs (Ryan, 1995).

Self-determination theorists posit that humans have three basic psychological needs: competence, autonomy, and relatedness (Deci & Ryan, 2000b). Competence "refers to feeling effective in one's interactions with the social environment—that is, experiencing opportunities and supports for the exercise, expansion, and expression of one's capacities and talents" (Deci & Ryan, 2017, p. 86). Autonomy is experienced when people perceive that "their actions stem from and are supported by volition and willingness versus feeling alien, forced, or compelled" (p. 51). Relatedness "refers to both experiencing others as responsive and sensitive and being able to be responsive and sensitive to them— that is, feeling connected and involved with others and having a sense of belonging" (p. 86). Environments can either support or thwart these needs, and people tend to flourish to the degree to which the needs are met and experience difficulties and distress when they are blocked (Deci & Ryan, 1987; Reis et al., 2000; Ryan & Deci, 2000). Competence needs might be supported through the provision of optimal challenges (tough enough to require effort but not impossible) and performance feedback. Autonomy needs

can be supported when people are given as much choice as possible and coerced as little as possible when being directed. Relatedness needs are supported when the lines of communication are open and interpersonal relationships are functioning well (Ryan, 1995). One key outcome of need satisfaction is intrinsic motivation, a form of motivation that is involved in pursuing goals and engaging in activities because we find the activities interesting and challenging by themselves, without their being necessarily connected to any concrete reward (Deci & Ryan, 1985; Ryan, 1995).

Self-determination theory is large and complex, encompassing multiple "mini theories" and decades of research, so I encourage readers to go beyond what we are covering in this chapter and seek out books such as Deci and Ryan's (2017) recent summary and update of SDT theory, research, and application. We will also discuss SDT in the workplace in chapter nineteen. At this point we will turn to a narrow consideration of SDT in the classroom.

Learning is marked by intrinsic motivation when students' curiosity and interest are engaged. "When the educational environment provides optimal challenges, rich sources of stimulation, and a context of autonomy, this motivational wellspring of learning is likely to flourish" (Deci & Ryan, 1985, p. 245). Koestner and colleagues (1984) investigated how classroom instruction might be delivered in such a way that autonomy is preserved. A sample of first-grade and second-grade students were given an art project (painting) and randomly assigned to one of three groups. Students in the control group were given no restrictions on their painting. Students in one of the experimental groups were told to keep their materials neat and tidy ("controlling" limits). Students in the third group were also told to keep their materials neat, but instead of just issuing commands, the researchers explained that while it might be fun to slop paint around, we need to keep the materials in good condition for the sake of other children who will be using them ("informational" limits). Afterward, students had the option of freely choosing an activity, with painting as one possible choice. Students in the controlling condition were less likely to choose painting, which showed that the external imposition of rules based on mere authority undermined intrinsic motivation. Students who were given the instructions in an informational manner were more likely to choose painting on their own and reported greater enjoyment of painting. Grolnick and Ryan (1989) examined the role parents can play in the educational motivation of their children (third through sixth graders). They focused on autonomy support (whether or not the parents encouraged their children's independent problem-solving, gave them choices, and involved them in family decision-making) and relatedness (using indicators of maternal involvement in the child's life). Positive need support was associated with better academic and personal outcomes.

The connection between need support and improved outcomes is the intrinsic motivation fostered in supportive environments. When teachers give positive feedback that encourages a sense of competence, students show greater intrinsic motivation (Vallerand & Reid, 1988). Deci and colleagues (1981) compared teachers who tended to be more controlling in their approach to those who tended to be more autonomy-supportive and found that students assigned to the autonomy-supportive teachers demonstrated more internalized motivation. Williams and colleagues (1997) examined medical students and found that those who experienced greater autonomy support in their internal medicine clerkships were more likely to select internal medicine as their specialization.

SDT researchers have examined the learning environment from a number of angles (Deci et al., 1991). Within the laboratory and field research surrounding need satisfaction, motivation, and performance in the classroom, with participants ranging from elementary school students to grad students, there are a number of practical tips we can assemble for creating schools that foster intrinsic motivation, superior performance, and enhanced student well-being.

First, we can support autonomy by giving students as much choice as possible (Deci & Ryan, 1985). Naturally, there needs to be some structure and limitations on classroom projects and assignments or else the goals of the class cannot be accomplished (Niemiec & Ryan, 2009). But autonomy support can harmoniously coexist with clear classroom structure (Vansteenkiste et al., 2012), so within the necessary limitations, it is possible to give students choice.

Projects should also hit the "sweet spot" of optimal challenge for students: those things that take effort and personal engagement but are not impossible. This level of challenge satisfies students' need for competence (Deci, Ryan, & Williams, 1996). Benware and Deci (1984) provided students with a task that increased challenge and personal engagement. Students in their study were taught neuropsychology material, with some told they were going to be tested on the material and others told they were going to teach the material later. Students who used their study time to prepare to teach showed greater understanding of the material. Providing structure in the form of clear goals, expectations, supervision, and positive feedback also fosters students' perceptions of competence (Vansteenkiste et al., 2012). Teachers can support students' need for relatedness by showing students they genuinely respect and value them (Niemiec & Ryan, 2009).

Teachers often have to field questions from students about the purpose of the topic being taught ("Why do I have to learn this?" and the many variations thereof). Answers about these goals can range from more extrinsic and controlling (grades, future salaries, social status, appeals to authority) to more intrinsic (connections to meaningful values, relationships, community, the inherently fascinating nature of the task). If we take the example of a student who is preparing for a career in medicine, an extrinsic goal would be the earning potential for doctors, while an intrinsic goal would be the nobility of saving lives and helping those who are hurting. Vansteenkiste et al. (2004) found that "when individuals learn concepts or activities for intrinsic goals, there will be deeper processing, better test performance, and greater persistence than when they learn for extrinsic goals" (p. 247), and when schools frame learning in more intrinsic

terms, students tend to respond with improved understanding, performance, and persistence (Vansteenkiste, Lens, & Deci, 2006). One practical tip educators can take from this research is to avoid placing too much emphasis on grades. Grades can be part of the necessary structure of a class, but overemphasis on grades (especially when communicated in a controlling manner) is associated with worse performance and student emotional well-being (Deci & Ryan, 1985).

THE PENN RESILIENCY PROGRAM

At this point we will start looking at some specific educational programs grounded in positive psychological theories and research. One of the most famous of these approaches is the Penn Resiliency Program (PRP), which is based mostly on Martin Seligman's optimism research and involves "teaching students to think more realistically and flexibly about the problems they encounter" (Seligman, 2011, p. 81). The PRP employs concepts and methods we saw in chapter seven, including the ABC (adversity, belief, consequence) method Seligman (1990) adapted from rational emotive behavior therapy (Gillham & Reivich, 2004). Guided by the idea that it is our beliefs about unhappy events that cause our emotional troubles rather than the events themselves, a student who is facing the disappointment of a bad grade would be taught to identify his or her attributional style (optimistic or pessimistic) and then look for an unstable and specific attribution for the event ("I didn't study enough") instead of a more stable global attribution ("I'm stupid"). Students are also taught realistic goal setting, the avoidance of worst-case thinking and catastrophizing, and social skills relating to assertiveness and communication. In an expanded version of the program, students are taught to identify and use their signature strengths (see chapter ten) and enhance gratitude (see chapter fourteen) with the "three good things" exercise (Seligman, 2011).

Thus far, the PRP has been shown to be effective. Brunwasser, Gillham, and Kim (2009) carried out a meta-analysis of PRP effectiveness studies, finding a significant (though small) effect of the training on students' depression scores. The program has also been shown to reduce behavior problems (Jaycox et al., 1994) and improve social skills and engagement with learning (Seligman et al., 2009). The success of the PRP has spawned a collection of spinoff programs in Britain, Australia, and New Zealand (Bowman et al., 2009). One of the most impressive projects to come out of this work took place in the Geelong Grammar School, a boarding school located in Australia south of Melbourne (Seligman et al., 2009). School administrators were willing to spend several million dollars to reorganize the entire curriculum around positive psychology, with Seligman and some colleagues living there for the entire school year and a "who's who" of positive psychologists flying in to teach and advise on their areas of specialization (Seligman, 2011). Faculty and staff were trained in positive psychology concepts and methods (with some receiving advanced training to themselves become trainers), with a focus on resilience, creativity, mindfulness, character strengths, self-efficacy, emotional competence, and gratitude (White, 2013). While no proper effectiveness research has been carried out on this experimental curriculum, Seligman (2011) and the principal of the school (Noorish, 2015) are confident that it has had a beneficial impact on the lives and characters of the students.

TEACHING FOR WISDOM

Back in chapter nine we looked at Sternberg's (1998) balance theory of wisdom, in which he describes the wise person as able to select a pathway to a good situational goal in a manner that balances intrapersonal (what's in it for me), interpersonal, (my friends and family), and extrapersonal (God, important values, and the good of the community) interests. This approach was put to work in the development of a wisdom-based approach to teaching American history to middle school students (Reznitskaya & Sternberg, 2004). History can be taught as a set of facts to memorize, or it can be seen as a story of people making decisions, trying to do the best they can with what they have and subject to all of the limitations and biases that affect the rest of us. It can also be an opportunity to *think* through the material by considering opposing perspectives, values, ends, and applications for the lessons students are learning. As the best way to cultivate practical wisdom is to engage in practices that require practical wisdom (Higgs, 2012), students in this program are "invited to experience and solve the problems faced by actual practitioners of the discipline of history" (Reznitskaya & Sternberg, 2004, p. 191) as they work through the material. Benjamin Franklin can serve as a source of wisdom when studying the American War of Independence. Students can stop and ponder what Franklin meant when he said, "Whatever is begun in anger ends in shame." Students can read selections from his autobiography, in which he attempted to design a method for achieving moral perfection in thirteen easy steps (turns out it was a bit harder than old Ben had planned) and keep a journal of their own attempts at self-improvement. Students can also learn from accounts of the Boston Massacre, as we have written accounts from the captain of the British troops who opened fire as well as accounts from the colonists. Was the Boston Massacre an instance of tyrannical enforcers gunning down peaceful demonstrators or of soldiers defending themselves from a violent mob? What might we learn about bias from reading these conflicting reports that we can apply in our own fake news–saturated context?

Guided by the notion that teaching wisdom is more about teaching students *how* to think than *what* to think, Sternberg (2001) offers several suggestions for teachers: (1) Students should read classic works and reflect on the lessons we can learn from the great thinkers of the past. (2) Students should be engaged in group discussion, dialogically (recognizing multiple points of view) and dialectically (trying to bring opposing views together in a coherent way) considering how lessons may apply to their own lives and the lives of others. (3) Students should be aware of the powerful role values play in wise decision-making and should understand what values they bring to the table. (4) Students should be encouraged to be creative in developing wise decisions that serve the common good, understanding that it matters to what ends our decisions

move us. (5) Teachers should model wise decision-making themselves. They might do this by adopting a more Socratic teaching method and by talking students through the decision-making process, saying things like "When I get into the situations like this, I try to . . . " (Sternberg, Reznitskaya, & Jarvin, 2007, p. 155).

STRENGTHS-BASED EDUCATION

In chapter ten we focused on positive psychological work involving character strengths and virtues and how one can identify and cultivate one's individual strengths. Applied to education, strengths-based teaching involves taking this approach to both teachers and students (Lopez & Louis, 2009). Those involved might take their guidance from the *CSV* (Peterson & Seligman, 2004) or the Clifton StrengthsFinder (Clifton, Anderson, & Schreiner, 2006), but the general strategy will be roughly the same. Teachers can discover their "signature strengths" by taking the VIA Inventory of Strengths and then look at how their top strengths can be applied in their classrooms. McGovern and Miller (2008) describe ways in which the twenty-four character strengths identified by the VIA-IS can be put to use by teachers. For example, someone who scores high on the character strength of creativity might excel at being an "innovator," developing and trying out new pedagogical methods, and this person would also likely find that activity deeply fulfilling. Someone who has a high degree of social intelligence is sensitive to the group dynamics in a classroom and would do well at flexibly responding to these dynamics to tailor the material to the emotional tone of the room.

A teacher who is very brave will stand up for what is right even at great personal risk and become known by students as someone who has their backs when troubles arise. Magyar-Moe (2015) describes possible approaches for teacher development using the Clifton Strengths-Finder. Those who take this measure are given their top five "talent themes," and teachers can find it helpful to see how capitalizing on their talents might lead to greater success and happiness in their careers. Someone who scores high on the "achiever" theme sets high standards and works hard to reach them, making an "achiever" teacher someone who is known to students as tough but dedicated to helping students reach those high standards. The talent of "connectedness" involves linking concepts together, and a teacher with this as a prominent theme will do well at helping students see connections between events (for example, how a story in today's news about a trial shows connections to Elizabeth Loftus's research on eyewitness testimony), ideas (how Stoicism influenced Albert Ellis), and practices (why Freud didn't want patients to see his face when they were talking).

Teachers can also identify and foster strengths in their students. Park and Peterson (2009b) report that students with higher scores on love, hope, and zest showed greater life satisfaction, students with more justice- and temperance-related strengths were more popular, and strengths such as perseverance, honesty, and hope were associated with higher grades. Magyar-Moe (2015) recommends "positive introductions," in which students prepare a brief story about "a time when they were at their best" (p. 143). Teachers can listen for strengths-related themes in these stories and provide helpful feedback. Lopez and Louis (2009) suggest that teachers provide (when possible) flexibility in assignment parameters, giving students the ability to find ways to complete class projects that allow them to employ their strengths. If we use the *CSV* categorization and apply it to a specific project (such as a paper for a Theories of Personality class), there are a number of possibilities. A student who has a high degree of appreciation for beauty and excellence might write the paper as a personality profile of a favorite artist. Those who score high on open-mindedness might enjoy diving into a critical assessment of a controversy within personality psychology. A student who has forgiveness as a signature strength might want to know how a knowledge of individual differences can be employed to resolve interpersonal conflicts. Wade (2015) discusses how students can be given career advice based on their strengths, looking for areas in which they have experienced flow (see chapter six), and how helping students create pathways for success that capitalize on their strengths establishes and affirms their sense of identity.

POSITIVE CAMPUS

Many positive psychologists have also looked at ways colleges and universities can be positive places (Wade, Marks, & Hertzel, 2015). "Flourishing individuals feel both empowered and confident in their learning and problem solving and feel a sense of belonging to their schools and their larger human community" (Ryan & Deci, 2017, p. 354), so it serves the purposes of colleges to foster students' well-being. Campus faith groups should be encouraged, as involvement in these groups is associated with improved mental and physical health (Frankel & Hewett, 1994), and information can be made available to students regarding healthy and unhealthy uses of social media (Kalpidou, Costin, & Morris, 2011; Twenge, 2017). Hodges and Kennedy (2015) argue that colleges can foster hope by communicating in ways that keep students aware of resources that can provide them with pathways to success. The material we covered in chapter seventeen involving sports and flourishing can be applied to college athletics. Extracurricular activities, including but not limited to athletics, provide opportunities for social engagement, relationship-building, and fun.

◆ ◆ ◆

Innovative thinkers in positive education (e.g., Schreiner, 2015) and in Christian education (e.g., Glanzer, Alleman, & Ream, 2017) share a desire to move education away from its current prioritization of economic instrumentalism over personal formation. Though we differ from our secular colleagues on the telos of human flourishing, there is much Christian educators can learn from the positive psychologists on how the virtues may be cultivated in schools and students made mentally stronger to deal with the strains they encounter in the education system.

SUGGESTIONS FOR FURTHER READING

Gilman, R., Huebner, E. S., & Furlong, M. J. (Eds.). (2009). *Handbook of positive psychology in schools.* Routledge.

Niemiec, C. P., & Ryan, R. M. (2009). Autonomy, competence, and relatedness in the classroom: Applying self-determination theory to educational practice. *Theory and Research in Education, 7*(2), 133-44.

Ryan, R. M., & Deci, E. L. (2017). *Self-determination theory: Basic psychological needs in motivation, development, and wellness.* Guilford Press.

Smith, D. I., & Smith, J. K. A. (2011). *Teaching and Christian practices: Reshaping faith and learning.* Eerdmans.

Sternberg, R. J. (2001). Why schools should teach for wisdom: The balance theory of wisdom in educational settings. *Educational Psychologist, 36*(4), 227-45.

Wade, J. C., Marks, L. I., & Hetzel, R. D. (Eds.). (2015). *Positive psychology on the college campus.* Oxford University Press.

Chapter Nineteen

A POSITIVE WORKPLACE

Pleasure in the job puts perfection in the work.

Aristotle

The story goes that Sigmund Freud was asked what was necessary for a good life. His answer was simple: love and work. In chapter thirteen we talked about love. In this chapter we will talk about work. The World Health Organization (1994) reports that the majority of the world's population will spend a third of their adult life at work. Given the proportion of our lives that we spend in the workplace, the role work plays in the good life is a very important topic. Some of the material presented here will look familiar, as many of the theories we have covered in earlier chapters have been applied in the workplace setting, but we will also be covering some workplace-specific scholarship within positive psychology.

Finding Your Job

Nathan and Hill (2006) define career counseling as "a process which enables people to recognise and utilise their resources to make career-related decisions and manage career-related issues" (p. 2). The current approach to career counseling is more flexible than the classic approach, in which clients were given assessments and then told what job best fit their profile of interests and aptitudes (rather like the

Sorting Hat scenes in the Harry Potter novels). In the newer, more client-centered approach, the career counselor offers guidance and support as clients figure out and take responsibility for their own career goals and plans.

Many of the approaches taken by career counselors involve the assessment of clients' personal strengths and working with clients to figure out ways to fruitfully make use of those strengths. Career counselors have been thinking about clients' strengths since long before positive psychology came along. Practitioners who use the Myers-Briggs Type Indicator (MBTI; developed in the 1940s), for example, place a heavy emphasis on the identification and development of individual strengths (Briggs Myers & Myers, 1995). Central to the MBTI approach is the idea that each of the sixteen personality types has its own set of strengths and weaknesses. Extraverts, for example, are good with people, while introverts tend to have difficulty in that arena. Introverts, though, are better than extraverts when it comes to solitary, focused activity. Many people take the MBTI for career guidance, a strategy that is based on encouraging people to capitalize on their strengths (Briggs Myers et al., 2003). When I took the MBTI, I was categorized as an INTJ (introverted, intuiting, thinking, judging), which meant I would probably shine in activities that involved quiet solitude, structure, and analysis of abstract ideas (one possible explanation for why I thoroughly enjoyed writing this book). Oswald and Kroeger (1988) apply the MBTI to religious leadership, and I drew heavily from their book back when I did assessments of Nazarene clergy candidates in Ontario. Ministry is a multiform career path, and the duties placed on pastors are many and varied. Consequently, while there is no single personality type best suited for ordination, people with different personalities may find that they flourish in different areas of ministry. Had I gone into ministry, my INTJ type would have inclined me to do well at preaching and theological instruction but not so well at the touchy-feely stuff like pastoral counseling.

Career counselors who actively associate themselves with the positive psychology movement often employ the Clifton StrengthsFinder (e.g., Clifton et al., 2006). Those who take this measure are given their top five (out of a list of thirty-four) "themes" (areas in which they are especially gifted), as well as practical guidance for putting these themes to work. Those who find that "strategic" is one of their dominant themes tend to be good at sizing up a situation and putting together a plan. Combine that theme with "analytical" (good at figuring out the causes of events), and such a person might do well in a career that involves a lot of problem-solving. I happened to glance at an online jobs board while writing this section and found that a major financial holdings company in Toronto is looking to hire someone for a strategy analyst position. Their ideal candidate is someone who has a business or finance degree, enjoys a fast-paced and flexible work environment, and has "excellent analytical and problem solving skills, with particular emphasis on financial analysis and strategic analysis." Sounds just about perfect for our hypothetical person with strengths in strategy and analysis.

Littman-Ovadia, Lazar-Butbul, and Benjamin (2014) constructed a strengths-based career counseling model based on the *CSV* (Peterson & Seligman, 2004) and Y. Joel Wong's strength-centered therapy (Wong, 2006). This approach is based on four sessions (Littman-Ovadia et al., 2014). In the first session, the counselor and client talk about the client's prior training and work experiences, articulate the client's career goals, and talk about personal strengths. The client then takes the VIA-IS at home between sessions. In the second session, the two talk about the client's top five "signature strengths" and how these strengths can be applied in the client's life. The third session involves more direct and explicit connections that link strengths to career performance and goals. In the fourth session, the counselor and client review and summarize, and they talk about how the strengths-based development went.

Seligman (2002) recommends that people find work that allows them to use their signature strengths on a daily basis. For example, if you took one of the VIA instruments and learned that "creativity," "appreciation of beauty," and "humility" were signature strengths, then you might enjoy a career in the arts, but not one that involved putting yourself forward as a "star." Working as a studio musician might be an appealing option; there is a lot of variety involved, and you would get to meet and make music with interesting and talented people. The military might be a good idea for those whose signature strengths include "bravery," "citizenship," and "leadership." You might recall from chapter ten that my signature strengths turned out to be "love of learning," "spirituality," "judgment," "curiosity," and "perseverance." Looking at that list, I think I made a good decision in opting for a career as a professor at a Christian college. Littman-Ovadia and colleagues (2014) found that their strengths-based career counseling model was effective, with more clients finding work within three months relative to a control group that received standard career counseling.

A Happy Worker Is a Productive Worker

The connection between employee happiness and employee performance is well-established within the organizational psychology research literature (e.g., Staw, 1986; Staw, Sutton, & Pelled, 1994; Wright & Staw, 1999). Fred Luthans (2002) brings together several areas of positive psychology and applies them in the workplace in an approach he calls "positive organizational behavior." Luthans's goal is to make use of scientific theorizing and research within positive psychology to identify "state-like strengths and positive capacities that can be developed and managed for performance improvement in the workplace" (p. 699), showing employers that investing in flourishing is a profitable

strategy. Luthans describes these capacities as psychological capital, which he says "is an individual's positive psychological state of development and is characterized by: (1) having confidence (self-efficacy) to take on and put in the necessary effort to succeed at challenging tasks; (2) making a positive attribution (optimism) about succeeding now and in the future; (3) persevering toward goals and, when necessary, redirecting paths to goals (hope) in order to succeed; and (4) when beset by problems and adversity, sustaining and bouncing back and even beyond (resiliency) to attain success" (Luthans, Youssef-Morgan, & Avolio, 2007, p. 3).

These are all concepts we have encountered within positive psychology. Self-efficacy (Bandura, 1997) has appeared in several chapters and refers to "beliefs in one's capacities to organize and execute the courses of action required to produce given attainments" (p. 3). People with a high degree of self-efficacy believe they are able to achieve their goals if they do a good job and work hard at it. Stajkovic and Luthans (1998) conducted a meta-analysis of self-efficacy in the workplace, finding that high self-efficacy was associated with superior overall workplace performance, especially when the tasks involved were of low complexity. People with high self-efficacy do better as managers (Wood, Bandura, & Bailey, 1990), adapt to workplace technological changes better (Hill, Smith, & Mann, 1987), and have a more entrepreneurial mindset (Zhao, Seibert, & Hills, 2005).

We discussed optimism in chapter seven. Someone with a high degree of optimism is more likely to attribute positive outcomes to their own effort or capabilities and is less likely to see failures or disappointments as global indictments of their intelligence or general competence (Seligman, 1990). Recall that Seligman advocates for a realistic optimism, in which the individual is able to wisely size up a situation and know when to employ more optimistic attributions and when to employ more pessimistic attributions. Unrealistic optimism has been shown to be associated with worse outcomes in terms of mental and physical health (Davidson & Prkachin, 1997; Peterson & Vaidya, 2001). Luthans and colleagues (2015) apply this to the workplace, arguing for the value of workers who are flexibly and realistically optimistic. Optimism shows strong overlaps with Snyder's (2002) hope theory, though Seligman's work on optimism is mostly focused on explaining the past, while hope is about the future. Snyder and colleagues (2005) define hope as "the belief that one can find pathways to desired goals and become motivated to use those pathways" (p. 257). Adams et al. (2010) review empirical research on hope in the workplace, showing that hopeful employees are happier, more productive, and more loyal to their employers.

The word *resilience* is used by different psychologists to mean different things, as we have seen in several chapters. When Luthans and colleagues (2007) talk about resilience in the workplace, they are referring to "everyday skills and psychological strengths that can be identified, measured, maintained, and nurtured in individuals of all ages and psychological conditions" (p. 111), and they use the term as a catch-all category for social and

psychological assets that help people bounce back from adversity, as well as pursue high levels of achievement. They include such things as sense of humor (see chapter five), self-regulation (chapter eleven), relationships (chapter thirteen), and personal morality (chapter ten). Luthans and colleagues encourage workplace leaders to do whatever is within their power to identify and foster these psychological capital factors, making their businesses both more productive and more pleasant places at which to work.

Sounds great. But what about those who do not work at pleasant places? Given current economic realities, it will not do to blithely tell people to just go find a better job. Shawn Achor is the co-founder of the Institute of Applied Positive Research and co-designer of Harvard's famous Happiness Course. In his book *The Happiness Advantage*, Achor (2010) offers advice from positive psychology for individuals who wish to flourish in spite of environmental impediments at work. Achor claims that "even in the midst of their heavy workloads and the tyranny of impossible expectations," the people with whom he has worked are "able to use the Happiness Advantage to reduce stress and achieve more in their academic and professional lives" (p. 22).

Achor (2010) focuses on seven key principles from positive psychology that he claims can be employed to flourish in trying circumstances. He begins by drawing from Fredrickson's (2000) broaden-and-build theory, as well as much of the research we covered in chapter four about the desirable effects of positive emotions. He recommends a variety of possible ways to increase one's reserves of positive emotion, including meditation, planned enjoyable activities, acts of kindness, exercise, and finding ways to make use of one's signature strengths (see chapter ten). Achor's second principle is the power of mindset, and in that chapter he pulls together a variety of cognitive theories, including Carol Dweck's work on entity versus incremental beliefs about the self (e.g., Dweck & Leggett, 1988), which we addressed in chapters seven, nine, and twelve, and the power of meaning (which we will deal with in some depth in chapter twenty-three) to transform a job into a calling. Third, Achor focuses on perception and the idea that we can train our brains to see what we practice looking for. He talks about Robert Emmons' gratitude research (e.g., Emmons & McCullough, 2003), which we covered in chapter fourteen, and Seligman's (1990) optimism research. Achor's fourth principle involves how we deal with failure. Here he again invokes Seligman and pessimistic versus optimistic attributions. He also brings in post-traumatic growth (Tedeschi & Calhoun, 2004) and rational emotive behavior therapy (Ellis, 1962). The fifth principle is about pursuing goals and involves culti-vating an internal locus of control (see chapter twelve). The sixth principle in-volves shaping our environments so that bad habits become more difficult (just to give a random example that is totally not about me in any way: someone who has a bad habit of wasting time arguing with people on the internet might delete all accounts on websites where these argu-ments happen since the added time to activate an account is enough of a pause to let this person, who is totally not me, cool

off enough to refrain from responding to every nitwit with a bad opinion) and our good habits easier. Finally, Achor discusses the power of social support to help us cope with the stresses of life.

There is a lot people can do to put positive psychology to work at their workplaces, turning a daily burden into a venue for positive adult development and flourishing (Nakamura, 2011).

How to Be a Good Boss

Leaders matter. The individual character-istics of leaders have been shown to in-fluence group effectiveness (e.g., Borgatta, Bales, & Couch, 1954; Hoffman et al., 2011), and bad leadership leads to a host of negative outcomes (Emler & Cook, 2001). Bad bosses, for example, are reported to be the largest contributor to stress in the workplace (Hertzberg, 1968; Moyle, 1998).

If bad bosses make a workplace toxic, what about good bosses? A large number of theories have been put forward to try to separate good leadership from bad; here we will focus on four major approaches with strong ties to the positive psychology movement. We will begin by looking at virtues. With the recent resurgence of virtue ethics and the influence of positive psychological volumes such as the *CSV* (Peterson & Seligman, 2004), the idea that good leadership requires certain moral strengths is becoming popular again. Research involving a virtue-based theory of leadership, though, is still young, and the available evidence base is limited at this time. Riggio and colleagues (2010) de-veloped the Leadership Virtues Question-naire, a nineteen-item self-report scale based on the four cardinal virtues of wisdom, courage, temperance, and justice (Pieper, 1965). Higher scores on all four virtues have been associated with higher scores on measures of ethical leadership, lower narcissism scores, and higher scores on indicators of effective leadership such as motivation, influence, intellectual stimulation, and empowerment of followers (Riggio et al., 2010). Models of leadership based on the cardinal virtues have also been put forward by Brown (2011) and Schiller (2013). Hackett and Wang (2012) add two "Confucian" virtues (humanity and truthfulness) to the cardinal virtues. In this model, virtuous leadership was found to be associated with charismatic leadership, ethical leadership, greater happiness and life satisfaction for both leaders and followers, and improved performance for both leaders and followers (Wang & Hackett, 2016). Other researchers have looked at specific virtues and character strengths without an overarching virtue theory to unify their thoughts on virtuous leadership. Ashford and Tsui (1991) found managerial effectiveness to involve self-regulation, and McClelland and Boyatzis (1982) found strong self-control to be a vital part of the "leadership motive pattern" that characterizes successful managers. Rosete and Carriochi (2005) found emotional intelligence to be associated with better performance among senior executives. Sosik, Gentry, and Chun (2012) found that integrity, bravery, and social intelligence were positively correlated with executive performance.

Another theory of leadership in which the character of the leader is vitally important is that of servant leadership (Spears, 2010). Beginning with the work of Robert Greenleaf (1970), servant leadership has developed as a kenotic, other-centered approach in which the leader prioritizes the good of his or her followers even above the good of the organization (van Dierendonck & Patterson, 2010). Less bullies and more persuaders (van Dierendonck, 2011), servant leaders see their role as one in which they encourage the flourishing of their followers by using minimally coercive methods to maximize their autonomy and cultivate their ability to think for themselves. Spears (2010) lists ten key characteristics of servant leaders: listening (good leaders value communication and follower input), empathy, healing (striving for the wholeness of followers), awareness, persuasion, conceptualization (big-picture thinking), foresight (long-term thinking), stewardship, commitment to the growth of people, and building community.

Researchers developing measures of servant leadership have generally ended up with dimensional scales that resemble Spears's (2010) list of characteristics but do not necessarily follow that list precisely. Barbuto and Wheeler (2006) began with an eleven-dimensional structure to their measure (Spears's ten plus a "calling" to serve) that reduced (via factor analysis) to five dimensions (wisdom, persuasion, stewardship, calling, and healing). Scores on this measure predicted greater transformational leadership (discussed below), employee satisfaction, effectiveness, and employee willingness to put in extra effort. Liden and colleagues (2008) ended up with seven factors (healing, creating value for the community, conceptual skills, empowering, helping subordinates, putting subordinates first, and ethical behavior).

Scores predicted transformational leadership, better relationships between followers and leaders, and better follower commitment and performance. Dirk van Dierendonck (van Dierendonck & Patterson, 2010) provides reviews of the empirical research involving servant leadership, showing it to produce improvements in the psychological climate of organizations, better leader-follower relationships, and superior organizational outcomes.

Stone, Russell, and Patterson (2003) argue that the core difference between servant leadership and transformational leadership is that, instead of a focus on the well-being of followers, transformational leaders focus on the good of the organization, igniting follower motivation to also pursue organizational goals. Bass and Riggio (2006) describe transformational leaders as "those who stimulate and inspire followers to both achieve extraordinary outcomes and, in the process, develop their own leadership capacity. Transformational leaders help followers grow and develop into leaders by responding to individual followers' needs by empowering them and by aligning the objectives and goals of the individual followers, the leader, the group, and the larger organization" (p. 3). This is contrasted with transactional leaders, who operate on a straightforward pay-for-work exchange.

Transformational leadership has been consistently associated with improved performance (Bass, 1999), whether the organization is athletic (Charbonneau, Barling, & Kelloway, 2001), military (Hardy et al., 2010), academic, (Koh, Steers, & Terborg, 1995), or a business (Barling, Weber, & Kelloway, 1996). Transformational

leadership includes four core components (Bass & Riggio, 2006): idealized influence (serving as a role model for followers), inspirational motivation (charismatic displays of enthusiasm and team spirit), intellectual stimulation (encouraging new ideas and creative problem-solving), and individualized consideration (being attentive to followers' needs and growth). Sivanathan and colleagues (2004) say that surprisingly little research has been done specifically looking at the effects of transformational leadership on follower flourishing, but they point to studies indicating that each component of transformational leadership can contribute to psychological well-being, and they identify psychological processes that facilitate this effect. More recently, a number of researchers have found links between transformational leadership and positive psychological capital (Gooty et al., 2009), as well as employee well-being (Arnold et al., 2007; Nielsen & Daniels, 2012).

Authentic leadership theory also involves strong connections between the leader's character and organizational outcomes. According to Avolio and Gardner (2005), authentic leaders are "deeply aware of how they think and behave," they are "perceived by others as being aware of their own and others' values/moral perspectives, knowledge, and strengths," they are "aware of the context in which they operate," and they are "confident, hopeful, optimistic, resilient, and of high moral character" (p. 321). Authentic leaders inspire followers because they value followers' contributions to organizational goals, work to have no gaps between their values and their behavior, are transparent toward followers, and "lead from the front, going in advance of others when there is a risk of doing so. They model confidence, hope, optimism, and resiliency, which inspire others to action" (Luthans & Avolio, 2003, p. 248). Researchers have found authentic leadership to predict a wide range of positive workplace outcomes, including improved psychological capital, employee satisfaction and performance, leader well-being, and organizational performance, as well as reduced follower burnout (see Gardner et al., 2011, for a review).

Positive Work Environments

While research and theories involving positive organizational behavior focus on positive variables at the level of the individual (employee or leader), the related field of positive organizational scholarship involves a focus on organizational context (Ko & Donaldson, 2011). We have frequently discussed virtues at the level of an individual. Can an organization be virtuous? Cameron, Bright, and Caza (2004) think so. They define organizational virtuousness in terms of "features of the organization that engender virtuousness on the part of members" (p. 768) and empower the flourishing of the group's members. Back in chapter four, we briefly touched on the idea that the good life for humans can take place only in social contexts that facilitate the good life (Stoner & James, 2015). Cameron (2011) examines businesses from this perspective, looking at practices (official and unofficial) that encourage such things as integrity, forgiveness, and gratitude. Virtuous businesses have been shown to perform better due to the effects of these practices in amplifying positive behavior and buffering against unfortunate occurrences (Cameron, Bright, & Caza, 2004).

In the previous chapter we spent some time with self-determination theory. Self-determination theorists (e.g., Ryan & Deci, 2000) consider the link between environments and flourishing in terms of the degree to which these environments satisfy the basic psychological needs of competence (seeing oneself as effective and having opportunities to expand capacities), autonomy (more freedom, less coercion), and relatedness (functioning social connections to other humans). Earlier, we looked at the application of SDT in the classroom. Now we turn to SDT in the workplace. A workplace in which basic needs are thwarted is a workplace in which we expect to find low productivity and miserable employees, while a need-satisfying workplace should foster both superior objective performance and employee well-being (Deci & Ryan, 2014). Slemp and colleagues (2018) conducted a meta-analysis in which they found that autonomy support in the workplace was associated with greater autonomous motivation and well-being among employees, as well as better employee performance and work engagement. A workplace is supportive of employee autonomy when there are opportunities for choice and input, initiative is encouraged, and the use of external rewards and punishments to shape behavior is minimized. Van den Broeck and colleagues (2016) conducted a meta-analysis of 119 studies looking at need-supportive versus need-thwarting workplace environments, and they found all three needs to show connections with workplace outcomes such as job satisfaction, work engagement, strain and burnout levels, and job performance. Autonomy-supportive environments were characterized by factors such as a less-crushing workload, less ambiguity and conflict between job roles, and greater opportunity for employee input into how the job is done. Competence-supportive environments included factors such as task feedback and social support so that one feels effective and has opportunities for growth. One of the variables that contributed to relatedness support in the workplace was less drama in "office politics." Relatedness involves feeling like others care about you and feeling like an integral part of an organization (Ryan & Deci, 2017), and workplaces where these connections are fostered (instead of an "everyone for himself" environment) are more likely to be places were employees are happy, motivated, and productive (e.g., Fernet, Austin, Trépanier, & Dussault, 2013; Van den Broeck, Vansteenkiste, De Witte, & Lens, 2008). Self-determination theorists have developed training programs aimed at showing managers the importance of need satisfaction at work and equipping them with the tools to craft those kinds of workplaces (e.g., Deci, Connell, & Ryan, 1989; Hardré & Reeve, 2009).

Most of the positive psychological theories and concepts we have seen in previous chapters have found applications in organizational psychology (Froman, 2010). Flow researchers (e.g., Csikszentmihalyi & LeFevre, 1989; Salanova, Bakker, & Llorens, 2006) have established that employees experience better psychological outcomes at work and are more productive when the workplace offers them opportu-

nities (e.g., optimal balance of skill and challenge) for flow experiences (Csikszentmihalyi, 2004). Luthans, Vogelgesang, and Lester (2006) focus on several ways businesses can foster resilience, including building trust between workers and leaders, providing social support, investing in developing employees' capabilities, providing opportunities to experience self-efficacy, increasing positive emotional experiences in the workplace, finding optimistic attributions, and helping workers discover meaning in their jobs. Adams and colleagues (2010) discuss ways businesses can be filled with the power of hope. Hope, "the belief that one can find pathways to desired goals and become motivated to use those pathways" (Snyder, Rand, & Sigmon, 2005, p. 257), can be cultivated by setting "stretch goals" for the organization, giving workers greater control over their tasks, establishing clear pathways to goals, and fostering the feeling that these goals are achievable.

Finally, there is the question of the physical workplace environment itself. Environmental psychology involves the study of the relationship between human thought-feeling-behavior and both the physical and social aspects of the surrounding environment (Bonnes, Lee, & Bonaiuto, 2003; Canter & Craik, 1981). Within that field, much of the work has focused on pro-environmental behavior (see Gifford, 2014), but some psychologists are interested in the impact the environment has on the humans who dwell within it. For example, Evans (2003) presents evidence that living in crowded, poor-quality housing units is bad for one's mental health, while Kaplan (1995) puts forward the theory that exposure to nature has restorative effects, undoing and preventing stress by replenishing cognitive resources. Davydenko and Peetz (2017) found that being indoors versus outdoors affects our perception of time.

Architectural structures are built around a certain set of assumptions about the nature of the humans who will be inside them and the kind of life they lead (de Botton, 2006). When those assumptions do not fit well with actual human nature and human flourishing, the outcomes are not good. Steven Pinker (2002) points to the totalitarian belief that human life is infinitely malleable (the "blank slate" view) and can therefore be shaped according to the utopian plans of the managing class. He argues that this attitude, when applied to architecture, resulted "in the glass-and-steel towers of multinational corporations and in the dreary high-rises of American housing projects, postwar British council flats, and Soviet apartment blocks" (p. 410), as well as in inhuman planned cities like Brasília and Chandigarh, where nobody wants to live other than technocratic middle managers.

Work environments are no exception, and many readers no doubt have had the unpleasant experience of entering a poorly designed office building that makes you feel like leaving as soon as possible. McCoy (2002) summarizes a wealth of research on the psychological effects of office designs on productivity, motivation, and employee well-being. Important details include layout (balancing the needs for individual space for uninterrupted solo work and shared space for collaborative teamwork), windows (always a plus), temperature and lighting (workers do better when they can

set these to their own preferences in their workspaces), good air quality, and the allowance for individual personalization of workspaces. Much of the emphasis on personal control over environment can be understood as a physical manifestation of the importance of autonomy that we saw in self-determination theory.

Some designers have been influenced by the "biophilic" school of thought in architecture, attempting to design workspaces that try to undo the separation between nature and everyday life in which so many of us spend our workdays. *Biophilia* comes from a 1984 book by sociobiologist E. O. Wilson in which he posits that humans have an innate connection to living things. Biophilic architects assert that the spaces in which we live and work should reflect this connection (Söderlund & Newman, 2015) and point to the work of psychologists who have shown that human well-being is enhanced by contact with nature (see Gillis & Gatersleben, 2015; Gullone, 2000; and Joye, 2007, for reviews). Biophilic designs include adding indoor plants, using wood wherever possible, incorporating water (ponds and fountains), and using structural designs that evoke natural shapes (one example might be interior columns that branch toward the top). Roelofsen (2002) points out that, since "personnel costs are substantially higher than the housing costs, investing in the quality of the working environment is the most effective way of combatting loss of performance" (p. 248). The field of architectural psychology is tiny at this time, and there is much work left to be done to understand how humans and our physical surroundings interact, but there is also great potential for positive psychologists to examine the ways in which physical space contributes to human flourishing.

SUGGESTIONS FOR FURTHER READING

Achor, S. (2010). *The happiness advantage: The seven principles of positive psychology that fuel success and performance at work.* Crown Business.

Cameron, K., Dutton, J., & Quinn, R. E. (Eds.). (2003). *Positive organizational scholarship: Foundations of a new discipline.* Berrett-Koehler Publishers.

Cameron, K. S., & Spreitzer, G. M. (Eds.). (2012). *Oxford handbook of positive organiza-tional scholarship.* Oxford University Press.

Froman, L. (2010). Positive psychology in the workplace. *Journal of Adult Development, 17*(2), 59-69.

Gagné, M. (Ed.). (2014). *Oxford handbook of work engagement, motivation, and self-deter-mination theory.* Oxford University Press.

Luthans, F., & Yousef, C. M. (2009). Positive workplaces. In S. J. Lopez & C. R. Snyder (Eds.), *Oxford handbook of positive psychology* (2nd ed.) (pp. 579-88). Oxford University Press.

van Dierendonck, D., & Patterson, K. (Eds.). (2010). *Servant leadership: Developments in theory and research.* Palgrave Macmillan.

Chapter Twenty

THE HAPPY WARRIOR

Who is the happy Warrior? Who is he
That every man in arms should wish to be?

WILLIAM WORDSWORTH

The true soldier fights not because he hates what is in front
of him, but because he loves what is behind him.

G. K. CHESTERTON

"A man was going down from Jerusalem to Jericho, when he was attacked by robbers. They stripped him of his clothes, beat him and went away, leaving him half dead" (Luke 10:30). This is the setup to one of Jesus' parables, typically referred to as the Good Samaritan, and Jesus is talking about what it means to love our neighbors. Christian ethicist Paul Ramsey (1950) suggests a thought experiment: How would Jesus' story be different if the Samaritan had come upon the scene while the violent robbery was still in progress? Would Jesus consider it "loving your neighbor" if the Samaritan had grabbed a stick and driven the robbers away from their victim, inflicting upon them a sound thrashing?

Can a follower of Jesus employ violence? In the third century, Tertullian declared that a Roman soldier who became a Christian had to resign immediately. He asked, "Shall it be held lawful to make an occupation of the sword, when the Lord proclaims that he who uses the sword shall perish by the sword?" (Holmes, 2005, p. 45). Augustine, on the other hand, said that in some circumstances wars are waged for the sake of justice and peace and that soldiers are peacemakers when they fight off barbarians so the rest of us can live in safety. Christians remain divided on the topic of warfare (Schlabach, 2004), with some (e.g., Hauerwas, 1983) arguing that violence never has a place in a Christian life, and others (e.g., O'Donovan, 2003) arguing that armed conflict is a theater in which believers can display justice, wisdom, and love. It is with an awareness, then, of the wide range of positions on this issue among sincere Christians that we enter into this chapter on the application of positive psychology to warfighting.

CALL TO ACTION

"I want to create an army that is just as psychologically fit as it is physically fit" (Seligman, 2011b, p. 127). These words were spoken in November of 2008 by General

George Casey, chief of staff of the US Army. Martin Seligman was at the Pentagon meeting with Army personnel who were concerned about the mental health of America's soldiers and looking for a new approach to addressing the problem. The result of that meeting was the Comprehensive Soldier Fitness (CSF) Program, the largest organization-wide application of positive psychology in the movement's history. At the time of this writing, the CSF Program is still underway, representing an investment of over $125 million and impacting the lives of over a million US soldiers.

In this chapter we will take a look at the idea of putting positive psychology to work in a military setting. We will focus on the CSF Program, compare and contrast the program with other approaches to psychological resilience training in military settings, and dive into the controversies that have surrounded the program since its beginning.

WHY TEACH SOLDIERS RESILIENCE?

In chapter one we saw a bit about the role the military played in psychology's shift toward the negative. In the aftermath of World War II, the existing psychiatric community was overwhelmed by the number of armed forces personnel who were returning from the front with combat-related psychological trauma. Although clinical psychologists rose to the challenge, there remains to this day a powerful need for trained clinicians to work with veterans. Suicide among US soldiers is higher than it has ever been, and posttraumatic stress disorder remains an ongoing problem (Casey et al., 2011). Hoge et al. (2004) found that 17% of returning Iraq War

veterans screened positive for PTSD, generalized anxiety, or depression. Comparable rates of psychological problems associated with deployment have been found among Canadian Forces personnel (Boulos & Zamorski, 2013; Zamorski et al., 2016) and United Nations peacekeepers (Broenéus, 2014; Weisaeth, Mehlum, & Mortensen, 1996).

While the majority of early and current work in military mental health involves helping armed forces personnel by providing psychological services after disorders occur, recently the focus has broadened to include the identification of resilience factors that can help reduce the chance of developing psychological problems in the first place (Meredith et al., 2011). Bryan and colleagues (2020), for example, found that happiness and meaning in life serve a protective function against the development of PTSD symptoms among National Guard personnel.

Britt, Sinclair, and McFadden (2013) define military resilience as "the demonstration of positive adaptation after exposure to significant adversity" (p. 4); it can generally be thought of as the ability to "bounce back" after experiencing a stressful event. Over the past few decades, a number of militaries have developed programs designed to foster resilience in their personnel (Fikretoglu & McCreary, 2012), including the Canadian Forces' Road to Mental Readiness program and the Australian Defense Forces BattleSMART program. We will discuss these programs below, comparing and contrasting their approaches. But first we begin with the US Army's Comprehensive Soldier Fitness program (renamed the Comprehensive Soldier and Family Fitness program, or CSF2, in 2012).

COMPONENTS OF THE CSF2

Cornum, Matthews, and Seligman (2011) claim that the military can "provide a natural home for positive psychology" (p. 5). Armed forces personnel tend to be physically fit and medically robust, are taught to value positive traits such as loyalty and integrity, and operate in an organization that promotes wellness and excellence. Based in large part on the Penn Resiliency Program (see our discussion of that in chapter eighteen), the CSF2 is intended to "to increase the resilience and performance of all soldiers and their families" (p. 6) and has four primary components. First, soldiers are administered the Global Assessment Tool (GAT), which is considered the heart of the program. Participants are assessed at enlistment and again annually across their careers, allowing for tracking of progress. Next, all soldiers are taught methods for cultivating resilience in themselves as well as fostering it in others. Active duty units are required to complete two hours of resilience training per quarter (Brazil, 2013). Third, soldiers access online training modules tailored to foster improvement in areas that need it as identified by the GAT. And finally, through a ten-day training program with four components (intro to resilience, mental toughness, character strengths, and strengthening relationships), soldiers can be certified as resilience teachers who then serve in their units, helping others develop resilience skills. The US Army's resilience training program is based out of Ft. Jackson, South Carolina.

THE GLOBAL ASSESSMENT TOOL

The GAT is a web-based program hosted on the secure ArmyFit platform that combines physical fitness and medical data with a 105-item self-report measure (Department of the Army, 2014). Guided by the five dimensions of health identified by the World Health Organization (Lester, McBride, & Cornum, 2013), the program is organized around five "dimensions of strength": (1) Physical: "Performing and excelling in physical activities that require aerobic fitness, endurance, strength, healthy body composition and flexibility derived through exercise, nutrition and training describes the physical dimension" (p. 7). This dimension is assessed using indicators such as the soldier's score on the Army Physical Fitness Test, blood pressure, and so on. (2) Emotional: This dimension is defined in terms of "approaching life's challenges in a positive, optimistic way by demonstrating self-control, stamina, and good character with your choices and actions" (p. 8). Soldiers are assessed based on their experiences of positive versus negative emotions, optimism, mental flexibility, engagement, and healthy coping (Peterson, Park, & Castro, 2011). They are also given an assessment of character strengths based on the six virtues found in the *CSV* (see chapter ten). (3) Social: Social fitness involves "developing and maintaining trusted, valued relationships and friendships that are personally fulfilling and foster good communication, including a comfortable exchange of ideas, views, and experiences" (Department of the Army, 2014, p. 8). Items that measure this dimension involve interpersonal trust, friendship, and morale (Peterson, Park, & Castro, 2011). (4) Spiritual: "Identifying one's purpose, core values, beliefs, identity, and life vision define the spiritual dimension" (Department of the Army, 2014, p. 8). As we will see in chapter twenty-one, the development of a robust and mature spiritual walk is associated with improved well-being at pretty much every level of human functioning, and the spiritual dimension is globally acknowledged as a core component of the human person. However, the US Army is not permitted to endorse religion. Further, the Army is a diverse population, and this program is intended for all soldiers. This means that it would not work to base the "spiritual fitness" component on an approach specific to one particular religion. It has to involve an approach to spirituality that is broad enough to encompass at least the great majority of faith traditions as well as forms of spirituality that would themselves reject the term *faith tradition* (see Hill et al., 2000, for a more in-depth discussion of these kinds of definitional difficulties). Guided by these two considerations, "spiritual fitness" is defined in terms of the capacity to "(a) identify one's core self and what provides life a sense of purpose and direction; (b) access resources that facilitate the realization of the core self and strivings, especially in times of struggle; and (c) experience a sense of connectedness with diverse people and the world" (Pargament & Sweeny, 2011, p. 59). (5) Family: "Family fitness refers to how one is faring in personal and familial relationships" (Peterson, Park, & Castro, 2011, p. 14). Soldiers are asked questions involving topics such as their home life, emotional support from family, and close friendships.

GAT scores are confidential. Different version of the tool exist for trainees, soldiers, civilian employees, and military families. After the GAT has been completed, soldiers are given access to online training modules designed to introduce key resilience concepts and skills (Lester, McBride, & Cornum, 2013).

MASTER RESILIENCE TRAINERS

The Master Resilience Trainer (MRT) course is based on a train-the-trainer model and is intended to teach Army noncommissioned officers (NCOs) resilience concepts and skills that they can then teach to others (Reivich, Seligman, & McBride, 2011). It is a ten-day program, with the first five days devoted to teaching resilience fundamentals and the next three focusing on how to teach these skills to others. Day nine focuses on military-specific applications, and day ten involves performance-enhancement material taken from sport psychology (Lester, McBride, & Cornum, 2013). The material covers a very wide range of positive psychology topics, from how to put the brakes on counterproductive thinking (see our material on optimism in chapter seven) to how to identify character strengths (see chapter ten) to how to build positive emotions (chapter four).

Potential MRTs are nominated by their commanding officers at the company or battalion level and are typically NCOs at the E-6 (staff sergeant) to E-8 (master sergeant/first sergeant) levels (Department of the Army, 2014). After passing their postcourse exam, graduates receive training materials and then work out a resilience training program with their unit leaders, dedicating at least two hours per quarter to teaching these skills to soldiers (Lester, McBride, & Cornum, 2013).

Outcome Research

Initial feedback to the program has been positive, with MRT graduates saying things like, "This training has been the most effective and professional training the Army has sent my way," and "This will be an invaluable asset to my soldiers, family members, and me" (Reivich, Seligman, & McBride, 2011, p. 33). However, actual data is better than appreciative quotes, and some initial empirical testing of the program has begun to be reported.

The first wave of data analysis was presented in a trio of Army documents. Lester, Harms, Bulling, Herian, and Spain (2011) looked at soldiers' GAT scores as indicators of psychological fitness and asked if they could predict mental health outcomes from GAT data. They found that those with higher resilience scores were less likely to commit suicide, had fewer drug problems, and committed fewer violent crimes, and they also experienced greater career success in the Army. Lester, Harms, Herian, Krasikova, and Beal (2011) reported the results of a fifteen-month longitudinal study comparing soldiers who took the MRT course against a control group who did not, finding that MRT training was associated with an improvement in GAT scores. It was noted by the authors of these studies that these were preliminary findings and that follow-up research was planned.

A fourth technical report (Harms et al., 2013) found that soldiers who served in units with MRTs were less likely to be diagnosed with anxiety, depression, PTSD, alcoholism, or drug abuse. The effect sizes were small, but the authors argue that this is par for the course for population-wide prevention programs. Griffith and West

(2013) give us the only research report (at the time of this writing) to be published in the scholarly literature. They looked at the application of MRT training to the Army National Guard and found the training to be associated with improved connection with others, optimism, mental agility, self-awareness, self-regulation, and character strengths. The increase in resilience was also shown to buffer against anxiety.

Although these early findings appear positive, they are still preliminary. Critics of the program (e.g., Denning, Meisnere, & Warner, 2014; Eidelson & Soldz, 2012) point to shortcomings in the studies' methodologies as well as the small size of the effects. Hopefully, given the large number of soldiers and family members affected by the CSF2 and the volume of resources dedicated to the program, in the future we will see the development of a rigorous body of research literature testing the effectiveness of this approach to resilience training.

Other Military Resilience Programs

While the CSF2 is the clearest example of positive psychology being put to use in the military, other resilience programs exist, and it is instructive to compare and contrast these approaches. Rather than positive psychology per se, most of these programs draw from work in health and stress research and also from sport psychology.

While the US Navy appears to be laying a foundation (at the time of this writing) for a resilience program modeled after the CSF2, programs already exist for the Navy and the Marine Corps (which falls within the Department of the Navy) that are based on stress-prevention literature. The Naval

Center for Combat and Operational Stress Control was launched in 2008 with the mission of providing resilience training and building psychological health among sailors and marines (Department of the Navy, 2015). Resilience is fostered through training that is intense and tough but not overwhelming, as well as the development of unit cohesion, inspirational leadership, willpower, and stress control techniques (Department of the Navy, 2010). A recent empirical evaluation of the program (Vaughan et al., 2015) indicates that the program has been generally well-received but is not necessarily achieving its goals. The authors of the study suggest a number of possible revisions that might enhance its effectiveness.

Until recently, the Canadian Forces used the US Army's Battlemind program as a part of its postdeployment transition program (Zamorski, Guest, Bailey, & Garber, 2012). This program sees psychological problems as the result of difficulties adapting to differences between what worked in deployment and what works at home. The new CF program, called Road to Mental Readiness (R2MR), has four major components. CF personnel are trained in healthy goal-setting (goals should be challenging but attainable), mental rehearsal (using visualization to imagine and prepare for possible outcomes), self-talk (identifying and overcoming unhealthy cognitive patterns), and arousal reduction (breathing techniques to reduce central nervous system excitation). Heavy emphasis is placed on social support from friends and leaders (National Defense, 2015). The program is delivered in a single 160-minute session during basic training

but is also intended to be integrated into all areas of training (Fikretoglu, Beatty, & Liu, 2014). At the time of this writing, the R2MR program is being adapted for use with police officers and emergency service workers in Canada.

The Australian Defense Forces' (ADF) BattleSMART program (SMART stands for Self-Management And Resilience Training) is a set of modules delivered at key points during a soldier's career (Moss, 2012). The program is strongly cognitive-behavioral in orientation, focusing on attribution and healthy thought patterns (Cohn, Hodson, & Crane, 2010) and also includes breathing and muscle relaxation techniques for arousal reduction (Moss, 2012). Preliminary testing of the program (e.g., Moss, 2013) shows that it is effective in teaching knowledge about mental health issues and methods of resilience to ADF personnel, but we are still awaiting empirical testing of the program's effectiveness at reducing psychological problems.

CSF2 CONTROVERSIES

In addition to criticisms of the CSF2 program that focus on the methodological side of the research, there are also criticisms based on conceptual and ethical grounds. When the January 2011 issue of *American Psychologist* was published, introducing us to the newly launched program, backlash was immediate, initially taking the form of letters of protest published in the October 2011 issue of the same journal. A theme that can be seen in more than one letter was, to use Lester, McBride, and Cornum's (2013) words: "War is bad, CSF helps soldiers fight war, so CSF must be bad, too" (p. 212). Phipps (2011) claimed that positive psychology in support of war was an oxymoron and that positive psychologists would be better off investing their time and effort speaking to public policy and diplomacy, reducing aggression, and increasing peaceful solutions to international conflicts, a position also put forward by Eidelson, Pilisuk, and Soldz (2011)—perhaps a position that also resonates with many pacifist Christians. Seligman (2011b) objects to this line of argument, describing it as psychologists withholding their knowledge and skills because of objection to US foreign policy. The situation, says Seligman, is not either-or. Psychologists can and do advocate for peace. We can also do what we can to provide the best prevention and treatment for American soldiers. Lester, McBride, and Corcum (2013) further argue that, as we clearly have not eradicated war from the human experience, it would be foolish not to prepare for war as best we can, equipping soldiers with the tools that can both reduce the likelihood of psychological trauma and also foster their flourishing in noncombat situations.

A second moral issue that has been brought up involves research ethics. Informed consent is one of the foundational ethical principles of psychological research (American Psychological Association, 2017; Canadian Institutes of Health Research et al., 2018). One aspect of the principle of informed consent is that research participants must have the right to decline to participate and the right to withdraw from a study at any time without penalty. Where does the CSF2 fall in relation to this principle? Novotny (2009) quotes Seligman as describing the program as "the largest study—1.1 million soldiers—psychology has

ever been involved in" (p. 40). Eidelson, Pilisuk, and Soldz (2011) argue that, if it is a study, then it should be subject to the same ethical restrictions as any other study. Making participation in a scientific study mandatory is a big ethical problem. Although he had previously described it as a study, Seligman (2011b) later denied that CSF2 data collection was in fact research. Rather, he said, it is an evaluation of training effectiveness. Lester, McBride, and Cornum (2013) compare it to the Army collecting and analyzing marksmanship or physical fitness scores. This kind of training outcome analysis does not fall in the same category as research, and as such it is not appropriate to hold it to the same ethical standards as research. To put it another way, professors do not need to consult with their universities' ethical review boards when creating final exams or looking at course evaluations.

Another source of difficulty for some is the "spiritual fitness" component of the CSF2 program. As we saw a bit earlier, the Army has to walk a fine line when it comes to this issue. Higher levels of religiosity and spirituality have consistently been associated with improved mental health outcomes and greater flourishing (e.g., Levin & Chatters, 1998; Myers, 2000), and spiritual well-being is one of the five foundations of health endorsed by the World Health Organization, which was a source of guidance in the creation of the program (Lester, McBride, & Cornum, 2013), so spiritual fitness may legitimately be seen as a vital component of military resilience (Pargament & Sweeney, 2011; Yeung & Martin, 2013). However, the Army is not allowed to violate religious freedom by requiring soldiers to engage in religious practices. According to some, by including spiritual fitness in the CSF2, the Army has done exactly that. Leopold (2011) argues that the spiritual fitness component of the GAT is a mere exercise in verbal "gymnastics," taking concepts that are grounded in religion and simply swapping out the word *spirituality* for *religion*. The program has been called "blatantly unconstitutional" by the founder of the Military Religious Freedom Foundation (Hagerty, 2011), with one senior member of that organization (Rodda, 2011) referring to it as overt evangelization of US soldiers. Anticipating this possible objection, program developers consulted Army chaplains and lawyers to ensure the legality of the program's spiritual fitness component (Peterson, Park, & Castro, 2011). Lester, McBride, and Cornum (2013) claim that the spiritual fitness component is about finding meaning and purpose, with religion presented as one of many possible pathways toward this goal. According to Pargament and Sweeney (2011), "The spiritual fitness component of the CSF program is not based on a particular stance or position on the ontological truth or validity of philosophical, non-religious, or religious frameworks of belief and practice" (p. 58), but instead focuses on spirituality as the search for what is sacred or essential in one's own life.

While this may satisfy the lawyers, the nonspecificity of the spiritual fitness component of the CSF2 may also be its weakness. When spirituality is defined so broadly that it encompasses anything the individual sees as meaningful, is it spirituality anymore? When Hill et al. (2000) examine the range of possible meanings of the word *spirituality*, they use examples

that include vegetarianism, gardening, and music, with some calling these their sources of spirituality. But, they argue, merely finding pleasure or meaning in something does not make it spiritual. What is missing from "spiritual fitness" is a concept of the sacred, the pursuit of which Hill and colleagues find to be the core concept in spirituality. Without a "transcendent" or "ultimate" toward which to strive, what if anything is actually being assessed and taught in the name of spiritual fitness? Christians in particular may find the spiritual fitness component of the CSF2 to be terribly anemic.

Finally, there is my (Hackney, 2014) criticism of the program (which naturally makes it the best criticism). The CSF2 is described as an example of "the relevance of contemporary psychological science to social issues at the macro level" (Cornum, Matthews, & Seligman, 2011, p. 8). However, the specific training modules developed to foster soldiers' flourishing are all about the transformation of individuals through assessment and training rather than any transformation of military policies, organizational structure, procedures, or cultural norms. This makes it a splendid example of Becker and Mareceks (2008) claim that positive psychologists "conceive of flourishing as something determined by individual choice and attained by private, self-focused effort" (p. 1777) rather than efforts toward social change. We will revisit this criticism in our final chapter. The CSF2 may be seen as one more example of the influence of Western individualism on positive psychology. When we look at the definition of spirituality given in the spiritual fitness component of the program, we see this individualism again, as spirituality is defined as the search for whatever the individual considers sacred (Bellah et al., 1985; Taylor, 2007), a move that will be familiar to us by now.

CSF2-style resilience programs appear to be spreading in the US military, replacing earlier resilience programs, just as the CSF2 replaced the Army's earlier Battlemind program. In 2014, the Air Force established a Comprehensive Airman Fitness program, including its own Master Resilience Trainers based on the four domains of mental, physical, social, and spiritual fitness (Department of the Air Force, 2014). The Navy has established a 21st Century Sailor Office, which includes a Total Sailor Fitness program (Department of the Navy, 2013). This expansion of programs follows a directive issued by the chairman of the Joint Chiefs of Staff (2011) titled "Total Force Fitness" (TFF). TFF is a framework for enhancing well-being along eight dimensions: physical, environmental, medical and dental, nutritional, ideological and spiritual, psychological, behavioral, and social (Defense Health Agency, 2020). The CSF2 is one of the core inspirations for TFF. These are quite recent innovations in military resilience training and a source of excitement for those of us who look forward to seeing empirical validation of the application of positive psychology to military contexts.

SUGGESTIONS FOR FURTHER READING

The January 2011 edition of *American Psychologist* (volume 66, issue 1).

Meredith, L. S., Sherbourne, C. D., Gaillot, S., Hansell, L., Ritschard, H. V., Parker, A. M., & Wrenn, G. (2011). *Promoting psychological resilience in the U.S. military*. The RAND Corporation.

Sinclair, R. R., & Britt, T. W. (Eds.). (2013). *Building psychological resilience in military personnel: Theory and practice*. American Psychological Association.

Chapter Twenty-One

GOOD RELIGION

I have come that they may have life, and have it to the full.

JOHN 10:10

The glory of God is man fully alive.

IRENAEUS

Religions around the world and across history have connected their doctrines and practices to flourishing and personal formation (Stalnaker, 2006; Yearley, 1990), and as we saw in chapter three, Christianity presents us with an especially compelling vision of the good life. In this chapter we will introduce the psychology of religion and connect this field to the positive psychology movement. We will cover a selection of core topics that connect religion to human flourishing and human flourishing to religion. We will cover a bit of research on the connection between religion and psychological well-being, then turn it around and look at some ideas given to us by psychologists of religion on what it means to be a highly functioning believer. Finally, we will look at some attempts to put positive psychology into practice in the life of the church.

WHAT IS "RELIGION," ANYWAY?

In order to study something, we have to measure it. In order to measure it, we need to know what it is. When I teach Psychology of Religion, the first project I give my students is deceptively simple: Define *religion*. One thing that makes it difficult is the variety of religions that exist. The definition produced needs to be wide enough to encompass the world's religions but narrow enough to exclude nonreligious activities such as belonging to a bowling league or attending Star Trek conventions (it is usually around this time that a student snickers and points out that, for some people, Star Trek is a religion, which only serves to further prove the point I am trying to make). The result of the project tends to be a jumbled mix of ideas that sometimes overlap and sometimes clash and sometimes seem to be going in opposite directions, which is what makes it a good project, since that is the state of affairs in the scholarly literature as well.

Some have claimed to have identified the core of religion as a social-psychological phenomenon, and their approaches have had an ongoing influence on the way psychologists define their terms and construct their measures. We will focus here on three of the major streams of thought on this topic. Emile Durkheim (1915) considered the core of religion to be the formation of a "moral community" centered around a common system of beliefs and practices related to "sacred things," while Immanuel Kant (1793/1960) said true religion was the end product of rational inquiry into universal principles of practical morality, and Friedrich Schleiermacher (1799/1958) claimed that rational principles were just the byproduct of the profound emotional experience of encountering the supernatural.

Those who hold to a more Durkheimian view of religion will see religion as a social organization and say that being a religious person is about membership and participation in that social organization. Such researchers are less likely to use established measures of religiosity, preferring to rely on either single items or a small set of items in which participants are asked if they belong to a denomination or how often they go to church or engage in public practices. This approach certainly captures a certain side of religion but leaves many scholars dissatisfied. Can the psychological impact of religion on a person's life really be captured by counting the number of times that person's backside has warmed a pew?

Researchers who are guided by a Kant-inspired view of religion tend to emphasize the "cognitive" side of the phenomenon, defining religion as a set of beliefs, an ideology, or an interpretive worldview. They are more likely to use measures of religiosity such as Degelman and Lynn's (1995) Belief in Divine Intervention Scale,

which emphasize the degree to which participants endorse the propositional truth claims in a religion. This approach seems to go for a more "internal" definition than the sociological definitions but is also unsatisfactory by itself, especially for those believers who remember the Lord's complaint in Isaiah 29:13 about those who honor God with their lips and follow human rules but whose hearts are far from him. And even demons can have accurate beliefs (James 2:19).

Opting for the "heart" approach might lead one to sympathy with Schleiermacher, preferring definitions of religiousness that emphasize personal devotion and other emotionally intensive approaches to religion. This would lead researchers toward measures of religiosity such as the Santa Clara Strength of Religious Faith Questionnaire (Plante & Boccaccini, 1997). On the other hand, there are many who find this approach also to be unsatisfactory by itself, as emotion-based measures might not distinguish between those who are truly "on fire for the Lord" and those who are happy to talk all about their feelings but haven't the faintest clue about the teachings of their faith and don't bother getting off their rumps and actually doing stuff. Some attempt to resolve this by combining multiple definitions and making multidimensional scales. Readers are directed to Hill and Hood's outstanding volume (1999) for a much more comprehensive presentation of available measurement options.[1] As we will see later, these questions of definition and measurement will have an impact on research into the role religion

---

[1] Peter Hill and Ralph Hood, if you are reading this, I love this book intensely, but it's been twenty years, and we need an updated edition!

can play in improving positive psycho-logical functioning.

And now for another thorny definitional question: What about the term *spirituality*? Many researchers differentiate between the two, creating the option to choose between "spiritual and religious," "spiritual but not religious," "religious but not spiritual," and "neither spiritual nor religious." In the *CSV*, Peterson and Seligman (2004) combine the two at first: "Spirituality and religiousness refer to beliefs and practices that are grounded in the conviction that there is a transcendent (nonphysical) dimension of life" (p. 600), but then they separate them, saying that "religiousness is believed to describe an individual's degree of accep-tance of the prescribed beliefs associated with the worship of a divine figure, and that individual's participation in public and private acts of worship. Spirituality, in contrast, is believed to describe both the private, intimate relationship between humans and the divine, and the range of virtues that result from that relationship" (p. 602). Note their use of the words "in contrast," indicating a separation between the concepts.

Pargament and Mahoney (2004) caution against this bifurcation, noting that both religion and spirituality are expressed socially and individually. Zinnbauer et al. (1997) found that most participants identify as both religious and spiritual, providing empirical support to the argument that religion and spirituality strongly overlap. Hill et al. (2000) attempt to show the overlap by claiming that religion has spirituality at its core, with spirituality defined as "the feelings, thoughts, experi-ences, and behaviors that arise from a

search for the sacred" (p. 66). Religion is grounded in that same search, but also includes the nonsacred goals that can be found in a religious context (such as identity and a sense of meaning) and "the means and methods (e.g., rituals or pre-scribed behaviors) of the search that receive validation and support from within an identifiable group of people" (p. 66). This approach preserves the idea that spirituality and religion are deeply inter-mixed while leaving open the possibility that someone might be spiritual but not religious (i.e., searching for the sacred outside of the context of a religious group) or religious but not spiritual (i.e., "doing religion" for reasons that are not about the search for the sacred, as we will see when we talk about intrinsic and extrinsic religious orientations).

RELIGION AND MENTAL HEALTH

Is it good for your mental health to be a religious person? Bad for it? No rela-tionship? This topic has been on the minds of psychologists who study religion since the beginning of the field. Literally. The official "first scholarly publication" in the psychology of religion was William James's (1902) *Varieties of Religious Experience*. In this book, James claims that the religious experience consists of overcoming the "wrongness" inherent to the human condition by establishing a proper con-nection to spiritual reality, resulting in a "new zest which adds itself like a gift to life" and an "assurance of safety and a temper of peace, and, in relation to others, a prepon-derance of loving affections" (p. 401). The "healthy-minded" (optimistic people) are able to gratefully enjoy the universe, and the "sick-souled" (pessimists) gain the strength to face and (to some extent) conquer the darkness.

Not everyone has been so positive about the psychological effects of religion. In his *Future of an Illusion* (1927/1989), Sigmund Freud describes religion as "the universal obsessional neurosis of humanity" (p. 55), which is based on the outworking of childhood parent issues and attempts by "our wretched, ignorant and downtrodden ancestors" (p. 42) to deal with the frightening and unpredictable nature of the world by projecting onto it a father figure who can protect and provide. Since he described religion as the result of infantile neuroses, Freud believed that religion was inherently toxic to proper psychological functioning and psychological growth was accompanied by the person walking away from religion. Freud's harsh attitude toward religion has influenced some of those who have followed his approach to psychology, which has resulted in a legacy of mistrust between believers and psychoanalysts (Burnham, 1985; Meissner, 1984). Post-Freudian psychoanalysts (particularly the ego psychologists and object-relations theorists) have been more nuanced and multidimensional in their approaches, resulting in less mutual antagonism between religion and psychoanalysis than used to be the case (Wallwork & Wallwork, 1990).

In chapter one we met Gordon Allport, one of the founding figures in personality psychology, and I described him as a forerunner of positive psychology. Allport is also a foundational scholar within the psychology of religion, with his book *The Individual and His Religion* (Allport, 1950). Allport was keenly interested in the role religion plays in peoples' lives, and he approached the topic both as a social scientist and as a believer (e.g., Allport, 1978). In *The Individual and His Religion*, Allport lays out his theory of religious maturity, which we will examine in more detail later. Though willing to admit the possibility of toxic forms of religion, Allport claimed that increases in religious maturity would be accompanied by increases in positive psychosocial functioning.

Another figure whom we have met before is Viktor Frankl. Placing himself (as did James and Allport) in opposition to the reductionism that still permeates much of psychology to this day, Frankl describes humans as self-transcending beings: "Three factors characterize human existence as such: man's spirituality, his freedom, his responsibility" (Frankl, 1969, p. xvi), asserting that a psychology that denies these factors denies the humanness of humans. With a strong emphasis on finding meaning by serving something beyond the self, Frankl's works contain multiple references to religion as a possible venue for the construction of a meaningful life and possessing enough positive psychological power to overcome such horrors as those found in the death camps of Nazi Germany (Frankl, 1984). Unlike Freud, Frankl (1967b) describes religion and psychotherapy as mutually reinforcing, as both involve learning to deal with issues such as suffering, human finitude, and mortality as well as the search for ultimate meaning: "Although religion may not aim at mental health it might result in it. Psychotherapy, in turn, often results in an analogous byproduct; while the doctor is not, and must not be, concerned with helping the patient to regain his belief in God, time and again this is just what occurs, unintended and unexpected as it is" (p. 33).

In general, higher religiosity scores tend to be associated with better mental health and well-being (e.g., Koenig, Al-Zaben, & VanderWeele, 2020; Sharma & Sing, 2019). However, between the conceptual difficulties surrounding definitions of religion and spirituality and the differing theoretical perspectives on the possible relationship between religiosity and mental health, the scholarly literature on the topic can get confusing (Koenig, 2018). In an attempt to obtain a little clarity and taking these difficulties into account, Glenn Sanders and I published a meta-analysis of the empirical research on the relationship between religiosity and mental health (Hackney & Sanders, 2003). We focused on the question of definitions not only of religion, but also of mental health (which is a whole other kettle of fish, one that I will not take space in this chapter addressing). We found that there was a relationship between the definitions employed by researchers and the outcomes of studies those researchers performed. Overall, with nothing else taken into account, there was a modest positive correlation between higher religiosity scores and better mental health. When we broke results down by definition of religion, we found the strongest correlations when researchers employed one of the "devotion"-oriented approaches, with "ideological" religion producing weaker correlations and "social" religion producing the weakest. See my chapter (Hackney, 2010d) on religion and mental health for a more detailed discussion of meta-analysis as a research tool in the psychology of religion. The psychology of religion is deeply complicated with few easy answers, so proceed with caution. And what we are covering in this chapter is not even the tip of the iceberg—more like the top of the tip.

RELIGION AND COPING

One of the major contributions made by psychologists of religion is their advancement of our understanding of the ways religion gives people the mental strength to deal with the difficulties of life (see our discussion of hardiness in chapter twelve). In this section we will look at the role of religion in the coping process, emphasizing the work of Kenneth Pargament.

Pargament (1997) has been studying religious coping for decades. His work is grounded in a cognitive approach to religion and also to coping. He defines religion as a part of a person's orienting system, "a general way of viewing and dealing with the world" (p. 99) that is primarily about one's "search for significance in ways related to the sacred" (p. 32). Pargament's approach to coping is guided by Lazarus and Folkman's (1984) appraisal theory, in which the process of sizing up a potentially stressful situation can be broken down into primary appraisal (what is happening?) and secondary appraisal (what can I do about it?). Religion can play a role at both steps in the process, and as in the upcoming material on religious maturity, the central question is not so much whether or not one is religious, but in what way (Pargament & Brant, 1998).

Religion has powerful resources believers can bring to bear in understanding what is happening during difficult times. We have already discussed the work of

Viktor Frankl (1984) and his observation that religion as a source of meaning can make the difference between one who has the mental resources to endure Nazi death camps and one who does not. Researchers have found that the ability to frame trying circumstances in terms of God's sovereignty makes tragedy comprehensible, which helps to make it endurable. Echterling (1993) interviewed people who were victims of a flood and found that the ability to find meaning in the disaster predicted positive coping and that "they became theologians by asking how God could have allowed such tragedies to occur to them and their loved ones" (p. 5). Jenkins and Pargament (1988) found that cancer patients who held to greater levels of belief that God was in control even in the midst of their suffering demonstrated better adjustment. Kuhn and Brulé (2019) found that religious resources, which give participants the ability to make sense of uncontrollable circumstances, provided a powerful buffer against the psychological consequences of negative life events.

However, not all religious appraisals are associated with the best outcomes. Pargament et al. (1998) did find that seeing your life as connected to the larger spiritual world and framing tragic events as intended by God for some good purpose (e.g., teaching some lesson) were associated with healthier outcomes. However, interpreting the stressful event as a demonic attack or as evidence that God has abandoned you, that he is powerless to stop tragedies, or that he is punishing you is associated with worse outcomes. Does this mean the psychologically healthy thing to do is assume that God never punishes anyone or that we should ignore spiritual warfare? Certainly not. But it is not the best idea to always jump to that conclusion. Back in chapter eight I told the story of my car breaking down in the middle of a snowstorm. That was a stressful situation, and as a Christian, I try to interpret events as a Christian. I believe that demons exist, but does that mean there was a demon in my transmission? I believe that sometimes God uses tragic events to correct sinful behaviors and attitudes, but does that mean my car broke down because I committed some sin and that if I had not sinned, my car would not have broken down? If I maintain moral purity, is God obligated to bless me with an eternal car? Jesus himself asked this question about the people who died when the tower of Siloam fell (Luke 13:4). He asked the people if, because a tower hadn't fallen on them, they were more righteous than the ones who happened to be in the tower when it collapsed. That's not the way it works. My car broke down because it was old and worn out. But that does not mean God was not present or that he was not in control of the situation. Maybe he allowed that situation to teach me about relying on others for help (which they did). Maybe there was another reason.

We now turn to the role of religion in secondary appraisal, which involves asking oneself what resources exist for dealing with a stressful situation. Pargament and colleagues (1988) looked at three possible approaches a believer can take in dealing with a problem. When someone engages in "self-directive" coping, that person intellectually acknowledges that God exists and technically is in charge of the universe, but that person then goes ahead and deals with the problem alone. A "deferring" style involves putting the situation entirely in God's hands and passively waiting for God to sort it out. In general, these two styles are not associated with the best psychological outcomes (though there are some exceptions). A "collaborative" approach, which involves God and the believer working together to deal with the problem, tends to get the best results (Wilt et al., 2019).

Religious resources abound for dealing with stressful situations. Prayer is associated with a range of beneficial health outcomes and is a common coping response (McCullough, 1995; Neighbors et al., 1983). One's congregation can be a source of emotional and practical support (Gibbs & Achterberg-Lawlis, 1978; Lasker, Lohmann, & Toedter, 1989), as can one's relationship with God (Cooper et al., 2009).

FLOURISHING FAITH

Too often, when psychologists look at the relationship between religiousness/spirituality and other variables (mental health, physical health, moral behavior, and so on), they take a "quantity" approach to religion, as if the only way to look at religion is to determine how much of it someone has. What is missing from this is a recognition that there is a right way and a wrong way to be religious, making the vital question not "how much" but "in what way" the person is religious. Jesus and the prophets were quite vocal in their condemnation of those who spoke religious words, attended religious gatherings, followed religious regulations for behavior, and even believed the correct religious teachings (none of which are bad things) but lacked anything

resembling genuine sanctification. In this section we will look at some ways psychologists of religion have attempted to describe and measure spiritual growth and maturation, looking at religious flourishing instead of the role religion plays in psychological flourishing.

Faith development. One prominent approach to spiritual growth is James Fowler's (1981) theory of faith development. If you have taken a developmental psychology course, you likely have been exposed to Lawrence Kohlberg's theory of moral development (e.g., Kohlberg, 1981), a neo-Piagetian theory in which people are described as progressing through stages from the most primitive stage of moral reasoning (avoid punishment) to the highest stage (abstract principles of universal justice). As Fowler began his work at Harvard Divinity School, he led discussions about spiritual growth, with readings from social scientists incorporated into the meetings, and students began asking him if he knew the new Harvard psychology professor Lawrence Kohlberg (Fowler, 2004). Through Kohlberg, Fowler began to apply principles of cognitive development to spiritual growth, eventually producing a theory of faith development that bears a striking resemblance to Kohlberg's theory of moral development.

Fowler (1974) shows his cognitive orientation by describing faith as "a way of knowing and construing" (p. 211). As is the case in Kohlberg's theory, Fowler describes advances in how we think about our faith, with an emphasis on how we form our personal identity, make decisions, and interpret the events in our lives (Fowler & Dell, 2006). Fowler's theory involves a series of stages, progressing from the most simple to the most complex forms of religious thought (Fowler, Streib, & Keller, 2004). Among young people, progression through the stages of faith is tied to general cognitive development. In toddlerhood and early childhood, children are ego-centric (unable to think beyond their own perspective) but draw their religious ideas from authority figures such as parents (Fowler, 1974) and have a preference for religious stories and symbols in which good and evil are presented unambiguously (Fowler & Dell, 2006). This parallels the overall pattern of their cognitive development, as described by Piagetian researchers, in that children tend to fail at tasks that demand thinking about things from another's perceptual point of view. In middle childhood, their thought processes are concrete and literal, and we see this played out in the way they think about religious topics. Children at this stage often think of God as the "first cause" of creation and as a ruler over a cosmic moral order in which good is rewarded and evil is punished. They tend not to handle complexity and contradiction well. As children enter adolescence, they begin to gain the ability to think about more abstract concepts and display a greater sophistication in their thought processes. At this stage of their faith development, young people's thinking is influenced by the social groups in which they move, and conflicts tend to be resolved by appealing either to consensus or to authority (Fowler, 1974). Religious symbols are seen as having multiple levels of meaning, but one's religious worldview is not critically evaluated at this stage (Fowler & Dell, 2006).

At this point we enter adulthood, and Fowler's (1981) theory becomes untethered from age. As is the case in Kohlberg's theory of moral development, it is entirely possible for someone to go through their entire adult life and remain at a simplistic level of thinking. Growth here is more a matter of choice and experience rather than innate maturational forces. Fowler attempts to be value-neutral at this point (I hear echoes of Seligman from one of our earlier chapters), claiming that evaluation of a person's faith does not imply any judgment about the sincerity or validity of that faith: "To identify a person's stage or stage transition does not imply that his or her spiritual life is better, more faithful, or desirable than anyone else's, whether in that stage or another. Faith development theory is not intended to be used, nor should it ever be used, as a measure of 'how good a Christian,' 'how good a Jew,' 'how good a Muslim,' or 'how good' anyone of any faith tradition may be. Making such judgments constitutes a major abuse of this theory" (Fowler & Dell, 2006, p. 40). However (and also reminiscent of criticisms of Seligman), such protestations appear (to me anyway) to mask an implicit telos and quite a few value judgments, as Fowler (1981) equates the pursuit of religious truth with the pursuit of the highest stage of development and specifically claims that his theory can contribute to religious life by "clarifying what might be meant by *good faith*" (p. 293). Elsewhere, Fowler claims that his work on faith development provides "evidence of what is optimally desirable for humanity" (Fowler, Streib, & Keller, 2004, p. 12), and on more than one occasion he makes the claim that progress from one stage to another is reflected in the transformation of cultures to more advanced levels of consciousness, even going so far as to employ his theory as a description of the work of the Holy Spirit in society (Fowler, 2001, 2004). So I will go ahead and ignore his claims that higher levels of faith development are not supposed to reflect greater degrees of spiritual maturity.

The most immature form of adult faith is "individualistic-reflective faith," in which adolescent literalness and rigidity are replaced by the beginnings of a process of critically examining one's prior assumptions and movement toward an internal, rather than external, focus on moral decision-making (Fowler & Dell, 2006). We see a movement away from "As a member of this group, what do I believe?" toward "As an individual, what do I believe?" When I was a young person being raised in a Baptist household, I took it for granted that the Baptist perspective on doctrinal issues was the one true approach and that non-Baptist denominations could be understood in terms of the nature and degree of their error. I believed that because I was an immature teenager. As I grew and increased my engagement with people from other denominational backgrounds, I began to understand that there is a difference between core issues (such as Christ as fully God and fully man) and peripheral issues (such as my Quaker friends holding to pacifism while Baptists tend toward the just-war tradition). The transition from adolescent faith (what Fowler called "synthetic-conventional") toward individualistic-reflective faith tends to occur as the individual realizes that compartmentalizing does not work as a way to deal with inconsistencies

(for example, what I believe as a Christian and what I believe as a member of a specific political party), and there is a growing awareness of the complexity and difficulty of forging a coherent worldview. This is a time when the beliefs and traditions held as a child are questioned and sometimes abandoned, but if the faith of one's childhood is retained, it is retained in a stronger and more sophisticated form.

While the individualistic-reflective stage of faith is more mature than the adolescent synthetic-conventional faith, it remains to a degree self-centered, as it is about me doing the homework to put together my ideas about what I believe for myself. The next stage, "conjunctive faith," involves moving beyond "either-or" thinking toward "both-and" thinking. Fowler (1981) compares it to physicists describing light as both a particle and a wave, or "looking at a field of flowers simultaneously through a microscope and a wide-angle lens" (p. 184). There is a greater openness to paradox and balance when dealing with the tensions that characterize life. There is a willingness to reach out to people of differing backgrounds (even non-Baptists!) and give them an honest hearing while still remaining solid in one's identity and adherence to one's home tradition. It is possible to tolerate and love others while still disagreeing with them. After all, as we see in this stage, the questions we must grapple with are not easy questions, and sincere people of faith can arrive at different answers.

The final and most mature stage (which also makes it the least populated) is "universalizing faith." One is so fully drawn out of one's egocentrism that one can be equally concerned with people of differing communities and backgrounds, even going so far as to embody Jesus' command to love our enemies (Fowler & Dell, 2006) to the point that we lay down our individual life for others. At this stage the inconsistencies in one's worldview have been resolved and there is a distinct lack of hypocrisy. Those who occupy this level of development are the "superstars" of faith, the exceptional people who end up being revered as great teachers and spiritual leaders. Daniel (2017) applies Fowler's theory to a series of case studies involving coping with loss, and Freund and Gill (2018) recommend that clinicians use Fowler's theory to help their clients grow as they struggle with faith-related issues.

The mature religious sentiment. As we saw earlier, Gordon Allport (1950) attempted to understand the paradox of religion's influence on people's lives. In some instances religion seems to make everything better; in others it seems to feed humanity's darkest impulses. How can it be both? Shouldn't religion be either a good thing or a bad thing? As both a scientist and a believer, Allport was distressed and perplexed by this seeming contradiction. His solution, derived from his studies of religiously active people, was to distinguish between the immature and mature "religious sentiment." As in Fowler's theory, Allport does not connect age and maturity: "A person of twenty, thirty, or even seventy, years of age does not necessarily have an adult personality. . . . In probably no region of personality do we find so many residues of childhood as in the religious attitudes of adults" (p. 59). Another similarity between Allport and Fowler is Allport's emphasis on complexity and sophistication of thought

as essential components of maturity. Allport described the religiously immature as characterized by a simplistic anthropomorphism (for example, thinking that God literally is a gray-bearded king who lives up in the sky) and lack of intellectual depth. When in 1961 cosmonaut Yuri Gagarin became the first human in space, it was reported (incorrectly) that he said, "I see no God up here." Even if it had been an actual quote, only an immature believer would find this in any way threatening. Okay, so he went into space and saw a bunch of stars. We already knew that. We've had telescopes for a while now.

The other component of Allport's description of religious immaturity is egocentric motivation. The immature believer is likely to think that the point of religion is to make oneself happy and comfortable and to look "spiritual" in the eyes of others and that the point of prayer is to get what one wants (I imagine Allport would have a few stern words for the peddlers of today's "prosperity gospel" malarkey). This egocentrism combines with the cognitive shallowness of the immature to produce self-justifying rationalizations ("God endorses the ideas put forward by my political party"), complacency ("Studying the Bible is too much work; I want to be told what to think and learn a few 'gotcha' quotes to score points against outsiders"), and fanaticism (Allport writes, "The religion of maturity makes the affirmation 'God is,' but only the religion of immaturity will insist, 'God is precisely what I say He is'" [Allport, 1950, p. 78]).

The religiously mature, on the other hand, are willing to put forth the effort to struggle through the process of developing intellectual depth. They also have better-organized motivations, with benefit to self located far down on the hierarchy. Rather than a means to one's own egocentric ends, "mature religion is less of a servant and more of a master" (p. 72), subordinating "what's in it for me" to "what is true" and "what is right." This produces a faith that is reflective and self-critical, morally consistent, and neither fanatic nor compulsive, without losing intensity of devotion. In another parallel to Fowler, Allport describes the mature believer as living within a set of seeming contradictions, possessing a faith that is cohesive but well-differentiated, confident but humble, stable but progressing, and perceiving shortcomings of traditions while recognizing their virtues. This maturity is fashioned in what Allport (1950) calls "the workshop of doubt" (p. 83). Maturity comes from dealing squarely with the struggles, difficulties, and doubts that accompany belief and emerging stronger on the other side.

In an attempt to empirically test this theory, Allport and Ross (1967) developed the Religious Orientation Scale, applying Allport's idea to the relationship between religion and racism. If Allport (1950) is correct that criticism of religion's bad influences is properly directed toward its immature forms, then we should see religious immaturity associated with greater prejudice and maturity associated with less prejudice. Allport and Ross (1960) focused on the motivational side, with "intrinsic orientation" representing the individual placing God at the top of the motivational hierarchy and forcing selfish motives into alignment with religious teachings. "Extrinsic orientation"

represented the individual pursuing religious activities for selfish reasons. So, if the question is, "Why do you go to church on Sundays?" the extrinsically oriented person might say something like, "The happy singing makes me feel good," while the intrinsically oriented person might say, "To worship and learn about God." Allport and Ross found that those who endorsed primarily intrinsic statements in the scale had the lowest prejudice scores, while those who primarily endorsed extrinsic statements had higher prejudice scores. The general pattern in the research literature has been for intrinsic orientation to be associated with better outcomes on a wide range of variables, while extrinsic orientation is associated with worse. Examples include altruism (Bernt, 1989), judgmentalism (Beck & Miller, 2000), gratitude (Watkins et al., 2003), and fear of death (Kahoe & Dunn, 1975).

However, things get more complicated in the religious orientation literature. When we looking more closely at the relationship between religious orientation and prejudice, higher extrinsic scores do tend to be associated with worse prejudice, but intrinsic scores tend to show no correlation at all, either positive or negative (Donahue, 1985), which makes it entirely possible to have a strong intrinsic orientation and still hold racist attitudes. Conceptually, there are those who wonder if intrinsic orientation properly captures Allport's ideas about religious maturity. C. Daniel Batson (1976) argues that, although Allport's original ideas involved the mature religious person as humble, self-critical, and thoughtful, "I" statements (such as, "My religious beliefs are what really lie behind my whole approach to life") can also be endorsed by one who is rigidly and unthinkingly orthodox. In order to capture the missing side of Allport's theory, Batson proposed a third orientation, which he called "quest." Those who score high on quest orientation (in honor of the movie *Galaxy Quest*, I will refer to these people as "questarians") view their faith "as an endless process of probing and questioning generated by the tensions, contradictions, and tragedies in their own lives and in society" (p. 32) and would likely agree with statements such as, "As I grow and change, I expect my religion also to grow and change." If you want a good idea of what a questarian's approach to the Christian life looks like, read the seventeenth-century classic *Pilgrim's Progress*. This book is an allegory in which the main character (named Christian, because it's an allegory) journeys to the cross and from there to the Celestial City, encountering equally allegorical characters (such as Mr. Worldly Wiseman, who tempts Christian to avoid the cross and tries to earn salvation through legalism) and allegorical dangers (such as the giant Despair). The point of me bringing this up is that *Pilgrim's Progress* is not the story of Christian effortlessly sliding through every temptation and easily answering every challenge. Half the time Christian seems not to know what he is doing. Sometimes he has to be rescued. He forgets things. He falls into traps. But he keeps going, drawing closer to the Celestial City. This is what a quest looks like. A questarian acknowledges creaturely finitude and personal ignorance but remains strong and confident in trusting God and tries to continually grow and

learn as he or she goes along. High quest scores have been shown to be associated with a number of desirable psychological outcomes (e.g., Batson & Raynor-Prince, 1983; Messay, Dixon, & Rye, 2012; Van Tongeren et al., 2016).

But there are also difficulties with quest scores as an adequate operationalization of Allport's theory of religious maturity. Conceptually there are some problems, as questarians tend to be comfortable with religious doubt, and Allport originally described the mature as having fought their way through doubt and conquered it, not having learned to happily coexist with it. Also, Donahue (1985) raises the question of how well quest describes the great religious figures and traditions. Quest may capture the humility in Allport's theory, but that humility was balanced with confidence. Exemplars of spiritual power are often humble, but they are also bold and unapologetic. No mature Christian would say, "I believe in God the Father almighty, creator of heaven and Earth, maybe, sorta, whatever floats your boat, I guess." Kojetin et al. (1987) found the score on Batson's quest measure to be associated with religious conflict and anxiety. Richard Beck has responded to problems such as these by exploring quest as a multidimensional construct, with some aspects of quest being correlated with positive outcomes and others with negative outcomes (Beck et al., 2001; Beck & Jessup, 2004). And the search for the perfect measure of religious maturity continues.

Positive psychology in the church. So far we have been examining the role religion can play in psychological and social flourishing. But the positive psychology of religion also includes attempts to put positive psychology to work in helping believers become more spiritually mature and to flourish within the church. Christopher Kaczor (2015) suggests that positive psychology provides empirical support for the formative power of traditional Christian practices such as prayer and forgiveness, and he recommends that Christians use the work of positive psychologists to get helpful, practical advice for cultivating Christian virtues, overcoming temptations, and serving our neighbors. Mark McMinn (2017) takes a similar approach, looking for ways "to make the tenets of Christian thought practical" (p. 9) when it comes to the nuts and bolts of how exactly to go about cultivating a Christlike character and lifestyle. He has also been involved in testing the effectiveness of church-based positive psychology programs involving the experience of grace (Bufford et al., 2017).

Living Your Strengths (Winseman, Clifton, & Liesveld, 2003) is based on the Gallup Organization's Clifton Strengths-Finder assessment tool. This tool is advertised to churches as a way to help believers select ministries in which they would do well, identify possible avenues for spiritual growth, and discover God's calling for their lives. Readers are given a code to enter at the StrengthsFinder website, and their top five strengths are identified and described. Based on that list, they are given tips for ministries to seek out (when I took the instrument, they suggested that I organize my church's library), careers to consider (I was encouraged to find a job with a religious organization; good thing I'm already a professor at a Christian college), ideas

that might foster spiritual growth (a trip to Israel was recommended for me), and team-building strategies (apparently, I need to partner with someone who can translate my ideas into concrete action). The authors of the book describe their approach as grounded in positive psychology research, and connections between positive psychology and the Gallup Organization are described. Winseman and colleagues describe a "strengths-based congregation" as one in which individuals' talents are identified and they are then helped to find a ministry that is well-suited to them.

So far, so good, but some of the implications and suggestions presented by the authors should be approached with caution. If you are experiencing church-related troubles such as discomfort with particular ministry activities, failure of your ministries, lack of joy and satisfaction, and boredom when studying the Bible, the authors explain those difficulties as the result of you either not properly applying your strengths or making the bigger mistake of attempting to correct your weaknesses (see our discussion in chapter ten on correcting weaknesses). The biggest element missing from their approach to church growth and spiritual formation is . . . God. According to Winseman and colleagues (2003), the reason the early church grew and succeeded was the fact that first-century Christians were enthusiastic and authentic and they maximized their talents. There is no discussion of the Holy Spirit as an active part of the process. Now, there is nothing wrong with identifying strengths (after all, I wrote an entire chapter on what a good idea this is). But over-focusing on one's own strengths to the exclusion of everything else, including the Lord, creates a problem for Christian positive psychologists.

This problem takes us back to one of my claims (Hackney, 2007, 2010b) about Christians and the positive psychology movement. We have to pay attention to what sets us apart from our secular colleagues as well as what we have in common. It is not enough to simply "baptize" positive psychology by saying, "Us too, but with Bible words added," and call it good. We have to pay attention to what is being assumed about the nature of the good life and the ways and means of moving toward that telos. For Christians, that means not ignoring our claim that flourishing is equally a work of the Holy Spirit and a work of responsible human participation.

SUGGESTIONS FOR FURTHER READING

Allport, G. W. (1950). *The individual and his religion*. Macmillan.

Fowler, J. W. (1981). *Stages of faith*. Harper-Collins.

Hackney, C. H. (2010). Religion and mental health: What do you mean when you say "religion?" What do you mean when you say "mental health?" In P. Verhagen, H. van Praag, J. Lopez-Ibor, J. Cox, & D. Moussaoui (Eds.), *Religion and psychiatry: Beyond boundaries* (pp. 343-60). John Wiley & Sons.

Hackney, C. H., & Sanders, G. S. (2003). Religiosity and mental health: A meta-analysis of recent studies. *Journal for the Scientific Study of Religion, 42*(1), 43-55.

Koenig, H. G. (2018). *Religion and mental health: Research and clinical applications*. Academic Press.

Miller-Perrin, C., & Mancuso, E. K. (Eds.). (2015). *Faith from a positive psychology perspective*. Springer.

Pargament, K. I. (1997). *The psychology of religion and coping*. Guilford Press.

Pargament, K. I., & Mahoney, A. (2004). Spirituality: Discovering and conserving the sacred. In C. R. Snyder & S. Lopez (Eds.), *Handbook of positive psychology* (pp. 646-62). Oxford University Press.

Part Seven

THE POSITIVE
IN THE NEGATIVE
AND
THE NEGATIVE
IN THE POSITIVE

Chapter Twenty-Two

GUILT IS GOOD

Lord Jesus Christ, Son of God, have mercy on me, a sinner.

ANCIENT CHRISTIAN PRAYER

With this chapter we start a pleasant journey into the darker side of positive psychology, guided by the idea that wholeness and maturity do not come from cutting negative experiences out of our lives and focusing exclusively on enhancing cheerfulness (Ivtzan et al., 2016; Kashdan & Biswas-Diener, 2014). If positive psychology is to be more than "happyology," we must look at those areas of psychological functioning that are unpleasant but still contribute to human flourishing and psychological health. Back in chapter seven, for example, we briefly discussed pessimism and the idea that there is a bad way to be optimistic and a good way to be pessimistic. Self-control in the face of temptation (chapter eleven) might not always be fun, but it is a powerful tool for flourishing. In this chapter we will talk about an actively unpleasant experience: guilt. There is such a thing as unhealthy guilt, but there is also a good and healthy place for guilt in the life of a flourishing person, and as positive psychologists, we have the task of discovering what that place is and encouraging its cultivation in our own lives and that of others.

DEFINING GUILT

In chapter four we briefly covered some theoretical concepts involving the purpose of emotions such as anger and fear (Izard, 1977). To begin with, guilt is one of the moral emotions, "those emotions that are linked to the interests or welfare either of society as a whole or at least of persons other than the judge or agent" (Haidt, 2003, p. 853). They influence our evaluations of behaviors (ours or someone else's) as moral or immoral and "provide the motivational force—the power and energy—to do good and to avoid doing bad" (Tangney, Stuewig, & Mashek, 2007a, p. 347). As we saw in chapter fourteen, gratitude is a moral emotion involving a recognition that one has benefited from the actions of another. Although anger is often produced as a reaction to a threat or to frustrated pursuit of goals (Izard, 1977), it is also a moral emotion, as we respond with anger when perceiving violations of justice and human rights (Haidt, 2003; Rozin et al., 1999). We might consider anger to be a "negative" moral emotion, as it involves responding to violations of moral standards, and gratitude to be a "positive" moral emotion, as it involves responding to excellent adherence to moral standards (if there is a second edition of this book, perhaps I should include a "healthy anger" chapter). This would make guilt one of the negative moral emotions as well, as it involves a recognition that one has behaved in a way that violated a moral obligation (Greenspan, 1995), produced an adverse effect on others (Tangney, 1991), or both.

Anger is often seen as an "other-condemning" moral emotion, as the primary focus is on a moral violation perpetrated by someone else (Haidt, 2003). Guilt, on the other hand, is a self-conscious emotion (Tracy, Robins, & Tangney, 2007). "As the self reflects upon the self, these emotions provide immediate punishment (or reinforcement) of behavior" (Tangney, Stuewig, & Mashek, 2007a, p. 347), helping keep the self on the right track. Other self-conscious emotions include pride (when described as an emotional reaction to triumph rather than as a vice) and embarrassment. Putting these components together, we can arrive at a definition of guilt as a negatively valenced self-conscious moral emotion involving the perception that one has violated a moral standard. "In the face of transgression or error, the self turns toward the self—evaluating and rendering judgment" (Tangney & Dearing, 2002, p. 2). This self-evaluation produces within the person an "unpleasant emotional state associated with possible objections to his or her actions, inactions, circumstances, or intentions . . . based on the possibility that one may be in the wrong" (Baumeister, Stillwell, & Heatherton, 1994, p. 245).

The way scholars describe us as seeing ourselves as "in the wrong" varies depending on their underlying theories of morality. A great deal of moral psychology is grounded in consequentialist thinking, with "good" defined in terms of behaviors that benefit others and "evil" defined in terms of behaviors that harm others (e.g., Miller, 2004). Following along these lines, Hoffman (1982) describes guilt as "the bad feeling one has about oneself because one is aware of actually doing harm to someone" (p. 297). An alternate approach, which we might connect to the deontological stream of moral thought, is about morality as a set of rules (e.g., Piaget, 1932). Those who assume that morality is about rules define guilt primarily in terms of perceived violations of moral obligations and standards of behavior (Eisenberg, 1982; Greenspan, 1995; Rushton, 1982; Tangney, Stuewig, & Mashek, 2007b).

Haidt and Kesebir (2010) present a social functionalist approach to morality, describing morality as a set of psychological mechanisms that bind societies together and promote individual functioning within those societies. This approach to morality can be seen in Baumeister and colleagues' (1994) review of research on guilt as an interpersonal phenomenon and Haidt's (2003) claim that "guilt is not just triggered by the appraisal that one has caused harm; it is triggered most powerfully if one's harmful action also creates a threat to one's communion with or relatedness to the victim" (p. 861).

If we are guided by a relational theory of the *imago Dei* (Grenz, 2001) and a vision of the human telos that encompasses our existing in loving relationships with God, creation, and each other (Balswick, King, & Reimer, 2016; Wright, 2010), then we should find ourselves in at least partial agreement with those moral psychologists who approach morality from a social functionalist approach and see immorality in terms of the disruption of proper relational functioning, though not ignoring other facets of sin such as lawbreaking (e.g., Blocher, 1997) and the harmful undoing of creation (e.g., Plantinga, 1995). So do not be surprised if all three approaches get woven together as we address the scholarly literature on the nature and functioning of guilt. As sin is multifaceted, so is guilt.

GUILT AND SHAME

Often one can find the words *guilt* and *shame* used interchangeably, and the two are similar in that they are negatively valenced self-conscious moral emotions involving the perception that one has failed or transgressed (Tangney & Dearing, 2002). There are some crucial differences, though, that are important for us to keep in mind. Helen Block Lewis (1971), in her psychoanalytic treatment of the topic, focuses on the specific target of the negative self-directed evaluations in shame and guilt: "The experience of shame is directly about the self, which is the focus of evaluation. In guilt, the self is not the central object of negative evaluation, but rather the thing done or undone is the focus" (p. 30).

There are a few connections we can make here with our earlier coverage of attributions as well as optimism and pessimism (see chapter seven). Recall that I might respond to a disappointment (such as a bad grade on an exam) in ways that implicate my entire self ("I'm a stupid loser") or are restricted to something more specific and possibly controllable ("I didn't study"). Similarly, I might respond to a

moral transgression such as lying with a negative self-evaluation that implicates the whole self ("I'm a dirty slimeball liar") or is restricted to the specific behavior ("I told a lie"). Interestingly, Tangney, Wagner, and Gramzow (1992) found that participants who were more prone to shame also tended to be more prone to "depressogenic" pessimistic attributions, and Tracy and Robins (2006) found that those who tended to make internal, stable, and uncontrollable attributions for their failures were more prone to shame, while those who tended to make internal, unstable, and controllable attributions for failure were more prone to guilt. The underlying cognitive processes that characterize shame and guilt are substantially different, with *shame* referring to the global evaluation of the self, and *guilt* referring to the specific evaluation of one's behavior (Tangney, 1991). The difference is between negatively evaluating "who I am" and "what I did" (Tangney & Dearing, 2002).

The findings of empirical researchers on this topic support Lewis's (1971) distinction between the core of these emotions. Wicker, Payne, and Morgan (1983) asked participants to recall a time when they either felt guilt or felt shame and to describe the experience. Both shame and guilt were reportedly tense and unpleasant, but guilt resulted in participants focusing to a greater degree on their behavior and in a feeling that that they should be punished for their actions. Shame, on the other hand, produced a greater desire to hide, a sense of inferiority and low status, and an "exposed" feeling (a biblically literate reader might be put in mind of a certain incident in a garden involving fig leaves). Lindsay-Hartz

(1984) interviewed participants about their experiences with shame and guilt. Shame produced a "shrinking" sensation and a desire to hide, while guilt produced a desire to confess and to set things right. Tangney, Miller, and colleagues (1996) asked participants to write about personal experiences of shame and guilt and what those experiences made them feel and think about themselves. Both shame and guilt were characterized by "substantial feelings of responsibility, regret, and desires to make amends" (p. 1260), but those recalling shame also felt small, isolated, and inferior, focused more on what others thought of them and wanting to hide and cover up their transgressions. The overall pattern in these and other studies is that guilt is primarily focused on the morally unacceptable nature of the transgression and on the suffering inflicted on the victim, while shame is "a self-focused, egocentric experience. The person in the midst of a shame reaction is concerned not so much with the implications for *others* of his or her failure or transgression; he or she is more concerned with the implications of negative events for the *self*" (Tangney & Dearing, 2002, p. 63).

There are connections between this line of research on shame and guilt and certain theological ideas about the nature of repentance. Berkhof (1986) claims that the core of repentance is that we deplore the action that disrupted the love relationship (echoing the "social" theory of guilt endorsed by many psychologists) and that repentance is different from self-hatred. "In repentance," says Berkhof, "we are not busy with ourselves, but with God" (p. 433). The idea that shame is a selfish reaction

revolving around an injury to one's pride is also seen in J. I. Packer's (1984) condemnation of a morbid preoccupation with one's own rottenness, which he saw as connected to legalism, overemphasizing human works in sanctification. If I begin with the erroneous notion that my standing before God is the result of my righteous acts, then a failure to act righteously is a tremendous blow to my self-concept. But if we flip that concept around, we find that awareness that any standing I may have is entirely due to God, which severs considerations of intrinsic worth from the relative rottenness of my specific behavior. This allows me to identify with my sin without turning my guilt into another opportunity to make it all about me (Berkhof, 1986).

ONLY THE PENITENT MAN WILL PASS

The outcomes of guilt and shame have been studied, with researchers examining guilt and shame both as temporary emotional states and as dispositional differences in guilt-proneness and shame-proneness. The overall pattern of research in guilt and shame as temporary states supports Tangney and Dearing's (2002) assertion that "on balance feelings of guilt are more adaptive than feelings of shame as we are confronted with our inevitable failures and transgressions" (p. 56). Guilt pushes us to confess, apologize, and make reparations, while shame pushes us to protect our pride and restore perceived lost status. To begin with, people who are made to feel shame tend to get more hostile toward others, possibly as a way of refocusing attention away from their own failings, "externalizing blame and anger outward onto a convenient scapegoat" (Tangney, Stuewig, & Mashek, 2007a, p. 352). Bennett, Sullivan, and Lewis (2005) found that children who were manipulated into feeling shame using a rigged game showed greater subsequent anger. Thomaes and colleagues (2011) found a similar pattern among young adolescents, and Thomaes et al. (2008) found that narcissistic young people were more likely to respond to induced shame with aggressive behavior. People can also defend their egos by withdrawing from others (part of the "hide" reaction). Chao, Cheng, and Chiou (2011) found that participants who were induced to feel shame (through bogus feedback to a competitive reaction-time test) chose to avoid cooperative tasks and were less likely to seek help when needed.

Researchers have found that external situations are not inherently shame-inducing or guilt-inducing (Tangney, Stuewig, & Mashek, 2007a). The same type of circumstance and the same type of moral offense can elicit either guilt or shame; it is the individual who makes the difference (Murrar et al., 2019). Individual differences in guilt-proneness and shame-proneness are assessed using measures such as Tangney's (1990) Self-Conscious Affect and Attribution Inventory (SCAAI) and the various variations of the Test of Self-Conscious Affect (TOSCA) (Tangney, Wagner, & Gramzow, 1989; see Tangney & Dearing, 2002, for a list and description of several TOSCA instruments), which are based on participants' responses to social scenarios. These scenarios involve some form of failure or transgression (such as spilling red wine on a coworker's cream-colored carpet), providing a list of possible responses, and asking which one the

participant thinks they are more likely to do (wanting to run away would indicate the "hide" part of a shame reaction, while staying after the party to help clean up the spill would indicate the desire to make amends seen in a guilt reaction). Studies involving the assessment of individual differences in guilt-proneness and shame-proneness make up the majority of research on the psychological outcomes of guilt and shame.

If it is the case that "guilt adds to our moral fiber, motivating us to be more socially sensitive and caring citizens than we might be otherwise" (Kashdan & Biswas-Diener, 2014, p. 82), while shame feeds selfishness and ego-defensive reactions, then we should see a consistent pattern of positive psychological and social functioning associated with greater guilt-proneness scores and worse psychosocial functioning associated with higher shame-proneness scores. Cândea and Szentagotai-Tăta (2018) found shame, but not guilt, to be associated with greater anxiety, and Tangney, Wagner, and Gramzow (1992) found shame-proneness to be associated with a number of negative mental health outcomes, including depression, anxiety, hostility, and psychoticism. Treeby and colleagues (2018) found guilt, but not shame, to buffer against alcoholism. Gramzow and Tangney (1992) found shame scores on the SCAAI and TOSCA to be associated with pathological narcissism, while guilt was uncorrelated with narcissism. Together with studies in which researchers found negative correlations between shame and empathy but positive correlations between guilt and empathy (e.g., Tangney, 1991), as well as Leith and Baumeister's (1998) finding that guilt-prone people are better at perspective-taking, we see empirical support for shame being self-concerned while guilt is other-concerned.

This egocentrism that is at the core of shame explains the existence of "shame-rage" cycles (Retzinger, 1991) in which a person who feels shame might lash out, looking for an excuse to blame and punish others. People who score high on shame-proneness are more likely to engage in "externalizing" reactions (Tangney & Dearing, 2002), blaming others for their failures or transgressions. When describing the assessment of guilt and shame a few paragraphs ago, I used the example of spilling red wine on a colleague's cream-colored carpet. An externalizing response would be something like saying the situation was my colleague's fault because he bought a light carpet and then served red wine to his guests. Griffin and colleagues (2016) found that those who felt more shame were more likely to come up with excuses for their wrongdoing, while those who felt more guilt were less likely to excuse themselves. Stuewig et al. (2010) found externalizing to be the link between shame and aggression. By redirecting hostility away from the self toward someone else, the shamed person is able to protect his or her damaged ego. Tangney et al. (1992) found shame-proneness to be associated with greater hostility and aggressive behaviour while guilt-proneness buffered against aggression, and Tangney, Wagner, and colleagues (1996) conducted a cross-sectional study in which they found shame-proneness to be associated with more unhealthy ways of dealing with anger (such as lashing out) and guilt-proneness to be associated with

healthier ways of dealing with anger (such as talking it out).

Social functioning is also connected to guilt and shame. Baumeister et al. (1994) point to three ways guilt fosters healthy relationships and flourishing communities: (1) Guilt "motivates relationship-enhancing patterns of behavior" (p. 247) by punishing transgressions and increasing motivation to pay attention to what the other person is feeling, (2) guilt can be employed (for example, by a less-powerful person) to get others (such as a more-powerful person who might not otherwise have reason to pay attention) to cooperate, and (3) guilt can restore relational balance by alleviating the victim's suffering and undoing the perpetrator's benefit. Turning to the empirical literature, Tangney (1994) found shame scores to be associated with worse self-reported moral behavior, while guilt was associated with greater moral behavior. Chrdileli and Kasser (2018) found that guilt-prone participants were more likely to apologize for being late. Stuewig et al. (2015) conducted a longitudinal study in which they found that children's guilt-proneness predicted a reduced probability of risky and illegal behavior, while shame-proneness increased the risk of engaging in risky and illegal behavior.

Speaking of illegal behavior, one of June Price Tangney's recent areas of emphasis is the study of guilt and shame in prison populations. Shame-proneness has been found to be associated with worse psychological outcomes among inmates as well as increased likelihood of recidivism, while guilt functions as a protective factor (Martinez, Stuewig, & Tangney, 2014; Tangney, Mashek, & Stuewig, 2007;

Tangney, Stuewig, & Hafez, 2011; Tangney, Stuewig, & Martinez, 2014; Tangney, Stuewig, Mashek, & Hastings, 2011; Tibbetts, 2003). This research led Tangney and colleagues to develop the Impact of Crime (IOC) workshop, which is specifically designed to induce guilt while reducing shame in inmates (Malouf et al., 2013). In the IOC workshop, the focus is shifted away from crime as an action against the law and toward crime as an action against the victims and the local community. Offenders are helped to take responsibility for their actions and work for restitution, and a part of that involves encouraging them to feel guilty for their actions while discouraging them from self-focused shame.

In another parallel between the psychology of guilt-proneness and the theology of repentance, we can find repentance also treated in dispositional terms by theologians as a habitual practice that one should maintain on a daily basis (Ames, 1629/1968), as an enduring attitude and emotional inclination that marks the believing soul (Murray, 1955), and as "the abiding undertone of all the Christian life" (Berkhof, 1986, p. 433). I have argued (Hackney, 2010b) that a Christian vision of flourishing will be inextricably tied up with the concept of sanctification, and Christians have long considered repentance to be a vital part of sanctification. Berkouwer (1952) considers "self-complaint" to be a natural product of communion with God, and he argues that the further we progress in sanctification, the more guilt-prone we are likely to become. Advancing this argument (Hackney, 2010b), I discuss penitence as "a dispositional tendency to feel sorrow when one has sinned, to turn again toward God, and to seek atonement and make reparation" (p. 202), including the idea that individuals can possess this tendency at lower or higher levels.

Penitence can be considered a virtue that facilitates the Christian's development toward greater Christlikeness as well as a situation-specific reaction. Roberts (2007) describes penitence as "a solidity of character nurtured by action after action, insight after insight, that consolidate the self in the terms of contrition" (p. 97). As believers grow in spiritual maturity, we come to understand God better and also to understand ourselves better. This should result in an increase in guilt-proneness and what Berkouwer (1952) called "the humility of the returning prodigal" (p. 129). "Litanies of guilt are spoken on the way of salvation," says Berkouwer, "not only during the first stage of conversion, but, as Christ becomes more wonderful to us, in crescendo" (p. 112). Christian penitence goes beyond simple guilt-proneness, though. As Roberts (2007) points out, it "is characterized by confident hope in God's mercy" and "can even shade into joy, the full perception of God's goodness to oneself, acceptance, and forgiveness" (p. 104). In Hebrews 4:16, we are told to "approach God's throne of grace with confidence, so that we may receive mercy and find grace to help us in our time of need." While guilt may motivate us to make reparations for our transgression, we also know that forgiveness by definition cannot be earned. It is a gift. Once again, we see the Christian "both-and" at work here, as we simultaneously refuse to excuse or minimize our failings and joyfully accept God's loving pardon. The "positive" and the "negative" operate together, again.

It Gets More Complicated

Now, after an extended discussion of the research (mostly Tangney's) demonstrating that guilt is good and shame is bad, I am about to complicate matters by talking about ways guilt can be bad and shame can be good. Tangney and Dearing (2002) do not deny the fact that sometimes guilt can be unhealthy, though their general take on the issue is that maladaptive guilt is probably guilt with shame mixed into it; they point out that in many of the studies linking guilt to pathology, the measures of guilt used conflate guilt and shame into a single score. Tangney, Stuewig, and Mashek (2007b) also note that guilt can become a mental health problem "when people have an exaggerated or distorted sense of responsibility for events" (p. 28). An example of this might be children dealing with their parents' divorce, as they can feel guilty due to the erroneous belief that they are responsible for the breakup (Henning & Oldham, 1977). Practitioners of rational emotive behavior therapy attribute un-healthy feelings of guilt in their clients to irrational beliefs such as overrigid moral standards and an exaggeration of the harm resulting from their behavior (Dryden, 2012), although the REBT literature is also vulnerable to Tangney and Dearing's (2002) criticism of psychologists conflating guilt and shame (for example, Dryden's treatment of guilt ties assessments of the behavior together with assessments of the self: "I did this thing; it was a bad thing; therefore, I am a terrible person").

There is also some evidence that shame, when correctly employed, can lead to beneficial outcomes and growth (Kelly & Lamia, 2018). Shame, as we have seen, is concerned with the self's loss of status (Tangney & Dearing, 2002). But it is important that we pay attention to what kind of status loss is involved and what kinds of behaviors are possible to restore that lost status. Gausel and Leach (2011) point out that the diminishment of the self that occurs when one feels shame could refer to a loss of status in the eyes of others (what we might call "face" or "social image"), or it could refer to a loss of status relative to one's own self-image. Think of it as the difference between "What would the neighbors think?" and "I thought I was a better person than that." These researchers argue that the "social image" side of shame is more likely to evoke defensive reactions such as escaping or blaming others, while the "self-image" side of shame is more likely to motivate us to reform the deficiencies in our character (for example, by vowing to become a better person) or restore our lost social status (for example, by trying again and doing it right this time). De Hooge, Zeelenberg, and Breugelmans (2010) found that inducing feelings of shame activated both the "protect" motivations (defensive reactions) and "restore" motivations (reforming deficiencies or repairing social status) but that different situations made it more likely that participants would seek one or the other forms of response. If the situation offered a clear opportunity to restore the self, then the prosocial reactions were more likely than the ego-defensive ones, especially if the opportunity directly connected back to the source of the shame (de Hooge, Breugelmans, & Zeelenberg, 2008). While guilt can motivate someone to apologize and seek restoration for a specific immoral action, shame can motivate global improvements to the self (Lickel et al., 2014). Braithwaite (1989) presents a criminological theory of rehabilitation in which shaming, when done properly, can reduce crime and facilitate healthy reintegration of perpetrators as well-functioning members of society (Ahmed et al., 2001). New Testament scholar Te-Li Lau (2017, 2020) looks at Paul's use of shame in Scripture, finding that shame, also when done properly, plays a valuable role in spiritual growth and maturity. So while we raise our two-and-a-half cheers for (healthy) guilt, we might consider keeping half a cheer available for the praise of (healthy) shame.

Guilt and Positive Psychology

Back in chapter one, part of the argument that psychology had become unbalanced involved how little we know about positive emotions compared to negative emotions. In chapter four we met Barbara Fredrickson, who has helped close that gap with her broaden-and-build theory of happiness and her research (e.g., Fredrickson & Branigan, 2005) on the opposing effects positive versus negative emotions have on our cognitions and behaviors. So positive psychologists have been making a distinction between positive and negative emotions since the beginning of the movement, which makes it a good idea to ask what standards are being applied. There is frequently confusion about what makes an emotion "positive" or "negative" (Parrott, 2014a). Solomon and Stone (2002) list over a dozen different ways people have classified emotions as positive or negative over the years. For example, sometimes an emotion is considered positive if it brings pleasure and negative if it brings pain.

Other times the question of whether an emotion is positive or negative is about whether it is associated with growth in virtue. Still other times an emotion is talked about as positive or negative if it is attached to an attitude of approval or disapproval. The idea that a positive emotion is a "healthy" emotion is another option.

W. G. Parrott (2014b) argues that the default assumptions about emotion in our contemporary Western society are that the "positive" in positive emotion refers to pleasure and also "that a person's goal in life is to experience pleasure and contentment" (p. 273). That is a teleological statement. Given the prevalent (sometimes unspoken) assumption by many positive psychologists that the telos of life is "to obtain abundant and authentic gratification" (Seligman, 2002, p. 249), which we also saw in chapter four in connection to proposals to shape public policy around subjective well-being scores, it is not surprising that the positive psychology movement has been slow to recognize the possibility that unpleasant emotions might be just as important as pleasant emotions in human flourishing.

A look at how guilt has been covered in the positive psychology literature is a good example of this skew away from the unpleasant. Guilt is not listed as one of the twenty-four strengths in the *CSV*. In that volume, Peterson and Seligman (2004) mention guilt as an unhealthy emotion in that it can disrupt creativity (p. 139) and misguide forgiveness (p. 432), and they only very briefly list guilt as a possible motivational component of prudence (p. 439). Seligman does not discuss guilt at all in *Authentic Happiness* (2002) and only mentions it in *Flourish* (2011) in the context of PTSD and survivor's guilt. In the *Handbook of Positive Psychology* (Snyder & Lopez, 2005), guilt is frequently treated as an impediment to be overcome (McCullough & Witvliet, 2005; Niederhoffer & Pennebaker, 2005) and associated with unhealthy outcomes (e.g., by Carver & Schier, 2005; Emmons & Shelton, 2005; Langer, 2005). Guilt is seen in a positive light by Schulman (2005) and Baumeister and Vohs (2005) only as a valuable motivator of moral action.

Within the two primary scholarly journals of the movement (the *Journal of Positive Psychology* and the *Journal of Happiness Studies*), the only studies in which guilt is not presented as a bad thing that should be reduced are Kim-Prieto and Eid's (2004) finding that some cultures value guilt more than others and Van Tongeren and colleagues' (2014) meta-analysis in which collective guilt is shown to play a role in intergroup forgiveness. Fortunately, there are some indications that this might be turning around, with three recent positive psychology books (Kashdan & Biswas-Diner, 2014; Kashdan & Ciarrochi, 2013; Parrott, 2014) containing sections in which the virtues of guilt are presented, so at least I am not alone in attempting to persuade positive psychologists that healthy psychological functioning will include the proper employment of the dark emotions as well as the light ones.

REPENT, FOR THE END (OF THIS CHAPTER) IS NEAR

As we saw in chapter three, the primary meaning of the word *sanctify* is to set something apart, with considerations of Christlike character flowing from that set-apart status. Bavinck (1899/2008) points out that early Christians endorsed and exercised a unique set of virtues, "aware that by these virtues they were distinguishing themselves from the world and called themselves the people of God" (p. 237). If the cultivation of Christian virtues within ourselves, especially "negative" virtues such as penitence, marks us out as distinct from the world and also makes us better fit to glorify God and live in relationship with him, then this satisfies both sides of the definition of "sanctification." A Christian approach to positive psychology also fulfills both sides of the definition, as it is an approach that is distinct from the positive psychology of our non-Christian colleagues and (if research into human flourishing is more coherent when set in the light of a biblically informed worldview) also makes us better equipped to account for the psychological data.

SUGGESTIONS FOR FURTHER READING

Baumeister, R. F., Stillwell, A. M., & Heatherton, T. F. (1994). Guilt: An interpersonal approach. *Psychological Bulletin, 115*(2), 243-67.

Parrott, W. G. (Ed.). (2014). *The positive side of negative emotions.* Guilford Press.

Tangney, J. P. (1991). Moral affect: The good, the bad, and the ugly. *Journal of Personality and Social Psychology, 61*(4), 598-607.

Tangney, J. P., & Dearing, R. L. (2002). *Shame and guilt.* Guilford Press.

Tangney, J. P., Wagner, P., & Gramzow, R. (1992). Proneness to shame, proneness to guilt, and psychopathology. *Journal of Abnormal Psychology, 101*(3), 469-78.

Chapter Twenty-Three

WE'RE ALL JUST GOING TO DIE ANYWAY

Life is hard. Then you die. Then they throw dirt in your face.
Then the worms eat you. Be grateful it happens in that order.

DAVID GERROLD

This chapter continues our look at the upside of the downside, focusing on the message that human flourishing involves darkness and discomfort as well as cheerfulness and gratification (Ivtzan et al., 2016; Kashdan & Biswas-Diener, 2014; Parrott, 2014a). Having looked at the benefits of guilt and shame (done properly), we now return for another drink from the well of existential psychology (see chapter twelve) as we explore matters relating to meaninglessness and death . . . in a positive psychology way.

WORLDVIEWS, SELF-ESTEEM, AND THE SEARCH FOR MEANING

The biblical book of Ecclesiastes is a story about the search for meaning in the face of inevitable mortality. The author (identified as Qohelet, a word meaning "teacher," "preacher," or "leader of the assembly") is an old man looking back at his life asking what it has all meant. The answer is twelve chapters of "not a whole heck of a lot." Qohelet is rich and powerful enough to do pretty much whatever he wants, and he sets out to try to answer the question of life's meaning. The results are depressing, and it's pretty much all because of death. He tries living as a party animal, he sets himself to study and increases in wisdom and knowledge, he amasses wealth, and he commissions great building projects (Ecclesiastes 2). What he finds is that it is all ultimately meaningless. Money is great, but then you die and everything you worked to accumulate goes to someone else. Wisdom is great, but then you die and you're just as dead as the biggest fool to ever walk the earth. Buildings with your name on them are great, but then you die and who knows what will happen to them? Pleasure is great, but it's a bit hard to enjoy the party knowing that the grim reaper is sitting there staring at you like Banquo's ghost. About the best thing you can do with life is try to chisel a few bits of fun out of this pathetic meaningless existence before you snuff it (Ecclesiastes 9:7-10).

The only thing that "saves" Ecclesiastes (and saves me from reacting to this teaching by developing a drinking problem) is the conclusion. Having examined and rejected all sorts of possible sources of meaning "under the sun," Qohelet finally finds something meaningful. He doesn't find it under the sun. Instead, what he says is:

> Now all has been heard;
> here is the conclusion of the matter:
> Fear God and keep his commandments,
> for this is the whole duty of man.
> For God will bring every deed into
> judgment,
> including every hidden thing,
> whether it is good or evil.
> (Ecclesiastes 12:13-14)

This is what matters, and this is what makes life matter.

Many psychologists have attempted to understand the human quest to make sense of the world and live a life that has meaning. Terror management theory (TMT; Solomon, Greenberg, & Pyszczynski, 1991) is an existential approach to understanding people based on the work of Ernest Becker, especially his classic book *The Denial of Death* (Becker, 1973). TMT is built on the idea that humans have the unique ability to contemplate the future. This is good, as it enables us to do things like plan ahead and prepare for possible difficulties. But it also leads us to an awareness of mortality. As we think about the future, we realize that sooner or later, one way or another, every one of us will eventually die. That part is less fun, but it is an unavoidable part of being human. The awareness of inevitable mortality clashes with our motivation for self-preservation and creates the "terror" we must find a way to "manage."

How do we deal with the unavoidable reality of mortality? We do it by pursuing a life that has meaning and value. The Austrian psychiatrist Viktor Frankl, whose work we have discussed a number of times in previous chapters, personally observed the connection between death and meaning during his time as a concentration camp prisoner in World War II. His observations can be found in his book *Man's Search for Meaning* (1984). Frankl saw that it was not always the weakest or sickest who died but the ones who had "lost faith" and saw their life as meaningless. Frankl is fond of quoting Nietzsche's saying: "He who has a *why* to live can bear with almost any *how*" (p. 84). A life of meaning is a life that is strong enough to withstand even the Nazi death camps.

As social psychologist Roy Baumeister (1991) points out, the modern notion of "creating your own meaning" in life is a fantasy. Our ideas about what life is, why we life, how we should live, and what has value are all given to us by society. We may not always be fully aware of it, but family, teachers, media, peers, politicians, activists, and all the other elements of the culture in which we live are teaching us what to believe about these things. Terror management theorists call this acquired way of looking at things the "shared cultural worldview."

The word *worldview* comes from the German *weltanschauung*, which was coined by the philosopher Immanuel Kant in 1790 (Naugle, 2002). *Worldview* is used by philosophers and psychologists to mean "sets of beliefs and assumptions that describe reality, . . . including human nature, the meaning and nature of life, and the composition of the universe itself, to name but a few issues" (Koltko-Rivera, 2004, p. 3). A person's worldview provides answers to questions such as where the universe came from, what a human is, why everything seems messed up, and what needs to be done to fix it. People's worldviews are frequently incoherent patchworks, picked up here and there as we deal with life's issues (Bibby, 1983), but they nevertheless have tremendous psychological power, "buffering" us from the anxiety that comes from being aware of death.

Worldviews serve as anxiety buffers by providing a description of what in life has meaning. Knowing what is meaningful gives us our standards of value, and living up to those standards of value is how we get self-esteem. So, for example, if you are a parent and you see taking care of your children as meaningful, then you will feel good about yourself when you are being a good parent. You will admire other good parents. You will be angry with the things in life that get in the way of being a good parent. Similarly, if you are an artist, and creative activity provides your life with meaning, then you will feel good about yourself when you are being a good artist. You will admire other good artists. You will be angry with the things in life that get in the way of being a good artist.

Terror management theorists argue that by doing things that are meaningful and living meaningful lives, people defeat existential "terror" by pursuing some form of immortality. There are two forms of immortality described by TMT: literal and symbolic. Literal immortality is often a component of religious worldviews that promise the survival of the individual beyond death, heaven and reincarnation being two major examples (Vail et al., 2010). Symbolic immortality comes from engaging in some kind of action that will "echo" beyond the individual's death.

Multiple examples exist of symbolic immortality. I mentioned parenting as a possible way to pursue meaning. Many parents find their "immortality" in the survival and success of their children. As long as the children are alive and well, death becomes less frightening for the parent to contemplate. Political activity is also a way to achieve symbolic immortality. An individual's political activity is typically aimed at making society better or protecting society from threats, and the effects of the activist on society will continue to be seen after the individual activist has died. Even better, though, is to engage in the kind of political activity that secures one's place in the history books. The motivation to engage in artistic creativity (Perach & Wisman, 2019) as well as scientific or scholarly activity can also be understood from this perspective. Creating a long-lasting work of art, having a theory named after you, being required reading in textbooks, or even having an article published in the research journals can all be pathways to immortality (so if anyone is reading this book after I am dead, mission accomplished!).

In summary, terror management theorists describe a wide range of human thought, feeling, and behavior in terms of our motivation to seek meaning in the face of inevitable mortality. Terror management theorists describe themselves as "experimental existential psychologists" (Pyszczynski et al., 2010), using the tools of experimental social psychology to examine how this connection between death and meaning operates in people's lives.

TMT research has centered on the mortality salience effect, which involves examining what happens when the researcher makes people think about their own death. The logic behind a mortality salience study goes like this: If motivation to seek a meaningful life as described by one's shared cultural worldview comes from our reaction to death-related anxiety, then making mortality salient should increase one's motivation to cling to the beliefs of the worldview and to do the things that make life meaningful. The first mortality salience study, conducted by researchers Rosenblatt, Greenberg, Solomon, Pyszczynski, and Lyon, was published in 1989. The researchers found that manipulating participants into contemplating their own eventual deaths caused them to be harsher in their treatment of those who violated standards of value and more generous in their treatment of those who upheld standards of value.

TMT researchers have used the mortality salience effect to examine motivation in a wide range of life domains. In the interest of buffering against death anxiety and upholding the shared cultural worldview, people will defend their national identity (Greenberg et al., 1990), intensify prejudice against foreigners (Nelson et al., 1997) and people of different religions (Greenberg et al., 1990), engage in aggression against people who have different political beliefs (McGregor et al., 1996), and avoid things that remind us of the animal nature of our physical bodies (Goldenberg et al., 2001).

HOW IS THIS POSITIVE?

TMT is frequently (and correctly) seen as a rather bleak look at the human condition.

By and large, existentialists are not known for being jolly. For example, when Pyszczynski, Greenberg, and Solomon (2000) wanted to examine the "upside" of humanity (our capacity for freedom and growth), they concluded that the best way to do this was to merge TMT with a more optimistic theory that we have encountered more than once in this book—self-determination theory (SDT)—rather than to employ the tools of TMT itself. This merger was intended to form a "dual-motive" approach, with SDT covering the light side and TMT covering the dark side. So what is a chapter on TMT doing in a text on positive psychology? So glad you asked. In line with our overall message that positive psychology is about achieving higher levels of human functioning, not necessarily just "happy feelings," terror management researchers have recently been examining the ways even the terrifying reality of unavoidable death can fuel the good life (Vail et al., 2012).

To begin with, while most TMT research has focused on defensive reactions such as aggression and harsh judgmentalism, the standards of value contained within a person's shared cultural worldview can also be entirely prosocial. Pyszczynski et al. (2006) found that the mortality salience manipulation caused Iranian participants to increase their support for "martyrdom attacks" on the US and also caused American participants to more strongly endorse extreme military solutions to the ongoing troubles in the Middle East, but that effect was not found among those for whom tolerance was a core value. Going further, Rothschild, Abdollahi, and Pyszczynski (2009) performed a similar study, examining the effect of mortality salience on a sample of American Christians and a sample of Iranian Shiite Muslims. When Christian participants were primed with biblical passages emphasizing compassion as a Christian value (such as, "Be kind and compassionate to one another, forgiving each other, just as in Christ God forgave you" [Ephesians 4:32]) before being exposed to the mortality salience manipulation, mortality salience no longer produced any increase in enthusiasm for extreme military action. Similarly, when Muslim participants were primed with passages from the Quran that emphasize universal compassion and goodness (e.g., Quran 4:36), the result was that the mortality salience manipulation produced a decrease in anti-Western attitudes. Looking at individual differences in religiosity, a number of researchers have found that intrinsic religious orientation (recall chapter twenty-one) can reverse the worldview defense effect and lead to less hostility toward outgroup members (e.g., Golec de Zavala et al., 2012). So our motivation to uphold our shared cultural worldview does not necessarily have to lead us down the path of hatred and violence. As Christians, we can uphold our shared cultural worldview by following the Prince of Peace.

Contemplating our mortality can also remind us of what is really important. Routledge and colleagues (2008) found that mortality salience can lead to enhanced prosocial creativity, and Blackie, Cozzolino, and Sedikides (2016) found that reflecting on one's mortality can lead to more coherent values and identity integration. In Ecclesiastes, Qohelet rejects all forms of symbolic immortality as ultimately unsatis-

fying. Only the literal immortality found in one's standing before God can truly "buffer" against the psychological threat posed by inevitable mortality. Another upside to this focus on literal immortality over symbolic immortality is that, once one's life is aligned with what really matters, the other goals (which had previously been declared meaningless) become infused with eternal meaning. Work, play, family, art, science, all of the things done "under the sun" suddenly find the meaning that otherwise disappears like a vapor when they are pursued as ends in themselves. As Frankl (1984) put it, "Self-actualization is possible only as a side-effect of self-transcendence" (p. 115).

The reality of death can also motivate us to reach out to each other (Plusnin, Pepping, & Kashima, 2018). Mikulincer and Florian (2000) found that participants who had secure attachment styles (see chapter thirteen) responded to the mortality salience manipulation with an increased desire for intimacy. Florian, Mikulincer, and Hirschberger (2002) followed up by arguing that close relationships serve many psychological functions that fit within TMT. First, having friends and family helps to buffer against our fear of death because friends and family offer the promise of help when we are in danger, making death a more remote possibility and therefore less threatening. Second, in line with attachment theory (Bowlby, 1969), and as we saw in chapter thirteen, we turn to close relationships when we are in distress, and this includes the distress that accompanies our own mortality. And third, close relationships are a source of self-esteem, which, as we saw earlier in this chapter, is a core component of TMT's "anxiety buffer." In a series of studies, Florian and colleagues (2002) found that reminding people of their mortality resulted in higher levels of romantic commitment, that getting people to think about their relationships resulted in less death-thought accessibility,[1] and that thinking about problems in relationships led to greater levels of death-thought accessibility.

Psychologists have followed this up with further studies, finding that mortality salience motivates people to initiate social relationships (Taubman Ben-Ari et al., 2002), to build families (Nobles, Frankenberg, & Thomas, 2015), and to seek out romantic partners who will support their worldview (Kosloff et al., 2010). Young people visualizing positive interactions with parents became immune to the mortality salience manipulation (Cox et al., 2008), and mortality salience made people in committed relationships more willing to forgive each other (Van Tongeren et al., 2013). So awareness of our mortality can also fuel the desire to seek out, establish, and maintain close relationships.

MEANING

One of the most central concepts in terror management theory is the idea that death is what motivates us to pursue a life that has meaning and value. The terror we must manage begins with the threat that mortality poses for meaning and leads to motivation to see ourselves as valuable members of a meaningful universe (Pyszczynski et al., 2010). Once this is done, seeing our lives as meaningful is associated with a wide range of desirable outcomes

(Batthyany & Russo-Netzer, 2014). People whose lives are meaningful are more mature and hopeful (Varahrami et al., 2010). They cope better with the inevitable trials and tragedies of life (e.g., Echterling, 1993; Fickova & Ruiselova, 1999; Park et al., 2008). They handle stress better (Halama, 2014). They are less prone to depression (Mascaro & Rosen, 2005) and more prone to happiness (Scannell et al., 2002). Meaning not only powerfully buffers against psychological dysfunction but also promotes well-being. When we have meaning in our lives, it carries the potential to be one of the greatest possible sources for human flourishing (Batthyany & Russo-Netzer, 2014; Steger, 2012; Wong, 2012a).

Positive existential psychologist Paul Wong (2016) says meaning in life involves seven related questions:

- *Who am I?* What defines me? Who am I when everything is stripped away from me and I am reduced to a naked lonely soul? Is there anything unique and special about me?

- *How can I be happy?* Why am I bored? Why am I so dissatisfied with life? What is the good life? Is this all there is to life?

- *What should I do with my life?* How shall I then live? What is my calling? To what should I devote the rest of my life?

- *How do I make the right choices?* How do I know that I am making the right decision regarding career and relationships? How can I tell right from wrong?

---

[1]Death-thought accessibility is an indicator of how well the person's unconscious mind is keeping thoughts of death at bay.

- *Where do I belong?* Why do I feel so alone in this world? How can I develop deep and meaningful relationships? Where can I find acceptance? Where is my home?

- *What is the point of striving when life is so short?* Why should I struggle to survive when life is transient and fragile? What is the point of building something only to see it swallowed up by death? (p. 1)

The vision of flourishing given to us by existential psychologists involves facing these hard questions without falling back on easy prepackaged answers. It is by struggling through these issues of death, freedom, isolation, and meaninglessness that we find life, responsibility, connection, and meaning. Although meaning and hedonic happiness (see chapter four) may overlap in a person's life, the meaningful life is not always the "happy" life (Baumeister et al., 2013). But it is a central component of the good life (Seligman, 2011; Wong, 2012c).

Psychologists have developed a number of different measures of meaning. Crumbaugh and Maholick (1964) based their Purpose in Life test on Frankl's logotherapy. This twenty-item test measures the degree to which individuals perceive their lives as having or lacking purpose. The PiL test has been widely used, and higher scores (indicating greater meaning) are associated with a number of positive outcomes (Crumbach & Maholick, 1964; Schulenberg & Melton, 2010), though Dyck (1987) criticizes the construct validity of the test. The Meaning in Life Questionnaire (Steger, Frazier, Oishi, & Kaler, 2006) gives us a two-dimensional motivational-cognitive approach, with subscales for the search for meaning and the presence of meaning. The two subscales are negatively correlated (those who see their lives as having meaning are less likely to be searching for it, and those who are searching are less likely to say they have it). Presence of meaning is associated with a number of positive variables, including life satisfaction, hope, gratitude, kindness, religiousness, bravery, social intelligence, sense of humor, and reduced likelihood of depression. Search for meaning, however, is either uncorrelated or is negatively correlated with desirable outcomes and is associated with more depression (Peterson & Park, 2012). Wong (2012b) chalks this up to the search for meaning being a multistep process that can take several forms, and the MiLQ is not sensitive to this kind of complexity. The Personal Meaning Profile (Wong, 1998; McDonald, Wong, & Gingras, 2012) is more about the possible domains within which a person can pursue meaning. Participants answer questions about the degree to which their sense of meaning comes from achievement, relationships, religion, self-transcendence, self-acceptance, intimacy, and fair treatment. Researchers who use the PMP have found scores on the measure to correlate with a wide range of positive variables (see McDonald, Wong, & Gingras, 2012, for a review).

Passing the Kobayashi Maru Test

Does the good life include the good death? In his *History* (fifth century BC), Heroditus tells the story of the wise Athenian Solon and his visit to the magnificently wealthy king Croesus. Croesus decides to go fishing for compliments and asks Solon who he thinks is the happiest of all men. Instead of giving the expected answer, Solon tells Croesus a story about an Athenian ruler who lived well, then died gloriously in battle and was posthumously honored. Hoping for the silver medal, Croesus asks who was the second happiest. Solon says the next place belongs to a pair of brothers who achieved glory for themselves and honor for their family and then died peacefully in their sleep. The lesson, Solon says, is that because we never know what tomorrow may bring, we do not know how happy someone's life is until we have seen how it ended. From this we get the saying, "Call no man happy until he dies." At a rather less highbrow level, we have the wisdom of Captain Kirk in *Star Trek II*: "How we deal with death is at least as important as how we deal with life."

Charles Taylor (2007) points out that "modern humanism tends to develop a notion of human flourishing which has no place for death. Death is simply the negation, ultimate negation, of flourishing; it must be combatted, and held off till the very last moment" (p. 320). Paul Wong (2008) pushes back against the modern denial of death, arguing that "death acceptance is one of the cornerstones for the good life" (p. 69). Wong, Reker, and Gesser (1994) identified five types of death attitudes. The first is fear of death. There is a long history of research on the experience of fear and anxiety over the prospect of one's eventual demise using measures such as Templer's (1970) Death Anxiety Scale. People with a high degree of fear of death would tend to agree with statements on Wong and colleagues' (1994) Death Attitude Profile such as, "I am disturbed by the finality of death," and are more likely to experience depression (Templer, 1971) and a sense of purposelessness in life (Bolt, 1978). Some people "deal" with death by not dealing with it, which Wong et al. (1994) identify as "death avoidance." Wong and colleagues found scores on death avoidance to be strongly associated with higher death anxiety scores, suggesting that trying not to think about death is not a very effective defense mechanism for the existential terror of life. Avoidance scores were also associated with greater psychological distress and depression among older adults.

In order to live fully, we have to face and deal with the reality of our mortality. "Positively oriented individuals are willing to confront the crisis and create opportunities for growth" (Wong & Tomer, 2011, p. 103), and Wong et al. (1994) identify three possible forms of death acceptance. "Neutral" acceptance involves facing death with rational indifference as a mere fact of life that is neither good nor bad. Higher scores on this subscale were associated with less fear of death, less vulnerability to depression, and greater well-being. "Approach" acceptance is the position of seeing death as a gateway to a better life. This necessarily involves the concept of an afterlife, so it is not surprising that Harding and colleagues (2005) found religious belief to predict greater death acceptance. Approach acceptance was strongly associated with less fear of death and with greater well-being among older adults (Wong et al., 1994). "Escape" acceptance involves seeing death as a release from the pain and suffering of life. This kind of attitude is more common among those who are dealing with ongoing pain and loss of function (Cicirelli, 2002). As this attitude is less about the goodness of death and more about the badness of life, Wong and colleagues (1994) found escape scores to be associated with worse physical well-being. They also found that escape scores were strongly positively correlated with approach scores, showing that many people combine a view of death as a release with a view of death as a door to a better existence. Monika Ardelt (2008) conducted a study of death attitudes among residents of nursing units, retirement communities, and hospice organizations. She found that participants who displayed greater wisdom (see chapter nine) showed less fear of death and lower escape scores. Religious orientation was another variable she measured. Recall from chapter twenty-one that extrinsic orientation (a less mature orientation) involves engaging in religious practices for self-centered reasons, while intrinsic orientation (more mature) involves participating in the religion for its own sake. In Ardelt's study, extrinsic orientation scores were associated with greater fear of death and death avoidance but also more neutral and escape acceptance. Intrinsic orientation scores were associated with the combination of greater escape and approach acceptance. Ardelt also administered Crumbaugh and Maholick's (1964) Purpose in Life test, finding that participants who experienced more purpose in their lives also tended to demonstrate less fear of death and death avoidance.

Despite its ancient roots, the idea of a good death "constitutes a new frontier of the current positive psychology movement" (Wong & Tomer, 2011, p. 101). Many traditions include practices that help cultivate a proper attitude toward one's death. In his *Meditations,* the Stoic emperor Marcus Aurelius encourages the reader to remember that "death hangs over you" in order to do good while you can and that your mindset should be shaped by the fact that you could leave life at any moment. Meditation on death is well established within Buddhism.

Christianity also contains a practice of contemplating one's eventual death. In the fifteenth century, the manuscript *Ars moriendi* ("the art of dying") presented readers with detailed advice for the spiritual health of those who are facing death as well as encouragement that believers should be prepared so they can die well at any moment. More broadly, there are a number of historical practices that fall within the *memento mori* ("remember that you must die") tradition stretching over many centuries. Believers are encouraged to consider the reality of mortality, the impermanence of life, and the importance of the afterlife. *Memento mori* themes can be found in Christian art, including skull motifs in paintings, *danse macabre* ("dance of death") woodcuts, morbid designs on tombs and tombstones, the famous Chapel of Bones in Portugal and the Capuchin Crypt in Rome, and numerous literary meditations on death. Overlapping with *memento mori* art are works classified as *vanitas* pieces, after the word in Ecclesiastes that is commonly translated as "vanity" or "meaningless." *Vanitas* artworks include many symbols of death (skulls, rotten fruit, and so on) and of the fleeting nature of life (bubbles, smoke), and they invite the viewer to contemplate mortality and meaninglessness. And for those believers who belong to more liturgical denominations,

Ash Wednesday services include the imposition of ashes on the forehead (in the form of a cross) with the instruction that we are to remember that we are dust and to dust we will return. Christians are blessed with an abundance of resources to help us cultivate a healthy attitude toward our eventual death and to give full consideration to the implications of mortality for the search for meaning.

A crucial question for Christians with an interest in existential psychology in general and TMT specifically is whether the meanings associated with our shared cultural worldviews are in fact true. When I was in graduate school, one of my colleagues decided she was unable to get on board with TMT because, as a Christian, she believed that life does in fact have a real meaning, while TMT posits that all worldviews are fictions invented to alleviate death anxiety. On the other hand, I, as a Christian, decided that TMT was awesome and wonderful because of the strong connections I saw with Ecclesiastes (and also because I am cheerfully morbid). Martin Seligman attempted to deal with the question of real meaning in *Flourish* (Seligman, 2011) but did not do a very good job of it. He gave the example of Abraham Lincoln, who sometimes felt that his life was meaningless, but argued that Lincoln's life was objectively meaningful because "we judge it pregnant with meaning" (p. 17), with the "we" being people who make logical judgments about history. Seligman does not mention whether it ever occurred to him that a society's assessments of meaning are not necessarily any more objective than an individual's. Solomon, Greenberg, and Pyszczynski (1991) also address this issue in a footnote (in the name

of symmetry, perhaps I should have addressed it in a footnote as well). They claim that while it might look at first like TMT requires that the universe be absurd and objectively meaningless, it is actually not vital to the theory to believe so. Therefore the meaning-motivation described in TMT can be seen as the *search* for meaning, the *creation* of meaning, or some combination of both.

As for me, I see it as both. As we discussed in chapter three, the Christian vision of flourishing that orients this text is one in which we see the telos of humanity in the glorification of God and the living out of relations with God and each other. This telos describes the meaning of life. When our lives are not properly aligned with this goal, we feel the existential vacuum sucking away at us and we come up with a plethora of artificial ways to fill it, like money, power, or pleasure (Frankl, 1984), the accumulation of facts, submission to a leader (Fromm, 1941), or the creation of works of art. In this way we create artificial meanings that we believe will fill the void and feel a certain sense of satisfaction in the attempt (though even that can turn out to be fleeting and unsatisfying; see Roberts, 2007, and Williams, 2011). When our lives are properly aligned with the genuine telos of existence, though, our lives are objectively meaningful as we seek first the kingdom of God (Matthew 6:33) and love our neighbors as ourselves (James 2:8).

SUGGESTIONS FOR FURTHER READING

Batthyany, A., & Russo-Netzer, P. (Eds.). (2014). *Meaning in positive and existential psychology.* Springer.

Frankl, V. (1984). *Man's search for meaning* (3rd ed). Simon & Schuster.

Rogers, R., Sanders, C. S., & Vess, M. (2019). The terror management of meaning and growth: How mortality salience affects growth-oriented processes and the meaningfulness of life. In C. Routledge & M. Vess (Eds.), *Handbook of terror management theory* (pp. 325-46). Academic Press.

Tomer, A., Eliason, G. T., & Wong, P. T. P. (Eds.). (2008). *Existential and spiritual issues in death acceptance.* Taylor & Francis.

Vail, K. E., Juhl, J., Arndt, J., Vess, M., Routledge, C., & Rutjens, B. T. (2012). When death is good for life: Considering the positive trajectories of terror management. *Personality and Social Psychology Review, 16*(4), 303-29.

Wong, P. T. P. (Ed.). (2012). *The human quest for meaning: Theories, research, and applications* (2nd ed). Routledge.

Wong, P. T. P. (2016). Existential positive psychology. *International Journal of Existential Psychology and Psychotherapy, 6*(1). http://journal.existentialpsychology.org/index.php/ExPsy/article/view/179.

Chapter Twenty-Four

CRITICISMS AND FUTURE DIRECTIONS FOR POSITIVE PSYCHOLOGY

"Where do we go from here?"

Buffy the Vampire Slayer, "Once More with Feeling"

Generally speaking, positive psychologists tend to be positive about positive psychology. Some are exceedingly positive. Alan Carr (2004) sees endless opportunities for research and application in positive psychology with the potential to create a new world. Csikszentmihalyi (1990) describes his flow research as contributing to the ascent of humanity to a higher level of evolution in which we merge with the flow of the universe. In *Authentic Happiness*, Seligman (2002) connects his advice for living an increasingly good life to a "nonzero" process of improving the universe, a process he thinks might ultimately create God (who, according to Seligman, does not exist yet).

While connections between positive psychology and cosmic ascent are the exception rather than the rule, the general sentiment within the movement is that positive psychology does in fact have "legs" (Lyubomirsky & Abbe, 2003) and will continue to make the world a better place. Snyder, Lopez, and Pedrotti (2011) asked a collection of positive psychologists what they think about positive psychology in the twenty-first century. Several of them looked forward to positive psychology becoming such an inextricable part of the mainstream that it would reorient clinical psychology, health care, and the social sciences in general. Aaron Jarden (2012) interviewed thirteen prominent positive psychologists and included questions about the future of positive psychology. Some respondents focused on the potential of positive psychology to shape public policy, and others were excited about all the remaining unexplored territory for researchers.

Not all feedback has been glowing, though. Some of Jarden's (2012) interviewees were concerned about positive psychologists' tendency to get excited and jump to applications and interventions before the science has been properly done. Others were critical of the lack of cross-cultural work. One of Snyder and colleagues' (2011) positive psychologists accused positive psychology of ignoring the darker sides of human existence. In this chapter, we will spend some time with scholars (and a few nonscholars) who criticize the positive psychology movement and examine a few ideas that have been put forward regarding how positive psychology might correct certain flaws and take the movement to the next level.

Writing about the current state of positive psychology and its possible future, Itai Ivtzan and colleagues (2016) employ the "thesis-antithesis-synthesis" cycle of Hegel's dialectic as their approach to analyzing the movement. In this dialectic, we begin with an idea or a social phenomenon (the thesis). People notice gaps and flaws in the thesis and put forward an idea that opposes the thesis (the antithesis). The antithesis is not perfect; it has its own gaps and flaws. Thesis and antithesis battle it out in a kickboxing extravaganza you won't want to miss. Thesis and antithesis both have some good points (or else not many people would be attracted to them), so eventually people start to think "why not both?" and combine thesis and antithesis into something new (the synthesis). The cycle then repeats, with the synthesis serving as the new thesis, which calls forth an antithesis, and so on.

Robert Sternberg (1998b) provides several examples of this dialectic in the history of psychology. For instance, psychoanalytic therapy focuses almost exclusively on internal dynamics (thesis). Behavior therapy rejects psychoanalysis, ignores internal states, and focuses entirely on external behavior patterns (antithesis). Cognitive-behavioral therapy takes into account both internal states and external behaviors (synthesis). Following the lead of Ivtzan et al. (2016) and Sternberg (1998b), I will structure this chapter along dialectical lines.

THESIS

For positive psychologists, the thesis in our story is mainstream twentieth-century psychology. As we saw all the way back in chapter one, Martin Seligman (1999) described post-World War II psychology as largely focused on the negative side of life. We see clinical psychologists treating clients with depression, social psychologists studying racism, developmental psychologists investigating ways to reduce juvenile criminal behavior, industrial psychologists studying workplace burnout, and so on. The thesis has a lot of good points; nobody in the positive psychology movement claims that wanting to help suffering people is bad. However, we see gaps and flaws in the thesis. There is more to life than dysfunction, and when we hold to theories that focus exclusively on problems, we end up seeing human nature as nothing but a bundle of problems.

ANTITHESIS

Positive psychology began as a reaction against the excessive negativity of mainstream psychology. Seligman and Csikszentmihalyi (2000) described psychology as a field that "concentrates on repairing damage within a disease model of human functioning" (p. 5) and contrasted it with positive psychology, which draws attention to strength, virtue, and flourishing. Seligman (2002) declared it his mission to combat and overthrow the "rotten-to-the-core dogma" of human nature (p. x). Berscheid (2003) presented a stark contrast between a "portrait that depicts the human as teeming with innate malignancies toward other humans" and "a portrait that depicts the human as eager to love other humans and to be loved by them" (p. 44). The *CSV* was explicitly created to be an "anti-*DSM*" (Peterson & Seligman, 2004). Lopez and Gallagher (2009) made the case for positive psychology courses in colleges by arguing that "since abnormal psychology courses, which are required for most psychology majors, are about fear, related negative emotions, and illness, a positive psychology course serves to round out a student's knowledge base with the study of hope, positive emotions, and health" (p. 4), framing the two courses as opposites of each other. With the lines thus drawn, we see positive psychology positioned as the antithesis to mainstream psychology's thesis.

Positive psychology has its own gaps and flaws, though, and the movement has been the target of much criticism. Some of these criticisms have been incisive and worthy of serious consideration, while others have been rather less valid. In this section, we will take a look at some of the criticisms that have been leveled against the positive psychology movement.

When positive psychology was introduced in the January 2000 issue of *American Psychologist*, several psychologists immediately responded, and some of their criticisms remain relevant two decades later (Brown, Lomas, & Eiroa-Orosa, 2017). Compton (2001) challenged Seligman's claims to study well-being in a value-neutral way, Ahuvia (2001) questioned the prominence given to individual happiness and unlimited choice in the definitions of well-being, and Walsh (2001) pointed out the lack of attention Seligman and company pay to non-Western approaches to psychology. We saw criticisms like these in some detail back in chapter two when we

looked at philosophical matters involving positive psychology's neo-Aristotelian roots. Sundararajan (2005b) and Kristjánsson (2013) point out that it is impossible to define flourishing without a moral vision of the good life (can't have *eudaimonia* without a telos), despite Seligman's (2002) attempts to do exactly that, and scholars such as Woolfolk and Wasserman (2005) and Fowers (2012a) accuse Seligman of sneaking an implicit telos in through the back door by defining the good life in terms of individual subjective gratification. A positive psychology that is grounded in a different vision of the good life would be a different positive psychology, as Wong (2009) demonstrates in his brief description of the contours of a "Chinese positive psychology." So it seems that many scholars saw immediately that the positive psychology movement rested on a questionable foundation.

One very public rebuke of positive psychology was issued by columnist and activist Barbara Ehrenreich in her 2009 book *Bright-Sided*. While some of her criticisms run parallel to those issued by serious scholars, the book itself is an intellectually thin hatchet job, relying heavily on emotional word choice and liberal use of scare quotes. Central to Ehrenreich's argument is the idea that Americans are addicted to the false notion that positive thinking will make us lastingly happier people, with positive psychology being just one more manifestation of the same pattern that gave us shallow self-help books, gormless gimcrack motivational speakers, and the prosperity gospel. While some sections of her book contain valuable criticism of broader trends in American culture, the chapter on positive psychology is largely an exercise in misrepresenting Seligman's (2002) *Authentic Happiness*, attacking Seligman personally, and engaging in a bit of conspiracy theorizing about the Templeton Foundation. The book received a lot of press, so I decided to mention it here, but we can look elsewhere for substantive criticisms of the positive psychology movement.

The idea that positive psychology is another manifestation of larger cultural phenomena does have some merit. Sociologist William Davies (2015) presents an argument that the project of solving moral and political problems "with an adequate science of human feelings" (p. 7) has been around since at least the French Revolution. He connects this project to Enlightenment philosophy, describing the application of psychological research to evidence-based policy decisions as "Benthamite," after the utilitarian philosopher Jeremy Bentham. Davies warns readers that proposals to monitor and increase people's happiness carry the risk of transferring ever more power to big business and big government, allowing them to employ the tools of surveillance and control to create "a society in which experts and authorities are able to divine what is good for us without our voices being heard" (p. 33), ostensibly for our benefit, but more often for the benefit of big business and big government.

Davies's book is littered with references to positive psychology, and his criticism echoes some of what we have seen in earlier chapters. In chapter two, for example, we looked at the individualism inherent in positive psychology, including the idea that flourishing is "something determined by individual choice and attained by private, self-focused effort" (Becker & Marecek, 2008, p. 1777). This focus on individual flourishing as the result of individual effort redirects blame away from those in power. When Shawn Achor (2010) tells us that "even in the midst of their heavy workloads and the tyranny of impossible expectations" (p. 22) employees can flourish if they learn to use the tools of positive psychology, one side effect is that the corporate overlords who laid the heavy workloads and impossible expectations on the employees are allowed to keep things going unchanged. And if the employees don't like it? Well, here's an example of what can happen if the employees don't like it: Dotcom millionaire Tony Hsieh took over the fashion company Zappos in 1999 and decided to run it on the principles of happiness. He began this happy process by firing the 10% of his employees who were the least enthusiastic about this happy process (Smedley, 2012). Hsieh found that the remaining 90% became "super-engaged" (as one might expect when the options are enthusiasm or termination).

In chapter four we looked at proposals to shape public policy around subjective well-being. Mulnix and Mulnix (2015) sound a note of alarm over the idea of giving governments authority over our happiness. Given that positive psychological research can be rallied in support of multiple political perspectives (Lomas, 2018), relying on the state to make us happy carries the potential for whoever happens to be in charge to use the science of well-being to justify overruling the will of the people (who are not deemed to be as knowledgeable as the experts) to advance their own agendas. When Barry Schwartz (2000) told us that too much freedom can be bad for our mental health, he was quick to clarify that he did not want the government deciding what freedoms to curtail (Schwartz, 2001). President Ronald Reagan once said, "The most terrifying words in the English language are: 'I'm from the government and I'm here to help.'" Many critics of positive psychology echo this sentiment, including the tyrannical implications of the alternate formulation: "I'm from a massive megacorporation and I'm here to help."

Speaking of tyranny, another early critic of positive psychology is Barbara Held (2002). She argues that, while America has always leaned toward the optimistic (see Samuel, 2018), our push for happiness by way of maintaining a positive attitude has exploded. This enthusiasm for accentuating the positive and putting on a happy face has, Held argues, crossed the line into moral demands that one be happy and positive, Seligman's objections that he is not trying to force a vision of the good life on anyone notwithstanding.

Despite my critical words earlier, one of the compelling sections in Ehrenreich's (2009) *Bright-Sided* is her account of her personal experience dealing with breast cancer and the sharp rebukes she faced when she entered an online forum for people with breast cancer and expressed frustration. Instead of receiving support, she was shamed and rejected. In chapter four we looked at research in support of the idea that positive emotions bring with them health benefits. Greer, Morris, and Pettingale (1979) conducted a study in which they found that breast cancer patients who

kept an upbeat "fighting spirit" were more likely to survive. This led many to advocate for positivity among cancer patients. This study had some methodological limitations, though, and better-run studies (e.g., Watson et al., 2005) found no effect. Coyne and colleagues (2007) also found no relationship between good spirits and survival among patients with head and neck cancer, and Schofield (2004) similarly found null results among lung cancer patients. It turns out that one cannot cure cancer through the power of cheerfulness. Reading the writeups of these null findings was an interesting experience, as it is the first time I have seen researchers express relief at finding nothing. Watson et al. (2005) hoped their null finding would "help to remove any continuing feelings of guilt or sense of blame for breast cancer relapse from those women who worry because they cannot always maintain a fighting spirit or a positive attitude" (p. 1713). It seems Ehrenreich (2009) got a faceful of that blame when she expressed her negative emotions online. Aspinwall and Tedeschi (2010) called this "the principal danger of popular versions of positive psychology" (p. 10). Kashdan and Biswas-Diener (2014) put it even more strongly, lamenting that "over the past fifteen years, positive psychology has been transformed from a reminder that 'positive experiences are important' to a kind of smiling fascism" (p. xii).

While I wouldn't go as far as "fascism," I do criticize positive psychology for fostering a judgmentalism toward the insufficiently happy, and I place the blame on the excessively positive view of human nature that pervades the movement (Hackney,

2014). If we believe that human nature is basically good, meaning that everyone can thrive if given the tools, then what are we to do when someone does not thrive after we equip them with the tools? It must be their fault for not trying hard enough. Talk show host Dennis Prager (2007) leveled an especially harsh attack on the insufficiently positive, posting a video on his website in which he stated, "Happiness is much more than a personal pursuit; it's a moral obligation," complete with a claim that unhappiness is the driving force behind cults, Islamic terrorism, and Nazis. J. P. Moroney, business coach and author of *Negative People Suck!* (Maroney, 2011) compares insufficiently positive people to a virus and encourages managers to fire them immediately. Many positive psychologists as well as critics of positive psychology warn of the downside of excessive focus on the positive and hope for a future positive psychology grounded in a view of humanity that incorporates both darkness and light (Aspinwall & Staudinger, 2003; Held, 2004; Ivtzan et al., 2016; Kashdan & Biswas-Diener, 2014; Larsen et al., 2003; Parrott, 2014a).

In our preceding chapters, as we examined specific topics within positive psychology, I often presented criticisms of positive psychology as we went along. In chapter one we saw the fissiparous tensions between positive psychology and humanistic psychology. In chapter two we saw several philosophical criticisms of positive psychology, including the lack of an explicit telos, the advancement of an implicit telos grounded in Western individualism, and the neglect of alternate cultural perspectives on the good life. In chapter seven Julie

Norem's defensive pessimism served as a counterpoint to Martin Seligman's learned optimism. And when appropriate, I pointed out the ways in which a Christian perspective on human nature puts us at odds with our secular colleagues.

SYNTHESIS

In keeping with our dialectical approach, we see that the thesis (mainstream psychology) has good points but also some gaps and flaws. We also see that the antithesis (positive psychology) has good points but also some gaps and flaws. In an approach that Paul Wong (2011) calls "positive psychology 2.0" and Ivtzan and colleagues (2016) call "second wave positive psychology," a movement is afoot in which we see scholars trying to create a synthesis that brings together good parts of mainstream psychology and positive psychology to create a more balanced and sophisticated understanding of human flourishing.

One key characteristic of second wave positive psychology is an integration of the darker parts of the human experience into our understanding of the good life. Barbara Held (2004) put forward a call for this kind of integrative project soon after the introduction of the positive psychology movement. Part of her criticism of positive psychology was that the prominent voices in the movement demonstrated a "negativity about negativity" (p. 10). Despite some statements by early positive psychologists cautioning us away from an unbalanced focus on optimism and positive emotions, the dominant message for living well has involved undoing negative emotion and avoiding pessimism by cultivating positive emotion and learning optimism (see our discussions of these in chapters four and seven). Recall as well that Ed Diener's recipe for the good life involves seeking that which produces higher levels of subjective well-being, defined in terms of fewer negative emotions and more positive emotions (also in chapter four).

Kashdan and Biswas-Diener (2014) chalk up this tendency to equate well-being with pleasantness to North Americans' "addiction to comfort" and argue (as do many other critics of positive psychology) that this message—that positive is good and negative is bad—is far too simplistic. In certain circumstances, optimism and positive emotion can lead to unhealthy outcomes, and pessimism and negative emotion can lead to healthy outcomes (Forgas, 2013; Norem, 2002; Parrott, 2014a). If we define flourishing in terms of being a highly functioning person, doing well that which humans do, instead of in terms of subjective individual gratification, then the central question for positive psychologists needs to be how to experience and employ both positive and negative variables in healthy ways.

Ryff and Singer (2003) bring the positive and negative together by arguing that wellness "comes from active encounters with life's challenges, setbacks, and demands, not from blissful, conflict-free, smooth sailing" (p. 279). Vohs, Aaker, and Catapano (2019) reviewed the research literature on negative experiences and found that these experiences have the potential to add greater meaning to life by activating cognitive processes related to comprehension and understanding. Eliminating the negative from life deprives us of the opportunity to grow through the

struggle. Wong (2011) reminds us that "too much emphasis on positive affect as the answer to all ills can be counterproductive because negative emotions, such as guilt, regret, frustration, and anger, can all motivate us toward positive change" (p. 70). Ahmed (2010) argues in favor of unhappiness as a spur that drives us to make revolutionary changes in society. In chapter twenty-two, we saw how guilt and even shame when correctly employed foster well-being and good relationships. In a review of the literature on the topic, Hess (2014) shows us that anger has a positive side as well, bestowing multiple cognitive, emotional, and social benefits when experienced and expressed correctly. In chapter eight we took a look at acceptance and commitment therapy, which is grounded in the idea that suffering is a part of normal life, and in chapter twenty-three, we even looked at the positive psychology of death. If suffering and death are an inextricable part of the human condition (this side of the eschaton, anyway), then part of living well includes knowing how to suffer and die well. As we've seen, very few positive psychologists are working on this.

If this unwillingness to integrate negative phenomena into our understanding of the good life is a product of Western modernity's cultural blind spots, then the second major theme in second wave positive psychology offers another bit of hope. This second theme is an attempt to correct mainstream positive psychology's West-centric bias by paying attention to other cultures in developing our understanding of flourishing.

As we saw in chapter two, Paul Wong has been working on this project for over a decade, describing what positive psychology would look like if it grew from the Confucian-Taoist-Buddhist soil of Chinese thought about the good life (Wong, 2009). A Chinese positive psychology would bring together the positive and the negative by starting from the beliefs that suffering is unavoidable, that much of life is uncontrollable, and that sometimes group harmony is more important than individual success, producing a vision of the good life in which virtues like acceptance, endurance, transcendence, flexibility, and responsibility are central to becoming a highly functioning person. Rao and Paranjpe (2016), in a section of their book about psychology in India, point to some parallels between mainstream positive psychology and Indian ideas about the good life, including altruism, the cultivation of the person so as to overcome the causes of suffering, and the powerful importance of meaning. However, they also argue that positive psychology pays insufficient attention to self-transcendence and the necessity of morality and that Indian psychology would include an emphasis on what happens between people as equally valid as what happens within the individual, as well as a willingness to look directly at the existential realities of the human condition. Marecek and Christopher (2018) contrast the vision of well-being that dominates mainstream positive psychology with conceptualizations of well-being in South Asia and Southeast Asia. The future for second wave positive psychology involves recognizing that Western individualist notions of the self and flourishing are not value-neutral statements of objective fact and also allowing psychologists from other cultures to have their own voices.

Does that inclusion of other voices include religious voices? Recall the material in chapter twenty-one about the difficulty distinguishing between religion and nonreligion. Outside of Western modernity the distinction makes little sense, as we have already seen with Wong's (2009) description of a Chinese positive psychology having religious roots. Similarly, Rao and Paranjpe (2016) present an Indian psychology that cannot be disconnected from Hindu ideas about the human condition. So a crosscultural positive psychology will already include religious ideas. We can already find psychologists drawing ideas about mental health from Muslim (Husain, 1998) and Buddhist (Sundararajan, 2005a) beliefs about the human condition.

Hill and Hall (2018) point to the unavoidable embeddedness of theories of flourishing in foundational beliefs about the human condition, arguing that the future of positive psychology is that it be reframed as "positive psychologies" (plural) in which "the socially constructed frameworks of worldviews are something not to be ignored or avoided, but rather embraced as theoretical frameworks that can account for the goodness and the unity of character" (p. 259). Perhaps this is the best way forward for us; rather than trying to force positive psychology to be a single school of thought united by a common vision of the good life, we embrace Peterson and Park's (2003) description of positive psychology as an "umbrella term" encompassing a plurality of schools of thought united only by our interest in human flourishing. In future works by positive psychologists, we might see a chapter on Buddhist positive psychology, a chapter on Aristotelian positive psychology, a chapter on Muslim positive psychology, a chapter on existential positive psychology, and a chapter on Christian positive psychology.

CHRISTIAN POSITIVE PSYCHOLOGY: WE WERE SECOND WAVE BEFORE SECOND WAVE WAS COOL

A few years ago I did a podcast interview with Mark McMinn, author of *The Science of Virtue* (McMinn, 2017), and we got to talking about the relationship between positive psychology and the church. He made the very good point that Christianity will likely always be on the margins of the positive psychology movement and that we should focus less on reforming the entire field and more on being faithful where we are. That may have been his Anabaptist roots showing through, but it lines up perfectly with the agenda of psychologists like Hill and Hall (2018). If second wave positive psychology will be about a plurality of voices explicitly speaking from differing pretheoretical viewpoints about the human condition, then all Christian positive psychologists really need is a metaphorical seat at the equally metaphorical table so we can go about our business of investigating the nature of flourishing and the conditions that help or hinder that process, guided by our theological notions about human nature and the good life.

It seems that those of us who have been working on constructing a Christian positive psychology have been doing second wave positive psychology all along. Despite the fact that Western Christians have been marinating in the cultural sauce of individualism our whole lives (Taylor,

2007), a biblically informed and theologically literate view of humanity provides us with resources for pushing back against the self-centeredness of Western modernity. As we saw in chapter three, the telos of human life is not to be found within ourselves (Hackney, 2007). Our true nature is inherently relational (Grenz, 2001), and as fallen creatures, we have hearts that are too corrupted to let "follow your heart" be an acceptable moral or psychological principle (Hackney, 2014). Christians can serve as a counterweight to the "Big Me" (McMinn, 2017) of mainstream Western positive psychology, especially as we are joined by an increasing number of non-Western theologians and biblical scholars who are speaking from their own perspectives about God and the Christian life (e.g., Chan, 2014). Christian ideas about the correct ways to experience and make use of negatively valenced phenomena such as guilt, repentance, sorrow, self-denial, anger, humility, and death also allow us to be a valuable voice for the role that the negative plays in flourishing.

So, in this way, this book has itself been an extended exercise in second wave positive psychology, as well as an attempt at presenting a Christian perspective on the positive psychology movement. Recent developments in this movement present us with a vast expanse of unexplored territory, and there is much more for us to talk about. In addition to the matters we have covered in this volume, positive psychologists are working in areas such as posttraumatic growth, humility, creativity, positive lifespan development, and a panoply of areas of application that we simply did not have space to adequately cover in this text.

And the task of developing an authentically Christian approach to positive psychology has only begun.

Suggestions for Further Reading

Ivtzan, I., Lomas, T., Hefferon, K., & Worth, P. (2016). *Second wave positive psychology: Embracing the dark side of life.* Routledge.

Kashdan, T. B., & Biswas-Diener, R. (2014). *The upside of your dark side.* Hudson Street Press.

Linley, P. A., Joseph, S., Harrington, S., & Wood, A. M. (2006). Positive psychology: Past, present, and (possible) future. *Journal of Positive Psychology, 1*(1), 3-16.

Parrott, W. G. (Ed.). (2014). *The positive side of negative emotions.* Guilford Press.

Wong, P. T. P. (2011). Positive psychology 2.0: Towards a balanced interactive model of the good life. *Canadian Psychology, 52*(2), 69-81.

REFERENCES

Abramson, L. Y., Seligman, M. E. P., & Teasdale, J. D. (1978). Learned helplessness in humans: Critique and reformulation. *Journal of Abnormal Psychology, 87*(1), 49-74.

Abuhamdeh, S., & Csikszentmihalyi, M. (2009). Intrinsic and extrinsic motivation orientations in the competitive context: An examination of person-situation interactions. *Journal of Personality, 77*(5), 1615-35.

Achor, S. (2010). *The happiness advantage: The seven principles of positive psychology that fuel success and performance at work.* Crown Business.

Acker, M., & Davis, M. H. (1992). Intimacy, passion and commitment in adult romantic relationships: A test of the triangular theory of love. *Journal of Social and Personal Relationships, 9*(1), 21-50.

Aczel, B. (2019). Low levels of wisdom: Foolishness. In R. J. Sternberg & J. Glück (Eds.), *Cambridge handbook of wisdom* (pp. 483-99). Cambridge University Press.

Adams, V. H., Snyder, C. R., Rand, K. L., O'Donnell, E. A., Sigmon, D. R., & Pulvers, K. M. (2010). Hope in the workplace. In R. A. Giacalone & C. L. Jurkiewicz (Eds.), *Handbook of workplace spirituality and organizational performance* (2nd ed.) (pp. 367-77). M. E. Sharpe.

Adie, J. W., Duda, J. L., & Ntoumanis, N. (2012). Perceived coach-autonomy support, basic need satisfaction and the well- and ill-being of elite youth soccer players: A longitudinal investigation. *Psychology of Sport and Exercise, 13*(1), 51-59.

Aelred of Rievaulx. (1977). *Spiritual friendship* (M. E. Laker, Trans.). Cistercian Publications. (Original work published 1167)

Ahmed, E., Harris, N., Braithwaite, J., & Braithwaite, V. (2001). *Shame management through reintegration.* Cambridge University press.

Ahmed, S. (2010). *The promise of happiness.* Duke University Press.

Ahuvia, A. (2001). Well-being in cultures of choice: A cross-cultural perspective. *American Psychologist, 56*(1), 77-78.

Al-Mabuk, R. H., Enright, R. D., & Cardis, P. A. (1995). Forgiveness education with parentally love-deprived late adolescents. *Journal of Moral Education, 24*(4), 427-44.

Alarcon, G., Eschleman, K. J., & Bowling, N. A. (2009). Relationships between personality variables and burnout: A meta-analysis. *Work & Stress, 23*(3), 244-63.

Alberts, J. K. (1992). An inferential/strategic explanation for the social organisation of teases. *Journal of Language and Social Psychology, 11*(3), 153-77.

Albrecht, F. M. (1970). A reappraisal of faculty psychology. *Journal of the History of the Behavioral Sciences, 6*(1), 36-40.

Algoe, S. B. (2012). Find, remind, and bind: The functions of gratitude in everyday relationships. *Social and Personality Psychology Compass, 6*(6), 455-69.

Algoe, S. B., Gable, S. L., & Maisel, N. C. (2010). It's the little things: Everyday gratitude as a booster shot for romantic relationships. *Personal Relationships, 17*(2), 217-33.

Algoe, S. B., Haidt, J., & Gable, S. L. (2008). Beyond reciprocity: Gratitude and relationships in everyday life. *Emotion, 8*(3), 425-29.

Allen, D. (1997). Ascetic theology and psychology. In R. C. Roberts & M. R. Talbot (Eds.), *Limning the psyche: Explorations in Christian psychology* (pp. 297-316). Eerdmans.

Allison, S. T. (2016). The initiation of heroism science. *Heroism Science, 1*(1), 1-9.

Allison, S. T., Goethals, G. R., & Kramer, R. M. (Eds.). (2017). *Handbook of heroism and heroic leadership.* Routledge.

Allport, G. W. (1921). Personality and character. *Psychological Bulletin, 18*(9), 441-55.

Allport, G. W. (1937). *Personality: A psychological interpretation.* Henry Holt.

Allport, G. W. (1950). *The individual and his religion.* Macmillan.

Allport, G. W. (1955). *Becoming: Basic considerations for a psychology of personality.* Yale University Press.

Allport, G. W. (1961). *Pattern and growth in personality.* Holt, Rinehart and Winston.

Allport, G. W. (1978). *Waiting for the Lord: 33 meditations on God and man* (P. A. Bertocci, Ed.). Macmillan.

Allport, G. W., & Ross, J. M. (1967). Personal religious orientation and prejudice. *Journal of Personality and Social Psychology, 5*(4), 432-43.

Allport, G. W., & Vernon, P. E. (1930). The field of personality. *Psychological Bulletin, 27*(10), 677-730.

American Psychiatric Association. (2013). *Diagnostic and statistical manual of mental disorders* (5th ed.).

American Psychological Association. (2017). *Ethical principals of psychologists and code of conduct.* www.apa.org/ethics/code

Ames, W. (1968). *The marrow of theology* (J. D. Eusden, Trans.). Baker Books. (Original work published 1629)

Anderson, A. R., & Fowers, B. J. (2020). An exploratory study of friendship characteristics and their relations with hedonic and eudaimonic well-being. *Journal of Social and Personal Relationships, 37*(1), 260-80.

Anderson, N. D., Lau, M. A., Segal, Z. V., & Bishop, S. R. (2007). Mindfulness-based stress reduction and attentional control. *Clinical Psychology and Psychotherapy, 14*(6), 449-63.

Anderson, N. H. (1968). Likableness ratings of 555 personality-trait words. *Journal of Personality and Social Psychology, 9*(3), 272-79.

Anglo, S. (2000). *The martial arts of renaissance Europe.* Yale University Press.

Ardelt, M. (2008). Wisdom, religiosity, purpose in life, and death attitudes of aging adults. In A. Tomer, G. T. Eliason, & P. T. P. Wong (Eds.), *Existential and spiritual issues in death attitudes* (pp. 65-87). Lawrence Erlbaum Associates.

Argyle, M. (1999). Causes and correlates of happiness. In D. Kahneman, E. Diener, & N. Schwartz (Eds.), *Well-being: The foundations of hedonic psychology.* Russell Sage Foundation.

Arnold, K. A., Turner, N., Barling, J., Kelloway, E. K., & McKee, M. C. (2007). Transformational leadership and psychological well-being: The mediating role of meaningful work. *Journal of Occupational Health Psychology, 12*(3), 193.

Asakawa, K. (2004). Flow experience and autotelic personality in Japanese college students: How do they experience challenges in daily life? *Journal of Happiness Studies, 5*(2), 123-54.

Asch, S. E. (1955). Opinions and social pressure. *Scientific American, 193*(5), 31-35.

Asch, S. E. (1956). Studies of independence and conformity: I. A minority of one against a unanimous majority. *Psychological Monographs: General and Applied, 7*(9), 1-70.

Ashford, S. J., & Tsui, A. S. (1991). Self-regulation for managerial effectiveness: The role of active feedback seeking. *Academy of Management Journal, 34*(2), 251-80.

Aspinwall, L. G., & Staudinger, U. M. (2003). A psychology of human strengths: Some central issues of an emerging field. In L. G. Aspinwall & U. M. Staudinger (Eds.), *A psychology of human strengths: Fundamental questions and future directions for a positive psychology* (pp. 9-22). American Psychological Association.

Aspinwall, L. G., & Tedeschi, R. G. (2010). The value of positive psychology for health psychology: Progress and pitfalls in examining the relation of positive phenomena to health. *Annals of Behavioral Medicine, 39*(1), 4-15.

Astin, J. A. (1997). Stress reduction through mindfulness meditation: Effects on psychological symptomatology, sense of control, and spiritual experiences. *Psychotherapy and Psychosomatics, 66*(2), 97-106.

Averill, J. R., & More, T. A. (2000). Happiness. In M. Lewis & J. M. Haviland-Jones (Eds.), *Handbook of emotions, second edition* (pp. 663-76). Guilford Press.

Avolio, B. J., & Gardner, W. L. (2005). Authentic leadership development: Getting to the root of positive forms of leadership. *The Leadership Quarterly, 16*(3), 315-38.

Ayduk, O., & Mischel, W. (2002). When smart people behave stupidly: Reconciling inconsistencies in social-emotional intelligence. In R. J. Sternberg (Ed.), *Why smart people can be so stupid* (pp. 86-105). Yale University Press.

Baer, R. A., & Lykins, E. L. M. (2011). Mindfulness and positive psychological functioning. In K. M. Sheldon, T. B. Kashdan, & M. F. Steger (Eds.), *Designing positive psychology: Taking stock and moving forward* (pp. 335-48). Oxford University Press.

Bahrke, M. S., & Morgan, W. P. (1978). Anxiety reduction following exercise and meditation. *Cognitive Therapy and Research, 2*(4), 323-33.

Baker, W. (2004). *The books of James & First and Second Peter: Faith, suffering, and knowledge.* AMG Publishers.

Baker, W. J. (2007). *Playing with God: Religion and modern sport.* Harvard University Press.

Bakker, A. B. (2005). Flow among music teachers and their students: The crossover of peak experiences. *Journal of Vocational Behavior, 66*(1), 26-44.

Bakker, A. B. (2008). The work-related flow inventory: Construction and initial validation of the WOLF. *Journal of Vocational Behavior, 72*(3), 400-414.

Bakker, A. B., Oerlemans, W., Demerouti, E., Slot, B. B., & Ali, D. K. (2011). Flow and performance: A study among talented Dutch soccer players. *Psychology of Sport and Exercise, 12*(4), 442-50.

Balswick, J. O., King, P. E., & Reimer, K. S. (2016). *The reciprocating self: Human development in theological perspective* (2nd ed.). IVP Academic.

Baltes, P. B., Glück, J., & Kunzmann, U. (2005). Wisdom: Its structure and function in regulating successful life span development. In C. R. Snyder & S. J. Lopez (Eds.), *Handbook of positive psychology* (pp. 327-50). Oxford University Press.

Baltes, P. B., & Smith, J. (1990). Toward a psychology of wisdom and its ontogenesis. In R. J. Sternberg (Ed.), *Wisdom: Its nature, origins, and development* (pp. 87-120). Cambridge University Press.

Baltes, P. B., Staudinger, U. M., Maercker, A., & Smith, J. (1995). People nominated as wise: A comparative study of wisdom-related knowledge. *Psychology and Aging, 10*(2), 155-66.

Bandura, A. (1973). *Aggression: A social learning analysis.* Prentice-Hall.

Bandura, A. (1997). *Self-efficacy: The exercise of control.* Freeman.

Barak, A. (1990). Counselor training in empathy by a game procedure. *Counselor Education and Supervision, 29*(3), 170-86.

Barber, L. K., Munz, D. C., Bagsby, P. G., & Powell, E. D. (2010). Sleep consistency and sufficiency: Are both necessary for less psychological strain? *Stress and Health, 26*(3), 186-93.

Barbuto, J. E., Jr., & Wheeler, D. W. (2006). Scale development and construct clarification of servant leadership. *Group & Organization Management, 31*(3), 300-26.

Barclay, J. (2015). *Paul and the gift.* Eerdmans.

Barling, J., Weber, T., & Kelloway, E. K. (1996). Effects of transformational leadership training on attitudinal and financial outcomes: A field experiment. *Journal of Applied Psychology, 81*(6), 827.

Barnum, D. D., Snyder, C. R., Rapoff, M. A., Mani, M. M., & Thompson, R. (1998). Hope and social

support in the psychological adjustment of pediatric burn survivors and matched controls. *Children's Health Care, 27*(1), 15-30.

Barrett, E. B. (1916). *Strength of will.* P. J. Kennedy & Sons.

Barth, K. (1961). *Church dogmatics: Vol. 3.4. The doctrine of creation* (A. T. Mackay, T. H. L. Parker, H. Knight, H. A. Kennedy, & J. Marks, Trans.; G. W. Bromiley & T. F. Torrance, Eds.). Hendrickson.

Bartholomew, K., & Horowitz, L. (1991). Attachment styles among young adults: A test of a four-category model. *Journal of Personality and Social Psychology, 61*(2), 226-44.

Bartholomew, K. J., Ntoumanis, N., Ryan, R. M., Bosch, J. A., & Thøgersen-Ntoumani, C. (2011). Self-determination theory and diminished functioning: The role of interpersonal control and psychological need thwarting. *Personality and Social Psychology Bulletin, 37*(11), 1459-73.

Bartholomew, K. J., Ntoumanis, N., & Thøgersen-Ntoumani, C. (2009). A review of controlling motivational strategies from a self-determination theory perspective: Implications for sports coaches. *International Review of Sport and Exercise Psychology, 2*(2), 215-33.

Bartlett, M. Y., & DeSteno, D. (2006). Gratitude and prosocial behavior: Helping when it costs you. *Psychological Science, 17*(4), 319-25.

Bartolo, A., Benuzzi, F., Nocetti, L., Baraldi, P., & Nichelli, P. (2006). Humor comprehension and appreciation: An fMRI study. *Journal of Cognitive Neuroscience, 18*(11), 1789-98.

Barton, B., & Hardesty, C. L. (2010). Spirituality and stripping: Exotic dancers narrate the body ekstasis. *Symbolic Interaction, 33*(2), 280-96.

Bartone, P. T. (1989). Predictors of stress-related illness in city bus drivers. *Journal of Occupational Medicine, 31*(8), 857-63.

Bartone, P. T. (1998). *Stress, hardiness & symptoms in Bosnia deployed soldiers.* [Paper Presentation]. American Psychological Association Convention, San Francisco, CA, United States.

Bartone, P. T. (1999). Hardiness protects against war-related stress in Army Reserve forces. *Consulting Psychology Journal: Practice and Research, 51*(2), 72-82.

Bartone, P. T., Eid, J., Helge Johnsen, B., Christian Laberg, J., & Snook, S. A. (2009). Big five personality factors, hardiness, and social judgment as predictors of leader performance. *Leadership & Organization Development Journal, 30*(6), 498-521.

Bartone, P. T., Eid, J., Hystad, S. W., Jocoy, K., Laberg, J. C., & Johnsen, B. H. (2015). Psychological hardiness and avoidance coping are related to risky alcohol use in returning combat veterans. *Military Behavioral Health, 3*(4), 274-82.

Bartone, P. T., Kelly, D. R., & Matthews, M. D. (2013). Psychological hardiness predicts adaptability in military leaders: A prospective study. *International Journal of Selection and Assessment, 21*(2), 200-210.

Bartone, P. T., Roland, R. R., Picano, J. J., & Williams, T. J. (2008). Psychological hardiness predicts success in US Army Special Forces candidates. *International Journal of Selection and Assessment, 16*(2), 78-81.

Bash, A. (2007). *Forgiveness and Christian ethics.* Cambridge University Press.

Baskin, T. W., & Enright, R. D. (2004). Intervention studies on forgiveness: A meta-analysis. *Journal of Counseling & Development, 82*(1), 79-90.

Bass, B. M. (1999). Two decades of research and development in transformational leadership. *European Journal of Work and Organizational Psychology, 8*(1), 9-32.

Bass, B. M., & Riggio, R. E. (2006). *Transformational leadership* (2nd ed.). Lawrence Erlbaum Associates.

Batson, C. D. (1976). Religion as prosocial: Agent or double agent? *Journal for the Scientific Study of Religion, 15*(1), 29-45.

Batson, C. D. (1991). *The altruism question: Toward a social-psychological answer.* Lawrence Erlbaum Associates.

Batson, C. D., & Ahmad, N. (2001). Empathy-induced altruism in a prisoner's dilemma II: What if the target of empathy has defected? *European Journal of Social Psychology, 31*(1), 25-36.

Batson, C. D., Ahmad, N., & Lishner, D. A. (2009). Empathy and altruism. In S. J. Snyder & C. R. Snyder (Eds.), *Oxford handbook of positive psychology* (pp. 417-26). Oxford University Press.

Batson, C. D., Klein, T. R., Highberger, L., & Shaw, L. L. (1995). Immorality from empathy-induced altruism: When compassion and justice conflict. *Journal of Personality and Social Psychology, 68*(6), 1042-54.

Batson, C. D., Lishner, D. A., Carpenter, A., Dulin, L., Harjusola-Webb, S., Stocks, E. L., Gale, S.,

Hassan, O., & Sampat, B. (2003). " . . . As you would have them do unto you": Does imagining yourself in the other's place stimulate moral action? *Personality and Social Psychology Bulletin, 29*(9), 1190-1201.

Batson, C. D., & Raynor-Prince, L. (1983). Religious orientation and complexity of thought about existential concerns. *Journal for the Scientific Study of Religion, 22*(1), 38-50.

Batson, C. D., & Shaw, L. L. (1991). Evidence for altruism: Toward a pluralism of prosocial motives. *Psychological Inquiry, 2*(2), 107-22.

Batthyany, A., & Russo-Netzer, P. (Eds.). (2014). *Meaning in positive and existential psychology.* Springer.

Bauer, S. W., & Wise, J. (2016). *The well-trained mind* (4th ed.). W. W. Norton.

Baumeister, R. F. (1991). *Meanings of life.* Guilford Press.

Baumeister, R. F. (1998). The self. In D. T. Gilbert, S. T. Fiske, & G. Lindzey (Eds.), *The handbook of social psychology* (pp. 680-740). McGraw-Hill.

Baumeister, R. F., & Alquist, J. L. (2009). Is there a downside to good self-control? *Self and Identity, 8*(2-3), 115-30.

Baumeister, R. F., Bratslavsky, E., Muraven, M., & Tice, D. M. (1998). Ego depletion: Is the active self a limited resource? *Journal of Personality and Social Psychology, 74*(5), 1252-65.

Baumeister, R. F., Campbell, J. D., Krueger, J. I., & Vohs, K. D. (2003). Does high self-esteem cause better performance, interpersonal success, happiness, or healthier lifestyles? *Psychological Science in the Public Interest, 4*(1), 1-44.

Baumeister, R. F., & Exline, J. J. (1999). Virtue, personality, and social relations: Self-control as the moral muscle. *Journal of Personality, 67*(6), 1165-94.

Baumeister, R. F., Exline, J. J., & Sommer, K. L. (1998). The victim role, grudge theory, and two dimensions of forgiveness. In E. L. Worthington Jr. (Ed.), *Dimensions of forgiveness: Psychological research & theological perspectives* (pp. 79-106). Templeton Foundation Press.

Baumeister, R. F., Gailliot, M., DeWall, C. N., & Oaten, M. (2006). Self-regulation and personality: How interventions increase regulatory success, and how depletion moderates the effects of traits on behavior. *Journal of Personality, 74*(6), 1773-802.

Baumeister, R. F., & Leary, M. R. (1995). The need to belong: Desire for interpersonal attachments as a fundamental human motivation. *Psychological Bulletin, 117*(3), 497-529.

Baumeister, R. F., Smart, L., & Boden, J. M. (1996). Relation of threatened egotism to violence and aggression: The dark side of high self-esteem. *Psychological Review, 103*(1), 5-33.

Baumeister, R. F., Tice, D. M., & Vohs, K. D. (2018). The strength model of self-regulation: Conclusions from the second decade of willpower research. *Perspectives on Psychological Science, 13*(2), 141-45.

Baumeister, R. F., & Tierney, J. (2011). *Willpower: Rediscovering the greatest human strength.* Penguin.

Baumeister, R. F., & Vohs, K. D. (2005). The pursuit of meaningfulness in life. In C. R. Snyder & S. J. Lopez (Eds.), *Handbook of positive psychology* (pp. 608-18). Oxford University Press.

Baumeister, R. F., Vohs, K. D., Aaker, J. L., & Garbinsky, E. N. (2013). Some key differences between a happy life and a meaningful life. *Journal of Positive Psychology, 8*(6), 505-16.

Baumsteiger, R., Mangan, S., Bronk, K. C., & Bono, G. (2019). An integrative intervention for cultivating gratitude among adolescents and young adults. *Journal of Positive Psychology, 14*(6), 807-19.

Bavinck, H. (2008). *Reformed dogmatics: Vol. 4. Holy Spirit, church, and new creation* (J. Bolt, Ed., J. Vriend, Trans.). Baker Academic. (Original work published 1899)

Baylus, N. (2004). Teaching positive psychology. In P. A. Linley & S. Joseph (Eds.), *Positive psychology in practice* (pp. 210-17). John Wiley & Sons.

Beaman, A. L., Barnes, P. J., Klentz, B., & Mcquirk, B. (1978). Increasing helping rates through information dissemination: Teaching pays. *Personality and Social Psychology Bulletin, 4*(3), 406-11.

Beck, R., Baker, L., Robbins, M., & Dow, S. (2001). A second look at quest motivation: Is quest unidimensional or multidimensional? *Journal of Psychology and Theology, 29*(2), 148-57.

Beck, R., & Jessup, R. K. (2004). The multidimensional nature of quest motivation. *Journal of Psychology and Theology, 32*(4), 283-94.

Beck, R., & Miller, C. D. (2000). Religiosity and agency and communion: Their relationship to religious judgmentalism. *Journal of Psychology, 134*(3), 315-24.

Becker, D., & Marecek, J. (2008). Dreaming the American dream: Individualism and positive psychology. *Social and Personality Psychology Compass, 2*(5), 1767-80.

Becker, E. (1973). *The denial of death.* Simon & Schuster.

Becker, H. S., & Geer, B. (1960). Latent culture: A note on the theory of latent social roles. *Administrative Science Quarterly, 5*(2), 304-13.

Beedie, C. J., & Lane, A. M. (2012). The role of glucose in self-control: Another look at the evidence and an alternative conceptualization. *Personality and Social Psychology Review, 16*(2), 143-53.

Bellah, R. N., Madsen, R., Sullivan, W. M., Swidler, A., & Tipton, S. M. (1985). *Habits of the heart: Individualism and commitment in American life.* University of California Press.

Beller, J. M., & Stoll, S. K. (1995). Moral reasoning of high school student athletes and general students: An empirical study versus personal testimony. *Pediatric Exercise Science, 7*(4), 352-63.

Ben-Shlomo, Y., Smith, G. D., Shipley, M., & Marmot, M. G. (1993). Magnitude and causes of mortality differences between married and unmarried men. *Journal of Epidemiology & Community Health, 47*(3), 200-205.

Bender, K., Thompson, S. J., McManus, H., Lantry, J., & Flynn, P. M. (2007). Capacity for survival: Exploring strengths of homeless street youth. *Child and Youth Care Forum, 36*(1), 25-42.

Bennett, D. S., Sullivan, M. W., & Lewis, M. (2005). Young children's adjustment as a function of maltreatment, shame, and anger. *Child Maltreatment, 10*(4), 311-23.

Benton, D. (1990). The impact of increasing blood glucose on psychological functioning. *Biological Psychology, 30*(1), 13-19.

Benton, D., Brett, V., & Brain, P. F. (1987). Glucose improves attention and reaction to frustration in children. *Biological Psychology, 24*(2), 95-100.

Benware, C. A., & Deci, E. L. (1984) Quality of learning with an active versus passive motivational set. *American Educational Research Journal, 21*(4), 755-65.

Bereczkei, T., Birkas, B., & Kerekes, Z. (2010). The presence of others, prosocial traits, Machiavellianism: A person x situation approach. *Social Psychology, 41*, 238-45.

Bergeman, C. S., Plomin, R., Pedersen, N. L., & McClearn, G. E. (1991). Genetic mediation of the relationship between social support and psychological well-being. *Psychology and Aging, 6*(4), 640-46.

Berger, B. G., & Motl, R. W. (2000). Exercise and mood: A selective review and synthesis of research employing the profile of mood states. *Journal of Applied Sport Psychology, 12*(1), 69-92.

Bergin, A. E. (1991). Values and religious issues in psychotherapy and mental health. *American Psychologist, 46*(4), 394-403.

Berk, L. S., Tan, S. A., Napier, B. J., & Eby, W. C. (1989). Eustress of mirthful laughter modifies natural killer cell activity. *Clinical Research, 37*(1), 115A.

Berkhof, H. (1986). *Christian faith* (rev. ed.) (S. Woudstra, Trans.). Eerdmans.

Berkouwer, G. C. (1952). *Faith and sanctification.* Eerdmans.

Bernt, F. M. (1989). Being religious and being altruistic: A study of college service volunteers. *Personality and Individual Differences, 10*(6), 663-69.

Berry, J. W., & Worthington, E. L., Jr. (2001). Forgivingness, relationship quality, stress while imagining relationship events, and physical and mental health. *Journal of Counseling Psychology, 48*(4), 447-55.

Berry, J. W., Worthington, E. L., Jr., Parrott, L., III, O'Connor, L. E., & Wade, N. G. (2001). Dispositional forgivingness: Development and construct validity of the Transgression Narrative Test of Forgivingness (TNTF). *Personality and Social Psychology Bulletin, 27*(10), 1277-90.

Berscheid, E. (2003). The human's greatest strength: Other humans. In L. S. Aspinwall & U. M. Staudinger (Eds.), *A psychology of human strengths: Fundamental questions and future directions for a positive psychology* (pp. 37-48). American Psychological Association.

Bibby, R. W. (1983). Searching for invisible thread: Meaning systems in contemporary Canada. *Journal for the Scientific Study of Religion, 22*(2), 101-19.

Biddle, S. J. H. (2000). Emotion, mood, and physical activity. In S. J. H. Biddle, K. R. Fox, & S. H. Boutcher (Eds.), *Physical activity and psychological well-being* (pp. 63-87). Routledge.

Biddle, S. J. H., & Mutri, N. (2008). *Psychology of physical activity: Determinants, well-being and interventions (2nd ed.).* Routledge.

Birren, J. E., & Fisher, L. M. (1990). The elements of wisdom: Overview and integration. In R. J. Sternberg (Ed.), *Wisdom: Its nature, origins, and development* (pp. 317-32). Cambridge University Press.

Birrer, D., Röthlin, P., & Morgan, G. (2012). Mindfulness to enhance athletic performance: Theoretical considerations and possible impact mechanisms. *Mindfulness, 3*(3), 235-46.

Biswas-Diener, R. (2008). Material wealth and subjective well-being. In M. Eid & R. J. Larsen (Eds.), *The science of subjective well-being* (pp. 307-22). Guilford Press.

Biswas-Diener, R. (2009). Diener, Ed. In S. J. Lopez (Ed.), *The encyclopedia of positive psychology* (pp. 287-288). Blackwell Publishing.

Biswas-Diener, R. (2012). *The courage quotient.* Jossey-Bass.

Biswas-Diener, R., Vittersø, J., & Diener, E. J. (2005). Most people are pretty happy, but there is cultural variation: The Inughuit, the Amish, and the Maasai. *Journal of Happiness Studies, 6*(3), 205-26.

Bjørnskov, C. (2012). Wellbeing and size of government. In P. Booth (Ed.), *. . . And the pursuit of happiness* (pp. 160-78). Institute of Economic Affairs.

Blackie, L. E., Cozzolino, P. J., & Sedikides, C. (2016). Specific and individuated death reflection fosters identity integration. *PloS one, 11*(5), e0154873.

Blocher, H. (1997). *Original sin: Illuminating the riddle.* Eerdmans.

Blumenthal, J. A., Babyak, M. A., Moore, K. A., Craighead, W. E., Herman, S., Khatri, P., . . . & Doraiswamy, P. M. (1999). Effects of exercise training on older patients with major depression. *Archives of Internal Medicine, 159*(19), 2349-56.

Boa, K. (2001). *Conformed to his image: Biblical and practical approaches to spiritual formation.* Zondervan.

Bodhi, B. (2011). What does mindfulness really mean? A canonical perspective. *Contemporary Buddhism, 12*(1), 19-39.

Boecker, H., & Dishman, R. K. (2013). Physical activity and reward: The role of endogenous opioids. In P. Ekkekakis (Ed.), *Routledge handbook of physical activity and mental health* (pp. 57-70). Routledge.

Boecker, H., Sprenger, T., Spilker, M. E., Henriksen, G., Koppenhoefer, M., Wagner, K. J., . . . & Tolle, T. R. (2008). The runner's high: Opioidergic mechanisms in the human brain. *Cerebral Cortex, 18*(11), 2523-31.

Bohart, A. C., & Greening, T. (2001). Humanistic psychology and positive psychology. *American Psychologist, 56*(1), 81-82.

Boice, J. M. (1986). *Foundations of the Christian faith* (rev. ed.). IVP Academic.

Bolt, M. (1978). Purpose in life and death concern. *Journal of Genetic Psychology, 132*(1), 159-60.

Bolt, M. (2004). *Pursuing human strengths: A positive psychology guide*. Worth Publishers.

Bolter, N. D., & Weiss, M. R. (2013). Coaching behaviors and adolescent athletes' sportspersonship outcomes: Further validation of the Sportsmanship Coaching Behaviors Scale (SCBS). *Sport, Exercise, and Performance Psychology, 2*(1), 32-47.

Bonnes, M., Lee, T., & Bonaiuto, M. (2003). Theory and practice in environmental psychology: An introduction. In M. Bonnes, T. Lee, & M. Bonaiuto (Eds.), *Psychological theories for environmental issues* (pp. 1-26). Routledge.

Bono, G., Froh, J. J., Disabato, D., Blalock, D., McKnight, P., & Bausert, S. (2019). Gratitude's role in adolescent antisocial and prosocial behavior: A 4-year longitudinal investigation. *The Journal of Positive Psychology, 14*(2), 230-243.

Bono, G., & McCullough, M. E. (2006). Positive responses to benefit and harm: Bringing forgiveness and gratitude into cognitive psychotherapy. *Journal of Cognitive Psychotherapy, 20*(2), 147-57.

Booth, P. (Ed.). (2012). . . . *And the pursuit of happiness*. The Institute of Economic Affairs.

Booth-Kewley, S., & Friedman, H. S. (1987). Psychological predictors of heart disease: A quantitative review. *Psychological Bulletin, 101*(3), 343-62.

Borgatta, E. F., Bales, R. F., & Couch, A. S. (1954). Some findings relevant to the great man theory of leadership. *American Sociological Review, 19*(6), 755-59.

Boulos, D., & Zamorski, M. A. (2013). Deployment-related mental disorders among Canadian Forces personnel deployed in support of the mission in Afghanistan, 2001–2008. *Canadian Medical Association Journal, 185*(11), E545-52.

Bourgeault, C. (2004). *Centering prayer and inner awakening*. Cowley Publications.

Bowlby, J. (1969). *Attachment and loss: Vol. 1. Attachment*. Basic Books.

Bowman, P., Furlong, M. J., Shochet, I., Lilles, E., & Jones, C. (2009). Optimism and the school context. In R. Gilman, E. S. Huebner, & M. J. Furlong (Eds.), *Handbook of positive psychology in schools* (pp. 51-64). Routledge.

Boyce, C. J., Daly, M., Hounkpatin, H. O., & Wood, A. M. (2017). Money may buy happiness, but often so little that it doesn't matter. *Psychological Science, 28*(4), 544-46.

Bradfield, M., & Aquino, K. (1999). The effects of blame attributions and offender likableness on forgiveness and revenge in the workplace. *Journal of Management, 25*(5), 607-31.

Braithwaite, J. (1989). *Crime, shame, and reintegration*. Cambridge University Press.

Brassard, A., & Johnson, S. M. (2016). Couple and family therapy: An attachment perspective. In J. Cassidy & P. R. Shaver (Eds.), *Handbook of attachment: Theory, research, and clinical applications* (3rd ed.) (pp. 805-823). Guilford Press.

Brazil, D. M. (2013). Comprehensive soldier fitness. In B. A. Moore & J. E. Barnett (Eds.), *Military psychologist's desk reference* (pp. 96-99). Oxford University Press.

Brehm, S. S., & Brehm, J. W. (1981). *Psychological reactance: A theory of freedom and control*. Academic Press.

Bretherton, I. (1992). The origins of attachment theory: John Bowlby and Mary Ainsworth. *Developmental Psychology, 28*(5), 759-75.

Breuer, J., & Freud, S. (1895). *Studies on hysteria* (J. Strachey, Trans.). Basic Books.

Brickman, P., Coates, D., & Janoff-Bulman, R. (1978). Lottery winners and accident victims: Is happiness relative? *Journal of Personality and Social Psychology, 36*(8), 917-27.

Briggs Myers, I., McCoulley, M. H., Quenk, N. L., & Hammer, A. L. (2003). *MBTI manual* (3rd ed.). CPP Inc.

Briggs Myers, I., & Myers, P. B. (1995). *Gifts differing: Understanding personality type*. Davies-Black Publishing.

Bright, P. (2008). Ascending to wisdom: A Christian pedagogy. In M. Ferrari & G. Potworowski (Eds.), *Teaching for wisdom: Cross-cultural perspectives on fostering wisdom* (pp. 163-76). Springer.

Britt, T. W., Sinclair, R. R., & McFadden, A. C. (2013). Introduction: The meaning and importance of military resilience. In R. R. Sinclair & T. W. Britt

(Eds.), *Building psychological resilience in military personnel: Theory and practice* (pp. 3-18). American Psychological Association.

Brodaty, H., Low, L. F., Liu, Z., Fletcher, J., Roast, J., Goodenough, B., & Chenoweth, L. (2014). Successful ingredients in the SMILE study: Resident, staff, and management factors influence the effects of humor therapy in residential aged care. *The American Journal of Geriatric Psychiatry, 22*(12), 1427-37.

Brounéus, K. (2014). On return from peacekeeping: A review of current research on psychological well-being in military personnel returning from operational deployment. *Journal of Military and Veterans' Health, 22*(1), 24-29.

Brower, A. M., & Ketterhagen, A. (2004). Is there an inherent mismatch between how Black and White students expect to succeed in college and what their colleges expect from them? *Journal of Social Issues, 60*(1), 95-116.

Brown, J. B. (2011). The building of a virtuous transformational leader. *Journal of Virtues & Leadership, 2*(1), 6-14.

Brown, K. W., & Holt, M. (2011). Experiential processing and the integration of dark and bright sides of the human psyche. In K. M. Sheldon, T. B. Kashdan, & M. F. Steger (Eds.). *Designing positive psychology: Taking stock and moving forward* (pp. 147-59). Oxford University Press.

Brown, K. W., & Ryan, R. M. (2003). The benefits of being present: Mindfulness and its role in psychological well-being. *Journal of Personality and Social Psychology, 84*(4), 822-48.

Brown, N. J. L., Lomas, T., & Eiroa-Orosa, F. J. (Eds.). (2017). *The Routledge international handbook of critical positive psychology.* Routledge.

Brown, N. J. L., Sokal, A. D., & Friedman, H. L. (2013). The complex dynamics of wishful thinking: The critical positivity ratio. *American Psychologist, 68*(9), 801-13.

Brown, R. P. (2003). Measuring individual differences in the tendency to forgive: Construct validity and links with depression. *Personality and Social Psychology Bulletin, 29*(6), 759-71.

Brown, R. P. (2004). Vengeance is mine: Narcissism, vengeance, and the tendency to forgive. *Journal of Research in Personality, 38*(6), 576-84.

Brown, W. P. (2012). Happiness and its discontents in the psalms. In B. A. Strawn (Ed.), *The Bible and the pursuit of happiness* (pp. 95-116). Oxford University Press.

Browning, D. S. (1987). *Religious thought and the modern psychologies.* Fortress.

Brunwasser, S. M., Gillham, J. E., & Kim, E. S. (2009). A meta-analytic review of the Penn Resiliency Program's effect on depressive symptoms. *Journal of Consulting and Clinical Psychology, 77*(6), 1042-54.

Bruya, B., & Ardelt, M. (2018). Fostering wisdom in the classroom, part 1: A general theory of wisdom pedagogy. *Teaching Philosophy, 41*(3), 239-53.

Bryan, C. J., Bryan, A., Rugo, K., Hinkson, K., & Leifker, F. (2020). Happiness, meaning in life, and PTSD symptoms among National Guard personnel: A multilevel analysis. *Journal of Happiness Studies, 21*, 1251-64.

Bryant, F. B., & Verhoff, J. (2007). *Savoring: A new model of positive experience.* Lawrence Erlbaum Associates.

Bufford, R. K., McMinn, M. R., Moody, J. A., & Geczy-Haskins, L. (2018). The effects of grace interventions in church communities. *Journal of Positive Psychology, 13*(5), 512-21.

Burke, C. (2015). *The theology of marriage: Personalism, doctrine, and canon law.* Catholic University of America Press.

Burnham, J. C. (1985). The encounter of Christian theology with deterministic psychology and psychoanalysis. *Bulletin of the Menninger Clinic, 49*(4), 321-52.

Burns, C. M., Morley, J., Bradshaw, R., & Domene, J. (2008). The emotional impact on and coping strategies employed by police teams investigating internet child exploitation. *Traumatology, 14*(2), 20-31.

Byng-Hall, J. (1999). Family and couple therapy: Toward greater security. In J. Cassidy & P. R. Shaver (Eds.), *Handbook of attachment: Theory, research, and clinical applications* (pp. 625-45). Guilford Press.

Cai, C., Yu, L., Rong, L., & Zhong, H. (2014). Effectiveness of humor intervention for patients with schizophrenia: A randomized controlled trial. *Journal of Psychiatric Research, 59*, 174-78.

Calvin, J. (1960). *Institutes of the Christian religion* (J. T. McNeil, Ed., F. L. Battles, Trans.). Westminster Press. (Original work published 1559)

Cameron, D. (2010). *PM speech on wellbeing.* www.gov.uk/government/speeches/pm-speech-on-wellbeing

Cameron, K. S. (2011). Effects of virtuous leadership on organizational performance. In S. I. Donaldson, M. Csikszentmihalyi, & J. Nakamura (Eds.), *Applied positive psychology: Improving everyday life, health, schools, work, and society* (pp. 171-183). Routledge.

Cameron, K. S., Bright, D., & Caza, A. (2004). Exploring the relationships between organizational virtuousness and performance. *American Behavioral Scientist, 47*(6), 766-90.

Canadian Institutes of Health Research, Natural Sciences and Engineering Research Council of Canada, Social Sciences and Humanities Research Council. (2018). *Tri-Council policy statement: Ethical conduct for research involving humans.* https://ethics.gc.ca/eng/policy-politique_tcps2 -eptc2_2018.html

Cândea, D. M., & Szentagotai-Tăta, A. (2018). Shame-proneness, guilt-proneness and anxiety symptoms: A meta-analysis. *Journal of Anxiety Disorders, 58,* 78-106.

Cann, A., & Calhoun, L. G. (2001). Perceived personality associations with differences in sense of humor: Stereotypes of hypothetical others with high or low senses of humor. *Humor: International Journal of Humor Research, 14*(2), 117-30.

Cann, A., Calhoun, L. G., & Banks, J. S. (1997). On the role of humor appreciation in interpersonal attraction: It's no joking matter. *Humor: International Journal of Humor Research, 10*(1), 77-89.

Canter, D. V., & Craik, K. H. (1981). Environmental psychology. *Journal of Environmental Psychology, 1*(1), 1-11.

Carlo, G., Okun, M. A., Knight, G. P., & de Guzman, M. R. T. (2005). The interplay of traits and motives on volunteering: Agreeableness, extraversion and prosocial value motivation. *Personality and Individual Differences, 38*(6), 1293-305.

Carr, A. (2004). *Positive psychology: The science of happiness and human strengths.* Brunner-Routledge.

Carse, A. L. (2005). The moral contours of empathy. *Ethical Theory and Moral Practice, 8*(1-2), 169-95.

Carson, J. W., Carson, K. M., Gil, K. M., & Baucom, D. H. (2006). Mindfulness-based relationship enhancement (MBRE) in couples. In R. A. Baer (Ed.), *Mindfulness-based treatment approaches: Clinician's guide to evidence base and applications* (pp. 309-32). Academic Press.

Carver, C. S., & Gaines, J. G. (1987). Optimism, pessimism, and postpartum depression. *Cognitive Therapy and Research, 11*(4), 449-62.

Carver, C. S., & Scheier, M. F. (1990). Origins and functions of positive and negative affect: A control-process view. *Psychological Review, 97*(1), 19-35.

Carver, C. S., & Scheier, M. F. (2005). Optimism. In C. R. Snyder & S. J. Lopez (Eds.), *Handbook of positive psychology* (pp. 231-243). Oxford University Press.

Carver, C. S., Scheier, M. F., Miller, C. J., & Fulford, D. (2009). Optimism. In S. J. Lopez & C. R. Snyder (Eds.), *The Oxford handbook of positive psychology* (pp. 303-11). Oxford University Press.

Casey, B. J., Somerville, L. H., Gotlib, I. H., Ayduk, O., Franklin, N. T., Askren, M. K., . . . & Glover, G. (2011). Behavioral and neural correlates of delay of gratification 40 years later. *Proceedings of the National Academy of Sciences, 108*(36), 14998-5003.

Casey, J. (1990). *Pagan virtue: An essay in ethics.* Clarendon Press.

Cassidy, J. (1999). The nature of the child's ties. In J. Cassidy & P. R. Shaver (Eds.), *Handbook of attachment: Theory, research, and clinical applications* (pp. 3-20). Guilford Press.

Casy, G. W., Jr. (2011). Comprehensive Soldier Fitness: A vision for psychological resilience in the U.S. Army. *American Psychologist, 66*(1), 1-3. doi: 10.1037/a0021930

Chairman of the Joint Chiefs of Staff. (2011). *CJCSI 3405.01: Chairman's total force fitness framework.* www.dtic.mil/cjcs_directives/cdata/unlimit/3405 _01.pdf

Chambers, R., Lo, B. C. Y., & Allen, N. B. (2008). The impact of intensive mindfulness training on attentional control, cognitive style, and affect. *Cognitive Therapy and Research, 32*(3), 303–322.

Chan, S. (2014). *Grassroots Asian theology: Thinking the faith from the ground up.* IVP Academic.

Chang, W. C., & Sivam, R. W. (2004). Constant vigilance: Heritage values and defensive pessimism in coping with severe acute respiratory syndrome in Singapore. *Asian Journal of Social Psychology, 7*(1), 35-53.

Chao, Y. H., Cheng, Y. Y., & Chiou, W. B. (2011). The psychological consequence of experiencing shame: Self-sufficiency and mood-repair. *Motivation and Emotion, 35*(2), 202-10.

Chaouloff, F. (1989). Physical exercise and brain monoamines: A review. *Acta Physiologica, 137*(1), 1-13.

Chapel, B. (1994). *Christ-centered preaching.* Baker Books.

Charbonneau, D., Barling, J., & Kelloway, E. K. (2001). Transformational leadership and sports performance: The mediating role of intrinsic motivation. *Journal of Applied Social Psychology, 31*(7), 1521-34.

Charry, E. (2010). *God and the art of happiness.* Eerdmans.

Chen, C. F., & Chen, C. W. (2011). Speeding for fun? Exploring the speeding behavior of riders of heavy motorcycles using the theory of planned behavior and psychological flow theory. *Accident Analysis & Prevention, 43*(3), 983-90.

Chen, J. Y. (2015). Virtue and the scientist: Using virtue ethics to examine science's ethical and moral challenges. *Science and engineering ethics, 21*, 75-94.

Chenoweth, L., Low, L. F., Goodenough, B., Liu, Z., Brodaty, H., Casey, A. N., . . . & Fleming, R. (2013). Something to SMILE about: Potential benefits to staff from humor therapy with nursing home residents. *Journal of Gerontological Nursing, 40*(2), 47-52.

Cherkas, L., Hochberg, F., MacGregor, A. J., Snieder, H., & Spector, T. D. (2000). Happy families: A twin study of humour. *Twin Research, 3*(1), 17-22.

Chrdileli, M., & Kasser, T. (2018). Guilt, shame, and apologizing behavior: A laboratory study. *Personality and Individual Differences, 135*, 304-6.

Christopher, J. C., & Hickinbottom, S. (2008). Positive psychology, ethnocentrism, and the disguised ideology of individualism. *Theory & Psychology, 18*(5), 563-89.

Cialdini, R. B., Brown, S. L., Lewis, B. P., Luce, C., & Neuberg, S. L. (1997). Reinterpreting the empathy-altruism relationship: When one into one equals oneness. *Journal of Personality and Social Psychology, 73*(3), 481-94.

Ciarrochi, J., Kashdan, T. B., & Harris, R. (2013). The foundations of flourishing. In T. B. Kashdan & J. Ciarrochi (Eds.), *Mindfulness, acceptance, and positive psychology* (pp. 1-29). Context Press.

Cicirelli, V. G. (2006). *Older adults' views on death.* Springer.

Clark, D. M., Ball, S., & Pape, D. (1991). An experimental investigation of thought suppression. *Behaviour Research and Therapy, 29*(3), 253-57.

Clark, R. D. (1975). The effects of reinforcement, punishment and dependency on helping behavior. *Bulletin of Personality and Social Psychology, 1*(4), 596-99.

Claxton, G., Owen, D., & Sadler-Smith, E. (2015). Hubris in leadership: A peril of unbridled intuition? *Leadership, 11*(1), 57-78.

Clements, M. L., & Mitchell, A. E. (2005). Noncoercion, nonviolence, and sacrifice: Applications in families. In A. Dueck & C. Lee (Eds.), *Why psychology needs theology: A radical-reformation perspective* (pp 79-98). William B. Eerdmans Publishing Company.

Clifton, D. O., Anderson, C. E., & Schreiner, L. A. (2006). *StrengthsQuest: Discover and develop your strengths in academics, career, and beyond* (2nd ed.). Gallup Press.

Coan, J. A., Schaefer, H. S., & Davidson, R. J. (2006). Lending a hand: Social regulation of the neural response to threat. *Psychological Science, 17*(12), 1032-39.

Cogan, R., Cogan, D., Waltz, W., & McCue, M. (1987). Effects of laughter and relaxation on discomfort thresholds. *Journal of Behavioral Medicine, 10*(2), 139-44.

Cohen, S., & Wills, T. A. (1985). Stress, social support, and the buffering hypothesis. *Psychological Bulletin, 98*(2), 310-57.

Cohn, A., Hodson, S., & Crane, M. (2010). Resilience training in the Australian Defense Force. *InPsych, 32*(2). www.psychology.org.au/publications/inpsych/2010/april/cohn

Cohn, M. A., & Fredrickson, B. L. (2009). Broaden-and-build theory of positive emotions. In S. J. Lopez (Ed.), *The encyclopedia of positive psychology* (pp. 105-10). Wiley-Blackwell.

Coke, J. S., Batson, C. D., & McDavis, K. (1978). Empathic mediation of helping: A two-stage model. *Journal of Personality and Social Psychology, 36*(7), 752-66.

Collini, S. (1985). The idea of "character" in Victorian political thought. *Transactions of the Royal Historical Society, 35*, 29-50.

Collins, J. D. (1962). *The lure of wisdom.* Marquette University Press.

Collins, N. L., & Feeney, B. C. (2000). A safe haven: An attachment theory perspective on support seeking and caregiving in intimate relationships. *Journal of Personality and Social Psychology, 78*(6), 1053-73.

Compton, W. C. (2001). The values problem in subjective well-being. *American Psychologist, 56*(1), 84.

Comte-Sponville, A. (2001). *A small treatise on the great virtues* (C. Temerson, Trans.). Henry Holt.

Conoley, C. W., & Conoley, J. C. (2009). Positive psychology for educators. In R. Gilman, E. S. Huebner, & M. J. Furlong (Eds.), *Handbook of positive psychology in schools* (pp. 463-76). Routledge.

Cooper, L. B., Bruce, A. J., Harman, M. J., & Boccaccini, M. T. (2009). Differentiated styles of attachment to God and varying religious coping efforts. *Journal of Psychology and Theology, 37*(2), 134-41.

Coover, J. E. (1916). *Formal discipline from the standpoint of experimental psychology.* Psychological Review Company.

Cornum, R., Matthews, M. D., & Seligman, M. E. P. (2011). Comprehensive soldier fitness: Building resilience in a challenging institutional context. *American Psychologist, 66*(1), 4-9.

Coutts, J. (2016). *A shared mercy: Karl Barth on forgiveness and the church.* IVP Academic.

Cox, C. R., Arndt J., Pyszczynski, T., Greenberg, J., Abdollahi, A., & Solomon, S. (2008). Terror management and adults' attachment to their parents: The safe haven remains. *Journal of Personality and Social Psychology, 94*(4), 696-717.

Coyne, J. C., Pajak, T. F., Harris, J., Konski, A., Movsas, B., Ang, K., & Watkins Bruner, D. (2007). Emotional well-being does not predict survival in head and neck cancer patients: A radiation therapy oncology group study. *Cancer, 110*(11), 2568-75.

Craft, L. L., & Landers, D. M. (1998). The effect of exercise on clinical depression and depression resulting from mental illness: A meta-analysis. *Journal of Sport and Exercise Psychology, 20*(4), 339-57.

Cramer, R. E., McMaster, M. R., Bartell, P. A., & Dragna, M. (1988). Subject competence and minimization of the bystander effect. *Journal of Applied Social Psychology, 18*(13), 1133-48.

Credé, M., Tynan, M. C., & Harms, P. D. (2017). Much ado about grit: A meta-analytic synthesis of the grit literature. *Journal of Personality and Social Psychology, 113*(3), 492-511.

Crisp, T. M., Porter, S. L., & Ten Elshof, G. A. (Eds.) (2019). *Psychology and spiritual formation in dialogue.* IVP Academic.

Crothers, M., & Shaw, G. (1999, August). *Validation of the Mutuality Assessment Questionnaire.* [Paper presentation]. Annual meeting of the American Psychological Association, Boston, MA, United States.

Crumbaugh, J. D., & Maholick, L. T. (1964). An experimental study in existentialism: The psychometric approach to Frankl's concept of noogenic neurosis. *Journal of Clinical Psychology, 20*(2), 200-207.

Csikszentmihalyi, M. (1975). *Beyond boredom and anxiety.* Jossey-Bass.

Csikszentmihalyi, M. (1990). *Flow: The psychology of optimal experience.* Harper & Row.

Csikszentmihalyi, M. (1999). If we are so rich, why aren't we happy? *American Psychologist, 54*(10), 821-27.

Csikszentmihalyi, M. (2000). Happiness, flow, and economic equality. *American Psychologist, 55*(10), 1163-64.

Csikszentmihalyi, M. (2004). *Good business: Leadership, flow, and the making of meaning.* Penguin.

Csikszentmihalyi, M. (2009). Flow. In S. J. Lopez (Ed.), *The encyclopedia of positive psychology* (pp. 394-400). John Wiley & Sons.

Csikszentmihalyi, M. (2014a). Play and intrinsic rewards. In M. Csikszentmihalyi (Ed.), *Flow and the foundations of positive psychology* (pp. 135-54). Springer.

Csikszentmihalyi, M. (2014b). Flow. In M. Csikszentmihalyi (Ed.), *Flow and the foundations of positive psychology* (pp. 227-38). Springer.

Csikszentmihalyi, M. (2014c). Toward a psychology of optimal experience. In M. Csikszentmihalyi (Ed.), *Flow and the foundations of positive psychology* (pp. 209-26). Springer.

Csikszentmihalyi, M., & Asakawa, K. (2016). Universal and cultural dimensions of optimal experiences. *Japanese Psychological Research, 58*(1), 4-13.

Csikszentmihalyi, M., & Csikszentmihalyi, I. (1988). *Optimal experience.* Cambridge University Press.

Csikszentmihalyi, M., & Hunter, J. (2003). Happiness in everyday life: The uses of experience sampling. *Journal of Happiness Studies, 4*(2), 185-99.

Csikszentmihalyi, M., & LeFevre, J. (1989). Optimal experience in work and leisure. *Journal of Personality and Social Psychology, 56*(5), 815-22.

Csikszentmihalyi, M., Rathunde, K., & Whalen, S. (1997). *Talented teenagers: The roots of success and failure.* Cambridge University Press.

Csikszentmihalyi, M., & Wong, M. M. H. (2014). The situational and personal correlates of happiness: A cross-national comparison. In M. Csikszentmihalyi (Ed.), *Flow and the foundations of positive psychology* (pp. 69-88). Springer.

Cupit, G. (1996). *Justice as fittingness.* Clarendon Press.

Curry, L. A., & Snyder, C. R. (2000). Hope takes the field: Mind matters in athletic performances. In C. R. Snyder (Ed.), *Handbook of hope: Theory, measures, and applications* (pp. 243-60). Academic Press.

Curry, L. A., Snyder, C. R., Cook, D. L., Ruby, B. C., & Rehm, M. (1997). The role of hope in student-athlete academic and sport achievement. *Journal of Personality and Social Psychology, 73*(6), 1257-67.

Curzer, H. J. (1990). A great philosopher's not so great account of great virtue: Aristotle's treatment of "greatness of soul." *Canadian Journal of Philosophy, 20*(4), 517-38.

Dahlsgaard, K., Peterson, C., & Seligman, M. E. P. (2005). Shared virtue: The convergence of valued human strengths across culture and history. *Review of General Psychology, 9*(3), 203-13.

Dalen, J., Smith, B. W., Shelley, B. M., Sloan, A. L., Leahigh, L., & Begay, D. (2010). Pilot study: Mindful Eating and Living (MEAL): Weight, eating behavior, and psychological outcomes associated with a mindfulness-based intervention for people with obesity. *Complementary Therapies in Medicine, 18*(6), 260-64.

Daniel, T. (2017). Grief as a mystical journey: Fowler's stages of faith development and their relation to post-traumatic growth. *Journal of Pastoral Care & Counseling, 71*(4), 220-29.

Daniels, B. C. (2008). Early modern Olympians: Puritan sportsmen in seventeenth-century England and America. *Canadian Journal of History, 43*(2), 253-63.

Danner, D. D., Snowdon, D. A., & Friesen, W. V. (2001). Positive emotions in early life and longevity: Findings from the Nun Study. *Journal of Personality and Social Psychology, 80*(5), 804-13.

Darby, B. W., & Schlenker, B. R. (1982). Children's reactions to apologies. *Journal of Personality and Social Psychology, 43*(4), 742-53.

Darley, J. M., & Latané, B. (1968). Bystander intervention in emergencies: Diffusion of responsibility. *Journal of Personality and Social Psychology, 8*(4), 377-83.

David, W. S., Simpson, T. L., & Cotton, A. J. (2006). Taking charge: A pilot curriculum of self-defense and personal safety training for female veterans with PTSD because of military sexual trauma. *Journal of Interpersonal Violence, 21*(4), 555-65.

Davidovitz, R., Mikulincer, M., Shaver, P. R., Izsak, R., & Popper, M. (2007). Leaders as attachment figures: Leaders' attachment orientations predict leadership-related mental representations and followers' performance and mental health. *Journal of Personality and Social Psychology, 93*(4), 632-50.

Davids, P. H. (1982). *The epistle of James: A commentary on the Greek text.* Eerdmans.

Davidson, K., & Prkachin, K. (1997). Optimism and unrealistic optimism have an interacting impact on health-promoting behavior and knowledge changes. *Personality and Social Psychology Bulletin, 23*(6), 617-25.

Davies, W. (2015). *The happiness industry: How the government and big business sold us well-being.* Verso.

Davydenko, M., & Peetz, J. (2017). Time grows on trees: The effect of nature settings on time perception. *Journal of Environmental Psychology, 54*, 20-26.

de Botton, A. (2006). *The architecture of happiness.* Vintage Books.

De Fruyt, F., De Bolle, M., McCrae, R. R., Terracciano, A., Costa Jr, P. T., & Collaborators of the Adolescent Personality Profiles of Cultures Project. (2009). Assessing the universal structure of personality in early adolescence: The NEO-PI-R and NEO-PI-3 in 24 cultures. *Assessment, 16*(9), 301-11.

De Hooge, I. E., Breugelmans, S. M., & Zeelenberg, M. (2008). Not so ugly after all: When shame acts as a commitment device. *Journal of Personality and Social Psychology, 95*(4), 933-43.

De Hooge, I. E., Zeelenberg, M., & Breugelmans, S. M. (2010). Restore and protect motivations following shame. *Cognition and Emotion, 24*(1), 111-27.

de Manzano, Ö., Cervenka, S., Jucaite, A., Hellenäs, O., Farde, L., & Ullén, F. (2013). Individual differences in the proneness to have flow experiences are linked to dopamine D2-receptor availability in the dorsal striatum. *Neuroimage, 67*, 1-6.

De Vos, M. (2012). The unbearable lightness of happiness policy. In P. Booth (Ed.), . . . *And the pursuit of happiness* (pp. 181-204). Institute of Economic Affairs.

Deci, E. L., Connell, J. P., & Ryan, R. M. (1989). Self-determination in a work organization. *Journal of Applied Psychology, 74*(4), 580-90.

Deci, E. L., & Ryan, R. M. (1985). *Intrinsic motivation and self-determination in human behavior.* Plenum Press.

Deci, E. L., & Ryan, R. M. (1987). The support of autonomy and the control of behavior. *Journal of Personality and Social Psychology, 53*(6), 1024-37.

Deci, E. L., & Ryan, R. M. (2000a) The darker and brighter sides of human existence: Basic psychological needs as a unifying concept. *Psychological Inquiry, 11*(4), 319-38.

Deci, E. L., & Ryan, R. M. (2000b). The "what" and "why" of goal pursuits: Human needs and the self-determination of behavior. *Psychological Inquiry, 11*(4), 227-68.

Deci, E. L., & Ryan, R. M. (2014). The importance of universal psychological needs for understanding motivation in the workplace. In M. Gagne (Ed.), *The Oxford handbook of work engagement, motivation, and self-determination theory* (pp. 13-32). Oxford University Press.

Deci, E. L., Ryan, R. M., & Williams, G. C. (1996). Need satisfaction and the self-regulation of learning. *Learning and Individual Differences, 8*(3), 165-83.

Deci, E. L., Schwartz, A. J., Sheinman, L., & Ryan, R. M. (1981). An instrument to assess adults' orientations toward control versus autonomy with children: Reflections on intrinsic motivation and perceived competence. *Journal of Educational Psychology, 73*(5), 642-50.

Deci, E. L., Vallerand, R. J., Pelletier, L. G., & Ryan, R. M. (1991). Motivation and education: The self-determination perspective. *Educational Psychologist, 26*(3-4), 325-46.

Deckers, L., & Ruch, W. (1992). Sensation seeking and the situational humour response questionnaire (SHRQ): Its relationship in American and German samples. *Personality and Individual Differences, 13*(9), 1051-54.

Defense Health Agency. (2020). *Total force fitness (TFF): Program update.* www.health.mil/Reference-Center/Presentations/2020/02/10/Total-Force-Fitness

Degelman, D., & Lynn, D. (1995). The development and preliminary validation of the belief in divine intervention scale. *Journal of Psychology and Theology, 23*(1), 37-44.

Dekeyser, M., Raes, F., Leijssen, M., Leysen, S., & Dewulf, D. (2008). Mindfulness skills and interpersonal behaviour. *Personality and Individual Differences, 44*(5), 1235-45.

del Valle, C. H. C., & Mateos, P. M. (2008). Dispositional pessimism, defensive pessimism and optimism: The effect of induced mood on prefactual and counterfactual thinking and performance. *Cognition and Emotion, 22*(8), 1600-12.

Delkeskamp-Hayes, C. (2007). Resisting the therapeutic reduction: On the significance of sin. *Christian Bioethics, 13*(1), 105-27.

Delle Fave, A., & Bassi, M. (2009). The contribution of diversity to happiness research. *Journal of Positive Psychology, 4*(3), 205-7.

Demerouti, E. (2006). Job characteristics, flow, and performance: The moderating role of conscientiousness. *Journal of Occupational Health Psychology, 11*(3), 266-80.

Denning, L. A., Meisnere, M., & Warner, K. E. (2014). *Preventing psychological disorders in service members and their families: An assessment of programs.* The National Academies Press.

Department of the Air Force. (2014). *Air Force instruction 90-506: Comprehensive airman fitness.* http://static.e-publishing.af.mil/production/1/saf_mr/publication/afi90-506/afi90-506.pdf

Department of the Army. (2014). *Comprehensive soldier and family fitness* (AR 350-53). https://armypubs.army.mil/epubs/DR_pubs/DR_a/pdf/web/r350_53.pdf

Department of the Navy. (2010). *Combat and operational stress control.* https://health.mil/Reference-Center/Policies/2010/12/01/US-Navy-US-Marine-Corps-COSC-Policy-Update

Department of the Navy. (2013). *Task Force Resilient final report.* www.hsdl.org/?view&did=752681

Department of the Navy. (2015). *OPNAVINST 6520.1: Operational stress control program.* www.secnav.navy.mil/doni/Directives/06000%20Medical%20and%20Dental%2Services/06-500%20Medical%20Research/6520.1A.pdf

Derks, P., & Berkowitz, J. (1989). Some determinants of attitudes toward a joker. *Humor: International Journal of Humor Research, 2*(4), 385-96.

Derks, P., Kalland, S., & Etgen, M. (1995). The effect of joke type and audience response on the reaction to a joker: Replication and extension. *Humor: International Journal of Humor Research, 8*(4), 327-37.

DeRobertis, E. M., & Bland, A. M. (2018). Tapping the humanistic potential of self-determination theory: Awakening to paradox. *The Humanistic Psychologist, 46*(2), 105-28.

Derryberry, D., & Tucker, D. M. (1994). Motivating the focus of attention. In P. M. Neidenthal & S. Kitayama (Eds.), *The heart's eye: Emotional influences in perception and attention* (pp. 167-96), Academic Press.

Detrick, P., Chibnall, J. T., & Luebbert, M. C. (2004). The revised NEO personality inventory as predictor of police academy performance. *Criminal Justice and Behavior, 31*(6), 676-94.

Devettere, R. J. (2002). *Introduction to virtue ethics: Insights of the ancient Greeks.* Georgetown University Press.

DeWall, C. N., Baumeister, R. F., Gailliot, M. T., & Maner, J. K. (2008). Depletion makes the heart grow less helpful: Helping as a function of self-regulatory energy and genetic relatedness. *Personality and Social Psychology Bulletin, 34*(12), 1653-62.

DeWall, C. N., Baumeister, R. F., Stillman, T. F., & Gailliot, M. T. (2007). Violence restrained: Effects of self-regulation and its depletion on aggression. *Journal of Experimental Social Psychology, 43*(1), 62-76.

Dews, S., Kaplan, J., & Winner, E. (1995). Why not say it directly? The social functions of irony. *Discourse Processes, 19*(3), 347-67.

Diener, E. (1984). Subjective well-being. *Psychological Bulletin, 95*(2), 542-75.

Diener, E. (1996). Subjective well-being in cross-cultural perspective. In H. Grad, A. Blanco, & J. Georgas (Eds.), *Key issues in cross-cultural psychology* (pp. 319-30). Swets & Zeitlinger.

Diener, E. (2000). Subjective well-being: The science of happiness and the proposal for a national index. *American Psychologist, 55*(1), 34-43.

Diener, E. (2008). One happy autobiography. In R. Levine, L. Zelezny, & A. Rodriques (Eds.), *Journeys in social psychology* (pp. 1-18). Psychology Press.

Diener, E., & Diener, C. (2011). Monitoring psycho-social prosperity for social change. In R. Biswas-Diener, (Ed.), *Positive psychology as social change* (pp. 53-72). Springer.

Diener, E., Gohm, C. L., Suh, E., & Oishi, S. (2000). Similarity of the relations between marital status and subjective well-being across cultures. *Journal of Cross-Cultural Psychology, 31*(4), 419-36.

Diener, E., Horwitz J., & Emmons, R. A. (1985). Happiness of the very wealthy. *Social Indicators Research, 16*(3), 263-74.

Diener, E., Lucas, R. E., Schimmack, U., & Helliwell, J. F. (2009). *Well-being for public policy.* Oxford University Press.

Diener, E., Oishi, S., & Lucas, R. E. (2003). Personality, culture, and subjective well-being: Emotional and cognitive evaluations of life. *Annual Review of Psychology, 54*(1), 403-25.

Diener, E., Oishi, S., & Lucas, R. E. (2009). Subjective well-being: The science of happiness and life satisfaction. In S. J. Lopez & C. R. Snyder (Eds.), *The Oxford handbook of positive psychology* (pp. 185-94). Oxford University Press.

Diener, E., & Seligman, M. E. P. (2002). Very happy people. *Psychological Science, 13*(1), 81-84.

Diener, E., & Seligman, M. E. P. (2004). Beyond money: Toward an economy of well-being. *Psychological Science in the Public Interest, 5*(1), 1-31.

Diener, E., & Suh, E. M. (Eds.). (2000). *Culture and subjective well-being.* MIT Press.

Dienstbier, R. A. (1995). The impact of humor on energy, tension, task choices, and attributions: Exploring hypotheses from toughness theory. *Motivation & Emotion, 19*(4), 255-67.

Dienstbier, R. A., & Zillig, L. M. P. (2002). Toughness. In Snyder, C. R., & Lopez, S. J. (Eds), *Handbook of positive psychology* (pp. 515-27). Oxford University Press.

Diessner, R., Solom, R. C., Frost, N. K., & Parsons, L. (2008). Engagement with beauty: Appreciating natural, artistic, and moral beauty. *Journal of Psychology, 142*(3), 303-29.

Dishman, R. K., & O'Connor, P. J. (2009). Lessons in exercise neurobiology: The case of endorphins. *Mental Health and Physical Activity, 2*(1), 4-9.

Donahue, M. J. (1985). Intrinsic and extrinsic religiousness: Review and meta-analysis. *Journal of Personality and Social Psychology, 48*(2), 400-419.

Dovidio, J. F., Gaertner, S. L., Isen, A. M., & Lowrence, R. (1995). Group representations and intergroup bias: Positive affect, similarity, and group size. *Personality and Social Psychology Bulletin, 21*(8), 856-65.

Dow, P. E. (2013). *Virtuous minds: Intellectual character development.* IVP Academic.

Dryden, W. (2012). *Understanding emotional problems: The REBT perspective.* Routledge.

Duckworth, A. (2016). *Grit: The power of passion and perseverance.* Scribner.

Duckworth, A., & Gross, J. J. (2014). Self-control and grit: Related but separable determinants of success. *Current Directions in Psychological Science, 23*(5), 319-25.

Duckworth, A. L., Kirby, T. A., Tsukayama, E., Berstein, H., & Ericsson, K. A. (2011). Deliberate practice spells success: Why grittier competitors triumph at the National Spelling Bee. *Social Psychological and Personality Science, 2* (2), 174-81.

Duckworth, A. L., Peterson, C., Matthews, M. D., & Kelly, D. R. (2007). Grit: Perseverance and passion for long-term goals. *Journal of Personality and Social Psychology, 92*(6), 1087-101.

Duckworth, A. L., & Quinn, P. D. (2009). Development and validation of the Short Grit Scale (GRIT–S). *Journal of Personality Assessment, 91*(2), 166-74.

Duckworth, A. L., Quinn, P. D., & Seligman, M. E. (2009). Positive predictors of teacher effectiveness. *Journal of Positive Psychology, 4*(6), 540-47.

Duckworth, A. L., & Seligman, M. E. (2005). Self-discipline outdoes IQ in predicting academic performance of adolescents. *Psychological Science, 16*(12), 939-44.

Dueck, A. C. (1995). *Between Jerusalem and Athens: Ethical perspectives on culture, religion, and psychotherapy.* Baker Books.

Dunn, E. W., Aknin, L. B., & Norton, M. I. (2008). Spending money on others promotes happiness. *Science, 319*(5870), 1687-88.

Dunn, J. D. C. (1999). Jesus: Teacher of wisdom or wisdom incarnate? In S. C. Barton (Ed.), *Where shall wisdom be found? Wisdom in the Bible, the church, and the contemporary world* (pp. 75-92). T&T Clark.

Dunn, J. R., & Schweitzer, M. E. (2005). Feeling and believing: The influence of emotion on trust. *Journal of Personality & Social Psychology, 88*(5), 736-48.

Durkheim, E. (1915). *The elementary forms of the religious life* (J. W. Swain, Trans.). The Free Press.

Dweck, C. S. (2002). Beliefs that make smart people dumb. In R. J. Sternberg (Ed.), *Why smart people can be so stupid* (pp. 24-41). Yale University Press.

Dweck, C. S., & Leggett, E. L. (1988). A social-cognitive approach to motivation and personality. *Psychological Review, 95*(2), 256-73.

Dyck, M. J. (1987). Assessing logotherapeutic constructs: Conceptual and psychometric status of the Purpose in Life and Seeking of Noetic Goals tests. *Clinical Psychology Review, 7*(4), 439-47.

Easterlin, R. A. (1974). Does economic growth improve the human lot? Some empirical evidence. In P. A. David & M. W. Reder (Eds.) *Nations and households in economic growth: Essays in honor of Moses Abramovitz* (pp. 98-125). Academic Press.

Easterlin, R. A. (1995). Will raising the income of all increase the happiness of all? *Journal of Economic Behavior and Organization, 27*(1), 35-47.

Eaton, J., & Struthers, C. W. (2006). The reduction of psychological aggression across varied interpersonal contexts through repentance and forgiveness. *Aggressive Behavior, 32*(3), 195-206.

Eaton, J., Struthers, C. W., & Santelli, A. G. (2006). Dispositional and state forgiveness: The role of self-esteem, need for structure, and narcissism. *Personality and Individual Differences, 41*(2), 371-80.

Echterling, L. G. (1993). *Making do and making sense: Long term coping of disaster survivors.* [Poster presentation]. American Psychological Association Annual Meeting, Toronto, ON, Canada.

Egli, T. J., & Hoven, M. (2019). Integrating faith: Sport psychology for Christian athletes and coaches. In M. Hoven, A. Parker, and N. J. Watson (Eds.), *Sport and Christianity: Practices for the twenty-first century* (pp. 109-18). T&T Clark.

Ehrenreich, B. (2009). *Bright-sided: How the relentless promotion of positive thinking has undermined America.* Thorndike Press.

Eidelson, R., Pilisuk, M., & Soldz, D. (2011). The dark side of comprehensive soldier fitness. *American Psychologist, 66*(7), 643-44.

Eidelson, R., & Soldz, D. (2012). *Does comprehensive soldier fitness work? CSF research fails the test (Coalition for an Ethical Psychology working paper no. 1).* www.ethicalpsychology.org/Eidelson-&-Soldz-CSF_Research_Fails_the_Test.pdf

Eisenberg, N. (1982). The development of reasoning regarding prosocial behavior. In N. Eisenberg (Ed.). *The development of prosocial behavior* (pp. 219-49). Academic Press.

Eisenberg, N., & Miller, P. A. (1987). The relation of empathy to prosocial and related behaviors. *Psychological Bulletin, 101*(1), 91-119.

Eisenberger, R. (1992). Learned industriousness. *Psychological Review, 99*(2), 248-67.

Elgee, N. J. (2003). Laughing at death. *Psychoanalytic Review, 90*(4), 475-97.

Ellens, J. H. (1989). A psychospiritual view of sin. In L. Aden & D. G. Benner (Eds.), *Counseling and the human predicament: A study of sin, guilt, and forgiveness*. Baker Book House.

Ellis, A. (1960). There is no place for the concept of sin in psychotherapy. *Journal of Counseling Psychology, 7*(3), 188-92.

Ellis, A. (1962). *Reason and emotion in psychotherapy*. Lyle Stuart.

Ellis, A. (1977). Fun as psychotherapy. *Rational Living, 12*(1), 2-6.

Ellis, A. (1980). Psychotherapy and atheistic values: A reply to A. E. Bergin's "Psychotherapy and religious values." *Journal of Consulting and Clinical Psychology, 48*(5), 635-39.

Ellis, A. (1987). The use of rational humorous songs in psychotherapy. In W. Fry & W. Salameh (Eds.), *Handbook of humor and psychotherapy* (pp. 265-86). Professional Resource Exchange.

Ellis, A. (2000). Can rational emotive behavior therapy (REBT) be effectively used with people who have devout beliefs in God and religion? *Professional Psychology: Research and Practice, 31*(1), 29-33.

Ellis, R. (2019). Creation, salvation, competition: Elements in a Christian doctrine of sport. In M. Hoven, A. Parker, & N. J. Watson (Eds.), *Sport and Christianity: Practices for the twenty-first century* (pp. 35-46). T&T Clark.

Elshaug, C., & Metzer, J. (2001). Personality attributes of volunteers and paid workers engaged in similar occupational tasks. *Journal of Social Psychology, 141*(6), 752-63.

Emler, N., & Cook, T. (2001). Moral integrity in leadership: Why it matters and why it may be difficult to achieve. In B. W. Roberts & R. Hogan (Eds.), *Personality psychology in the workplace* (pp. 277-98). American Psychological Association.

Emmons, R. A. (2000). Personality and forgiveness. In M. E. McCullough, K. I Pargament, & C. E. Thoresen (Eds.), *Forgiveness: Theory, research, and practice* (pp. 156-75). Guilford Press.

Emmons, R. A., & McCullough, M. E. (2003). Counting blessings versus burdens: An experimental investigation of gratitude and subjective well-being in daily life. *Journal of personality and social psychology, 84*(2), 377-89.

Emmons, R. A., & McCullough, M. E. (Eds.). (2004). *The psychology of gratitude*. Oxford University Press.

Emmons, R. A., & Shelton, C. M. (2005). Gratitude and the science of positive psychology. In C. R. Snyder & S. J. Lopez (Eds.), *Handbook of positive psychology* (pp. 459-71). Oxford University Press.

Enright, R. D., & Coyle, C. T. (1998). Researching the process model of forgiveness within psychological interventions. In E. L. Worthington Jr. (Ed.), *Dimensions of forgiveness: Psychological research & theological perspectives* (pp. 139-61). Templeton Foundation Press.

Enright, R. D., & the Human Development Study Group. (1996). Counseling within the forgiveness triad: On forgiving, receiving forgiveness, and self-forgiveness. *Counseling and Values, 40*(2), 107-26.

Ericsson, K. A., Krampe, R. T., & Tesch-Römer, C. (1993). The role of deliberate practice in the acquisition of expert performance. *Psychological Review, 100*(3), 363-406.

Erikson, E. H. (1963). *Childhood and society* (2nd ed.). W. W. Norton & Company.

Eronen, S., Nurmi, J. E., & Salmela-Aro, K. (1998). Optimistic, defensive-pessimistic, impulsive and self-handicapping strategies in university environments. *Learning and Instruction, 8*(2), 159-177.

Escolas, S. M., Pitts, B. L., Safer, M. A., & Bartone, P. T. (2013). The protective value of hardiness on military posttraumatic stress symptoms. *Military Psychology, 25*(2), 116-23.

Eskreis-Winkler, L., Duckworth, A. L., Shulman, E. P., & Beal, S. (2014). The grit effect: Predicting retention in the military, the workplace, school and marriage. *Frontiers in Psychology, 5*, 36.

Etchegoyen, R. H., & Nemas, C. R. (2003). Salieri's dilemma: A counterpoint between envy and appreciation. *The International Journal of Psychoanalysis, 84*(1), 45-58.

Evans, G. W. (2003). The built environment and mental health. *Journal of Urban Health, 80*(4), 536-55.

Evans, R. I. (1971). *Gordon Allport: The man and his ideas.* E. P. Dutton & Co.

Evdokimov, P. (1985). *The sacrament of love* (A. P. Gythiel & V. Steadman, Trans). St. Vladimir's Seminary Press.

Exline, J. J., & Baumeister, R. F. (2000). Expressing forgiveness and repentance: Benefits and barriers. In M. E. McCullough, K. I. Pargament, & C. E. Thoresen (Eds.), *Forgiveness: Theory, research, and practice* (pp. 133-55). Guilford Press.

Exline, J. J., Baumeister, R. F., Bushman, B. J., Campbell, W. K., & Finkel, E. J. (2004). Too proud to let go: Narcissistic entitlement as a barrier to forgiveness. *Journal of Personality and Social Psychology, 87*(6), 894-912.

Exline, J. J., & Martin, A. (2005). Anger toward God: A new frontier in forgiveness research. In E. L. Worthington, Jr. (Ed.), *Handbook of forgiveness* (pp. 73-88). Routledge.

Exline, J. J., Park, C. L., Smyth, J. M., & Carey, M. P. (2011). Anger toward God: Social-cognitive predictors, prevalence, and links with adjustment to bereavement and cancer. *Journal of Personality and Social Psychology, 100*(1), 129-48.

Exline, J. J., & Rose, E. (2005). Religious and spiritual struggles. In R. F. Paloutzian & C. L. Park (Eds.), *Handbook of the psychology of religion and spirituality* (pp. 315-30). Guilford Press.

Exline, J. J., Worthington, E. L., Jr., Hill, P., & McCullough, M. E. (2003). Forgiveness and justice: A research agenda for social and personality psychology. *Personality and Social Psychology Review, 7*(4), 337-48.

Exline, J. J., Yali, A. M., & Lobel, M. (1999). When God disappoints: Difficulty forgiving God and its role in negative emotion. *Journal of Health Psychology, 4*(3), 365-79.

Fagin-Jones, S., & Midlarsky, E. (2007). Courageous altruism: Personal and situational correlates of rescue during the Holocaust. *Journal of Positive Psychology, 2*(2), 136-47.

Fairclough, S. H., & Houston, K. (2004). A metabolic measure of mental effort. *Biological Psychology, 66*(2), 177-90.

Farias, M., & Wikholm, C. (2015). *The Buddha pill: Can meditation change you?* Watkins.

Farrell, S. (2010). Sir Aristotle and the code of chivalry. In G. Priest & D. Young (Eds.), *Martial arts and philosophy: Beating and nothingness* (pp. 179-88.). Open Court.

Fatfouta, R., Gerlach, T. M., Schröder-Abé, M., & Merkl, A. (2015). Narcissism and lack of interpersonal forgiveness: The mediating role of state anger, state rumination, and state empathy. *Personality and Individual Differences, 75*, 36-40.

Feeney, B. C. (2004). A secure base: Responsive support of goal strivings and exploration in adult intimate relationships. *Journal of Personality and Social Psychology, 87*(5), 631-48.

Feeney, B. C., & Collins, N. L. (2015a). Thriving through relationships. *Current Opinion in Psychology, 1*, 22-28.

Feeney, B. C., & Collins, N. L. (2015b). A new look at social support: A theoretical perspective on thriving through relationships. *Personality and Social Psychology Review, 19*(2), 113-47.

Feeney, J. A. (1999). Adult romantic attachment and couple relationships. In J. Cassidy & P. R. Shaver (Eds.), *Handbook of attachment: Theory, research, and clinical applications* (pp. 355-77). Guilford Press.

Feltz, D. L., Short, S. E., & Sullivan, P. J. (2008). *Self-efficacy in sport.* Human Kinetics.

Fenell, D. L. (1993). Characteristics of long-term first marriages. *Journal of Mental Health Counseling, 15*(4), 446-60.

Fernet, C., Austin, S., Trépanier, S. G., & Dussault, M. (2013). How do job characteristics contribute to burnout? Exploring the distinct mediating roles of perceived autonomy, competence, and relatedness. *European Journal of Work and Organizational Psychology, 22*(2), 123-37.

Fickova, E., & Ruiselova, Z. (1999). Preference for coping strategies in adolescents in relation to the sense of coherence. *Psychologia-a-Patopsychologia-Dietata, 34*(4), 291-301.

Fikretoglu, D., Beatty, E., & Liu, A. (2014). *Comparing different versions of Road to Mental Readiness to determine optimal content: Testing instruction type, homework, and intelligence effects at two timepoints (Scientific Report DRDC-RDDC-2014-R164).* Defense Research and Development Canada.

Fikretoglu, D., & McCreary, D. R. (2012). *Psychological resilience: A brief review of definitions, and key theoretical, conceptual, and methodological issues (Technical Report 2012-012).* Defence Research and Development Canada.

Fincham, F. (2000). Optimism and the family. In J. Gillham (Ed.), *The science of optimism and hope* (pp. 271-98). Templeton Foundation Press.

Fincham, F. D., & May, R. W. (2019). Self-forgiveness and well-being: Does divine forgiveness matter? *Journal of Positive Psychology, 14*(6), 854-59.

Fincham, F. D., May, R. W., & Carlos Chavez, F. L. (2020). Does being religious lead to greater self-forgiveness? *Journal of Positive Psychology, 15*(3), 400-406.

Fincham, F. D., Paleari, F. G., & Regalia, C. (2002). Forgiveness in marriage: The role of relationship quality, attributions, and empathy. *Personal Relationships, 9*(1), 27-37.

Findley, M. J., & Cooper, H. M. (1983). Locus of control and academic achievement: A literature review. *Journal of Personality and Social Psychology, 44*(2), 419-27.

Fine, G. A., & De Soucey, M. (2005). Joking cultures: Humor themes in social regulation in group life. *Humor, 18*(1), 1-22.

Finkel, E. J., Rusbult, C. E., Kumashiro, M., & Hannon, P. A. (2002). Dealing with betrayal in close relationships: Does commitment promote forgiveness? *Journal of Personality and Social Psychology, 82*(6), 956-74.

Finkenberg, M. F. (1990). Effect of participation in taekwondo on college women's self-concept. *Perceptual and Motor Skills, 71*(3), 891-94.

Finley, J. A. (2016). Adult romantic attachment: Developments in the study of couple relationships. In J. Cassidy & P. R. Shaver (Eds.), *Handbook of attachment: Theory, research, and clinical applications* (3rd ed.) (pp. 435-63). Guilford Press.

Fischer, P., Krueger, J. I., Greitemeyer, T., Vogrincic, C., Kastenmüller, A., Frey, D., . . . & Kainbacher, M. (2011). The bystander-effect: A meta-analytic review on bystander intervention in dangerous and non-dangerous emergencies. *Psychological Bulletin, 137*(4), 517-37.

Fisher, S., & Fisher, R. L. (1981). *Pretend the world is funny and forever: A psychological analysis of comedians, clowns, and actors.* Erlbaum.

Florian, V., Mikulincer, M., & Hirschberger G. (2002). The anxiety-buffering function of close relationships: Evidence that relationship commitment acts as a terror management mechanism. *Journal of Personality and Social Psychology, 82*(4), 527-42.

Florian, V., Milkulincer, M., & Taubman, O. (1995). Does hardiness contribute to mental health during a stressful real life situation? The roles of appraisal and coping. *Journal of Personality and Social Psychology, 68*(4), 687-95.

Floyd, R. K., & McDermott, D. (1998, August). *Hope and sexual risk-taking in gay men.* [Paper presentation]. American Psychological Association, San Francisco, CA, United States.

Focht, B. C., Bouchard, L. J., & Murphey, M. (2000). Influence of martial arts training on the perception of experimentally induced pressure pain and selected psychological responses. *Journal of Sport Behavior, 23*(3), 232-44.

Fodor, J. A. (1983). *The modularity of mind.* MIT Press.

Fontaine, K. R., & Cheskin, L. J. (1999). Optimism and obesity treatment outcomes. *Journal of Clinical Psychology, 55*(1), 141-43.

Foot, P. (1978). *Virtues and vices and other essays in moral philosophy.* University of California Press.

Foot, P. (2001). *Natural goodness.* Clarendon Press.

Forabosco, G. (2008). Is the concept of incongruity still a useful construct for the advancement of humor research? *Lodz Papers in Pragmatics, 4*(1), 45-62.

Ford, B. Q., Mauss, I. B., & Gruber, J. (2015). Valuing happiness is associated with bipolar disorder. *Emotion, 15*(2), 211-22.

Ford, B. Q., Shallcross, A. J., Mauss, I. B., Floerke, V. A., & Gruber, J. (2014). Desperately seeking happiness: Valuing happiness is associated with symptoms and diagnosis of depression. *Journal of Social and Clinical Psychology, 33*(1), 890-905.

Forgas, J. P. (2013). Don't worry, be sad! On the cognitive, motivational, and interpersonal benefits of negative mood. *Current Directions in Psychological Science, 22*(3), 225-32.

Foster, R. (1998). *Streams of living water: Essential practices of six great traditions of Christian faith.* HarperCollins.

Fowers, B. J. (1998). Psychology and the good marriage: Social theory as practice. *American Behavioral Scientist, 41*(4), 516-41.

Fowers, B. J. (2000). *Beyond the myth of marital happiness.* Jossey-Bass.

Fowers, B. J. (2001). The limits of a technical concept of a good marriage: Examining the role of virtues in communication skills. *Journal of Marital and Family Therapy, 27*(3), 327-40.

Fowers, B. J. (2005). *Virtue and psychology: Pursuing excellence in ordinary practices.* American Psychological Association.

Fowers, B. J. (2012a). Placing virtue and the human good. *Journal of Theoretical and Philosophical Psychology, 32*(1), 1-9.

Fowers, B. J. (2012b). An Aristotelian framework for the human good. *Journal of Theoretical and Philosophical Psychology, 32*(1), 10-23.

Fowers, B. J. (2015). *The evolution of ethics: Human sociality and the emergence of ethical mindedness.* Palgrave Macmillan.

Fowers, B. J., Laurenceau, J. P., Penfield, R. D., Cohen, L. M., Lang, S. F., Owenz, M. B., & Pasipandoya, E. (2016). Enhancing relationship quality measurement: The development of the Relationship Flourishing Scale. *Journal of Family Psychology, 30*(8), 997-1007.

Fowers, B. J., & Owenz, M. B. (2010). A eudaimonic theory of marital quality. *Journal of Family Theory and Review, 2*(4), 334-52.

Fowers, B. J., Richardson, F. C., & Slife, B. D. (2017). *Frailty, suffering, and vice: Flourishing in the face of human limitations.* Psychological Association.

Fowler, J. W. (1974). Toward a developmental perspective on faith. *Religious Education, 69*(2), 207-19.

Fowler, J. W. (1981). *Stages of faith.* HarperCollins.

Fowler, J. W. (2001). *Weaving the new creation: Stages of faith and the public church.* Wipf & Stock.

Fowler, J. W. (2004). Faith development at 30: Naming the challenges of faith in a new millennium. *Religious Education, 99*(4), 405-21.

Fowler, J. W., & Dell, M. L. (2006). Stages of faith from infancy through adolescence: Reflections on three decades of faith development theory. In E. C. Roehlkepartain, P. E. King, L. Wagener, & P. L. Bensen (Eds.), *The handbook of spiritual development in childhood and adolescence* (pp. 34-45). Sage Publications.

Fowler, J. W., Streib, H., & Keller, B. (2004). *Manual for faith development research.* Center for Research in Faith and Moral Development.

Fraley, B., & Aron, A. (2004). The effect of a shared humorous experience on closeness in initial encounters. *Personal Relationships, 11*(1), 61-78.

Framson, C., Kristal, A. R., Schenk, J., Littman, A. J., Zeliadt, S., & Benitez, D. (2009). Development and validation of the Mindful Eating Questionnaire. *Journal of the American Dietetic Association, 109*(8), 1439-44.

Franco, Z. E., Blau, K., & Zimbardo, P. G. (2011). Heroism: A conceptual analysis and differentiation between heroic action and altruism. *Review of General Psychology, 15*(2), 99-113.

Franco, Z. E., Efthimiou, O., & Zimbardo, P. G. (2016). Heroism and eudaimonia: Sublime actualization through the embodiment of virtue. In J. Vitterso (Ed.), *Handbook of eudaimonic well-being* (pp. 337-48). Springer.

Franco, Z., & Zimbardo, P. (2006). The banality of heroism. *Greater Good, 3*(2), 30-35.

Frankel, B. G., & Hewitt, W. E. (1994). Religion and well-being among Canadian university students: The role of faith groups on campus. *Journal for the Scientific Study of Religion, 33*(1), 62-73.

Frankl, V. (1967a). *Psychotherapy and existentialism.* Penguin.

Frankl, V. (1967b). Existential dynamics and neurotic escapism. In V. E. Frankl (Ed.) *Psychotherapy and existentialism: Selected papers on logotherapy* (pp. 19-51). Simon and Schuster.

Frankl, V. (1969). *The doctor and the soul* (R. Winston & C. Winston, Trans.). Bantam Books. (Original work published 1946)

Frankl, V. (1984). *Man's search for meaning* (3rd ed.). Simon & Schuster.

Franz, C. E., McClelland, D. C., Weinberger, J., & Peterson, C. (1994). Parenting antecedents of adult adjustment: A longitudinal study. In C. Perris, W. A. Arrindell, & M. Eisemann (Eds.), *Parenting and psychopathology* (pp. 127-44). Academic Press.

Fredrickson, B. L. (1998). What good are positive emotions? *Review of General Psychology, 2*(3), 300-319.

Fredrickson, B. L. (2000). The role of positive emotions in positive psychology: The broaden-and-build theory of positive emotions. *American Psychologist, 56*(3), 218-26.

Fredrickson, B. L. (2004). Gratitude, like other positive emotions, broadens and builds. In R. A. Emmons & M. E. McCullough (Eds.), *The psychology of gratitude* (pp. 145-66). Oxford University Press.

Fredrickson, B. L. (2013). Updated thinking on positivity ratios. *American Psychologist, 68*(9), 814-22.

Fredrickson, B. L., & Branigan, C. (2005). Positive emotions broaden the scope of attention and thought-action repertoires. *Cognition & Emotion, 19*(3), 313-32.

Fredrickson, B. L., & Joiner, T. (2002). Positive emotions trigger upward spirals toward emotional well-being. *Psychological Science, 13*(2), 172-75.

Fredrickson, B. L., & Levenson, R. W. (1998). Positive emotions speed recovery from the cardiovascular sequelae of negative emotions. *Cognition and Emotion, 12*(2), 191-220.

Fredrickson, B. L., & Losada, M. F. (2005). Positive affect and the complex dynamics of human flourishing. *American Psychologist, 60*(7), 678-86.

Fredrickson, B. L., & Losada, M. F. (2013). "Positive affect and the complex dynamics of human flourishing": Correction to Fredrickson and Losada (2005). *American Psychologist, 68*(9), 822.

Fredrickson, B. L., Mancuso, R. A., Branigan, C., & Tugade, M. M. (2000). The undoing effect of positive emotions. *Motivation and Emotion, 24*(4), 237-58.

Fretheim, T. E. (2012). God, creation, and the pursuit of happiness. In B. A. Strawn (Ed.), *The Bible and the pursuit of happiness* (pp. 33-56). Oxford University Press.

Freud, S. (1928). Humor. *The International Journal of Psychoanalysis, 9,* 1-6.

Freud, S. (1960). *Jokes and their relation to the unconscious* (J. Strachey, Trans.). W. W. Norton & Company. (Original work published 1905)

Freud, S. (1989). *The future of an illusion* (J. Strachey, Trans.). W. W. Norton & Company. (Original work published 1927)

Freund, R., & Gill, C. S. (2018). Understanding the development of spirituality, religion, and faith in the client's life. In C. S. Gill & R. R. Freund (Eds.), *Spirituality and religion in counseling: Competency-based strategies for ethical practice* (pp. 51-63). Routledge.

Frewen, P. A., Evans, E. M., Maraj, N., Dozois, D. J. A., & Partridge, K. (2008). Letting go: Mindfulness and negative automatic thinking. *Cognitive Therapy and Research, 32*(6), 758-74.

Frey, B. S., & Stutzer, A. (2002). What can economists learn from happiness research? *Journal of Economic Literature, 40*(2), 402-35.

Frias, A., Watkins, P. C., Webber, A. C., & Froh, J. J. (2011). Death and gratitude: Death reflection enhances gratitude. *Journal of Positive Psychology, 6*(2), 154-62.

Frise, N. R., & McMinn, M. R. (2010). Forgiveness and reconciliation: The differing perspectives of psychologists and Christian theologians. *Journal of Psychology and Theology, 38*(2), 83-90.

Froh, J. J., Sefick, W. J., & Emmons, R. A. (2008). Counting blessings in early adolescents: An experimental study of gratitude and subjective well-being. *Journal of School Psychology, 46*(2), 213-33.

Froman, L. (2010). Positive psychology in the workplace. *Journal of Adult Development, 17*(2), 59-69.

Fromm, E. (1941). *Escape from freedom.* Avon.

Fruzzetti, A. E., & Erikson, K. R. (2010). Mindfulness and acceptance interventions in cognitive-behavioral therapy. In K. S. Dobson (Ed.), *Handbook of cognitive-behavioral therapies (3rd ed.)* (pp. 347-72). Guilford Press.

Fujita, K., Trope, Y., Liberman, N., & Levin-Sagi, M. (2006). Construal levels and self-control. *Journal of Personality and Social Psychology, 90*(3), 351-67.

Funk, S. C, & Houston, B. K. (1987). A critical analysis of the Hardiness Scale's validity and utility. *Journal of Personality and Social Psychology, 53*(3), 572-78.

Gable, S. L., & Haidt, J. (2005). What (and why) is positive psychology? *Review of General Psychology, 9*(2), 103-10.

Gagne, M. (2003). Autonomy support and need satisfaction in the motivation and well-being of gymnasts. *Journal of Applied Sport Psychology, 15*(4), 372-90.

Gailliot, M. T., & Baumeister, R. F. (2007a). Self-regulation and sexual restraint: Dispositionally and temporarily poor self-regulatory abilities contribute to failures at restraining sexual behavior. *Personality and Social Psychology Bulletin, 33*(2), 173-86.

Gailliot, M. T., & Baumeister, R. F. (2007b). The physiology of willpower: Linking blood glucose to self-control. *Personality and Social Psychology Review, 11*(4), 303-27.

Gailliot, M. T., Baumeister, R. F., DeWall, C. N., Maner, J. K., Plant, E. A., Tice, D. M., . . . & Schmeichel, B. J. (2007). Self-control relies on glucose as a limited energy source: Willpower is more than a metaphor. *Journal of Personality and Social Psychology, 92*(2), 325-36.

Gailliot, M. T., Plant, E. A., Butz, D. A., & Baumeister, R. F. (2007). Increasing self-regulatory strength can reduce the depleting effect of suppressing stereotypes. *Personality and Social Psychology Bulletin, 33*(2), 281-94.

Gardner, W. L., Cogliser, C. C., Davis, K. M., & Dickens, M. P. (2011). Authentic leadership: A review of the literature and research agenda. *The Leadership Quarterly, 22*(6), 1120-45.

Garzon, F., & Ford, K. (2016). Adapting mindfulness for conservative Christians. *Journal of Psychology & Christianity, 35*(3), 263-68.

Gausel, N., & Leach, C. W. (2011). Concern for self-image and social image in the management of moral failure: Rethinking shame. *European Journal of Social Psychology, 41*(4), 468-78.

Gebauer, J. E., Nehrlich, A. E., Stahlberg, D., Sedikides, C., Hackenschmidt, A., Schick, D., Stegmaier, C. A., Windfelder, C. C. Bruk, A., & Mander, J. V. (2018). Mind-body practices and the self: Yoga and meditation do not quiet the ego, but instead boost self-enhancement. *Psychological Science, 29*(8), 1299-1308.

Gesch, C. B., Hammond, S. M., Hampson, S. E., Eves, A., & Crowder, M. J. (2002). Influence of supplementary vitamins, minerals and essential fatty acids on the antisocial behaviour of young adult prisoners: Randomised, placebo-controlled trial. *British Journal of Psychiatry, 181*(1), 22-28.

Gibbons, S. L., & Ebbeck, V. (1997). The effect of different teaching strategies on the moral development of physical education students. *Journal of Teaching in Physical Education, 17*(1), 85-98.

Gibbs, H. W., & Achterberg-Lawlis, J. (1978). Spiritual values and death anxiety: Implications for counseling with terminal cancer patients. *Journal of Counseling Psychology, 25*(6), 563-69.

Gifford, R. (2014). Environmental psychology matters. *Annual Review of Psychology, 65,* 541-79.

Gillham, J., & Reivich, K. (2004). Cultivating optimism in childhood and adolescence. *The Annals of the American Academy of Political and Social Science, 591*(1), 146-63.

Gillis, K., & Gatersleben, B. (2015). A review of psychological literature on the health and wellbeing benefits of biophilic design. *Buildings, 5*(3), 948-63.

Gilman, R., Huebner, E. S., & Furlong, M. J. (Eds.) (2009). *Handbook of positive psychology in schools.* Routledge.

Ginis, K. A. M., Jetha, A., Mack, D. E., & Hetz, S. (2010). Physical activity and subjective well-being among people with spinal cord injury: A meta-analysis. *Spinal Cord, 48*(1), 65-72.

Girgis, S., Anderson, R. T., & George, R. P. (2012). *What is marriage? Man and woman: A defense.* Encounter Books.

Gismero-González, E., Jódar, R., Martínez, M. P., Carrasco, M. J., Cagigal, V., & Prieto-Ursúa, M. (2020). Interpersonal offenses and psychological well-being: The mediating role of forgiveness. *Journal of Happiness Studies, 21*(1), 75-94.

Glanzer, P., Alleman, N. F., & Ream, T. C. (2017). *Restoring the soul of the university.* IVP Academic.

Gleser, J. M., Margulies, J. Y., Nyeska, M., Porat, S., Mandelberg, H., & Wertman, E. (1992). Physical and psychosocial benefits of modified judo practice for blind, mentally retarded children: A pilot study. *Perceptual and Motor Skills, 74*(3), 915-25.

Goble, F. G. (1970). *The third force: The psychology of Abraham Maslow.* Pocket Books.

Gold, G. J., & Weiner, B. (2000). Remorse, confession, group identity, and expectancies about repeating a transgression. *Basic and Applied Social Psychology, 22*(4), 291-300.

Goldenberg, J. L., Pyszczynski, T., Greenberg, J., Solomon, S., Kluck, B., & Cornwell, R. (2001). I am not an animal: Mortality salience, disgust, and the denial of human creatureliness. *Journal of Experimental Psychology: General, 130*(3), 427-35.

Goldstein, J. H. (1982). A laugh a day. *The Sciences, 22*(6), 21-25.

Golec de Zavala, A., Cichocka, A., Orehek, E., & Abdollahi, A. (2012). Intrinsic religiosity reduces intergroup hostility under mortality salience. *European Journal of Social Psychology, 42*(4), 451-61.

Goodenough, B., Low, L. F., Casey, A. N., Chenoweth, L., Fleming, R., Spitzer, P., . . . & Brodaty, H. (2012). Study protocol for a randomized controlled trial of humor therapy in residential care: The Sydney Multisite Intervention of Laughter-Bosses and ElderClowns (SMILE). *International Psychogeriatrics, 24*(12), 2037-44.

Gooty, J., Gavin, M., Johnson, P. D., Frazier, M. L., & Snow, D. B. (2009). In the eyes of the beholder: Transformational leadership, positive psychological capital, and performance. *Journal of Leadership & Organizational Studies, 15*(4), 353-67.

Gordon, A. M., Impett, E. A., Kogan, A., Oveis, C., & Keltner, D. (2012). To have and to hold: Gratitude promotes relationship maintenance in intimate bonds. *Journal of Personality and Social Psychology, 103*(2), 257-74.

Gordon, C. L., Arnette, R. A., & Smith, R. E. (2011). Have you thanked your spouse today? Felt and expressed gratitude among married couples. *Personality and Individual Differences, 50*(3), 339-43.

Gordon, K. C., Baucom, D. H. & Snyder, D. K. (2005). Forgiveness in couples: Divorce, infidelity, and couples therapy. In E. L. Worthington Jr. (Ed.), *Handbook of forgiveness* (pp. 407-22). Routledge.

Gorsuch, R. L., & Hao, J. Y. (1993). Forgiveness: An exploratory factor analysis and its relationship to religious variables. *Review of Religious Research, 34*(4), 333-47.

Goud, N. H. (2005). Courage: Its nature and development. *Journal of Humanistic Counseling, Education and Development, 44*(1), 102-16.

Gouldner, A. W. (1960). The norm of reciprocity: A preliminary statement. *American Sociological Review, 25*(2), 161-78.

Gove, W. R. (1973). Sex, marital status, and mortality. *American Journal of Sociology, 79*(1), 45-67.

Gove, W. R., Hughes, M., & Style, C. B. (1983). Does marriage have positive effects on the psychological well-being of the individual? *Journal of Health and Social Behavior, 24*(2), 122-31.

Gowan, D. E. (2010). *The Bible on forgiveness.* Pickwick Publications.

Grammer, K. (1990). Strangers meet: Laughter and nonverbal signs of interest in opposite-sex encounters. *Journal of Nonverbal Behavior, 14*(4), 209-36.

Gramzow, R., & Tangney, J. P. (1992). Proneness to shame and the narcissistic personality. *Personality and Social Psychology Bulletin, 18*(3), 369-76.

Grant, A. M., & Schwartz, B. (2011). Too much of a good thing: The challenge and opportunity of the inverted U. *Perspectives on Psychological Science, 6*(1), 61-76.

Graziano, W. G., & Eisenberg, N. (1997). Agreeableness: A dimension of personality. In R. Hogan, J. Johnson, & S. Briggs (Eds.), *Handbook of personality psychology* (pp. 795-824). Academic Press.

Greenberg, J., Pyszczynski, T., Solomon, S., Rosenblatt, A., Veeder, M., Kirkland, S., & Lyon, D. (1990). Evidence for terror management theory: II. The effects of mortality salience on reactions to those who threaten or bolster the cultural worldview. *Journal of Personality and Social Psychology, 58*(2), 308-18.

Greenleaf, R. K. (1970). *The servant as leader.* Paulist Press.

Greenspan, P. S. (1995). *Practical guilt.* Oxford University Press.

Greer, S., Morris, T., & Pettingale, K. W. (1979). Psychological response to breast cancer: Effect on outcome. *The Lancet, 314*(8146), 785-87.

Grenz, S. J. (1990). *Sexual ethics: A biblical perspective.* Word Publishing.

Grenz, S. J. (1994). *Theology for the community of God.* Eerdmans.

Grenz, S. J. (2001). *The social God and the relational self: A trinitarian theology of the imago Dei.* Westminster John Knox.

Griffin, B. J., Moloney, J. M., Green, J. D., Worthington, E. L., Jr., Cork, B., Tangney, J. P., . . . & Hook, J. N. (2016). Perpetrators' reactions to perceived interpersonal wrongdoing: The associations of guilt and shame with forgiving, punishing, and excusing oneself. *Self and Identity, 15*(6), 650-61.

Griffin, B. J., Toussaint, L. L., Zoelzer, M., Worthington Jr, E. L., Coleman, J. A., Lavelock, C. R., . . . & Rye, M. S. (2019). Evaluating the effectiveness of a community-based forgiveness campaign. *Journal of Positive Psychology, 14*(3), 354-61.

Griffith, J., & West, C. (2013). Master resilience training and its relationship to individual well-being and stress buffering among Army National Guard soldiers. *Journal of Behavioral Health Services & Research, 40*(2), 140-55.

Grolnick, W. S., & Ryan, R. M. (1989). Parent styles associated with children's self-regulation and competence in school. *Journal of Educational Psychology, 81*(2), 143-54.

Grossman, D. (1995). *On killing: The psychological cost of learning to kill in war and society.* Back Bay Books.

Grossman, P., Kappos, L., Gensicke, H., D'Souza, M., Mohr, D. C., Penner, I. K., & Steiner, C. (2010). MS quality of life, depression, and fatigue improve after mindfulness training: A randomized trial. *Neurology, 75*(13), 1141-49.

Grover, S., & Helliwell, J. F. (2019). How's life at home? New evidence on marriage and the set point for happiness. *Journal of Happiness Studies, 20*(2), 373-90.

Grubbs, J. B., Exline, J. J., & Campbell, W. K. (2013). I deserve better and God knows it! Psychological entitlement as a robust predictor of anger at God. *Psychology of Religion and Spirituality, 5*(3), 192-200.

Guilford, J. P. (1950). Creativity. *American Psychologist, 5,* 444-54.

Guivernau, M., & Duda, J. L. (2002). Moral atmosphere and athletic aggressive tendencies in young soccer players. *Journal of Moral Education, 31*(1), 67-85.

Gullone, E. (2000). The biophilia hypothesis and life in the 21st century: Increasing mental health or increasing pathology? *Journal of Happiness Studies, 1*(3), 293-322.

Guthrie, D. (1981). *New testament theology.* IVP Academic.

Gutman, J., & Priest, R. F. (1969). When is aggression funny? *Journal of Personality and Social Psychology, 12*(1), 60-65.

Haas, J. (1972). Binging: Educational control among high steel ironworkers. *American Behavioral Scientist, 16*(1), 27-34.

Hackett, R. D., & Wang, G. (2012). Virtues and leadership: An integrating conceptual framework founded in Aristotelian and Confucian perspectives on virtues. *Management Decision, 50*(5), 868-99.

Hackney, C. H. (2007). Possibilities for a Christian positive psychology. *Journal of Psychology & Theology, 35*(3), 211-21.

Hackney, C. H. (2009a, October). *Pride kills wisdom* [Paper presentation]. Educating for Successful Intelligence and Creativity Symposium, Ancaster, ON, Canada.

Hackney, C. H. (2009b). The Aristotelian philosophy of the martial arts. *Journal of Asian Martial Arts, 18*(4), 8-17.

Hackney, C. H. (2010a). Positive psychology and Vanhoozer's theodramatic model of flourishing. *Edification: The Transdisciplinary Journal of Christian Psychology, 4*(1), 24-27.

Hackney, C. H. (2010b). Sanctification as a source of theological guidance in the construction of a Christian positive psychology. *Journal of Psychology and Christianity, 29*(3), 195-207.

Hackney, C. H. (2010c). *Martial virtues.* Charles E. Tuttle Publications.

Hackney, C. H. (2010d). Religion and mental health: What do you mean when you say "religion?"

What do you mean when you say "mental health?" In P. Verhagen, H. van Praag, J. Lopez-Ibor, J. Cox, & D. Moussaoui (Eds.), *Religion and psychiatry: Beyond boundaries* (pp. 343-60). John Wiley & Sons.

Hackney, C. H. (2011). The effect of mortality salience on the evaluation of humorous material. *Journal of Social Psychology, 151*(1), 51-62.

Hackney, C. H. (2013). Martial arts as a pathway to flourishing. In J. Sinott (Ed.), *Positive psychology: Advances in understanding adult motivation* (pp. 145-58). Springer Publishing.

Hackney, C. H. (2014) Imperfectible: Why positive psychology needs original sin. *Christian Psychology, 8*(1), 5-14.

Hackney, C. H., & Sanders, G. S. (2003). Religiosity and mental health: A meta-analysis of recent studies. *Journal for the Scientific Study of Religion, 42*(1), 43-55.

Hagerty, B. B. (2011, January 13). Army's "spiritual fitness" test angers some soldiers. *National Public Radio.* www.npr.org/2011/01/13/132904866/armys-spiritual-fitness-test-angers-some-soldiers

Hagger, M. S. (2010). Sleep, self-regulation, self-control and health. *Stress and Health, 26*(3), 181-85.

Hagger, M. S., & Chatzisarantis, N. L. D. (Eds.). (2007). *Intrinsic motivation and self-determination in exercise and sport.* Kinetics.

Hagger, M. S., Wood, C., Stiff, C., & Chatzisarantis, N. L. (2010). Ego depletion and the strength model of self-control: A meta-analysis. *Psychological Bulletin, 136*(4), 495-525.

Haidt, J. (2002). *It's more fun to work on strengths than weaknesses (but it may not be better for you).* http://wsrv.clas.virginia.edu/~jdh6n/strengths_analysis.doc

Haidt, J. (2003). The moral emotions. In R. J. Davidson, K. R. Scherer, & H. H. Goldsmith (Eds.), *Handbook of affective sciences* (pp. 852-70). Oxford University Press.

Haidt, J. (2006). *The happiness hypothesis: Finding modern truth in ancient wisdom.* Basic Books.

Haidt, J., & Kesebir, S. (2010). Morality. In S. T. Fiske, D. T. Gilbert, & G. Lindzey (Eds.), *Handbook of social psychology* (pp. 797-832). John Wiley & Sons.

Halama, P. (2014). Meaning in life and coping: Sense of meaning as a buffer against stress. In A. Batthyany & P. Russo-Netzer (Eds.), *Meaning in positive and existential psychology* (pp. 239-50). Springer.

Hall, G. S. (1882). The education of the will. *Princeton Review, 2*, 306-25.

Halpern, D. F. (2002). Sex, lies, and audiotapes: The Clinton-Lewinsky scandal. In R. J. Sternberg (Ed.), *Why smart people can be so stupid* (pp. 106-23). Yale University Press.

Hamilton, W. D. (1964). The genetical evolution of social behaviour. II. *Journal of Theoretical Biology, 7*(1), 17-52.

Hanek, K. J., Olson, B. D., & McAdams, D. P. (2011). Political orientation and the psychology of Christian prayer: How conservatives and liberals pray. *International Journal for the Psychology of Religion, 21*(1), 30-42.

Haney, C., Banks, C., & Zimbardo, P. (1973). Interpersonal dynamics in a simulated prison. *International Journal of Criminology and Penology, 1*(1), 69-97.

Hannon, P. A. (2001). *Perpetrator behavior and forgiveness in close relationships* [Unpublished doctoral dissertation]. University of North Carolina at Chapel Hill.

Harari, Y. N. (2008). Combat flow: Military, political, and ethical dimensions of subjective well-being in war. *Review of General Psychology, 12*(3), 253-64.

Harding, S. R., Flannelly, K. J., Weaver, A. J., & Costa, K. G. (2005). The influence of religion on death anxiety and death acceptance. *Mental Health, Religion & Culture, 8*(4), 253-61.

Hardman, A. R., & Jones, C. (2011). Sports coaching and virtue ethics. In A. R. Hardman & C. Jones (Eds.), *The ethics of sports coaching* (pp. 72-84). Routledge.

Hardman, A. R., Jones, C., & Jones, R. (2010). Sports coaching, virtue ethics and emulation. *Physical Education and Sport Pedagogy, 15*(4), 345-59.

Hardré, P. L., & Reeve, J. (2009). Training corporate managers to adopt a more autonomy-supportive motivating style toward employees: An intervention study. *International Journal of Training and Development, 13*(3), 165-84.

Hardy, L., Arthur, C. A., Jones, G., Shariff, A., Munnoch, K., Isaacs, I., & Allsopp, A. J. (2010). The relationship between transformational leadership behaviors, psychological, and training outcomes in elite military recruits. *The Leadership Quarterly, 21*(1), 20-32.

Harker, L., & Keltner, D. (2001). Expressions of positive emotion in women's college yearbook pictures and their relationship to personality and life outcomes across adulthood. *Journal of Personality and Social Psychology, 80*(1), 112-24.

Harms, P. D. (2011). Adult attachment styles in the workplace. *Human Resource Management Review, 21*(4), 285-96.

Harms, P. D., Herian, M. N., Krasikova, D. V., Vanhove, A., & Lester, P. B. (2013). *The Comprehensive Soldier and Family Fitness Program evaluation report #4: Evaluation of resilience training and mental and behavioral health outcomes.* http://csf2.army.mil /supportdocs/TR4.pdf

Harpham, E. J. (2004). Gratitude in the history of ideas. In R. A. Emmons & M. E. McCullough (Eds.), *The psychology of gratitude* (pp. 19-36). Oxford University Press.

Harrington, D., & Keenan, J. (2005) *Jesus and virtue ethics: Building bridges between New Testament studies and moral theology.* Sheed and Ward.

Harris, R. (2006). Embracing your demons: An overview of acceptance and commitment therapy. *Psychotherapy in Australia, 12*(4), 2-8.

Harrison, P. R., Smith, J. L., & Bryant, F. B. (2013). The savoring expedition: An exercise to cultivate savoring. In J. J. Froh & A. C. Parks (Eds.), *Activities for teaching positive psychology: A guide for instructors* (pp. 149-52). American Psychological Association.

Harter, S. (1999). *The construction of the self: A developmental perspective.* Guilford Press.

Harvey, L. (2014). *A brief theology of sport.* SCM Press.

Harwood, A., Lavidor, M., & Rassovsky, Y. (2017). Reducing aggression with martial arts: A meta-analysis of child and youth studies. *Aggression and Violent Behavior, 34*, 96-101.

Hathaway, A. D., & Sharpley, J. (2010). The cannabis experience: An analysis of "flow." In D. Jacquette (Ed.), *Philosophy for everyone. Cannabis: What were we just talking about?* (pp. 50-61). Wiley-Blackwell.

Hathaway, W., & Tan, E. (2009). Religiously oriented mindfulness-based cognitive therapy. *Journal of Clinical Psychology, 65*(2), 158-71.

Hatsumi, M., & Cole, B. (2001). *Understand? Good. Play!* Bushin Books.

Hauerwas, S. (1975). *Character and the Christian life: A study in theological ethics.* Trinity University Press.

Hauerwas, S. (1983). *The peaceable kingdom: A primer in Christian ethics.* University of Notre Dame Press.

Hayes, S. C. (2005). *Get out of your mind and into your life: The new acceptance and commitment therapy.* New Harbinger Publications.

Hayes, S. C., Strosahl, K. D., & Wilson, K. G. (2012). *Acceptance and commitment therapy: The process and practice of mindful change.* Guilford Press.

Hazan, C., & Shaver, P. (1987). Romantic love conceptualized as an attachment process. *Journal of Personality and Social Psychology, 52*(3), 511-24.

Hebl, J., & Enright, R. D. (1993). Forgiveness as a psychotherapeutic goal with elderly females. *Psychotherapy: Theory, Research, Practice, Training, 30*(4), 658-67.

Hefferon, K., & Mutrie, N. (2012). Physical activity as a "stellar" positive psychology intervention. In E. O. Acevedo (Ed.), *Oxford handbook of exercise psychology* (pp. 117-28). Oxford University Press.

Heine, C. (1996). *Flow and achievement in mathematics* [Unpublished doctoral dissertation]. University of Chicago.

Held, B. S. (2002). The tyranny of the positive attitude in America: Observation and speculation. *Journal of Clinical Psychology, 58*(9), 965-92.

Held, B. S. (2004). The negative side of positive psychology. *Journal of Humanistic Psychology, 44*(1), 9-46.

Held, V. (2006). *The ethics of care: Personal, political, and global.* Oxford University Press.

Henman, L. D. (2001). Humor as a coping mechanism: Lessons from POWs. *Humor, 14*(1), 83-94.

Henning, J. S., & Oldham, J. T. (1977). Children of divorce: Legal and psychological crises. *Journal of Clinical Child Psychology, 6*(2), 55-58.

Henry, C. F. H. (1957). *Christian personal ethics.* Eerdmans.

Herdt, J. A. (2015). Frailty, fragmentation, and social dependency in the cultivation of Christian virtue. In N. E. Snow (Ed.), *Cultivating virtue: Perspectives from philosophy, theology, and psychology* (pp. 227-49). Oxford University Press.

Herman, C. P., & Mack, D. (1975). Restrained and unrestrained eating. *Journal of Personality, 43*(4), 647-60.

Hertzberg, F. (1968). One more time: How do you motivate employees? *Harvard Business Review, 46*, 53-62.

Hess, U. (2014). Anger is a positive emotion. In W. G. Parrott (Ed.), *The positive side of negative emotions* (pp. 55-75). Guilford Press.

Heuer, R. J., Jr. (1999). *Psychology of intelligence analysis.* Center for the Study of Intelligence.

Hickey, W. S. (2010). Meditation as medicine: A critique. *CrossCurrents, 60*(2), 168-84.

Hicks, D. J., & Stapleford, T. A. (2016). The virtues of scientific practice: MacIntyre, virtue ethics, and the historiography of science. *Isis, 107*(3), 449-72.

Higgins, C. (2003). MacIntyre's moral theory and the possibility of an aretaic ethics of teaching. *Journal of Philosophy of Education, 37*(2), 279-92.

Higgs, J. (2012). Realising practical wisdom from the pursuit of wise practice. In A. E. Kinsella & A. Pitman (Eds.), *Phronesis as professional knowledge: Practical wisdom in the professions* (pp. 73-86). Sense Publishers.

Higgs, R. J. (1995). *God in the stadium: Sports and religion in America.* University Press of Kentucky.

Highland, J. (2005). Transformation to eternity: Augustine's conversion to mindfulness. *Buddhist-Christian Studies, 25*(1), 91-108.

Hilbig, B. E., Zettler, I., Leist, F., & Heydasch, T. (2013). It takes two: Honesty-humility and agreeableness differentially predict active versus reactive cooperation. *Personality and Individual Differences, 54*(5), 598-603.

Hill, P. C., & Hall, M. E. L. (2018). Uncovering the good in positive psychology: Toward a worldview conception that can help positive psychology flourish. In N. J. L. Brown, T. Lomas, & F. J. Eiroa-Orosa (Eds.), *Routledge international handbook of critical positive psychology* (pp. 245-62). Routledge.

Hill, P. C., & Hood, R. W. (Eds.). (1999). *Measures of religiosity.* Religious Education Press.

Hill, P. C., Pargament, K. I., Hood, R. W., Jr., McCullough, M. E., Swyers, J. P., Larson, D. B., & Zinnbauer, B. J. (2000). Conceptualizing religion and spirituality: Points of commonality, points of departure. *Journal for the Theory of Social Behaviour, 30*(1), 51-77.

Hill, T., Smith, N. D., & Mann, M. F. (1987). Role of efficacy expectations in predicting the decision to use advanced technologies: The case of computers. *Journal of Applied Psychology, 72*(2), 307-13.

Hill, W. (2015). *Spiritual friendship: Finding love in the church as a celibate gay Christian.* Brazos.

Hodge, C. (2001). *Systematic theology: Vol. 3. Soteriology.* Hendrickson Publishers. (Original work published 1872)

Hodge, K., & Lonsdale, C. (2011). Prosocial and antisocial behavior in sport: The role of coaching style, autonomous vs. controlled motivation, and moral disengagement. *Journal of Sport & Exercise Psychology, 33*(4), 527-47.

Hodges, T., & Kennedy, J. (2015). Creating a positive campus culture. In J. C. Wade, L. I. Marks, & R. D. Hetzel (Eds.), *Positive psychology on the college campus* (pp. 343-57). Oxford University Press.

Hoekema, A. (1987). The Reformed perspective. In S. N. Gundry (Ed.), *Five views on sanctification* (pp. 61-90). Zondervan.

Hoff, F. (2002). *Kyudo: The way of the bow* (S. C. Kohn, Trans). Shambhala Publications.

Hoffman, B. J., Woehr, D. J., Maldagen-Youngjohn, R., & Lyons, B. D. (2011). Great man or great myth? A quantitative review of the relationship between individual differences and leader effectiveness. *Journal of Occupational and Organizational Psychology, 84*(2), 347-81.

Hoffman, M. L. (1982). Development of prosocial motivation: Empathy and guilt. In N. Eisenberg (Ed.). *The development of prosocial behavior* (pp. 281-313). Academic Press.

Hoffmann, P. (1997). The endorphin hypothesis. In W. P. Morgan (Ed.), *Physical activity and mental health* (pp. 163-77). Taylor & Francis.

Hoffman, S. G., Sawyer, A. T., Witt, A. A., & Oh, D. (2010). The effect of mindfulness-based therapy on anxiety and depression: A meta analytic review. *Journal of Consulting and Clinical Psychology, 78*(2), 169-83.

Hoffman, S. J. (2010). *Good game: Christianity and the culture of sports.* Baylor University Press.

Hofmann, W., Vohs, K. D., & Baumeister, R. F. (2012). What people desire, feel conflicted about, and try to resist in everyday life. *Psychological Science, 23*(6), 582-88.

Hoge, C. W., Castro, C. A., Messer, S. C., McGurk, D., Cotting, D. I., & Koffman, R. L. (2004). Combat duty in Iraq and Afghanistan, mental health problems, and barriers to care. *New England Journal of Medicine, 351*(1), 13-22.

Hojjat, M., & Cramer, D. (Eds.). (2013). *Positive psychology of love.* Oxford University Press.

Holdaway, S. (1988). Blue jokes: Humour in police work. In C. Powell & G. E. C. Paton (Eds.), *Humour in society: Resistance and control* (pp. 106-22). Macmillan.

Holladay, C. R. (2012). The beatitudes: Happiness and the kingdom. In B. A. Strawn (Ed.), *The Bible and the pursuit of happiness* (pp. 141-68). Oxford University Press.

Holmes, A. F. (Ed.). (2005). *War and Christian ethics* (2nd ed.). Baker Academic.

Hoover, J. (2018). Can Christians practice mindfulness without compromising their convictions? *Journal of Psychology & Christianity, 37*(3), 247-55.

Horton, M. (2011). *The Christian faith: A systematic theology for pilgrims on the way.* Zondervan.

Houston, J. M., & Hindmarsh, B. (2013). *For Christ and his kingdom: Inspiring a new generation.* Regent College Publishing.

Howell, A. J., & Passmore, H. A. (2019). Acceptance and commitment training (ACT) as a positive psychological intervention: A systematic review and initial meta-analysis regarding ACT's role in well-being promotion among university students. *Journal of Happiness Studies, 20,* 1-16.

Huggins, M. K., Haritos-Fatouros, M., & Zimbardo, P. G. (2002). *Violence workers: Police torturers and murderers reconstruct Brazilian atrocities.* University of California Press.

Hughes, P. E. (1989). *The true image: The origin and destiny of man in Christ.* Eerdmans.

Hursthouse, R. (1999). *On virtue ethics.* Oxford University Press.

Husain, S. A. (1998). Religion and mental health from the Muslim perspective. In H. G. Koenig (Ed.), *Handbook of religion and mental health* (pp. 279-91). Academic Press.

Huston, T. L., Ruggiero, M., Conner, R., & Geis, G. (1981). Bystander intervention into crime: A study based on naturally occurring episodes. *Social Psychology Quarterly, 44*(1), 14-23.

Huynh, A. C., Oakes, H., Shay, G., & McGreggor, I. (2017). The wisdom in virtue: Pursuit of virtue predicts wise reasoning about personal conflicts. *Psychological Science, 28*(12), 1848-56.

Hyman, R. (2002). Why and when are smart people stupid? In R. J. Sternberg (Ed.), *Why smart people can be so stupid* (pp. 1-23). Yale University Press.

Hystad, S. W., Eid, J., Laberg, J. C., & Bartone, P. T. (2011). Psychological hardiness predicts admission into Norwegian military officer schools. *Military Psychology, 23*(4), 381-89.

Inglehart, R. (1990). *Culture shift in advanced industrial society.* Princeton University Press.

Isen, A. M., & Daubman, K. A. (1984). The influence of affect on categorization. *Journal of Personality and Social Psychology, 47*(6), 1206-17.

Isen, A. M., Daubman, K. A., & Nowicki, G. P. (1987). Positive affect facilitates creative problem solving. *Journal of Personality and Social Psychology, 52*(6), 1122-31.

Isen, A. M., Niedenthal, P. M., & Cantor, N. (1992). An influence of positive affect on social categorization. *Motivation and Emotion, 16*(1), 65-78.

Ivtzan, I., & Lomas, T. (Eds.). (2016). *Mindfulness in positive psychology: The science of meditation and wellbeing*. Routledge.

Ivtzan, I., Lomas, T., Hefferon, K., & Worth, P. (2016). *Second wave positive psychology: Embracing the dark side of life*. Routledge.

Izard, C. (1977). *Human emotions*. Plenum Press.

Jackson, S. A., & Csikszentmihalyi, M. (1999). *Flow in sports*. Human Kinetics.

Jackson, S. A., Thomas, P. R., Marsh, H. W., & Smethurst, C. J. (2001). Relationships between flow, self-concept, psychological skills, and performance. *Journal of Applied Sport Psychology, 13*(2), 129-53.

James, W. (1890). *The principles of psychology*. Encyclopedia Britannica.

James, W. (1902). *The varieties of religious experience*. Penguin Putnam.

Jarden, A. (2012). Positive psychologists on positive psychology. *International Journal of Wellbeing, 2*(2), 70-149.

Jaycox, L. H., Reivich, K. J., Gillham, J., & Seligman, M. E. P. (1994). Preventing depressive symptoms in school children. *Behaviour Research and Therapy, 32*(8), 801-16.

Jeal, R. R. (2010). Preface. In R. R. Jeal (Ed.), *Human sexuality and the nuptial mystery* (pp. xii-xviii). Cascade Books.

Jebb, A. T., Tay, L., Diener, E., & Oishi, S. (2018). Happiness, income satiation and turning points around the world. *Nature Human Behaviour, 2*(1), 33-38.

Jenkins, R. A., & Pargament, K. I. (1988). Cognitive appraisals in cancer patients. *Social Science & Medicine, 26*(6), 625-33.

Joeckel, S. (2014). Christianity. In S. Attardo (Ed.), *Encyclopedia of humor studies* (pp. 127-29). Sage.

Johnson, D. C., Thom, N. J., Stanley, E. A., Haase, L., Simmons, A. N., Shih, P. B., Thomson, W. K.,

Potterat, E. G., Minor, T. R., & Paulus, M. P. (2014). Modifying resilience mechanisms in at-risk individuals: A controlled study of mindfulness training in Marines preparing for deployment. *American Journal of Psychiatry, 171*(8), 844-53.

Johnson, E. L. (Ed.). (2010). *Psychology and Christianity: Five views*. IVP Academic.

Johnson, J. A., Keiser, H. N., Skarin, E. M., & Ross, S. R. (2014). The dispositional flow scale-2 as a measure of autotelic personality: An examination of criterion-related validity. *Journal of Personality Assessment, 96*(4), 465-70.

Johnson, K. J., & Fredrickson, B. L. (2005). "We all look the same to me": Positive emotions eliminate the own-race bias in face recognition. *Psychological Science, 16*(11), 875-81.

Johnson, M., Dose, A. Pipe, T., Petersen, W., Huschka, M., Gallenberg, M., et al. (2009). Centering prayer for women receiving chemotherapy for recurrent ovarian cancer: A pilot study. *Oncology Nursing Forum, 36*(4), 421-28.

Jones, L. G. (1995). *Embodying forgiveness: A theological analysis*. Eerdmans.

Jones, L. G., & Musekura, C. (2010). *Forgiving as we've been forgiven: Community practices for making peace*. InterVarsity Press.

Jordan, R. D. (1989). *The quiet hero: Figures of temperance in Spenser, Donne, Milton, and Joyce*. Catholic University of America Press.

Jørgensen, I. S., & Nafstad, H. E. (2004). Positive psychology: Historical, philosophical, and epistemological perspectives. In P. A. Linley & S. Joseph (Eds.), *Positive psychology in practice* (pp. 15-34). John Wiley and Sons.

Joshanloo, M. (2014). Eastern conceptualizations of happiness: Fundamental differences with Western views. *Journal of Happiness Studies, 15*(2), 475-93.

Joye, Y. (2007). Architectural lessons from environmental psychology: The case of biophilic architecture. *Review of General Psychology, 11*(4), 305-28.

Kabat-Zinn, J. (1990). *Full catastrophe living: Using the wisdom of your body and mind to face stress, pain, and illness*. Delta Trade Paperbacks.

Kabat-Zinn, J. (1994). *Wherever you go, there you are: Mindfulness meditation in everyday life*. Hyperion.

Kabat-Zinn, J. (2003). Mindfulness-based interventions in context: Past, present, and future. *Clinical Psychology: Science and Practice, 10*(2), 144-56.

Kabat-Zinn, J. (2011). Some reflections on the origins of MBSR, skillful means, and the trouble with maps. *Contemporary Buddhism, 12*(1), 281-306.

Kaczor, C. (2015). *The gospel of happiness: Rediscover your faith through spiritual practice and positive psychology*. Image.

Kahoe, R. D., & Dunn, R. F. (1975). The fear of death and religious attitudes and behavior. *Journal for the Scientific Study of Religion, 14*(4), 379-82.

Kale, D. W. (2003). *Managing conflict in the church*. Beacon Hill.

Kalpidou, M., Costin, D., & Morris, J. (2011). The relationship between Facebook and the well-being of undergraduate college students. *CyberPsychology, Behavior, and Social Networking, 14*(4), 183-89.

Kamins, M., & C. S. Dweck (2000). *Theories of intelligence, contingent self-worth, and coping*. Unpublished manuscript, Columbia University.

Kano, J. (1986). *Kodokan judo*. Kodansha America.

Kant, I. (1960). *Religion within the limits of reason alone* (2nd ed.) (T. M. Greene & H. H. Hudson, Trans.). Open Court Publishing. (Original work published 1793)

Kaplan, S. (1995). The restorative benefits of nature: Toward an integrative framework. *Journal of Environmental Psychology, 15*(3), 169-82.

Kashdan, T. B., & Biswas-Diener, R. (2014). *The upside of your dark side*. Hudson Street Press.

Kashdan, T. B., & Ciarrochi, J. (Eds.). (2013). *Mindfulness, acceptance, and positive psychology*. Context Press.

Kashdan, T. B., Mishra, A., Breen, W. E., & Froh, J. J. (2009). Gender differences in gratitude: Examining appraisals, narratives, the willingness to express emotions, and changes in psychological needs. *Journal of Personality, 77*(3), 691-730.

Kasser, T., & Ahuvia, A. C. (2002). Materialistic values and well-being in business students. *European Journal of Social Psychology, 32*(1), 137-46.

Kasser, T., Dungan, N., Rosenblum, K. L., Sameroff, A. J., Deci, E. L., Niemiec, C. P., Ryan, R. M., Osp, A., Bond, R., & Dittmar, H. (2014). Changes in materialism, changes in psychological well-being: Evidence from three longitudinal studies and an intervention experiment. *Motivation and Emotion, 38*(1), 1-22.

Kasser, T., & Ryan, R. M. (1993). A dark side of the American dream: Correlates of financial success as a central life aspiration. *Journal of Personality and Social Psychology, 65*(2), 410-422.

Keane, A., Ducette, J., & Adler, D. (1985). Stress in ICU and non-ICU nurses. *Nursing Research, 34*(4), 231-36.

Keen, M. (1984). *Chivalry*. Yale University Press.

Keenan, J. F. (2016). Virtues. In P. McCoster & D. Turner (Eds.), *The Cambridge companion to the Summa Theologiae* (pp. 194-205). Cambridge University Press.

Keener, C. S. (1999). *A commentary on the gospel of Matthew*. Eerdmans.

Keith-Spiegel, P. (1972). Early conceptions of humor: Varieties and issues. In J. H. Goldstein & P. E. McGhee (Eds.) *The psychology of humor: Theoretical perspectives and empirical issues* (pp. 4-42). Academic Press.

Keller, J., & Bless, H. (2008). Flow and regulatory compatibility: An experimental approach to the flow model of intrinsic motivation. *Personality and Social Psychology Bulletin, 34*(2), 196-209.

Keller, J., & Blomann, F. (2008). Locus of control and the flow experience: An experimental analysis. *European Journal of Personality, 22*(7), 589-607.

Keller, J., Ringelhan, S., & Blomann, F. (2011). Does skills-demands-compatibility result in intrinsic motivation? Experimental test of a basic notion proposed in the theory of flow-experiences. *Journal of Positive Psychology, 6*(5), 408-17.

Kelly, D. R., Matthews, M. D., & Bartone, P. T. (2014). Grit and hardiness as predictors of performance among West Point cadets. *Military Psychology, 26*(4), 327-42.

Kelly, V. C., & Lamia, M. C. (2018). *The upside of shame: Therapeutic interventions using the positive aspects of a "negative" emotion*. W. W. Norton & Company.

Keng, S., Smoski, M. J., & Robins, C. J. (2011). Effects of mindfulness on psychological health: A review of empirical studies. *Clinical Psychology Review, 31*(6), 1041-56.

Khoshaba, D. M., & Maddi, S. R. (1999). Early experiences in hardiness development. *Consulting Psychology Journal, 51*(2), 106-16.

Kiecolt-Glaser, J. K., & Newton, T. L. (2001). Marriage and health: His and hers. *Psychological Bulletin, 127*(4), 472-503.

Kierkegaard, S. (1941a). *Concluding unscientific postscript* (D. Swenson & W. Lowrie, Trans.).

Princeton University Press. (Original work published 1846)

Kierkegaard, S. (1941b). *Fear and trembling and the sickness unto death* (W. Lowrie, Trans.). Princeton University Press. (Original work published 1849)

Kierkegaard, S. (1944). *The concept of dread* (W. Lowrie, Trans.). Princeton University Press. (Original work published 1844)

Kim-Prieto, C., & Eid, M. (2004). Norms for experiencing emotions. *Journal of Happiness Studies, 5*(3), 241-268.

Kimball, B. A. (1986). *Orators and philosophers: A history of the idea of liberal education.* Teachers College Press.

Kimball, C. N. (2005). Radical-reformation theology and the recovery of the proper incarnational view of the self. In A. Dueck & C. Lee (Eds.), *Why psychology needs theology: A radical-reformation perspective* (pp. 99-118). Eerdmans.

King, L. A., Eells, J. E., & Burton, C. M. (2004). The good life, broadly and narrowly considered. In P. A. Linley & S. Joseph (Eds.), *Positive psychology in practice* (pp. 35-54). John Wiley & Sons.

Kinsella, E. L., Ritchie, T. D., & Igou, E. R. (2015). Zeroing in on heroes: A prototype analysis of hero features. *Journal of Personality and Social Psychology, 108*(1), 114-27.

Kirk, D., & Kinchin, G. (2003). Situated learning as a theoretical framework for sport education. *European Physical Education Review, 9*(3), 221-35.

Kiyota, M. (2002). *The shambhala guide to kendo.* Shambhala Publications.

Kipp, L. E., & Weiss, M. R. (2013). Social influences, psychological need satisfaction, and well-being among female adolescent gymnasts. *Sport, Exercise, and Performance Psychology, 2*(1), 62-75.

Kirk, D., & Kinchin, G. (2003). Situated learning as a theoretical framework for sport education. *European Physical Education Review, 9*(3), 221-35.

Kirkpatrick, L. A., & Shaver, P. R. (1990). Attachment theory and religion: Childhood attachments, religious beliefs, and conversion. *Journal for the Scientific Study of Religion, 29*(3), 315-34.

Knabb, J. J. (2012). Centering prayer as an alternative to mindfulness-based cognitive therapy for depression relapse prevention. *Journal of Religion and Health, 51*(3), 908-24.

Knabb, J. J., Welsh, R. K., & Alexander, P. (2012). Towards an integrated view of the necessity of human interdependence: Perspectives from theology, philosophy, and psychology. *Journal of Spirituality in Mental Health, 14*(3), 166-80.

Ko, I., & Donaldson, S. I. (2011). Applied positive organizational psychology: The state of the science and practice. In S. I. Donaldson, M. Csikszentmihalyi, & J. Nakamura (Eds.), *Applied positive psychology: Improving everyday life, health, schools, work, and society* (pp. 137-154). Routledge.

Kobasa, S. C. (1979). Stressful life events and health: An inquiry into hardiness. *Journal of Personality and Social Psychology, 37*(1), 1-11.

Kobasa, S. C. (1982). Commitment and coping in stress resistance among lawyers. *Journal of Personality and Social Psychology, 42*(4), 707-17.

Kobasa, S. C., Maddi, S. R., & Courington, S. (1981). Personality and constitution as mediators of the stress-illness relationship. *Journal of Health and Social Behavior, 22*(4), 368-78.

Kobasa, S. C., Maddi, S. R., & Kahn, S. (1982). Hardiness and health: A prospective study. *Journal of Personality and Social Psychology, 42*(1), 884-90.

Kobasa, S. C., Maddi, S. R., & Puccetti, M. C. (1982). Personality and exercise as buffers in the stress-illness relationship. *Journal of Behavioral Medicine, 5*(4), 391-404.

Kobasa, S. C., Maddi, S. R., Puccetti, M., & Zola, M. (1986). Relative effectiveness of hardiness, exercise, and social support as resources against illness. *Journal of Psychosomatic Research, 29*(5), 525-33.

Koch, A. (2012). Biblical and patristic foundations for sport. In K. Lixey, C. Hübenthal, D. Mieth, & N. Müller (Eds.), *Sport and Christianity: A sign of the times in the light of faith* (pp. 81-103). Catholic University of America Press.

Koenig, H. G. (2018). *Religion and mental health: Research and clinical applications.* Academic Press.

Koenig, H. G., Al-Zaben, F., & VanderWeele, T. J. (2020). Religion and psychiatry: Recent developments in research. *BJPsych Advances, 26*, in press.

Koestner, R., Ryan, R. M., Bernieri, F., & Holt, K. (1984). Setting limits on children's behavior: The differential effects of controlling vs. informational styles on intrinsic motivation and creativity. *Journal of Personality, 52*(3), 233-48.

Koh, W. L., Steers, R. M., & Terborg, J. R. (1995). The effects of transformational leadership on teacher attitudes and student performance in Singapore. *Journal of Organizational Behavior, 16*(4), 319-33.

Kohlberg, L. (1981). *Essays on moral development: Vol. 1. The philosophy of moral development.* Harper & Row.

Kojetin, B. A., McIntosh, D. N., Bridges, R. A., & Spilka, B. (1987). Quest: Constructive search or religious conflict? *Journal for the scientific study of Religion, 26*(1), 111-15.

Koltko-Rivera, M. E. (2004). The psychology of worldviews. *Review of General Psychology, 8*(1), 3-58.

Koltyn, K. F. (1997). The thermogenic hypothesis. In W. P. Morgan (Ed.), *Physical activity and mental health* (pp. 213-26). Taylor and Francis.

Kosits, R. D. (2004). Of faculties, fallacies, and freedom: Dilemma and irony in the secularization of American psychology. *History of Psychology, 7*(4), 340-66.

Kosloff, S., Greenberg, J., Sullivan, D., & Weise, D. (2010). Of trophies and pillars: Exploring the terror management functions of short-term and long-term relationship partners. *Personality and Social Psychology Bulletin, 36*(8), 1037-51.

Kotva, J. J., Jr. (1996). *The Christian case for virtue ethics.* Georgetown University Press.

Koyzis, D. (2019). *Political visions and illusions* (2nd ed.). IVP Academic.

Krause, N., & Ingersoll-Dayton, B. (2001). Religion and the process of forgiveness in late life. *Review of Religious Research, 42*(3), 252-76.

Kreighbaum, A. (2018, June 22). An "education and the workforce" agency? *Inside Higher Ed.* www.insidehighered.com/news/2018/06/22/white-house-merger-plan-reignites-debate-education-training

Kristjánsson, K. (2010). Positive psychology, happiness, and virtue: The troublesome conceptual issues. *Review of General Psychology, 14*(4), 296-310.

Kristjánsson, K. (2013). *Virtue and vices in positive psychology: A philosophical critique.* Cambridge University Press.

Krizan, A., & Hisler, G. (2016). The essential role of sleep in self-regulation. In K. D. Vohs & R. F. Baumeister (Eds.), *Handbook of self-regulation: Research, theory, and applications* (3rd ed.), (pp. 182-202), Guilford Press.

Krumrei-Mancuso, E. J., Haggard, M. C., LaBouff, J. P., & Rowatt, W. C. (2020). Links between intellectual humility and acquiring knowledge. *Journal of Positive Psychology, 15*(2), 155-70.

Kubitz, K. A., Landers, D. M., Petruzzello, S. J., & Han, M. (1996). The effects of acute and chronic exercise on sleep. A meta-analytic review. *Sports Medicine, 21*(4), 277-91.

Kuhlman, T. L. (1988). Gallows humor for a scaffold setting: Managing aggressive patients on a maximum-security forensic unit. *Psychiatric Services, 39*(10), 1085-90.

Kuhn, T. S. (1996). *The structure of scientific revolutions* (3rd ed.). University of Chicago Press.

Kuhn, U., & Brulé, G. (2019). Buffering effects for negative life events: The role of material, social, religious and personal resources. *Journal of Happiness Studies, 20*(5), 1397-1417.

Kuiper, N. A. (2012). Humor and resiliency: Towards a process model of coping and growth. *Europe's Journal of Psychology, 8*, 475-91.

Kuiper, N. A., & Martin, R. A. (1998). Is sense of humor a positive personality characteristic? In V. Raskin & W. Ruch (Eds.), *The sense of humor: Explorations of a personality characteristic* (pp. 159-178). Mouton de Gruyter.

Kuiper, N. A., Martin, R. A., & Dance, K. A. (1992). Sense of humour and enhanced quality of life. *Personality and Individual Differences, 13*(12), 1273-83.

Kuiper, N. A., Martin, R. A., & Olinger, L. J. (1993). Coping humour, stress, and cognitive appraisals. *Canadian Journal of Behavioural Science 25*(1), 81-96.

Kuiper, N. A., McKenzie, S. D., & Belanger, K. A. (1995). Cognitive appraisals and individual differences in sense of humor: Motivational and affective implications. *Personality and Individual Differences, 19*(3), 359-72.

Kurian, M., Caterino, L. C., & Kulhavy, R. W. (1993). Personality characteristics and duration of ATA taekwondo training. *Perceptual and Motor Skills, 76*(2), 363-66.

Kurian, M., Verdi, M. P., Caterino, L. C., & Kulhavy, R. W. (1994). Rating scales on the children's personality questionnaire to training time and belt rank in ATA taekwondo. *Perceptual and Motor Skills, 79*(2), 904-6.

Ladd, T., & Mathisen, J. A. (1999). *Muscular Christianity: Evangelical protestants and the development of American sport.* Baker Books.

Lakes, K. D., & Hoyt, W. T. (2004). Promoting self-regulation through school-based martial arts training. *Applied Developmental Psychology, 25*(3), 283-302.

Lamb, S. (2002). Women, abuse, and forgiveness: A special case. In S. Lamb & J. G. Murphy (Eds.), *Before forgiving: Cautionary views of forgiveness in psychotherapy* (pp. 155-71). Oxford University Press.

Lambert, R. B., & Lambert, N. K. (1995). The effects of humor on secretory immunoglobulin A levels in school-aged children. *Pediatric Nursing, 21*(1), 16-19.

Lancer, K. (2000). *Hardiness and Olympic women's synchronized swim team* [Paper presentation]. Conference on Improving Performance in Sports, Las Vegas, NV, United States.

Landhäußer, A., & Keller, L. (2012). Flow and its affective, cognitive, and performance-related consequences. In S. Engeser (Ed.), *Advances in flow research* (pp. 65-86). Springer.

Langer, E. (2005). Well-being: Mindfulness versus positive evaluation. In C. R. Snyder & S. J. Lopez (Eds.), *Handbook of positive psychology* (pp. 214-30). Oxford University Press.

Langer, E. (2009). Mindfulness versus positive evaluation. In S. J. Lopez & C. R. Snyder (Eds.), *Oxford handbook of positive psychology* (pp. 279-94). Oxford University Press.

Laporte, J. (1997). Kenosis as a key to maturity of personality. In R. C. Roberts & M. R. Talbot (Eds.), *Limning the psyche: Explorations in Christian psychology* (pp. 229-44). Eerdmans.

Lapsley, J. (2012). A happy blend: Isaiah's vision of happiness (and beyond). In B. A. Strawn (Ed.), *The Bible and the pursuit of happiness* (pp. 75-94). Oxford University Press.

Larsen, J. T., Hemenover, S. H., Norris, C. J., & Cacioppo, J. T. (2003). Turning adversity to advantage: On the virtues of the coactivation of positive and negative emotions. In L. G. Aspinwall & U. M. Staudinger (Eds.), *A psychology of human strengths: Fundamental questions and future directions for a positive psychology* (pp. 211-25). American Psychological Association.

Larsen, R. J., & Eid, M. (2008). Ed Diener and the science of subjective well-being. In M. Eid & R. J. Larsen (Eds.), *The science of subjective well-being* (pp. 1-16). Guilford Press.

Larson, R., & Csikszentmihalyi, M. (1983). The experience sampling method. In H. T. Reid (Ed.), *New directions for methodology of social and behavioral science: Vol. 15* (pp. 41-56). Jossey-Bass.

Las Vegas Sun. (2011, March 8). *UNLV president presents cuts, says they are "a tragic loss and a giant step backward for Nevada"*. https://lasvegassun.com /blogs/ralstons-flash/2011/mar/08/unlv-president -presents-cuts-says-they-are-tragic-/

Lasker, J. N., Lohmann, J., & Toedter, L. (1989, October). *The role of religion in bereavement: The case of pregnancy loss* [Paper presentation]. Annual Meeting of the Society for the Scientific Study of Religion, Salt Lake City, UT, USA.

Latané, B., & Nida, S. (1981). Ten years of research on group size and helping. *Psychological Bulletin, 89*(2), 308-24.

Latourette, K. S. (2000). *A history of Christianity: Vol. I. Beginnings to 1500* (rev. ed.). Prince Press.

Lau, T. L. (2017). I write these things not to shame you. *Journal of the Evangelical Theological Society, 60*(1), 105-24.

Lau, T. L. (2020). *Defending shame: Its formative power in Paul's letters*. Baker Academic.

Lawlor, D. A., & Hopker, S. W. (2001). The effectiveness of exercise as an intervention in the management of depression: Systematic review and meta-regression analysis of randomised controlled trials. *British Medical Journal, 322*(7289), 1-8.

Lawrence, C. (2010). Why practice an unmartial martial art? In G. Priest & D. Young (Eds.), *Martial arts and philosophy: Beating and nothingness* (pp. 203-210). Open Court.

Lawrence, E. M., Rogers, R. G., Zajacova, A., & Wadsworth, T. (2019). Marital happiness, marital status, health, and longevity. *Journal of Happiness Studies, 20*(5), 1539-61.

Layard, R. (2005). *Happiness: Lessons from a new science*. Penguin.

Layman, F. D. (1982) Theology and humor. *The Asbury Seminarian, 38*, 3-25.

Layton, C. (1988). The personality of black-belt and nonblack-belt traditional karateka. *Perceptual and Motor Skills, 67*(1), 218.

Layton, C. (1990). Anxiety in black-belt and nonblack-belt traditional karateka. *Perceptual and Motor Skills, 71*(3), 905-6.

Lazarus, R. S., & Folkman, S. (1984). *Stress, appraisal, and coping*. Springer.

Lazarus, R. S., & Lazarus, B. N. (1994). *Passion and reason: Making sense of our emotions*. Oxford University Press.

Ledyard, G. S. (2002, April 9). *Appropriate ukemi. AikiWeb.* www.aikiweb.com/training/ledyard1 .html

Lee, M., Zimbardo, P. G., & Bertholf, M. J. (1977, November). Shy murderers. *Psychology Today, 76*(11), 68-70, 76, 148.

Lee, P., & George, R. P. (2014). *Conjugal union: What marriage is and why it matters.* Cambridge University Press.

Lefcourt, H. M. (2004). Humor. In C. R. Snyder and S. J. Lopez (Eds.), *Handbook of positive psychology* (pp. 619-31). Oxford University Press.

Lefcourt, H. M., Davidson, K., Shepherd, R., Phillips, M., Prkachin, K., & Mills, D. (1995). Perspective-taking humor: Accounting for stress moderation. *Journal of Social and Clinical Psychology, 14*(4), 373-91.

Lefcourt, H. M., Davidson-Katz, K., & Kueneman, K. (1990). Humor and immune system functioning. *Humor, 3*(3), 305-21.

Lehrer, J. (May 18, 2009). Don't! The secret of self-control. *The New Yorker.* www.newyorker .com/magazine/2009/05/18/dont-2

Leith, K. P., & Baumeister, R. F. (1998). Empathy, shame, guilt, and narratives of interpersonal conflicts: Guilt-prone people are better at perspective taking. *Journal of Personality, 66*(1), 1-37.

Leith, L. M., Kerr, G. A., & Faulkner, G. E. (2011). Exercise and mental health. In P. R. E. Crocker (Ed.), *Sport and exercise psychology: A Canadian perspective* (2nd ed.) (pp. 306-36). Pearson.

Leithart, P. J. (2014). *Gratitude: An intellectual history.* Baylor University Press.

Leopold, L. (2011, January 5). *Army's "spiritual fitness" test comes under fire. Truthout.* https://truthout .org/articles/armys-spiritual-fitness-test-comes -under-fire

Lester, P. B., Harms, P. D., Bulling, D. J., Herian, M. N., & Spain, S. M. (2011). *Evaluation of relation-ships between reported resilience and outcomes— Report #1: Negative outcomes (suicide, drug use, & violent crimes).* Defense Technical Information Center. www.dtic.mil/dtic/tr/fulltext/u2/a538618 .pdf

Lester, P. B., Harms, P. D., Bulling, D. J., Herian, M. N., Beal, S. J., & Spain, S. M. (2011). *Evaluation of relationships between reported resilience and outcomes—Report #2: Positive performance outcomes in officers (promotions, selections, & professions).* Defense Technical Information Center. https://apps.dtic.mil/dtic/tr/fulltext/u2 /a542229.pdf

Lester, P. B., Harms, P. D., Herian, M. N., Krasikova, D. V., & Beal, S. J. (2011). *The Comprehensive Soldier Fitness program evaluation—Report #3: Longitudinal analysis of the impact of Master Resilience Training on self-reported resilience and psychological health data.* Comprehensive Soldier & Family Fitness. https://readyandresilient.army .mil/CSF2/supportdocs/TR3.pdf

Lester, P. B., McBride, S., & Cornum, R. L. (2013). Comprehensive soldier fitness: Understanding the facts, dismantling the fiction. In R. R. Sinclair & T. W. Britt (Eds.), *Building psychological resilience in military personnel: Theory and practice* (pp. 193-220). American Psychological Association.

Leventhal, H., & Patrick-Miller, L. (2000). Emotions and physical illness: Causes and indicators of vulnerability. In M. Lewis & J. M. Haviland-Jones (Eds.), *Handbook of emotions (2nd ed.)* (pp. 523-37). Guilford Press.

Levin, J. S., & Chatters, L. M. (1998). Research on religion and mental health: An overview of empirical findings and theoretical issues. In H. G. Koenig (Ed.) *Handbook of religion and mental health* (pp. 34-51). Academic Press.

Levine, M., & Wilson, N. (2016). Bystanders and emergencies: Why understanding group processes is key to promoting prosocial behavior. In A. G. Miller (Ed.), *The social psychology of good and evil* (2nd ed.) (pp. 345-66). Guilford Press.

Lewis, C. S. (1960). *The four loves.* Harcourt Brace Jovanovich.

Lewis, C. S. (2002). On the reading of old books. In W. Hooper (Ed.), *God in the dock: Essays on theology and ethics* (pp. 200-207). Eerdmans. (Original work published 1944)

Lewis, H. B. (1971). *Shame and guilt in neurosis.* Inter-national Universities Press.

Lickel, B., Kushlev, K., Savalei, V., Matta, S., & Schmader, T. (2014). Shame and the motivation to change the self. *Emotion, 14*(6), 1049-61.

Liden, R. C., Wayne, S. J., Zhao, H., & Henderson, D. (2008). Servant leadership: Development of a multidimensional measure and multi-level assessment. *The Leadership Quarterly, 19*(2), 161-77.

Lifton, D. E., Seay, S., & Bushke, A. (2000). Can student "hardiness" serve as an indicator of likely persistence to graduation? Baseline results from a longitudinal study. *Academic Exchange Quarterly, 4*(2), 73-81.

Lindsay-Hartz, J. (1984). Contrasting experiences of shame and guilt. *American Behavioral Scientist, 27*(6), 689-704.

Linley, P. A., & Joseph, S. (2004). Toward a theoretical foundation for positive psychology in practice. In P. A. Linley & S. Joseph (Eds.), *Positive psychology in practice* (pp. 713-731). John Wiley & Sons.

Littman-Ovadia, H., Lazar-Butbul, V., & Benjamin, B. A. (2014). Strengths-based career counseling: Overview and initial evaluation. *Journal of Career Assessment, 22*(3), 403-419.

Lixey, K. (2012). Sport in the magisterium of Pius XII. In K. Lixey, C. Hübenthal, D. Mieth, & N. Müller (Eds.), *Sport and Christianity: A sign of the times in the light of faith* (pp. 81-103). Catholic University of America Press.

Lomas, T. (2018). Positive politics: Left-wing versus right-wing policies, and their impact on the determinants of well-being. In N. J. L. Brown, T. Lomas, & F. J. Eiroa-Orosa (Eds.), *Routledge international handbook of critical positive psychology* (pp. 351-67). Routledge.

Lomas, T., Medina, J. C., Ivtzan, I., Rupprecht, S., & Eiroa-Orosa, F. J. (2019). Mindfulness-based interventions in the workplace: An inclusive systematic review and meta-analysis of their impact upon wellbeing. *Journal of Positive Psychology, 14*(5), 625-40.

Long, B. C., & Van Stavel, R. (1995). Effects of exercise training on anxiety: A meta-analysis. *Journal of Applied Sport Psychology, 7*(2), 167-89.

Long, D. L., & Graesser, A. C. (1988). Wit and humor in discourse processing. *Discourse Processes, 11*(1), 35-60.

Lopez, S. J., & Gallagher, M. W. (2009). A case for positive psychology. In S. J. Lopez & C. R Snyder (Eds.), *Oxford handbook of positive psychology* (2nd ed.) (pp. 3-6). Oxford University Press.

Lopez, S. J., & Louis, M. C. (2009). The principles of strengths-based education. *Journal of College and Character, 10*(4), 1-8.

Lopez, S. J., Rose, S., Robinson, C., Marques, S. C., & Pais-Ribiero, J. (2009). Measuring and promoting hope in schoolchildren. In R. Gilman, E. S. Huebner, & M. J. Furlong (Eds.), *Handbook of positive psychology in schools* (pp. 37-50). Routledge.

Lopez, S. J., Snyder, C. R., Magyar-Moe, J. L, Edwards, L. M., Pedrotti, J. T., Jankowski, K., Turner, J. L., & Pressgrove, C. (2004). Strategies for accentuating hope. In P. A. Linley & S. Joseph (Eds.), *Positive psychology in practice* (pp. 388-404). John Wiley & Sons.

Low, L. F., Brodaty, H., Goodenough, B., Spitzer, P., Bell, J. P., Fleming, R., . . . & Chenoweth, L. (2013). The Sydney Multisite Intervention of Laughter-Bosses and ElderClowns (SMILE) study: Cluster randomised trial of humour therapy in nursing homes. *BMJ Open, 3*(1), e002072.

Low, L. F., Goodenough, B., Fletcher, J., Xu, K., Casey, A. N., Chenoweth, L., . . . & Brodaty, H. (2014). The effects of humor therapy on nursing home residents measured using observational methods: The SMILE cluster randomized trial. *Journal of the American Medical Directors Association, 15*(8), 564-69.

Luthans, F. (2002). The need for and meaning of positive organizational behavior. *Journal of Organizational Behavior, 23*(6), 695-706.

Luthans, F., & Avolio, B. J. (2003). Authentic leadership: A positive developmental approach. In K. S. Cameron, J. E. Dutton, & R. E. Quinn (Eds.), *Positive organizational scholarship* (pp. 241-61). Barrett-Koehler.

Luthans, F., Vogelgesang, G. R., & Lester, P. B. (2006). Developing the psychological capital of resiliency. *Human Resource Development Review, 5*(1), 25-44.

Luthans, F., Youssef-Morgan, C. M., & Avolio, B. J. (2007). *Psychological capital.* Oxford University Press.

Luthans, F., Youssef-Morgan, C. M., & Avolio, B. J. (2015). *Psychological capital and beyond.* Oxford University Press.

Lykken, D. (1999). *Happiness: What studies on twins show us about nature, nurture, and the happiness set-point.* Golden Books.

Lykken, D., & Tellegan, A. (1996). Happiness is a stochastic phenomenon. *Psychological Science, 7*(3), 186-89.

Lyubomirsky, S., & Abbe, A. (2003). Positive psychology's legs. *Psychological Inquiry, 14*(2), 132-36.

Lyubomirsky, S. King, L., & Diener, E. (2005). The benefits of frequent positive affect: Does happiness lead to success? *Psychological Bulletin, 131*(6), 803-55.

Lyubomirsky, S., Sheldon, K. M., & Schkade, D. (2005). Pursuing happiness: The architecture of sustainable change. *Review of General Psychology, 9*(2), 111-31.

MacDonald, N. (2012). Is there happiness in the Torah? In B. A. Strawn (Ed.), *The Bible and the pursuit of happiness* (pp. 57-74). Oxford University Press.

MacIntyre, A. (2007). *After virtue* (3rd ed.). University of Notre Dame Press.

MacIntyre, A. (1988). *Whose justice? Which rationality?* University of Notre Dame Press.

MacIntyre, A. (1990). *The rival version of moral enquiry: Encyclopaedia, genealogy, and tradition.* University of Notre Dame Press.

MacIntyre, A. (1999). *Dependent rational animals: Why human beings need the virtues.* Open Court.

MacIntyre, A. (2016). *Ethics in the conflicts of modernity.* Cambridge University Press.

MacInnis-Hackney, A. (2017). "Unity-in-distinction": Toward a model for understanding the relationship between faith practice and academic practice. *Didaskalia, 27,* 99-114.

Madden, M. E. (1990). Attributions of control and vulnerability at the beginning and end of a karate course. *Perceptual and Motor Skills, 70*(3), 787-94.

Madden, M. E. (1995). Perceived vulnerability and control of martial arts and physical fitness students. *Perceptual and Motor Skills, 80*(3), 899-910.

Maddi, S. R. (1987). Hardiness training at Illinois Bell Telephone. In J. Opatz (Ed.), *Health promotion evaluation* (pp. 101-15). National Wellness Institute.

Maddi, S. R. (1999). The personality construct of hardiness, I. Effects on experiencing, coping, and strain. *Consulting Psychology Journal: Practice and Research, 51*(2), 83-94.

Maddi, S. R. (2002). The story of hardiness: Twenty years of theorizing, research, and practice. *Consulting Psychology Journal: Practice and Research, 54*(3), 175-85.

Maddi, S. R. (2004). Hardiness: An operationalization of existential courage. *Journal of Humanistic Psychology, 44*(3), 279-98.

Maddi, S. R. (2006). Hardiness: The courage to grow from stresses. *Journal of Positive Psychology, 1*(3), 160-68.

Maddi, S. R. (2008). The courage and strategies of hardiness as helpful in growing despite major, disruptive stresses. *American Psychologist, 63*(6), 563-64.

Maddi, S. R. (2013). *Hardiness: Turning stressful circumstances into resilient growth.* Springer.

Maddi, S. R., Harvey, R. H., Khoshaba, D. M., Fazel, M., & Resurreccion, N. (2009a). The personality construct of hardiness, IV: Expressed in positive cognitions and emotions concerning oneself and developmentally relevant activities. *Journal of Humanistic Psychology, 49*(3), 292-305.

Maddi, S. R., Harvey, R. H., Khoshaba, Fazel, M., & Resurreccion, N. (2009b). Hardiness training facilitates performance in college. *Journal of Positive Psychology, 4*(6), 566-77.

Maddi, S. R., Harvey, R. H., Khoshaba, D. M., Lu, J. L., Persico, M., & Brow, M. (2006). The personality construct of hardiness, III: Relationships with repression, innovativeness, authoritarianism, and performance. *Journal of Personality, 74*(2), 575-98.

Maddi, S. R., Harvey, R. H., Resurreccion, R., Giatras, C. D., & Raganold, S. (2007). Hardiness as a performance enhancer in firefighters. *International Journal of Fire Service Leadership and Management, 1*(2), 3-9.

Maddi, S. R., & Hess, M. (1992). Personality hardiness and success in basketball. *International Journal of Sports Psychology, 23*(4), 36-68.

Maddi, S. R., Kahn, S., & Maddi, K. L. (1998). The effectiveness of hardiness training. *Consulting Psychology Journal: Practice and Research, 50*(2), 78-86.

Maddi, S. R., & Khoshaba, D. M. (1994). Hardiness and mental health. *Journal of Personality Assessment, 63*(2), 265-74.

Maddi, S. R., Khoshaba, D. M., Harvey, R. H., Fazel, M., & Resurreccion, N. (2011). The personality construct of hardiness, V: Relationships with the construction of existential meaning in life. *Journal of Humanistic Psychology, 51*(3), 369-88.

Maddi, S. R., Khoshaba, D. M., Jensen, K., Carter, E., Lu, J., & Harvey, R. H. (2002). Hardiness training for high-risk undergraduates. *NACADA Journal, 22*(1), 45-55.

Maddi, S. R., Khoshaba, D. M., Persico, M., Lu, J., Harvey, R., & Bleecker, F. (2002). The personality construct of hardiness, II. Relationships with comprehensive tests of personality and psychopathology. *Journal of Research in Personality, 36*(1), 72-85.

Maddi, S. R., Erwin, L. M., Carmody, C. L., Villarreal, B. J., White, M., & Gundersen, K. K. (2013). Relationship of hardiness, grit, and emotional intelligence to internet addiction, excessive consumer spending, and gambling. *Journal of Positive Psychology, 8*(2), 128-34.

Maddi, S. R., Wadhwa, P., & Haier, R. J. (1996). Relationship of hardiness to alcohol and drug use in adolescents. *American Journal of Drug and Alcohol Abuse, 22*(2), 247-57.

Magyar-Moe, J. L. (2015). Positive psychology in the classroom. In J. C. Wade, L. I. Marks, & R. D. Hetzel (Eds.), *Positive psychology on the college campus* (pp. 133-66). Oxford University Press.

Maier, G. J., Bernstein, M., & Musholt, E. A. (1989). Personal coping mechanisms for prison clinicians: Toward transformation. *Journal of Prison & Jail Health, 8*(1), 29-39.

Maier, S. F., & Seligman, M. P. (1976). Learned helplessness: Theory and evidence. *Journal of Experimental Psychology: General, 105*(1), 3-46.

Malcolm, W., Warwar, S., & Greenberg, L. (2005). Facilitating forgiveness in individual therapy as an approach to resolving interpersonal injuries. In E. L. Worthington Jr. (Ed.), *Handbook of forgiveness* (pp. 407-22). Routledge.

Maliszewski, M. (1996). *Spiritual dimensions of the martial arts.* Charles E. Tuttle.

Malouf, E., Youman, K., Harty, L., Schaefer, K., & Tangney, J. P. (2013). Accepting guilt and abandoning shame: A positive approach to addressing moral emotions among high-risk, multineed individuals. In T. B. Kashdan & J. Ciarrochi (Eds.), *Mindfulness, acceptance, and positive psychology* (pp. 215-39). Context Press.

Malouff, J. M., & Schutte, N. S. (2017). Can psychological interventions increase optimism? A meta-analysis. *Journal of Positive Psychology, 12*(6), 594-604.

Maltby, J., Day, L., & Barber, L. (2005). Forgiveness and happiness: The differing contexts of forgiveness using the distinction between hedonic and eudaimonic happiness. *Journal of Happiness Studies, 6*(1), 1-13.

Mangan, J. A., & Hickey, C. (2008). An exceptional pioneer: Be strong for Christ. *Soccer & Society, 9*(5), 671-89.

Marciniak, P. (2014). Byzantine humor. In S. Attardo (Ed.), *Encyclopedia of humor studies* (pp. 98-102). Sage.

Marecek, J., & Christopher, J. C. (2018). Is positive psychology an indigenous psychology? In N. J. L. Brown, T. Lomas, & F. J. Eiroa-Orosa (Eds.), *Routledge international handbook of critical positive psychology* (pp. 84-98). Routledge.

Markus, H. R., & Kitayama, S. (1991). Culture and the self: Implications for cognition, emotion, and motivation. *Psychological Review, 98*(2), 224-53.

Marlatt, G. A., & Kristeller, J. (1999). Mindfulness and meditation. In W. R. Miller (Ed.), *Integrating spirituality into treatment* (pp. 67-84). American Psychological Association.

Maroney, J. P. (2011). *Negative people suck!* https://web.archive.org/web/20110125055200/http://www.negativepeoplesuck.com:80/jp-maroney-negative-people-suck.pdf

Martin, R. A. (1996). The Situational Humor Response Questionnaire (SHRQ) and Coping Humor Scale (CHS): A decade of research findings. *Humor: International Journal of Humor Research, 9*(3-4), 251-72.

Martin, R. A. (2001). Humor, laughter, and physical health: Methodological issues and research findings. *Psychological Bulletin, 127*(4), 504-19.

Martin, R. A. (2008). Humor and health. In V. Raskin, (Ed.), *Primer of humor research* (pp. 479-522). Mouton de Gruyter.

Martin, R. A. (2010). *The psychology of humor: An integrative approach.* Elsevier.

Martin, R. A., & Lefcourt, H. M. (1983). Sense of humor as a moderator of the relation between stressors and moods. *Journal of Personality & Social Psychology, 45*(6), 1313-24.

Martineau, W. H. (1972). A model of the social functions of humor. In J. H. Goldstein & P. E. McGhee (Eds.), *The psychology of humor: Theoretical perspectives and empirical issues* (pp. 101-28). Academic Press.

Martinez, A. G., Stuewig, J., & Tangney, J. P. (2014). Can perspective-taking reduce crime? Examining a pathway through empathic-concern and guilt-proneness. *Personality and Social Psychology Bulletin, 40*(12), 1659-67.

Mascaro, N., & Rosen, D. H. (2005). Existential meaning's role in the enhancement of hope and prevention of depressive symptoms. *Journal of Personality, 73*(4), 985-1014.

Masicampo, E. J., & Baumeister, R. F. (2008). Toward a physiology of dual-process reasoning and judgment: Lemonade, willpower, and expensive rule-based analysis. *Psychological Science, 19*(3), 255-60.

Maslow, A. H. (1962). *Toward a psychology of being.* D. Van Nostrum Company.

Massimini, F., Csikszentmihalyi, M., & Carli, M. (1987). The monitoring of optimal experience: A tool for psychiatric rehabilitation. *Journal of Nervous and Mental Disease, 175*(9), 545-49.

Mastekaasa, A. (1994). Marital status, distress, and well-being: An international comparison. *Journal of Comparative Family Studies, 25*(2), 183-205.

Masten, A. S. (1986). Humor and competence in school-aged children. *Child Development, 57*(2), 461-73.

Mathewes, C. (2015). Toward a theology of joy. In M. Volf & J. E. Crisp (Eds.), *Joy and human flourishing: Essays on theology, culture and the good life* (pp. 63-96). Fortress Press.

Mathisen, J. A. (2008). A brief history of Christianity and sport: Selected highlights of a puzzling relationship. In D. Deardorff II & J. White (Eds.), *The image of God in the human body: Essays on Christianity and sports* (pp. 9-41). Edwin Mellen Press.

Mattison, W. C., III (2008). *Introducing moral theology: True happiness and the virtues.* Brazos.

Mauss, I. B., Savino, N. C., Anderson, C. L., Weisbuch, M., Tamir, M., & Laudenslager, M. L. (2011). The pursuit of happiness can be lonely. *Emotion, 12*(5), 908-12.

Mauss, I. B., Tamir, M., Anderson, C. L., & Savino, N. C. (2011). Can seeking happiness make people unhappy? Paradoxical effects of valuing happiness. *Emotion, 11*(4), 807-15.

Maxwell, N. (1984). *From knowledge to wisdom.* Basil Blackwell.

Maxwell, W. (2003). The use of gallows humor and dark humor during crisis situations. *International Journal of Emergency Mental Health, 5*(2), 93-98.

May, R. (1967). *Psychology and the human dilemma.* Van Norstrand Reinhold.

McAdams, D. P. (1997). A conceptual history of personality psychology. In R. Hogan, J. Johnson, & S. Briggs (Eds.), *Handbook of personality psychology* (pp. 3-39). Academic Press.

McCall, T. D., Waters, L. E., & White, M. A. (2015). A comparison between theological Christian approaches to wisdom and Peterson and Seligman's classification of character strengths and virtues. In M. A. White & A. S. Murray (Eds.), *Evidence-based approaches in positive education* (pp. 27-41). Springer.

McCauley, C., Woods, K., Coolidge, C., & Kulick, W. (1983). More aggressive cartoons are funnier. *Journal of Personality and Social Psychology, 44*(4), 817-23.

McClelland, D. C., & Boyatzis, R. E. (1982). Leadership motive pattern and long-term success in management. *Journal of Applied Psychology, 67*(6), 737-43.

McClelland, D. C., & Cheriff, A. D. (1997). The immunoenhancing effects of humor on secretory IgA and resistance to respiratory infections. *Psychology and Health, 12*(3), 329-44.

McCoy, J. M. (2002). Work environments. In R. B. Bechtel & A. Churchman (Eds.), *Handbook of environmental psychology* (pp. 443-60). John Wiley & Sons.

McCracken, B. (2017). Church shopping with Charles Taylor. In C. Hansen (Ed.), *Our secular age: Ten years of reading and applying Charles Taylor* (pp. 75-86). The Gospel Coalition.

McCrae, R. R., & Costa, P. T. (2003). *Personality in adulthood: A five-factor theory perspective* (2nd ed.). Guilford Press.

McCrae, R. R., Costa, P. T., Jr., & Martin, T. A. (2005). The NEO-PI-3: A more readable revised NEO personality inventory. *Journal of Personality Assessment, 84*(3), 261-70.

McCullough, M. E. (1995). Prayer and health: Conceptual issues, research review, and research agenda. *Journal of Psychology and Theology, 23*(1), 15-29.

McCullough, M. E., Bono, G., & Root, L. M. (2005). Religion and forgiveness. In R. F. Paloutzian & C. L. Park (Eds.), *Handbook of the psychology of religion and spirituality* (pp. 394-411). Guilford Press.

McCullough, M. E., Emmons, R. A., Kilpatrick, S. D., & Mooney, C. N. (2003). Narcissists as "victims": The role of narcissism in the perception of transgressions. *Personality and Social Psychology Bulletin, 29*(7), 885-93.

McCullough, M. E., Emmons, R. A., & Tsang, J. A. (2002). The grateful disposition: A conceptual and empirical topography. *Journal of Personality and Social Psychology, 82*(1), 112-27.

McCullough, M. E., Fincham, F. D., & Tsang, J. (2003). Forgiveness, forbearance, and time: The temporal unfolding of transgression-related interpersonal motivations. *Journal of Personality and Social Psychology, 84*(3), 540-57.

McCullough, M. E., Kilpatrick, S. D., Emmons, R. A., & Larson, D. B. (2001). Is gratitude a moral affect? *Psychological Bulletin, 127*(2), 249-66.

McCullough, M. E., Kimeldorf, M. B., & Cohen, A. D. (2008). An adaptation for altruism: The social causes, social effects, and social evolution of gratitude. *Current Directions in Psychological Science, 17*(4), 281-85.

McCullough, M. E., Pargament, K. I., & Thoresen, C. E. (2000). The psychology of forgiveness: History, conceptual issues, and overview. In M. E. McCullough, K. I. Pargament, & C. E. Thoresen (Eds.), *Forgiveness: Theory, research, and practice* (pp. 1-14). Guilford Press.

McCullough, M. E., Root, L. M., Tabak, B. A., & Witvliet, C. V. (2009). Forgiveness. In S. J. Lopez & C. R Snyder (Eds.), *Oxford handbook of positive psychology* (pp. 427-36). Oxford University Press.

McCullough, M. E., & Witvliet, C. V. (2005). The psychology of forgiveness. In C. R. Snyder & S. J. Lopez (Eds.), *Handbook of positive psychology* (pp. 446-58). Oxford University Press.

McCullough, M. E., & Worthington, E. L., Jr. (1999). Religion and the forgiving personality. *Journal of Personality, 67*(6), 1141-64.

McCullough, M.E., Worthington, E. L., Jr., & Rachal, K.C. (1997). Interpersonal forgiving in close relationships. *Journal of Personality and Social Psychology, 73*(2), 321-36.

McDonald, H. D. (1981). *The Christian view of man.* Crossway Books.

McDonald, M. J., Wong, P. T. P., & Gingras, D. T. (2012). Meaning-in-life measures and development of a brief version of the Personal Meaning Profile. In P. T. P. Wong (Ed.), *The human quest for meaning* (2nd ed.) (pp. 357-82). Routledge.

McGhee, P. E. (1971). Development of the humor response: A review of the literature. *Psychological Bulletin, 76*(5), 328-48.

McGhee, P. E. (1974). Cognitive mastery and children's humor. *Psychological Bulletin, 81*(10), 721-30.

McGhee, P. E. (1979). *Humor: Its origin and development.* W. H. Freeman and Company.

McGhee, P. E., Bell, N. J., & Duffey, N. S. (1986). Generational differences in humor and correlates of humor development. In L. Nahemow, K. A. McCluskey-Fawcett, & P. E. McGhee (Eds.), *Humor and aging* (pp. 253-63). Academic Press.

McGovern, L. P., Ditzian, J. L., & Taylor, S. P. (1975). The effect of one positive reinforcement on helping with cost. *Bulletin of the Psychonomic Society, 5*(5), 421-23.

McGovern, T. V., & Miller, S. L. (2008). Integrating teacher behaviors with character strengths and virtues for faculty development. *Teaching of Psychology, 35*(4), 278-85.

McGregor, H., Lieberman, J., Greenberg, J., Solomon, S., Arndt, J., & Simon, L. (1996). Terror management and aggression: Evidence that mortality salience promotes aggression against worldview-threatening individuals. *Journal of Personality and Social Psychology, 74*(3), 590-605.

McKee, P. (1990). Philosophy and wisdom. *Teaching Philosophy, 13*(4), 325-330.

McMinn, M. R. (2017). *The science of virtue: Why positive psychology matters to the church.* Brazos.

McNamee, M. (2008). *Sports, virtues and vices: Morality plays.* Routledge.

McNamee, M., Jones, C., & Duda, J. L. (2003). Psychology, ethics, and sports: Back to an Aristotelian "museum of normalcy." *International Journal of Sport and Heath Science, 1*(1), 61-75.

McReynolds, P. (1987). Lightner Witmer: Little-known founder of clinical psychology. *American Psychologist, 42*(9), 849-58.

McWilliams, N., & Lependorf, S. (1990). Narcissistic pathology of everyday life: The denial of remorse and gratitude. *Contemporary Psychoanalysis, 26*(3), 430-51.

Meacham, J. A. (1990). The loss of wisdom. In R. J. Sternberg (Ed.) *Wisdom: Its nature, origins, and development* (pp. 181-211). Cambridge University Press.

Mead, N. L., Baumeister, R. F., Gino, F., Schweitzer, M. E., & Ariely, D. (2009). Too tired to tell the truth: Self-control resource depletion and dishonesty. *Journal of Experimental Social Psychology, 45*(3), 594-97.

Meeusen, R., & De Meirleir, K. (1995). Exercise and brain neurotransmission. *Sports Medicine, 20*(3), 160-88.

Meilaender, G. C. (1984). *The theory and practice of virtue.* University of Notre Dame Press.

Meissner, W. W. (1984). *Psychoanalysis and religious experience.* Yale University Press.

Meredith, L. S., Sherbourne, C. D., Gaillot, S., Hansell, L., Ritschard, H. V., Parker, A. M., & Wrenn, G. (2011). *Promoting psychological resilience in the U.S. military.* The RAND Corporation.

Messay, B., Dixon, L. J., & Rye, M. S. (2012). The relationship between Quest religious orientation, forgiveness, and mental health. *Mental Health, Religion & Culture, 15*(3), 315-33.

Metcalfe, J., & Mischel, W. (1999). A hot/cool system analysis of delay of gratification: Dynamics of willpower. *Psychological Review, 106*(1), 3-19.

Meyer, A. R. (2019). Historical relationship between sport and Christianity. In M. Hoven, A. Parker, & N. J. Watson (Eds.), *Sport and Christianity: Practices for the twenty-first century* (pp. 59-70). T&T Clark.

Middleton, R. (1959). Negro and white reactions to racial humor. *Sociometry, 22,* 175-83.

Mikulincer, M., & Florian, V. (2000). Exploring individual differences in reactions to mortality salience: Does attachment style regulate terror management mechanisms? *Journal of Personality and Social Psychology, 79*(2), 260-73.

Milgram, S. (1963). Behavioral study of obedience. *Journal of Abnormal and Social Psychology, 67*(4), 371-78.

Milgram, S. (1965). Some conditions of obedience and disobedience to authority. *Human Relations, 18*(1), 57-76.

Miller, A. G. (2004). Introduction and overview. In A. G. Miller (Ed.), *The social psychology of good and evil* (pp. 1-17). Guilford Press.

Miller, C. K., Kristeller, J. L., Headings, A., & Nagaraja, H. (2014). Comparison of a mindful eating intervention to a diabetes self-management intervention among adults with type 2 diabetes: A randomized controlled trial. *Health Education & Behavior, 41*(2), 145-54.

Miller, D. N., Nickerson, A. B., & Jimerson, S. R. (2009). Positive psychology and school-based interventions. In R. Gilman, E. S. Huebner, & M. J.

Furlong (Eds.), *Handbook of positive psychology in schools* (pp. 293-304). Routledge.

Miller, P. A., & Eisenberg, N. (1988). The relation of empathy to aggressive and externalizing/antisocial behavior. *Psychological Bulletin, 103*(3), 324-44.

Mischel, W. (1966). Theory and research on the antecedents of self-imposed delay of reward. *Progress in Experimental Personality Research, 3,* 85-132.

Mischel, W. (1996). From good intentions to willpower. In P. Gollwitzer & J. A. Bargh (Eds.), *The psychology of action: Linking cognition and motivation to behavior* (pp. 197-218). Guilford Press.

Mischel, W., & Ayduk, O. (2011). Willpower in a cognitive affective processing system: The dynamics of delay of gratification. In K. D. Vohs & R. F. Baumeister (Eds.), *Handbook of self-regulation: Research, theory, and applications* (2nd ed.) (pp. 83-105). Guilford Press.

Mischel, W., Ayduk, O., Berman, M. G., Casey, B. J., Gotlib, I. H., Jonides, J., . . . & Shoda, Y. (2010). "Willpower" over the life span: Decomposing self-regulation. *Social Cognitive and Affective Neuroscience, 6*(2), 252-56.

Mischel, W., & Baker, N. (1975). Cognitive appraisals and transformations in delay behavior. *Journal of Personality and Social Psychology, 31*(2), 254-61.

Mischel, W., & Ebbesen, E. B. (1970). Attention in delay of gratification. *Journal of Personality and Social Psychology, 16*(2), 329-37.

Mischel, W., Ebbesen, E. B., & Zeiss, A. R. (1972). Cognitive and attentional mechanisms in delay of gratification. *Journal of Personality and Social Psychology, 21*(2), 204-18.

Mischel, W., Shoda, Y., & Peake, P. (1988). The nature of adolescent competencies predicted by preschool delay of gratification. *Journal of Personality and Social Psychology, 54*(4), 687-96.

Mischel, W., Shoda, Y., & Rodriguez, M. L. (1989). Delay of gratification in children. *Science, 244*(4907), 933-38.

Moffitt, T. E., Arseneault, L., Belsky, D., Dickson, N., Hancox, R. J., Harrington, H., . . . & Sears, M. R. (2011). A gradient of childhood self-control predicts health, wealth, and public safety. *Proceedings of the National Academy of Sciences, 108*(7), 2693-98.

Mohler, R. A., Jr. (1992). A theology of preaching. In M. Duduit (Ed.), *Handbook of contemporary preaching* (pp. 13-20). Broadman & Holman.

Molden, D. C., Hui, C. M., Noreen, E. E., Meier, B. P., Scholer, A. A., D'Agostino, P. R., & Martin, V. (2012). The motivational versus metabolic effects of carbohydrates on self-control. *Psychological Science, 23*(1), 1130-37.

Moldoveanu, M., & Langer, E. (2002). When "stupid" is smarter than we are: Mindlessness and the attribution of stupidity. In R. J. Sternberg (Ed.), *Why smart people can be so stupid* (pp. 212-31). Yale University Press.

Moltmann, J. (1967). *Theology of hope* (J. W. Leitch, Trans.). Harper & Row.

Moltmann, J. (2015). Christianity: A religion of joy. In M. Volf & J. E. Crisp (Eds.), *Joy and human flourishing: Essays on theology, culture, and the good life* (pp. 1-16). Fortress.

Moneta, G. B. (2004a). The flow experience across cultures. *Journal of Happiness Studies, 5*(2), 115-21.

Moneta, G. B. (2004b). The flow model of intrinsic motivation in Chinese: Cultural and personal moderators. *Journal of Happiness Studies, 5*(2), 181-217.

Moneta, G. B., & Csikszentmihalyi, M. (1996). The effect of perceived challenges and skills on the quality of subjective experience. *Journal of Personality, 64*(2), 275-310.

Monroe, K. R. (1996). *The heart of altruism: Perceptions of a common humanity.* Princeton University Press.

Moo, D. J. (2000). *The letter of James.* Eerdmans.

Moorhead, G., Ference, R., & Neck, C. P. (1991). Group decision fiascoes continue: Space shuttle Challenger and a revised groupthink framework. *Human Relations, 44*(6), 539-50.

Moran, C. C. (1996). Short-term mood change, perceived funniness, and the effect of humor stimuli. *Behavioral Medicine, 22*(1), 32-38.

Morf, C. C., & Mischel, W. (2012). The self as a psycho-social dynamic processing system. In M. R. Leary & J. P. Tangney (Eds.), *Handbook of self and identity* (2nd ed.) (pp. 21-49). Guilford Press.

Moroney, S. K. (2000). *The noetic effects of sin: A historical and contemporary exploration of how sin affects our thinking.* Lexington Books.

Morreall, J. (2008). Philosophy and religion. In V. Raskin (Ed.), *Primer of humor research* (pp. 211-42). Mouton de Gruyter.

Mosing, M. A., Magnusson, P. K., Pedersen, N. L., Nakamura, J., Madison, G., & Ullén, F. (2012). Heritability of proneness for psychological flow experiences. *Personality and Individual Differences, 53*(5), 699-704.

Moss, A. (2012). *JHC Technical Brief R11047793: Evaluation of the ab initio officer BattleSMART module at the RAAF officer training school.* Australian Government Department of Defence. www.defence.gov.au/FOI/Docs/Disclosures /318_1314_Documents.pdf

Moss, A. (2013). *JHC Technical Brief R10895451: Evaluation of the BattleSMART predeployment module September 2011.* Australian Government Department of Defence. www.defence.gov.au/FOI /Docs/Disclosures/ 318_1314_Documents.pdf

Moss, M. K., & Page, R.A. (1972). Reinforcement and helping behavior. *Journal of Applied Social Psychology, 2*(4), 360-71.

Moyle, P. (1998). Longitudinal influences of managerial support on employee well-being. *Work & Stress, 12*(1), 29-49.

Muller, C. M., & Dweck, C. S. (1998). Praise for intelligence can undermine children's motivation and performance. *Journal of Personality and Social Psychology, 75*(1), 32-52.

Mullet, E., Barros, J., Frongia, L., Usai, V., Neto, F., & Shafihi, S. R. (2003). Religious involvement and the forgiving personality. *Journal of Personality, 71*(1), 1-19.

Mullet, E., Neto, F., & Riviére, S. (2005). Personality and its effects on resentment, revenge, forgiveness, and self-forgiveness. In E. L. Worthington Jr. (Ed.), *Handbook of forgiveness* (pp. 159-81). Routledge.

Mulnix, J. W., & Mulnix, M. J. (Eds.). (2015). *Theories of happiness: An anthology.* Broadview Press.

Mugno, D. A., & Feltz, D. L. (1985). The social learning of aggression in youth football in the United States. *Canadian Journal of Applied Sport Sciences, 10*(1), 26-35.

Muraven, M., Baumeister, R. F., & Tice, D. M. (1999). Longitudinal improvement of self-regulation through practice: Building self-control through strength through repeated exercise. *Journal of Social Psychology, 139*(4), 446-57.

Muraven, M., Collins, R. L., & Nienhaus, K. (2002). Self-control and alcohol restraint: An initial application of the self-control strength model. *Psychology of Addictive Behaviors, 16*(2), 113-20.

Muraven, M., Tice, D. M., & Baumeister, R. F. (1998). Self-control as a limited resource: Regulatory depletion patterns. *Journal of Personality and Social Psychology, 74*(3), 774-89.

Murdoch, I. (1970). *The sovereignty of good.* Routledge & Kegan Paul.

Murphy, N. (1997). Introduction. In N. Murphy, B. J. Kallenberg, & M. T. Nation (Eds.), *Virtues and practices in the Christian tradition: Christian ethics after MacIntyre* (pp. 1-3). University of Notre Dame Press.

Murphy, N. (2005a). Philosophical resources for integration. In A. Dueck & C. Lee (Eds.), *Why psychology needs theology: A radical-reformation perspective* (pp. 3-27). Eerdmans.

Murphy, N. (2005b). Theological resources for integration. In A. Dueck & C. Lee (Eds.), *Why psychology needs theology: A radical-reformation perspective* (pp. 28-52). Eerdmans.

Murphy, N. (2005c). Constructing a radical-reformation research program in psychology. In A. Dueck & C. Lee (Eds.), *Why psychology needs theology: A radical-reformation perspective* (pp. 53-76). Eerdmans.

Murphy, N., & Ellis, G. F. R. (1996). *On the moral nature of the universe: Theology, cosmology, and ethics.* Fortress.

Murphy, N., & Hackney, C. H. (2011). An interview with Nancey Murphy: Constructing an Anabaptist vision of ideal psychological functioning. *Edification: The Transdisciplinary Journal of Christian Psychology, 4*(1), 73-78.

Murphy, N., Kallenberg, B. J., & Nation, M. T. (1997). *Virtues and practices in the Christian tradition: Christian ethics after MacIntyre.* University of Notre Dame Press.

Murphy, R. E. (2002). *The tree of life: An exploration of biblical wisdom literature* (3rd ed.). Eerdmans.

Murrar, S., Isenberg, N., Niedenthal, P., & Brauer, M. (2019). Shame and guilt among ice hockey players in the penalty box. *Motivation and Emotion, 43*(6), 940-47.

Murray, J. (1955). *Redemption accomplished and applied.* Eerdmans.

Mutrie, N., & Faulkner, G. (2004). Physical activity: Positive psychology in motion. In P. A. Linley & S. Joseph (Eds.), *Positive psychology in practice* (pp. 146-64). John Wiley & Sons.

Myers, D. G. (1992). *The pursuit of happiness.* Avon Books.

Myers, D. G. (2000). The friends, funds, and faith of happy people. *American Psychologist, 55*(1), 56-67.

Myers, D. G., & Diener, E. (1995). Who is happy? *Psychological Science, 6*(1), 10-19.

Nakamura, J. (2011). Contexts of positive adult development. In S. I. Donaldson, M. Csikszentmihalyi, & J. Nakamura (Eds.), *Applied positive psychology: Improving everyday life, health, schools, work, and society* (pp. 185-202). Routledge.

Nakamura, J., & Csikszentmihalyi, M. (2005). The concept of flow. In C. Snyder & S. Lopez (Eds.), *Handbook of positive psychology* (pp. 89-105). Oxford University Press.

Nathan, R., & Hill, L. (2006). *Career counselling* (2nd ed.). Sage Publications.

National Defense. (2015). *Road to mental readiness aide memoir (DGM-10-07-00285).* www.scribd.com/doc/153155052/Road-to-Mental-Readiness-Aide-Memoire

Naugle, D. K. (2002). *Worldview: The history of a concept.* Eerdmans.

Neighbors, H. W., Jackson, J. S., Bowman, P. J., & Gurin, G. (1983). Stress, coping, and black mental health: Preliminary findings from a national study. *Prevention in Human Services, 2*(3), 5-29.

Nelson, J. M., & Slife, B. D. (2017). A new positive psychology: A critique of the movement based on early Christian thought. *Journal of Positive Psychology, 12*(5), 459-67.

Nelson, L. J., Moore, D. L., Olivetti, J., & Scott, T. (1997). General and personal mortality salience and nationalistic bias. *Personality and Social Psychology Bulletin, 23*(8), 884-92.

Nettleship, R. L. (1961). *Lectures on the Republic of Plato* (2nd ed.). St Martin's Press. (Original work published 1901)

Nevo, O., Keinan, G., & Teshimovsky-Arditi, M. (1993). Humor and pain tolerance. *Humor: International Journal of Humor Research, 6*(1), 71-88.

Nezu, A. M., Nezu, C. M., & Blissett, S. E. (1988). Sense of humor as a moderator of the relation between stressful events and psychological distress: A prospective analysis. *Journal of Personality & Social Psychology, 54*(3), 520-25.

Nicholson, I. A. (1998). Gordon Allport, character, and the "culture of personality," 1897–1937. *History of Psychology, 1*(1), 52-68.

Nicholson, I. A. M. (2003). *Inventing personality: Gordon Allport and the science of selfhood.* American Psychological Association.

Niebuhr, R. (1946). *Discerning the signs of the times.* Charles Scribner's Sons.

Niederhoffer, K. G., & Pennebaker, J. W. (2005). Sharing one's story: On the benefits of writing or talking about emotional experience. In C. R. Snyder & S. J. Lopez (Eds.), *Handbook of positive psychology* (pp. 573-83). Oxford University Press.

Nielsen, K., & Daniels, K. (2012). Does shared and differentiated transformational leadership predict followers' working conditions and well-being? *The Leadership Quarterly, 23*(3), 383-97.

Nielsen, S. L. (1994). Rational-emotive behavior therapy and religion: Don't throw the therapeutic baby out with the holy water! *Journal of Psychology and Christianity, 13*(4), 312-22.

Niemiec, C. P., & Ryan, R. M. (2009). Autonomy, competence, and relatedness in the classroom: Applying self-determination theory to educational practice. *Theory and Research in Education, 7*(2), 133-44.

Niemiec, R. M. (2013). VIA character strengths: Research and practice (the first 10 years). In H. H. Knoop & A. Delle Fave (Eds.), *Well-being and cultures: Perspectives on positive psychology* (pp. 11-29). Springer.

Niemiec, R. M. (2017). *Character strengths interventions: A field guide for practitioners.* Hogrefe.

Nobles, J., Frankenberg, E., & Thomas, D. (2015). The effects of mortality on fertility: Population dynamics after a natural disaster. *Demography, 52*(1), 15-38.

Noorish, J. M. (2015). *Positive education: The Geelong Grammar School journey.* Oxford University Press.

Norcross, J. C., & Vangarelli, D. J. (1988). The resolution solution: Longitudinal examination of New Year's change attempts. *Journal of Substance Abuse, 1*(2), 127-34.

Norem, J. K. (2001). Defensive pessimism, optimism, and pessimism. In E. C. Chang (Ed.), *Optimism & pessimism: Implications for theory, research, and practice* (pp. 77-100). American Psychological Association.

Norem, J. K. (2002). *The positive power of negative thinking: Using defensive pessimism to harness anxiety and perform at your peak.* Basic Books.

Norem, J. K. (2014). The right tool for the job: Functional analysis and evaluating positivity/negativity. In W. G. Parrott (Ed.), *The positive side of negative emotions* (pp. 247-72). Guilford Press.

Norem, J. K., & Cantor, N. (1986). Defensive pessimism: Harnessing anxiety as motivation. *Journal of Personality and Social Psychology, 51*(6), 1208-17.

Norem, J. K., & Chang, E. C. (2002). The positive psychology of negative thinking. *Journal of Clinical Psychology, 58*(9), 993-1001.

North, H. F. (1979). *From myth to icon: Reflections of Greek ethical doctrine in literature and art.* Cornell University Press.

Novotny, A. (2009). Strong in mind and body: With help from psychologists, a new U.S. Army program puts psychological well-being on par with physical fitness. *Monitor on Psychology, 40,* 40.

Nozick, R. (2015). Happiness. In J. W. Mulnix & M. J. Mulnix (Eds.), *Theories of happiness: An anthology* (pp. 246-62). Broadview Press.

Ntoumanis, N., & Standage, M. (2009). Morality in sport: A self-determination theory perspective. *Journal of Applied Sport Psychology, 21*(4), 365-80.

Nussbaum, M. C. (2001). *The fragility of goodness: Luck and ethics in Greek tragedy and philosophy* (rev. ed.). Cambridge University Press.

Nussbaum, M. C. (2010). *Not for profit: Why democracy needs the humanities.* Princeton University Press.

Nussbaum, M. C. (2015). Who is the happy warrior? Philosophy, happiness research, and public policy. In J. W. Mulnix & M. J. Mulnix (Eds.), *Theories of happiness: An anthology* (pp. 219-45). Broadview Press.

Oaten, M., & Cheng, K. (2006). Longitudinal gains in self-regulation from regular physical exercise. *British Journal of Health Psychology, 11*(4), 717-33.

Oaten, M., & Cheng, K. (2007). Improvements in self-control from financial monitoring. *Journal of Economic Psychology, 28*(4), 487-501.

Obrdlik, A. J. (1942). "Gallows humor": A sociological phenomenon. *American Journal of Sociology, 47*(5), 709-16.

O'Brien, E., & Smith, R. W. (2019). Unconventional consumption methods and enjoying things consumed: Recapturing the "first-time" experience. *Personality and Social Psychology Bulletin, 45*(1), 67-80.

O'Donovan, O. (2003). *The just war revisited.* Cambridge University Press.

Oepke, A. (1964). Κενός (G. Bromiley, Trans.). In G. Kittel (Ed.). *Theological dictionary of the New*

Testament: Vol. 3 (pp. 662-69). Eerdmans. (Original work published 1933)

Oh, D. (2007, January). *The relevance of virtue ethics and application to the formation of character development in warriors* [Paper presentation]. International Symposium for Military Ethics, Springfield, IL, USA.

Okazaki, T. (2006). *Perfection of character: Guiding principles for the martial arts & everyday life.* GMW Publishing.

O'Keefe, P. A., & Dweck, C. S. (2018). Implicit theories of interest: Finding your passion or developing it? *Psychological Science, 29*(10), 1653-64.

Oman, D., Shapiro, S. L., Thoresen, C. E., Plante, T. G., & Flinders, T. (2008). Meditation lowers stress and supports forgiveness among college students. *Journal of American College Health, 56*(5), 569-78.

Osborne, K. P. (1979). *Aristotle's conception of megalopsychia* [Doctoral dissertation, City University of New York]. http://academicworks .cuny.edu/gc_etds/2202

Osbourne, G. R. (2010). *Matthew: Zondervan exegetical commentary on the New Testament.* Zondervan.

Osofsky, M. J., Bandura, A., & Zimbardo, P. G. (2005). The role of moral disengagement in the execution process. *Law and Human Behavior, 29*(4), 371-93.

Ostenfeld, I. (1978). *Soren Kierkegaard's psychology* (A. McKinnon, Trans.). Wilfrid Laurier University Press. (Original work published 1972)

O'Sullivan, S. (2004). *Early medieval glosses on Prudentius' psychomachia: The Weitz tradition.* Brill.

Oswald, R. M., & Kroeger, O. (1988). *Personality type and religious leadership.* Alban Institute.

Ozer, E. M., & Bandura, A. (1990). Mechanisms governing empowering effects: A self-efficacy analysis. *Journal of Personality and Social Psychology, 58*(3), 472-86.

Packer, J. I. (1984). *Keep in step with the Spirit.* F. H. Revell.

Palmer, C. T. (1993). Anger, aggression, and humor in Newfoundland floor hockey: An evolutionary analysis. *Aggressive Behavior, 19*(3), 167-73.

Pargament, K. I. (1997). *The psychology of religion and coping.* Guilford Press.

Pargament, K. I., & Brant, C. R. (1998). Religion and coping. In H. G. Koenig (Ed.), *Handbook of religion and mental health* (pp. 111-29). Academic Press.

Pargament, K. I., Kennell, J., Hathaway, W., Grevengoed, N., Newman, J., & Jones, W. (1988). Religion and the problem-solving process: Three styles of coping. *Journal for the Scientific Study of Religion, 27*(1), 90-104.

Pargament, K. I., & Mahoney, A. (2004). Spirituality: Discovering and conserving the sacred. In C. R. Snyder & S. Lopez (Eds.), *Handbook of positive psychology* (pp. 646-62). Oxford University Press.

Pargament, K. I., & Rye, M. S. (1998). Forgiveness as a method of religious coping. In E. L. Worthington Jr. (Ed.), *Dimensions of forgiveness: Psychological research & theological perspectives* (pp. 59-78). Templeton Foundation Press.

Pargament, K. I., Smith, B. W., Koenig, H. G., & Perez, L. (1998). Patterns of positive and negative religious coping with major life stressors. *Journal for the Scientific Study of Religion, 37*(4), 710-24.

Pargament, K. I., & Sweeney, P. J. (2011). Building spiritual fitness in the army: An innovative approach to a vital aspect of human development. *American Psychologist, 66*(1), 58-64.

Park, C. L., Malone, M. R., Suresh, D. P., Bliss, D., & Rosen, R. I. (2008). Coping, meaning in life, and quality of life in congestive heart failure patients. *Quality of Life Research, 17*(1), 21-26.

Park, N., & Peterson, C. (2008). The cultivation of character strengths. In M. Ferrari & G. Potworowski (Eds.), *Teaching for wisdom: Cross-cultural perspectives on fostering wisdom* (pp. 59-78). Springer.

Park, N., & Peterson, C. (2009a). Character strengths: Research and practice. *Journal of College and Character, 10*(4), 1-10.

Park, N., & Peterson, C. (2009b). Strengths of character in school. In R. Gilman, E. S. Huebner, & M. J. Furlong (Eds.), *Handbook of positive psychology in schools* (pp. 65-76). Routledge.

Park, N., & Peterson, C. (2010). Does it matter where we live? The urban psychology of character strengths. *American Psychologist, 65*(6), 535-47.

Park, N., Peterson, C., & Seligman, M. E. (2004). Strengths of character and well-being. *Journal of Social and Clinical Psychology, 23*(5), 603-19.

Parrott, W. G. (Ed.). (2014a). *The positive side of negative emotions.* Guilford Press.

Parrott, W. G. (2014b). Feeling, function, and the place of negative emotions in a happy life. In W. G. Parrott (Ed.), *The positive side of negative emotions* (pp. 273-96). Guilford Press.

Pasupathi, M., Staudinger, U. M., & Baltes, P. B. (2001). Seeds of wisdom: Adolescents' knowledge and judgment about difficult life problems. *Developmental Psychology, 37*(3), 351-61.

Patchell-Evans, D. (2004). *Living the good life: Your guide to health and success.* ECW Press.

Paxson, A. A., & Shapiro, S. L. (2013). Love and physical health. In M. Hojjat & D. Cramer (Eds.), *Positive psychology of love* (pp. 191-202). Oxford University Press.

Peale, N. V. (1952). *The power of positive thinking.* Ballantine Books.

Pennington, J. T., & Hackney, C. H. (2017). Re-sourcing a Christian positive psychology from the Sermon on the Mount. *Journal of Positive Psychology, 12*(5), 427-435.

Perach, R., & Wisman, A. (2019). Can creativity beat death? A review and evidence on the existential anxiety buffering functions of creative achievement. *Journal of Creative Behavior, 53*(2), 193-210.

Pervin, L. A. (1960). Existentialism, psychology, and psychotherapy. *American Psychologist, 15*(5), 305-9.

Peterson, C. (1991). Meaning and measurement of explanatory style. *Psychological Inquiry, 2*(1), 1-10.

Peterson, C. (2006). *A primer in positive psychology.* Oxford University Press.

Peterson, C. (2013). *Pursuing the good life: 100 reflections on positive psychology.* Oxford University Press.

Peterson, C., & Barrett, L. (1987). Explanatory style and academic performance among university freshmen. *Journal of Personality and Social Psychology, 53*(3), 603-7.

Peterson, C., Maier, S. F., & Seligman, M. E. P. (1993). *Learned helplessness: A theory for the age of personal control.* Oxford University press.

Peterson, C., & Park, N. (2003). Positive psychology as the evenhanded positive psychologist views it. *Psychological Inquiry, 14*(2), 143-47.

Peterson, C., & Park, N. (2004). Classification and measurement of character strengths: Implications for practice. In P. A. Linley & S. Joseph (Eds.), *Positive psychology in practice* (pp. 433-46). John Wiley & Sons.

Peterson, C., & Park, N. (2012). Character strengths and the life of meaning. In P. T. P. Wong (Ed.), *The human quest for meaning* (2nd ed.) (pp. 277-95). Routledge.

Peterson, C., Park, N., & Castro, C. A. (2011). Assessment for the U.S. Army Comprehensive Soldier Fitness Program: The Global Assessment Tool. *American Psychologist, 66*(1), 10-18.

Peterson, C., Ruch, W., Beermann, U. Park, N., & Seligman, M. E. P. (2007). Strengths of character, orientations to happiness, and life satisfaction. *Journal of Positive Psychology 2*(3), 149-56.

Peterson, C., & Seligman, M. E. P. (1984). Causal explanations as a risk factor for depression: Theory and evidence. *Psychological Review, 91*(3), 347-74.

Peterson, C., & Seligman, M. E. P. (2004). *Character strengths and virtues: A handbook and classification.* American Psychological Association.

Peterson, C., & Steen, T. A. (2005). Optimistic explanatory style. In C. R. Snyder & S. J. Lopez (Eds.), *Handbook of positive psychology* (pp. 244-56). Oxford University Press.

Peterson, C., & Vaidya, R. S. (2001). Explanatory style, expectations, and depressive symptoms. *Personality and Individual Differences, 31*(7), 1217-23.

Peterson, E. H. (2000). *A long obedience in the same direction: Discipleship in an instant society* (2nd ed.). InterVarsity Press.

Peterson, E. H. (2005). *Christ plays in ten thousand places: A conversation in spiritual theology.* Eerdmans.

Peterson, E. H. (2006). *Eat this book: A conversation in the art of spiritual reading.* Eerdmans.

Petruzzello, S. J., Landers, D. M., Hatfield, B. D., Kubitz, K. A., & Salazar, W. (1991). A meta-analysis on the anxiety-reducing effects of acute and chronic exercise: Outcomes and mechanisms. *Sports Medicine, 11*(3), 143-82.

Phillips A., & Brown R. (2002). *The power of apology: Reality and perception* [Paper presentation]. Society for Personality and Social Psychology, Savannah, GA, USA.

Phipps, S. (2011). Positive psychology and war: An oxymoron. *American Psychologist, 66*(7), 641-42.

Piaget, J. (1932). *The moral judgment of the child.* Kegan, Paul, Trench, Trubner & Co.

Pieper, J. (1965). *The four cardinal virtues.* Harcourt, Brace & World.

Piet, J., & Hougaard, E. (2011). The effect of mindfulness-based cognitive therapy for prevention of relapse in recurrent major depressive disorder: A systematic review and meta-analysis. *Clinical Psychology Review, 31*(6), 1032-40.

Pinches, C. (2014). On hope. In K. Timpe & C. A. Boyd (Eds.), *Virtues and their vices* (pp. 349-68). Oxford University Press.

Pinker, S. (2002). *The blank slate: The modern denial of human nature.* Penguin.

Plante, T. G., & Boccaccini, M. T. (1997). The Santa Clara Strength of Religious Faith Questionnaire. *Pastoral Psychology, 45*(5), 375-87.

Plantinga, C., Sr. (1995). *Not the way it's supposed to be: A breviary of sin.* Eerdmans.

Plusnin, N., Pepping, C. A., & Kashima, E. S. (2018). The role of close relationships in terror management: A systematic review and research agenda. *Personality and Social Psychology Review, 22*(4), 307-46.

Pohls, H., & Oak, S. (2007). War & military mental health: The US psychiatric response in the 20th century. *American Journal of Public Health, 97*(12), 2132-42.

Polanin, J. R., Espelage, D. L., & Pigott, T. D. (2012). A meta-analysis of school-based bullying prevention programs' effects on bystander intervention behavior. *School Psychology Review, 41*(1), 47-65.

Polivy, J. (1976). Perception of calories and regulation of intake in restrained and unrestrained subjects. *Addictive Behaviors, 1*(3), 237-43.

Porter, J. (2016). Happiness. In P. McCosker & D. Turner (Eds.), *The Cambridge companion to the Summa Theologiae* (pp. 181-93). Cambridge University Press.

Post, S. G. (2002). The tradition of agape. In S. G. Post, L. G. Underwood, J. P. Schloss, & W. B. Hurlbut (Eds.), *Altruism and altruistic love: Science, philosophy, & religion in dialogue* (pp. 51-64). Oxford University Press.

Prager, D. (2007, February 20). *Happiness is a moral obligation. The Dennis Prager Show.* www.dennis prager.com/column/happiness-is-a-moral -obligation

Pretz, J. E., Naples, A. J., & Sternberg, R. J. (2003). Recognizing, defining, and representing problems. In J. E. Davidson & R. J. Sternberg (Eds.), *The psychology of problem solving* (pp. 3-30). Cambridge University Press.

Priest, R. F. (1966). Election jokes: The effects of reference group membership. *Psychological Reports, 18*(2), 600-602.

Privette, G. (1983). Peak experience, peak performance, and flow: A comparative analysis of positive human experiences. *Journal of Personality and Social Psychology, 45*(6), 1361-68.

Procksch, O., & Kuhn, K. G. (1964). ἅγιος. (G. Bromiley, Trans.). In G. Kittel (Ed.), *Theological dictionary of the New Testament: Vol. 1* (pp. 88-115). Eerdmans. (Original work published 1933)

Pyszczynski, T., Abdollahi, A., Solomon, S., Greenberg, J., Cohen, F., & Weise, D. (2006). Mortality salience, martyrdom, and military might: The Great Satan versus the Axis of Evil. *Personality and Social Psychology Bulletin, 32*(4), 525-37.

Pyszczynski, T., Greenberg, J., Koole, S., & Solomon, S. (2010). Experimental existential psychology: Coping with the facts of life. In S. T. Fiske, D. T. Gilbert, & G. Lindzey (Eds.), *Handbook of social psychology: Vol. 1* (5th ed.) (pp. 724-57). John Wiley & Sons.

Pyszczynski, T., Greenberg, J., & Solomon, S. (2000). Toward a dialectical analysis of growth and defensive motives. *Psychological Inquiries, 11*(4), 301-5.

Quested, E., & Duda, J. L. (2011). Antecedents of burnout among elite dancers: A longitudinal test of basic needs theory. *Psychology of Sport and Exercise, 12*(2), 159-67.

Rackl, L. (2003, September). But seriously folks: Humor can keep you healthy. *Reader's Digest,* 62-71.

Radner, E. (2010). The nuptial mystery: The historical flesh of procreation. In R. R. Jeal (Ed.), *Human sexuality and the nuptial mystery* (pp. 85-115). Cascade Books.

Ramsey, P. (1950). *Basic Christian ethics.* Charles Scribner's Sons.

Rao, K. R., & Paranjpe, A. C. (2016). *Psychology in the Indian tradition.* Springer.

Rashid, T., & Anjum, A. (2005). *340 ways to use VIA character strengths.* Action for Happiness. www .actionforhappiness.org/media/52486/340_ways _to_use_character_strengths.pdf

Rasmussen, H. N., Scheier, M. F., & Greenhouse, J. B. (2009). Optimism and physical health: A meta-analytic review. *Annals of Behavioral Medicine, 37*(3), 239-56.

Rathunde, K. (1996). Family context and talented adolescents' optimal experience in school-related activities. *Journal of Research on Adolescence, 6*(4), 605-28.

Reis, H. T., Sheldon, K. M., Gable, S. L., Roscoe, J., & Ryan, R. M. (2000). Daily well-being: The role of autonomy, competence, and relatedness. *Personality and Social Psychology Bulletin, 26*(4), 419-35.

Reiss, S. (2000). Human individuality, happiness, and flow. *American Psychologist, 55*(10), 1161-62.

Reivich, K. J., Seligman, M. E. P., & McBride, S. (2011). Master resilience training in the U.S. Army. *American Psychologist, 66*(1), 25-34.

Rejeski, W. J., Shelton, B., Miller, M., Dunn, A. L., King, A. C., & Sallis, J. F. (2001). Mediators of increased physical activity and change in subjective well-being: Results from the activity counseling trial (ACT). *Journal of Health Psychology, 6*(2), 159-68.

Retzinger, S. M. (1991). *Violent emotions: Shame and rage in marital quarrels.* Sage Publications.

Reynolds, J. M. (2009). *When Athens met Jerusalem.* IVP Academic.

Reznitskaya, A., & Sternberg, R. J. (2004). Teaching students to make wise judgments: The "teaching for wisdom" program. In P. A. Linley & S. Joseph (Eds.), *Positive psychology in practice* (pp. 181-96). John Wiley & Sons.

Rice, E. (1958). *The renaissance idea of wisdom.* Harvard University Press.

Rich, G. J. (2013). Finding flow: The history and future of a positive psychology concept. In J. D. Sinnott (Ed.), *Positive psychology: Advances in understanding adult motivation* (pp. 43-60). Springer.

Richardson, K., & Norgate, S. H. (2015). Does IQ really predict job performance? *Applied Developmental Science, 19*(3), 153-69.

Richman, C. L., & Rehberg, H. (1986). The development of self-esteem through the martial arts. *International Journal of Sport Psychology, 17*(3), 234-39.

Riggio, R. E., Zhu, W., Reina, C., & Maroosis, J. A. (2010). Virtue-based measurement of ethical leadership: The Leadership Virtues Questionnaire. *Consulting Psychology Journal: Practice and Research, 62*(4), 235-50.

Rind, B., & Bordia, P. (1995). Effect of server's "thank you" and personalization on restaurant tipping. *Journal of Applied Social Psychology, 25*(9), 745-51.

Robb, H. (1988). *How to stop driving yourself crazy: With help from Christian scriptures.* Albert Ellis Institute.

Roberts, R. C. (1995). Forgivingness. *American Philosophical Quarterly, 32*(4), 289-306.

Roberts, R. C. (1997). Attachment: Bowlby and the Bible. In R. C. Roberts & M. R. Talbot (Eds.), *Limning the psyche: Explorations in Christian psychology.* Eerdmans.

Roberts, R. C. (2000). A Christian psychology view. In E. L. Johnson & S. L. Jones (Eds.), *Psychology and Christianity: Four views* (pp. 148-77). InterVarsity Press.

Roberts, R. C. (2007). *Spiritual emotions: A psychology of Christian virtues.* Eerdmans.

Robertson-Kraft, C., & Duckworth, A. L. (2014). True grit: Trait-level perseverance and passion for long-term goals predicts effectiveness and retention among novice teachers. *Teachers College Record, 116*(3), 1-24.

Robinson, D. N. (1990). Wisdom through the ages. In R. J. Sternberg (Ed.) *Wisdom: Its nature, origins, and development* (pp. 13-24). Cambridge University Press.

Rodda, C. (2011, August 21). Why is the military spending millions on Christian contractors bent on evangelizing US soldiers? *AlterNet.* www.alternet.org/2011/08/why_is_the_military_spending_millions_on_christian_contractors_bent_on_evangelizing_us_soldiers

Roelofsen, P. (2002). The impact of office environments on employee performance: The design of the workplace as a strategy for productivity enhancement. *Journal of Facilities Management, 1*(3), 247-64.

Rogers, C. R. (1961). *On becoming a person: A therapist's view of psychotherapy.* Houghton Mifflin.

Rokeach, M. (1973). *The nature of human values.* Free Press.

Rosenblatt, A., Greenberg, J., Solomon, S., Pyszczynski, T., & Lyon, D. (1989). Evidence for terror management theory: I. The effects of mortality salience on reactions to those who violate or uphold cultural values. *Journal of Personality and Social Psychology, 57*(4), 681-90.

Rosete, D., & Ciarrochi, J. (2005). Emotional intelligence and its relationship to workplace performance outcomes of leadership effectiveness. *Leadership & Organization Development Journal, 26*(5), 388-99.

Ross, S. R., & Keiser, H. N. (2014). Autotelic personality through a five-factor lens: Individual differences in flow-propensity. *Personality and Individual Differences, 59,* 3-8.

Rothschild, Z., Abdollahi, A., & Pyszczynski, T. (2009). Does peace have a prayer? The effect of mortality salience, compassionate values, and religious fundamentalism on hostility toward out-groups. *Journal of Experimental Social Psychology, 45*(4), 816-27.

Rotter, J. B. (1966). Generalized expectancies for internal versus external control of reinforcement. *Psychological Monographs: General and Applied, 80*(1), 1-28.

Rotter, J. B. (1990). Internal versus external control of reinforcement: A case history of a variable. *American Psychologist, 45*(4), 489-93.

Rousseau, J. J. (1993). *Emile* (B. Foxley, Trans.). Charles E. Tuttle. (Original work published 1762)

Routledge, C., Arndt, J., Vess, M., & Sheldon, K. M. (2008). The life and death of creativity: The effects of mortality salience on self versus social-directed creative expression. *Motivation and Emotion, 32*(4), 331-38.

Rozin, P., Lowery, L., Imada, S., & Haidt, J. (1999). The CAD triad hypothesis: A mapping between three moral emotions (contempt, anger, disgust) and three moral codes (community, autonomy, divinity). *Journal of Personality and Social Psychology, 76*(4), 574-86.

Ruch, W. (1994). Temperament, Eysenck's PEN system, and humor-related traits. *Humor: International Journal of Humor Research, 7*(3), 209-44.

Ruch, W. (1997). State and trait cheerfulness and the induction of exhilaration: A FACS study. *European Psychologist, 2*(4), 328-41.

Ruch, W. (1998). Foreword and overview. Sense of humor: A new look at an old concept. In W. Ruch (Ed.), *The sense of humor: Explorations of a personality characteristic* (pp. 3-14). Mouton de Gruyter.

Ruch, W., & Köhler, G. (1998). A temperament approach to humor. In V. Raskin & W. Ruch (Eds.), *The sense of humor: Explorations of a personality characteristic* (pp. 203-28). Mouton de Gruyter.

Ruch, W., Proyer, R. T., Harzer, C., Park, N., Peterson, C., & Seligman, M. E. (2010). Values in Action Inventory of Strengths (VIA-IS): Adaptation and validation of the German version and the

development of a peer-rating form. *Journal of Individual Differences, 31*(3), 138-49.

Runco, M. A., & Acar, S. (2012). Divergent thinking as an indicator of creative potential. *Creativity Research Journal, 24*(1), 66-75.

Rusbult, C. E., Hannon, P. A., Stocker, S. L., & Finkel, E. J. (2005). Forgiveness and relational repair. In E. L. Worthington Jr. (Ed.), *Handbook of forgiveness* (pp. 185-206). Routledge.

Rushton, J. P. (1982). Social learning theory and the development of prosocial behavior. In N. Eisenberg (Ed.), *The development of prosocial behavior* (pp. 77-105). Academic Press.

Rushton, J. P., Chrisjohn, R. D., & Fekken, G. C. (1981). The altruistic personality and the self-report altruism scale. *Personality and Individual Differences, 2*(4), 293-302.

Rust, T., Diessner, R., & Reade, L. (2009). Strengths only or strengths and relative weaknesses? A preliminary study. *The Journal of Psychology, 143*(5), 465-476.

Ryan, R. M. (1995). Psychological needs and the facilitation of integrative processes. *Journal of Personality, 63*(3), 397-427.

Ryan, R. M., Chirkov, V. I., Little, T. D., Sheldon, K. M., Timoshina, E., & Deci, E. L. (1999). The American dream in Russia: Extrinsic aspirations and well-being in two cultures. *Personality and Social Psychology Bulletin, 25*(12), 1509-24.

Ryan, R. M., & Deci, E. L. (2000). Self-determination theory and the facilitation of intrinsic motivation, social development, and well-being. *American Psychologist, 55*(1), 68-78.

Ryan, R. M., & Deci, E. L. (2001). On happiness and human potentials: A review of research on hedonic and eudaimonic well-being. *Annual Review of Psychology, 52,* 141-66.

Ryan, R. M., & Deci, E. L. (2007). Active human nature: Self-determination theory and the promotion and maintenance of sport, exercise, and health. In M. S. Hagger & N. L. D. Chatzisa-rantis (Eds.), *Intrinsic motivation and self-determination in exercise and sport* (pp. 1-19). Human Kinetics.

Ryan, R. M., & Deci, E. L. (2017). *Self-determination theory: Basic psychological needs in motivation, development, and wellness.* Guilford Press.

Ryff, C. D., & Singer, B. (2003). Ironies of the human condition: Well-being and health on the way to mortality. In L. G. Aspinwall & U. M. Staudinger (Eds.), *A psychology of human strengths: Fundamental questions and future direction for a positive psychology* (pp. 271-88). American Psychological Association.

Sabates, A. M. (2012). *Social psychology in Christian perspective*. IVP Academic.

Sacks, D. W., Stevenson, B., & Wolfers, J. (2012). Subjective wellbeing, income, economic development and growth. In P. Booth (Ed.), . . . *And the pursuit of happiness* (pp. 59-97). Institute of Economic Affairs.

Salanova, M., Bakker, A. B., & Llorens, S. (2006). Flow at work: Evidence for an upward spiral of personal and organizational resources. *Journal of Happiness Studies, 7*(1), 1-22.

Samuel, L. R. (2018). *Happiness in America: A cultural history*. Rowman & Littlefield.

Sandvik, A. M., Bartone, P. T., Hystad, S. W., Phillips, T. M., Thayer, J. F., & Johnsen, B. H. (2013). Psychological hardiness predicts neuroimmunological responses to stress. *Psychology, Health & Medicine, 18*(6), 705-13.

Sartre, J. P. (1956). *Being and nothingness* (H. E. Barnes, Trans.). Philosophical Library.

Scannell, E. D., Allen, F. C., & Burton, J. (2002). Meaning in life and positive and negative well-being. *North American Journal of Psychology, 4*(1), 93-111.

Scheier, M. F., & Carver, C. S. (1988). A model of behavioral self-regulation: Translating intention into action. *Advances in experimental social psychology, 21*, 303-46.

Scheier, M. F., Carver, C. S., & Bridges, M. W. (2001). Optimism, pessimism, and psychological well-being. In E. C. Chang (Ed.), *Optimism and pessimism: Implications for theory, research, and practice* (pp. 189-216). American Psychological Association.

Schiller, J. L., II (2013). Cardinal virtue and the well of fortitude. *Journal of Virtues & Leadership, 3*(1), 43-52.

Schlabach, G. W. (2004). Breaking bread: Peace and war. In S. Hauerwas & S. Wells (Eds.), *The Blackwell companion to Christian ethics* (pp. 360-74). Blackwell Publishing.

Schleiermacher, F. (1958). *On religion: Speeches to its cultured despisers* (J. Oman, Trans.). Harper & Row. (Original work published 1799)

Schmeichel, B. J., Vohs, K. D., & Baumeister, R. F. (2003). Intellectual performance and ego depletion: Role of the self in logical reasoning and other information processing. *Journal of Personality and Social Psychology, 85*(1), 33-46.

Schnitker, S. A., & Richardson, K. L. (2019). Framing gratitude journaling as prayer amplifies its hedonic and eudaimonic well-being, but not health, benefits. *Journal of Positive Psychology, 14*(4), 427-39.

Schofield, P., Ball, D., Smith, J. G., Borland, R., O'Brien, P., Davis, S., . . . & Joseph, D. (2004). Optimism and survival in lung carcinoma patients. *Cancer, 100*(6), 1276-82.

Schreiner, L. A. (2015). Positive psychology and higher education: The contribution of positive psychology to student success and institutional effectiveness. In J. C. Wade, L. I. Marks, & R. D. Hetzel (Eds.), *Positive psychology on the college campus* (pp. 1-26). Oxford University Press.

Schulman, M. (2005). How we become moral: The sources of moral motivation. In C. R. Snyder & S. J. Lopez (Eds.), *Handbook of positive psychology* (pp. 499-512). Oxford University Press.

Schulman, P., Keith, D., & Seligman, M. E. P. (1993). Is optimism heritable? A study of twins. *Behavior Research and Therapy, 31*(6), 569-74.

Schutte, N. S., & Malouff, J. M. (2019). The impact of signature character strengths interventions: A meta-analysis. *Journal of Happiness Studies, 20*(4), 1179-96.

Schwartz, B. (2000). Self-determination: The tyranny of freedom. *American Psychologist, 55*(1), 79-88.

Schwartz, B. (2001). Freedom and tyranny: Descriptions and prescriptions. *American Psychologist, 56*(1), 80-81.

Schwartz, B., & Sharpe, K. (2010). *Practical wisdom: The right way to do the right thing*. Riverhead Books.

Schwartz, B., & Sharpe, K. E. (2019). Practical wisdom: What Aristotle might add to psychology. In R. J. Sternberg & J. Glück (Eds.), *Cambridge handbook of wisdom* (pp. 226-48). Cambridge University Press.

Schwartz, P. (2012). Happiness is not within the government's remit: The philosophical flaw in happiness economics. In P. Booth (Ed.), . . . *And the pursuit of happiness* (pp. 222-45). Institute of Economic Affairs.

Schwarz, N. (2002). Situated cognition and the wisdom in feelings: Cognitive tuning. In L. F. Barrett & P. Salovey (Eds.), *The wisdom in feeling: Psychological processes in emotional intelligence* (pp. 144-66). Guilford Press.

Scruton, R. (2011). *Beauty: A very short introduction.* Oxford University Press.

Segal, Z. V., Williams., J. M. G., & Teasdale, J. D. (2002). *Mindfulness-based cognitive therapy for depression.* Guilford Press.

Seligman, M. E. P. (1975). Depression and learned helplessness in man. *Journal of Abnormal Psychology, 84*(3), 228-38.

Seligman, M. E. P. (1990). *Learned optimism.* Knopf.

Seligman, M. E. P. (1999). The president's address. *American Psychologist, 54*(8), 559-62.

Seligman, M. E. P. (2002). *Authentic happiness: Using the new positive psychology to realize your potential for lasting fulfillment.* Free Press.

Seligman, M. E. P. (2011a). *Flourish: A visionary new understanding of happiness and well-being.* Free Press.

Seligman, M. E. P. (2011b). Helping American soldiers in time of war: Reply to comments on the Comprehensive Soldier Fitness special issue. *American Psychologist, 66*(7), 646-47.

Seligman, M. E. P., Abramson, L. Y., Semmel, A., & von Baeyer, C. (1979). Depressive attributional style. *Journal of Abnormal Psychology, 88*(3), 242-47.

Seligman, M. E. P., & Csikszentmihalyi, M. (2000). Positive psychology: An introduction. *American Psychologist, 55*(1), 5-14.

Seligman, M. E. P., & Csikszentmihalyi, M. (2001). Reply to comments. *American Psychologist, 56*(1), 89-90.

Seligman, M. E., Ernst, R. M., Gillham, J., Reivich, K., & Linkins, M. (2009). Positive education: Positive psychology and classroom interventions. *Oxford Review of Education, 35*(3), 293-311.

Seligman, M. E. P., & Maier, S. F. (1967). Failure to escape traumatic shock. *Journal of Experimental Psychology, 74*(1), 1-9.

Seligman, M. E. P., Nolan-Hoeksma, S., Thornton, N., & Thornton, K. M. (1990). Explanatory style as a mechanism of disappointing athletic performance. *Psychological Science, 1*(2), 143-46.

Seligman, M. E. P., Peterson, C., Kaslow, N. J., Tanenbaum, R. L., Alloy, L.B., & Abramson, L. Y. (1984). Attributional style and depressive symptoms among children. *Journal of Abnormal Psychology, 93*(2), 235-38.

Seligman, M. E., & Schulman, P. (1986). Explanatory style as a predictor of productivity and quitting among life insurance sales agents. *Journal of Personality and Social Psychology, 50*(4), 832-38.

Seligman, M. E. P., Steen, T. A., Park, N., & Peterson, C. (2005). Positive psychology progress: Empirical validation of interventions. *American Psychologist, 60*(5), 410-21.

Shapiro, J., Morrison, E. H., & Boker, J. R. (2004). Teaching empathy to first year medical students: Evaluation of an elective literature and medicine course. *Education for Health, 17*(1), 73-84.

Shapiro, J., & Rucker, L. (2004). The Don Quixote effect: Why going to the movies can help develop empathy and altruism in medical students and residents. *Families, Systems, & Health, 22*(4), 445-52.

Shapiro, S. B. (2001). Illogical positivism. *American Psychologist, 56*(1), 82.

Shapiro, S. L., Schwartz, G. E. R., & Santerre, C. (2005). Meditation and positive psychology. In C. R. Snyder & S. J. Lopez (Eds.), *Handbook of positive psychology* (pp. 632-45). Oxford University Press.

Shapiro, S. L., & Mariels, T. R. (2013). Cultivating mindfulness through listening. In J. J. Froh & A. C. Parks (Eds.), *Activities for teaching positive psychology: A guide for instructors* (pp. 99-103). American Psychological Association.

Sharma, S., & Singh, K. (2019). Religion and well-being: The mediating role of positive virtues. *Journal of Religion and Health, 58*(1), 119-31.

Sheldon, K. M., & Lyubomirsky, S. (2006). How to increase and sustain positive emotion: The effects of expressing gratitude and visualizing best possible selves. *Journal of Positive Psychology, 1*(2), 73-82.

Sheldon, K. M., & Ryan, R. M. (2011). Positive psychology and self-determination theory: A natural interface. In V. I. Chirkov, R. M. Ryan, & K. M. Sheldon (Eds.), *Human autonomy in cross-cultural context* (pp. 33-44). Springer.

Shepperd, J. A., Maroto, J. J., & Pbert, L. A. (1996). Dispositional optimism as a predictor of health changes among cardiac patients. *Journal of Research in Personality, 30*(4), 517-34.

Sherlock, C. (1996). *The doctrine of humanity.* IVP Academic.

Shields, D. L., LaVoi, N. M., Bredemeier, B. L., & Power, F. C. (2007). Predictors of poor sportspersonship in youth sports: Personal attitudes and social influences. *Journal of Sport and Exercise Psychology, 29*(6), 747-62.

Shiota, M. N., Campos, B., Keltner, D., & Hertenstein, M. J. (2004). Positive emotion and the regulation of interpersonal relationships. In P. Philippot & R. S. Feldman (Eds.), *The regulation of emotion* (pp. 127-55). Lawrence Erlbaum Associates.

Shoda, Y., Mischel, W., & Peake, P. (1990). Predicting adolescent cognitive and self-regulatory competencies from preschool delay of gratification: Identifying diagnostic conditions. *Developmental Psychology, 26*(6), 978-86.

Showers, C., & Ruben, C. (1990). Distinguishing defensive pessimism from depression: Negative expectations and positive coping mechanisms. *Cognitive Therapy and Research, 14*(4), 385-99.

Shulenberg, S. E., & Melton, A. M. A. (2010). A confirmatory factor-analytic evaluation of the Purpose in Life Test: Preliminary psychometric support for a replicable two-factor model. *Journal of Happiness Studies, 11*(1), 95-111.

Shurcliff, A. (1968). Judged humor, arousal, and the relief theory. *Journal of Personality and Social Psychology, 8*(4), 360-63.

Shuster, M. (2004). *The fall and sin: What we have become as sinners.* Eerdmans.

Siegel, R. D., Germer, C. K., & Olendzki, A. (2009). Mindfulness: What is it? Where did it come from? In F. Didonna (Ed.), *Clinical handbook of mindfulness* (pp. 17-36). Springer.

Silvas, A. M. (2005). *The asketikon of St Basil the Great.* Oxford University Press.

Simon, Z. (2018, May 14). *Machida says he's "back," explains post-Belfort KO pose at UFC 224 was incidental. Bloody Elbow.* www.bloodyelbow.com/2018/5/14/17352758/ufc-224-lyoto-machida-video-interview-vitor-belfort-karate-kid-ko-pose-back-mma-news

Sinclair, R. R., & Britt, T. W. (Eds.). (2013). *Building psychological resilience in military personnel: Theory and practice.* American Psychological Association.

Sivanathan, N., Arnold, K. A., Turner, N., & Barling, J. (2004). Leading well: Transformational leadership and well-being. In P. A. Linley & S. Joseph (Eds.), *Positive psychology in practice* (pp. 241-55). John Wiley & Sons.

Skinner, B. F. (1953). *Science and human behavior.* Macmillan.

Skinner, B. F. (1971). *Beyond freedom and dignity.* Knopf.

Slater, J., & Hunt, H. T. (1997). Postural-vestibular integration and forms of dreaming: A preliminary report on the effects of brief t'ai chi chuan training. *Perceptual and Motor Skills, 85*(1), 97-98.

Slemp, G.R., Kern, M. L., Patrick, K. J., & Ryan, R. M. (2018). Leader autonomy support in the workplace: A meta-analytic review. *Motivation and Emotion, 42*(5), 706-24.

Sliter, M., Kale, A., & Yuan, Z. (2014). Is humor the best medicine? The buffering effect of coping humor on traumatic stressors in firefighters. *Journal of Organizational Behavior, 35*(2), 257-72.

Smedes, L. B. (1984). *Forgive and forget: Healing the hurts we don't deserve.* Harper and Row.

Smedley, T. (2012, June 20). Can happiness be a good business strategy? *The Guardian.* www.theguardian.com/sustainable-business/happy-workforce-business-strategy-wellbeing

Smid, H. G., Trümper, B. G., Pottag, G., Wagner, K., Lobmann, R., Scheich, H., . . . & Heinze, H. J. (1997). Differentiation of hypoglycaemia induced cognitive impairments. An electrophysiological approach. *Brain: A Journal of Neurology, 120*(6), 1041-56.

Smith, D. I., & Smith, J. K. A. (2011). *Teaching and Christian practices: Reshaping faith and learning.* Eerdmans.

Smith, J. K. A. (2009). *Desiring the kingdom: Worship, worldview, and cultural formation.* Baker Academic.

Smith, P. D. (2002). *The virtue of civility in the practice of politics.* University Press of America.

Smith, T. (2000). Cultural values and happiness. *American Psychologist, 55*(1), 1162.

Snyder, C. R. (2000a). Hypothesis: There is hope. In C. R. Snyder (Ed.), *Handbook of hope: Theory, measures, and applications* (pp. 3-21). Academic Press.

Snyder, C. R. (2000b). Genesis: The birth and growth of hope. In C. R. Snyder (Ed.), *Handbook of hope: Theory, measures, and applications* (pp. 25-38). Academic Press.

Snyder, C. R. (2002). Hope theory: Rainbows in the mind. *Psychological Inquiry, 13*(4), 249-75.

Snyder, C. R., Harris, C., Anderson, J. R., Holleran, S. A., Irving, L. M., Sigmon, S. T., et al. (1991). The will and the ways: Development and validation of an individual-differences measure of hope. *Journal of Personality and Social Psychology, 60*(4), 570-85.

Snyder, C. R., Hoza, B., Pelham, W. E., Rapoff, M., Ware, L., Danovsky, M., . . . & Stahl, K. J. (1997). The development and validation of the Children's Hope Scale. *Journal of Pediatric Psychology, 22*(3), 399-421.

Snyder, C. R., & Lopez, S. J. (Eds.). (2005). *Handbook of positive psychology.* Oxford University Press.

Snyder, C. R., Lopez, S. J., Aspinwall, L. Fredrickson, B. L., Haidt, J., Keltner, D., Robitschek, C., Wehmeyer, M., & Wrzesniewski, A. (2005). The future of positive psychology: A declaration of independence. In C. R Lopez & S. J. Snyder (Eds.), *Handbook of positive psychology* (pp. 751-68). Oxford University Press.

Snyder, C. R., Lopez, S. J., & Pedrotti, J. T. (2011). *Positive psychology: The scientific and practical explorations of human strengths* (2nd ed.). SAGE Publications.

Snyder, C. R., McDermott, D., Cook, W., & Rapoff, M. A. (1997). *Hope for the journey: Helping children through good times and bad.* Basic Books.

Snyder, C. R., Rand, K. L., & Sigmon, D. R. (2005). Hope theory: A member of the positive psychology family. In C. R. Snyder & S. J. Lopez (Eds.), *Handbook of positive psychology* (pp. 257-76). Oxford University Press.

Söderlund, J., & Newman, P. (2015). Biophilic architecture: A review of the rationale and outcomes. *AIMS Environmental Science, 2*(4), 950-69.

Solomon, R. C., & Stone, L. D. (2002). On "positive" and "negative" emotions. *Journal for the Theory of Social Behaviour, 32*(4), 417-35.

Solomon, S., Greenberg, J., & Pyszczynski, T. (1991). A terror management theory of social behavior: The psychological functions of self-esteem and cultural worldviews. *Advances in Experimental Social Psychology, 24*, 93-159.

Sosik, J. J., Gentry, W. A., & Chun, J. U. (2012). The value of virtue in the upper echelons: A multi-source examination of executive character

strengths and performance. *The Leadership Quarterly, 23*(3), 367-82.

Spears, L. C. (2010). Character and servant leadership: Ten characteristics of effective, caring leaders. *Journal of Virtues & Leadership, 1*(1), 25-30.

Spilka, B., & Ladd, K. L. (2013). *The psychology of prayer: A scientific approach.* Guilford Press.

Sprecher, S., & Regan, P. C. (2002). Liking some things (in some people) more than others: Partner preferences in romantic relationships and friendships. *Journal of Social and Personal Relationships, 19*(4), 463-81.

Stahl, B., & Goldstein, E. (2010). *A mindfulness-based stress reduction workbook.* New Harbinger Publications.

Stajkovic, A. D., & Luthans, F. (1998). Self-efficacy and work-related performance: A meta-analysis. *Psychological Bulletin, 124*(2), 240-61.

Stalnaker, A. (2006). *Overcoming our evil: Human nature and spiritual exercises in Xunzi and Augustine.* Georgetown University Press.

Stanovich, K. E., & West, R. F. (2008). On the relative independence of thinking biases and cognitive ability. *Journal of Personality and Social Psychology, 94*(4), 672-95.

Stark, S. (2004). A change of heart: Moral emotions, transformation, and moral virtue. *Journal of Moral Philosophy, 1*(1), 31-50.

Stathi, A., Fox, K. R., & McKenna, J. (2002). Physical activity and dimensions of subjective well-being in older adults. *Journal of Aging and Physical Activity, 10*(1), 76-92.

Staudinger, U. M., & Baltes, P. B. (1996). Interactive minds: A facilitative setting for wisdom-related performance? *Journal of Personality and Social Psychology, 71*(4), 746-62.

Staudinger, U. M., & Glück, J. (2011). Psychological wisdom research: Commonalities and differences in a growing field. *Annual Review of Psychology, 62*, 215-41.

Staudinger, U. M., Maciel, A. G., Smith, J., & Baltes, P. B. (1998). What predicts wisdom-related performance? A first look at personality, intelligence, and facilitative experiential contexts. *European Journal of Personality, 12*(1), 1-17.

Staudinger, U. M., Smith, J., & Baltes, P. B. (1992). Wisdom-related knowledge in a life review task: Age differences and the role of professional specialization. *Psychology and Aging, 7*(2), 271-81.

Stavrou, N. A., Jackson, S. A., Zervas, Y., & Kartero-liotis, K. (2007). Flow experience and athletes' performance with reference to the orthogonal model of flow. *Sport Psychologist, 21*(4), 438-57.

Staw, B. M. (1986). Organizational psychology and the pursuit of the happy/productive worker. *California Management Review, 28*(4), 40-53.

Staw, B. M., Sutton, R. I., & Pelled, L. H. (1994). Employee positive emotion and favorable outcomes at the workplace. *Organizational Science, 5*(1), 51-71.

Steger, M. F. (2012). Experiencing meaning in life: Optimal functioning at the nexus of well-being, psychopathology, and spirituality. In P. T. P. Wong (Ed.), *The human quest for meaning* (2nd ed.) (pp. 165-84). Routledge.

Steger, M. F., Frazier, P., Oishi, S., & Kaler, M. (2006). The Meaning in Life Questionnaire: Assessing the presence of and search for meaning in life. *Journal of Counseling Psychology, 53*(1), 80-93.

Steger, M. F., Kashdan, T. B., & Oishi, S. (2008). Being good by doing good: Daily eudaimonic activity and well-being. *Journal of Research in Personality, 42*(1), 22-42.

Steindl-Rast, D. (1984). *Gratefulness, the heart of prayer.* Paulist Press.

Steindl-Rast, D. (2004). Gratitude as thankfulness and as gratefulness. In R. A. Emmons & M. E. McCullough (Eds.), *The psychology of gratitude* (pp. 282-90). Oxford University Press.

Stenling, A., Lindwall, M., & Hassmén, P. (2015). Changes in perceived autonomy support, need satisfaction, motivation, and well-being in young elite athletes. *Sport, Exercise, and Performance Psychology, 4*(1), 50-61.

Stephens, D. E. (2000). Predictors of likelihood to aggress in youth soccer: An examination of coed and all-girls teams. *Journal of Sport Behavior, 23*(3), 311-25.

Stephens, D., & Bredemeier, B. (1996). Moral atmosphere and judgments about aggression in girls' soccer: Relationships among moral and motivational variables. *Journal of Sport and Exercise Psychology, 18*(2), 158-73.

Stephens, D., & Kavanagh, B. (1997). Predictors of aggression and cheating in youth ice hockey. *Journal of Sport and Exercise Psychology, 19(Suppl.)*, S110.

Sterba, J. P. (1988). *How to make people just: A practical reconciliation of alternate conceptions of justice.* Rowman & Littlefield.

Sternberg, R. J. (1985). Implicit theories of intelligence, creativity, and wisdom. *Journal of Personality and Social Psychology, 49*(3), 607-27.

Sternberg, R. J. (1986). A triangular theory of love. *Psychological Review, 93*(2), 119-35.

Sternberg, R. J. (Ed.). (1990). *Wisdom: Its nature, origins, and development.* Cambridge University Press.

Sternberg, R. J. (1997). Construct validation of a triangular love scale. *European Journal of Social Psychology, 27*(3), 313-35.

Sternberg, R. J. (1998a). A balance theory of wisdom. *Review of General Psychology, 2*(4), 347-65.

Sternberg, R. J. (1998b). The dialectic as a tool for teaching psychology. *Teaching of Psychology, 25*(3), 177-80.

Sternberg, R. J. (2001). Why schools should teach for wisdom: The balance theory of wisdom in educational settings. *Educational Psychologist, 36*(4), 227-45.

Sternberg, R. J. (Ed.). (2002). *Why smart people can be so stupid.* Yale University Press.

Sternberg, R. J. (2004). Why smart people can be so foolish. *European Psychologist, 9*(3), 145-50.

Sternberg, R. J. (2005). Foolishness. In R. J. Sternberg & J. Jordan (Eds.), *A handbook of wisdom: Psychological perspectives* (pp. 331-52). Cambridge University Press.

Sternberg, R. J. (2019). Race to Samarra: The critical importance of wisdom in the world today. In R. J. Sternberg & J. Glück (Eds.), *Cambridge handbook of wisdom* (pp. 3-9). Cambridge University Press.

Sternberg, R. J., & Glück, J. (Eds.). (2019). Wisdom, morality, and ethics. In R. J. Sternberg & J. Glück (Eds.), *Cambridge handbook of wisdom* (pp. 551-74). Cambridge University Press.

Sternberg, R. J., Reznitskaya, A., & Jarvin, L. (2007). Teaching for wisdom: What matters is not just what students know, but how they use it. *London Review of Education, 5*(2), 143-58.

Stephens, D. E., & Kavanagh, B. (2003). Aggression in Canadian youth ice hockey: The role of moral atmosphere. *International Sports Journal, 7*(2), 109–119.

Stevenson, B., & Wolfers, J. (2013). Subjective well-being and income: Is there any evidence of satiation? *American Economic Review, 103*(3), 598-604.

Stevenson, R. G. (1993). We laugh to keep from crying: Coping through humor. *Loss, Grief & Care, 7*(1-2), 173-79.

Stokker, K. (1991). Heil Hitler; God save the king: Jokes and the Norwegian resistance 1940–1945. *Western Folklore, 50*(2), 171-90.

Stone, G. A., Russell, R. F., & Patterson, K. (2004). Transformational versus servant leadership: A difference in leader focus. *Leadership & Organization Development Journal, 25*(4), 349-61.

Stone, T. L., & Watkins, P. C. (2001, May). *Does the expression of gratitude improve mood?* [Paper presentation]. 81st Annual Convention of the Western Psychological Association, Maui, HI, USA.

Stoner, J. R., Jr., & James, H. (Eds.). (2015). *The thriving society: On the social conditions of human flourishing*. Witherspoon Institute.

Storr, W. (2014, February 25). The man who destroyed America's ego. *Medium.* https://medium.com/matter/the-man-who-destroyed-americas-ego-94d214257b5

Strawn, B. A. (Ed.). (2012). *The Bible and the pursuit of happiness*. Oxford University Press.

Strube, M. J. (1986). An analysis of the self-handicapping scale. *Basic and Applied Social Psychology, 7*(3), 211-24.

Strudler Wallston, B., & Wallston, K. A. (1978). Locus of control and health: A review of the literature. *Health Education Monographs, 6*(1), 107-17.

Struthers, C. W., Eaton, J., Santelli, A. G., Uchiyama, M., & Shirvani, N. (2008). The effects of attributions of intent and apology on forgiveness: When saying sorry may not help the story. *Journal of Experimental Social Psychology, 44*(4), 983-92.

Stuewig, J., Tangney, J. P., Heigel, C., Harty, L., & McCloskey, L. (2010). Shaming, blaming, and maiming: Functional links among the moral emotions, externalization of blame, and aggression. *Journal of Research in Personality, 44*(1), 91-102.

Suh, E., Diener, E., Oishi, S., & Triandis, H. C. (1998). The shifting basis of life satisfaction judgments across cultures: Emotions versus norms. *Journal of Personality and Social Psychology, 74*(2), 482-93.

Suls, J., Witenberg, S., & Gutkin, D. (1981). Evaluating reciprocal and nonreciprocal prosocial behavior: Developmental changes. *Personality and Social Psychology Bulletin, 7*(1), 25-31.

Suls, J. M. (1972). A two-stage model for the appreciation of jokes and cartoons: An information-processing analysis. In J. H. Goldstein & P. E. McGhee (Eds.), *The psychology of humor: Theoretical perspectives and empirical issues* (pp. 81-100). Academic Press.

Sundararajan, L. (2005a, August). *Beyond hope: The Chinese Buddhist notion of emptiness* [Paper presentation]. Annual Convention of the American Psychological Association, Washington, DC, USA.

Sundararajan, L. (2005b). Happiness donut: A Confucian critique of positive psychology. *Journal of Theoretical and Philosophical Psychology, 25*(1), 35-60.

Susman, W. (2012). *Culture as history*. Pantheon.

Swann, W. B., Jr., & Bosson, J. K. (2010). Self and identity. In S. T. Fiske, D. T. Gilbert, & G. Lindzey (Eds.), *Handbook of social psychology* (5th ed.) (pp. 589-628). John Wiley & Sons.

Swartley, W. M. (2007). Peacemaking pillars of character formation in the new testament. In R. L. Brawley (Ed.), *Character ethics and the new testament: Moral dimensions of scripture* (pp. 225-43). Westminster John Knox.

Swartwood, J., & Tiberius, V. (2019). Philosophical foundations of wisdom. In R. J. Sternberg & J. Glück (Eds.), *Cambridge handbook of wisdom* (pp. 10-39). Cambridge University Press.

Sweeney, P. D., Anderson, K., & & Bailey, S. (1986). Attributional style in depression: A meta-analytic review. *Journal of Personality and Social Psychology, 50*(5), 974-91.

Symington, S. H., & Symington, M. F. (2012). A Christian model of mindfulness: Using mindfulness principles to support psychological well-being, value-based behavior, and the Christian spiritual journey. *Journal of Psychology and Christianity, 31*(1), 71-77.

Szabo, A. (2000). Physical activity as a source of psychological dysfunction. In S. J. H. Biddle, K. R. Fox, & S. H. Boutcher (Eds.), *Physical activity and psychological well-being* (pp. 130-53). Routledge.

Szabo, A. (2003). The acute effects of humor and exercise on mood and anxiety. *Journal of Leisure Research, 35*(2), 152-62.

Tan, E. S. N., & Yarhouse, M. A. (2010). Facilitating congruence between religious beliefs and sexual identity with mindfulness. *Psychotherapy: Theory, Research, Practice, Training, 47*(4), 500-511.

Tan, S. Y. (2011). Mindfulness and acceptance-based cognitive behavioral therapies: Empirical evidence and clinical applications from a Christian perspective. *Journal of Psychology and Christianity, 30*(3), 243-49.

Tangney, J. P. (1990). Assessing individual differences in proneness to shame and guilt: Development of the Self-Conscious Affect and Attribution Inventory. *Journal of Personality and Social Psychology, 59*(1), 102-11.

Tangney, J. P. (1991). Moral affect: The good, the bad, and the ugly. *Journal of Personality and Social Psychology, 61*(4), 598-607.

Tangney, J. P. (1994). The mixed legacy of the superego: Adaptive and maladaptive aspects of shame and guilt. In J. M. Masling & R. F. Bornstein (Eds.), *Empirical perspectives on object relations theory* (pp. 1-28). American Psychological Association.

Tangney, J. P., Baumeister, R. F., & Boone, A. L. (2004). High self-control predicts good adjustment, less pathology, better grades, and interpersonal success. *Journal of Personality, 72*(2), 271-324.

Tangney, J. P., Boone, A. L., & Dearing, R. (2005). Forgiving the self: Conceptual issues and empirical findings. In E. L. Worthington Jr. (Ed.), *Handbook of forgiveness* (pp. 143-58). Routledge.

Tangney, J. P., Mashek, D., & Stuewig, J. (2007). Working at the social-clinical-community-criminology interface: The George Mason University inmate study. *Journal of Social and Clinical Psychology, 26*(1), 1-21.

Tangney, J. P., Miller, R. S., Flicker, L., & Barlow, D. H. (1996). Are shame, guilt and embarrassment distinct emotions? *Journal of Personality and Social Psychology, 70*(6), 1256-69.

Tangney, J. P., Stuewig, J., & Hafez, L. (2011). Shame, guilt, and remorse: Implications for offender populations. *Journal of Forensic Psychiatry & Psychology, 22*(5), 706-23.

Tangney, J. P., Stuewig, J., & Martinez, A. G. (2014). Two faces of shame: The roles of shame and guilt in predicting recidivism. *Psychological Science, 25*(3), 799-805.

Tangney, J. P., Stuewig, J., & Mashek, D. J. (2007a). Moral emotions and moral behavior. *Annual Review of Psychology, 58*, 345-72.

Tangney, J. P., Stuewig, J., & Mashek, D. J. (2007b). What's moral about the self-conscious emotions?

In J. L. Tracy, R. W. Robins, & J. P. Tangney (Eds.), *The self-conscious emotions: Theory and research* (pp. 21-37). Guilford Press.

Tangney, J. P., Stuewig, J., Mashek, D., & Hastings, M. (2011). Assessing jail inmates' proneness to shame and guilt: Feeling bad about the behavior or the self? *Criminal Justice and Behavior, 38*(7), 710-34.

Tangney, J. P., Wagner, P., Fletcher, C., & Gramzow, R. (1992). Shamed into anger? The relation of shame and guilt to anger and self-reported aggression. *Journal of Personality and Social Psychology, 62*(4), 669-75.

Tangney, J. P., Wagner, P. E., & Gramzow, R. (1989). *The Test of Self-Conscious Affect (TOSCA)*. George Mason University.

Tangney, J. P., Wagner, P., & Gramzow, R. (1992). Proneness to shame, proneness to guilt, and psychopathology. *Journal of Abnormal Psychology, 101*(3), 469-78.

Tangney, J. P., Wagner, P. E., Hill-Barlow, D., Marschall, D. E., & Gramzow, R. (1996). Relation of shame and guilt to constructive versus destructive responses to anger across the lifespan. *Journal of Personality and Social Psychology, 70*(4), 797-809.

Tani, F., Greenman, P. S., Schneider, B. H., & Fregoso, M. (2003). Bullying and the Big Five: A study of childhood personality and participant roles in bullying incidents. *School Psychology International, 24*(2), 131-46.

Tao, H. L. (2019). Marriage and happiness: Evidence from Taiwan. *Journal of Happiness Studies, 20*(6), 1843-61.

Taubman Ben-Ari, O., Findler, L., & Mikulincer, M. (2002). The effects of mortality salience on relationship strivings and beliefs: The moderating role of attachment style. *British Journal of Social Psychology, 41*(3), 419-41.

Taylor, C. (2007). *A secular age*. Belknap Press.

Taylor, E. (2001). Positive psychology and humanistic psychology: A reply to Seligman. *Journal of Humanistic Psychology, 41*(1), 13-29.

Teasdale, J. D., Segal, Z. V., Williams, J. M. G., Ridgeway, V. A., Soulsby, J. M., & Lau, M. A. (2000). Prevention of relapse/recurrence in major depression by mindfulness-based cognitive therapy. *Journal of Consulting and Clinical Psychology, 68*(4), 615-23.

Tedeschi, R. G., & Calhoun, L. G. (2004). Posttraumatic growth: Conceptual foundations and empirical evidence. *Psychological Inquiry, 15*(1), 1-18.

Tellegen, A., Lykken, D. T., Bouchard, T. J., Wilcox, K. J., Segal, N. L., & Rich, S. (1988). Personality similarity in twins reared apart and together. *Journal of Personality and Social Psychology 54*(6), 1031-39.

Templer, D. (1970). The construction and validation of the Death Anxiety Scale. *Journal of General Psychology, 82*(2), 165-77.

Templer, D. (1971). Death anxiety as related to depression and health of retired persons. *Journal of Gerontology, 26*(4), 521-23.

ten Boom, C. (1971). *The hiding place.* Fleming J. Revell.

Terrion, J. L., & Ashforth, B. E. (2002). From "I" to "we": The role of putdown humor and identity in the development of a temporary group. *Human Relations, 55*(1), 55-88.

Tetlock, P. E. (2005). *Expert local judgment: How good is it? How can we know?* Princeton University Press.

Thayer, R. E., Newman, J. R., & McClain, T. M. (1994). Self-regulation of mood: Strategies for changing a bad mood, raising energy, and reducing tension. *Journal of Personality and Social Psychology, 67*(5), 910-25.

Thomaes, S., Bushman, B. J., Stegge, H., & Olthof, T. (2008). Trumping shame by blasts of noise: Narcissism, self-esteem, shame, and aggression in young adolescents. *Child Development, 79*(6), 1792-1801.

Thomaes, S., Stegge, H., Olthof, T., Bushman, B. J., & Nezlek, J. B. (2011). Turning shame inside-out: "Humiliated fury" in young adolescents. *Emotion, 11*(4), 786-93.

Thorne, G. (2010). Friendship: The end of marriage. In R. R. Jeal (Ed.), *Human sexuality and the nuptial mystery* (pp. 45-64). Cascade Books.

Thorson, J. A. (1985). A funny thing happened on the way to the morgue: Some thoughts on humor and death, and a taxonomy of the humor associated with death. *Death Studies, 9*(3-4), 201-16.

Tibbetts, S. G. (2003). Self-conscious emotions and criminal offending. *Psychological Reports, 93*(1), 101-26.

Titus, C. S., & Moncher, F. (2009). A Catholic Christian positive psychology: A virtue approach. *Edification: The Transdisciplinary Journal of Christian Psychology, 3*(1), 57-63.

Tjeltveit, A. C. (2003). Implicit virtues, divergent goods, multiple communities: Explicitly addressing virtues in the behavioral sciences. *American Behavioral Scientist, 47*(4), 395-414.

Tomer, A. (2012). Meaning and death attitudes. In P. T. P. Wong (Ed.), *The human quest for meaning: Theories, research, and applications* (pp. 209-32). Routledge.

Tomlinson, J. M., & Aron, A. (2013). The positive psychology of romantic love. In H. Hojjat & D. Cramer (Eds.), *The positive psychology of love* (pp. 3-15). Oxford University Press.

Toner, C. (2006). Military service as a practice: Integrating the sword and shield approaches to military ethics. *Journal of Military Ethics, 5*(3), 183-200.

Toussaint, L., & Friedman, P. (2009). Forgiveness, gratitude, and well-being: The mediating role of affect and beliefs. *Journal of Happiness Studies, 10*(6), 635-55.

Tracy, J. L., & Robins, R. W. (2006). Appraisal antecedents of shame and guilt: Support for a theoretical model. *Personality and Social Psychology Bulletin, 32*(10), 1339-51.

Tracy, J. L., Robins, R. W., & Tangey, J. P. (2007). *The self-conscious emotions: Theory and research.* Guilford Press.

Trammel, R. C. (2015). Mindfulness as enhancing ethical decision-making and the Christian integration of mindful practice. *Social Work & Christianity, 42*(2), 165-77.

Treasure, D. (2002). Teaching ethics via sports. *The Futurist, 36*, 2-3.

Treeby, M. S., Rice, S. M., Cocker, F., Peacock, A., & Bruno, R. (2018). Guilt-proneness is associated with the use of protective behavioral strategies during episodes of alcohol use. *Addictive Behaviors, 79*, 120-23.

Triandis, H. C. (2000). Cultural syndromes and subjective well-being. In E. Diener & E. M. Suh (Eds.), *Culture and subjective well-being* (pp. 13-36). MIT Press.

Triandis, H. C. (2001). Individualism-collectivism and personality. *Journal of Personality, 69*(6), 907-24.

Trivers, R. L. (1971). The evolution of reciprocal altruism. *Quarterly Review of Biology, 46*(1), 35-57.

Trulson, M. E. (1989). Martial arts training: A novel "cure" for juvenile delinquency. *Human Relations, 39*(12), 1131-40.

Tsang, J. (2006). Gratitude and prosocial behaviour: An experimental test of gratitude. *Cognition and Emotion, 20*(1), 138-48.

Tsang, J. A., & Martin, S. R. (2019). Four experiments on the relational dynamics and prosocial consequences of gratitude. *Journal of Positive Psychology, 14*(2), 188-205.

Tsang, J. A., McCullough, M. E., & Fincham, F. D. (2006). The longitudinal association between forgiveness and relationship closeness and commitment. *Journal of Social and Clinical Psychology, 25*(4), 448-72.

Tsang, J. A., McCullough, M. E., & Hoyt, W. T. (2005). Psychometric and rationalization accounts of the religion-forgiveness discrepancy. *Journal of Social Issues, 61*(4), 785-805.

Twemlow, S. W., & Sacco, F. C. (1998). The application of traditional martial arts practice and theory to the treatment of violent adolescents. *Adolescence, 33*(131), 505-18.

Twenge, J. (2006). *Generation me.* Free Press.

Twenge, J. (2017). *iGen.* Atria Books.

Uchida, Y., Unkit, V. N., & Kitayama, S. (2004). Cultural constructions of happiness: Theory and empirical evidence. *Journal of Happiness Studies, 5*(3), 223-39.

Uekermann, J., Daum, I, & Channon, S. (2007). Toward a cognitive and social neuroscience of humor processing. *Social Cognition, 25*(4), 553-72.

Ullén, F., de Manzano, Ö., Almeida, R., Magnusson, P. K., Pedersen, N. L., Nakamura, J., . . . & Madison, G. (2012). Proneness for psychological flow in everyday life: Associations with personality and intelligence. *Personality and Individual Differences, 52*(2), 167-72.

Vail, K. E., Juhl, J., Arndt, J., Vess, M., Routledge, C., & Rutjens, B. T. (2012). When death is good for life: Considering the positive trajectories of terror management. *Personality and Social Psychology Review, 16*(4), 303-29.

Vail, K. E., Rothschild, Z. K., Weise, D. R., Solomon, S., Pyszczynski, T., & Greenberg, J. (2010). A terror management analysis of the psychological functions of religion. *Personality and Social Psychology Review, 14*(1), 84-94.

Vaillant, G. E. (1977). *Adaptation to life.* Cambridge University Press.

Vaillant, G. E. (1992). *Ego mechanisms of defense: A guide for clinicians and researchers.* American Psychiatric Press.

Vaillant, G. (1993). *The wisdom of the ego.* Harvard University Press.

Vaillant, G. (2000). Adaptive mental mechanisms: Their role in a positive psychology. *American Psychologist, 55*(1), 89-98.

Vallerand, R. J., & Reid, G. (1988). On the relative effects of positive and negative verbal feedback on males' and females' intrinsic motivation. *Canadian Journal of Behavioural Science, 20*(3), 239-50.

Van Belle, H. A. (1980). *Basic intent and therapeutic approach of Carl R. Rogers.* Wedge Publishing Foundation.

Van Boven, L., & Gilovich, T. (2003). To do or to have? That is the question. *Journal of Personality and Social Psychology, 85*(6), 1192-1202.

Van den Berghe, L., Vansteenkiste, M., Cardon, G., Kirk, D., & Haerens, L. (2014). Research on self-determination in physical education: Key findings and proposals for future research. *Physical Education and Sport Pedagogy, 19*(1), 97-121.

Van den Broeck, A., Ferris, D. L., Chang, C. H., & Rosen, C. C. (2016). A review of self-determination theory's basic psychological needs at work. *Journal of Management, 42*(5), 1195-229.

Van den Broeck, A., Vansteenkiste, M., De Witte, H., & Lens, W. (2008). Explaining the relationships between job characteristics, burnout, and engagement: The role of basic psychological need satisfaction. *Work & Stress, 22*(3), 277-94.

Van Dierendonck, D. (2011). Servant leadership: A review and synthesis. *Journal of Management, 37*(4), 1228-61.

van Dierendonck, D. & Patterson, K. (2010). Servant leadership: An introduction. In D. van Dierendonck & K. Patterson (Eds.), *Servant leadership: Developments in theory and research* (pp. 3-10). Palgrave Macmillan.

Van Leeuwen, M. S. (1979). The behaviorist bandwagon and the body of Christ I: A critique of ontological behaviorism from a Christian perspective. *Journal of the American Scientific Affiliation, 31,* 88-91.

Van Tongeren, D. R., Burnette, J. L., O'Boyle, E., Worthington, E. L., Jr., & Forsyth, D. R. (2014). A meta-analysis of intergroup forgiveness. *Journal of Positive Psychology, 9*(1), 81-95.

Van Tongeren, D. R., Green, J. D., Davis, D. E., Worthington, E. L., & Reid, C. A. (2013). Till death do us part: Terror management and forgiveness in close relationships. *Personal Relationships, 20*(4), 755-68.

Van Tongeren, D. R., Hakim, S., Hook, J. N., Johnson, K. A., Green, J. D., Hulsey, T. L., & Davis, D. E. (2016). Toward an understanding of religious tolerance: Quest religiousness and positive attitudes toward religiously dissimilar others. *The International Journal for the Psychology of Religion, 26*(3), 212-24.

Vandenberghe, L., & Costa-Prado, F. (2009). Law and grace in Augustine: A fresh perspective on mindfulness and spirituality in behavior therapy. *Mental Health, Religion & Culture, 12*(6), 587-600.

Vanhoozer, K. J. (2010). Forming the performers: How Christians can use canon sense to bring us to our (theodramatic) senses. *Edification, 4*(1), 5-16.

Vansteenkiste, M., Duriez, B., Simons, J., & Soenens, B. (2006). Materialistic values and well-being among business students: Further evidence for their detrimental effect. *Journal of Applied Social Psychology, 36*(12), 2892-2908.

Vansteenkiste, M., Lens, W., & Deci, E. L. (2006). Intrinsic versus extrinsic goal contents in self-determination theory: Another look at the quality of academic motivation. *Educational Psychologist, 41*(1), 19-31.

Vansteenkiste, M., Sierens, E., Goossens, L., Soenens, B., Dochy, F., Mouratidis, A., Aelterman, N., Haerens, L., & Beyers, M. (2012). Identifying configurations of perceived teacher autonomy support and structure: Associations with self-regulated learning, motivation and problem behavior. *Learning and Instruction, 22*(6), 431-39.

Vansteenkiste, M., Simons, J., Lens, W., Sheldon, K. M., & Deci, E. L. (2004). Motivating learning, performance, and persistence: The synergistic role of intrinsic goals and autonomy-support. *Journal of Personality and Social Psychology, 87*(2), 246-60.

Varahrami, A., Arnau, R. C., Rosen, D. H., & Mascaro, N. (2010). The relationships between meaning, hope, and psychosocial development. *International Journal of Existential Psychology and Psychotherapy, 3*(1). http://journal.existential psychology.org/index.php /ExPsy/article/view/136

Vaughan, C. A., Farmer, C. M., Breslau, J., & Burnette, C. (2015). *Evaluation of the Operational Stress Control and Readiness (OSCAR) program.* The RAND Corporation.

Vilaythong, A. P., Arnau, R. C., Rosen, D. H., & Mascaro, N. (2003). Humor and hope: Can humor increase hope? *Humor: International Journal of Humor Research, 16*(1), 79-89.

Vinton, K. L. (1989). Humor in the workplace: It is more than telling jokes. *Small Group Behavior, 20*(2), 151-66.

Visser, M. (2008). *The gift of thanks: The roots, persistence, and paradoxical meanings of a social ritual.* HarperCollins.

Vohs, K. D., Aaker, J. L., & Catapano, R. (2019). It's not going to be that fun: Negative experiences can add meaning to life. *Current Opinion in Psychology, 26*, 11-14.

Vohs, K. D., & Faber, R. J. (2007). Spent resources: Self-regulatory resource availability affects impulse buying. *Journal of Consumer Research, 33*(4), 537-47.

Vohs, K. D., & Heatherton, T. F. (2000). Self-regulatory failure: A resource-depletion approach. *Psychological Science, 11*(3), 249-54.

Vohs, K. D., Redden, J. P., & Rahinel, R. (2013). Physical order produces healthy choices, generosity, and conventionality, whereas disorder produces creativity. *Psychological Science, 24*(9), 1860-67.

Volf, M. (1996). *Exclusion and embrace: A theological exploration of identity, otherness, and reconciliation.* Abingdon Press.

Volf, M. (2015). The crown of the good life: A hypothesis. In M. Volf & J. E. Crisp (Eds.), *Joy and human flourishing: Essays on theology, culture, and the good life* (pp. 127-35). Fortress.

Von Culin, K. R., Tsukayama, E., & Duckworth, A. L. (2014). Unpacking grit: Motivational correlates of perseverance and passion for long-term goals. *Journal of Positive Psychology, 9*(4), 306-12.

Wade, J. C., Marks, L. I., & Hetzel, R. D. (2015). *Positive psychology on the college campus.* Oxford University Press.

Wade, N. G., Worthington, E. L., Jr., & Meyer, J. E. (2005). But do they work? A meta-analysis of group interventions to promote forgiveness. In E. L. Worthington Jr. (Ed.), *Handbook of forgiveness* (pp. 423-40). Routledge.

Wallwork, E., & Wallwork, A. S. (1990). Psychoanalysis and religion: Current status of an old antagonism. In J. H. Smith & S. A. Handelman (Eds). *Psychoanalysis and religion* (pp. 160-73). John Hopkins University Press.

Walsh, R. (2001). Positive psychology: East and west. *American Psychologist, 56*(1), 83-84.

Wanden-Berghe, R. G., Sanz-Valero, J., & Wanden-Berghe, C. (2010). The application of mindfulness to eating disorders treatment: A systematic review. *Eating Disorders, 19*(1), 34-48.

Wandzilak, T., Carroll, T., & Ansorge, C. J. (1988). Values development through physical activity: Promoting sportsmanlike behaviors, perceptions, and moral reasoning. *Journal of Teaching in Physical Education, 8*(1), 13-22.

Wang, G., & Hackett, R. D. (2016). Conceptualization and measurement of virtuous leadership: Doing well by doing good. *Journal of Business Ethics, 137*(2), 321-45.

Waterman, A. S. (1993). Two conceptions of happiness: Contrasts of personal expressiveness (eudaimonia) and hedonic enjoyment. *Journal of Personality and Social Psychology, 64*(4), 678-91.

Waterman, A. S. (2013). The humanistic psychology–positive psychology divide: Contrasts in philosophical foundations. *American Psychologist, 68*(3), 124-33.

Watkins, P. C. (2014). *Gratitude and the good life: Toward a psychology of appreciation.* Springer.

Watkins, P. C., Woodward, K., Stone, T., & Kolts, R. L. (2003). Gratitude and happiness: Development of a measure of gratitude, and relationships with subjective well-being. *Social Behavior and Personality: An International Journal, 31*(5), 431-51.

Watson, D., & Pennebaker, J. W. (1989). Health complaints, stress, and distress: Exploring the central role of negative affectivity. *Psychological Review, 96*(2), 234-54.

Watson, M., Homewood, J., Haviland, J., & Bliss, J. M. (2005). Influence of psychological response on breast cancer survival: 10-year follow-up of a population-based cohort. *European Journal of Cancer, 41*(12), 1710-14.

Watson, N. J., Wier, S., & Friend, S. (2005). The development of muscular Christianity in Victorian Britain and beyond. *Journal of Religion and Society, 7*, 1-21.

Watson, R. I. (1961). A brief history of educational psychology. *Psychological Record, 11*(3), 209-42.

Watts, F. (2004). Relating the psychology and theology of forgiveness. In F. Watts & L. Gulliford (Eds.), *Forgiveness in context: Theology and psychology in creative dialogue* (pp. 1-10). T&T Clark.

Weary, G., & Williams, J. P. (1990). Depressive self-presentation: Beyond self-handicapping. *Journal of Personality and Social Psychology, 58*(5), 892-98.

Wegner, D. M., Schneider, D. J., Carter, S. R., & White, T. L. (1987). Paradoxical effects of thought suppression. *Journal of Personality and Social Psychology, 53*(1), 5-13.

Weir, S. (2008). Competition as relationship: Sport as a mutual quest towards excellence. In D. Deardorff II & J. White (Eds.), *The image of God in the human body: Essays on Christianity and sports* (pp. 101-21). Edwin Mellen Press.

Weisaeth, L., Mehlum, L., & Mortensen, M. (1996). Peacekeeper stress: New and different? *National Center for Post-Traumatic Stress Disorder Clinical Quarterly, 6*(1), 12-15.

Weise, D. R., Pyszczynski, T., Cox, C. R., Arndt, J., Greenberg, J., Solomon, S., & Kosloff, S. (2008). Interpersonal politics: The role of terror management and attachment processes in shaping political preferences. *Psychological Science, 19*(5), 448-55.

Weisenberg, M., Raz, T., & Hener, T. (1998). The influence of film induced mood on pain perception. *Pain, 76*(3), 365-75.

Weiser, M., Kutz, I., Kutz, S. J., & Weiser, D. (1995). Psychotherapeutic aspects of the martial arts. *American Journal of Psychotherapy, 49*(1), 118-27.

Weissman, M. M., Bland, R. C., Canino, G. J., Faravelli, C., Greenwald, S., Hwu, H., Joyce, P. R., . . . & Yeh, E. K. (1996) Cross-national epidemiology of major depression and bipolar disorder. *JAMA, 276*(4), 293-99.

Wegner, J. H. (1999). Lost and found fragments of Egyptian wisdom. *Expedition, 41*(2), 46-47.

Wenke, D., & Frensch, P. A. (2003). Is success or failure at solving complex problems related to intellectual ability? In J. E. Davidson & R. J. Sternberg (Eds.), *The psychology of problem-solving* (pp. 87-126). Cambridge University Press.

Westman, M. (1990). The relationship between stress and performance: The moderating effect of hardiness. *Human Performance, 3*(3), 141-55.

Westhusing, T. (2003). A beguiling military virtue: honor. *Journal of Military Ethics, 2*(3), 195-212.

Whalen, S. P., & Csikszentmihalyi, M. (1991). *Putting flow theory into educational practice: The Key School's flow activities room. Report to the Benton*

Center for Curriculum and Instruction, University of Chicago. ERIC Institute of Education Sciences. https://files.eric.ed.gov/fulltext/ED338381.pdf

White, M. A. (2013). Positive education at Geelong Grammar School. In S. A. David, I. Boniwell, & A. C. Ayers (Eds.), *Oxford handbook of happiness* (pp. 708-20). Oxford University Press.

Whitley, B. E., Jr. (1993). Reliability and aspects of the construct validity of Sternberg's Triangular Love Scale. *Journal of Social and Personal Relationships, 10*(3), 475-80.

Wicker, E. W., Payne, G. C., & Morgan, R. D. (1983). Participant descriptions of guilt and shame. *Motivation and Emotion, 7*(1), 25-39.

Wieselquist, J. (2009). Interpersonal forgiveness, trust, and the investment model of commitment. *Journal of Social and Personal Relationships, 26*(4), 531-48.

Wilkens, S. (2019). *What's so funny about God? A theological look at humor.* IVP Academic.

Williams, C. (2011). *Existential reasons for belief in God.* IVP Academic.

Williams, G. C., Saizow, R., Ross, L., & Deci, E. L. (1997). Motivation underlying career choice for internal medicine and surgery. *Social Science and Medicine, 45*(11), 1705-13.

Williams, R. B., Barefoot, J. C., Califf, R. M., Haney, T. L., Saunders, W. B., Pryor, D. B., Hlatky, M. A., Siegler, I. C., & Mark, D. B. (1992). Prognostic importance of social and economic resources among medically treated patients with angiographically documented coronary artery disease. *JAMA, 267*(4), 520-24.

Wilson, E. O. (1984) *Biophilia.* Harvard University Press.

Wilson, G. S., Raglin, J. S., & Pritchard, M. E. (2002). Optimism, pessimism, and precompetition anxiety in college athletes. *Personality and Individual Differences, 32*(5), 893-902.

Wilson, J. R. (1997). *Living faithfully in a fragmented word: Lessons for the church from MacIntyre's After Virtue.* Trinity Press.

Wilson, K. G., & Murrell, A. R. (2004). Values work in acceptance and commitment therapy: Setting a course for behavioral treatment. In S. C. Hayes, V. M. Follette, & M. M. Linehan (Eds.), *Mindfulness and acceptance: Expanding the cognitive-behavioral tradition* (pp. 120-51). Guilford Press.

Wilson, R. I. (1978). *The great psychologists* (4th ed.). J. B. Lippincott.

Wilson, R. S. (1985). Risk and resilience in early mental development. *Developmental Psychology, 21*(5), 795-805.

Wilt, J. A., Stauner, N., Harriott, V. A., Exline, J. J., & Pargament, K. I. (2019). Partnering with God: Religious coping and perceptions of divine intervention predict spiritual transformation in response to religious-spiritual struggle. *Psychology of Religion and Spirituality, 11*(3), 278-90.

Wink, P., & Helson, R. (1997). Practical and transcendent wisdom: Their nature and some longitudinal findings. *Journal of Adult Development, 4*(1), 1-15.

Winseman, A. L., Clifton, D. O., & Liesveld, C. (2003). *Living your strengths: Discover your God-given talents and inspire your community.* Gallup Press.

Wittmer, M. (2008). A Christian perspective on sport. In D. Deardorff II & J. White (Eds.), *The image of God in the human body: Essays on Christianity and sports* (pp. 43-55). Edwin Mellen Press.

Witvliet, C. V. O., Ludwig, T. E., & Laan, K. L. V. (2001). Granting forgiveness or harboring grudges: Implications for emotion, physiology, and health. *Psychological Science, 12*(2), 117-23.

Witvliet, C. V., Richie, F. J., Root Luna, L. M., & Van Tongeren, D. R. (2019). Gratitude predicts hope and happiness: A two-study assessment of traits and states. *Journal of Positive Psychology, 14*(3), 271-82.

Wolfe, R. N., & Johnson, S. D. (1995). Personality as a predictor of college performance. *Educational and Psychological Measurement, 55*(2), 177-85.

Wolff, H. A., Smith, C. E., & Murray, H. A. (1934). The psychology of humor: 1. A study of responses to race-disparagement jokes. *Journal of Abnormal and Social Psychology, 28*, 341-65.

Woolfolk, R. L., & Wasserman, R. H. (2005). Count no one happy: Eudaimonia and positive psychology. *Journal of Theoretical and Philosophical Psychology, 25*(1), 81-90.

Wolters, A. M. (1985). *Creation regained.* Eerdmans.

Wong, P. T. P. (1998). Implicit theories of meaningful life and the development of the Personal Meaning Profile (PMP). In P. T. P. Wong & P. S. Fry (Eds.), *The human quest for meaning* (pp. 111-40). Erlbaum.

Wong, P. T. P. (2008). Meaning management theory and death acceptance. In A. Tomer, G. T. Eliason, & P. T. P. Wong (Eds.), *Existential and spiritual issues in death attitudes* (pp. 65-87). Lawrence Erlbaum Associates.

Wong, P. T. P. (2009). Chinese positive psychology. In S. J. Lopez (Ed.), *The encyclopedia of positive psychology* (pp. 148-56). John Wiley & Sons.

Wong, P. T. P. (2011). Positive psychology 2.0: Towards a balanced interactive model of the good life. *Canadian Psychology, 52*(2), 69-81.

Wong, P. T. P. (Ed.). (2012a). *The human quest for meaning: Theories, research, and applications* (2nd ed.). Routledge.

Wong, P. T. P. (2012b). Introduction. In P. T. P. Wong (Ed.), *The human quest for meaning* (2nd ed.) (pp. xxix-xlvi). Routledge.

Wong, P. T. P. (2012c). Toward a dual-systems model of what makes life worth living. In P. T. P. Wong (Ed.), *The human quest for meaning* (2nd ed.) (pp. 3-22). Routledge.

Wong, P. T. P. (2016). Existential positive psychology. *International Journal of Existential Psychology and Psychotherapy, 6*(1). http://journal.existential psychology.org/index.php/ExPsy/article/view/179

Wong, P. T. P., Reker, G. T., & Gesser, G. (1994). Death Attitude Profile-Revised: A multidimensional measure of attitudes toward death. In R. A. Neimeyer (Ed.), *Death anxiety handbook: Research instrumentation and application* (pp. 121-48). Taylor and Francis.

Wong, P. T., & Tomer, A. (2011). Beyond terror and denial: The positive psychology of death acceptance. *Death Studies, 35*(2), 99-106.

Wong, P. T., & Wong, L. C. J. (2012). A meaning-centered approach to building youth resilience. In P. T. P. Wong (Ed.), *The human quest for meaning: Theories, research, and applications* (pp. 585-618). Routledge.

Wong, Y. J. (2006). Strength-centered therapy: A social constructionist, virtues-based psychotherapy. *Psychotherapy: Theory, Research, Practice, Training, 43*(2), 133-46.

Wood, A. M., Froh, J. J., & Geraghty, A. W. (2010). Gratitude and well-being: A review and theoretical integration. *Clinical Psychology Review, 30*(7), 890-905.

Wood, A. M., Joseph, S., & Linley, P. A. (2007). Gratitude: The parent of all virtues. *The Psychologist, 20*(1), 18-21.

Wood, A. M., Joseph, S., & Maltby, J. (2008). Gratitude uniquely predicts satisfaction with life: Incremental validity above the domains and facets of the five factor model. *Personality and Individual Differences, 45*(1), 49-54.

Wood, A. M., Linley, P. A., Maltby, J., Baliousis, M., & Joseph, S. (2008). The authentic personality: A theoretical and empirical conceptualization and the development of the Authenticity Scale. *Journal of Counseling Psychology, 55*(3), 385-99.

Wood, A. M., Maltby, J., Stewart, N., Linley, P. A., & Joseph, S. (2008). A social-cognitive model of trait and state levels of gratitude. *Emotion, 8*(2), 281-90.

Wood, R., Bandura, A., & Bailey, T. (1990). Mechanisms governing organizational performance in complex decision-making environments. *Organizational Behavior and Human Decision Processes, 46*(2), 181-201.

Woodyatt, L., Wenzel, M., & Griffin, B. J. (Eds.). (2017). *Handbook of the psychology of self-forgiveness*. Springer International Publishing.

World Health Organization. (1994). *Global strategy on occupational health for all: The way to health at work*. www.who.int/occupational_health /publications/globstrategy/en/index2.html

Worthington, E. L., Jr. (1998). An empathy-humility-commitment model of forgiveness applied within family dyads. *Journal of Family Therapy, 20*(1), 59-76.

Worthington, E. L., Jr. (2001). *Five steps to forgiveness: The art and science of forgiving*. Crown.

Worthington, E. L., Jr. (2003). *Forgiving and reconciling: Bridges to wholeness and hope*. InterVarsity Press.

Worthington, E. L., Jr. (2006). *Forgiveness and reconciliation: Theory and application*. Routledge.

Worthington, E. L., Jr. (2010). Surprised by grace: God's faithfulness in developing a Christian psychologist. In G. L. Moritarty (Ed.), *Integrating faith and psychology: Twelve psychologists tell their stories* (pp. 28-42). IVP Academic.

Worthington, E. L., Jr. (2013). *Moving forward: Six steps to forgiving yourself and breaking free from the past*. Waterbrook Press.

Worthington, E. L., Jr. (2019). A campaign for forgiveness research: Lessons in studying a virtue. *Journal of Psychology and Christianity, 38*(3), 184-90.

Worthington, E. L., Jr., Griffin, B. J., & Lavelock, C. R. (2019). Cultivating the fruit of the Spirit: Contributions of positive psychology to spiritual formation. In T. M. Crisp, S. L. Porter, & G. A. Ten Elshof (Eds.), *Psychology and spiritual formation in dialogue* (pp. 206-34). IVP Academic.

Worthington, E. L., Jr., & Sandage, S. J. (2016). *Forgiveness and spirituality in psychotherapy.* American Psychological Association.

Worthington, E. L., Jr., & Scherer, M. (2004). Forgiveness is an emotion-focused coping strategy that can reduce health risks and promote health resilience: Theory, review, and hypotheses. *Psychology & Health, 19*(3), 385-405.

Worthington, E. L., Jr., Sharp, C. B., Lerner, A. J., & Sharp, J. R. (2006). Interpersonal forgiveness as an example of loving one's enemies. *Journal of Psychology and Theology, 34*(1), 32-42.

Wright, N. T. (2008). *Surprised by hope.* HarperCollins.

Wright, N. T. (2010). *After you believe: Why Christian character matters.* HarperCollins.

Wright, T. A., & Staw, B. M. (1999). Affect and favorable work outcomes: Two longitudinal tests of the happy-productive worker thesis. *Journal of Organizational Behavior, 20*(1), 1-23.

Wu, C. H. J., & Liang, R. D. (2011). The relationship between white-water rafting experience formation and customer reaction: A flow theory perspective. *Tourism Management, 32*(2), 317-25.

Yalom, I. D. (1980). *Existential psychotherapy.* Basic Books.

Yaryura-Tobias, J. A., & Neziroglu, F. A. (1975). Violent behavior, brain dysrhythmia, and glucose dysfunction: A new syndrome. *Journal of Orthomolecular Psychiatry, 4*(3), 182-88.

Yearley, C. (1990). *Mencius and Aquinas: Theories of virtue and conceptions of courage.* State University of New York Press.

Yeung, D., & Martin, M. T. (2013). *Spiritual fitness and resilience: A review of relevant constructs, measures, and links to well-being.* The RAND Corporation.

Younger, J., Aron, A., Parke, S., Chatterjee, N., & Mackey, S. (2010). Viewing pictures of a romantic partner reduces experimental pain: Involvement of neural reward systems. *PloS ONE, 5*(10), e13309.

Zabelina, D. L., Robinson, M. D., & Anicha, C. L. (2007). The psychological tradeoffs of self-control: A multi-method investigation. *Personality and Individual Differences, 43*(3), 463-73.

Zamorski, M. A., Bennett, R. E., Rusu, C., Weeks, M., Boulos, D., & Garber, B. G. (2016). Prevalence of past-year mental disorders in the Canadian Armed Forces, 2002–2013. *Canadian Journal of Psychiatry, 61(Supplement)*, 26S-35S.

Zamorski, M. A., Guest, K., Bailey, S., & Garber, B. G. (2012). Beyond Battlemind: Evaluation of a new mental health training program for Canadian Forces personnel participating in third-location decompression. *Military Medicine, 177*(11), 1245-53.

Zettle, R. D. (2007). *ACT for depression: A clinician's guide to using acceptance and commitment therapy in treating depression.* New Harbinger Publications.

Zhao, H., Seibert, S. E., & Hills, G. E. (2005). The mediating role of self-efficacy in the development of entrepreneurial intentions. *Journal of Applied Psychology, 90*(6), 1265-72.

Zimbardo, P. G. (1969). The human choice: Individuation, reason, and order versus deindividuation, impulse, and chaos. *Nebraska Symposium on Motivation, 17,* 237-307.

Zimbardo, P. G. (2004). A situationist perspective on the psychology of evil: Understanding how good people are transformed into perpetrators. In A. G. Miller (Ed.), *The social psychology of good and evil* (pp. 21-50). Guilford Press.

Zimbardo, P. (2007). *The Lucifer effect: Understanding how good people turn evil.* Random House.

Zimbardo, P., & Hartley, C. (1985). Cults go to high school. *The Cultic Studies Journal, 2,* 91-147.

Zimmermann, J. (2017). Christian humanism: Christ-centred education by another name. *Didaskalia, 27,* 1-30.

Zinnbauer, B. J., Pargament, K. I., Cole, B., Rye, M. S., Butter, E. M., Belavich, T. G., . . . & Kadar, J. L. (1997). Religion and spirituality: Unfuzzying the fuzzy. *Journal for the Scientific Study of Religion, 36*(4), 549-64.

Zivin, G., Hassan, N. R., DePaula, G. F., Monti, D. A., Harlan, C., Hossain, K. D., & Patterson, K. (2001). An effective approach to violence prevention: Traditional martial arts in middle school. *Adolescence, 36*(143), 443-59.

Zullow, H., & Seligman, M. E. P. (1990). Pessimistic rumination predicts defeat of presidential candidates, 1900 to 1984. *Psychological Inquiry, 1*(1), 52-61.

INDEX

An Association for Christian Psychologists,
Therapists, Counselors and Academicians

CAPS is a vibrant Christian organization with a rich tradition. Founded in 1956 by a small group of Christian mental health professionals, chaplains and pastors, CAPS has grown to more than 2,100 members in the U.S., Canada and more than 25 other countries.

CAPS encourages in-depth consideration of therapeutic, research, theoretical and theological issues. The association is a forum for creative new ideas. In fact, their publications and conferences are the birthplace for many of the formative concepts in our field today.

CAPS members represent a variety of denominations, professional groups and theoretical orientations; yet all are united in their commitment to Christ and to professional excellence.

CAPS is a non-profit, member-supported organization. It is led by a fully functioning board of directors, and the membership has a voice in the direction of CAPS.

CAPS is more than a professional association. It is a fellowship, and in addition to national and international activities, the organization strongly encourages regional, local and area activities which provide networking and fellowship opportunities as well as professional enrichment.

To learn more about CAPS, visit www.caps.net.

The joint publishing venture between IVP Academic and CAPS aims to promote the understanding of the relationship between Christianity and the behavioral sciences at both the clinical/counseling and the theoretical/research levels. These books will be of particular value for students and practitioners, teachers and researchers.

For more information about CAPS Books, visit InterVarsity Press's website at www.ivpress.com/christian-association-for-psychological-studies-books-set.

Finding the Textbook You Need

The IVP Academic Textbook Selector
is an online tool for instantly finding the IVP books
suitable for over 250 courses across 24 disciplines.

---

ivpacademic.com